Political Economy, Public Policy and Monetary Economics

Austrian economist, Ludwig von Mises, was one of the most original and controversial economists of the twentieth century, both as a defender of free-market liberalism and a leading opponent of socialism and the interventionist-welfare state. He was both the grand designer of a political economy of freedom and a trenchant, detailed critic of government regulatory and monetary policies in the first half of the twentieth century.

This fascinating book explores the cultural currents of anti-Semitism in Austria before and after World War I that Mises confronted as an Austrian Jew; his analysis of Austria-Hungary's establishment of a gold standard; Mises' multi-sided activities in the years after the War in stemming a hyperinflation, opposing government fiscal mismanagement, and resisting misguided policies during the Great Depression; and his analysis of how Europe plunged into World War II and the policies to restore freedom and prosperity in the post-war period. It also discusses the confrontation between the Austrian Economists and the Keynesians over the causes and cures for the Great Depression, as well as how Mises' "Austrian" approach to money and the business cycle contrasted with both the ideas of Joseph A. Schumpeter and the Swedish Economists of the interwar period.

This volume breaks new ground in placing Ludwig von Mises' many original views on political economy, public policy and monetary economics in the historical context of his time, especially during the interwar period when he was a senior economic analyst for the Vienna Chamber of Commerce and after his arrival in America during World War II. The book will therefore be of interest to students and researchers in monetary economics, political economy, expectations theory and the market process, and the history of economic thought.

Richard M. Ebeling is Professor of Economics at Northwood University in Midland, Michigan. He was previously the president of the Foundation for Economic Education in Irvington, New York.

Routledge studies in the history of economics

Political Economy, Public Policy and Monetary Economics

Ludwig von Mises and
the Austrian Tradition

Richard M. Ebeling

Routledge
Taylor & Francis Group

LONDON AND NEW YORK

First published 2010
by Routledge
4 Park Square, Milton Park, Abingdon, Oxon OX14 4RN
605 Third Avenue, New York, NY 10017

Routledge is an imprint of the Taylor & Francis Group, an informa business

© 2010 Richard M. Ebeling

Typeset in Times by Wearset Ltd, Tyne and Wear
First issued in paperback in 2013

British Library Cataloguing in Publication Data
A catalogue record for this book is available from the British Library

Library of Congress Cataloging in Publication Data
A catalog record for this book has been requested

ISBN13: 978-0-415-74552-9 (pbk)
ISBN13: 978-0-415-77951-7 (hbk)
ISBN13: 978-0-203-86148-6 (ebk)

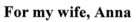
For my wife, Anna

Contents

xiv *Contents*

Acknowledgments

The chapters included in this volume were mostly written during the time when I was the Ludwig von Mises Professor of Economics at Hillsdale College in Hillsdale, Michigan (1988–2003) or when I served as the president of the Foundation for Economic Education (FEE) in Irvington-on-Hudson, New York (2003–2008).

Chapter 1, "Austrian Economics and the Political Economy of Freedom," Chapter 2, "Ludwig von Mises: The Political Economist of Liberty," and Chapter 3, "Ludwig von Mises and the Vienna of His Time," originally appeared in FEE's monthly publication, *The Freeman: Ideas on Liberty*, after being delivered as lectures, respectively, at the Ludwig von Mises Institute in Auburn, Alabama, Hillsdale College, and the Austrian Colloquium at New York University.

Chapter 4, "Austria-Hungary's Economic Policies in the Twilight of the 'Liberal' Era: Ludwig von Mises' Writings on Monetary and Fiscal Policy Before World War I," was delivered as a paper at the Austrian Colloquium at New York University and the Workshop on Philosophy, Politics and Economics at George Mason University.

Chapter 5, "The Economist as the Historian of Decline: Ludwig von Mises and Austria Between the Two World Wars," Chapter 6, "Planning for Freedom: Ludwig von Mises as Political Economist and Policy Analyst," Chapter 7, "The Austrian Economists and the Keynesian Revolution: The Great Depression and the Economics of the Short Run," and Chapter 8, "Two Variations on the Austrian Monetary Theme: Ludwig von Mises and Joseph A. Schumpeter on the Business Cycle" were first delivered at Hillsdale College's Ludwig on Mises Lecture Series. They then appeared in Hillsdale College's *Champions of Freedom* book series.

Chapter 9, "Money, Economics Fluctuations, Expectations and Period Analysis: The Austrian and Swedish Economists in the Interwar Period," was presented as a paper at a conference on Austrian Economics held at the Tinbergin Institute in Amsterdam, the Netherlands. It was then published in *Austrian Economics in Debate*, edited by Willem Keizer, Bert Tieben and Rudy van Zijp (London: Routledge, 1997).

Chapter 10, "Human Action, Ideal Types, and the Market Process: Alfred Schutz and the Austrian Economists," was delivered at a symposium on Alfred Schutz and the Methods of the Social Sciences held on the campus of Florida

Atlantic University, Boca Raton, Florida. It was then published in *Schutzian Social Science* edited by Lester Embree (New York: Springer Publishers, 1999).

I wish to thank *The Freeman*, Hillsdale College Press, Routledge, and Springer for kindly granting permission for essays originally published under their auspices to appear in this volume.

These chapters are part of a long intellectual journey that began decades ago, indeed, when I was a teenager and had already developed an interest in Austrian Economics. I never had the opportunity to meet Ludwig von Mises, who passed away in 1973 when I was still an undergraduate at California State University, Sacramento.

But the following year I had the good fortune to be invited by the Institute for Humane Studies to attend the first Austrian Economics conference held in South Royalton, Vermont in June 1974. There I had the opportunity to meet three of the leading figures of the Austrian School: Israel M. Kirzner, Ludwig M. Lachmann, and Murray N. Rothbard, whose writings have greatly influenced my thinking on both economic theory and policy, as well as the wider issues of human liberty in the free society.

During the summers of 1975 and 1977 I was a summer fellow at the Institute for Humane Studies when they were headquartered in Menlo Park, California. During most of those two summers, Austrian Economist and Nobel Laureate, Friedrich A. Hayek, was also in residence at IHS. Being in Hayek's company some part of almost every day for weeks at a time was one the most memorable events in my life, and has left a permanent imprint in my mind. He truly was one of the greatest social philosophers and political economists of the twentieth century. His patience and generosity in giving of his time and knowledge to a young and insistent student, who constantly bombarded him with questions about economic theory, classical liberalism, and the old Vienna days, will forever remain with me.

Not long after I moved to New York to begin my graduate studies in 1976, Murray Rothbard and his wife, JoAnn, very kindly introduced me to Ludwig von Mises' widow, Margit, shortly after I wrote a review of her book, *My Years with Ludwig von Mises*. I frequently visited the Mises' apartment at 777 West End Avenue on the Upper Westside of Manhattan to have afternoon tea with Margit. It gave me the chance to learn from her much about Mises the man behind the public persona of a famous economist and champion of liberty, as well as a better feel for everyday life in the Vienna between the two world wars as seen through her eyes.

It was also through the kindness of Margit Mises that I was given an introduction to meet Alfred Schutz's widow, Ilse, who also lived in Manhattan. She, too, told me about the old Vienna and her husband's work and his relationships with some of the Austrian Economists, especially their close friendship with Fritz Machlup. I also remember her kindness in giving me copies of Schutz's collected works in three volumes, when as a rather poor graduate student at the time their price seemed far beyond my very limited budget.

When I briefly studied at New York University and then, later, as a research fellow with the Austrian program at NYU for a year, I took the opportunity to sit in classes offered by Israel Kirzner, Ludwig Lachmann, Fritz Machlup and Oskar Morgenstern. Besides anything I may have learned from their masterful presentations in class, I absorbed far more from the chance to have numerous and long conversations with each of them.

Machlup and Morgenstern both had their own forms of old-world Viennese charm, and a generous willingness to share their ideas and recollections of Vienna and the Austrian School in those now very far bygone days of the 1920s and 1930s. Machlup, in particular, shared fascinating and often amusing and funny stories of the intellectual environment among the academics at the University of Vienna, and about the circle of scholars who made up the membership of Mises' "private seminar."

Conversations with Ludwig Lachmann were always a great and challenging delight. I would enter his NYU office, and immediately after closing the door, he would say in his slightly gravelly and sing-song German accent, "Well, Mr. Ebeling, in these four walls we can speak our mind." Soon we were lost in fascinating talk about the trials and tribulations of the economics profession, and its failure to successfully grapple with the dilemmas of radical uncertainty, kaleidic expectations, and disequilibrium dynamics.

I especially wish to thank Israel Kirzner who, since those NYU days, has served as a role model for me for what scholarship and intellectual integrity should mean. The weekly Austrian Colloquium, under Dr. Kirzner's chairmanship at NYU, was an extremely valuable experience that deepened my knowledge and understanding of both Austrian and mainstream economics. For his support at various times as well as his friendship I shall always be most deeply grateful.

Those years in the second half of the 1970s and the early 1980s in New York resulted in many friendships that are now decades old, a good number of them having begun at that Austrian conference in South Royalton in 1974. Among those many people whose writings and conversations have had a great impact on me are, especially, Walter Block, John Egger, Roger Garrison, Jack High, Gerald O'Driscoll, Mario Rizzo, Joseph Salerno, George Selgin, and Lawrence H. White. I would be remiss if I did not also at least mention two of our circle who have passed away – Don Lavoie and Sudha Shenoy – who were inspiring scholars and warm human beings. I met both of them at South Royalton, and they, too, influenced me a great deal over the years.

I also owe sincere thanks to Mr. John Battalana, who I met in New York in the 1970s when I was working at the Center for Libertarian Studies. We have shared an intense interest in Austrian Economics over the decades from which I've learned many valuable things. And we have shared a common excitement in finding rare and often forgotten books and articles on Austrian Economic and classical liberal themes that has greatly increased my knowledge over the years.

After my New York days, there have been other "Austrian" friends whose writings and conversations have enriched my thoughts on the ideas contained in this volume including Peter Boettke, Samuel Bostaph, Bruce Caldwell, Wolfgang Grassl, Steven Horwitz, Sandy Ikeda, Roger Koppl, Ivan Pongracic, and Mark Skousen.

Among these friends are some of my former students from Hillsdale College who are pursuing successful academic and scholarly careers: Peter Calcagno, Paul Cwik, Peter Leeson, Robert Murphy, and Ryan Oprea. While I have only named these few, I owe an immense debt to the many students who passed through my Austrian Economics and History of Economic Thought classes during my fifteen years at Hillsdale College. Their questions, comments, and conversations helped a great deal in the clarification of my ideas and understanding. To all of them I say, thank you.

The chapters contained in this volume were revised into their finished forms during the academic year, 2008–2009, when I was the Shelby Cullom Davis Visiting Professor of American Business and Economic Enterprise at Trinity College in Hartford, Connecticut. I am grateful to my friends and colleagues during this year, Gerald Gunderson, William Butos, and Adam Grossburg, who made it an especially delightful environment in which to teach and write and share ideas.

I have also been greatly stimulated in my work by another group of individuals with whom I have interacted during this same time frame at the American Institute for Economic Research in Great Barrington, Massachusetts, where I served as a senior research fellow. Preparing a variety of commentaries and studies on themes relating to the financial and economic crisis of 2008–2009 for the Institute has reinforced my confidence that the "Austrian" analysis of money and the business cycle remains as relevant and applicable today as when the theory was developed by Mises and Hayek in the first half of the twentieth century.

In addition, I want to thank Thomas Sutton, associate editor at Routledge, for supporting the publication of this volume.

Finally, my greatest debt is to my wife, Anna, who for almost two decades, now, has supported and encouraged me in everything I have done. I cannot imagine my life without her. It was through her efforts in the mid-1990s that we were able to gain access to Ludwig von Mises' "lost papers" in a formerly secret KGB archive in her native city of Moscow, Russia. Several of the chapters in this volume could not have been written the way they have been if not for access to Mises' "lost papers."

It is for these and many, many other reasons far too numerous to name that I dedicate this volume to her, and say – for everything – *Spasibo!*

Introduction

The following chapters offer an analysis of the political economy, public policy conceptions and monetary economics of the Austrian School, especially as developed in the writings of Ludwig von Mises, the most influential and original member of the school during the last one hundred years. The Austrian School had its origin in the late nineteenth century contributions of Carl Menger, Eugen von Böhm-Bawerk, and Friedrich von Wieser. They and other proponents of the "Austrian" approach in the years before World War I developed a uniquely "subjectivist" approach to marginal utility theory, opportunity cost doctrine, the theories of capital, interest and rent, and the theory of price formation in the market process.

By "subjectivist" the Austrians almost always meant something more and deeper than the "subjectivity" of given tastes and preferences. Austrian "subjectivism" referred to the meanings and expectations of the individual human actors in a world of imperfect knowledge, uncertainty and change. The focus of their analysis usually was on, or at least always included an interest in, an understanding of the processes of market adjustment that may lead to a state of economic equilibrium, rather than merely a description of the conditions for and the unique properties of a general equilibrium state.[1]

These themes became the hallmark of the Austrian School even more explicitly in the years between the two world wars. One of the reasons for this was the radically different political-economic climate that emerged during and out of the ashes of World War I. Though it may be with some exaggeration, it can be said that the world before 1914 was one in which the liberal institutions of private property, limited constitutional government, and relatively free enterprise at home and free trade among nations were not merely philosophically taken for granted but actually served as the basis of much of the political-economic and social order. They were most certainly the normative standards of "civilized" nations, even if in fact not always fully practiced by the leading governments of Europe and North America.[2]

These norms all fell by the wayside during the war and certainly after 1918 in many parts of Europe, especially as the 1920s and 1930s progressed. In their place there arose the new ideologies of political and economic collectivism in the form of communist and fascist dictatorships and the ideal of government central planning.[3] In the remaining Western democracies, the ideas of individual freedom and limited government were replaced with the new notions of government intervention and the welfare state.[4] Throughout the world, liberal internationalism was replaced by political and economic nationalism.[5] With this new nationalist spirit came an accompanying monetary nationalism that resulted in the demise of the gold standard and its function as an international monetary system anchored in fixed exchange rates.[6]

These changes in the political and economic environment suddenly raised important issues that captured the attention of social scientists in general and economists in particular. The socialist promise of a realizable paradise on earth was no longer an intellectual plaything of some academics and radical dreamers. During the Great War governments in all the belligerent countries imposed economy-wide regulations and planning systems in the name of winning the war. When the conflict ended the world did not return to the preceding relatively laissez faire social order. Instead, the paternalist state became – whether in its extreme or moderate forms – the new standard guiding political decision-making.[7]

In this new world of the regulated and planned society among the burning issues were: how would such systems function? Could the planned society generate outcomes superior to the levels of production and income experienced in a liberal free market economy, and with a greater degree of "social" fairness? What would be the place and role of the individual in these brave new socially engineered worlds? What were the likely economic consequences from politically controlled and manipulated monetary systems? Additionally the world seemed to increasingly lose its memory of the benefits of a market-based international order, the explanation and understanding of which had been one of the great achievements of the classical economists of the nineteenth century and which had brought about the demise of Mercantilism, the eighteenth century version of the planned economy.[8]

Among the Austrian Economists of the interwar period, Ludwig von Mises most especially devoted a great deal of time focusing on these momentous issues. He was an uncompromising advocate of classical liberalism and the free market. But Mises viewed himself as an economist, first and foremost. He believed that the economist's role was to approach questions of both economic theory and policy dispassionately and without bias. He once expressed this very clearly in the early 1930s:

> I am an economist, not a preacher of morality who wishes to judge, avenge, or punish. I do not look for guilty parties but for causal connections. And if I speak of interventionism, I am not making accusations against the "state" or against "labor." I only attempt to point out to what consequences a system, a policy, an ideology must necessarily lead.[9]

He believed that the practical usefulness of economics was precisely to enable informed discussion about the likely outcomes from the implementation of various public policies or institutional changes to the social order. His strong and even sharp tone in many of his writings on socialism and the interventionist state were based upon his belief that too many advocates of these systems failed to consider the economist's logical and "value-free" analysis concerning the likely results from their introduction in place of a competitive free market economy.[10]

Part of Mises' "impatience" with much of the economic policy discussions in the years following World War I had to do with the intellectual environment in the German-speaking world in which he lived at this time. For decades before and then after the war, the German Historical School dominated these discussions. They rejected the idea of a general theory of economic decision-making and conduct that would be universal and applicable to all individuals at all times and in all places. For them any and all economic theory was period specific. They insisted that any supposed "laws" of economics set forth by the British Classical Economists in the early years of the nineteenth century might have had validity for the Great Britain of the 1820s. But there could be no a priori justification to assume that any such "laws" would be or were relevant to the Germany of the 1870s or 1890s.

Particularly some leaders of the German Historical School such as Gustav von Schmoller insisted that the first task of any "real" political-economic study was for detailed historical and statistical investigation of the social and political institutions of a nation, people, or *Volk*. From such studies there might be derived insights into various "laws" of the economic relationships between the members of that nation during a particular period of time. Such laws could claim no universality, either across nations and people or even for the same nation at different historical moments. All claims of such universality were really only rationalizations by British political economists to further the commercial and trading interests of their own country over other nations.

The German historicists asserted that there were no "laws of economics" from which might be deduced an understanding of how markets work in general, and what consequences would follow from various types of government intervention and regulation of the citizens' affairs. All matters of policy were to be determined and decided on the basis of pragmatism, expediency, and the opportunism of what seemed to serve the changing interests of the nation-state at a particular time.[11]

Thus, Mises' sometimes strident insistence on the universal and "apodictic certainty" of economic theory was an attempt to fight back against an approach that was essentially "anti-economics." Often the Historicists seemed to be offering merely rationales and justifications for various implicit nationalist and ideological goals in Germany, and the government policies considered useful to advance them. They helped to lay the groundwork for an historical chain of events that finally culminated in the triumph of Hitler and the Nazi movement in the 1930s.[12]

Another outgrowth of World War I was a far more activist approach to monetary management and planning. Certainly the late nineteenth century gold standard had been a "managed" monetary system under which national central banks were expected to use policy tools to maintain gold parity and currency stability. But during the war all the major belligerent powers had ended gold convertibility, resorted to paper money to fund war expenditures, and generated huge inflations.[13]

In the aftermath of the war, even as most of these nations attempted to return to some form of a gold-backed currency in the 1920s, the "policy-orientation" about the role and purpose of monetary management had significantly changed. A central figure, though certainly not the only one during this period, was British economist, John Maynard Keynes. He became the most recognized advocate of monetary and fiscal policies that started from the assumption that markets were inherently unstable and open to wide fluctuations in output and employment that could leave an economy operating below its productive potential for prolonged periods of time.

It was in this climate of opinion that Mises made his contributions to the debate over alternative social institutional orders – capitalism versus socialism versus the interventionist state – and to the problems of monetary theory and policy in the years between the two world wars. Mises and his younger Austrian colleague, Friedrich A. Hayek, offered a fundamentally different conception of the economic system, its self-coordinating potential, and the monetary causes behind the occurrence of business cycles. They argued that an extended social system of division of labor was made possible through the emergence of markets, the evolution of a medium of exchange that facilitated economic calculation, and a competitive price system that integrated multitudes of people divided by time, space, and dispersed knowledge.

There was nothing inherent in the nature of a developed market order or a commodity-backed monetary system that had to lead to the business cycle pattern of booms and busts. They turned their attention, therefore, to the question of how central bank policy might serve and had served as the conduit through which monetary changes and resulting interest rate and price distortions could bring about imbalances between savings and investment, and misdirections of capital and labor, that eventually required a "correction" to restore sustainable coordination in the market.

They were, of course, not alone in the interwar period in offering a non-Keynesian conception of this process. Two approaches parallel to, though distinct from, that of Mises and Hayek were that of Joseph A. Schumpeter and those of the Swedish Economists. They, too, focused on how monetary impulses and interest rate distortions could bring about discoordination on the basis of a far more microeconomic process analysis than Keynes' macro-aggregate method. The Swedish Economists, in particular, emphasized the role of expectations for understanding the source and potential for economy-wide imbalances.

The Austrians and, again, especially Mises, developed a particular methodological subjectivist approach to understanding the formation and functioning of expectations in the market. Mises derived this approach from the earlier writings of the German sociologist, Max Weber, and which was extended by a younger colleague of Mises', the phenomenological sociologist, Alfred Schutz.

The task of the following chapters is to explain some of these "Austrian" ideas, particularly in the forms in which Ludwig von Mises developed them in the historical context of his life and of his time.

Chapter 1, on "Austrian economics and the political economy of freedom," offers an overview of what I see as some of the unique aspects of the Austrian approach in comparison to positivism, historicism and the narrowly equilibrium-focused approach of mainstream, neo-classical economics for understanding the nature of human action and the market process.

Chapter 2, "Ludwig von Mises: political economist of liberty" offers a similar overview of Mises' life, ideas, and place in the flow of twentieth century political and economic events. It first explains the ideological and political currents of historicism, socialism, interventionism, and waning liberalism in late nineteenth and early twentieth century Europe that was the historical setting in which Mises lived and wrote. It then explains the alternative conception of a free, liberal and prosperous society that Mises presented in several of his most important books in the interwar period as a response to these collectivist trends.

Then Chapter 3, "Ludwig von Mises and the Vienna of his time," turns to an understanding of the socio-political environment in which Mises was born in late nineteenth century Austria-Hungary. He came from a prominent Jewish family in the Galician capital of Lemberg (Lvov). I explain the triumph and tragedy of the Austrian and Viennese Jews who were liberated and prospered in the more liberal environment of the last half-century of the Hapsburg monarchy, and then who suffered their terrible fate with the rise of political anti-Semitism that culminated in Hitler's coming to power. I then discuss in some detail Mises' analysis and critique of the origin and consequence of anti-Semitism in Europe in general and particularly in the German-speaking part of the continent including in his native Austria.

The focus of Chapter 4, "Austria-Hungary's economic policies in the twilight of the 'liberal' era: Ludwig von Mises' writings on monetary and fiscal policy before World War I," is on the political and economic inconsistencies in the liberalism of the Hapsburg Empire and the events behind the establishment of a formal gold standard in Austria-Hungary in the 1890s. This is the context for discussing some of Mises' first serious writings as a young economist on monetary and fiscal issues. Mises presented a Public Choice-like analysis of the changing currents of special interest politics that culminated in the instituting of a gold standard. He then argued for the policy of full, legal gold-convertibility by the Austro-Hungarian Central Bank, and found himself challenged not by facts and arguments, but by those who personally gained by keeping the country only on an informal gold convertibility. Mises then analyzed the growth in Austrian government spending and fiscal mismanagement that was threatening the long-run financial stability of the monarchy even before the Great War began.

Chapter 5, "The economist as the historian of decline: Ludwig von Mises and Austria between the two world wars," discusses what was most certainly the most politically active and productive period of Mises' life. Serving as one of the most senior economic analysts at the Vienna Chamber of Commerce, he was at the center of many of the economic and political events and crises that plagued Austria in the 1920s and 1930s. I first explain the history of post-World War I Austria following the disintegration of the Empire in 1918: the hyperinflation and fiscal madness of the early 1920s; the illusionary political stability after monetary stabilization in 1924; the economic and political problems during the

Great Depression that lead to dictatorship even before Hitler's annexation of the country in 1938. In this period, Mises is not simply the "armchair" theorist, but the detailed policy analyst who is attempting to devise strategies to stop or at least limit the consequences from the collapse of the Austrian currency; who is presenting proposals for fiscal restraint and administrative reorganization to reduce the financial burdens facing the government; who explains the causes of excessive government expenditures even before the Great Depression set in; and then faces the policy issues after the depression began, in an attempt to reduce the impact of the policies that he considers are only making the economic crisis worse.

In 1934, Mises left Vienna to accept an appointment at the Graduate Institute of International Studies in Geneva, Switzerland, a position that he held until he moved to the United States in 1940. He lived the rest of his life in America, and for most of those years he was a Visiting Professor in the School of Business Administration at New York University.

In Chapter 6, "Planning for freedom: Ludwig von Mises as political economist and policy analyst," we look at Mises' wider conceptions of social philosophy and the economic order, and his proposals for post-World War II reform and reconstruction. The core of Mises' theory of society was what he called the "Ricardian Law of Association" – the discovery of the far greater productivity that men can experience from the permanent social system of division of labor that has created all that we call the achievements of modern civilization. The chapter discusses why Mises considered only a widely free and competitive market order could serve as the basis for such a civilization, and how the implementations of socialism or aggressive political interventionism threatened to weaken and undermine the social order. In this context, Mises analyzed how Europe came to the abyss of destruction for a second time in the twentieth century, and what policies were needed to assure peace and prosperity when World War II had ended. He then developed reconstruction programs for three situations: the revival of a small, export-dependent nation like his native Austria; a political-economic union for Eastern Europe to reduce the likelihood of nationalist antagonisms and war; and the policies most appropriate for an underdeveloped country such as Mexico to become a more prosperous nation.

Central to much of Mises' theoretical and policy analysis was the belief that sounder economic policies needed to be based on a more stable monetary system than the ones experienced during and after World War I. Already before World War I he had developed a theory of money and the business cycle that was refined in the 1920s, 1930s, and 1940s. The next three chapters focus on Mises' "Austrian" views on monetary matters.

Chapter 7, "The Austrian economists and the Keynesian revolution: the Great Depression and the economics of the short run," offers a detailed exposition of the Austrian theory of money and the business cycle, the Austrian analysis of the causes and consequences of the Great Depression, and a critique of the alternative Keynesian approach that was the rival to Austrian policy proposals in the 1930s for escaping from the depression.

In Chapter 8, "Two variations on the Austrian monetary theme: Ludwig von Mises and Joseph A. Schumpeter on the business cycle," Mises' view of the nature of money and credit and their role in the economic system is contrasted with one of Austria's other famous economists, Joseph Schumpeter. Both thinkers focused on microeconomic dynamics of how monetary changes impact on the structures of relative prices and production that results in waves of booms and busts. But Schumpeter considered credit expansion often to be essential for dramatic economic development and innovation; Mises considered inflationary credit expansion to be inherently destabilizing and actually undermining sound economic development in the longer run.

In Chapter 9, "Money, economic fluctuations, expectations and period analysis: the Austrian and Swedish economists in the interwar period," the discussion turns to the similarities and differences in the approaches of the Austrian and Swedish Economists in the 1930s and 1940s. Both groups of economists had their ideas grounded in the earlier contributions of Eugen von Böhm-Bawerk and Knut Wicksell on capital, interest and money. In his earlier writings Erik Lindahl, in particular, followed an analysis paralleling that of Mises and Hayek on how monetary changes distorted relative sectors in the economy that are unsustainable. But Gunner Myrdal and Lindahl in his later writings moved in directions more in line with the macro approach developed by Keynes. The Swedes pioneered an emphasis on the role of expectations in market processes, but theirs was a mechanical "period analysis" that explained little about how expectations were formed. This leads us to Mises' formulation of a version of Max Weber's ideal types for understanding how actors construct and utilize expectations in market interactions.

Finally, Chapter 10, "Human action, ideal types, and the market process: Alfred Schutz and the Austrian economists," looks at the development of an "Austrian" theory of expectations and expectations-formation. It explains the limits of the Neo-Classical economic approach to the problem of understanding market coordination, and discusses the particular dynamic subjectivist approach in Mises and the Austrians that affords a better starting point for economic analysis. Mises' younger colleague, Alfred Schutz, developed Weber's conception of ideal typifications precisely for comprehending processes of interpersonal coordination, including in the market arena. I elaborate on Mises' and Schutz's ideas to tease out the logic of their arguments for a fuller economic application for understanding the workings of the market as a starting point for a possible "research program" for other Austrians.

It is hoped that through these chapters there will be a better understanding and appreciation for the unique contributions of one of the more original economists of the last one hundred years. Mises was the broad and general economic theorist who offered a grand vision of the nature and workings of the market system. But he was also an applied economist in the Austria of his time who dealt with some of the most momentous economic problems of modern times – runaway inflations, mismanaged socialist and interventionists systems, and the quagmire of a Great Depression. His work in this capacity has often not been known or fully appreciated, including what we may learn from it for our own economic times.

This most especially applies to issues surrounding business cycle crises and monetary theory and policy. Here, too, there was a unique originality to Mises' writings in developing a microeconomic process analysis for understanding the origins and phases of economic fluctuations. The resulting policy conclusions that Mises, Hayek and other Austrians reached in the 1930s may have been "defeated" by the emerging Keynesian Revolution. But they nonetheless point us in the direction of remembering that economy-wide economic stability is dependent upon microeconomic coordination that is easily overlooked when focusing only on the aggregated macroeconomic surface. The Austrian theory of money and the business cycle shows how monetary factors that distort interest rates from their market-determined levels potentially bring about an imbalance between savings and investment that can result in misdirections of capital, resources, and labor. Monetary influences do not only impact upon the general scale of prices, but upon the structure of relative prices as well, and this latter microeconomic process through time and across markets represents the real significance of the "non-neutrality of money" within the economy.

The "Austrian" method and approach, therefore, still offer valuable insights for the problems of economic theory and policy in the twenty-first century.

Notes

1 See, Richard M. Ebeling, *Austrian Economics and the Political Economy of Freedom* (Northampton, MA: Edward Elgar, 2003), Ch. 2: "The Significance of Austrian Economics in 20th Century Economic Thought," pp. 14–60; and Ludwig M. Lachmann, "The Significance of the Austrian School of Economics in the History of Ideas," [1966] reprinted in, Richard M. Ebeling, ed., *Austrian Economics a Reader* (Hillsdale, MI: Hillsdale College Press, 1990), pp. 17–39.

2 See, Richard M. Ebeling, "1914 and the World We Lost," *The Freeman: Ideas on Liberty* (June 2004), pp. 2–3.

3 See, for example, William Henry Chamberlin, *Collectivism: A False Utopia* (New York: Macmillan Co., 1936), pp. 1–2:

> Before the World War it would have seemed banal and superfluous to make out a case for human liberty, so far as North America and the greater part of Europe were concerned. Such things as regular elections, freedom of press and speech, security against arbitrary arrest, torture, and execution, were taken for granted in almost all leading countries. People could travel freely in foreign lands without worrying overmuch about passports and were not liable to be arrested by the police of one insolvent country if they failed to declare a few bills of the currency of its equally insolvent neighbor at the border. Concentration camps for political recalcitrants and the wholesale conscription of forced labor as a means of getting public works done were unknown ... It is an ironical sequel to the war that was supposed to safeguard the world for democracy that today the European picture is entirely different. The history of the postwar phase in Europe has been one of severe and unbroken defeats for the ideals of democracy and individual liberty. The revolutions of the twentieth century, unlike those of the eighteenth and nineteenth, have led to the contraction, not the expansion, of freedom. The two main governmental philosophies which have emerged since the war, fascism and communism, are based, in practice, on the most rigid regimentation of the individual.

Also, Ramsay Muir, "Civilization and Liberty," *Nineteenth Century and After* (September 1934), pp. 213–225.

4 William E. Rappard, "The Relation of the Individual to the State," *Annals of the American Academy of Political and Social Science* (January 1937), pp. 215–218:

> The revolutions at the end of the eighteenth century … were essentially revolts of the individual against the traditional state – expressions of his desire to emancipate himself from the ties and inhibitions which the traditional state had imposed on him … After the rise of individualism, which one may define as the emancipation of the individual from the state, we had the rise of democracy, which one may define as the subjection of the state to the will of the individual. In the latter half of the nineteenth century and up to the present, the individual, having emancipated himself from the state and having subjected the state to his will, has furthermore demanded of the state that it serve his material needs. Thereby he has complicated the machinery of the state to such a degree that he has again fallen under the subjection of it and he has been threatened with losing control over it … The individual has increasingly demanded of the state services which the state is willing to render. Thereby, however, he has been led to return to the state an authority over himself which it was the main purpose of the revolutions in the beginning of the nineteenth century to shake and break … The individual demanding that the state provide him with every security has thereby jeopardized his possession of that freedom for which his ancestors fought and bled.

5 On the meaning of and dangers from economic nationalism as understood as this time, see, T.E. Gregory, "Economic Nationalism," *International Affairs* (May 1931), pp. 289–306; Lionel Robbins, "The Economic Consequences of Economic Nationalism," *Lloyd's Bank Limited Review* (May 1936), pp. 226–239; William E. Rappard, "Economic Nationalism," in *Authority and the Individual, Harvard Tercentenary Conference of Arts and Sciences* (Cambridge, MA: Harvard University Press, 1937), pp. 74–112; and, Michael A. Heilperin, *Studies in Economic Nationalism* (Geneva: Liberaire E. Droz, 1962).

6 See, Moritz J. Bonn, "The Gold Standard in International Relations," in, William E. Rappard, ed., *Problems of Peace*, 8th Series [1934] (Freeport, NY: Books for Libraries, 1968), pp. 163–179; and T.E Gregory, *The Gold Standard and Its Future* (New York: E.P. Dutton, 1935), pp. 1–21.

7 See, Gustav Stolper, "Lessons of the World Depression," *Foreign Affairs*, Vol. 9, No. 2 (1931), pp. 244–245; and Stolper, "Politics versus Economics," *Foreign Affairs*, Vol. 12, No. 3 (1934), pp. 365–366.

8 See, J.B. Condliffe, "The Value of International Trade," *Economica* (May 1938), pp. 123–137; and Frederic Benham, "The Muddle of the Thirties," *Economica* (February 1945), pp. 1–9.

9 Ludwig von Mises, "Interventionism as the Causes of the Economic Crisis" [1932] in, Richard M. Ebeling, ed., *Selected Writings of Ludwig von Mises, Vol. 2: Between the Two World Wars: Monetary Disorder, Interventionism, Socialism, and the Great Depression* (Indianapolis, IN: Liberty Fund, 2002), p. 201.

10 As one of Mises' most thoughtful students, Israel M. Kirzner, pointed out in his introduction to the reprint of Mises' *The Ultimate Foundations to Economic Science: An Essay on Method* [1962] (Irvington-on-Hudson, NY: Foundation for Economic Education, 2002), p. xii:

> Mises would surely have conceded that his lifelong pursuit and teaching of economics was motivated by values, themselves necessarily outside the scope of science. Certainly these values included the intellectual's unreasoned passion for truth and the yearning of the lover of liberty for the free society. But Mises would have dismissed with proud (and deserved) contempt any questioning of the disinterestedness of his scientific conclusions. *Precisely because* he believed that economic science has a crucial role to play in the struggle for freedom,

Mises saw how necessary it is for the economist to be incorruptible in his disinterested pursuit of scientific truth … If economics is to fulfill its wholesome potential in the battle of ideas and ideologies, this can be made possible only by adhering rigorously to standards of intellectual honesty and objectivity impervious to corruption of any kind. Only in this way can we understand the apparently imperturbable calm with which Mises continued his own scientific work despite decades of inglorious academic neglect. Mises' austere scientific *Wertfreiheit* drew its source from the very passion with which he held to his basic convictions (Emphasis in the original).

11 As examples, the following passages from two of their American followers who were filled with that enthusiasm of having recently finished their graduate studies under the tutorship of leading members of the Historical School in Germany; first, Edwin R.A. Seligman, "Change in the Tenets of Political Economy with Time," *Science* (April 23, 1886), p. 375:

The modern school, the historical and critical school, holds that the economic theories of any generation must be regarded primarily as the outgrowth of the peculiar conditions of time, place, and nationality, under which the doctrines were evolved, and that no particular set of tenets can arrogate to itself the claim of immutable truth, or the assumption of universal applicability to all countries or epochs.

Second, Richard T. Ely, "The Past and the Present in Political Economy," *The Overland Monthly* (September 1883), pp. 233–234:

These [German] professors rejected, not merely a few incidental conclusions of the English school, but its method and assumptions, or major premises – that is to say, its very foundation. They took the name Historical School … Account is taken of time and place; historical surroundings and historical development are examined. Political economy … is not regarded as something fixed and unalterable, but as a growth and development, changing with society. It is found that the political economy of today is not the political economy of yesterday; while the political economy of Germany is not identical with that of England or America. All *a priori* doctrines or assumptions are cast aside, or at least their acceptance is postponed until external observation has proved them correct. The first thing is to gather facts. It has, indeed, been claimed that for an entire generation no attempt should be made to discover laws, but this is an extreme position … We must observe to theorize and theorize in order to observe."

On the German Historical School's view that the hallmark of statesmanship and economic policy should be pragmatism, expediency, and opportunism, see, Richard M. Ebeling, *Austrian Economics and the Political Economy of Freedom*, Ch. 7: "The Political Myths and Economic Realities of the Welfare State," pp. 179–202.

12 For summaries of the ideas of three prominent members of this direction in German thinking, see, Barth Landheer, "Othmar Spann's Social Theories," *Journal of Political Economy* (April 1931), pp. 239–248; Evalyn A. Clark, "Adolf Wagner: From National Economist to National Socialist" *Political Science Quarterly* (September 1940), pp. 378–411; and Abram L. Harris, "Sombart and German (National) Socialism," *Journal of Political Economy* (December 1942), pp. 805–835.

13 For a brief summary of the great German and Austrian inflations during and then after the Great War, see, Richard M. Ebeling, "The Lasting Legacies of World War I: Big Government, Paper Money and Inflation" *Economic Education Bulletin*, Vol. XLVIII, No. 11 (Great Barrington, MA: American Institute for Economic Research, November 2008).

1 Austrian economics and the political economy of freedom

The revival of the modern Austrian School of Economics may be said to have begun over thirty-five years ago, during the week of June 15–22, 1974, when the Institute for Humane Studies sponsored a conference on "Austrian Economics" for about forty participants in the small New England town of South Royalton, Vermont.

In 1974, the Austrian School had been in hiatus for almost a quarter of a century. During the more than sixty years before the 1940s, the Austrian Economists had been considered some of the most original contributors to economic theory and policy. They were among the leading developers of the theory of marginal utility, opportunity cost, value and price, capital and interest, markets and competition, money and business cycle theory, and comparative economic systems – capitalism versus socialism versus the interventionist-welfare state.

But the rise and then triumph in the late 1930s and 1940s of the Keynesian explanation of and policy prescription for the Great Depression eclipsed all competing approaches to the problems of economic depressions and high unemployment. This included the Austrian theory of the business cycle, which in the first half of the 1930s had been a leading alternative to the emerging Keynesian macroeconomics.[1]

At the same time, there developed what came to be called the Neo-Classical approach in microeconomics. The study of the logic of individual decision-making, the allocation of scarce resources among competing uses, and the distribution of income among the factors of production – land, labor and capital – became increasingly an exercise in mathematical optimization under conditions of various quantitative constraints. The focus of attention was on the specification and determination of the narrow and often highly artificial conditions under which a market economy might be in general equilibrium.

This, too, was in stark contrast to the approach of almost all of the Austrian economists, who attempted to explain the logic and processes of market competition in a world of constant change. The Austrians, unlike their Neo-Classical rivals, emphasized imperfect knowledge, the pervasive role of time in all market decision-making, and the nature of market coordination through continual adaptation to changing circumstances.[2]

Eight months before that conference in South Royalton, in October 1973, the most important contributor to Austrian economics in the twentieth century,

Ludwig von Mises, had died at the age of ninety-two.[3] The second most prominent member of the Austrian School at that time, Friedrich A. Hayek, had been invited to attend the conference, but had declined due to health problems that made it impossible for him to travel to America from Europe. No one at the conference anticipated that only four months later, in October 1974, Hayek would be awarded the Nobel Prize in Economics.[4]

The speakers at the conference were three other leading figures in Austrian economics: Ludwig M. Lachmann, who had studied with Hayek at the London School of Economics in the 1930s; Israel M. Kirzner, who had studied with and written his dissertation under Mises at the New York University in the late 1950s;[5] and Murray N. Rothbard, who had attended Mises' New York University seminar for many years beginning in the late 1940s and had received his doctoral degree in economics from Columbia University.

One evening during the conference, Milton Friedman came from his summer home in Vermont to join us for dinner and make a few remarks after the meal. Friedman commented that he was delighted to be with us and recalled he had long known both Mises and Hayek, having himself been one of the founding members of the Mont Pelerin Society and present at its first meeting in Switzerland in April 1947.[6] But what stood out in his remarks for many of us who were there was his statement that there is no such thing as different schools of thought in economics; there are only good economics and bad economics. Clearly, therefore, in Friedman's mind, we were on a fool's errand attending a conference on something called "Austrian" economics.

Acting man as the core of Austrian economics

Yet most of us attending that conference did not consider ourselves on a fool's errand. We just considered Austrian economics to be "good economics."[7] At its most fundamental level, Austrians see the individual as "acting man." This was already clearly stated by Ludwig von Mises in 1933:

> In our view the concept of man is, above all else, also the concept of the being who acts. Our consciousness is that of an ego which is capable of acting and does act. The fact that our deeds are intentional makes them actions. Our thinking about men and their conduct, and our conduct toward men and toward our surroundings in general presuppose the category of action.[8]

The Austrian view of man runs counter to the positivist, historicist, and Neo-Classical conceptions of man as a mere physical, quantitative object, or as a passive subject controlled by the dark forces of history, or as a "dependent variable" in a system of mathematical equations. Positivism tried to reduce man and his mind to merely magnitudes to be measured, studied and manipulated like the inanimate matter experimented on in some of the natural sciences. Historicism claimed that man is determined and molded by external laws of history that shape his thoughts, actions and destiny, with little latitude for the individual to design and guide his own future.[9] Neo-Classical Economics treats man as a mathematical function possessing given tastes and preferences, which are themselves induced by his surrounding environment and on the basis of which he responds in predictable ways when confronted with various constraining and objective trade-offs in the form of market prices.[10]

For Austrians, on the other hand, man is an intentional and purposeful being. He thinks, plans and acts. Man may be made up of matter, but he possesses consciousness. He has the capacity to imagine, create and initiate. His mind is not simply reducible to lifeless matter. He has spirit and will. Man reflects upon the circumstances in which he finds himself. He judges aspects of his physical and social surroundings less than satisfactory. He imagines states of affairs that would be more to his liking. He creates in his mind plans of action that would bring those preferred states of affairs into existence. He discovers that things in his world that he can use as means to the achievement of *some* of his ends are insufficient to achieve *all* his ends. He has to weigh the alternatives and decide in his own mind which of those possible states of affairs he prefers more and which he prefers less, since some of them, in the face of scarcity, will have be foregone for today or forever. He, therefore, has to decide on the trade-offs he is willing to make, and as a result he determines the costs of his own choices in the form of desired goals he is willing give up so as to pursue others that he considers more important.

Those "ends" and "means" that Neo-Classical Economics take as "given" are, in fact, created and compared in the actor's mind. They change and are modified as man experiences successes and failures. They are not static. Nor is man a hopeless victim or captive of history. He makes his own history by reflecting on what has happened in the past and mentally projecting himself into the future. He decides what past course of action is worth trying to continue and what might be a better course of action as he looks ahead.

Imperfect knowledge and market opportunities

This is why Mises insisted that in every man there is the element of entrepreneurship. In all his actions, man searches for and creates profitable opportunities to improve his lot and tries to avoid losses, that is, circumstances worse than they need to be. By necessity, man is therefore a speculator in everything he does.[11]

Creating profitable opportunities and avoiding losses are concepts that have no meaning in the traditional Neo-Classical conception of "perfect competition" in which every market participant is assumed to possess perfect or sufficient knowledge of all possibilities that might be relevant to his decisions. What is the meaning to "opportunities discovered" or "losses avoided" when the actors already know from the beginning what are the best and indeed the only optimal options that should be followed, given that perfect and sufficient knowledge of all relevant circumstances?[12]

From the Austrian perspective, to choose is to select from alternatives; and to select from alternatives must mean that, at least from the individual's perspective, the future is not preordained. If that future is not preordained, but can be

influenced by the choices he makes, then perfect knowledge is logically inconsistent with the very concept of acting and choosing man. Otherwise, man would
know already all the decisions he will make and their necessary outcomes. But
what then remains of any commonsensical notion of what it means for man to
choose?[13] Even if we assume only knowledge of objective probabilities and not
absolute certainties about the future, every man would still know what is the
precise set of options from which he has to choose and the exact weight he
should assign to each possible outcome; then, given his tastes and preferences
for risk, he would again know from the start the only courses of action he could
and should logically follow.[14]

Many Neo-Classical Economists may despair of a world in which imperfect
knowledge and uncertainty prevail, a world in which their mathematically deter-
ministic models lose their force. But for Austrians, this reality of the human condition is a reason for optimism about man and his world. The fact that man does
not know for certain what the future holds in store, including what his own
future actions may be, means that the world in which he lives is one of wondrous
possibility. Individuals have incentives to experiment with creative new ideas
precisely because they do not know for sure or with any probabilistic degree of
certainty how many of those ideas may actually turn out. It is this element of
uncertainty about the future that opens a vista for imagination and action to influence the shape of things-to-come – and through them all the advancements in the
social, economic and cultural condition of mankind.[15]

For the Neo-Classical Economists, the market is reduced to a series of simultaneous equations of supply-and-demand functions, the properties of which
specify whether a general equilibrium "solution" exists for the market as a
whole, and whether that solution is "unique" and "stable." Prices are the quantitative ratios of exchange at which goods may be bought and sold, and which
"objectify" the trade-offs at which alternatives in the market may be obtained.
Likewise, the theory of comparative advantage, in this Neo-Classical framework,
merely determines the relative opportunity costs of potential trading partners for
determination of their highest-valued roles in the division of labor. In addition,
property rights, money, and the social and political institutions are usually
treated as "givens," in Neo-Classical analysis. They are merely the background
in front of which the supply and demand functions interact.[16]

Minds, markets and the entrepreneur

For Austrians, the essence of the market is missed when reduced to a skeletal
representation in the form of mathematical functions. The market is where the
minds and the meanings of men meet. It is the place where the plans of multitudes of individuals overlap, enabling people mutually to improve their situations through discovered and created gains from trade. It is where the wants of
men find greater degrees of fulfillment and satisfaction than in isolated self-
sufficiency, and where achieving things never conceived of before is practicable.
In the Austrian conception of the market, prices are not simply quantitative ratios
of exchange; they are the encapsulation of the market participants' valuations

and appraisements, which result from their buying and selling.[17] Carl Menger, the founder of the Austrian School, expressed it in 1871,

> Prices ... are by no means the most fundamental feature of the economic phenomenon of exchange. This central feature lies rather in the better provision two persons can make for the satisfaction of their needs by trade ... Prices are only incidental manifestations of these activities, symptoms of an economic equilibrium between the economies of individuals, and consequently are of secondary interest for the economic subjects ... The force that drives [prices] to the surface is the ultimate and general cause of all economic activity, the endeavor of men to satisfy their needs as completely as possible, to better their economic positions.[18]

In Neo-Classical theory prices are usually taken as "given," with any changes in prices coming, somehow, from the "outside" and to which the market participants respond accordingly. In the Austrian approach, prices emerge out of the interactions of the market actors. They initiate price bids and offers, and competitively move prices up or down. In Eugen von Böhm-Bawerk's famous horse market, any resulting equilibrium between suppliers and demanders arises out of their efforts to attract trading partners by offering better terms of exchange than their rivals.[19]

Thus the Austrian focus is on *the logic and sequential process of price formation*, rather than only on any final equilibrium price that may result from this active market rivalry. It is why one prominent member of the Austrian School, in the period between the two world wars, referred to the Austrian theory of price as *the causal-genetic approach*: the purpose of the theory is to explain "causal origin" of prices in the valuations and actions of market actors, as well as the sequential changes and adjustments through time that may bring about a final equilibrium.[20]

The theory is also the basis for the later Austrian emphasis on the role and significance of the entrepreneur. In the division of labor, the entrepreneurs are not only the "undertakers of enterprise" who imagine the patterns of future consumer demand, conceive of ways of organizing production processes to better satisfy that demand, oversee the stages of production to the completion of finished goods, and then who bring the goods to market. They also set and change consumer prices on the market when they discover that they have over- or underestimated how intensely consumers want the goods.[21]

It is the "promoting and speculating entrepreneurs" who are "the driving force of the market," wrote Mises. Their "social function" is to coordinate the use of resources, capital, and labor with the demands of the consuming public through the rewards of profits and the penalties of losses.[22] Again, as Mises concisely put it,

> It is the entrepreneurial decision that creates either profit or loss. It is mental acts, the mind of the entrepreneur, from which profits ultimately originate. Profit is a product of the mind, of success in anticipating the future state of the market. It is a spiritual and intellectual phenomenon.[23]

The intentionality of entrepreneurship, the creative mental processes that are the essence of the enterpriser's activities, is drained of all understanding if the market is reduced to a simplified and barren mathematical functional form.

Economic calculation and the market process

The social institutions of private property and monetary exchange are not simply conceptual backdrops to the determination of equilibrium prices and outputs, as has tended to be the view in Neo-Classical Economics. In the standard text-books, from which most economists learn the core concepts of their discipline, private property is described as an "incentive mechanism" for work and the con-serving of scarce resources; and money is explained to be a "unit of account" that serves as a common denominator for comparing the value of goods bought and sold in the market. Both descriptions are true and important. But they fail to capture the institutions' profundity for the functioning and coordinating of the complex and ever-changing market order.

Private property and money are, instead, the core – the indispensable features – of the market economy and the civilization that develops with it. The evolution of private property rights and a medium of exchange has made possible the eco-nomic calculation without which rational market decision-making would be impossible. And, again, it is Mises who has articulated this most clearly:

> Monetary calculation is the guiding star of action under the social system of division of labor. It is the compass of the man embarking upon production. He calculates in order to distinguish the remunerative lines of production from the unprofitable ones ... Monetary calculation is the main vehicle of planning and acting in the social setting of a society of free enterprise directed and controlled by the market and prices ... We can view the whole market of material factors of production and of labor as a public auction. The bidders are the entrepreneurs. Their highest bids are limited by their expectation of the prices the consumers will be ready to pay for the products ... The competition between the entrepreneurs reflects these prices of con-sumers' goods in the formation of the prices of the factors of production ... To the entrepreneur of capitalist society a factor of production through its price, sends out a warning: Don't touch me, I am earmarked for the satisfac-tion of another, more urgent need.[24]

Only private property enables all marketable commodities and means of pro-duction to be open for sale and purchase in the arena of exchange. Only a medium of exchange provides the means by which all the heterogeneous com-modities and supplies on the market may be reduced to a valuational common denominator. Only the competitive market enables every participant in the society to contribute to the formation of prices through his bids and offers.[25] Only economic calculation enables the integration of billions of people's actions in a global network of mutually beneficial market relationships and coordinated plans.

Yet every man is free to make his own decisions, guided by his own hopes, dreams, goals and plans. The money prices that make economic calculation possible are used by each individual for his own purposes. He weighs their significance and relevance for the ends he has in mind. He uses them to evaluate his past actions and plan his future actions.[26] He is at liberty to integrate himself in the division of labor on the basis of his own evaluations of the costs and benefits of alternative courses of action – while bearing the consequences, for good or ill, for the choices he makes.

It is through economic calculation in the free market that individual freedom is made compatible with social order. It is through economic calculation that billions of individual plans are combined into patterns of rational social coordination. No wonder that Mises concluded that "Our civilization is inseparably linked with our methods of economic calculation. It would perish if we were to abandon this most precious intellectual tool of acting."[27]

The "law of association" as the foundation of society

In a similar fashion, the Austrians see more in the theory of division of labor and comparative advantage than simply the determination of the specialization of tasks at various relative prices, given the quantities of capital and labor available. Once again, it was Ludwig von Mises who insightfully clarified the implications of the eighteenth and nineteenth century Classical Economists' views on the benefits from a system of division of labor. The theory of comparative advantage, Mises explained, is really the basis of what he called the *law of human association* and therefore the foundation of a theory of society. Based on Adam Smith's and David Ricardo's expositions of the benefits from specialization, it was possible to show how society emerged and had taken form over the centuries as the result of individuals discovering the mutual benefits from trade.[28] The additional gains through specialization resulted in an expanding network of interdependent human relationships. The theory of the division of labor, therefore, is able to serve as the analytical tool for explaining the emergence of society as the result of human actions but not of any prior human design. As Mises explained this process:

> The law of association makes us comprehend the tendencies that resulted in the progressive intensification of human cooperation. We conceive what incentive induced people to not consider themselves simply as rivals in a struggle for the appropriation of limited supplies of means of subsistence made available by nature. We realize what has impelled them and permanently impels them to consort with one another for the sake of cooperation ... Thus we are in a position to comprehend the course of human evolution.[29]

The theory of division of labor and comparative advantage become the basis for a "science of society." A foundation is laid for the theory of market relationships, the interconnections between supply and demand, and the network of market prices for finished goods and the factors of production. The way is opened to an understanding of the "inevitable laws of the market and exchange," which is "one of the greatest achievements of the human mind."[30]

Out of the Classical Economists' theory of division of labor there now comes the Classical Liberal "philosophy of peace and social cooperation" that is the basis "for the astonishing development of the economic civilization of [our] age."[31] The greater material productivity of a peaceful division of labor, Mises explained, provides the means for the development of what we call civilization. The means are now provided that enable leisure and the peace of mind required for art, literature, and scientific and philosophic reflection.

Men increasingly become differentiated from each other, but not only in the specialized tasks and skills through which they find their place in the division of labor. They also differentiate themselves by developing their distinct individual personalities thanks to the greater abundance of resources and free time with which they can cultivate the pursuits that most interest them. Individualism, meaning man as distinct from the tribal mass and unique in his character and qualities as a singular human being, is a product of the evolution of society through the extension and intensification of the system of division of labor.[32]

At the same time, the division of labor and its law of association becomes the foundation for a social philosophy of world peace. In the collaborative efforts of interdependent specialization and exchange men become allies against the niggardliness of nature. No longer are individuals and nations opponents, where the improvement of one requires a loss to another. Instead, all benefit from everyone's talents, industry, and creativity.

Competition, both within and between nations, is no longer a life-and-death struggle for survival. The competitive market process becomes the peaceful procedure through which each member of society finds his most productive and profitable niche for improving his own circumstances by furthering the ends of others. Again, Mises captured the essence of this great social process:

> All collaborate and cooperate, each in the particular role he has chosen for himself in the framework of the division of labor. Competing in cooperation and cooperating in competition all people are instrumental in bringing about the result, viz., the price structure of the market, the allocation of the factors of production to the various lines of want-satisfaction, and the determination of the share of each individual.[33]

The world, therefore, becomes one integrated community of free men who, though separated by time, distance and interest, are peacefully guided to assist one another by the information and incentives supplied by the global structure of market prices. People's buying and selling determines the patterns of production and the allocation of the means of production that best serve the wants and needs of humanity. The value that all of us place on the productive services that each individual performs in the market process determines the relative income he earns, so he in turn can obtain from others what he desires to buy as a consumer. The market economy thus is the means that gives reality to the peaceful unity of mankind.

The political economy of freedom

None of these Austrian insights about man and the market is compatible with the positivist, historicist, and Neo-Classical Economic views of the world. Reduced to physical object or mathematical function, man is stripped of his most essential human qualities. What are intention and imagination, choice and creativity, if the human mind is banished from the realm of social and economic analysis? What meaning, therefore, does freedom have when man is merely a measured magnitude or a dependent variable in a system of simultaneous equations?

It should not be surprising that so many members of the Austrian School of Economics have also been Classical Liberals – defenders of individual liberty, private property and the market economy. Once you see the individual as a thinking, creating, and acting man, with so many potentials within him, who can tolerate the idea of making him the slave to another's will – of denying him his humanness? Once you comprehend the majesty of the market order, in which each man is free to follow his own purposes and plans, while advancing the welfare of others, who would want to restrict him to the dictates of a central planner or political intervener? Once you understand the significance of prices for social coordination within the market process, who can presume to have the knowledge and ability to command humanity's consumption and production?[34]

It is no wonder, therefore, that so many of freedom's friends have been influenced by the contributions of the Austrian Economists. For almost a century and a half they have been the true political economists of liberty. The Austrian School of Economics has enriched our understanding of the market economy and advanced the cause of freedom in our time.

Notes

1 For an exposition and contrast of the Austrian and Keynesian explanations of and policy prescriptions for the Great Depression of the 1930s, see, Ch. 7: "The Austrian Economists and the Keynesian Revolution: The Great Depression and the Economics of the Short Run" in the present volume. See, also, Richard M. Ebeling, "John Maynard Keynes: The Damage Still Done by a Defunct Economist," *The Freeman: Ideas on Liberty* (May 2006), pp. 2–3; and Richard M. Ebeling, "Henry Hazlitt and the Failure of Keynesian Economics," *The Freeman: Ideas on Liberty* (November 2004), pp. 15–19.

2 For an overview of many of the theoretical and policy themes in the writings of the Austrian Economists, see, Richard M. Ebeling, *Austrian Economics and the Political Economy of Freedom* (Northampton, MA: Edward Elgar, 2003), Ch. 2: "The Significance of Austrian Economics in 20th Century Economic Thought," pp. 34–60; also, Ludwig M. Lachmann, "The Significance of the Austrian School of Economics in the History of Ideas" [1966] reprinted in, Richard M. Ebeling, ed., *Austrian Economics: A Reader* (Hillsdale, MI: Hillsdale College Press, 1991), pp. 17–39.

3 For expositions of Mises' many contributions to economic theory and policy, see, Richard M. Ebeling, "A Rational Economist in an Irrational Age: Ludwig von Mises," *Austrian Economics and the Political Economy of Freedom*, pp. 61–100; also, see, Ch. 6: "Planning for Freedom: Ludwig von Mises as Political Economist and Policy Analyst," and Ch. 5, "The Economist as the Historian of Decline: Ludwig von Mises and Austria Between the Two World Wars," in the present volume. In addition, Murray N. Rothbard, *Ludwig von Mises: Scholar, Creator, Hero* (Auburn, AL: Ludwig von Mises Institute, 1988); and Israel M. Kirzner, *Ludwig von Mises* (Wilmington, DE: ISI Books, 2001).

4 For a summary of Hayek's life and contributions to economics, see, Richard M. Ebeling, "Friedrich A. Hayek: A Centenary Appreciation," *The Freeman: Ideas on Liberty* (May 1999), pp. 28–32; also, Bruce Caldwell, *Hayek's Challenge: An Intellectual Biography of F.A. Hayek* (Chicago: University of Chicago Press, 2004).

5 For a summary of Kirzner's contributions to Austrian Economics, see, Richard M. Ebeling, "Israel M. Kirzner and the Austrian Theory of Competition and Entrepreneurship" *Freedom Daily* (August 2001), pp. 8–14.

6 See, R.M. Hartwell, *A History of the Mont Pelerin Society* (Indianapolis, IN: Liberty Fund, 1995).

7 For a summary of the conference's events, see, Richard M. Ebeling, "Austrian Economics on the Rise," *Libertarian Forum* (October 1974), pp. 3–6; the lectures delivered by Lachmann, Kirzner and Rothbard at South Royalton were later published in Edwin G. Dolan, ed., *The Foundations of Modern Austrian Economics* (Kansas City, KS: Sheed & Ward, 1976).

8 Ludwig von Mises, *Epistemological Problems of Economics* [1933] (New York: New York University Press, 1981), p. 14.

9 One of Ludwig von Mises' most insightful but unfortunately highly neglected works was devoted to critically evaluating the assumptions and absurdities in both positivism and historicism; see, Ludwig von Mises, *Theory and History: An Interpretation of Social and Economic Evolution* [1957] (Auburn, AL: Ludwig von Mises Institute, 1985); also, F.A. Hayek, *The Counter-Revolution of Science* [1955] (Indianapolis, IN: Liberty Fund, 1980); and Murray N. Rothbard, *Individualism and the Philosophy of the Social Sciences* (San Francisco, CA: Cato Institute, 1979).

10 For a contrast of the Austrian and Neo-Classical conceptions of man in relation to action and choice, see, Richard M. Ebeling, *Austrian Economics and the Political Economy of Freedom*, pp. 3–7.

11 Ludwig von Mises, *Human Action: A Treatise on Economics* (Irvington-on-Hudson, NY: Foundation for Economic Education, 1996), p. 254: "Entrepreneur means acting man in regard to the changes occurring in the data of the market." And Mises, *The Ultimate Foundations of Economic Science* [1962] (Irvington-on-Hudson, NY: Foundation for Economic Education, 2002), p. 51: "Every action is a speculation, i.e., guided by a definite opinion concerning the uncertain conditions of the future."

12 For the classic Austrian criticisms of the Neo-Classical mathematical general equilibrium approach, and the theory of perfect competition, see, Hans Mayer, "The Cognitive Value of Functional Theories of Price" [1932] in Israel M. Kirzner, ed., *Classics of Austrian Economics: A Sampling in the History of a Tradition* (London: William Pickering, 1994), pp. 55–168; F.A. Hayek, "The Meaning of Competition" [1946] *Individualism and Economic Order* (Chicago: University of Chicago Press, 1948), pp. 92–106; Ludwig von Mises, *Human Action: A Treatise on Economics*, pp. 350–357, and Mises, "Comments on the Mathematical Treatment of Economic Problems," [1953] *Journal of Libertarian Studies*, Vol. I No. 2 (1977), pp. 97–100.

13 See, Richard M. Ebeling, "Freedom and the Pitfalls of Predicting the Future," *The Freeman: Ideas on Liberty* (June 2006), pp. 2–3.

14 For a very insightful analysis of the assumptions and inescapable limits to both general equilibrium theory and statistical probability theory in economics, see, Jack High, *Maximizing, Action, and Market Adjustment: An Inquiry into the Theory of Economic Disequilibrium* (Munich: Philosophia Verlag, 1990).

15 Mises, *Human Action*, p. 105:

> The uncertainty of the future is already implied in the very notion of action. That man acts and that the future is uncertain are by no means two independent matters. They are only two different modes of establishing one thing.

16 It should be pointed out that there has developed what is now referred to as the "new institutional economics" that attempts to explain the emergence, evolution and significance of the underlying institutional order in which market processes actually operate.

And some of these economists have consciously incorporated elements of the Austrian perspective in their theories; see, especially, Wolfgang Kasper and Manfred E. Steit, *Institutional Economics: Social Order and Public Policy* (Northampton, MA: Edward Elgar, 1998), and, also, Eirik G. Furubotn and Rudolf Richter, *Institutions and Economic Theory: The Contribution of the New Institutional Economics* (Ann Arbor: University of Michigan Press, 1998).

17 Mises, *Human Action*, pp. 327–333.

18 Carl Menger, *Principles of Economics* [1871] (New York: New York University Press, 1981), pp. 191–192; and Menger, *Grundsätze der Volkswirtschaftslehre* (Vienna: Holder-Pichler-Tempsky, 2nd ed., 1923), pp. 182–183.

19 Eugen von Böhm-Bawerk, *Capital and Interest, Vol. 2: The Positive Theory of Capital* (South Holland, IL: Libertarian Press, 1959), pp. 115–124.

20 Hans Mayer, "The Cognitive Value of Functional Theory of Price" [1932], p. 57.

21 See the much neglected analysis on this point by Philip Wicksteed, *The Common Sense of Political Economy* [1910], Vol. 1 (London: Routledge & Kegan Paul, 1933), pp. 212–237.

22 Mises, *Human Action*, pp. 328–329.

23 Ludwig von Mises, "Profit and Loss," [1951] in his *Planning for Freedom* (South Holland, IL: Libertarian Press, 1980), p. 120.

24 Mises, *Human Action*, pp. 229–230; Ludwig von Mises, *Bureaucracy* [1944] (New Rochelle, NY: Arlington House, 1969), pp. 28–29.

25 Ludwig von Mises, *Liberalism in the Classical Tradition* [1927] (Irvington-on-Hudson, NY: Foundation for Economic Education, 1985), pp. 71–72, 75:

> This is the decisive objection that economics raises against the possibility of a socialist society. It must forego the intellectual division of labor that consists in the cooperation of all entrepreneurs, landowners, and workers as producers and consumers in the formation of market prices. But without it, rationality, i.e., the possibility of economic calculation, is unthinkable.

26 Mises, *Human Action*, p. 229:

> Monetary calculation is entirely inapplicable and useless for any consideration which does not look at things from the point of view of individuals ... The premeditation of planned action becomes commercial pre-calculation of expected costs and expected proceeds. The retrospective establishment of the outcome of past action becomes accounting of profit and loss.

27 Mises, *Human Action*, p. 230.

28 Adam Smith, *The Wealth of Nations* [1776] (New York: The Modern Library, 1937) Book I, Chapters 1–3, pp. 3–21; Piero Sraffa, ed., *The Works and Correspondence of David Ricardo, Vol. I: On the Principles of Political Economy and Taxation* [1821] (Cambridge: Cambridge University Press, 1951), pp. 128–149; Jean-Baptiste Say, *A Treatise on Political Economy, or the Production, Distribution, and Consumption of Wealth* [1821] (New York: Augustus M. Kelley, 1971), pp. 90–99; John R. McCulloch, *The Principles of Political Economy, with Some Inquiries Respecting Their Applications* [1864] (New York: Augustus M. Kelley, 1965), pp. 37–46, 85–116.

29 Mises, *Human Action*, pp. 160–161.

30 Ludwig von Mises, *Interventionism: An Economic Analysis* [1941] (Irvington-on-Hudson, NY: Foundation for Economic Education, 1998), p. 24.

31 Ludwig von Mises, *Socialism: An Economic and Sociological Analysis* [1922] (Indianapolis, IN: Liberty Classics, 1981), pp. 55–56, 268–269.

32 Mises, *Socialism*, pp. 256–272; *Human Action*, 157–174.

33 Mises, *Human Action*, p. 338.

34 See, F.A. Hayek, "The Use of Knowledge in Society," [1945] *Individualism and Economic Order*, pp. 77–91; reprinted in, Richard M. Ebeling, ed., *Austrian Economics: A Reader*, pp. 247–263.

2 Ludwig von Mises
Political economist of liberty

Over a professional career that spanned almost three-quarters of the twentieth century, Austrian economist, Ludwig von Mises, was without any exaggeration one of the leading and most important defenders of economic liberty. The ideas of individual freedom, the market economy, and limited government that he defended in the face of the rising tide of socialism, fascism, and the interventionist welfare state have had few champions as clear and persuasive as Mises. He was the most comprehensive and consistent critic of all forms of modern collectivism. Furthermore, his numerous writings on the political, economic, and social principles of classical liberalism and the market order remain as fresh and relevant as when he penned them decades ago.[1]

Born in the city of Lemberg in the old Austro-Hungarian Empire on September 29, 1881, Mises came from a prominent family of Jewish merchants and businessmen. His great-grandfather, Mayer Rachmiel Mises, was honored with a nobility title for his service to the Emperor, Francis Joseph, as a leader of the Jewish community in Lemberg, a few months before Ludwig was born.[2]

Ludwig's father, Arthur, moved his family to Vienna in the early 1890s where he worked as a civil engineer for the Imperial railway system. Ludwig attended one of the city's leading academic *gymnasiums* as preparation for university studies. He entered the University of Vienna in 1900, and received his doctoral degree in jurisprudence in 1906. In 1909, he was employed by the Vienna Chamber of Commerce, Crafts, and Industry, and continued to work at the Chamber as a senior economic analyst until he left Vienna in 1934 to accept a full-time teaching position at the Graduate Institute of International Studies in Geneva, Switzerland. Besides his work at the Chamber, Mises also taught at the University of Vienna, led an internationally renowned interdisciplinary private seminar, and founded the Austrian Institute for Business Cycle Research in 1927, with a young Friedrich A. Hayek as its first director.[3]

It was during his years in Geneva, between 1934 and 1940, that Mises wrote his greatest work in economics, the German-language version of what became in English, *Human Action: A Treatise on Economics*.[4] In the summer of 1940, as the Nazi war machine was finishing its conquest of Western Europe, Mises and his wife made their way to the United States from Switzerland, where he spent the rest his life continuing his writings and also teaching for most of those years at New York University, until his death on October 10, 1973 at the age of ninety-two.

In addition, in both Vienna between the two world wars and then again in post-World War II America, Mises demonstrated a unique ability to attract intellectually creative students around him, thus fostering new generations of scholars to continue the ideas of the Austrian School of Economics.[5]

Ludwig von Mises and the historical context of his time

An appreciation of Mises' defense of freedom requires an understanding of the political and ideological trends of the first half of the twentieth century. Throughout most of the nineteenth century, "liberalism" had meant belief in and devotion to personal freedom, constitutionally limited government, the sanctity of private property, as well as freedom of enterprise at home and free trade among the nations of the world.

But even before the Great War many of those who labeled themselves "liberals" were in fact advocates of what a few decades earlier had been called "state socialism" in prewar Imperial Germany. For almost forty years before World War I, many of the leading German economists, historians, and political scientists – who became widely known as members of the German Historical School – had argued that the socialists had been correct in their criticisms of free-market capitalism. The unregulated market, they said, resulted in an exploitation of the workers and a disregard of the "national interest." Where the socialists had gone wrong, they insisted, was in their radical demand for a revolutionary overthrow of the entire existing social order.

What Germany needed instead, they stated, was "state socialism," under which social reforms would be introduced to ameliorate the supposed "excesses" of unbridled laissez faire. The German Historical School supported and encouraged the imposition of the modern welfare state by the German "Iron Chancellor," Otto von Bismarck, in the 1880s and 1890s. Socialized medicine, state-managed old-age pensions, minimum-wage laws, and government-sponsored public housing and recreational facilities would provide "cradle to grave" security for the "working classes," and would thus lure them away from the more radical proposals of the Marxian socialists.[6]

At the same time, government regulation of industry and agriculture through tariffs, cartels, and subsidies, as well as production and price controls, would assure that the activities of the "capitalist class" would be harnessed to what the political authorities considered to be in the "national interest," especially in the preparation for inevitable and desirable wars of conquest and global power. Pragmatism and expediency in all economic and social policy decisions were hailed as the highest forms of political wisdom and "statesmanship," in place of "inflexible" constitutional restraints that limited the discretionary power for government intervention.

Members of the German Historical School argued that old-fashioned classical liberalism had been purely "negative" in its understanding of freedom, and in advocating that government's role was simply to secure the life, liberty, and property of the citizenry from violence, aggression, and fraud. Government, they said, had to be more "positive" and active in providing social safety nets for the masses against the uncertainties of life. Hence, they and their "progressive" followers in England, France, and especially the United States soon were referring to their ideas as a newer and more-enlightened "liberalism," which would create a truer and more complete "freedom" from want and worry.[7] The concept of liberalism, most particularly in the United States, was changing from a political and economic philosophy of individual liberty and free enterprise under the rule of law and limited government, to a notion of political paternalism with an increasingly intrusive hand of government in the social and commercial affairs of its citizens.[8]

The last decades of the nineteenth century also saw the growth of two other modern forms of collectivism: socialism and nationalism. Their common premise was that the individual and his interests were always potentially in conflict with the best interests of society as a whole. The Marxists claimed to have discovered the inescapable "laws of history," which demonstrated that the emergence of the division of labor and private property split society into inherently antagonistic social "classes." Those who owned the means of production earned rent and profit by extracting a portion of the wealth produced by the non-owning workers whom the owners of productive property employed in agriculture and industry.

Eventually, this class conflict would lead, through a process of historical evolution, to a radical and revolutionary change in which the workers would rise up and expropriate the property of the capitalists. After having socialized the means of production, the new workers' state would introduce central planning in place of the previous decentralized and profit-oriented production plans of the now expropriated capitalists. Socialist central planning, it was claimed, would generate a level of production and a rising standard of living far exceeding anything experienced during the "capitalist phase" of human history. This process would culminate in a "post-scarcity" world in which all of man's wants and wishes would be fully satisfied, with selfishness and greed abolished from the face of the earth.[9]

The proponents of aggressive nationalism, among whom were many of the members of the German Historical School, argued that there was, indeed, an inherent conflict among men in the world.[10] This antagonism, however, was not based on social classes as the Marxian socialists defined them. Instead, these conflicts were between nations and national groups. Unfortunately, the nationalist ideologues said, individuals within nations often acted in ways inconsistent with the best interests of the nation to which they belonged. Thus the particular interests of businessmen, workers, and those in various professional groups had to be regulated and controlled for the furtherance of the greater national good. As a result, aggressive nationalism dovetailed – especially, though certainly not exclusively, in Imperial Germany – with the interventionist and welfare-statist policies of state socialism and the newer "progressive" liberalism.

Commercial and military conflict between the nations of the world was inevitable in the eyes of these nationalists. The prosperity of any one nation could only come at the expense of other nations. Hence, the task of all national statesmen was to foster the power and triumph of their own national group through the conquest and impoverishment of others around the world. Since no nation would willingly accept its own political and material destruction, war was an inescapable aspect of the human condition. Militarism and the martial spirit were likewise hailed as both necessary and superior to the "individualistic" and "pacifistic" spirit of production and trade.[11]

The culmination of these collectivist tendencies was the outbreak of World War I in 1914, an analysis of the causes and consequences of which Ludwig von Mises offered in his 1919 volume, *Nation, State, and Economy*.[12] The Great War, as it was called, not only brought forth the triumph of the nationalistic spirit; it also saw the imposition of various forms of socialist central planning as virtually all the belligerent nations either nationalized or thoroughly controlled private industry and agriculture in the name of the wartime national emergency. The governments at war also established welfare-statist rationing and regulation of all consumer production since the needs of total war required total state responsibility for the supposed well-being of entire populations.

Out of the ashes of the Great War there arose new totalitarian states, first with the establishment of a communist dictatorship in Russia following the Bolshevik Revolution of 1917 under Lenin's leadership, and then with the rise to power of Mussolini and his Fascist Party in Italy in 1922. Both the communists and the fascists rejected the ideas and the institutions of classical liberalism. Constitutional government, the rule of law, civil liberties, and economic freedom were declared by both these variations on the collectivist theme as reactionary hindrances to the success of, respectively, the worker's state in Soviet Russia and national greatness in Fascist Italy. Both communism and fascism insisted that the individual needed to be "reeducated" and made to conform to the wider socialist or nationalist good. The individual was to be reduced to a cog in the machinery of the all-powerful and all-planning state.[13]

Germany's defeat in the war had resulted in political and economic chaos, which culminated in the disastrous hyperinflation of the early 1920s.[14] Many of the social and cultural anchors of German society were torn away by the war and the inflation.[15] A growing number of Germans longed for a "Leader" to guide them out of the morass of political instability and economic hardship. In 1925, Mises analyzed these trends in Germany and concluded that they were leading the German people toward a "national socialism," instead of either classical liberalism or Marxian socialism.[16] Anticipating the triumph of Hitler and his National Socialist (Nazi) movement in 1933, Mises warned in 1926 that many Germans were "setting their hopes on the coming of the 'strong man' – the tyrant who will think for them and care for them."[17]

In later years, Mises emphasized that while the Marxists in the Soviet Union used the tools of central planning to culturally redesign a socialist "new man" through various methods of indoctrination and thought control, the National Socialists in Nazi Germany took this a step further with their scheme of centrally planning the racial breeding of a new "master race."[18]

Capitalism, socialism, and interventionism

This was the historical context in which Mises published some of his most important works in the period between the two world wars: *Socialism*, (1922) *Liberalism* (1927) and *Critique of Interventionism* (1929). The task he set himself was to offer a radically different vision of man in society from that presented by the socialists, nationalists, and interventionists. In place of their starting premise of inescapable conflicts among men in terms of "social class," nationality and race, or narrow group interest, Mises insisted that reason and experience demonstrated that all men could associate in peace for their mutual material and cultural betterment. The key to this was an understanding and appreciation of the benefits of a division of labor. Through specialization and trade the human race has the capacity to lift itself up from both poverty and war.

Men become associates in a common process of social cooperation, instead of antagonists with each attempting to rule over and plunder the others. Indeed, all that we mean by modern civilization, and the material and cultural comforts and opportunities that it offers man, is due to the highly productive benefits and advantages made possible by a division of labor. Men participated in this associative collaboration in the arena of competitive market exchange.

The confusion, Mises pointed out, is the failure to view this cooperative social process from a longer-run perspective than the changing circumstances of everyday life. In the rivalries of the market, there are always some who earn profits and others who suffer losses in the interactive and competitive processes of supply and demand. But what needs to be understood is that these changes in the short-run fortunes of various participants in the division of labor are the method through which each participant is informed and nudged into either doing more of some things or less of others. This process brings about the necessary adjustment of society's productive activities in order to assure that they tend to match and reflect the market pattern of consumer demand.[19]

Of course, political force can be substituted for the "reward" of profits and the "punishment" of losses. However, the costs of this substitution are extremely high, Mises argued. First, men are less motivated to apply themselves with intelligence and industry when forced to work under the lash of servitude and compulsion, and thus society loses what their free efforts and invention might have produced.[20] Second, men are forced to conform to the values and goals of those in command, and thus they lose the liberty of following their own ends and purposes, with no certainty that those who rule over them know better what may give them happiness and meaning in life.

And, third, socialist central planning and political intervention in the market, respectively, abolish or distort the functioning of social cooperation. A sustained and extended system of specialization for mutual improvement is only possible under a unique set of social and economic institutions. Without private ownership in the means of production, the coordination of multitudes of individual activities in the division of labor is impossible. Indeed, Mises' analysis of the "impossibility" of a socialist order being able to match the efficiency and productivity of a free market economy was the basis for his international stature and reputation as one of the most original economists of his time, and was the center-piece of his book on *Socialism.*[21]

Private ownership and competitive market exchange enable the formation of prices for both consumer goods and the factors of production, expressed in the common denominator of a medium of exchange – money. On the basis of these money prices, entrepreneurs can engage in economic calculation to determine the relative costs and profitability of alternative lines of production. Without these market-generated prices, there would be no rational way to allocate resources among their competing uses to assure that those goods most highly valued by the buying public were produced in the least-costly and therefore most economical manner. Economic calculation, Mises demonstrated, guarantees that the scarce means available are utilized to best serve the ends of the members of society.

Such rationality in the use of means to satisfy ends is impossible in a compre-hensive system of socialist central planning. How, Mises asked, will the socialist planners know the best uses for which the factors of production under their central control should be applied without such market-generated money prices? Without private ownership of the means of production there would be nothing (legally) to buy and sell. Without the ability to buy and sell, there will be no bids and offers, and therefore no haggling over terms of trade among competing buyers and sellers. Without the haggling of market competition there would, of course, be no agreed-upon terms of exchange. Without agreed-upon terms of exchange, there are no actual market prices. And without such market prices, how will the central planners know the opportunity costs and therefore the most highly valued uses for which those resources could or should be applied? With the abolition of private property, and therefore market exchange and prices, the central planners would lack the necessary institutional and informational tools to determine what to produce and how, in order to minimize waste and inefficiency.

Socialists and many non-socialist economists claimed over the decades that Mises was "wrong," when he said that Socialism was "impossible." They pointed to the Soviet Union and said it existed and operated. However in numer-ous places in his various writings, beginning from the early 1920s, Mises insisted that he was not saying that a socialist system could not exist. Of course, the factors of production could be nationalized and a central planning agency could be delegated the responsibility to direct all the production activities of the society.

But any supposed rationality and seeming degree of efficiency observed in the workings of the Soviet and similar socialist economies was due to the fact that such socialist planning systems existed in a world in which there were still functioning market societies. The existing market economies provided various "shadow prices" that the socialist planners could try to use as proxies and bench-marks for evaluating their own allocation and production decisions. However, since the actual economic circumstances in such a socialist economy would never be an exact duplicate of the conditions in the neighboring market societies – resources availabilities, labor skills, the quantity and qualities of capital equipment, the fertility and variety of land, the patterns of consumer demand – such proxy prices could never completely "solve" the economic calculation problem for the socialist planners in places like the Soviet Union.[22]

Therefore, Mises declared in 1931,

> From the standpoint of both politics and history, this proof [of the "impossibility" of socialist planning] is certainly the most important discovery by economic theory ... It alone will enable future historians to understand how it came about that the victory of the socialist movement did not lead to the creation of the socialist order of society.[23]

At the same time, Mises demonstrated the inherent inconsistencies in any system of piecemeal political intervention in the market economy. Price controls and production restrictions on entrepreneurial decision-making bring about distortions and imbalances in the relationships of supply and demand, as well as constraints on the most efficient use of resources in the service of consumers. The political intervener is left with the choice of either introducing new controls and regulations in an attempt to compensate for the distortions and imbalances the prior interventions have caused, or repealing the interventionist controls and regulations already in place and allowing the market once again to be free and competitive. The path of one set of piecemeal interventions followed by another entails a logic in the growth of government that eventually would result in the entire economy coming under state management. Hence, interventionism consistently applied could lead to socialism on an incremental basis.[24]

The most pernicious form of government intervention, in Mises' view, was political control and manipulation of the monetary system. Contrary to both the Marxists and the Keynesians, Mises did not consider the fluctuations experienced over the business cycle to be an inherent and inescapable part of the free market economy. Waves of inflations and depressions were the product of political intervention in money and banking. And this included the Great Depression of the 1930s, Mises argued.

Under various political and ideological pressures, governments had monopolized control over the monetary system. They used the ability to create money out of thin air through the printing press or on the ledger books of the banks to finance government deficits and to artificially lower interest rates to stimulate unsustainable investment booms. Such monetary expansions always tended to distort market prices resulting in misdirections of resources, including labor, and malinvestments of capital. The inflationary upswing that is caused by an artificial expansion of money and bank credit sets the stage for an eventual economic downturn. By distorting the rate of interest, the market price for borrowing and lending, the monetary authority throws savings and investment out of balance, with the need for an inevitable correction. The "depression" or "recession" phase of the business cycle occurs when the monetary authority either slows downs or stops any further increases in the money supply. The imbalances and distortions become visible, with some investment projects having to be written down or written off as losses, with reallocations of labor and other resources to alternative more profitable employments, and sometimes significant adjustments and declines in wages and prices to bring supply and demand back into proper order.[25]

The Keynesian Revolution of the 1930s, which then dominated economic policy discussions for decades following World War II, was based on a fundamental misconception of how the market economy worked, in Mises' view. What Keynes called "aggregate demand failures," to explain the reason for high and prolonged unemployment, distracted attention away from the real source of less than full employment: the failure of producers and workers on the "supply-side" of the market to price their products and labor services at levels that potential demanders would be willing to pay. Unemployment and idle resources were a pricing problem, not a demand management problem. Mises considered Keynesian Economics basically to be nothing more than a rationale for special interest groups, such as trade unions, who didn't want to adapt to the reality of supply and demand and what the market viewed as their real worth.[26]

Thus Mises' conclusion from his analysis of socialism and interventionism, including monetary manipulation, was that there is no alternative to a thoroughgoing unhampered free-market economy, and one that included a market-based monetary system such as the gold standard.[27] Both socialism and interventionism are, respectively, unworkable and unstable substitutes for capitalism. The classical liberal defends private property and the free-market economy, he insisted, precisely because it is the only system of social cooperation that provides wide latitude for freedom and personal choice to all members of society, while generating the institutional means for coordinating the actions of billions of people in the most economically rational manner.

Classical liberalism, freedom, and democracy

Mises' defense of classical liberalism against these various forms of collectivism, however, was not limited to the "merely" economic benefits from the private-property order. Property also provides man with that most valuable and cherished object – *freedom*. Property gives the individual an arena of autonomy in which he may cultivate and live out his own conception of the good and meaningful life. It also protects him from dependency on the state for his existence; through his own efforts and voluntary exchange with other free men, he is not beholden to any absolute political authority that would dictate the conditions of his life. Freedom and property, if they are to be secure, require *peace*. Violence and fraud must be outlawed if each man is to take full advantage of what his interests and talents suggest would be the most profitable avenues to achieve his goals in consensual association with others.

The classical liberal ideal also emphasizes the importance of *equality before the law*, Mises explained. Only when political privilege and favoritism are eliminated can each man have the latitude to use his own knowledge and talents in ways that benefit himself and also rebound, through the voluntary transactions of the market, to the betterment of society as a whole. This means, at the same time, that a liberal society is one that accepts that *inequality of income and wealth* is inseparable from individual freedom. Given the diversity of men's natural and acquired abilities and volitional inclinations, the rewards earned by people in the marketplace will inevitably be uneven. Nor can it be otherwise if we are not to diminish or even suffocate the incentives that move men to apply themselves in creative and productive ways.

The role of government, therefore, in the classical liberal society is to respect and protect each individual's right to his life, liberty, and property. The significance of *democracy*, in Mises' view, is not that majorities are always right or should be unrestrained in what they may do to minorities through the use of political power. Elected and representative government is a means of changing those who hold political office without resort to revolution or civil war. It is an institutional device for maintaining social peace. It was clear to Mises from the experience of communism and fascism, as well as from the many tyrannies of the past, that without democracy the questions of who shall rule, for how long, and for what purpose would be reduced to brute force and dictatorial power. Reason and persuasion should be the methods that men use in their dealings with one another – both in the marketplace and the social and political arenas – and not the bullet and the bayonet.[28]

In his book on classical liberalism, Mises bemoaned the fact that people are all too willing to resort to state power to impose their views of personal conduct and morality whenever their fellow human beings veer from their own conception of the "good," the "virtuous" and the "right." He despaired,

> The propensity of our contemporaries to demand authoritarian prohibition as soon as something does not please them ... shows how deeply ingrained the spirit of servility still remains in them ... A free man must be able to endure it when his fellow men act and live otherwise than he considers proper. He must free himself from the habit, just as soon as something does not please him, of calling for the police.[29]

What, then, should guide social policy in determining the limits of government action? Mises was a utilitarian who argued that laws and institutions should be judged by the standard of whether and to what extent they further the goal of peaceful social cooperation. Society is the most important means through which men are able to pursue the ends and purposes that give meaning to their lives. But Mises was not what has become known in philosophical discussion as an "act-utilitarian," i.e., one who believes that a course of action or a policy is to be determined on an ad hoc, case-by-case basis. Rather, he was a "rule-utilitarian," i.e., one who believes that any particular course of action or policy must be evaluated in terms of its consistency with general rules of personal and social conduct that reason and experience have accumulated as guides to conduct. Any action's long-run influences and consequences must be taken into consideration in terms of its consistency with and relationship to the preservation of the institutions essential for successful social interaction.[30] This is the meaning of the phrase Mises often used: the "rightly understood long-run interests" of the members of society.[31]

Thus his defense of democracy and constitutional limits on the powers of government was based on the reasoned judgment that history has demonstrated far too many times that the resort to non-democratic and "extra-constitutional" means has led to violence, repression, abrogation of civil and economic liberties, and a breakdown of respect for law and the legal order, which destroys the long-run stability of society. The apparent "gains" and "benefits" from "strong men" and "emergency measures" in times of seeming crisis have always tended to generate costs and losses of liberty and prosperity in the longer run that more than exceed the supposed "short run" stability, order, and security promised by such methods.

Classical liberalism and international peace

The benefits from social cooperation through a market-based division of labor, Mises argued, are not limited to a country's borders. The gains from trade through specialization extend to all corners of the globe. Hence, the classical liberal ideal is inherently cosmopolitan. Aggressive nationalism, in Mises' view, not only threatens to bring death and destruction through war and conquest, it also denies all men the opportunity to benefit from productive intercourse by imposing trade barriers and various other restrictions on the free movement of goods, capital, and people from one country to another. Prosperity and progress are artificially constrained within national boundaries. This perversely can create the conditions for war and conquest as some nations conclude that the only way to obtain the goods and resources available in another country is through invasion and violence. Eliminate all trade barriers and restrictions on the free movement of goods, capital, and men, and limit governments to the securing of each individual's life, liberty, and property, and most of the motives and tensions that can lead to war will have been removed.

Mises also suggested that many of the bases for civil wars and ethnic violence would be removed if the right of self-determination was recognized in determining the borders between countries. Mises took great care to explain that by "self-determination" he did not mean that all those belonging to a particular racial, ethnic, linguistic, or religious group are to be forced into the same nation-state. He clearly stated that he meant the right of individual self-determination through plebiscite. That is, if the individuals in a town or region or district vote to join another nation, or wish to form their own independent country, they should have the freedom to do so.

There still may be minorities within these towns, regions, or districts, of course, that would have preferred to remain part of the country to which they had belonged, or would have preferred to join a different country. But however imperfect self-determination may be, it would at least potentially reduce a good amount of the ethnic, religious, or linguistic tensions. The only lasting solution, Mises said, is the reduction of government involvement to those limited classical liberal functions, so the state may not be used to impose harm or disadvantage on any individual or group in society for the benefit of others.[32]

Classical liberalism and the general welfare

Finally, Mises also discussed the question: for whose benefit does the classical liberal speak in society? Unlike virtually all other political and ideological movements, liberalism is a social philosophy of the common good. Both at the time that Mises wrote many of his works and now, political movements and parties often resort to the rhetoric of the common good and the general welfare, but in fact their goals are to use the power of government to benefit some groups at the expense of others.

Government regulations, redistributive welfare programs, trade restrictions and subsidies, tax policies, and monetary manipulation are employed to grant profit and employment privileges to special-interest groups that desire positions in society they are unable to attain on the open, competitive market. Corruption, hypocrisy, and disrespect for the law, as well as abridgements on the freedom of others, naturally follow from this.

What liberalism offers as an ideal and as a goal of public policy, Mises declared, is an equality of individual rights for all under the rule of law, with privileges and favors for none. It speaks for and defends the freedom of each individual and therefore is the voice of liberty for all. It wants every person to be free to apply himself in the pursuit of his own goals and purposes, so he and others can benefit from his talents and abilities through the peaceful transactions of market exchange. Classical liberalism wants elimination of government intervention in human affairs, so political power is not abusively applied at the expense of anyone in society.[33]

Mises was not unaware of the power of special-interest-group politics and the difficulty of opposing the concentrated influence of such groups in the halls of political power.[34] But he insisted that the ultimate power in society resides in the power of ideas. It is ideas that move men to action, that make them bare their chests at barricades, or that embolden them to oppose wrongheaded policies and resist even the strongest of vested interests. It is ideas that have achieved all the victories that have been won by freedom over the centuries.

Neither political deception nor ideological compromise can win liberty in the twenty-first century. Only the power of ideas, clearly stated and forthrightly presented, can do so. And that is what stands out in Mises' books and make them one of the enduring sources of the case for freedom.

When Mises wrote many of his books in the 1920s, 1930s, and 1940s, communism and fascism seemed irresistible forces in the world. Since then, their ideological fire has been extinguished in the reality of what they created and the unwillingness of tens of millions to live under their yoke. Nonetheless, many of their criticisms of the free market continue to serve as the rationales for the intrusions of the interventionist welfare state in every corner of society. And many of the contemporary arguments against "globalization" often resemble the criticisms leveled against free markets and free trade by European nationalists and socialists a hundred years ago.[35]

Mises' arguments for individual freedom and the market economy in the pages of *Socialism, Liberalism, Critique of Interventionism, Omnipotent Gov-*

ernment, Bureaucracy, Planned Chaos, Human Action, and many others continue to ring true and remain relevant to our own times. It is what makes his
works as important now as when he wrote them across the decades of the twentieth century.

Notes

1 On Mises' life and contributions to economics and the philosophy of freedom, see,
Richard M. Ebeling, *Austrian Economics and the Political Economy of Freedom*
(Northampton, MA: Edward Elgar, 2003), Ch. 3, "A Rational Economist in an Irra-
tional Age: Ludwig von Mises," pp. 61–99; and Ch. 2: "The Significance of Austrian
Economics in 20th Century Economic Thought," pp. 34–60; see, also, Murray N.
Rothbard, *Ludwig von Mises: Scholar, Creator, Hero* (Auburn, AL: Ludwig von
Mises Institute, 1988), and Israel M. Kirzner, *Ludwig von Mises* (Wilmington, DE:
ISI Books, 2001).
2 On Mises' family background and the cultural climate of Vienna and Austria in terms
of the Jews and anti-Semitism, see, Ch. 3: "Ludwig von Mises and the Vienna of His
Time," in the present volume.
3 On Mises' work as policy analyst and advocate in the Austria of the interwar period,
see, Ch. 5: "The Economist as the Historian of Decline: Ludwig von Mises and
Austria Between the Two World Wars," in the present volume.
4 Ludwig von Mises, *Human Action: A Treatise on Economics* [1949] (Irvington-on-
Hudson, NY: Foundation for Economic Education, [3rd revised ed., 1966] 1996).
5 In a review of Mises' *Omnipotent Government,* one of the leading figures of the older
Chicago School of Economics, Henry Simons, in *The Annual of the American Academy
of Political and Social Science* (November 1944), p. 192, pointed out that, "Professor
Mises, patriarch of the modern Austrian School, is the greatest living teacher of economics – if one may judge by the contributions of his many distinguished students and
protégés." Among these students and protégés in the interwar period were: F.A. Hayek,
Gottfried Haberler, Fritz Machlup, Oskar Morgenstern, and Lionel Robbins.
6 Bismarck told an American admirer, "My idea was to bribe the working class, or shall
I say, to win them over, to regard the state as a social institution existing for their sake
and interested in their welfare." See, William H. Dawson, *The Evolution of Modern
Germany,* Vol. II (New York: Charles Scribner's Sons, 1914), p. 349. See, Richard
M. Ebeling, "Marching to Bismarck's Drummer: The Origin of the Modern Welfare
State," *The Freeman: Ideas on Liberty* (December 2007), pp. 2–3.
7 On the ideas and development of the German welfare state and regulated economy in
the late nineteenth and early twentieth centuries, see, Richard M. Ebeling, *Austrian
Economics and the Political Economy of Freedom,* Ch. 7: "The Political Myths and
Economic Realities of the Welfare State," pp. 179–202, especially, pp. 179–184; and,
Ebeling, "National Health Care and the Welfare State," in Jacob G. Hornberger and
Richard M. Ebeling, eds., *The Dangers of Socialized Medicine* (Fairfax, VA: The
Future of Freedom Foundation, 1994), pp. 25–37; see also, Mises' criticisms of the
German Historical School in, "The Historical Setting of the Austrian School of Eco-
nomics" [1969], reprinted in Bettina Bien Greaves, ed., *Austrian Economics: An
Anthology* (Irvington-on-Hudson, NY: Foundation for Economic Education, 1996),
pp. 53–76, especially pp. 60–69.
8 See, Richard M. Ebeling, "Free Markets, the Rule of Law, and Classical Liberalism"
The Freeman: Ideas on Liberty (May 2004), pp. 8–15.
9 Ludwig von Mises analyzed the inherent flaws and contradictions in the Marxian
theory of history and class conflict in *Socialism: An Economic and Sociological Analysis* [1922; revised eds., 1932, 1951] (Indianapolis, IN: Liberty Classics, 1981),
pp. 279–320; and *Theory and History: An Interpretation of Social and Economic Evolution* [1957] (Indianapolis, IN: Liberty Fund, 2005), pp. 102–158.

10 On the evolution and meanings of nationality and nationalism, see, Carlton J.H. Hayes, *The Historical Evolution of Modern Nationalism* (New York: Richard R. Smith, 1931); Hayes, *Essays on Nationalism* (New York: Macmillan, 1928); Walter Sulzbach, *National Consciousness* (Washington, DC: American Council on Public Affairs, 1943); Frederick Hertz, *Nationality in History and Politics* (New York: Oxford University Press, 1944); and, Hans Kohn, *The Idea of Nationalism* (New York: Macmillan, 1944).

11 Ludwig von Mises, "Autarky and Its Consequences" [1943] in Richard M. Ebeling, ed., *Money, Method and the Market Process: Essays by Ludwig von Mises* (Norwell, MA: Kluwer Academic Press, 1990), p. 138:

> *Aggressive or militaristic nationalism* aims at conquest and the subjugation of other nations by arms. *Economic Nationalism* aims at the furthering the well-being of one's own nation or some of its groups through inflicting harm upon foreigners by economic measures, for instance: trade and migration barriers, expropriation of foreign investments, repudiation of foreign debts, currency devaluation, and foreign exchange control.

12 Ludwig von Mises, *Nation, State, and Economy: Contributions to the Politics and History of Our Time* [1919] (New York: New York University Press, 1983).

13 See, Richard M. Ebeling, *Austrian Economics and the Political Economy of Freedom*, Ch.6: "Classical Liberalism and Collectivism in the 20th Century," pp. 159–178, especially pp. 159–163; on the political and ideological similarities of communism, fascism, and Nazism, see, Ludwig von Mises, *Planned Chaos* (Irvington-on-Hudson, NY: Foundation for Economic Education, 1947), pp. 62–79; also, see, Richard Overy, *The Dictators: Hitler's Germany, Stalin's Russia* (New York: W.W. Norton, 2004); A. James Gregor, *The Faces of Janus: Marxism and Fascism in the Twentieth Century* (New Haven, CT: Yale University Press, 2000); Francois Furet, *The Passing of an Illusion: The Idea of Communism in the Twentieth Century* (Chicago: University of Chicago Press, 1999); and, Richard Pipes, *Russia Under the Bolshevik Regime* (New York: Alfred A. Knopf, 1993), pp. 240–281.

14 For Mises' analysis of the Great German Inflation, see his monograph, "Stabilization of the Monetary Unit – From the Viewpoint of Theory" [1923], in Percy L. Greaves, ed., *Ludwig von Mises, On the Manipulation of Money and Credit* (Dobbs Ferry, NY: Free Market Books, 1978), pp. 1–49, and Ludwig von Mises, "Business Under German Inflation" [1946], reprinted in *Ideas on Liberty* (November 2003), pp. 10–13; also, Richard M. Ebeling, "The Great German Inflation," *Ideas on Liberty* (November 2003), pp. 4–5.

15 See Albrecht Mendelssohn Bartholdy, *The War and German Society: The Testament of a Liberal* [1937] (New York: Howard Fertig, 1971), and, Mortiz J. Bonn, *Wandering Scholar* (London: Cohen & West, Ltd., 1949), pp. 273–290.

16 Ludwig von Mises, "Anti-Marxism" [1925] in *Critique of Interventionism* [1929] (Irvington-on-Hudson, NY: Foundation for Economic Education, 1996), pp. 71–95.

17 Ludwig von Mises, "Social Liberalism," [1926] in *Critique of Interventionism*, p. 67.

18 Mises, *Planned Chaos*, pp. 77–78.

19 Mises, *Socialism*, pp. 256–278; *Human Action*, pp. 143–176.

20 Mises, *Human Action*, pp. 628–634.

21 Ludwig von Mises, "Economic Calculation in the Socialist Commonwealth" [1920], in F.A. Hayek, *Collectivist Economic Planning: Critical Studies on the Possibilities of Socialism* (London: George Routledge & Sons, 1935), pp. 87–130, reprinted in Israel M. Kirzner, ed., *Classics in Austrian Economics: A Sampling in the History of a Tradition*, Vol. 3 (London: William Pickering, 1994), pp. 3–30, and Mises, *Socialism*, pp. 95–194; *Bureaucracy* (New Haven, CT: Yale University Press, 1944), pp. 20–56; *Human Action*, pp. 689–715; also, Richard M. Ebeling, "Why Socialism is 'Impossible,'" *The Freeman: Ideas on Liberty* (October 2004), pp. 8–12.

22 Ludwig von Mises, *Socialism*, p. 102; *Liberalism: The Classical Tradition* [1927]

(Irvington-on-Hudson, NY: Foundation for Economic Education, 1996), p. 74; *Omnipotent Government*, p. 55; *Bureaucracy* (New Haven, CT: Yale University Press, 1944), pp. 58–59; *Planned Chaos* (Irvington-on-Hudson, NY: Foundation for Economic Education, 1947), p. 84; *Human Action*, pp. 258–259, 702–703.

23 Ludwig von Mises, "On the Development of the Subjective Theory of Value," [1931] *Epistemological Problems of Economics* [1933] (New York: New York University Press, 1981), p. 157.

24 Mises, *Critique of Interventionism*, pp. 1–31, 97–106; *Interventionism: An Economic Analysis* [1941] (Irvington-on-Hudson, NY: Foundation for Economic Education, 1996); *Human Action*, pp. 716–779; *Planning for Freedom* (South Holland, IL: Libertarian Press, 4th ed., 1980), pp. 1–49.

25 Ludwig von Mises, *The Theory of Money and Credit* [1912; revised eds., 1934, 1953] (Indianapolis, IN: Liberty Classics, 1981); "Monetary Stabilization and Cyclical Policy" [1928] reprinted in Kirzner, ed., *Classics in Austrian Economics*, Vol. 3, pp. 33–111; *Human Action*, pp. 398–478, 538–586, 780–803.

26 For Mises' analysis of the causes and cures for the Great Depression, see, Ludwig von Mises, "The Causes of the Economic Crisis" [1931] in, Greaves, ed., *Ludwig von Mises, On the Manipulation of Money and Credit*, pp. 173–203; and on Keynesian Economics, see, Mises, "Stones into Bread, The Keynesian Miracle" [1948] and "Lord Keynes and Say's Law" [1950], in *Planning for Freedom*, pp. 50–71; for a detailed comparison of the Austrian and Keynesian analyses of the Great Depression, see, Ch 7: "The Austrian Economists and the Keynesian Revolution: The Great Depression and the Economics of the Short Run" in the present volume.

27 See, Ebeling, *Austrian Economics and the Political Economy of Freedom*, Ch. 5: "Ludwig von Mises and the Gold Standard," pp. 136–158.

28 *Socialism*, pp. 58–73; *Liberalism*, pp. 18–42; *Human Action*, pp. 150–153, 264–289.

29 Mises, *Liberalism*, p. 55.

30 Ludwig von Mises, *Human Action*, pp. 664–88; *Theory and History*, pp. 44–61; and, Henry Hazlitt, *The Foundations of Morality* [1964] (Irvington-on-Hudson, NY, Foundation for Economic Education, 1998), pp. 55–61. See also, Leland B. Yeager, *Ethics as Social Science: The Moral Philosophy of Social Cooperation* (Northampton, MA: Edward Elgar, 2001), pp. 81–97.

31 Mises, *Human Action*, pp. 664–688.

32 Mises, *Nation, State, and Economy*, pp. 31–56; *Liberalism*, pp. 105–121; *Omnipotent Government*, pp. 79–93.

33 Mises, *Liberalism*, pp. 155–187.

34 See, for example, his essay, "The Clash of Group Interests" [1945] reprinted in, Ebeling, ed., *Money, Method and the Market Process*, pp. 202–214.

35 See, Jerry Z. Muller, *The Mind and the Market: Capitalism in Modern European Thought* (New York: Alfred A. Knopf, 2002), and, Ian Buruma and Avishai Margalit, *Occidentalism: The West in the Eyes of Its Enemies* (New York: The Penguin Press, 2004).

3 Ludwig von Mises and the Vienna of his time

Ludwig von Mises was a passionate advocate of reason who deeply believed in the value of human freedom. He also was a patriotic cosmopolitan; that is, in the years before he left Europe in 1940, Mises was deeply loyal to the Austria of his birth, while adhering to a philosophy and an outlook on life that was universalistic in its principles. In other words, Ludwig von Mises was an Austrian Jew.[1]

This may seem like a strange statement to anyone familiar with Mises' writings. In his memoirs, *Notes and Recollections*, he never once mentions the faith of his ancestors.[2] Nor does he speak in favor of Judaism – indeed, in his treatise on *Socialism*, he refers to Orthodox Judaism as one of the stagnant and backward religions.[3] And only in *Omnipotent Government*, written during World War II from his exile in America, does he discuss and criticize anti-Semitism in Germany in particular and Europe in general.[4] Yet, Friedrich A. Hayek once commented that Mises considered himself to have been a victim of anti-Semitism in having never been awarded the academic position at the University of Vienna for which he considered himself rightfully qualified.[5]

But in many ways Mises' life from his birth in Lemberg in the old Austro-Hungarian Empire to his departure from the Austria of the interwar period reflects and parallels the triumphs and tragedies of the Jews of Austria. Mises was born on September 29, 1881, in Austrian Poland, or Galicia, as it was called. In the last decades of the nineteenth century, more than 50 percent of the population of some parts of Galicia was Jewish, with the center of Jewish life and culture being in the province's capital of Lemberg, Mises' birthplace.[6]

The documents that Ludwig von Mises' great-grandfather, Mayer Rachmiel Mises, prepared as background for his ennoblement by the Austrian Emperor Francis Joseph in June 1881 (just a few months before Ludwig was born), record the history of the Mises family in Lemberg going back to the 1700s. Mayer's father, Fischel Mises, had been a wholesaler and real estate owner who had received permission to live and conduct business in the so-called "restricted district" reserved for non-Jews. At the age of eighteen, Mayer married a daughter of Hirsch Halberstamm, the leading Russian-German export trader in the Galician city of Brody.

Mayer took over the family business following his father's death and also served for twenty-five years as a commissioner in the commercial court of Lemberg. For a period of time he also was on the city council and a full member of the Lemberg Chamber of Commerce. He also was a co-founder of the Lemberg Savings Bank, and later was a member of the board of the Lemberg branch of the Austrian National Bank. In addition, he was a founder of a Jewish orphanage, a reform school, a secondary education school, a charitable institution for infant orphans, and a library in the Jewish community. Some of these charities were begun with funds provided by Mayer for their endowment. Indeed, it was for his service to the Emperor as a leader of the Jewish community in Lemberg that Mayer Mises, great-grandfather of Ludwig von Mises, was ennobled.

Mayer's oldest son, Abraham Oscar Mises, ran the Vienna office of the family business until he was appointed, in 1860, the director of the Lemberg branch of the CreditAnstalt bank. Abraham also was the director of the Galician Carl-Ludwig Railroad. It is perhaps because of Abraham's connection with this railroad that his own son, Arthur Edler Mises, took up civil engineering with a degree from the Zurich Polytechnic in Switzerland, and then worked for the Lemberg-Czernowitz Railroad Company. Arthur married Adele Landau, the granddaughter of Moses Kallir and the grandniece of Mayer Kallir, a prominent Jewish merchant family in the city of Brody. Arthur and Adele had three sons, of whom Ludwig was the oldest. His brother, Richard, became an internationally renowned mathematician who later taught at Harvard University. The third child died at an early age.

Members of the Mises family also were devout practitioners of their Jewish faith. The vast majority of the Galician Jews were Hasidic, with all the religious customs and rituals that entailed.[7] But the Mises family was part of that movement in the Jewish community devoted to theological and cultural reform, and participated in the liberal-oriented political activities that were attempted in nineteenth century Galicia. As a small boy, Ludwig would have heard and spoken Yiddish, Polish, and German, and studied Hebrew in preparation for his bar mitzvah.

Ludwig's father, Arthur, like many of his generation, chose to leave Galicia and make his life and career in the secular and German cultural world of Vienna. But from the documents among Ludwig von Mises' "lost papers" in the Moscow archives,[8] it is clear that his mother maintained ties to her birthplace, contributing money to several charities in Brody, including a Jewish orphanage.[9] In Vienna in the 1890s, Arthur was an active member of the Israelite Community's Board, a focal point for Jewish cultural and political life in the Austrian capital.[10]

Civil rights and the liberation of the Austrian Jews

Until the early and middle decades of the nineteenth century, Jews throughout many parts of Europe were denied civil liberties, often being severely restricted in their economic freedom, and especially in Eastern Europe, confined to certain geographical areas. In the 1820s it was still not permitted for Jews to unrestrictedly live and work in Vienna; this required the special permission of the Emperor.[11] Commercial and civil liberation of the Austrian Jews only occurred in the aftermath of the Revolution of 1848, and most especially with the new constitution of 1867, which created the Austro-Hungarian Dual Monarchy following Austria's defeat in its 1866 war with Prussia.[12] The spirit and content of the 1867 constitution, which remained the fundamental law of the Empire until the collapse of Austria-Hungary in 1918, reflected the classical liberal ideas of the time.[13] Every subject of the Emperor was secure in his life and private property; freedom of speech and the press was guaranteed; freedom of occupation and enterprise was permitted; all religious faiths were respected and allowed to be practiced; freedom of movement and residence within the Empire was a guaranteed right; and all national groups were declared to have equal status before the law.[14]

No group within the Austro-Hungarian Empire took as much advantage of the new liberal environment as the Jews. In the early decades of the nineteenth century a transformation had begun among the Jewish community in Galicia. Reformers arose arguing for a revision in the practices and customs of Orthodox Jewry. Jews needed to enter the modern world and to secularize in terms of dress, manner, attitudes and culture. The faith had to be stripped of its medieval characteristics and ritualism. Jews should immerse themselves in the German language and German culture. All things "German" were distinguished as representing freedom and progress.[15]

With the freedoms of the 1867 constitution, Austrian and especially Galician Jews began a cultural as well as a geographical migration. In 1869, Jews made up about 6 percent of the population of Vienna. By the 1890s, when the young Ludwig von Mises moved to Vienna from Lemberg with his family, Jews made up 12 percent of the Vienna population. In District I, the center of the city around where the Mises family lived, Jews made up over 20 percent of the population. In the neighboring District II, the percentage was over 30 percent.[16]

But in the late nineteenth and early twentieth centuries, there was a stark contrast between these two districts of the city. In the central district I, the vast majority of the Jewish population had attempted to assimilate with their non-Jewish neighbors in dress, manners, and cultural outlook. In District II, bordering on the Danube, on the other hand, the Jewish residents were more likely to have retained their Hasidic practices and orthodox manners, including their traditional dress. It was the visible difference of these Jews, who often had more recently arrived from Galicia, which so revolted the young Adolf Hitler – who was shocked, and wondered how people acting and appearing as they did could ever be considered "real Germans." They seemed such an obviously alien element in Hitler's eyes.[17]

The characteristic mark of most of the Jews who migrated to Vienna (and other large cities of the Empire such as Budapest or Prague) was their desire and drive for assimilation; in many ways they tried to be more German than the German-Austrians.[18] The Czechs, the Hungarians, and the Slavs, on the other hand, often were still focused on their traditional ways; the Hungarians in particular were suspicious of the Enlightenment, civil liberties, and equality – these threatened their dominance over the subject peoples in their portions of the Empire (the Slovaks, Romanians, and Croats). To constrain the Hungarians, the Emperor increasingly put the Czechs, Poles, and Slavs under direct Imperial administration on an equal legal footing with the German-Austrians.[19] For the Jews, Austrian Imperial policy meant the end of official prejudice and legal restrictions, and a securing of civil rights and educational opportunities.[20] Their continuing and generally steadfast loyalty to the Hapsburgs, however, led many of the other nationalities to be suspicious and anti-Semitic as the years went by. The Jews were viewed as apologists and blind supporters of the Hapsburg emperor, without whose indulgence and protection the Jews might have been kept within the ghetto walls.[21]

Civil liberties and practically unrestrained commercial and professional opportunity soon saw the Jews rise to prominence in a wide array of areas of Viennese life.[22] By the beginning of the twentieth century more than 50 percent of the lawyers and medical doctors in Vienna were Jewish. The leading liberal and socialist newspapers in the capital were either owned or edited by those of Jewish descent, including the *New Free Press*, the Viennese newspaper for which Mises often wrote in the 1920s and 1930s. The membership of the journalists' association in Vienna was more than 50 percent Jewish. At the University of Vienna, in 1910, professors of Jewish descent constituted 37 percent of the law faculty, 51 percent of the medical faculty and 21 percent of the philosophy faculty. At the time Mises attended the University in the first decade of the twentieth century almost 21 percent of the student body was Jewish. The proportion of Jews in literature, theatre, music and the arts was equally pronounced.[23]

The main avenue for social and professional advancement was education in the Gymnasium system – the high school system in the German-speaking world. But the Gymnasium education not only offered the path to higher education and a university degree for many Jews, it also was an avenue for acculturation and assimilation into European and especially German culture. For example, Mises and his fellow student Hans Kelsen (who later became an internationally renowned philosopher of law and the author of the 1920 constitution of the Republic of Austria) attended the *Akedemisches Gymnasium* in the center of Vienna. It was meant for students preparing for the university and professional careers. Here a wide liberal arts education was acquired with mandatory courses in Latin, Greek, German language and literature, history, geography, mathematics, physics, and religion, with electives in either French or English – Mises selected French. At the core of the curriculum also was the study of the ancient Greek and Roman classics. Mises and other Jewish students at the *Akedemisches Gymnasium*, as a part of their religion training, had courses in Hebrew.[24]

According to memoirs written by people who attended the *Akademisches Gymnasium* in the 1880s and 1890s, most of the students ridiculed the religion classes as "superstition." The Greek and Roman classics were considered as literary avenues for entering the mainstream of modern European and Western culture. And while it was not assigned, the students absorbed on their own contemporary writings in history, social criticism, literature, and the sciences as their way to integrate themselves into modern and "progressive" society.[25]

In the 1890s, during Mises' time at the *Akademisches Gymnasium*, 44 percent of the student body was Jewish. But there were some Gymnasiums at which

Jewish admission was informally restricted. For example, the Maria Theresa Academy of Knights in Vienna was reserved for the children of the nobility and senior officials. Joseph Schumpeter attended it in the 1890s, but only because his stepfather was a Lieutenant Field-Marshal. No matter what his academic qualification, Mises would have had virtually no chance to have been accepted there. The result was that there were clusters of these Gymnasiums that were clearly closed to Jews, even if they were converts to Christianity, while other clusters represented the high schools where middle-class Jewish businessmen, professionals and civil servants sent their children.[26]

But for all their assimilationist strivings – their conscious attempts to be German-Austrians in thought, philosophy, outlook, and manner – they remained distinct and separate. Not only was this because they belonged to schools, professions, and occupations in which they as Jews were concentrated, but because non-Jewish German-Austrians viewed them as separate and distinct. However eloquent and perfect their German in literature and the spoken word, no matter how contributing they were to the improvement of Viennese society and culture, most non-Jewish Viennese considered these to be Jewish contributions to and influences on German-Austrian corners of cultural life.

Name, family history, gossip, and mannerisms made it clear to most people who were Jewish and who were not. The wide and pronounced success of so many Viennese Jews made non-Jews conscious of their preponderance and presence in many visible works of life. And it served as the breeding ground for anti-Semitism.[27]

Anti-Jewish sentiment in the Austro-Hungarian empire

In the Hapsburg domains part of this anti-Semitism was fed by conservative and reactionary forces in society who often resented the Emperor's diminishment or abolition of the privileges, favors, and status of the Catholic Church and the traditional landed aristocracy. The high proportion of Austrian Jews involved in liberal or socialist politics made them targets of the conservatives who said they were carriers of modernity, with its presumption of civil equality, unrestrained market competition, and a secularization that was said to be anti-Christian and therefore immoral and decadent. Preservation and restoration of traditional and Christian society, it was claimed, required opposition to and elimination of the Jewish influence on society. Jews were the rootless "peddlers" who undermined traditional occupations and ways of earning a living, as well as the established social order of things. They pursued profit. Honor, custom, and faith were willingly traded away by them for a few pieces of gold, it was said. Craft associations became leading voices of anti-Semitism, especially when economic hard times required small craftsmen and businessmen to go hat in hand to Jewish bankers for the borrowed sums to tide them over these times of economic trouble.[28]

German nationalism also was a vehicle for growing anti-Jewish sentiment. The paradox here is that in the 1860s and 1870s a sizable number of Jewish intellectuals were founders and leaders in the Austrian and German nationalist

movements. German culture and society were viewed as representing the universal values of reason, science, justice and openness in both thought and deed.
German culture and political predominance within the Austro-Hungarian Empire
held back the backward-looking forces of darkness, i.e., the Hungarian, Czech,
and Slavic threats. At the same time, German culture in Central Europe offered
rays of enlightenment in the regions of Eastern Europe.

Mises estimated that before World War II, Jews made up 50 percent of the
business community in Central Europe and 90 percent of the business community in Eastern Europe.[29] Indeed, in *Omnipotent Government* he asserted that in
Eastern Europe "modern civilization was predominantly an achievement of
Jews."[30] What the Jews in these parts of Europe introduced and represented, at
least in their own minds, was the enlightened German mind, with its culture and
institutions. But to those other nationalities being introduced to and "threatened"
by this German cultural influence, it was perceived as Jewish as much as being
German – a dominating, imperial, and "foreign" culture.

At the same time, in both Germany and German-Austria, the Jews in the fore-
front of the Pan-German nationalist movements were viewed as interlopers by
many of the Christian German nationalists. As a consequence, there emerged in
the second half of the nineteenth century rationalizations to justify the rejection
of Jewish participation in the cause of German nationalism and culture. First, it
was said that only Christians and the Christian faith were consistent with true
German life and culture. But when a significant number of German and Austrian
Jews converted to Christianity, it still was found not to be enough. Now it was
claimed that to be a true German it was not sufficient to be a convert to Christianity. "Germanness" was a culture, an attitude towards life and a certain sense of
belonging to the *Volk* community.

As a growing number of Jews immersed themselves into all things German –
language, philosophy, literature, dress and manner – it was found, again, not to
be enough. Really to be a German was to share a common ancestry, a heritage of
a common blood lineage.[31] This was one barrier the German and Austrian Jews
could not overcome. In the emergence of racial anti-Semitism in the 1880s and
1890s, there were laid the seeds of the "final solution."

In Vienna, Karl Lueger, who was mayor of the capital city in the first decade
of the twentieth century and a leader of the Christian Social Party, represented
the spirit of anti-Semitism. He insisted that only "fat Jews" could weather the
storm of capitalist competition. Anti-Semitism, Lueger said, "is not an explosion
of brutality, but the cry of oppressed Christian people for help from church and
state."[32] He blended anti-Semitism with social-left reforms, which included civil
service and municipal government restrictions on Jewish access to city jobs or
contracts. On the other hand, when Lueger was challenged as to why he had
Jewish friends and political associates, he replied, "I decide who is a Jew."[33]

But in spite of the presence and growth of anti-Semitic attitudes in the late
nineteenth and early twentieth centuries in Austria in general and Vienna in particular, Mises' lack of attention to his own Jewish family background or any hint
of the impact of anti-Semitism around him – there were anti-Jewish student riots
at the University of Vienna during the years when he was a student there around

the turn of the century – was in fact not uncommon. One can read Stefan Zweig's fascinating account of everyday life in the Vienna of this time, and have the distinct impression that anti-Semitic attitudes or municipal government policy were virtually non-existent.[34]

Yet the circles in which people moved in Viennese society both before and after World War I existed with many invisible walls. Traditional or Orthodox Jews lived and worked within a world of their own in the city.[35] Secular and assimilated Jews, like Ludwig von Mises and Hans Kelsen, moved in circles of both Jews and non-Jews; but even the non-religious and German-acculturated Jews clustered together. A review of the list of participants in Mises' famous private seminar in Vienna, for example, shows a high proportion of Jews.[36] And even after Mises had moved to Geneva, Switzerland in 1934, his agenda books for this time show that many of his social engagements were with other Jews residing in that country.

The end of the nineteenth century and the beginning of the twentieth saw the eclipse of liberalism in Austria and the rise of socialism in its place, centered in the political ascendancy of the Social Democratic Party. A sizable number of Jews were prominent in the Austrian Socialist movement; they were anti-capitalist and viewed the entrepreneurial segment of the society as exploiters and economic oppressors. The capitalist class would to be swept away in the trans-formation to socialism, including the Jewish capitalists in the "ruling class." Most of the Jews in the socialist movement were not only secular and considered themselves as harbingers of the worker's world to come; they were contemptu-ously opposed to cultural and religious Judaism as well.[37]

These three political movements in Austria and Vienna when Mises was a young man – conservatism, German nationalism, and radical socialism – were, each for its own reasons, enemies of liberal society, opponents of free-market capitalism, and therefore threats to the ideas and occupations of those middle class, or "bourgeois," walks of life heavily populated by the Jews of Austria and Vienna.

The history of Austrian Jewry during this time is a story of triumph and tragedy. The winds of nineteenth century liberalism freed the Austrian Jewish community, both internally and externally. Internally, the liberal idea pried open Orthodox Jewish society in places such as Austrian Galicia. It heralded reason over ritual; greater individualism over religious collectivism; open-minded modernity over the strictures of traditionalism. Externally, it freed the Jewish community from legal and political restraints and restrictions. The right of freedom of trade, occupation, and profession opened wide many opportunities for social improvement, economic betterment, and political acceptance.[38]

Within two generations this transformed Austrian Jewish society. And within that same span of time it saw the rise of many Jews to social and economic prominence, with greater political tolerance than ever known before. If these two liberating forces had not been at work, there would not have been Ludwig von Mises – the economist, the political and social philosopher, and the notable public figure in the Austria between the two world wars.[39]

At the same time these two liberating forces set the stage for the tragedy of the German and Austrian Jews. Their very successes in the arts and the sciences, in academia, and in commerce fostered the animosity and resentment of those less successful in the arenas of intellectual, cultural, and commercial competition. It set loose the emotion of envy, the terror of failure, and the psychological search for scapegoats and excuses. It ended at the gates to the Nazi death camps.[40]

Classical liberalism, interventionism, and anti-Semitism

From the time of the Great War, Ludwig von Mises' writings expressed the classical liberal cosmopolitan conception of man, society, and freedom. Throughout the period between the two world wars his works on the general principles of the liberal free market order, or on the dangerous dead end to which socialist society would lead, or on the contradictions and corrupting influences of economic interventionism, all represented attempts to stem the tide of anti-Enlightenment thought – to hold back what he referred to as the "revolt against reason."[41]

For Mises, classical liberalism is the world view that liberates mankind from the ancient regime, with its systems of caste and class, favors and privileges, inequalities and injustices.[42] If groups of individuals wish to cling to their traditional conceptions of identity, and a longing for custom, tradition, and religious ritual, they are free to do so in the liberal society. But they are prevented, or at least greatly hindered, from any harm they may do to others, since the agency of government is limited to the securing of peaceful cooperation through a rule of law with equal treatment for all. Under limited-government liberalism, the resentments, envies, and angers of some cannot be transformed into political malice and abuse toward others.

In the face of the ascending influence of socialist ideas, liberalism is the world view and economic system, in Mises' eyes, that can forestall the establishment of a terrible collectivist tyranny, which can only produce stagnation and poverty. Socialism is merely the old petty resentments and personal envies now cloaked in the rhetoric of a grandiose theory of economic and institutional exploitation and injustice. Worse, the triumph of socialism will introduce an economic system without a rational method for economic calculation. Thus, socialism also will lead to waste, inefficiency, and standards of living far below that of the market order it will have replaced.

All of these anti-liberal forces were set loose by World War I: socialism, nationalism, racism, and fascism. Together they cumulatively represented a counter-revolution against all that classical liberalism had advocated and succeeded in creating in the eighteenth and nineteenth centuries. They are man's return to the master and to chains. They herald the end of the free man.

What was behind the anti-Semitic aspect of collectivism's counter-revolution, Mises believed, was envy and resentment against those who had succeeded socially and economically in the arena of free market opportunity. While Mises does not discount the role of non-economic factors in generating anti-Jewish sentiments, especially in earlier ages, he was persuaded that the most important factor behind it in modern times was the frustration of those who had failed in the face of competitors who happened to be Jewish, or of Jewish ancestry.

Nazi race doctrine was unable to scientifically define and classify the incontestable characteristics of a "Jew" or an "Aryan." Indeed, in the context of Europe's long history of conquest and mixings of multitudes of groups of various ethnic and racial backgrounds there was no scientific meaning to a "pure" race in virtually any part of the continent. And after enumerating the many negative meanings that had been given to "Jewish" culture, attitudes, behavior, and influence on German society, Mises concluded that the only thing that could be found in common among them was that the critic did not like them. For example, the Jews were criticized for being either economic liberals in favor of rugged individualism or communists desiring the nationalization of the individual; for being either warmongers for profits or dangerous pacifists unwilling to fight for their country; for being either Zionist nationalists or rootless cosmopolitans with loyalty to no one; for being either crude materialist or utopian idealists; for being either advocates of democracy or agents of dictatorship. "Jew" was simply the covering term for whatever was disliked or considered undesirable in society.[43]

Yet it was a fact, as Mises pointed out, and as we have mentioned earlier, the Jews played a pivotal role in the cultural and economic development of Central and Eastern Europe in the second half of the nineteenth century and the early decades of the twentieth century. Those who resented the passing of older and more traditional forms of social order or who were unable to as easily adapt to the rising currents of market competition saw the Jew as the cause of their "misfortune." The Jews were central to industrialization, modern commerce, railway infrastructure, and raw material and resource development, especially in Imperial Germany and Austria-Hungary – even though at no time did the Jews represent more than 1 percent of the entire population of the German Empire, and scarcely 5 percent of the population of the Austro-Hungarian Empire.

For traditionalist Germans, the Jews represented "modernity" and secularization – especially in its free-market manifestation. For the various non-German nationalities in eastern Germany and Austria-Hungary, the Jews represented "German" cultural and economic domination, especially since the German and Austrian Jews saw German "culture" as the most enlightened and progressive force that a large majority of them wanted to assimilate into and be part of.[44]

But the fact remained that in the market, individuals continued to patronize the suppliers who could provide the better products and services, and less expensive goods. People demonstrated their preferences and voted with their money in terms of with whom they found it advantageous to do business. As Mises explained it:

> Many decades of intensive anti-Semitic propaganda did not succeed in preventing German "Aryans" from buying in shops owned by Jews, from consulting Jewish doctors and lawyers, and from reading books by Jewish authors. They did not patronize the Jews unawares – "Aryan" competitors were careful to tell them again and again that these people were Jews. Whoever wanted to get rid of his Jewish competitors could not rely on an alleged hatred of Jews; he was under the necessity of asking for legal dis-

crimination against them. Such discrimination is not the result of nationalism or of racism. It is basically – like nationalism – a result of
interventionism and the policy of favoring the less efficient producer to the
disadvantage of the consumer.[45]

And if the Jews were to be blamed for bringing anti-Semitism on themselves
it would have to be for their most meritorious qualities:

> But if the cause of anti-Semitism were really to be found in distinctive fea-
> tures of the Jews, these properties would have to be extraordinary virtues
> and merits that would qualify the Jews as the elite of mankind. If the Jews
> themselves are to blame for the fact that those whose ideal is perpetual war
> and bloodshed, who worship violence and are eager to destroy freedom,
> consider them the most dangerous opponents of their endeavors, it must be
> because the Jews are foremost among the champions of freedom, justice,
> and peaceful cooperation among nations. If the Jews incurred the Nazis'
> hatred through their conduct, it is no doubt because what was great and
> noble in the German nation, all the immortal achievements of Germany's
> past, were either accomplished by the Jews or congenial to the Jewish mind.
> As the parties seeking to destroy modern civilization and return to barba-
> rism have put anti-Semitism at the top of their programs, this civilization is
> apparently a creation of the Jews. Nothing more flattering could be said of
> an individual or a group than that the deadly foes of civilization have well-
> founded reasons to persecute them.[46]

Mises did not assert that the civilization was the result of the Jews. He pointed
out that the anti-Semites greatly exaggerated the contribution of the Jews to
modern society and its accomplishments. What was distinct about the German
and Austrian Jews was that they were small minorities in the greater society who
could easily be targeted for economic discrimination through interventionism,
with no ability to politically prevent more powerful special-interest groups from
using the State at their expense. And "the Jews" were able to serve as a convenient hook upon which could be hung all the excuses for individual disappointment
and national humiliation, especially in the wake of the defeat in the Great War.[47]

What the Vienna of Mises' time demonstrated, especially in the decades
before World War I, is that classical liberalism in practice means the protection
of freedom in reality. The reawakening of Jewish life in Germany and Austria
was made possible by the Enlightenment culture of reason, experience, and individualism in place of superstition, blind faith, and cultural collectivism. The
spirit of individualism fostered a growing environment of self-education and
self-improvement in the Jewish community. However, that spiritual individualism would have been stymied if it had not coincided with the new epoch of political and economic liberalism in which the individual could apply his liberated
mind to the external world.

But it was the ideology of interventionism and socialism put into practice in
the period between the two world wars that enabled the prejudices of the envious

and the resentful to be applied against their more successful competitors. Mises explained the methods by which the power of the interventionist state could be turned against a minority group such as the Jews:

> If, for instance, members of the minority are alone engaged in a specific branch of business, the government can ruin them by means of customs provisions. In other words, they can raise the price of raw materials and machinery. In these countries [in post-World War I Central and Eastern Europe], every measure of government interference – taxes, tariffs, freight rates, labor policy, monopoly and price control, foreign exchange regulations – were used against minorities. If you wish to build a house or use the services of an architect from the minority group, then you find yourself beset by difficulties raised by the departments of building, of health, of fire. You will wait longer to receive your telephone, gas, electric, and water connections from the municipal authorities. The department of sanitation will discover some irregularities in your building. If members of your minority group are injured or even killed for political reasons, the police are slow in finding the culprit. Against such obstacles all provisions of minority protection are useless. Think of the assessment of taxes. In those countries, Chief Justice Marshall's dictum "The power to tax is the power to destroy" was practiced against the minorities. Or think of the power that [occupational] licensing gives to a government.[48]

In the two decades following the Great War, the governments of Central and Eastern Europe, especially in countries such as Poland, Lithuania, Hungary, and Romania, used these types of interventionist policies to prohibit and restrict economic opportunities for the Jewish populations in their lands. This was often accompanied with brutal acts of violence against the lives and property of Jews.[49]

Nazism and the end of the Austrian Jews

It was precisely through such interventionist policies that the Jews were increasingly excluded from German social and economic life in the years following the triumph of Hitler's National Socialist movement in 1933. During the first five years of the Nazi regime, restrictions, regulations and prohibitions were imposed on the German Jewish community that completely reversed the previous hundred years of economic and social liberalization. Step by step Jews were legally banned from the professions, academia, the arts and sciences, and commerce, industry and trade. This was matched by savage physical attacks on Jews throughout the country, in which thousands were killed, beaten, or arrested and imprisoned in the new system of concentration camps.[50]

What had taken five years to accomplish in Nazi Germany itself was achieved within weeks and months in Austria following its annexation to the Third Reich in March of 1938. The following passages from Bruce Pauley's book on the history of Austrian anti-Semitism gives a chilling sense of the tragedy that befell the Jews of Vienna in the days and months after the *Anschluss*:

The night of 11–12 March 1938 marked the dramatic end of a thousand years of Austro-Jewish history. On Friday, 11 March, all the Jewish newspapers of Vienna published their usual weekly editions. By the next day their offices and those of other Jewish organizations had been seized by Nazis. Within a matter of days, or at most a few months, nearly all Austrian Jews had lost their means of livelihood and in many cases their homes as well ...

Gangs of Nazis invaded Jewish department stores, humble Jewish shops in the Leopoldstadt, the homes of Jewish bankers, as well as the apartments of middle-class Jews, and stole money, art treasures, furs, jewelry, and even furniture. Some Jews were robbed of their money on the street. All automobiles owned by Jews were confiscated immediately. Jews who complained to the police about the thefts were lucky if they escaped arrest or physical violence ...

SA men stood at the entrances of Jewish shops; Christians who entered the stores were arrested and forced to wear signs saying they were "Christian pigs." ... Within a few hours or at most a few days all Jewish actors, musicians and journalists lost their jobs. By mid-June 1938, just three months after the *Anschluss*, Jews had already been more thoroughly purged from public life in Austria than in the five years following Hitler's takeover of power in Germany. Tens of thousands of Jewish employees had lost their jobs. Only rarely were they given any warning or severance pay. Among those dismissed were all state and municipal employees (what few there were), including 183 public schools teachers, and employees of banks, insurance companies, theaters, and concert halls. Meanwhile, private Jewish businesses large and small were either confiscated outright or their owners were paid only a small fraction of the property's true value. Jews were also excluded from most areas of public entertainment and to some extent even public transportation by the early summer of 1938; similar rules were not imposed on German Jews until November. Austrian Jews were also subjected to all kinds of personal insults and indignities that were not the result of official Nazi legislation. If a gentile streetcar passenger did not like the looks of a Jewish fellow passenger in the summer of 1938, he could have the trolley stopped and the Jew thrown off. The number of coffeehouses and restaurants that would not serve Jews grew from day to day. All of the public baths and swimming pools were closed to the Jews. Park benches all over the city had the words "Juden verboten" stenciled on them. Jews were not admitted to theater performances, concerts, or the opera. Numerous cinemas had notices saying that Jewish patronage was not wanted. Sometimes Jews were ejected from a motion picture theater in the middle of a performance if gentiles complained about them. SA men at times even stood at the last tramway stop in the suburb of Neuwaldegg in order to prevent Jews from strolling in the nearby Vienna Woods ...[51]

In the spring of 1940, shortly before Mises left Geneva to come to the United States, he pointed out that Austria had had one thousand outstanding entrepreneurs before the *Anschluss* in 1938. Of these at least two-thirds had been Jews.

Now, two years later, all of these Jews either had been tortured and murdered, or sent off to concentration camps, or expelled from the country. The supposed gains to the remaining Austrian population through confiscation and expulsion of their Jewish neighbors were all illusionary, Mises insisted, based on the crudest of Marxian fallacies:

> The so-called Aryanization of firms was based on the Marxist idea that capital (machinery and raw material) and the labor input of workers were the only vital ingredients of an enterprise, whereas the entrepreneur was an "exploiter." An enterprise without entrepreneurial spirit and creativity, however, is nothing more than a pile of rubbish and iron. Today the Aryanized firms, one and all, contribute nothing to exports. They are either working for the military or they have been liquidated. Commercial ties abroad, built up by more than one hundred years of unrelenting effort, have been broken. The core of skilled workers have been dispersed and displaced from its traditional skills.[52]

Thus, the ideology of envy and the interventionist policies of discrimination under German National Socialism brought to a disastrous close the liberal epoch of freedom for the Jews in Austria. In 1938, Austria's Jewish population had numbered around 250,000. By May of 1939 only 121,000 were still in Austria, with most of the rest having emigrated. Those who were not able to leave ended up in the inferno of the Holocaust.[53] According to one estimate less than 300 survived the war in hiding in Austria.

Among those who left before or immediately after Germany's annexation of Austria were many members of the Austrian School of Economics or Mises' private seminar circle (both Jews and non-Jews): Martha Steffy Browne, Gottfried Haberler, Friedrich A. Hayek, Felix Kaufmann, Fritz Machlup, Ilse Mintz, Oscar Morgenstern, Paul N. Rosenstein-Rodan, Alfred Schutz, Erich Voegelin, to name just a few.

Mises had departed in the autumn of 1934 for a teaching position at the Graduate Institute of International Studies in Geneva, when it was clear that the collectivist darkness was starting to fall over the center of Europe. Mises made a new life for himself after 1940 in the United States, like many of his Austrian colleagues and friends did, where the spirit of freedom was not yet in the same shadow of tyranny as their native Austria. America, for them, was still a land where Austrian Jews such as Mises could still breathe the air of liberty.

For many Austrians, and especially Austrian Jews, there long remained a nostalgia for the old Vienna before the Great War. It represented peace, freedom, security and certainty with its liberal values and apparent tolerant atmosphere in which a vast diversity of peoples lived and worked, and culturally gained from each other. As the Austrian writer Stefan Zweig expressed it, "It was sweet to live here, in this atmosphere of spiritual conciliation, and subconsciously every citizen became supernational, cosmopolitan, a citizen of the world."[54]

Yet, this appearance was deceiving. Beneath the surface anti-liberal currents were at work that brought this idyllic epoch to an end. In too many people's hearts and minds, collectivist attitudes and sentiments dominated their conduct and desires. Ludwig von Mises explained the problem and danger in the years immediately after World War I. The mentalities of people had lagged behind the political and economic changes in nineteenth century society. Institutions had been transformed more rapidly than the everyday psychologies of men. And a counter-revolution against freedom had emerged. It was characterized by the migrations of a growing multitude of people from the countryside to the cities, from traditional society to urban life, Mises argued:

> Immigrants soon find their place in urban life, they soon adopt, externally, town manners and opinions, but for a long time they remain foreign to civic thought. One cannot make a social philosophy one's own as easily as a new costume. It must be earned – earned with the effort of thought ... The growth of the towns and of the town life was too rapid. It was more extensive than intensive. The new inhabitants of the towns had become citizens superficially, but not in ways of thought ... More menacing than barbarians storming the walls from without are the seeming citizens within – those who are citizens in gesture, but not in thought.[55]

Classical liberalism requires not only a political and economic philosophy. Its survivability is also dependent upon an attitude and a philosophy of life: the accepting of self-responsibility for both successes and failures; a respect for others as individuals; a realization that peace of mind comes only from within, and that purpose and meaning cannot be bought at others' expense; and that one's own freedom, and that of others, should not be traded away for a few pieces of silver and a false sense of security through political paternalism.

Men's unwillingness or inability to adapt to this wider and deeper sense of a true citizenship of liberty brought all the ruin of the last one hundred years, including the barbaric extermination of the Jews of Europe and the destruction of an entire continent in World War II. After analyzing the collectivist roots of Nazism and the anti-Jewish attitudes of both Germans and many others at that time, Mises concluded: "Mankind has paid a high price indeed for anti-Semitism."[56]

Notes

1 On the general meaning of liberalism among many of the Austrian Jews in the late nineteenth and early twentieth centuries as representing a belief in the importance and role of reason in human affairs, a universal or cosmopolitan philosophy of individual rights and equality before the law, an advocacy of voluntary association outside of state regulation and control, and a loyalty to a multinational political authority (the Hapsburg emperor) as a defender and protector of these ideas, see, Pieter M. Judson, "Rethinking the Liberal Legacy" and Malachi Haim Hacohen, "Popper's Cosmopolitanism" in Steven Beller, ed., *Rethinking Vienna, 1900* (New York: Berghahn Books, 2001), pp. 57–79, 171–194; and, Marsha L. Rozenblit, *Reconstructing a National Identity: The Jews of Habsburg Austria During World War I* (New York: Oxford University Press, 2001), pp. 14–38.

2 Ludwig von Mises, *Notes and Recollections* [1940] (South Holland, IL: Libertarian

Press, 1978); these memoirs were written in the autumn of 1940 shortly after Mises and his wife, Margit, had arrived in the United States from war-torn Europe.

3 Ludwig von Mises, *Socialism: An Economic and Sociological Analysis* [1922; revised ed., 1932] (Indianapolis, IN: Liberty Classics, 1981), p. 370:

> Today the Islamic and Jewish religions are dead. They offer their adherents nothing more than ritual. They know how to prescribe prayers and fasts, certain foods, circumcision and the rest; but that is all. They offer nothing to the mind. Completely despiritualized, all they teach and preach are legal forms and external rule. They lock their follower into a cage of traditional usages, in which he is often hardly able to breathe; but for his inner soul they have no message. They suppress the soul, instead of elevating and saving it ... Today the religion of the Jews is just as it was when the Talmud was drawn up. The religion of Islam has not changed since the days of the Arab conquests ... But it is otherwise in the living [Christian] Church of the West. Here, where faith is not yet extinct, where it is not merely external form that conceals nothing but the priest's meaningless ritual, where, in a word, it grips the whole man, there is a continuous striving after a social ethic. Again and again do its members go back to the Gospels to renew their life in the Lord and His message.

4 Ludwig von Mises, *Omnipotent Government: The Rise of the Total State and Total War* (New Haven, CT: Yale University Press, 1944), pp. 169–192, a chapter on "Anti-Semitism and Racism."

5 F.A. Hayek, "Ludwig von Mises (1881–1973)" in, Peter G. Klein, ed., *The Collected Works of F.A. Hayek, Vol. 4: The Fortunes of Liberalism: Essays on Austrian Economics and the Ideal of Freedom* (Chicago: University of Chicago Press, 1992), p. 128.

6 See, William O. McCagg, Jr., *A History of Habsburg Jews, 1670–1918* (Bloomington, IN: Indiana University Press, 1989), pp. 105–122, 181–200.

7 But it is clear that Mayer Mises' family was active in the Jewish reform movement in Galicia, including the assimilation into German culture through the learning and use of the German language, as well as a desire to politically and socially cooperate with the ethnic Poles in the neighboring Galician community. See, McCagg, *A History of Habsburg Jews*, pp. 114–117.

8 See, Richard M. Ebeling, "Mission to Moscow: The Mystery of the 'Lost Papers' of Ludwig von Mises," *Notes from FEE* (Irvington-on-Hudson, NY: Foundation for Economic Education, July 2004).

9 In the late 1920s, Adele Mises dictated her memoirs about her life in Galicia and Vienna. She refers to the emphasis on charitable work within her family in Brody, saying that "the memories of my youth all relate to charitable activities. They occupied our parents' lives so completely that we children naturally became involved with them as well from an early age." And she recalled

> my aunt Halberstamm angrily remarking to her sister (my dear mother-in-law): 'You heartless Lembergers' (there was always an antagonism between Brody and Lemberg) 'you sit behind closed doors and care about nothing at all!' Actually, my mother-in-law also came from Brody and was compassionate and charitable. The accusation was most unjust. Of course, in Lemberg people had bells and locked their front doors, but the back door to the kitchen remained open just as in Brody"

to the poor and orphaned who need charitable assistance.

10 Robert S. Wistrich, *The Jews of Vienna in the Age of Franz Joseph* (New York: Oxford University Press, 1990), p. 165.

11 On the history of the Jews in the Austro-Hungarian Empire, see Wistrich, *The Jews of Vienna in the Age of Franz Joseph*; McCagg, *A History of Habsburg Jews, 1670–1918*; Steven Beller, *Vienna and the Jews, 1867–1938: A Cultural History*

(Cambridge, MA: Cambridge University Press, 1989); George E. Berkley, *Vienna and Its Jews: The Tragedy of Success, 1880s-1980s* (Lanham, MD: Madison Books, 1988); and, Max Grunwald, *History of the Jews in Vienna* (Philadelphia: Jewish Publication Society of America, 1936).

12 Full legal and economic rights were extended to Jews in Germany only in 1871, following the Franco-Prussian War and the unification of the German Empire under Prussian leadership.

13 In 1867, the Lower Austrian Chamber of Commerce located in Vienna (where Ludwig von Mises was to work as an economic analyst from 1909 until he left Austria in 1934) declared that

> The state has fulfilled its task if it removes all obstacles to the free, orderly activity of its citizens. Everything else is achieved by the considerateness and benevolence of the factory owners and above all by the personal efforts and thriftiness of the workers.

See, Robin Okey, *The Habsburg Monarchy: From Enlightenment to Eclipse* (New York: St. Martin's Press, 2001), p. 206.

14 The Fundamental Law Concerning the General Rights of Citizens from the Austrian Constitution of 1867 may be found at: www.h-net.org/~habsweb/ sourcetexts/auscon. htm.

15 This transformation of the Jewish communities in Central and Eastern Europe, especially in the German-speaking lands, is usually associated with the influence of Moses Mendelssohn beginning in the middle of the eighteenth century. See, Marvin Lowenthal, *The Jews of Germany: A Story of 16 Centuries* (Philadelphia, PA: The Jewish Publication Society of America, 1938), pp. 197–216; Ruth Gay, *The Jews of Germany: A Historical Portrait* (New Haven, CT: Yale University Press, 1992), pp. 98–117; Nachum T. Gidal, *Jews in Germany: From Roman Times to the Weimar Republic* (Köln, Germany: Konemann Verglagsgesellshcaft mbH, 1998), pp. 118–123; Amos Elon, *The Pity of It All: A History of the Jews in Germany, 1743–1933* (New York: Metropolitan Books, 2002), pp. 1–64.

16 On the demographics of the Jewish community in Vienna, see, Marsha L. Rozenblit, *The Jews of Vienna, 1867–1914: Assimilation and Identity* (Albany, NY: State University of New York Press, 1983).

17 Adolf Hitler, *Mein Kampf* [1925] (Boston: Houghton Mifflin, 1943), p. 56:

> Once as I was walking through the Inner City [of Vienna before World War I] I suddenly encountered an apparition in a black caftan and black hair locks. Is this a Jew? was my first thought. For, to be sure, they had not looked like that in Linz. I observed the man furtively and cautiously, but the longer I stared at this foreign face, scrutinizing feature after feature, the more the first question assumed a new form: Is this a German?

18 On the parallel process of Jewish assimilation and resistance from non-Jews in Prague and Bohemia, see the autobiographical recollections of this period in, Hans Kohn, *Living in a World Revolution: My Encounters with History* (New York: Trident Press, 1964), pp. 1–46.

19 On the "nationalities problem" and their respective goals and perspectives, see, Robert A. Kann, *The Multinational Empire: Nationalism and National Reform in the Habsburg Monarchy, 1848–1918*, 2 Vols. (New York: Columbia University Press, 1964); Oscar Jaszi, *The Dissolution of the Habsburg Monarchy* (Chicago: University of Chicago Press, 1928); and, Hans Kohn, *The Habsburg Empire, 1804–1918* (New York: D. Van Nostrand Reinhold, 1961), pp. 49–71.

20 Hapsburg enlightenment was more advanced in many ways over that of the German government. For example, before World War I it was virtually impossible for a Jew to be commissioned as an officer in the German Army, no matter what his qualifications and merit. On the other hand, Jews were accepted as officers in the Austrian Army

with no similar prejudice, and is what enabled Ludwig von Mises to be commissioned as a reserve officer in the Austrian Army as a young man, and serve with distinction in the Great War on the Russian front. See, Wistrich, *The Jews of Vienna in the Age of Franz Joseph*, pp. 174–175:

> In striking contrast to the Prussian regiments, there was no deliberate exclusion of Jewish officers and anti-Semitism was not officially tolerated. Indeed, anti-Semitism appears to have been notably weaker in the army than in many other sectors of Austrian society in spite of persistent nationalist agitation and the fact that most officers were Roman Catholic Germans ...In this supranational institution *par excellence* which was loyal to the Emperor and the dynasty alone, Jews were by and large treated on equal terms with other ethnic and religious groups. The army could simply not tolerate open racial or religious discrimination which would only undermine morale and patriotic motivation.

21 On the perception of the Jews before World War I by the various nationalities of the Austro-Hungarian Empire, including the Austrian-Germans, see, Henry W. Steed, *The Hapsburg Monarchy* [1913] (New York: Howard Fertig, 1969), pp. 145–194.

22 See, Jerry Z. Muller, *The Mind and the Market: Capitalism in Modern European Thought* (New York: Alfred A. Knopf, 2002) pp. 350–352.

23 On the occupational demographics, see, Rozenblit, *The Jews of Vienna, 1867–1914*, pp. 47–70; Beller, *Vienna and the Jews, 1867–1938*, pp. 165–187.

24 On the Vienna gymnasiums, and Jewish assimilation and social and economic advancement, see, Rozenblit, *The Jews of Vienna, 1867–1914*, pp. 99–126; Beller, *Vienna and the Jews, 1867–1938*, pp. 49–70.

25 See, Arthur Schnitzler, *My Youth in Vienna* (New York: Holt, Rinehart and Winston, 1970), for a rich memoir on the *Akademisches Gymnasium* in Vienna a few years before Mises attended as a student. Also, see, the fascinating account of Viennese gymnasium life during this time in, Stefan Zweig, *The World of Yesterday* (New York: Viking Press, 1943), pp. 28–66.

26 On the Maria Theresa Academy of Knights in Vienna during the time when Schumpeter attended, see, Robert Loring Allen, *Opening Doors: The Life and Work of Joseph Schumpeter*, Vol. 1 (Brunswick, NJ: Transaction Books, 1991) pp. 18–22; and, Richard Swedberg, *Schumpeter: A Biography* (Princeton, NJ: Princeton University Press, 1991), pp. 10–12.

27 On the nature and evolution of anti-Semitism in Germany and Austria, see, Peter G.J. Pulzer, *The Rise of Political Anti-Semitism in Germany and Austria* (New York: John Wiley, 1964); and Bruce F. Pauley, *From Prejudice to Persecution: A History of Austrian Anti-Semitism* (Chapel Hill: University of North Carolina Press, 1992).

28 That the real target behind much of the anti-Semitism in Germany and Austria was economic liberalism has been suggested by, Frederick Hertz, *Nationality in History and Politics* (New York: Oxford University Press, 1944), p. 403:

> It was rightly felt by many that the real object of [anti-Semitic attacks such as those by the Germany historian Heinrich von Treitschke, who coined the phrase, "The Jews are our misfortune"] was not the Jews, but liberalism, and that the Jews were only used as a means for working up public opinion against its fundamental principles.

And by, Hans Kohn, "Treitschke: National Prophet," *Review of Politics* (October 1945), pp. 434–435:

> Treitschke's words, 'The Jews are our misfortune,' served as a rallying banner for the German anti-Semitic movements for the next sixty years. Though the Jews were the immediate goal of the agitation, it ultimately aimed at the liberalism which had brought about Jewish emancipation. Treitschke hated the liberal middle-class society of the West and despised its concern for trade, prosperity

and peace ... In view of the apparent decay of the Western world through liberalism and individualism, only the German mind with its deeper insight and its
higher morality could regenerate the world.

See, also, F.A. Hayek, *The Road to Serfdom* (London: George Routledge and Sons,
Ltd, 1944), p. 104:

> In Germany and Austria the Jew had come to be regarded as the representative
> of capitalism because a traditional dislike of large classes of the population for
> commercial pursuits had left these more readily accessible to a group that was
> practically excluded from the more highly esteemed occupations. It is the old
> story of the alien race being admitted only to the less respected trades, and then
> being hated still more for practicing them. The fact that German anti-Semitism
> and anti-capitalism spring from the same root is of great importance for the
> understanding of what has happened there, but this is rarely grasped by foreign
> observers.

And, Fritz Stern, *The Politics of Cultural Despair: A Study in the Rise of Germanic
Ideology* (Berkeley: University of California Press, 1961), pp. 142–143:

> Of course, the Jews favored liberalism, secularism, and capitalism. Where else
> but in the cities, in the free professions, in an open society, could they escape
> from the restrictions and prejudices that lingered on from the closed, feudal
> society of an earlier era? They were, and in a sense had to be, the promoters and
> profiteers of modernity, and for this ... [many Germans] could not forgive the
> Jews.

29 Ludwig von Mises, "Postwar Economic Reconstruction of Europe" [1940] in, Richard
M. Ebeling, ed., *Selected Writings of Ludwig von Mises, Vol. 3: The Political Economic of International Reform and Reconstruction* (Indianapolis, IN: Liberty Fund
2000), p. 27.
30 Mises, *Omnipotent Government: The Rise of the Total State and Total War*, p. 185.
31 This attitude was expressed, as one example, during the 1930s by the ardent National
Socialist Adolf Bertels, who said about Heinrich Heine, possibly, after Goethe, the
greatest German writer of the nineteenth century, that "however well he handles the
German language and German poetical forms, however much he knows the German
way of life, it is impossible for a Jew to be a German." Quoted in, Alistair Hamilton,
The Appeal of Fascism: A Study of Intellectuals and Fascism, 1919–1945 (London:
Anthony Blond, 1971), p. 109.
32 Quoted in, J. Sydney Jones, *Hitler in Vienna, 1907–1913: Clues to the Future* (New
York: Cooper Square Press, 2002), p. 155.
33 Ibid., p. 157; also, Berkley, *Vienna and Its Jews*, pp. 103–111; on the history of the
Christian Social movement and Lueger's role and participation in it, see, John W.
Boyer, *Political Radicalism in Late Imperial Vienna: Origins of the Christian Social
Movement, 1848–1897* (Chicago: University of Chicago Press, 1981), and, John W.
Boyer, *Culture and Political Crisis in Vienna: Christian Socialism in Power,
1897–1918* (Chicago: University of Chicago Press, 1995).
34 Stefan Zweig, *The World of Yesterday*. Zweig was born the same year as Mises, 1881,
and was forced to leave Vienna with the rise of Nazi power in Austria. He went into
exile in Brazil, where he committed suicide in 1942.
35 Harriet Pass Freidenreich, *Jewish Politics in Vienna, 1918–1938* (Bloomington:
Indiana University Press, 1991), pp. 138.
36 Mises, *Notes and Recollections*, p. 100.
37 See, Robert S. Wistrich, *Socialism and the Jews* (East Brunswick, NJ: Associated
University Presses, 1982).
38 Many of the Jews in Germany and Austria understood that connection between economic liberalism and individual opportunity that had enabled so many in the Jewish

community to prosper in spite of anti-Semitic sentiments. Thus, for example, in 1897, Emil Lehmann, head of the Dresden Jewish community argued against the Social Democrats,

> In the Mosaic teaching the ideals of justice and equality before the law find their substantiation just as envy and hatred – which the Social Democracy share with the anti-Semites – receives the sharpest condemnation. Thou shalt not covet! Other demands contrary to civilization such as the abolition of the family, State education of children, etc. etc, which are desired by the Social Democrats, are firmly rejected in the Ten Commandments.
> Quoted in, Wistrich, *Socialism and the Jews*, p. 69.

39 On Mises' role and prominence in the Austria of the interwar period, see, Ch. 5: "The Economist as the Historian of Decline: Ludwig von Mises and Austria between the Two World Wars," in the present volume.

40 That the loss due to anti-Semitism did not only fall upon the Jews who were robbed of their property, exiled, imprisoned, or murdered in the concentration and death camps was pointed out by Hugo Bettauer in his fictional account *The City Without Jews: A Novel of Our Time* (New York: Bloch Publishing, 1926). Originally published in German in Vienna in 1923, it imagines a complete expelling of the Jews from Vienna at some future point in the city's history. And with the Jews goes much of the city's cultural, social, and economic achievement and potential. Indeed, the city decays in cultural and economic poverty without the contribution of Vienna's former Jewish citizens.

41 Mises' monumental work on *Socialism: An Economic and Sociological Analysis* (Indianapolis, IN: Liberty Classics, 1981), originally published in 1922, is not merely a logical argument against the possibility for socialist central planning – which of course is a centerpiece of the book. It is also a sweeping and majestic analysis of the social, cultural and political potential of a free and [classical] liberal community, and the poverty and destructive tendencies of all forms of collectivism. His 1927 volume, *Liberalism* (Irvington-on-Hudson, NY: Foundation for Economic Education, 2004), presents an integrated and coherent exposition of the truly humane world that a liberal society can bring mankind. All of these themes on the nature of the free society were brought together in his masterful treatise, *Human Action* [1949] (Irvington-on-Hudson, NY: Foundation for Economic Education, 1996). On Mises as social and political philosopher, see, Ch. 6: "Planning for Freedom: Ludwig von Mises as Political Economist and Policy Analyst" in the present volume.

42 See, Ludwig von Mises, "The Clash of Group Interests" [1945] in Richard M. Ebeling, ed., *Money, Method and the Market Process: Essays by Ludwig von Mises* (Norwell, MA: Kluwer Academic Press, 1990), pp. 202–214; and Ludwig von Mises, *Theory and History: An Interpretation of Social and Economic Evolution* (New Haven, CT: Yale University Press, 1957), pp. 112–122.

43 Ludwig von Mises, *Omnipotent Government: The Rise of the Total State and Total War* (New Haven, CT: Yale University Press, 1944), pp. 171–177.

44 Many of these assimilated Jews were embarrassed and ashamed of their "eastern cousins" who continued to follow more traditional Jewish cultural and religious forms. Their physical appearance and religious practices seemed a reminder of that which they had chosen to escape. And the arrival of these more orthodox Jews in Berlin and Vienna in the years both before and after the Great War was viewed with great unease. Indeed, the assimilated Jews were fearful that their country orthodox cousins would make them look "bad" in the eyes of their non-Jewish neighbors. They would be tarred with the negative impressions these Orthodox Jews would (and did often) create in the minds of non-Jewish Germans and Austrians. See, Jack Wertheimer, *Unwelcome Strangers: Eastern European Jews in Imperial Germany* (New York: Oxford University Press, 1987); Derek J. Penslar, *Shylock's Children: Economics and Jewish Identity in Modern Europe* (Berkeley: University of California

Press, 2001), pp. 195–205; and, Amos Elon, *The Pity of It All: A History of the Jews in Germany, 1743–1933* (New York: Metropolitan Books, 2002), pp. 231–257.
45 Mises, *Omnipotent Government*, p. 184.
46 Ibid., pp. 184–185.
47 Indeed, though Mises does not draw attention to this point, what most German and Austrian Jews shared with their non-Jewish countrymen was an enthusiasm for Germany imperialism on the eve of World War I, and they served in the German Army in a proportion far in excess of their percentage in the general population. They also shared the same resentments and feelings of humiliation with the defeat of the German and Austrian armies at the end of the war, especially in the wake of the peace terms imposed by the Allied powers in 1919. See, Amos Elon, *The Pity of It All*, pp. 297–354; Howard M. Sachar, *Dreamland: Europeans and Jews in the Aftermath of the Great War* (New York: Alfred A. Knopf, 2002), pp. 205–282; and, Marsha L. Rozenblit, *Reconstructing a National Identity: The Jews of Habsburg Austria During World War I*. The perversity, as Mises does point out, is that many of the non-Jews in Germany tried to maintain their mental equilibrium in the face of Germany's defeat by looking for a scapegoat for the humiliation of 1919 and found it in a Jewish "stab in the back," see, Mises, *Omnipotent Government*, p. 187:

> It was salvation for the self-esteem of all these disheartened souls when some generals and nationalist leaders found a justification and an excuse: it had been the work of the Jews. Germany was victorious by land and sea and air, but the Jews had stabbed the victorious forces in the back. Whoever ventured to refute this legend was himself denounced as a Jew or a bribed servant of the Jews. No rational argument could shake the legend … It must be realized that German nationalism managed to survive the defeat in the First World War only by means of the legend of the stab in the back.

Mises later developed the theme of envy and resentment as the foundation for anti-capitalist attitudes; see, Ludwig von Mises, *The Anti-Capitalistic Mentality* (Princeton, NJ: D. Van Nostrand, 1956).
48 Mises, "Postwar Reconstruction" [1941] in, Richard M. Ebeling, ed., *Selected Writings of Ludwig von Mises, Vol. 3: The Political Economic of International Reform and Reconstruction*, p. 13.
49 On how such interventionist policies were used against the Jews in the countries of Central and Eastern Europe in the period between the two world wars, see, Sachar, *Dreamland*, and Ezra Mendesohn, *The Jews of East Central Europe Between the World Wars* (Bloomington: Indiana University Press, 1983); see, also, P.G.J. Pulzer, "The Development of Political Antisemitism in Austria" in, Josef Fraenkel, ed., *The Jews of Austria: Essays on Their Life, History and Destruction* (London: Vallentine, Mitchell, 1967), pp. 429–443.
50 For detailed accounts of the growing political and interventionist discrimination and prohibition on the social, civil and economic liberties of the Jews in Nazi Germany during the 1930s, see, Raul Hilberg, *The Destruction of the European Jews* (Chicago: Quadrangle Books, 1967), pp. 43–105; Lucy S. Dawidowicz, *The War Against the Jews, 1933–1945* (New York: Bantam Books), pp. 48–69; J. Noakes and G. Pridham, *Nazism, 1933–1945, Vol. 2: State, Economy and Society, 1933–1939* (Exeter: University of Exeter Press, 1984), pp. 521–567; Arno J. Mayer, *Why Did the Heavens Not Darken? The "Final Solution" in History* (New York: Pantheon, 1988), pp. 113–158; Saul Friedlander, *Nazi Germany and the Jews, Vol. I: The Years of Persecution, 1933–1939* (New York: Harper/Collins, 1997); Deborah Dwork and Robert Jan van Pelt, *Holocaust: A History* (New York: Norton, 2002), pp. 82–102; also, Stephen Roberts, *The House that Hitler Built* (New York: Harper & Brothers, 1938), pp. 258–267; and, Marvin Lowenthal, *The Jews of Germany: A Story of Sixteen Centuries* (Philadelphia: The Jewish Publications Society of America, 1938), pp. 392–421. On anti-Semitism in Germany in the 1920s, see, Donald L. Niewyk, *The Jews in*

Weimar Germany (New Brunswick, NJ: Transaction Books, 2001), pp. 43–81. And on the response of the Jews in Germany to mounting interventionist discrimination and violence in the 1930s, see, John V.P. Dippel, *Bound Upon a Wheel of Fire: Why So Many German Jews Made the Tragic Decision to Remain in Nazi Germany* (New York: Basic Books, 1996).

51 Pauley, *From Prejudice to Persecution: A History of Austrian Anti-Semitism*, pp. 275, 280–284.

52 Mises, "A Draft of Guidelines for the Reconstruction of Austria" [1940] in, Richard M. Ebeling, ed., *Selected Writings of Ludwig von Mises, Vol. 3: The Political Economic of International Reform and Reconstruction*, pp. 135–136.

53 For an account of how it was the rise of immigration barriers across Europe and North America in the post-World War I period that closed the door and determined the fate of many German and Austrian Jews who therefore had no route of escape from the Nazis, see, Deborah Dwork and Robert Jan van Pelt, *Holocaust: A History*, pp. 103–132; also, Arthur D. Morse, *While Six Million Died: A Chronicle of American Apathy* (New York: Random House, 1967); and David S. Wyman, *Paper Walls: America and the Refugee Crisis, 1938–1941* (New York: Pantheon Books, 1968). On the general development and effects of immigration restrictions, see, John Torpey, *The Invention of the Passport: Surveillance, Citizenship and the State* (Cambridge, MA: Cambridge University Press, 2000).

54 Stefan Zweig, *The World of Yesterday* [1943] (Lincoln: University of Nebraska Press, 1964), p. 13.

55 Mises, *Socialism*, p. 38.

56 Mises, *Omnipotent Government*, p. 192.

4 Austria-Hungary's economic policies in the twilight of the "liberal" era

Ludwig von Mises' writings on monetary and fiscal policy before World War I

Austria-Hungary and the nineteenth-century liberal era

Those who lived through the Great War and then experienced the rise of political and economic collectivism in the years following 1918 often had a deep nostalgia for the epoch that came to an end in 1914. They looked back at that earlier liberal era with remembrance of a time of international peace, growing economic prosperity, and wide respect for the liberty of the individual. There was a sense that man, before the opening shots of those guns of August in 1914, had freed himself from the old political and social superstitions of the past; and with all of his very human frailties was on the path of slow but certain improvement.

For example, in 1934, the famous British historian, G.P. Gooch, expressed this nostalgia with a lament about the world in which he now lived:

> Only men and women who, like myself, were adult citizens at the turn of the [twentieth] century can realize the enormous contrast between the years preceding and following the World War. I grew to manhood in an age of sensational progress and limitless self-confidence. Civilization was spreading across the earth with giant strides; science was tossing us miracle after miracle; wealth was accumulating at a pace undreamed of in earlier generations; the amenities of life were being brought within the range of an ever greater number of our fellow-creatures ... There was a robust conviction that we were on the right track; that man was a teachable animal who would work out his salvation if given his chance; that the nations were on the march toward a larger freedom and a fuller humanity; that difficulties could be taken in their stride ... Some of the ruling conceptions of the time, such as national and political liberty, equality before the law, religious toleration and a minimum standard of life, were the ripe fruit of a long process of evolution ... No one spoke of a possible return to the Dark Ages or wondered whether we could keep civilization afloat. We realize today that we were living in a fool's paradise ... The Europe that emerged from the four years of carnage contrasted sensationally from that which we had known ... Half of Europe is ruled by dictators who scoff at democracy and trample human rights under their feet. Meanwhile the Communists look on with grim satisfaction awaiting their hour.[1]

The decades before World War I *were* a liberal epoch. The people of nineteenth century Europe, particularly after the 1850s, enjoyed a degree of freedom and prosperity unimaginable under the Mercantilism of the eighteenth century. It was a period of the "three freedoms," as German economist Gustav Stolper expressed it: the free movement of goods, the free movement of money, and the free movement of men.[2]

Wars still occurred in nineteenth century Europe, though they were usually limited and of relatively short duration, and increasingly constrained by international agreements on the "rules of war" and the treatment of non-combatants, at least when fought among the European powers. However, political corruption continued to exist, and interest groups still plied the halls of power for favors and privileges. Censorship, taxes, and regulations still pinched the freedoms of thought and enterprise. And as the century progressed, friends of liberty increasingly expressed concerns that the interventionist state was making a comeback, along with the appeal and demands of the new collectivisms – nationalism and socialism.[3] This was even true in the home of liberalism, in Great Britain.[4]

Certainly Europe before 1914 offered far more personal, political, and economic liberty than was then experienced in the years following 1918, after the triumph of communism, fascism, Nazism, and an array of other authoritarian regimes throughout Central and Eastern Europe. Yet, this liberal epoch had been drawing to a close for a long time even before the Great War made it clear for even the most optimistic to finally see and understand. This trend was partly due to the fact that the monarchical and paternalistic "old regimes" of the eighteenth and early nineteenth centuries had never been fully overthrown.[5] So in Europe the liberal ideals had only partly replaced the absolutism and political paternalism of the past; in fact, liberal policies and changes were frequently simply overlaid onto the political institutions of the pre-liberal era. It was this incomplete and often thwarted liberalism-in-practice that was then challenged by the rising ideas of nineteenth century socialism and nationalism.

A particular example of these mixings of the older monarchical absolutism with elements of political and economic liberalism was Austria-Hungary before the World War I. But in spite of all of its inconsistencies and contradictions, the Hapsburg Empire was considered by many to be crucial to the stability of the pre-1914 political and economic order.

In 1900, a correspondent for *The Economist* summed up the nature and significance of the Hapsburg Monarchy, as the new century was about to begin. Another constitutional crisis was at hand in Vienna, he explained. The dozen or so national and linguistic groups comprising the peoples of the Empire – Germans, Hungarians, Czechs, Slovaks, Croatians, Romanians, Italians, Poles, Bulgarians, Serbians, Slovenians, Ruthenians – were once more at each other's throats, each wanting more political and cultural autonomy (if not outright independence) for themselves at the economic and social expense of other groups within the Hapsburg domain.

The Hungarians, in particular, wanted more sovereignty outside of the periodically revised provisions of the Dual Monarchy of Austria-Hungary that had been established in 1867, in the wake of Austria's defeat at the hands of Bismarck's Prussian Armies the year before. *The Economist* correspondent explained:[6]

> When the relations between two allied countries are whittled down gradually to bare matters of finance, and those countries differ in language, race and feeling, one doubts the permanence of the union. And such is the condition of Austria-Hungary at the present time,

Yet, he said, "somehow" the machinery of government in Vienna and Budapest went on. Compromises, shortcuts, and evasions kept "the noisy, creaking and grinding" wheels of the political process functioning without breaking asunder. "How long Austria-Hungary will hold together we do not know." But, he continued, if the Austrian Empire

> had not existed, it would have been necessary to invent her, for she alone, so far as one can see, can render the common service of welding together certain diverse elements of race, language, creed, and separate interest, which would otherwise be flying at one another's throats, and so perpetuating anarchy and bloodshed over a large portion of Europe.

What held the Austro-Hungarian Empire together was its Emperor, Francis Joseph. *The Economist*'s writer said that it was the Emperor's "daily practical wisdom – not the wisdom of the great genius, but of a good-natured, commonsense mind which is gifted with one quality of genius, i.e., the faculty of seeing things as they are ... combined with his long experience" that was "the reason why the Dual Monarchy is enabled to continue on its way under conditions which would probably wreck any other state on earth." Whether or not the Empire would survive the Emperor was unknown. But, "[s]erious as is the condition of Europe, it would be rendered ten times more serious by the collapse of Austria-Hungary."

Born in 1830, Francis Joseph had ascended the Austrian throne in 1848 when he was eighteen years old, and ruled for sixty-eight years until his death in 1916 during the Great War. Those who had lived a good part of their lives under his reign – even if they found fault with many aspects of his rule – still held him in high reverence and great awe long after he had died. Joseph Redlich (1869–1936), one of the great Austrian liberals before and after World War I, who had served as finance minister in the last Austro-Hungarian cabinet before the end of the war, and who again was minister of finance in the Austrian Republic from 1931 to 1934, spoke with just such reverence for the Emperor on the occasion of what would have been Francis Joseph's hundredth birthday in 1930:

> When all of us who lived many decades under this old man's scepter now remember the hundredth anniversary of his birth, we unavoidably fall into a kind of historic reverie and of a sudden that whole world of old Austria rises up before us quick and vivid. And instantly we feel what a short time indeed a century is. Our whole life and the lives of our fathers and grandfathers fill

that century almost to overflowing. We have lived through all that and still we are alive. For us that whole world of great events in peace and war, of great names and powerful men and of the rivalry of so many races and peoples united into one empire ... this is the historic Austria, our old world which bred us and shaped us and made our life what it has become. And always Francis Joseph stands in the midst of this many-colored, fine old picture that our memory retains – piously and cynically – just as we have known him from the old-fashioned likenesses of his childhood and the first years of his reign; and then recollect him as he was later almost to the last of his days, standing tall, erect, and almost invisibly distancing himself from everybody, watchful and never shrinking his royal work, a dignified figure, every inch a ruler of men and lands.[7]

Not that liberals like Redlich failed to see the shortcoming and fatal mistakes in the Emperor's rule. Francis Joseph, Redlich explained, had "a cool and sober mind, almost wholly devoid of imaginative power, a realist, looking dryly at the world and at his work." (Other historians have suggested that Francis Joseph's idea of exciting and adventurous reading was spending the night with the Austrian military manual of arms!) What he had inherited from his ruling ancestors was a belief in "his divine right of unlimited monarchical power," tempered with the idea

> that his rule must, before all, produce the best possible results for the peoples of his realm ... Yet, up to the end he did not doubt that his empire, composed of so many different races and lands, could be governed successfully only by a hereditary monarch and according to his absolute will.[8]

Both Redlich and other Austrian liberals who had lived a part of their mature life under the long reign of the last but one of the Hapsburg emperors, believed that Francis Joseph had twice missed the opportunity to make his domain a truly multi-national liberal society.[9] Shortly after becoming Emperor, Francis Joseph renounced a liberal democratic constitution that he had initially endorsed in the immediate aftermath of the revolution of 1848.

> He never realized that his empire could be best safeguarded by a perfect system of administrative decentralization and by the fullest realization of the principles of equality of all nations on the basis of local autonomy. Thus he closed the door to a reconciliation of the struggling nationalities of his empire,

at the very time that radical nationalism was beginning to rise in revolutionary importance throughout Central and Eastern Europe.[10]

The second lost opportunity occurred following his defeat at the hands of the Prussians in 1866. Bismarck pushed Austria out of the German confederation, which the Hapsburgs had dominated for centuries. Fearful of the Hungarians taking advantage of the Empire's postwar weakness to claim full independence,

Francis Joseph agreed to the *Ausgleich*, the "Compromise," of 1867 that transformed the Austrian Empire into the Austro-Hungarian Empire. While Francis Joseph remained Emperor of both halves of his domain, Hungary became widely independent in many of its domestic affairs. Only a common customs and monetary system and a shared military and foreign policy completely linked it to the Austrian "Crownlands" directly ruled by Francis Joseph's government in Vienna.

This also meant that the Hungarians had wide powers over the subject peoples in their half of the Empire – Romanians, Slovaks, and Croats – who were denied autonomy in many aspects of local, economic or cultural life. The Hungarians were determined to prevent these groups from enjoying any of the new political liberty they claimed for themselves.

As Hans Kohn, one of the twentieth century's leading experts on the history and philosophy of nationalism, and who had grown up under the rule of Francis Joseph in Prague,[11] explained:

> In the Compromise with the Hungarian nobility in 1867, the aspirations of the Czechs, Slovaks, Serbs, Croats, and Romanians, who in large majority were then still loyal to the dynasty, were sacrificed for the purpose of winning the assent of the Magyars to a common foreign and military policy on the part of what now became the Dual Monarchy.[12]

But not only the Hungarians were the problem; the German-Austrians were, too.

> The spread of democracy, literacy, and economic well-being in the western half of the monarchy after 1867 strengthened the non-German nationalities there at the expense of the Germans. The result was that many Germans in the monarchy lost their faith in an Austrian idea as much as many Slavs and other non-Germanic peoples did ... By the end of the nineteenth century many Austrian Germans looked to the Prussian German Reich as their real home and venerated Bismarck.

As a result, again, the chance for a decentralized federalist system in which all of the linguistic and national groups would have been treated with complete political equality before the law was lost. Kohn concluded that due to this Francis Joseph missed the opportunity to unify the "polyglot" empire along "Swiss-type" lines that might very well have saved and even reinforced the unity of the Hapsburg Empire as a truly liberal multi-national state.[13]

Looking back at the events that brought about the demise of the Hapsburg Empire in the immediate aftermath of the Great War, Ludwig von Mises explained why many German-Austrians turned against liberalism as a foundation for the preservation of the monarchy and the Austro-Hungarian state. Over the centuries German-Austrian settlers had made their homes in the eastern reaches of the Empire. They brought with them the German language, culture, literature, commercial knowledge and knowhow. They viewed themselves as a "civilizing force" among the lesser advanced nationalities, especially the Slavic peoples.

And, indeed, many of these subject peoples became acculturated into German-Austrian life, since the latter was the dominant group; the German language in particular became the venue for social and economic advancement. But as literacy and national consciousness awakened among these other peoples in the nineteenth century, loyalties to and identification with German-Austria and the Hapsburg dynasty were replaced with a growing allegiance and sense of belonging to their own ethnic and linguistic groups.

Furthermore, birth rates were higher among these peoples than that among the Germans living among them. Cities and towns that had been settled and predominantly populated by Germans for centuries became increasingly Czech or Hungarian, or Polish or Romanian, or Slovenian communities. German-Austrians found themselves shrinking minorities in lands that they long considered to be their own politically, culturally, and commercially. This was especially true in the Czech lands with Prague at its center.

As the nineteenth century progressed, German-Austrians discovered that adherence to liberal principles of representative government and full individual and cultural equality before the law meant the demise of these German communities sprinkled across the Hapsburg domains. For many German-Austrian liberals the choice was between a liberalism that would logically mean the decentralization and possible eventual break-up of the Empire along nationalist lines, or advocacy of centralized political control, monarchical dictate when required, and subversion of democratic aspirations among the non-German peoples.

The first course meant the eventual loss of German political and culture domination in the non-German lands; the second meant holding on to both political and cultural power as long as possible in the non-German areas of the Empire but only by increasingly alienating the other subject peoples. As Mises explained, part of the German-Austrian tragedy was that national and linguistic imperialism won over liberal idealism.[14]

As a result, this meant that from the 1880s until the disintegration of the Hapsburg Empire in 1918, the history of the country was one of liberal freedoms that were introduced after 1867 being undermined by nationalist discord, periods of rule by central government decree, and the continuation or introduction of interventionist policies that merely intensified the antagonisms among the subject peoples.[15]

The only group that predominantly remained loyal to the Emperor virtually to the end was the Jews of the Austro-Hungarian Empire. As late as the 1820s, no Jew could reside in Vienna without permission of the Emperor. They lived ghettoized lives throughout the Empire. But the Constitution of 1867, which accompanied the creation of "Austria-Hungary," was imbued with the spirit of the classical liberal ideas that were then at their zenith in Europe.[16] Every subject of the Hapsburg Emperor was guaranteed freedom of religion, language, association, profession, and occupation. Any subject might live wherever he chose throughout the Emperor's domain. Private property was secure and relative free trade prevailed within the boundaries of the Empire.[17]

Among all of his subject peoples none took as much advantage of this new freedom as the Jews of Austria. Within two generations, following the repeal of the legal and many of the informal barriers to personal improvement and economic opportunity, they attained a good number of the most prominent positions in a wide variety of walks of life. They owed all this, they sincerely believed, to the guardianship of Francis Joseph.[18] He protected them from the anti-Semitism of the rural peasants and priests, and from the envious urban businessmen and professionals who resented their more successful Jewish rivals. (But as the nineteenth century became the twentieth, a growing number in the Jewish community turned their voting loyalty to the Social Democrats in the Austrian parliament.)[19]

Out of all of these political, social, and economic currents came that liberal postwar nostalgic imagery of an Austria-Hungary before 1914, in which the most diverse populations intermingled, in cities like Vienna, Budapest, and Prague, in apparent peace and growing prosperity in an environment of high culture and intellectual creativity. One voice that attempted to capture this "lost world" was that of Stefan Zweig (1881–1942), a renowned Austrian novelist and essayist who fled Vienna in 1934 and committed suicide in Brazil during World War II out of despair for all that was happening in the European world that he had known. In his posthumous work, *The World of Yesterday*, he said:

> One lived well and easily and without cares in that old Vienna ... "Live and let live" was the famous Viennese motto, which today still seems to me more humane than all the categorical imperatives, and it maintained itself throughout all classes. Rich and poor, Czechs and Germans, Jews and Christians, lived peaceably together in spite of occasional chafing, and even the political and social movements were free of the terrible hatred which has penetrated the arteries of our time as a poisonous residue of the First World War. In the old Austria they still strove chivalrously, they abused each other in the news and in the parliament, but at the conclusion of their ciceronian tirades the selfsame representatives sat down together in friendship with a glass of beer or a cup of coffee, and called each other Du [the "familiar" in the German language] ... The hatred of country for country, for nation for nation, of one table for another, did not yet jump at one daily from the newspaper, it did not divide people from people and nations from nations; not yet had every herd and mass feeling become so disgustingly powerful in public life as today. Freedom in one's personal affairs, which is no longer considered comprehensible, was taken for granted. One did not look down upon tolerance as one does today as weakness and softness, but rather praised it as an ethical force ... For the genius of Vienna – a specifically musical one – was always that it harmonized all the national and lingual contrasts. Its culture was a synthesis of all Western cultures. Whoever lived there and worked there felt himself free of all confinement and prejudice.[20]

It was, of course, only an illusion. That liberal era about which Zweig was so nostalgic had never been as pure and perfect as his mind recalled it. It was certainly true that liberal ideals had been established in the constitution of 1867, and that they were implemented and enforced for the most part, especially in the Crownlands more directly under Emperor Francis Joseph's imperial authority. But beneath the surface of tolerance, civility, and cosmopolitanism were all the undercurrents of racial and nationalist bigotry, economic collectivism, and political authoritarianism that poured forth like destructive lava from an exploding volcano during and in the aftermath of the Great War.

The Austrian monetary system, 1867–1914

One of the institutions of nineteenth century Western liberalism that Austria-Hungary adopted, in 1892, was the establishment of the gold standard as the basis of the Empire's monetary system. It was the culmination of a century of disastrous Austrian monetary policy. The story of the Austrian currency in the late eighteenth century and the first two-thirds of the nineteenth century is one of almost continual financial mismanagement. The government would debase the currency to cover its expenses, followed by promises to put its budget on a sound footing, only to see another crisis arise requiring once again turning the handle on the monetary printing press.[21]

The Austrian government made several experiments with state-chartered banks in the 1700s. But each of these banks soon collapsed or was closed due to lack of public confidence following large quantities of paper monies being issued to cover government expenditures.[22] These expenditures reached huge proportions during the long years of war between the Austrian Empire and first Revolutionary and then Napoleonic France.

Between 1797 and 1811, the supply of government paper money increased from 74,200,000 florins to 1,064,000,000 florins, or a fourteen-fold increase over this period. Not surprisingly, whereas the price of silver coin expressed in paper money was 118 in 1800, it rose to 203 by 1807, then to 500 by 1810, and reached 1,200 by 1811.

The government announced its intention in 1811 to stop the printing presses and issue a new currency that would be converted at the ratio of five old florins for one new florin, with the total amount of paper money in circulation to be reduced to 212,800,000 florins. But the renewal of the war with Napoleon in 1812 resulted in the new currency being increased to 678,716,000 florins by 1816, a near tripling of the "reformed" currency in five years.

With the final defeat of Napoleon, the Austrian government announced that it would use a portion of the war reparations being paid by France to retire about 131,829,900 florins from circulation, leaving the paper money supply outstanding at around 546,886,000 florins. This process was assisted with the establishment of a new National Bank of Austria, with the Bank withdrawing government paper money in circulation in exchange for its own bank notes, until by the early 1848, the total currency supply in circulation had been reduced to 241,240,000 florins, or an almost two-thirds reduction in the paper money supply over a thirty-year period. The National Bank, in February 1848, had silver reserves of about 65,000,000 florins, i.e., an approximate 25 percent specie cover for its outstanding currency in circulation.

But all of these monetary reforms began to unravel with the outbreak of the revolution of 1848, especially the Hungarian revolt against Austrian rule. Within days, panic runs on the Bank reduced its silver reserves to 35,023,000 florins, a 53 percent loss in specie. The Austrian government suspended silver redemption, and banned the exporting of silver and gold. Putting down the revolution forced the government to again borrow heavily from the National Bank. As a result, confidence in the Bank fell so low that in 1849 the government publicly promised to stop borrowing and cease increasing the currency.

But the process started again in a few years with Austria's participation in the Crimean War, and then its wars against Italian nationalists and their French ally in a vain attempt to maintain control of portions of northern Italy. In 1850 government indebtedness to the National Bank had stood at 205,300,000 florins. With the Crimean War of 1854, the government's debt increased to 294,200,000 florins. It was reduced to 145,700,000 florins by 1859. But the start of the Italian campaigns that year pushed it up again to 285,800,000 florins, along with a renewed suspension of specie payments as the public wished to redeem the paper currency representing the value of this enlarged debt.

In 1863, an attempt was made, once again, to introduce a currency reform – the Plener Act – this time along the lines of Britain's Peel's Bank Act of 1844. But Austria's disastrous war with Prussia in 1866 pushed the supply of paper money in circulation from 80,000,000 florins before the conflict to 300,000,000 florins at its end.

The Compromise of 1867 that formally created the Austro-Hungarian Empire granted Hungary its own parliament, government, and domestic budget. It established a customs union and a common military and foreign policy between the two parts of the Hapsburg domain, and a monetary union with the Austrian National Bank retaining its monopoly of note issue throughout Francis Joseph's domain. Some of the Hungarian liberals had advocated a system of competitive note-issuing private banks in place of the National Bank, but secret agreements between the Emperor's government and the Hungarian nobility eliminated this as an option.[23]

On July 1, 1878, the Austrian National Bank was transformed into the Austro-Hungarian Bank. The Emperor, under joint nomination of the Austrian and Hungarian parliaments, appointed its Governor. He was assisted by two Vice-Governors – one Austrian and the other Hungarian – appointed by the respective governments. The Banks operating privileges were renewed in 1887, 1899, and in 1910, with few substantial changes in their detail.

Formally, from 1816, Austria had been on a silver standard. But as we saw the Austrian National Bank only maintained unofficial specie redemption for limited periods of time, soon interrupted usually by another war crisis requiring currency expansion to fund the government's expenditures.

The paper currency florin, not surprisingly, traded at a significant discount against the silver coin florin. Between 1848 and 1870, this discount was never less than about 14 percent and was often between 20 and 23 percent. But restrictions on note issuance under the operating rules of the Bank limited the expansion of the supply of bank notes. The provisions of the 1863 Bank Act limited the circulation of "uncovered" florins to 200,000,000. Any amount above that had to be covered by gold or silver coin or bullion. Any additional "uncovered" bank note issuance was subject to a penalty tax against the Bank of 5 percent.

With many of the major governments of Europe and North America establishing or reestablishing their economies on a gold basis in place of silver in the 1870s, the world price of silver began to fall.[24] After the Austro-Prussian War of 1866, the government's pressures on the Bank to fund deficits were greatly reduced, and the Bank could more or less follow the rules against uncovered note issuance. As a result, the paper florin's discount relative to silver disappeared by 1878. Silver began to flow into Austria-Hungary in such quantities that the Bank was instructed by the government to end the free minting of silver.

The paper florin actually rose to a premium against silver, as a result. As Friedrich von Wieser expressed it, "Silver had become of less value than paper!"[25] In addition, the florin was significantly appreciating in value against gold. The price in paper florins for one hundred gold florins between 1887 and 1892 was:

Average for the year	Austrian florin notes
1887	125.25
1888	122.87
1889	118.58
1890	115.48
1891	115.83

The major monetary issue, therefore, during these years was to bring a halt to any further increase in the value of the Austrian paper currency. In February 1892, the Austrian and Hungarian governments invited a group of professional and academic experts to meet and address a set of questions relating to: whether a gold standard should be adopted; if so, should it be monometallic or partly bimetallic with silver; what should be the status of government notes in circulation; how should the conversion from the existing florin to a gold standard be undertaken; and what monetary unit should be chosen?

Some of the most illustrious people in the field were brought together to offer their views and opinions on these questions. Thirty years later Ludwig von Mises described them in the following manner:

> From March 8 to March 17, 1892 the Currency Inquiry Commission convened by the government met in Vienna. The chairman was Finance Minister [Emil] Steinbach; beside him stood the memorable [Eugen von] Böhm-Bawerk as section head. Thirty-six experts appeared in order to answer the five questions that the government had posed. No Austrian was left off the list of members at the assembly who had anything of importance to say about currency matters. Along with Carl Menger, the founder of the Austrian School of Economics, there was Wilhelm von Lucam, the highly honored long-time general secretary of the Austro-Hungarian Bank; Moriz Benedikt, the publisher of *Neue Freie Presse* [New Free Press]; Theodor

Thaussig, the spiritual leader of the Viennese banking world; and Theodor Hertzka, the writer on monetary matters and social policy-thinker. The thick quarto volume of the stenographic minutes of these sessions is still today a source for the best teachings in all matters relating to monetary policy.[26]

Virtually all of the participants spoke in favor of Austria's adoption of a gold standard. Menger, for example, at one point said:

> Gold is the money of advanced nations in the modern age. No other money can provide the convenience of a gold currency in our age of rapid and massive commodity exchanges. Silver has become a troublesome tool of trade. Even paper money must yield to gold when it comes to monetary convenience in everyday life … Moreover, under present conditions only a gold currency constitutes hard money. Neither a bank note and treasury note nor a silver certificate can take the place of gold, especially in moments of crisis.[27]

Later summarizing the work of the commission, Wieser supported the adoption of the gold standard in colorful language:

> Money is like speech; it is a means of intercourse. He who would have dealings with others must speak their language, however irrational he may find it. Language is rational by the very fact that it is intelligible to others, and more rational in proportion as it is intelligible to more people or to all. There can no more be an independent money system than independent speech; indeed, the more universal character of money, as compared with language, appears in this, that while a national language has its justification and significance in the intercourse of the world, there is no place for a national monetary system in the world's intercourse. If Europe errs in adopting gold, we must still, for good or evil, join Europe in her error, and we shall thus receive less injury than if we insist on being "rational" all by ourselves.[28]

The Currency Commission, in its official report to the Upper House of the Austrian Parliament, was no less adamant that gold, and only gold, was the recognized and essential international money. For that reason Austria-Hungary needed to adopt gold as the nation's standard if it was to successfully participate in the commerce and trade of the world.[29]

The Commission proposed and the government accepted that the monetary unit would be renamed the *krone* (the Crown), with the new Crown being equal to one-half the replaced florin. Standard coins would be gold pieces of ten and twenty Crowns, each one being of 900 parts gold to 100 parts copper. The twenty-Crown coin would have a full weight of 6.775067 grams, and a fine weight of 6.09756 grams. In 1892 an exchange rate for the Crown was fixed at 1.05 Swiss Francs and 0.8505 German Marks.

Silver was kept as a secondary medium of exchange for smaller transactions and limited legal tender status. Government paper money was temporarily kept in circulation up to a certain maximum, but with the expectation of its eventual retirement. For the transition to a full gold standard with legally mandated redemption of banknotes for specie, it was expected that the Austro-Hungarian Bank would continue to accumulate sufficient supplies of gold until at an unspecified date formal redemption would be instituted.

A legal obligation to redeem Crowns for gold was, in fact, never made into law. Yet, from 1896 and most certainly after 1900, the Austro-Hungarian Bank acted as if it now had that obligation and did pay in gold for its banknotes presented for redemption. Indeed, the oversight of this "shadow" gold standard (as it was called) by the Austro-Hungarian Bank, with maintenance of the exchange rate within a margin not much off the "gold points" was praised by authorities at the time as an exemplary case of a highly successful "managed currency."[30]

Ludwig von Mises and Austrian monetary and fiscal controversies before World War I

Though the Gold Commission of 1892 had proposed conversion to a legally mandated gold standard with full convertibility, and successive Austrian governments had endorsed the goal of full convertibility by the Austro-Hungarian Bank, it was never implemented up to 1914. After that, the financing of much of the government's war expenditures through a huge monetary expansion brought the Bank's unofficial policy of gold convertibility to a halt.[31]

Ludwig von Mises' earliest writings on monetary and fiscal policy were published between 1907 and 1914,[32] and focused on these monetary and related issues. He devoted a chapter in his memoirs, *Notes and Recollections*, in explaining the background behind some of these articles.[33] He details his frustrations when the articles resulted in him coming face-to-face for the first time with opposition by government officials to reasonable and publicly endorsed policies due to political corruption and misappropriation of "secret" slush funds that would be threatened by implementing a fully convertible gold standard.

But he does not go into very great detail about the content of these early essays. They may be grouped under two headings. The first consists of articles concerning the political pressures that finally lead to putting Austria formally on the path of a gold standard in 1892, and the reasons for the resistance and delay in legally establishing gold convertibility up to the beginning of World War I. The second group deals with fiscal extravagance and the regulatory and redistributive intrusiveness of the Austro-Hungarian government, which was leading the country to a potential financial and economic crisis. Even if the events of the World War had not intervened to accelerate the process that culminated in an end to the more than 600 year reign of the Hapsburgs, the growth of the interventionist state was weakening the foundations of the country.

The earliest of the essays was concerned with "The Political-Economic Motivations for the Regulation of the Austrian Currency"[34] It is primarily an analysis of the changing factors influencing various interest groups that finally lead to a sufficient coalition of these interests endorsing the move toward a gold standard, and therefore it has an implicit public choice-like flavor to it. It highlights the fact that a major shift in economic policy is often dependent upon the vagaries of unique historical events, without which such a change might never have the chance to be implemented.[35]

After discussing the factors behind the appreciation of the Austrian currency during the second half of the 1880s and the early 1890s, and the difficulty of historically differentiating and quantitatively estimating the influence of each of these factors on the supply and demand sides of the market, Mises turned to the resulting changing views of various interest groups.

From 1872 to 1887, the Austrian currency continuously depreciated against gold, and therefore

> functioned like a protective tariff against the import of manufactured goods, and assisted the export of domestic products like an export premium, and benefited the debtors, as well. Under these circumstances, support for plans to stabilize the value of the currency could not be counted upon from the industrial and agricultural circles.

But after 1887, the process was reversed, with the currency gaining value on the international exchanges.

> The exporter who had received 50.6 florins for 100 francs in February 1887 only received 44.54 florins in September 1890. The farmer received 10 percent less for his [exported] produce than only two years previously, but his taxes and mortgage interest had to be paid at the old levels.

A growing number of people began to expect that the currency appreciation was not likely to be reversed in any immediate future, but instead was probably going to continue. As a consequence, "The demand for regulation of the value of the currency became general." The Austro-Hungarian Export Association appealed for all members to advocate currency reform. And rallies in support of such reform were held from one end of the Empire to the other.

Of particular importance were the actions of the Hungarian government. When the currency had been depreciating in the 1880s, the authorities in Budapest opposed any stabilization of the currency, since the depreciation was viewed as beneficial to the agricultural interests in that part of the Empire, especially for wheat exporters. Indeed, in late 1890 when the florin was now appreciating in value, the Hungarian finance ministry, Mises said, began to buy gold on the foreign exchange to push down the value of the florin, purchasing forty-five million florins in gold exchange in the process.

But what especially motivated the Hungarians to join the chorus in favor of currency reform was their belief that it could serve as a means of establishing a greater degree of financial independence from Vienna. Mises explained:

> In the introduction of a gold currency and the implementation of specie payments, those in Budapest saw their most secure means of freeing themselves financially from the Viennese banks, increasing the prestige of Hungarian

national credit abroad, and acquiring the required means from international capital that were necessary for economic war with Austria.

Indeed, the degree to which the Hungarian political leadership was able to rally virtually the entire nation behind currency reform was "truly an example of political discipline worthy of awe" and "the fate of currency reform was decided."

In addition, most of those in the banking and financial sectors also came out in favor of a reformed, gold-backed currency. Austrian industry had never fully recovered from the "depression" of 1873. Placing Austria-Hungary on a sound gold basis was expected to increase international confidence in the country's finances, and as a result improve the prospects for foreign investment and the terms under which foreign capital was borrowed.

On the other hand, there were those who gained from an appreciation of the currency, including bondholders and other creditors who received their payments in money experiencing an increase in its real value. They were unable, however, to make a persuasive claim "that the country should allow the favorable situation of the monetary system to continue unchanged for their interests alone."

Even many of the conservatives in the German part of Austria-Hungary were won over to currency reform due to their core constituency being in the country-side where the appreciating currency was financially pinching the farmers.

The primary opposition came from the Christian-Socialist Party. They argued that the gold standard would only further the interests of "international commerce" and those who have "an interest in the development and construction of the global economy." This would run counter, the Christian-Socialists claimed, to "the correctly understood interests of all working classes" whose well being depended upon "the development of the fatherland as an autonomous national economic state, as an autonomous national customs and commercial space."

The Christian-Socialists drew much of their support from small manufacturers and retail businessmen. Claiming to be the friend of "the little guy," the Christian-Socialist Party argued that an easy money policy would increase buying power in the economy and improve the business environment. Thus, they were not for stabilization of the currency, but renewed depreciation.

"All of these arguments," Mises said,

> which had been brought forward by inflationists in all countries and at all times, were accepted by the friends of "our father's paper florin" to defend their point of view. The weapons with which these battles were fought were not always genteel; opponents did not lack for suspicions of and insults directed at the "liberal, usurious, capitalistic economic system."

While the opponents of currency reform may have only called for a "moderate" inflation as a continuous "stimulus" for business, Mises pointed out that they were not able to formulate a persuasive alternative to the gold standard because they could not specify what a "moderate" rate of inflation would be and how it could be sustained within that "moderate" range.

Thus, Mises summed up:

> The power relations of the currency policy parties at the time of tack-
> ling the regulation of the currency were generally favorable to the introduc-
> tion of a gold currency. Unimportant in number and influence were those
> who advocated the continuation of the monetary system then current,
> because they expected a continuing increase in the value of money. To wit,
> these were solely the possessors of claims to money. All the other groups in
> society desired a change in the currency that would offer, at a minimum, a
> halt in the continuing appreciation of the currency; all manufacturers
> belonged to this group, and also the workers whose interests here went
> hand-in-hand with those of their employers. Even "high finance," which had
> a substantial say on currency questions, was found to be on this side. Admit-
> tedly, the opponents of the then existing currency system were not united in
> their views about the shape of a future monetary system. However their
> efforts to create a "national," inflationist monetary system were completely
> futile ... Thus, the question over a metallic currency was already decided
> before the actual discussions about the project for currency regulation had
> even begun.

By the time the Austrian Currency Commission convened in early 1892, the
general discussion was already focused on "the so-called relation," i.e., the rate
at which the new currency would be stabilized and fixed in relation to gold. The
heated debate was over whether the new parity would be "lighter" or "heavier"
than the prevailing market rate at which the florin was then exchanging for gold.
The outcome would differently influence the economic position of the various
interest groups who had been more or less united in wanting a gold-based stabilization of the currency.

Mises pointed out that what those on different sides of this debate failed to
understand was that regardless of what the actual parity rate turned out to be, any
"gain" expected from it by a particular group would be transitory.

> Sooner or later, the prices of all domestic goods and services will be
> adjusted to the change in the value of the monetary unit, and the 'advan-
> tages' that a devalued currency offers to production, and the obstacles that
> an over-valued one sets against production will disappear. This is because
> the agio as such does not function as an export premium or as a protective
> tariff; rather, it is merely the increasing agio, or inversely only the decreas-
> ing agio, not the low agio in itself, that is able to check exports and boost
> imports.

As it was, when the reform came into effect after 1892, only an upper limit
was placed on the extent to which the new Crown could vary from its parity,
thus protecting the currency from any further appreciation. What was not initially set was a lower limit, so in principle the currency could depreciate –
clearly a "victory" for those who wanted currency reform but who would not

mind if the currency varied in value in a way that "stimulated" exports and "retarded" imports. But after 1896 and until the outbreak of World War I, the Austro-Hungarian Bank also set a lower limit to fluctuations in the Crown from parity. In effect, from 1896 the Bank managed the Crown within a band set by the "gold points," beyond which it would become profitable to either import or export gold.

But since the Austro-Hungarian Bank was managing the Crown after 1896 "as if" it was legally bound to redeem gold for currency, why did the government and the Bank not in fact just take the formal and official step to declare the legal requirement for convertibility? This was the theme of four of Mises' articles from this period: "The Foreign Exchange Policy of the Austro-Hungarian Bank,"[36] "The Problem of Legal Resumption of Specie Payments in Austria-Hungary,"[37] "About the Problem of Legal Resumption of Specie Payments in Austria-Hungary,"[38] and "The Fourth Privilege of the Austro-Hungarian Bank."[39]

In the 1920s Mises explained that when the gold standard was implemented in Germany in the 1870s, one of the guiding ideas

> was the view that in everyday commercial transactions wider scope needed to be assigned to the use of gold coins ... In Germany things were never carried as far as in England, where all bank-note denominations under five pounds was suppressed. Nevertheless, all regulations concerning bank-note denominations and German Imperial Treasury certificates were clearly based on the idea that paper-money substitutes did not belong in the hands of the farmer, the worker, the craftsman, and the subordinate. It was considered an important task of the new German Imperial monetary policy to "satisfy" the demand for gold, for which considerable material sacrifices were made.[40]

The same idea was followed when the gold standard was being established in Austria-Hungary. Indeed, the government and the Bank expected that many in the society would enthusiastically accept the newly coined Crowns in place of the paper florins that carried the legacy of an inflationary past. "To the great surprise of the government and the Bank, the public's opinion about the gold coins appeared quite negative," Mises explained.

> The people, who had grown to adulthood under the rule of paper money, found the use of gold coins to be uncomfortable. The 5 Crown coins, the silver florins, and the 1 Crown coins, which had been placed in circulation after 1892, could only be kept in circulation because the 1 and 5 florin state notes had been withdrawn at the same time. Everyone who received the gold coins in payment attempted to exchange them for notes as quickly as they could, so the gold soon flowed back into the Bank.[41]

Notwithstanding the lack of enthusiasm for coined money by the Austro-Hungarian populace, the Bank imported large quantities of gold as a reserve backing for the banknotes in circulation and for the eventual legal requirement for specie redemption. Positive trade balances throughout this period made it relatively easy to finance the gold importations.[42] By 1900 Austria-Hungary had a "gold standard without gold in circulation," as Mises put it.

But gold bullion was not the only reserve supporting Austria-Hungary's currency or eventual convertibility. The Bank Act of 1863 permitted the Austrian National Bank to ship bullion abroad and use it to purchase foreign bills and other interest-earning assets that were payable in gold, a rule applied also to the new Austro-Hungarian Bank. Thus, from its beginning the Austro-Hungarian gold standard was in fact a gold-exchange standard.

The advantage from the Bank's point of view was that it enabled it to earn significant income from its gold reserve without having to let the bullion sit "idle" in vaults in Vienna. It also enabled the Bank to intervene in the foreign exchange market and buy or sell foreign bills representing gold held abroad to counteract any movements in the foreign exchange rate before such movements were anywhere near the upper or lower gold points.

Leon von Bilinski, governor of the Austro-Hungarian Bank during part of this period, considered the policy to be a great success. "[The Bank's] action in either direction must, however, be so exerted, that the metallic stock of the bank shall remain as far as possible undisturbed," Balinski said.

> Foreign bills are to be used to the greatest practicable extent in international payments, and compensatory payments from abroad are to be made to take the place of gold so often as possible, so that, in spite of all efflux and reflux in international payments, any unfavorable change in the value of the standard coin of the country relative to foreign money (in other words, a premium on foreign coin), bringing a rise in the rate of discount, may be averted.

The Bank's task was to make the management of its foreign bill holdings a "constant and daily concern" to assure the success of this policy.[43]

The critics of formal convertibility argued that making redemption official would require the Bank to possibly lose its vital gold reserves rather than being able to "merely" pay out in foreign bills. The necessity to meet all claims only in bullion would mean that the Bank would have to resort far more frequently to changes in the discount rate to counteract adverse gold flows. Raising the discount rate would ripple through the economy and restrict investment and business activity, thus placing an undesirable burden on the domestic economy in the name of defending the foreign exchange rate.

Mises' response, in a nutshell, was that the Bank was already accepting gold and redeeming gold when demanded by holders of banknotes and other redeemable claims to specie. Legal convertibility, therefore, would only be formalizing what it already was doing according to the "rules" of the gold standard. Furthermore, this in no way would interfere with the Bank continuing to buy and sell foreign bills on the market to head off movements in the foreign exchange rate within the gold-point band. After all, it was usual practice in the market for bills of exchange to be bought and sold to avoid incurring the costs of gold shipment in foreign transactions. As long as the Bank continued to accept and provide gold at the official parity, market transactions would normally remain within the gold points. And, he said, during the years since the Bank had informally followed the "rules" of the gold standard starting in 1896 the exchange rate had rarely moved much more than one-fourth of a percent above or below the parity rate.[44]

What would be gained, therefore, by establishing formal and legal redemption?

> The monarchy will profit immensely by a legally prescribed gold payment, for its international credit, which it urgently needs for its enormous foreign debts, would considerably improve. For only *de jure* gold payments would clearly convince everyone abroad that Austria-Hungary enjoys nowadays a perfectly regulated currency.[45]

In *Notes and Recollections*, Mises explained that behind the scenes the opposition to formal convertibility was partly due to the fact that a portion of the rather large funds earned by foreign exchange dealings were hidden away in a secret account from which senior political and ministerial officials could draw for various "off the books" purposes, including influencing the media of the time. He learned about this special fund from Böhm-Bawerk, who told him about it off the record, and who was disgusted by the whole business and frustrated by the fact that even when he was finance minister (1900–1904), he had not been able to abolish the fund. A good part of the opposition and anger expressed against Mises' defense of legal convertibility was the fear by those accessing these special funds that this source of money would dry up under the more transparent accounting procedures that would come with legal redemption.[46]

But in 1909, Mises also pointed out that another reason behind the opposition to legal convertibility was the resistance of the Hungarians, who wanted to weaken the power of the joint Austro-Hungarian Bank as a way to continue their drive for independence from the Hapsburg monarchy:

> Since the Compromise of 1867, Hungarian politics have ceaselessly endeavored to loosen the common bond that binds that country to Austria. The achievement of economic independence from Austria has appeared as a singular goal of Hungarian policy, and as a preliminary step on the way to political autonomy. The national rebirth of the non-Magyar peoples of Hungary – Germans, Serbo-Croatians, Romanians, Ruthenians, and Slovaks – will, however, pull the rug out from under these endeavors and contribute to the strengthening of the national ideal of Greater Austria. At the moment, however, Hungarian policy is still determined by the views of the Hungarian nobility and the power of the government rests in the hands of the intransigent Independent Party.[47]

The nationalistic "rebirth" of these peoples under the often oppressive control of the Hungarians did not "strengthen the ideal of Greater Austria" as Mises assumed and clearly hoped. Instead, the appeal of nationalism over liberty and liberalism that had been developing throughout the Empire for decades finally led to the death of the Hapsburg dynasty in 1918.

But if the centrifugal forces of nationalism were pulling the Empire apart from within, it was also being undermined by the fiscal cost and growth of the State. This was the second theme in Mises' writings before the Great War, in two essays on "Fiscal Reform in Austria"[48] and "Disturbances in the Economic Life of the Austro-Hungarian Empire during the Years 1912–1913."[49]

Years before the crushing tax burden and extensive network of wartime controls that began in 1914,[50] Austria-Hungary was on a path of fiscal extravagance. After nearly twenty years of relative fiscal responsibility between 1889 and 1909, the Austrian government was dramatically increasing taxing and spending in the Empire, Mises pointed out.[51]

During the first decade of the twentieth century government expenditures increased 53 percent. And its spending was likely to continue increasing in the years to come, Mises warned. First, the European arms race was compelling the Austro-Hungarian government to implement a huge growth in spending on both the army and the navy. Second, growth in social insurance obligations was going to result in rising government expenditures in the years to come. The difference between Austria-Hungary and, say, Germany, France, or Britain, was that their financial difficulties were due to the pressures that high military and welfare costs were already placing upon their societies. "In Austria, on the other hand," Mises emphasized, "the [government's budget] deficit already exists even though the State has up to now fulfilled its military and social obligations to only a minor degree."

Working in the Vienna Chamber of Commerce as an expert analyst on financial matters, Mises possessed detailed information about the fiscal policies and plans of the Austrian government. In every direction, the government had or was implementing huge tax increases. A progressive tax on inheritance and gifts was to be put into place. By today's standards, of course, the proposed inheritance tax is all part of the nostalgic imagery of that bygone world of pre-1914.

The law already in effect in 1909 set the rate of the inheritance tax on the basis of the relation of the recipient to the deceased. It was 1.25 percent when the money had been left to members of the immediate family. It went to 5 percent when the money was left to, say, a niece or nephew. And it would be as high as 10 percent when the beneficiary was not a relative. Under the proposed law, a bequest of less than 500 Crowns to an immediate relative would be tax-exempt (about $100 at that time). Between 500 and 1,000 Crowns, the tax would come into effect at the rate of 1.25 percent, and could increase to as much as 4 percent(!) when the bequest was for more than two million Crowns (or $400,000). For other relatives and non-relatives the inheritance tax rate progressively rose until reaching between 13 and 18 percent when the inheritance was 2,000 Crowns or more. A separate real estate inheritance tax would go to a maximum rate of 2 percent on property valued above 20,000 Crowns.

New taxes were planned for alcohol, soda-water and mineral water. And the match industry was to be nationalized so the government could have a monopoly position in this vital sector of the economy! The personal income tax was to be raised from the then current highest rate of 5 percent on income over 20,000 Crowns to 6.5 percent.

Corporate profit taxes, however, were already significantly high in the Austria of 1909. "In Austria," Mises said,

> stock corporations are taxed at the enormous base rate of 10 percent of profits. To this tax the state adds supplements for the benefit of the provinces and municipalities, so that it often it reaches the rate of 20 percent to 30 percent.

In addition, dividends above 10 percent of the invested capital were subject to a supplementary tax, and then progressively increased on larger dividends. And a new "innovation" was to be a tax on directors' profit shares. But one new proposal was meeting

> vigorous opposition in commercial and industrial circles: in the future, according to the plan, fiscal authorities will have the right to inspect the books of businesses and industries. Austrian entrepreneurs rightly see in this arrangement an intensification of the harassing attitude which the authorities display toward them.

In addition, within the Austrian parliament, Mises explained, the agrarian regions of the Hapsburg Crownlands held a disproportional representation. They also formed alliances with small and medium size business associations to shift the tax burden to the shoulders of the larger urban industrial enterprises. Landed interests in the countryside were able to assure that the tax incidence was lower on themselves (often through various production subsidies), while the higher taxes on urban industry throttled the development of manufacturing and capital investment. The government imposed "crushing" taxes on urban buildings, while lowering taxes on buildings in the countryside. Even the proposed taxes on alcohol, soda-water and mineral water were skewed against the urban populations, since the greatest consumption of these beverages were in the cities.

The essence of all these fiscal forces, Mises concluded, was a deep dislike for modern capitalist society:

> In Austria, public opinion is hostile to the capitalist system of production in contrast to the dominant opinion in the Western countries. This trend in Austria should not be compared to that which is called anti-capitalism in England, the United States, and other Western countries. In the countries of Western Europe and America the large profits of capitalist enterprises are not, of course, looked upon favorably, but nobody would like to bring about a reversal of industrial evolution in those places. In Austria, the most influential political parties are firm adversaries of the entire modern economic system. The agrarian parties dislike industry because it raises wages. Big industry and big commerce irritate the *petite-bourgeoisie* parties – those to

which the small artisans and small businessmen belong – because they have the upper hand in commerce. But these parties, the petite bourgeoisie and the agrarians, have a huge majority in the Austrian parliament; on the one side, hundreds of representatives of agriculture and small business; on the other side, some twenty representatives of big industry. This state of affairs is aggravated by the fact that the bureaucracy exercises an excessive influence in the administration, and that the free initiative of the individual is constantly frustrated.[52]

In the long run, Mises stated, such policies could not continue if the economic development of the country was to occur.

In the spring of 1914, just before the clouds of war were to darken the skies over Europe for four years, Mises wrote the last of the articles on these themes. Austria-Hungary had been experiencing a serious economic recession in 1912–1913 that negatively impacted industry, trade, and employment. Many pointed to threats or actual wars that had broken out among some of the Balkan states in 1912 as the cause of the economic downturn. But whatever influence these events in areas bordering on the Hapsburg Empire may have contributed to the country's difficulties, in Mises' view, they were not at the heart of the problem. Mises quoted from a series of articles that Böhm-Bawerk had written in January of 1914 (the last major statement on public affairs from that great Austrian Economist's pen before his untimely death in August of that year):[53]

We have seen innumerable variations of the vexing game of trying to generate political contentment through material concessions. If formerly the Parliaments were the guardians of thrift, they are today far more like its sworn enemies. Nowadays the political and nationalist parties … are in the habit of cultivating a greed of all kinds of benefits for their co-nationals or constituencies that they regard as a veritable duty, and should the political situation be correspondingly favorable, that is to say correspondingly unfavorable for the Government, then political pressure will produce what is wanted. Often enough, though, because of the carefully calculated rivalry and jealousy between parties, what has been granted to one has also to be conceded to others – from a single costly concession springs a whole bundle of costly concessions.

Böhm-Bawerk accused the Austrian government of having "squandered amidst our good fortune [of economic prosperity] everything, but everything, down to the last penny, that could be grabbed by tightening the tax-screw and anticipating future sources of income to the upper limit" by borrowing in the present at the expense of the future. For some time, he said, "a very large number of our public authorities have been living beyond their means." Such a fiscal policy, Böhm-Bawerk feared, was threatening the long-run financial stability and soundness of the entire country.[54]

Mises added to Böhm-Bawek's argument by saying that the central government's extravagance and excessive spending had been matched if not exceeded by all levels of the government. Mises said:

In Austria and Hungary, too much is consumed, or as can be said in a different way, too little is produced. The country, the provinces, and the municipalities have been led astray by the ease with which the modern banking system and financial technologies issue loans.

"In the decade from 1902 to 1912, the country's debt (for the Crownlands and provinces represented in parliament), increased from 3,640 million Crowns to 7,240 million Crowns (or a near doubling of the government's debt)." The monetary expansion to feed these expenditures had negative effects on those with fixed pensions and on the incentives for savings due to inflation.

The growth in total government expenditures was exacerbated by the multiple layers of government at the federal, provincial, and local levels that were often duplicative in their activities and contradictory in many of their policies. The expenses of government were also increased due to inefficiencies of nationalized industries, the most costly and unproductive of which was the national railroad system. It was a drain on the federal government's budget since its sizable deficit had to be covered from general revenues. Its labor force was half as productive as even those who worked for the nationalized railway system in neighboring Imperial Germany.

Similar inefficiencies were visible in the private sector due to protective tariffs for agriculture that resulted in lower productivity in both the growing of food and the raising of cattle. For example, Mises pointed out, in Germany 58.9 cows were raised and grazed on one square kilometer of productive land; in Austria only 32.5 cows were maintained on comparable land. Shielded from international competition, many farming enterprises used "the government's leisurely and unimaginative method of business administration as a model."

The situation was no better in industry.

> The Austrian worker (and the same is true for the Hungarians to an even greater extent) labors less intensively than, e.g., the Germans or even the Americans. Only the slightest tendency exists for entrepreneurial activity; and what there is, is impeded at every turn by a legislature that, to the best of its ability, has set itself the goal of inhibiting the development of large enterprises.

What was the attitude of the population?

> The farmer, the tradesman, the worker, and above all the civil servant work and earn little; however, they still desire to live comfortably, and thus they spend more than their circumstances would allow. The frivolity of the Austrians and the Hungarians set them sharply apart from the sober thriftiness of the Western Europeans. There appears little concern for the future, and new debts are added to old ones as long as the willing lenders can be found.

This, Mises said, was the crux of the problem

Rather than cash payments for goods and services bought and sold, virtually everyone in Austrian society lived on credit: From the manufacturer or merchant extending credit to those further down the wholesale chain leading to the retail level, to the retailers extending credit to their "regular" customers with no consideration of their ability to pay the mounting debts accumulating on their books. Everyone was living far beyond their means with little thought of anyone's longer-term "credit worthiness." The day of reckoning had to finally arrive and, Mises explained,

> The 1912–1913 crises bought about the liquidation of some of the unsustainable borrowing system of previous years ... Sooner or later, the day had to come on which it became clear that a large portion of these outstanding loans that had been posted in the merchant's books as assets were irrecoverable. All these officials, employees, functionaries of the public administration and local governments, and all these farmers and craftsmen had been living far beyond their means. They had taken on debts that they were neither willing nor capable of repaying ... The scope of the restrictions and divestments of credit, which resulted in the first months of the crisis, were highly exaggerated; yet, they were indeed large enough to be the final straw. The retail merchant, for whom credit was impeded, began to measure his outstanding loans and must have recognized, to his horror, that a portion of them were irrecoverable. In many cases, the retailer saw himself now forced to suspend payments himself; this functioned retroactively from the end consumers step-by-step back to the producers. Credits, which had for years been entered into the account books as "good," were revealed at one stroke to be rotten. The businessman recognized too late that he had already lost a majority of that which he thought he had earned through years of hard work.[55]

What could bring recovery and sustainable prosperity? "Only one possibility could help," Mises concluded, "the radical elimination of all of those barriers placed in the path of the development of productive forces by economic policy." Even if his argument had been listened to, the Great War that began in the summer of 1914 made following any such advice impossible.

Conclusion: from the afterglow of the liberal era to the new reality of postwar collectivism

Reality fades into memory, and what really was becomes what one wishes it had been. The second half of the nineteenth century was never really the idyllic liberal epoch that those who lived in it came to recall it to be when it had passed away. It was more than anything else the stark contrast of the new reality of totalitarian collectivism and the interventionist-welfare state in the period between the two world wars that made what preceded 1914 seem so "wondrous" in comparison to what was then being lived through.

The "demons" that were set loose by "war socialism" during 1914–1918 had been ideologically maturing for decades before that conflict began. The economic policies that Ludwig von Mises analyzed and opposed in the first years of the twentieth century were the early manifestations of these ideas. The impediments to individual initiative and enterprise, the manipulations of the monetary system, and the resulting credit-based boom and recession that followed the Austrian government's extravagance and easy monetary policy had had their intellectual origin in Austria's neighbor, Imperial Germany, in those last decades of the nineteenth century.

Since the defeat of Napoleon, the anti-liberal spirit had been strongest and most successful in the German States. German Romanticism had started as a literary and poetic movement extolling the "spirit" over the intellect and the connectedness of man to nature. But in the hands of a growing number of German thinkers it was turned into a revolt against the Enlightenment, reason, liberalism, and free trade.[56]

It was most strongly represented by those who became known as members of the German Historical School. It is difficult to appreciate today the full flavor of the ideas of these German historicists. It was not only that they rejected much of economic theory as it had developed from the time of Adam Smith and David Ricardo, including the ideas that emerged out of the "marginalist" revolution of the late nineteenth century. Nor that they insisted upon and erroneously believed that they were actually following a "theory-free" approach to historical and statistical investigations in trying to unearth period-specific "laws" of economics.

It was also, and crucially, their philosophical and ideological collectivism that rejected methodological, epistemological and ethical individualism. Social analysis did not begin with the individual, but with the collective whole. What defined the collective were such things as nation, race, genetics, and intuitive insight belonging to a select and chosen few who "understood" the true meaning and real interests of the German people, the *Volk*. In their view the role of economic policy, including monetary policy, was to help prepare the nation for war and conquest as the path to "national greatness."[57]

In the years before the Great War, Ludwig von Mises confronted these ideas as a young member of the Austrian School of Economics attending the annual meetings of the *Verein für Sozialpolitik* [Society of Social Policy], the leading association of academics and scholars in the German-speaking world. Forty years after the Great War, Mises recollected the mentality of these German historicists and their attitude toward ideas of the Austrian School and economic theory in general:

> Böhm-Bawerk, my conversation partners remarked, is without doubt an honorable seeker of truth. Nevertheless, his deplorable errors resulted in an unacceptable justification of the worst form of unearned income – interest on capital. According to them, it was required of a moral State to use governmental measures to lower high market rates of interest. The most absurd book in economic literature is, they said, Bentham's *Defense of Usury* ... They charged that Böhm-Bawerk's allegations against the Marxian exploitation theory were foolish. No matter how much Marx may have been mistaken in his criticism of modern society, he nevertheless had the merit of having revealed the motives of British economists. Compared with the con-

tributions of the German Historical School, Böhm-Bawerk was a stubborn reactionary ...

The same thing was allegedly true about my theory of money. The periodic reoccurrence of economic crises was a phenomenon inherent in the nature of capitalism, they said ... Strict supervision and skillful regulation of market activities by a super-party government would free the economy of economic crises. It was pointless, they thought, to try to explain economic fluctuations on the basis of monetary and credit policies. The real causes must be sought at a deeper level, they said ...

The monetary system, they said, is not an end in itself. Its purpose is to serve the state and the people. Financial preparations for war must continue to be the ultimate and highest goal of monetary policy, as of all policy. How could the state conduct war, after all, if every self-interested citizen retained the right to demand redemption of bank notes in gold? It would be blindness not to recognize that only full preparedness for war – not only in the military sense but also with regard to the economy – could ensure the maintenance of peace. It was admitted that the Historical School has long neglected the treatment of monetary problems. Yet, with Knapp's *State Theory of Money*, they said, the German spirit has finally rejected the destructive theories of the English economists ...

There could be only one excuse for my errors, namely, that they were the logical results of the subversive ideas that the "Austrian School" had taken over from the doctrines of the Manchester men. Thinking in a vacuum was characteristic of Menger, Wieser, and Böhm-Bawerk, and was my error too. What would the monetary system be like if the State did not stand behind it with all its power? It was fortunate, they alleged, that even in Austria only a small group of naïve authors shared the views of the "Austrian School." ...

They were ready to grant me that I wrote in good faith. But they were convinced that my book only served the interests of unpatriotic and subversive speculators. They never entered into any kind of process of theoretical thinking. The quantity theory of money and the theories of the Currency School were, in their eyes, nothing but curiosities in the historical literature. One of these gentlemen remarked that a colleague of his had asked whether I was not also an adherent of the phlogiston theory. Another gentleman suggested that he considered my "Austrianness" to be a mitigating circumstance; with a citizen of Germany he wouldn't even discuss such questions ...

Such were the opinions of my interlocutors during the last five years before the First World War.[58]

These years were the intellectual battleground that prepared Ludwig von Mises for the fights to come, and those first articles of his on monetary and fiscal policy in Austria-Hungary were the opening shots in a war of ideas that he continued to participate in through seven decades of the twentieth century.

Notes

1 G.P. Gooch, "The Lessons of 1914–1918," *Current History* (August 1934), pp. 513–514, 516, 520; see the similar sentiment expressed by internationally respected Italian philosopher, Benedetto Croce, "Of Liberty," *Foreign Affairs* (October 1932), pp. 1–2:

> We remember the old Europe with its riches, its flourishing trade, its abundance of goods, its ease of life, its bold sense of security; we see today the new Europe – impoverished, discouraged, crisscrossed with high tariff walls, each nation occupied solely with its own affairs, too distraught to pay heed to the things of the spirit and tormented by the fear of worse to come. Gone is the gay international society once the pride of Europe's capitals; extinct, or almost so, is the old community of thought, art, civilization.

Croce despaired, as well, that,

> Impatience with free institutions has led to open or masked dictatorships, and, where dictatorships do not exist, to the desire for them. Liberty, which before the war was a faith, or at least a routine acceptance, has now departed from the hearts of men even if it still survives in certain institutions.

2 Gustav Stolper, *This Age of Fable: The Political and Economic World We Live In* (New York: Reynal & Hitchcock, 1942), pp. 1, 7–8.

3 Shortly before World War I the trend was summarized by German historian Hermann Levy, *Economic Liberalism* (London: Macmillan, 1913), p. 1:

> The Manchester School of laissez faire has of recent years been brought face to face with two very momentous phenomena – Socialism and Neo-Mercantilism. These two very different tendencies have a common element in their opposition to the individualist doctrines of political economy. Socialism is concerned with the division of the product according to certain principles of "justice," rather than the development of potential production. Mercantilism is the most complete expression of an all-embracing regulation of industrial conditions by political wisdom and administrative practice. But both agree that industry must be organized by the State. Manchester Liberalism has been undermined bit by bit by the union of these two forces.

4 See, Francis W. Hirst, "Liberalism and Wealth," *Essays in Liberalism by Six Oxford Men* (London: Cassel and Co., 1897), pp. 33, 51:

> A sneer at Cobden, a contemptuous allusion to Manchesterism and the "dismal science" help nowadays to make up that small but choice reservoir of blind abuse, upon which the Social Democrats ... draw for the great work of irrigating electoral ignorance.

Hirst for one made no apology for the preceding

> half-century of free trade and free enterprise ... The nation has largely been freed from private monopoly; for fifty years it has made uninterrupted and unprecedented progress in culture, power, and comfort. Will not Englishmen think once, twice, and thrice before they exchange the assurance of increased and increasing prosperity for the dim Utopias of State monopoly depicted by a gentleman known to Social Democrats as "our local horganizer"?

And, of course, Herbert Spencer had warned of these growing anti-liberal forces even earlier in his collection of essays on *Man vs. the State* (London: Williams & Norgate, 1885), in which he spoke of "The Coming Slavery" and "The New Toryism" of increasing government control over people's personal and commercial lives.

5 A reasoned case for this interpretation can be found in, Arno Mayer, *The Persistence of the Old Regime: Europe to the Great War* (New York: Pantheon, 1982).

6 This, and the next series of quotations are taken from "Austria-Hungary," *The Economist* reprinted in *Living Age* (February 10, 1900), pp. 399–400.
7 Joseph Redlich, "The End of the House of Austria," *Foreign Affairs* (July 1, 1930), p. 599.
8 Redlich, p. 605; see, also, Hans Kohn, *The Habsburg Empire, 1804–1918* (New York: Van Nostrand Reinhold, 1961), p. 49:

> Like a good eighteenth century monarch, [Francis Joseph] regarded himself as the first servant of the nation, but he identified the nation with himself and his dynasty. He worked indefatigably for the good of his people, but they were *his* people and *he* interpreted what was good for them.

9 See, also, Hans Kohn, "The Viability of the Habsburg Monarchy," *Slavic Review* (March 1963), pp. 37–42.
10 Redlich, p. 606; see, also, Joseph Redlich, *Emperor Francis Joseph of Austria: A Biography* (New York: Macmillan, 1929).
11 Hans Kohn, *Living in a World Revolution: My Encounters with History* (New York: Trident Press Book, 1964), pp. 1–19, for his recollections of those years of his youth in Prague under Hapsburg rule.
12 Kohn, "The Viability of the Habsburg Monarchy," p. 38.
13 Kohn, "The Viability of the Habsburg Monarchy," p. 39; on the mutual benefits to be derived from a state that incorporates a variety of different national groups, see the classic essay by Lord Acton, "Nationality," [1862] in *The History of Freedom and Other Essays* (London: Macmillan, 1907), pp. 270–300.
14 Ludwig von Mises, *Nation, State, and Economy: Contributions to the Politics and History of Our Time* [1919] (New York: New York University Press, 1983), pp. 106–131. A somewhat similar view was expressed by Friedrich von Wieser, one of the leading figures of the early Austrian School, in 1905:

> In Austria, the term nationalities some decades ago referred, in fact, only to the non-German peoples, but today it must be extended to the German people ... The Germans developed national sensitiveness only gradually and slowly. They began to consider the concessions to the alien nationalities as a lowering of their national status. Finally, they arrived at the doctrine of national assets, which they had to defend. They were pushed forward one step further in Bohemia, where they saw themselves curtailed as a minority. Here they changed from a policy of mere defense to one of raising demands of their own to restore the balance which had been disturbed to their disadvantage. They asked for assurance of their equality in all national affairs ... They asked for the German state language; they asked for a German-led Austria as historic development had created it in the period from the awakening of the national spirit onwards. They asked for it now in regard to the accomplished self-assurance of the alien nationalities as a German national claim.

Quoted in, Robert A. Kann, *The Multinational Empire: Nationalism and National Reform in the Habsburg Monarchy, 1848–1918* (New York: Columbia University Press, 1950), p. 51. On the historical shift from the classical liberal ideal of individual liberty, limited government, equality before the law, and voluntary and peaceful association to the collectivist conceptions of aggressive political and economic nationalism with its emphasis on group identity and compulsory allegiance based on common language, race, religion and geography, and radical socialism with its idea of class conflict and violent revolution in Europe in general in the second half of the nineteenth century, see, Hans Kohn, *The Twentieth Century: The Challenge to the West and Its Response* (New York: Macmillan, 2nd ed., 1957), pp. 3–72; and Hans Kohn, *Nationalism: Its Meaning and History* (Princeton, NJ: D. Van Nostrand, 2nd ed., 1965).
15 The interventionist and regulatory policies of the government in the Hapsburg domains only served both to aggravate and create antagonisms among the linguistic and national groups. See, A.J.P. Taylor, *The Habsburg Monarchy, 1809–1918:*

A History of the Austrian Empire and Austria-Hungary (Chicago: University of Chicago Press, 1948), p. 173:

> In another way, the Austrian state suffered from its strength: it never had its range of activity cut down during a successful period of laissez faire, and therefore the openings for national conflict were far greater. There were no private schools or hospitals, no independent universities; and the state, in its infinite paternalism, performed a variety of services from veterinary surgery to the inspecting of buildings. The appointment of every schoolteacher, of every railway porter, of every hospital doctor, of every tax collector, was a signal of national struggle. Besides, private industry looked to the state for aid from tariffs and subsidies; these, in every country, produce "log-rolling," and nationalism offered an added lever with which to shift the logs. German industries demanded state aid to preserve their privileged position; Czech industries demanded state aid to redress the inequalities of the past. The first generation of national rivals had been the products of universities and fought for appointments at the highest professional level; their disputes concerned only a few hundred state jobs. The generation which followed them was the result of universal elementary education and fought for the trivial state employment which existed in every village; hence, the more popular national conflicts at the end of the century.

16 See, Hans Kohn, *The Habsburg Empire, 1804–1918*, p. 72:

> Amidst all the controversies and upheavals caused by the growing conflict of nationalities and by the vain search for an Austrian idea, the Austrian Constitution of December 31, 1867, which was a document of mid-century liberalism, remained in force for over half a century.

The Fundamental Law Concerning the General Rights of Citizens from the Austrian Constitution of 1867 may be found at: www.h-net.org/~habsweb/ sourcetexts/auscon. htm.

17 In 1867, the Lower Austrian Chamber of Commerce located in Vienna (where Ludwig von Mises was to work as an economic analyst from 1909 until he left Austria in 1934) declared,

> The state has fulfilled its task if it removes all obstacles to the free, orderly activity of its citizens. Everything else is achieved by the considerateness and benevolence of the factory owners and above all by the personal efforts and thriftiness of the workers.

See, Robin Okey, *The Habsburg Monarchy: From Enlightenment to Eclipse* (New York: St. Martin's Press, 2001), p. 206.

18 On the liberation and successes of the Austrian and Viennese Jews in the era of nineteenth century classical liberalism, and their demise with the counter-revolution of national and racial collectivism in the twentieth century, see, Ch, 3, "Ludwig von Mises and the Vienna of His Time," in this volume.

19 Mark Twain, "Stirring Times in Austria," *Harper's New Monthly Magazine* (March 1898), p. 533, in his witty and insightful account of Viennese politics, he described the makeup of the Austrian parliament:

> As to the makeup of the House, it is this: the deputies come from all the walks of life and from all the grades of society. There are princes, counts, barons, priests, peasants, mechanics, laborers, lawyers, judges, physicians, professors, merchants, bankers, shopkeepers. They are religious men, they are earnest, sincere, devoted, and they all hate the Jews.

20 Stefan Zweig, *The World of Yesterday* (New York: The Viking Press, 1943), pp. 24–25.

21 The following brief account of the history of the Austrian currency is taken primarily from, Charles A. Conant, *A History of Modern Banks of Issue*, 5th ed. (New York G.P.

Putnam's Sons, 1915), pp. 219–250; J. Laurence Laughlin, *History of Bimetallism in the United States* (New York: Appleton, 1898), pp. 189–197, 331–337; Robert Zuckerkandl, "The Austro-Hungarian Bank" in *Banking in Russia, Austro-Hungary, the Netherlands, and Japan* (Washington, DC: Government Printing Office, 1911), pp. 55–118. Also, specifically on the currency reform of 1892 and its implementation, "The Gold Standard in Austria" [Translation of the Report of the Special Currency Commission to the Upper House of the Austrian Parliament], *Quarterly Journal of Economics* (January 1893), pp. 225–254; "Reform of the Currency in Austria-Hungary," *Journal of the Royal Statistical Society* (June 1892), pp. 333–339; Friedrich von Wieser, "Resumption of Specie Payments in Austria-Hungary," *Journal of Political Economy* (June 1893), pp. 380–405; and Wesley C. Mitchell, "Resumption of Specie Payments in Austria-Hungary," *Journal of Political Economy* (December 1898), pp. 106–113.

22 See, Edwin R.A. Seligman, *Currency Inflation and Public Debt* (New York: Equitable Trust Co., 1921), p. 35: "Austria was the first of the European countries to issue paper money in the eighteenth century."

23 Jurgen Nautz, *Austrian Exchange Rate and Interest Rate Policies in Ethnic Conflicts, 1867–1914*, p. 8, a paper prepared for an international conference on the Political Economy of Currency Unions in a Globalized World, in Jerusalem, Israel, April 30 – May 1, 2006.

24 For example, following the Franco-Prussian War of 1870–1871, the German Empire was proclaimed, unifying under Prussian leadership the various German states and principalities. In 1871 and 1873, legislation was passed formally putting Imperial Germany on the gold standard. See, *The Reichbank, 1876–1900* (Washington, DC: Government Printing Office, 1910).

25 Wieser, "Resumption of Specie Payments in Austria-Hungary," p. 386.

26 Ludwig von Mises, "Das österreichische Währungsproblem vor 30 Jahren und heute: ein Gedenkblatt" ["The Austrian Currency Problem Thirty Years Ago and Today,"] *Neue Freie Presse* (March 12, 1922). An English-language translation of this article will appear in, Richard M. Ebeling, ed., *Selected Writings of Ludwig von Mises Vol. I* (Indianapolis, IN: Liberty Fund, forthcoming).

27 Quoted in Hans Sennholz, "The Monetary Writings of Carl Menger," in Llewellyn H. Rockwell, ed., *The Gold Standard: Perspectives in the Austrian School* [1985] (Auburn, AL: The Ludwig von Mises Institute 1992), p. 26; see, also, Günther Chaloupek, "Carl Menger's Contributions to the Austrian Currency Debate (1892) and His Theory of Money," paper presented to the 7th ESHET Conference, in Paris, France, January 30 – February 1, 2003.

28 Wieser, "Resumption of Specie Payments in Austria-Hungary," pp. 387–388.

29 "The Gold Standard in Austria," p. 230.

30 More recently, the Austro-Hungarian Bank's exchange rate policy has been praised as an example of successful "target zone" management of an exchange rate band; see, Marc Flandreau and John Komlos, "Target Zone in History and Theory: Lessons from an Austro-Hungarian Experiment (1896–1914)," Discussion Paper No. 18 (July 2003), Department of Economics, University of Munich, Germany.

31 For a brief summary of the inflation in Austria during and after World War I, and its disastrous consequences, see, Richard M. Ebeling, "The Great Austrian Inflation," *The Freeman: Ideas on Liberty* (April 2006), pp. 2–3; also Richard M. Ebeling, "The Lasting Legacies of World War I: Big Government, Paper Money and Inflation" *Economic Education Bulletin*, Vol. XLVIII, No. 11 (Great Barrington, MA: American Institute for Economic Research, November 2008).

32 Ludwig von Mises was between twenty-six and thirty-three years old when he wrote these articles.

33 Ludwig von Mises, *Notes and Recollections* [1940] (South Holland, IL: Libertarian Press, 1978), pp. 43–53.

34 The next series of quotations comes from: Ludwig von Mises, "Die wirtschaftspolitischen Motive der österreichischen Valuta-regulierung" ["The Political-Economic

86   *Austrian policies*

Motivations for Regulating the Austrian Currency"] *Zeitschrift für Volksvirtschaft, Sozialpolitik und Verwaltung*, Vol. 16 (1907), pp. 561–582. An English-language translation of this article will appear in, Ebeling, ed., *Selected Writings of Ludwig von Mises Vol. I.*

35 For example, the classical economist, Henry Fawcett argued in *Free Trade and Protection* (London: Macmillan 1878), pp. 17–47, that if not for the fact that in the winter of 1845–1846 there had been such a great famine due to the failure of many of the crops and therefore such a large portion of the population in England and Ireland simultaneously threatened with starvation, the pressure for the unilateral repeal of agricultural protectionism (the Corn Laws) might never have otherwise occurred. It was unlikely that the same passion for a radical change to free trade would have been stimulated by the existing industrial and manufacturing protectionism that only affected different, diverse and limited sub-groups of the consuming public.

36 Ludwig von Mises, "The Foreign Exchange Policy of the Austro-Hungarian Bank, *Economic Journal* (June 1909), pp. 201–211.

37 Ludwig von Mises, "Das Problem gesetzlicher Aufnahme der Barzahlungen in Österreich-Ungarn" ["The Problem of Legal Resumption of Specie Payments by the Austro-Hungarian Bank,"] *Jahrbuch für Gesetzgebug, Verwaltung und Volkswirtschaft*, Vol. 33 No. 3 (1909), pp. 895–1037. An English-language translation of this article will appear in, Ebeling, ed., *Selected Writings of Ludwig von Mises Vol. I.*

38 Ludwig von Mises, "Zum Problem gesetzlicher Aufnahme der Barzahlungen in Oesterreich-Ungarn" ["About the Problem of the Legal Resumption of Specie Payments in Austria- Hungary,"] *Jahrbuch für Gesetzgebug, Verwaltung und Volkswirtschaft*, Vol. 34, No. 3–4 (1910), pp. 1877–1884. An English-language translation of this article will appear in, Richard M. Ebeling, ed., *Selected Writings of Ludwig von Mises Vol. I.*

39 Ludwig von Mises, "Das vierte Privilegium der Österreichisch-Ungarischen Bank" ["The Fourth Privilege of the Austro-Hungarian Bank,"] *Zeitschrift für Volkswirtschaft, Sozialpolitik und Verwaltung*, Vol. 21 (1912), pp. 11–24. An English-language translation of this article will appear in, Ebeling, ed., *Selected Writings of Ludwig von Mises Vol. I.*

40 Ludwig von Mises, "Die Goldkernwährung" ["The Gold-Exchange Standard,"] *Deutsche allgemeine Zeitung* (February 24, 1925). An English-language translation of this article will appear in, Ebeling, ed., *Selected Writings of Ludwig von Mises Vol. I.*

41 Mises, "The Problem of Legal Resumption of Specie Payments by the Austro-Hungarian Bank."

42 See, Leo Pasvolsky, *Economic Nationalism of the Danubian States* (New York: Macmillan, 1928), p. 7, for the data on Austria-Hungary's trade balance and its bullion flows during the period 1894–1914.

43 Quoted in, Robert Zuckerkindl, "The Austro-Hungarian Bank," pp. 112–113.

44 Mises, "About the Problem of Legal Resumption of Specie Payments in Austria-Hungary."

45 Mises, "The Foreign Exchange Policy of the Austro-Hungarian Bank," p. 211. A large part of Mises' arguments in this group of articles relating to legal convertibility involved the historical and institutional details of how, when, and why the Austro-Hungarian Bank had followed various courses of action concerning gold purchases, foreign bills, and the costs and profits connected with it. He also attempted to show why arguments against the Bank's redemption of gold were often theoretically wrong and factually inaccurate.

46 Mises, *Notes and Recollections*, pp. 48–51; for a brief account of some of Böhm-Bawerk's accomplishments as finance minister of Austria-Hungary, see, Richard M. Ebeling, "Eugen von Böhn-Bawerk: A Sesquicentennial Appreciation," *The Freeman: Ideas on Liberty* (February 2001), pp. 36–41.

47 Mises, "The Problem of Legal Resumption of Specie Payments by the Austro-Hungarian Bank."

48 Ludwig von Mises, "La Réforme financière en Autriche" ["Financial Reform in Austria,"] *Revue Economique Internationale*, Vol. 7, No. 4 (October 1910). pp. 39–59. An English-language translation of this article will appear in, Ebeling, ed., *Selected Writings of Ludwig von Mises Vol. I.*

49 Ludwig von Mises, "Die Störungen im Wirtschaftsleben der österreichisch-ungarischen Monarchie während der Jahre 1912/1913" ["Disturbances in the Economic Life of the Austro-Hungarian Empire during the Years 1912–1913,"] *Archiv für Sozialwissenschaft und Sozialpolitik*, Vol. 39 (1914–1915), pp. 174–186. An English-language translation of this article will appear in, Richard M. Ebeling, ed., *Selected Writings of Ludwig von Mises Vol. I.*

50 See, Joseph Redlich, *Austrian War Government* (New Haven, CT: Yale University Press, 1929), for a detailed history of the fiscal costs and war economy of planning and control in Austria-Hungary in World War I.

51 The four years when Böhm-Bawerk was minister of finance (1900–1904) were especially notable for the fact that they were the years when the rate of annual tax increases were virtually the lowest in terms of the twenty-year period between 1894 and 1913; Böhm-Bawerk's tenure in office also saw the only two years over the period 1894–1913 when government spending actually decreased compared to the preceding year; see, B.R. Mitchell, *European Historical Statistics, 1750–1970* (New York: Cambridge University Press, 1979), pp. 372, 376.

52 Mises, "Financial Reform in Austria."

53 Eugen von Böhm-Bawerk, "Our Negative Balance of Trade" *Neue Freie Presse* (January 6, 8, and 9, 1914).

54 Quoted in, Eduard Marz, *Austrian Banking and Financial Policy: Creditanstalt at the Turning Point, 1913–1923* (New York: St. Martin's Press, 1984), pp. 26–27.

55 Mises, "Disturbances in the Economic Life of the Austro-Hungarian Empire during the Years 1912–1913."

56 See, Hans Kohn, "Romanticism and the Rise of German Nationalism," *Review of Politics* (October 1950), pp. 442–472.

57 For a thoughtful discussion of the evolution of these ideas from the late eighteenth century through World War II, see, Hans Kohn, *The Mind of Germany: The Education of a Nation* (New York: Harper Torchbooks, 1965); also by Hans Kohn, "Treitschke: National Prophet," *Review of Politics* (October 1945), pp. 433, 435:

> The "socialists of the chair" desired a benevolent paternal socialism to strengthen Germany's national unity. Their leaders, Adolf Wagner and Gustav von Schmoller, [Heinrich von] Treitschke's colleagues at the University of Berlin and equally influential in molding public opinion, shared Treitschke's faith in the German power state and its foundations. They regarded the struggle against English and French political and economic liberalism as the German mission, and wished to substitute the superior and more ethical German way for the individualistic economics of the West ... In view of the apparent decay of the Western world through liberalism and individualism, only the German mind with its deeper insight and its higher morality could regenerate the world.

58 Ludwig von Mises, "Bemerkungen über die ideologischen Wurzeln der Währungskatastrophe von 1923" ["Remarks Concerning the Ideological Roots of the Monetary Catastrophe of 1923,"] in *Freundesgabe zum 12. Oktober 1959 für Albert Hahn.* [Homage by Friends for Albert Hahn on October 12, 1959] (Frankfurt am Main: Fritz Knapp, 1959), pp. 54–58. An English-language translation of this article will appear in, Ebeling, ed., *Selected Writings of Ludwig von Mises Vol. I.* The phlogiston theory originated in 1667 with Johann Joachim Becher; it posited that inside flammable substances was a special element without odor, color, taste, or mass that is freed by the burning process, and is what caused the burning process. It was refuted in the eighteenth century through a variety of quantitative experiments.

5 The economist as the historian of decline

Ludwig von Mises and Austria between the two World Wars

Ludwig von Mises and his place in Austria between the two World Wars

In the months immediately after he arrived in the United States in the summer of 1940, Ludwig von Mises set down on paper his reflections on his life and contributions to the social sciences. But his *Notes and Recollections* is less a detailed autobiography and more a restatement of his most strongly held ideas in the context of the times in which he had lived in Europe. It carries in it a tone of despair and dismay about the direction in which European civilization seemed to be moving at the end of the first four decades of the twentieth century. In clear anguish and frustration, he summarized how he viewed his efforts as an economist in Europe in general and Austria in particular during those years between the two world wars:

> Occasionally I entertained the hope that my writings would bear practical fruit and show the way for policy. Constantly I have been looking for evidence of a change in ideology. But I have never allowed myself to be deceived. I have to come realize that my theories explain the degeneration of a great civilization; they do not prevent it. I set out to be a reformer, but only became the historian of decline.[1]

In the years between 1918 and 1938 Mises' activities were divided into two interrelated categories: his scholarly writings on various themes in economic theory and political economy, and his work as an economic policy analyst and advocate for the Vienna Chamber of Commerce, Crafts, and Industry.[2] Even before World War I, he had already established himself as a leading monetary theorist with the publication of *The Theory of Money and Credit* in 1912. Besides its many other theoretical contributions, Mises formulated what became known as the Austrian theory of the business cycle. Inflation and depression were not inherent to a capitalist economy, but were the result of government control and mismanagement of the monetary system through manipulation of market rates of interest.[3]

In the months following the end of the war in November 1918, Mises wrote *Nation, State and Economy*. He attempted to present a classical liberal analysis of and explanation for the problems of nationality and nationalism, the failures of German and Austrian liberalism that culminated in the Great War, and the economic consequences from the implementation of wartime collectivism and socialism in Imperial Germany and the Austro-Hungarian Empire. He ended the book with an appeal for reason and rationality in designing postwar policies in Germany that would enable an enduring peace and a renewal of prosperity through a return to a regime of economic liberalism and a political philosophy of individualism under the rule of law.[4]

But an article he published in April 1920, and which two years later he expanded into a book-length treatise on *Socialism,* caused the whirlwind of debate that surrounded him for the rest of his life. In this work, Mises demonstrated that the central planners of a socialist state would have no way of knowing how to use the resources of the society at their disposal for least-cost and efficient production. Without market-generated prices, the planners would lack the necessary tools for "economic calculation." The reality of the promised socialist utopia would be poverty, economic imbalance, and social decay. Furthermore, Mises argued that any type of collectivism that was applied comprehensively would result in a terrible tyranny, since the state would monopolize control over everything needed for human existence. While written as a response to those who were advocates of socialist central planning in general, it is also worth keeping in mind that his 1920 article, in particular, was written – and first delivered as a lecture at the Austrian Economic Society – against the backdrop of the proposals being made for "nationalization" and "socialization" of the means of production in Austria and Germany during the year following the end of the war, when Social Democrats were in positions of power in both countries.[5]

In 1927, Mises published *Liberalism,* in which he presented the classical liberal vision of the free and prosperous society, one in which individual freedom would be respected, the market economy would be free, open, and unregulated, and government would be limited to the primary functions of protecting life, liberty, and property.[6] He followed this work with *Critique of Interventionism* in 1929, a collection of essays in which he tried to explain that the interventionist-welfare state was not a "third way" between capitalism and socialism, but a set of contradictory policies that, if fully applied, would eventually lead to socialism through incremental increases in government regulation and control over the economy – and that Germany in the 1920s was heading down a dangerous political road that would lead to the triumph of national socialism.[7]

Not surprisingly, both Marxists and Nazis viewed Ludwig von Mises as a serious intellectual enemy. In fact, in 1925, the Soviet journal *Bolshevik* published an article calling him a "theorist of fascism."[8] What was Mises' "crime" deserving of such a charge? In a 1925 article, "Anti-Marxism," Mises explained the process by which Marxian thought came to have such a strong hold on German intellectuals and the division of these intellectuals into different anti-capitalist camps. Looking over the ideological and political landscape of Germany in the middle of the 1920s, Mises argued that the rising force in opposition to Marxian socialism was "national socialism." The national socialists argued that "proletarian interests" had to be submerged in the wider interests of the "fatherland." The strong state would control and repress the profit motive of the private sector and pursue an aggressive foreign policy. Mises also said in this article that Marxist Russia and a "national socialist" Germany would be natural allies in a war in Eastern Europe – thereby anticipating the infamous Nazi–Soviet Pact of August 1939, which served as the prelude to the beginning of World War II.[9]

In an accompanying article, "Social Liberalism," which Mises published the following year, 1926, he warned that a growing number of people in Germany were "setting their hopes on the coming of the 'strong man' – the tyrant who will think for them and care for them."[10] What Mises clearly saw and explained in the mid-1920s were the political, cultural, and ideological forces at work in Germany that were creating the conditions for the victory of Adolf Hitler and the Nazi movement in 1933.

Mises' efforts in various areas of public policy in Austria grew out of his position at the Vienna Chamber of Commerce where he was hired in October 1909, first as an assistant for the drafting of documents and then in 1910 as a deputy secretary. Mises was promoted to "first secretary" of the Vienna Chamber *(Leitenden Kammerssekertars)* when he returned to his duties after his service as an officer in the Austrian Army during the Great War. He was in charge of the Chamber's finance department, which was responsible for banking and insurance questions, currency problems, foreign exchange regulations, and public finance and taxation. He also consulted on issues relating to civil, administrative, and constitutional law. Indeed, because of his wide interests and knowledge, practically every facet of the Chamber's activities concerning public policy and regulation fell within his expertise.[11]

Mises also was assigned special tasks. From November 1918 to September 1919, he was responsible for financial matters relating to foreign affairs at the Chamber. In 1919–1921, he was in charge of the section of the Austrian Reparations Commission for the League of Nations concerned with the settling of outstanding prewar debt.[12] His activities in these assignments were highly regarded and praised for their accomplishments. For example, after he stepped down as one of the directors of the Office of Accounts for the settlement of these prewar debts, *The Laws for Peace,* a publication reporting on matters relating to the execution of the terms of the Treaty of St. Germain that ended the war between Austria and the Allied Powers, summarized his contribution in the following way:

> Due to his responsibilities as a deputy director in the offices of the Vienna Chamber of Commerce, Crafts and Industry, he has had to resign from his activities in the Office of Accounts. As an economic theorist, Professor Mises has made a name for himself in the German-speaking scientific world far beyond the boundaries of Austria. His wide knowledge and his accurate, clear way of thinking are combined with an extraordinary, practical understanding and a detailed knowledge of the economic life in Vienna and Austria. Given Austria's present economic and financial difficulties, that the

arranging of the debentures for the settlement of prewar debts has been facilitated under such comparatively favorable conditions we owe to his far-seeing and able handiwork. With foresight into the requirements necessary for success, he sketched out the rules for the committee overseeing the settlement of the debentures. And it was his proposals for the issuance of the debentures that were adopted by the consortium of nations. It was just as important and beneficial for the work of the Office of Accounts that Mises applied, in a strictly objective way, his knowledge of the economic situation in the selection of the Office's personnel. Already as a staff member of the Chamber of Commerce, he had won the confidence of wide circles in the business world, and he has kept that confidence in his work with the Office of Accounts.[13]

At the Chamber, Mises explained, "I created a position for myself." While always having a superior nominally above him, he basically came to operate on his own with the assistance of a few colleagues. Though he felt that his advice was not often taken, he viewed himself as "the economist of the country," whose efforts were "concentrated on the crucial economic political questions" and that "[i]n the Austria of the postwar period I was the economic conscience."[14]

Friends often suggested to him that he could have had more of a positive impact on Austrian economic policy if he had been willing to give a little and modify his principled stance on various issues. But Mises' only regret, as he looked back on his years at the Chamber, was that he often felt that he compromised too much, though he stated that he had always clearly understood that in politics compromise was inevitable. The challenge was to "give" on the less important issues so as to have a better chance to succeed on the essential ones. This is how he viewed the positions he often took within the Chamber so as to get the organization to publicly back policies that he considered crucial at various times during these years.[15]

By the early 1930s, Mises understood that a Nazi victory in Germany would threaten Austria. As a classical liberal and a Jew, he could be certain that after a Nazi takeover of Austria the Gestapo would come looking for him. So when in March 1934 he was offered a way out by William E. Rappard, co-founder and director of the Graduate Institute of International Studies in Geneva, Switzerland, who offered him a position as Professor of International Economic Relations, Mises readily accepted and moved to Geneva in October 1934.[16] After he accepted the appointment in Geneva he went on extended leave from the Chamber, though he continued to return to Vienna periodically to consult on various policy matters until February 1938.[17]

But by the time he left Vienna in October 1934, Mises believed that he had done little more than fight a series of rear-guard actions to delay the decay and destruction of his beloved Austria. "For sixteen years I fought a battle in the Chamber in which I won nothing more than a mere delay of the catastrophe ... Even if I had been completely successful, Austria could not have been saved," Mises forlornly admitted. "The enemy who was about to destroy it came from abroad [Hitler's Nazi Germany]. Austria could not for long withstand the onslaught of the National-Socialists who soon were to overrun all of Europe." But he had no regrets over the efforts he had made. "I could not act otherwise. I fought because I could do no other."[18]

Austria between the two World Wars, 1918–1938

One day in 1927, Ludwig von Mises stood at the high window of his office at the Vienna Chamber of Commerce. Looking out over the *Ringstrasse* (the main grand boulevard in the center of Vienna), he said to his young friend and former student Fritz Machlup, "Maybe grass will grow there, because our civilization will end."[19] To understand why Mises would have drawn such a dark picture of Vienna's and Austria's future, and his attempts to influence Austrian economic policy during this period between the two world wars, requires an appreciation of the political and economic catastrophe that followed from World War I in this part of the European continent.[20]

Prewar Austria-Hungary under the Hapsburg monarchy had been a vast polyglot empire in Central and Eastern Europe encompassing a territory of approximately 415,000 square miles with a population of over fifty million. The two largest linguistic groups in the Empire were the German-speaking and Hungarian populations, each numbering about ten million. The remaining thirty million were Czechs, Slovaks, Poles, Romanians, Ruthenians, Croats, Serbs, Slovenes, Italians, and a variety of smaller groups of the Balkan region.

During the last decades of the nineteenth and the opening decade and a half of the twentieth centuries, the Empire increasingly came under the strain of nationalist sentiments by these various groups, each desiring greater autonomy and some forcefully demanding independence. The Great War brought the 700-year-old Hapsburg dynasty to a close.[21] The war had put severe political and economic strains on the country. Power was centralized in the hands of the military command, civil liberties were greatly curtailed, and the economy was controlled and regulated.[22] But the more that power was concentrated and the more that the fortunes of war turned against the Empire, the more the national groups – most insistently the Hungarians and then the Czechs, Croats, and Poles – demanded self-determination to form their own nation states.[23]

The Empire formally began to disintegrate in October 1918, when first the Czechs declared their independence, followed by the Hungarians and the Croats and Slovenes. On November 11, 1918, the last of the Hapsburg emperors, Karl, stepped down from the throne, and on November 12, a provisional national assembly in Vienna proclaimed a republic in German Austria, as this remnant of the Empire was now named. But in the second article of the document of independence, it was stated that "German Austria is an integral part of the German Republic." Thus the new Austria was born – reduced to 32,370 square miles with a population of 6.5 million inhabitants, one-third of whom resided in Vienna – with a significant portion of the population not wishing their country to be independent but unified (an *Anschluss*) with the new republican Germany.

From the moment the new Austria was born, it was plagued by three problems: the disintegration of the Austro-Hungarian monetary system; socialist-welfare programs, budget deficits, and inflation; and threatened political disintegration within the boundaries of the new smaller Austrian state.

For almost five months after the Empire had politically broken apart, the Austro-Hungarian National Bank continued to operate as the note-issuing central bank within German Austria, Czechoslovakia, and Hungary. The Czechs, however, increasingly protested that the Bank was expanding the money supply to cover the expenses and food subsidies of the German Austrian government in Vienna. In January 1919, the new Yugoslavian government declared that all notes of the Austro-Hungarian Bank on their territory would be stamped with a national mark, and only such stamped money would then be legal tender. The Czech government announced the same in late February 1919. The Czech border was sealed to prevent smuggling notes into the country and the notes on Czechoslovakian territory were stamped between March 3 to 10. Soon after, both Yugoslavia and Czechoslovakia began to issue their own national currencies and exchange the stamped Austrian notes for their new monetary units.

In Hungary the situation was more chaotic. In March 1919 a Bolshevik government took power in Budapest, and began printing huge quantities of small denomination notes with Austro-Hungarian Bank plates in their possession, as well as larger notes of their own design, causing a severe inflation. The Bolshevik government was overthrown in August 1919 by invading Romanian armies. The Austrian Bank notes were not embossed with a national stamp until March 1920, and a separate national currency was introduced in Hungary in May 1921.

The Austrian government, in response, to the monetary decisions by the Yugoslavians and the Czechs, began their own official stamping of Austro-Hungarian Bank notes within its territory between March 12 and 24, 1919.[24] But the limiting of notes considered legal tender in the new Austria did not end the problem of monetary inflation. In a matter of weeks after the declaration of the Austrian Republic, the coalition government made up of the Social Democrats, the Christian Socials, and the Pan-German Nationalists began introducing a vast array of social welfare programs. They included a mandatory eight-hour workday, a guaranteed minimum one-to-two-week holiday for industrial employees, a continuation and reinforcement of the wartime system of rent controls in Vienna, centrally funded unemployment and welfare payments, and price controls on food supplies that were supplemented with government rationing and subsidies.[25] The cost for these latter programs was huge and kept growing. In 1921, half of the Austrian government's budget deficit was caused by the food subsidies.[26]

To cover these expenditures the Austrian government resorted to the printing press.[27] Between March and December 1919, the paper money of the Austrian Republic increased from 831.6 million crowns to 12.1 billion crowns. By December 1920, it had increased to 30.6 billion crowns; by December 1921 to 174.1 billion crowns; by December 1922 to 4 trillion crowns; and to 7.1 trillion crowns by the end of 1923. Prices rose dramatically through this period. A cost of living index, excluding housing, (with July 1914 =1) stood at 28.37 in January 1919; by January 1920 it had risen to 49.22; by January 1921 it had gone up to 99.56; in January 1922 it stood at 830; by January 1923 it had shot up to 11,836; and in April 1924 it was at 14,850.

The foreign exchange value of the Austrian Crown also dramatically fell during this period. In January 1919, one dollar could buy 16.1 crowns in the Vienna foreign exchange market; by May of 1923, a dollar traded for 70,800 crowns.[28]

Adding to the monetary and financial chaos was the virtual political disintegration of what remained of Austria. Immediately after the declaration of the Austrian Republic, political power devolved to the provinces and the local communities; the provinces showed little loyalty to the new national government and great animosity toward the capital city of Vienna. In 1919 some provinces even entered into independent negotiations with Switzerland and Bavaria about possible political incorporation into these neighboring countries.[29] But a primary motivation for this provincial "nationalism" or "particularism" (as it was called) was the food and raw materials crisis.

The imperial government had forcefully requisitioned food from the agricultural areas of German Austria during the war. The new republican government in Vienna continued the practice of forced requisition at artificially low prices, using a newly formed *Volkswehr* (People's Defense Force) to seize the food supplies sold in Vienna at controlled prices for ration tickets.[30] The provincial governments used their local power to prevent the export of their agricultural products to Vienna at these below-market prices. The governments in the provinces blockaded the provincial borders and imposed passport controls to enter or exit their respective jurisdictions, with baggage and body searches at the provincial checkpoints to determine whether food or other "contraband" were being smuggled between the regions of Austria. But in spite of this, Vienna received food from the countryside through a vast black market network that operated throughout the country. Anything could be had – for (illegal) market prices.[31]

Men, women, and children would scrape together enough money to make weekly railway trips to the countryside to beg and buy food from the farmers in the outlying areas. They would also make excursions to the Vienna Woods to bring back firewood to heat their apartments, hauling on their backs heavy cords of wood they had chopped down. One observer described seeing

> men and women of all ages, children as young as five struggling under crushing loads of wood, fighting their way into the trains, falling exhausted upon the roads and incidentally ruining by ignorant felling the timber resources of the country. Moreover this daily migration into the country means withdrawal from productive labor of thousands of the best workers in Vienna.[32]

The food crisis was reinforced by an economic blockade, one that was continued for a brief time after the armistice by the Allied powers, but mostly imposed by the Czechs, Hungarians, and Yugoslavians. Coal supplies throughout 1919 and early 1920 were often very scarce. The Czechs and Hungarians refused to supply coal and other resources unless they received payment in manufactured goods in trade or the hard currencies of the Western powers. But the inability to acquire coal and other essential raw materials resulted in Austrian, and especially Viennese, industry grinding to a halt, with no way to produce the goods necessary to pay for the resources required for production.

Throughout 1919 to 1922, Vienna was on the verge of mass starvation, with food and milk rations almost nonexistent except for the very young. The streets of central Vienna often saw children of all ages begging for food at the entrances to restaurants and hotels. Only relief supplies provided by both the Allied powers and private charities saved thousands of lives in the city. How desperate the economic condition was in Vienna at this time was described by Austrian economist Friedrich von Wieser in a paper he wrote in the autumn of 1919 for a conference on famine in Europe:

> Milk can only be supplied to babies and invalids. In peacetime the daily consumption in Vienna amounted to between 800,000 and 900,000 liters. Now, barely 70,000 liters are available, because Hungary and Czechoslovakia have completely stopped their milk supply to Vienna, and milk production in the Austrian provinces are much reduced. In Vienna today no milk can be given to children over two years of age. Children up to one year receive one liter a day, and those between one and two years receive three-quarters of a liter. We need not dwell on the horrible effects on child mortality ... The nourishment of the population is extremely inadequate, the state of public health very low, and death claims many victims. The number of crimes committed in this extremity, and the number of suicides is extraordinarily high ... The coal shortage and the transport difficulty connected therewith are so severe that we fear we may not be able to forward in time, to the consumer, even the foodstuffs which can be procured. The railroads have no stocks of coal, and when the lines will be blocked by the winter snow, traffic will have to cease everywhere ... Shortage of coal and the transport crisis hamper our industrial production. Even the farmer has to wait for the coal that he needs to thrash his harvest. In the towns, especially Vienna, the supply of gas and electric light is reduced to a minimum, and we fear from day to day that it may have to be stopped altogether. For the two million inhabitants of Vienna, there is at present [autumn of 1919] only enough coal to cover the most urgent kitchen requirements. Till now no supplies are available for the heating of rooms ... Deprived of millions of her own race, who have been assigned as subjects to alien national States; cut off from her industrial undertakings, which she had established and guided throughout the former empire; without food for more than half her inhabitants, almost without coal, without raw materials from abroad – with her railways and workshops worn out, bowed down under the burdens of the War and under those of the Peace Treaty – we [Austrians] must indeed doubt whether she [Austria] will be capable of surviving when once the time has come when she may use her powers in peaceful and free competition.[33]

In October 1920 a new constitution was promulgated as the law of the land. Written primarily by the Austrian legal philosopher Hans Kelsen, it defined the lines of authority between the central government and the provinces. The

provinces were given wide powers at the local and regional level but the constitution established the supremacy of the federal authority over essential political
and economic matters that ended the provincial nationalism and "particularism."[34] One new element resulting from the constitution was that the city of
Vienna was now administratively recognized as having a separate "provincial"
status. So neither the surrounding province of Lower Austria nor the federal government located in Vienna had jurisdiction over the affairs of the city. From
1920 until 1934, the city became known as "Red Vienna."

Throughout the interwar period, Austrian politics were dominated by the
battle between the Social Democrats and the Christian Socials. The Social
Democrats, while rejecting the Bolshevik tactic of dictatorship to achieve their
ends, were dedicated to the ideal of marching to a bright socialist future. But
outside Vienna (where they consistently won a large electoral majority) they
were thwarted in this mission by the Christian Socials who held the majority in
the Alpine provinces of Austria, and therefore in the National Assembly that
governed the country as a whole. The Christian Socials based their support in the
agricultural regions of the country where there was a suspicion and dislike for
socialist radicalism. The Christian Socials, however, were willing to use, in turn,
domestic regulations, trade restrictions, and income transfer programs to benefit
segments of the rural population at the expense of the larger municipalities, and
especially Vienna.

The battle between these two parties had first been fought out in 1921 and
1922 when government expenditures and the mounting increases in the money
supply to pay for them were threatening runaway inflation and financial and economic collapse. International loans totaling over 170 million US dollars and
charitable expenditures of about fifty million US dollars provided temporary
support. In May 1922, Monsignor Ignaz Seipel of the Christian Social Party
became Chancellor of Austria. After several appeals to the Allied powers, Seipel
made a dramatic appearance at the League of Nations in Geneva in August 1922
and arranged for the League to extend a 131.7 million US dollar loan to the Austrian government to repay outstanding debts left over from the war and to temporarily cover current expenditures.[35]

In return the League supervised a demanding austerity plan that required
sizable cuts in government spending, including the end of expensive food subsidies for the urban population and the firing of 80,000 civil servants. In addition,
the League assisted in the construction of a new Austrian National Bank, for
which Mises played a central role in the writing of the charter and bylaws. In
November 1922 the new Bank was established and the inflation of bank notes
was soon ended. By November 1923, the Austrian Federal budget had been
brought into balance, a half year earlier than called for under the terms of the
loan from the League of Nations. In March 1925, a new Austrian schilling was
introduced to replace the old inflated Austrian crown, and it became redeemable
in gold in June 1925.

But in Vienna the Social Democrats were determined to press on with
creating a model socialist community. Huge sums of money were spent in the
1920s on building dozens of schools, kindergartens, libraries, and hospitals in

the "working class" districts of the city. They also constructed vast new housing complexes, sometimes built literally like fortresses ready to be defended against any counter-revolutionary attacks; one of the most famous of these complexes was *Karl Marx Hof* three-fifths of a mile long and containing almost 1,400 apartments. In other parts of the city rent control kept the cost of apartment housing artificially low at the expense of the landlords. Municipal social and medical insurance programs provided cradle-to-grave protection – including free burials – for the constituents of the Social Democratic Party in Vienna.[36]

To pay for these programs and projects, the Social Democrats imposed a "soak the rich" tax system. Among them were eighteen categories of "luxury" taxes, including entertainment levies that placed a 10 percent tax on opera, theater, and concert tickets and a 40 percent tax on movie theater tickets, which was meant to induce the "working class" to listen to classical music rather than watch Hollywood films. The tax for attending horse races or boxing matches was 50 percent, under the presumption that these were the spectator sports of the wealthy and the comfortable middle class. There was a 33 percent tax levied on any person giving a luncheon or dinner party, or if music was played at a funeral, again under the assumption that only the rich had such parties or could afford to hire musicians. There were heavy taxes on "luxury" apartments and automobiles, as well as on horses used for riding or for drawing a carriage. There was a tax on the employment of more than one servant in a household, with the rate set at fifty schillings a year for the second servant, if female, 300 schillings for the third, and an extra 250 schillings per year for each additional servant after that. There were steep taxes for food and drink served to patrons in bars, cabarets, variety clubs, concert cafes and restaurants, *Huerigen and Buschenschenken* (popular taverns and inns in the suburbs of Vienna), and liqueur and breakfast houses; the tax rates on these establishments were set anywhere between 2 and 15 percent at the discretion of the tax officials, depending on how they classified the income categories of the clientele in each.[37] One newspaper referred to the city's fiscal system as "the success of the tax vampires," especially since to cover these municipal expenditures the tax base and rates soon enveloped a large portion of Vienna's middle class as well as "the rich."[38]

Parallel to the electoral combat between Social Democrats and the Christian Socials were paramilitary battles around the country. In 1919 and 1920, under the threat of foreign invaders, especially the Yugoslavian armed forces along Austria's ill-defined southern border, and the plundering expeditions of private gangs and the government's *Volkswehr,* who attempted to seize food supplies from the rural population, the farming communities created a *Heimwehr* (Home Defense Force). It soon became the paramilitary army of the Christian Socials. In turn, the Social Democrats created the *Schutzbund* (Protection League), as their private armed force. Armed with war surplus and other weaponry, they both had training camps, parades, and military drills, and held maneuvers in the countryside, during which they would sometimes engage in actual combat. By 1931, the *Heimwehr* had an armed force of 60,000 men, while the *Schutzbund* had an armed and trained membership of 90,000. In comparison, under the peace treaty that ended the Great War, the Austrian Army was limited to a force of 30,000 men.[39]

One of the most serious of these clashes occurred in January 1927 in a town near the Hungarian border southeast of Vienna. Several people were killed in the fighting, including a small child. In July 1927, three members of the local *Heimwehr* where the combat occurred were put on trial in Vienna but soon were acquitted. Mobs from the "working class" districts of the city, who were led by known communists, rampaged through parts of the center of Vienna; they burned the Federal Palace of Justice, requiring the police to use deadly force to put down the violence; in the end, eighty-nine people died and 1,057 were wounded in the street fighting. In response, the Social Democratic mayor of the city declared the police "incompetent" and set up a new parallel police force, the *Wiener Gemiendewache* (Vienna Municipal Guard); it was manned mostly by recruits from the Social Democrat's *Schutzbund,* all at the taxpayers' extra expense.

Throughout the 1920s, Austria lived a precarious economic existence. Heavy taxes and domestic regulations hampered private investment in the country with both the private sector and the municipal authorities dependent upon foreign lenders and domestic credit expansion for financing many of their activities. Indeed, the burden of rising taxes and social insurance costs, increasing wage demands by labor unions, and tariff regulations actually resulted in *capital consumption* in the Austrian economy through the 1920s.[40] In a report for the Austrian government that Ludwig von Mises had co-authored in 1931, it was shown that between 1925 and 1929 taxes had risen by 32 percent, social insurance by 50 percent, industrial wages by 24 percent, agricultural wages by 13 percent, and transportation costs by 15 percent. Meanwhile, an index of the prices of manufactured goods bearing these costs had increased only 4.74 percent between 1925 and early 1930.[41]

This was the political and economic situation in the country as Austria entered the Great Depression in 1929. Austria's crises in the early 1930s were both political and economic. Between 1929 and 1932, Austria had four changes in the government, with Engelbert Dollfuss becoming Chancellor in May 1932. The economic crisis became especially severe after May 1931. One of Austria's old imperial-era banks, the *CreditAnstalt,* had taken over the *Boden-KreditAnstalt* in October 1929. The latter bank had branches throughout Central Europe and suffered heavy financial losses through most of 1929 into 1930. To sustain the *Boden-KreditAnstalt* and its own financial position, *CreditAnstalt* borrowed heavily in the short-term market. In May 1931, panic set in that *CreditAnstalt* would not be able to meet its financial obligations, which precipitated a run on the bank. At the same time, there was a rush to exchange Austrian schillings for foreign currencies and gold.

The Austrian government responded by passing a series of emergency measures between May and December 1931. Concerned about continuing losses of hard currency reserves, the Austrian government instituted foreign exchange control. But distortions, imbalances, and corruption resulting from the law lead to three revisions during the first year, each one loosening the controls a little bit more.

In February 1932, for example, the Austrian National Bank permitted the use of a system of "private clearings:" exporters earning foreign currency from sales abroad could sell at least a portion of their foreign exchange holdings directly to Austrian importers of foreign raw materials, and at a rate of exchange above the official rate. Also that same month, the Austrian National Bank, in cooperation with the Vienna Chamber of Commerce, established a "certificate system." The Chamber was permitted to issue "certificates" allowing exporters of manufactured goods to retain the foreign currency proceeds they had earned from sales abroad so that they would have the necessary funds to purchase the imported raw materials essential to the continuation of production in their enterprises. The controls were phased out in 1933 and 1934 after the Austrian government received loans from a group of foreign sources.[42]

In June of 1931, Austria appealed for financial assistance to provide funds needed to stem the massive loss of gold and foreign exchange following the collapse of the *CreditAnstalt* bank in May. On June 16, the Bank of England provided a 150 million schilling credit to the Austrian National Bank. This was immediately followed by a hundred million schilling credit from the Bank for International Settlements in Basel, Switzerland. In August 1931, the Austrian government appealed to the League of Nations in Geneva for a 250 million schilling loan. Representatives of the Financial Section of the League traveled to Vienna to evaluate the situation. On October 15, 1931, the Bank of England and the Bank for International Settlements postponed repayment of their loans. On May 9, 1932, Austria sent another appeal to the League of Nations for a loan.

After Austria declared a partial moratorium on payment of its international debts, the League signed the Geneva Protocol on July 15, 1932, stating a willingness on the part of Great Britain, France, and Italy to extend a loan to the Austrian National Bank. But the actual loan, in the amount of 296 million schillings (237.4 million in devalued schillings), was not transferred to the National Bank until August 1933. It enabled the Bank to repay the hundred million schillings owed to the Bank of England and the ninety million schillings owed to the Bank for International Settlements, as well as fifty million schillings still owed to the League from 1923. Refinancing the loan a short time later at a lower rate of interest significantly reduced Austria's total foreign debt.

But the events that were to seal Austria's fate were being played out in the political arena. The League loan, like the one in 1922, required that a League representative supervise the allocation and use of the funds and imposed austerity measures to reduce government expenditures, in addition to a renewal of the pledge against an *Anschluss* with Germany.[43] The Social Democrats and Pan-German Nationalists in the Austrian Parliament unsuccessfully attempted to block passage of the loan bill, which left a bitter and tense relationship between these two parties and Dollfuss' Christian Socials.

In March 1933, a procedural argument arose during a parliamentary vote and the leading members of each major party stepped down from the rostrum, bringing the proceedings to a halt. The next day, Chancellor Dollfuss used this as an excuse to suspend the parliament and announce that he was going to rule by decree. In May 1933, Dollfuss decreed a new constitution for Austria that established a fascist-type corporatist political structure in place of the constitution written by Hans Kelsen in 1920.[44]

Tensions continued to mount for the next year until the situation exploded into civil war in February 1934. Based on information that units of the *Schutzbund,* the paramilitary arm of the Social Democratic Party, were going to initiate a coup attempt, the Christian Socials' *Heimwehr* attempted to disarm them in several cities around the country, including Linz. When fighting broke out, the Austrian Army was called into action to put down the combat.

In Vienna, the Social Democrats called for armed insurrection in "self-defense" against the "reactionary" forces of the Austrian Army and the *Heimwehr.* For four days deadly and destructive fighting went on in the outer districts of Vienna, with hundreds either killed or wounded and the government forces using artillery pieces to bombard Social Democratic strongholds. When the fighting ended, the Social Democratic forces were completely defeated, most of its leadership fled the country, and the party was declared illegal.

Then in July 1934, a group of Austrian Nazis, inspired by Hitler's rise to power in Germany the preceding year, attempted a coup. They seized the Chancellery building in Vienna, captured and killed Dollfuss, and proclaimed a National Socialist government. They were swiftly defeated by forces loyal to the Austrian government, as was another Nazi-led uprising in the region of Styria at the same time. When Mussolini declared Italy's intention to preserve Austria's independence by sending military forces to the Brenner Pass at the Italian-Austrian border, Hitler repudiated his Austrian followers (for the time being).

Kurt von Schuschnigg became Chancellor following Dollfuss' death, continuing to rule in the same authoritarian manner as his predecessor until early 1938, when he succumbed to Hitler's threats and agreed to the *Anschluss,* the German annexation of Austria. On March 12, 1938, the German Army crossed the Austrian border. When Adolf Hitler arrived in Vienna on March 15, he announced that his native Austria had been incorporated into Nazi Germany.[45] Over the next several weeks the Gestapo arrested tens of thousands of Viennese. An estimated seventy thousand were soon imprisoned or sent to concentration camps, including Schuschnigg. Among the immediate victims were the Jews of Vienna, who were harassed, beaten, tortured, murdered, or humiliated by being made to scrub the streets of Vienna on their hands and knees with tooth-brushes while surrounded by tormenting crowds of onlookers.[46] Thus ended Austria's tragic twenty-year history between the two world wars.

Monetary disintegration, inflation, and institutional reform, 1918–1923

When World War I ended, Ludwig von Mises was serving as an economic consultant with the Austrian General Staff in Vienna. He had seen action on the Russian front as an artillery officer, three times decorated for bravery under fire. Following the signing of the Treaty of Brest-Litovsk in March 1918, which ended the war between Imperial Germany and Austria-Hungary and Lenin's new Bolshevik government in Russia, Mises was appointed the officer in charge of currency control in Austrian-occupied Ukraine, with his headquarters in Odessa. He was transferred to Vienna in the summer of 1918. Back in the capital, he picked up his writings on policy matters, when not occupied with his military responsibilities.

For the General Staff, he prepared a paper in which he offered some "Remarks Concerning the Establishment of a Ukrainian Note-Issuing Bank." In February 1918, an independent Ukraine had been declared in Kiev, and Mises outlined the institutional rules that should be followed by a Ukrainian central bank. All bank notes issued and outstanding should be at all times covered with gold or foreign exchange redeemable in gold equal to one-third of the bank's liabilities. Bank assets in the form of secure short-term loans should back the remaining two-thirds of the notes in circulation. Mises admitted that there were particular institutional and historical circumstances that would have to be taken into consideration in setting the conditions under which certain types of borrowers might have access to the lending facilities of the Ukrainian central bank. What was crucial for Ukraine to have a sound monetary system were relatively high reserves for assured redemption of bank notes on demand and limits on the term-structure of the loans made by the central bank.[47]

But the more important problem, looking forward to the end of the war and a return to peacetime economic conditions, was the reestablishment of the Austrian monetary system. On July 23, 1914, the Austro-Hungarian National Bank had 2,130 million crown notes in circulation with a 74.6 percent cover in gold. Shortly after the war began in August 1914, the government suspended gold redemption for crown notes, and turned to the central bank to finance a large proportion of the wartime expenses. By October 26, 1918, crown notes in circulation had increased to 33,529 million with only a 1 percent gold cover. The actual state of the bank's financial condition was not widely known due to wartime censorship. [48]

In two published articles in the autumn of 1918 that were subject to the censor's red pen,[49] Mises restated the quantity theory of money, explained the inherent non-neutrality of money on the structure of prices, argued against those who claimed that the general rise in prices was singularly due to the decrease in the quantities of goods and services available on the market during wartime; he reasoned that a general and sustained rise in prices during the war could only have come about from a sizable expansion of the money supply.

The task ahead would be to end the inflation and restore the soundness and stability of the Austrian currency when the fighting stopped. Mises made clear that monetary theory, as a social scientific endeavor, offered no answer to the question as to which policy was best to follow in the postwar period. One option would be to end the printing of bank notes and allow the value of the Austrian crown to stabilize in terms of its current depreciated market value in exchange for gold and foreign currencies. A new fixed rate of exchange could be established, Mises suggested, say, one year from the day the war ended. If, on the other hand, there were a strong preference to return to the status before the war began in 1914, including a restoration of the prewar foreign exchange value of the Austrian crown, it would be necessary for the government to run a budget surplus and pay off its debt to the Austro-Hungarian Bank, which would then take the bank notes out of circulation. The monetary contraction would have to continue until the value of the crown had once again risen to its prewar parity.

Mises emphasized that such a monetary deflation would have various disruptive social consequences in the transition to the higher foreign exchange rate for the crown. Whether to contract the money supply or stabilize the value of the crown at its depreciated value was a political question that economic theory could not answer, other than to explain the consequences that were likely to follow from either course of action.[50]

These essays looked forward to a return of peace, but they contain nothing suggesting the actual cataclysm of events that were to follow. Indeed they almost have a surrealistic quality to them in suggesting a postwar period in which there would be a calm, stable, and relatively smooth transition to a restructured monetary system as a complement to the return to a tranquil peacetime economy. Instead, the problems that Mises attempted to grapple with when the war was over in November 1918 concerned the actual situation of monetary disintegration, high inflation, political disorder, and general economic chaos.

With the end of the war, Mises returned to his position with the Vienna Chamber of Commerce. And he was shortly to take on responsibility for the Austrian Section of the League of Nations Reparations Commission. His written contributions during the next year and a half seem almost Herculean, considering that he was working far more than a nine-to-five day. His two most well-known works from this period are *Nation, State and Economy* and his essay on "Economic Calculation in the Socialist Commonwealth." People who knew Mises at this time suggested that there was, also, the possibility that he might have been called to serve as Austrian Finance Minister.[51] But he was not. Instead, through most of 1919, the Austrian Minister of Finance was Joseph A. Schumpeter.

But, nonetheless, he formulated several possible monetary policies during the first half of 1919, meant to deal with the onrush of events during those uncertain months. In three fairly lengthy papers he dealt with three distinct but interrelated questions. How shall a previously unified monetary system be separated into different national currencies? How might the private banking sector create a transition to a new currency after government mismanagement of the monetary system will have brought about a sudden inflationary collapse of the currency? And, how might two separate national currency systems be unified or reunified into a single monetary regime?

As we have seen, the first monetary crisis in early 1919 was the disintegration of the unified monetary system of the now collapsed Austro-Hungarian Empire. The newly independent successor states had started embossing official stamps on Austro-Hungarian bank notes on their territories, declaring that only these would be considered legal tender within their respective nation-states.

In April 1919, shortly before the Austrian delegation left for France to be given the formal terms for peace from the Allied Powers, Mises prepared a paper titled "The Austrian Currency Problem Prior to the Peace Conference,"[52] in his role as the senior economist responsible for financial matters relating to foreign affairs at the Chamber of Commerce. He outlined alternative possibilities that might be followed in establishing a new monetary order in the wake of the collapse of the Austro-Hungarian Empire and its unified currency system. He discussed the possibilities of maintaining a common single currency area with a single central bank, or a monetary union with independent central banks, or completely independent national currencies issued and managed by separate central banks.

Mises assumed that none of the successor states would opt for the first alternative. So, whether the successor states were to finally adopt a monetary union of national central banks or national central banks each making independent monetary policies, the matter concerned how all the people presently holding notes issued by the Austro-Hungarian National Bank would convert them into units of the respective new national currencies. He suggested that those residing in the respective successor states should have the freedom of converting their old notes into either the national currency of the new country in which they resided or into the currency of any other of the successor states as they found most convenient and useful. The same free choice of currency conversion should apply to those holding quantities of the old notes in countries outside the territory of the former Empire, as well.

The additional problem to which the currency conversion would be tied, Mises said, was the distribution of the Austro-Hungarian prewar and wartime debt among the successor states. He offered a detailed formula of how the distribution of this debt and the conversion of the old notes into new currencies might be reasonably balanced without an undue financial burden on any one of the new countries.[53]

But in the spring of 1919, a far greater problem confronted the new Austria: the danger of runaway or hyperinflation. With state spending seemingly out of control because of the welfare-redistributive programs introduced by the Social Democratic and Christian Social coalition government, and especially the cost of subsidized food for the urban populations, the monetary system seemed headed for collapse. In the first half of 1919, the Austrian money supply increased from 831.6 million crowns in March to 8.3 billion crowns in July. The note issue reached twelve billion crowns by December 1919. In a paper marked "confidential" that he prepared in May 1919 for the bankers and businessmen connected with the Chamber, Mises presented a proposal "On the Actions to be Taken in the Face of Progressive Currency Depreciation."[54] He was cautious to say that it was neither certain nor inevitable that a currency collapse had to occur. But if it did, Austria, and particularly Vienna with its large urban population, could be faced with social disintegration, food riots, and mass destruction and theft of property as the value of the medium of exchange fell to zero.

Such violence had already been seen on the streets of Vienna. In an account given by the Austrian Social Democrat Otto Bauer, on April 18, 1919, Austrian communists had instigated a riot by "a few hundred hungry, ignorant, and despairing unemployed and disabled men" to attack the parliament buildings.

At the same time the incident threw ghastly light upon the terrible privation which existed in Vienna. The demonstrators threw themselves upon the fallen horses of the police, tore out pieces of flesh from the still warm bodies of the dead animals, and carried them home as delicacies which had not been enjoyed for a long time.[55]

If the currency were to suffer a rapid collapse, the government would have lost all legitimacy and trust in relation to monetary matters. It would fall on the shoulders of the private sector – banks and businesses – to devise the mechanism to bridge the gap between any such dramatic and rapid collapse of the old currency and the spontaneous shift to the use of alternative monies by the citizens of the society.

Why did the private sector have to prepare for such a contingency? Because, Mises said, "We can hardly expect the government to be of any help." For five years they had done nothing but follow "a disastrous inflationary course." Therefore, he stated,

> It is up to us citizens to try to do on our own what the government is failing to do for us. All we can hope from the government is that it will not stymie the endeavors of its private citizens. In their own interest and in the interest of the community, the banks as well as large industrial and commercial enterprises must take the necessary preparatory steps to avert the catastrophic consequences that will follow from the collapse of the currency.[56]

Mises presented a plan to these elements in the private sector to use export revenues and sales of assets to accumulate cash reserves of small denomination units of Swiss money to use as the temporary emergency medium of exchange. He estimated that the amount needed for the purpose was approximately thirty million Swiss francs. There were approximately 1.5 million employees who were neither self-employed nor working in the agriculture or timber sectors of the economy. Assuming that the average monthly income was 1,500 crowns, the total monthly income to be covered would be 2,250 million crowns. At the going exchange rate that came to 22.5 million Swiss francs. Assuming a need for an additional 150 million for government monthly subsistence, unemployment and pension incomes, that added another 1.5 million Swiss francs. To meet any unplanned contingencies, Mises suggested adding an extra 25 percent, to be on the safe side, for a total of thirty million Swiss francs.

The money would be used to pay salaries and pensions and to loan to the government and other employers in the market so that the population would have access to a medium of exchange in which they could have confidence. This would be necessary only until normal export sales and capital transfers supplied the required quantities of gold or foreign currencies to use as the permanent substitute monies in a post-inflationary Austrian economy.

These were "expedients for the moment of the collapse," Mises explained. Because,

> As soon as government interference in the monetary system is eliminated by the collapse of the currency, free market forces will automatically come into

play that will supply the economy with the exact amount of money it needs. Sales to other countries will build up at that moment, and will attract the requisite money into the country.

Goods might have to be sold at very low prices on the world market, "but that is the inescapable consequence of the disastrous currency policy that will have been pursued earlier."[57]

He also explained the process by which private banks could form an informal consortium to jointly cover the costs and clearings of providing alternative small-note private currencies. "The collapse of the currency will almost certainly have so thoroughly undermined general confidence in the state's monetary system," Mises suggested, "that it will take some length of time before the public will again be willing to use any form of money issued by the state."[58]

While Mises alluded to the possibility of a private monetary order without a central bank in the wake of a currency collapse, realistically central banking was and would remain the prevailing monetary regime. The question then arose as to whether the new Austria should have its own independent central bank and national currency or instead should be integrated into a common currency area with the new postwar Germany. Indeed, Mises stated that, "It is beyond doubt that some day we will carry through a political union with Germany. It is perfectly clear that at such a time the fusion of the Austrian and the German currency systems will take place." But he also said, "We must remember that the time of such a currency merger is especially critical," for various political and international reasons.[59]

We pointed out that when Austria was declared to be a republic in November 1918, the second article of the document stated that "German Austria is an integral part of the German Republic." Both inside Austria and among the Allied Powers, there was a strong opinion that an independent Austria as it had been constituted with the break-up of the Austro-Hungarian Empire was not viable as a separate political entity. The Pan-German Nationalist Party in Austria believed that race, language, and culture required the unification of all German people in one German Reich. Many Social Democrats – the most vocal being Otto Bauer, who served as Foreign Minister in the first coalition government – desired unification because it would strengthen the socialist cause in Austria if the country was joined with the new German Republic, which possessed a large Social Democratic movement. The Christian Socials were more reluctant to endorse Austro-German unification, but found it a useful ploy in bargaining for aid, loans, and political support from the Western Allied Powers.

When he looked back at this period immediately after World War I in his *Notes and Recollections,* written in 1940, Mises said that on the issue of Austrian unification with Germany,

The situation [of Austria's apparently paralyzed political and economic situation at this time] sometimes made me vacillate in my position on the annexation program. I was not blind regarding the danger to Austrian culture in a union with the German Reich. But there were moments in which

I asked myself whether the annexation was not a lesser evil than the continuation of a policy that inescapably had to lead to catastrophe."[60]

Yet in certain passages in essays written in 1919 it is clear that at the time Mises was persuaded that unification with Germany was a "political and moral necessity."[61]

In 1919, he said that Germany was in the throes of its own inflationary disaster. This made it wiser at this moment to devise a way for Austria to find its own way out of the monetary collapse that might be in front of it. "We are not abandoning the idea of a Greater Germany when we envision a currency merger as a means to a joint ascension rather than a means to a joint decline." If Austria solved its monetary problem it would be offering to Germany "an example for the proper conduct in critical times like these."[62]

In spite of the fact that in the Treaty of St. Germain, which was presented by the Allied Powers to the Austrian delegation in France in June 1919, it was stated directly that Austria was barred from unification with the new German Republic, the sentiment for *Anschluss* persisted. At the end of June 1919, Mises finished a lengthy paper on the very theme of "The Reentry of German-Austria into the German Reich and the Currency Question."[63]

Here one sees Mises as not only a monetary theorist but as the monetary historian. He first lays out a detailed account of how the Austrian monetary system had evolved, from it earlier monetary linkage with the German principalities to its monetary expulsion from the German Confederation in the 1860s after Austria's war with Prussia in 1866, and to its establishment of a gold standard in the 1890s and on through to the inflationary funding of Austria-Hungary's war expenditures between 1914 to 1918.

Political unification of Austria with Germany necessarily would mean monetary unification, as well. If the two countries were respectively on the gold standard, the unification would be relatively simple; but the dilemma, Mises pointed out, was that both countries were on paper currencies. No successful unification would be possible until Austria and Germany had abandoned inflationary methods of financing their government expenditures. But this, in turn, would require a coordination of fiscal policies, and in Mises' view this meant a subordination of Austrian financial policy to that of Germany's. "This agreement can hardly be conceived as determining anything but a settlement under which Germany assumes over German-Austria all those powers of expenditure and revenue that she has in the other federal [German] states," including the conversion of Austrian debt into the national debt of Germany.[64] Independent budgetary policies, including deficit spending during the period leading up to conversion of the currencies, could only create pressures for inflationary policies or continuing accumulations of debt that would only forestall the unification process.

Another central reason for the ending of inflationary policies in both countries leading up to unification, Mises argued, was that monetary expansions were non-neutral and took time to work their full effect through the structure of prices.[65] For the market to settle upon a rate of exchange for purposes of the currency conversion between the Austrian crown and the German mark, which would more or less reflect their equilibrium purchasing power parities, there needed to be a period during which the inflationary influences would have worked their final effects on the respective price systems in Austria and Germany.

For the transition to a common currency, Mises suggested the German mark could first be introduced as a "core" or reserve currency in Austria, with a specified ratio of exchange at which the Austrian bank would be obliged to redeem Austrian notes for German marks, and vice versa.[66] Increases and decreases in the number of units of Austrian currency in circulation would be dependent upon deposits or withdrawals of marks from the Austrian banking system. The Austrian National Bank would no longer be an independent authority that determined the quantity of money in the country (similar to the idea behind a currency board). Final unification would then come through the German central bank redeeming all Austrian bank notes for marks at a specified ratio of conversion, after which there would be only one monetary system and one currency in use in both countries.

But no great advantage would accrue from monetary unification for either Austria or Germany unless it was permanently joined by a renunciation of inflationary monetary policies. "The positive effects of having overcome the pernicious effects of monetary 'particularism,'" Mises concluded, "will not be enjoyed by the entire German people unless in matters of currency policy they will have taken a stance in favor of renouncing any inflationary measures."[67]

But a far more immediate problem in 1919 was the disintegration of trade and commerce between the provinces and regions making up the new Austria, a disintegration that threatened the very existence of the country as a political entity. Mises offered his analysis and solutions for Austria's economic future in his paper titled "Vienna's Political Relationship with the Provinces in the Light of Economics," delivered as a lecture at the Association of Austrian Economists in December 1919.[68] The causes behind the problem, he argued, were preferential abuse of the fiscal structure through the system of differential tax incidence borne by the rural areas in comparison to the urban population, and Vienna in particular. The price controls on food supplies and the government's subsidies for Vienna's residents at the financial expense of the farmers reinforced the tension.

Throughout the war, rural property owners had borne a differentially smaller fraction of the costs of the war. While the prices of agricultural goods rose from forty to a hundred times what they had been before the war, the tax on land had not even doubled. Even the income taxes paid by landowners did not keep up with the rental price on land. The agrarian sector in general had been left financially no worse off than they had been before the war.

The tax burden for the war had fallen predominantly on the shoulders of commercial and industrial sectors situated in the cities, especially in Vienna. Not only did taxes go up dramatically, but the government took no account of the effects of inflation on the real cost of assets and their maintenance. They taxed away as "war profits" the greater nominal sums that the entrepreneurs and businessmen needed merely to maintain their capital intact, given the higher crown expense of replacement and repair, and replenishment of inventory and stock. Capital, in other words, was consumed.[69] "Thus, the result from this fiscal policy followed during the war," Mises said, "is that primarily the agrarian provinces received tax relief, while on the other hand the greater part of all liquid capital was seized by the state, transformed into consumer goods, and used for non-productive purposes during the war."[70]

What the farmers objected to and revolted against was the requisitioning policy introduced during the war, under which, rather than pay higher taxes from the sale of their agricultural goods, the government demanded in-kind payments at implicitly far-below market prices calculated on the basis of gross revenues earned from the land. "The farmers of the Alpine provinces sent their sons willingly into the hopeless war from which many were never to return," Mises explained.

> But their loyalty to the Emperor quickly made an about-face the moment the military commercial inspectors for the district began the forced collection of the imposed quota. In the struggle between the brute force of the military and the cunning of the peasantry, the latter won. The collection results worsened from day to day.[71]

From the perspective of the landowners and the peasants, they were being made to sacrifice the means of their livelihood at the point of a gun or a bayonet to feed the middle class and the well-off workers of the factories in the cities – especially Vienna – about whom they had always been suspicious.

On the other hand, in the cities – and especially in Vienna – both the working and middle classes were so captured by the myth of class conflict and the supposed exploiting aspect to wartime profits and speculation that they supported the far-below-market imposed maximum prices that both reduced the supplies of food coming into the city and only enflamed the anger and resentment of the farmers in the rural provinces from whence the city's food needed to come. These same segments of the urban population, enthusiastically supporting the taxing of wartime and inflationary profits, did not realize that,

> In light of the depreciation of our national currency, taxing away war profits signifies that owners of liquid capital, i.e., capital that is recorded in the books of businesses or represented in the form of securities, will be divested through taxation of their financial means for investment ... The city's working population is so much under the spell of the ideas of class struggle and irreconcilable differences of interest between the entrepreneur and the worker, that they do not realize that due to this fiscal policy the basis of their very existence is being reduced through the erosion of liquid capital. The difficulties with which our industry has to struggle nowadays are primarily due to the fact that because of the lack of liquid capital they cannot successfully compete against foreign industry. The level of real wages in our country will have to be kept below that of the foreign worker until, as the result of many years of hard work and economizing, we will again be financially sound and, thus, more competitive.[72]

The central government was reduced to either attempting to use force to requisition food supplies from the outlying provinces, which only served to drive the provincial governments further away from wanting to be politically a part of the new Austria, or go begging for rations of food from the countryside. Either method was a path to political disintegration and economic destruction.

Matching this, considering that Vienna was on the verge of mass starvation, was the loss of the bourgeois spirit of enterprise and work that is both the hallmark and the necessity of city life:

> City residents have to live on what they make through commerce and trade. This is already reflected in the very concept and nature of the city … If we, the Viennese, want to eat, then we must do business and produce and sell commercial products, so that we can use the profits to procure what we are not able to produce ourselves, namely raw materials and foodstuffs … Our public's opinion and our ideas about economic policy regarding raw material supplies are completely untenable. We demand from our farmer that he supply us with foodstuffs at a price that is below the price quoted on the world market, and we demand from foreign countries that they make us a present of their foodstuffs and raw materials … Our ideas about supplying our cities do not correspond to the reality of a city whose working population is made up of entrepreneurs and workers, but reflects the notion of an idle city proletariat that wants to live off the fruits of the farmer's diligence.[73]

A city must be open to commerce and trade. Because the Austrian provinces attempted to economically lock themselves away through provincial trade restrictions and passport controls did not mean that it was in the interest of Vienna to do so in retaliation. "But it is definitely a mistake when the city of Vienna retaliates by restricting entry into Vienna," Mises insisted.

> A city whose livelihood depends on commerce and selling industrial products has to rely on visits by people from elsewhere; it must desire and foster such visits and not restrict it under any circumstances … It is village politics of the worst kind that we are pursuing and not by any means the policy of a great city.[74]

All of Vienna's and Austria's economic difficulties would be gone with a return to a free market. "All these conflicts of interest that exist today between Vienna and the provinces would disappear under free trade," Mises explained.

> There would be no conflict over the seizure of grain, the supply of foodstuffs, entry visas, nationalization questions, compensations, and similar matters. As soon as we get rid of the idea that a city can obtain its foodstuffs by means other than commerce and industry, as soon as we understand once again that we have to produce and sell, then foreign countries will perceive us in a completely different light.[75]

Vienna had been reduced to this state of affairs, Mises argued, due to the loss of the spirit of enterprise.

> What we lack are not foodstuffs and raw materials, but the spirit that has to pervade a non-agrarian population if it wants to survive, and that is the modern, capitalist spirit of profit-making commerce ... An industrial state can survive without coal, but not without the spirit of a modern economy.

The Viennese were living by selling the accumulated wealth of the past. And if their civilization collapsed, Mises concluded, "we will not have perished due to a lack of coal and food, but because we lacked the spirit that builds cities and makes them flourish: the bourgeois spirit."[76] Free trade and division of labor on the basis of market prices was the only path to salvation if the new Austria was to survive.

In February 1921, an Austrian politician asked Mises to present an outline of a reform program that could save the country from economic disaster. The objective conditions for Austria's postwar revival were not the problem, in Mises' view. In principle Austria had the ability to earn the export revenues to pay for raw material and consumer goods imports upon which the country's economic prosperity would be based.

What was hampering recovery and revival were the "subjective" factors – people's attitudes and ideological beliefs that failed to see that prosperity could only come through private enterprise and free competition, not through national-ized industries and government food subsidies. Mises then presented the follow-ing reform proposal:

1 The progressive devaluation of the crown, which manifests itself in a rise in both the foreign exchange rate and in prices and wages, is a consequence of bank note inflation. *It can only be brought to a standstill if we succeed in eliminating the government's budget deficit.*

2 The federal, provincial and municipality budget deficits principally all spring from the same two sources: The inefficient management of public enterprises and the food subsidy scheme. At the present time the number of public enterprises is growing through nationalization; and the food subsidy scheme is being expanding.

3 If things continue to be managed in this way, *then inevitably the time will come when the currency will collapse,* i.e., the crown will become com-pletely worthless. Then there will be a frightful catastrophe. Suddenly the country will no longer be in a position to maintain these public enterprises or to sustain the food subsidies. If dismantling both of these occurs in time, then it will be possible to avoid such a collapse and it will be possible to reduce the difficulties in making the transition to a normal economy.

4 The goal should be to transfer the public enterprises into the hands of private businessmen and to dismantle the food subsidies. *The government manage-ment of food supplies is to be abolished.* For the indigent who are incapable

of working government financial support is to be introduced. This would be incomparably less costly.

5 The attempt must be made to stabilize the value of the currency, with the establishment of a fixed rate of exchange between the crown and either gold or the dollar. The new parity should be set at a level that corresponds to the domestic purchasing power of the crown. To go beyond this parity would be injurious to the economy; any further rise in the foreign exchange value of the currency beyond this point would only hamper exports and stimulate imports, with severely harmful consequences, i.e., unemployment. The catchphrase of a fall in prices is absurd. Those who are today most loudly demanding a reduction in prices would be hardest hit by such a fall in prices. We do not need decreasing prices, but incomes that are increasing. That, however, can only be achieved by a rise in industrial and business activity.

6 *Currency trading is to be decontrolled.* Foreign trade has an incomparably greater importance for a small country [like Austria] than for a large one. Businesses should have the chance to free themselves from some of the speculative risks that are connected with foreign trade when there are large fluctuations in the values of currencies. *The prohibition against the importing and exporting of crowns from the country should be ended.* It is only an illusion that such prohibitions succeed in raising the foreign exchange value of the crown. In reality it has depressed the crown's exchange rate since *foreign speculators no longer want to have anything to do with the crown.*

7 *All import prohibitions are to be lifted.* Such prohibitions are worthless for purposes of monetary policy. Moreover, they stimulate retaliatory measures by foreign countries, which only succeed in seriously hampering our exports, and as a consequence paralyze our industry. Austria can cover its need for raw materials and foodstuffs only by importing them. In order to pay for imports it must export finished products, on the basis of which businesses may earn profits. *Austria needs free trade.*

8 *The Central Foreign Exchange Office,* the Central Office for Import, Export and Transfers, and all offices that do not appear necessary for the carrying out of the above principles *are to be abolished.* The officials who are relieved of their duties are to be put on leave and, within a foreseeable time, dismissed. They will easily find jobs in a thriving market.

9 *All obstacles to traffic within the Austrian federation are to be removed.* If the provinces should resist, then nothing stands in the way of Vienna going first with lifting all entry and residency restrictions for citizens and foreigners. A city based on commerce and trade should not impede entry and the sojourning of visitors in any way.

10 Government oversight of industrial production of manufactured goods and the use of raw materials is to be *ended.* It is impossible to attract foreign capital into the country as long as the illusionary profits arising from devaluation of the currency are subject to taxation. Stabilizing the value of the currency will provide the necessary remedy. In order not to waste time, tax breaks should be granted for new industrial plants.

Mises admitted that, "I scarcely believe that there is a party in the country today that would be inclined to carry out this program. Nevertheless, I hope that that which is sensible and necessary will prevail."[77]

What brought Austria back from the precipice was the appointment of Monsignor Ignaz Seipel as Chancellor of Austria in May 1922. In *Notes and Recollections,* Mises describes his interactions with "this noble priest whose world view and conception of life remained alien to me," but whom Mises considered "a great personality." Seipel's "ignorance in economic affairs was that which only a cleric could have," Mises said. "He saw inflation as an evil, but otherwise was rather unacquainted with financial policy." Mises explained to the Monsignor that following the end of the inflation there would come an unavoidable "stabilization crisis" that no doubt would be blamed on Seipel's Christian Socials, with the inevitable short-run negative effects for his party. The Chancellor replied that a policy that was necessary had to be undertaken even if it injured his party's standing. "There were not many politicians in Austria who thought that way," Mises declared.[78]

Seipel did bear severe criticism, both from outside and inside his party, for following this economic policy. The Social Democrats ridiculed his "conversion" to "Manchester liberalism," with an underlying anti-Semitic tone by suggesting a Jewish element at work behind him. His own Christian Socials accused him of moving from a socialist course to "a consciously and deliberately capitalistic" one. In reply, Seipel said, "A people does not just perish, however, desperate its economic situation." "Spend less and save more" was the remedy for Austria's economic ills.[79]

As we explained earlier, through the assistance of the League of Nations in 1922 to 1923, the Austrian inflation was stopped before a total collapse (as did happen in Germany during this time).[80] The Austrian federal budget was balanced ahead of schedule (in fact, in 1924 and 1925 the budget went into a modest surplus), and a new Austrian central bank was instituted on a gold basis with redeemability. Over 85,000 government jobs were eliminated by 1925, and modest progress was made in revising the tax schedules.[81]

Monetary policy, interventionism, and fiscal policy, 1924–1930

But Mises' fight against interventionism, socialism, and fiscal mismanagement did not end, especially after the League's supervision of Austrian finances under the terms of the loan agreement expired in 1926. In this period of the mid- to late 1920s, he recalled that his work at the Chamber "was even more routine than during the earlier periods. It was a daily fight against ignorance, inability, indolence, malice, and corruption."[82]

In the area of monetary policy Mises was heartened by "The Return to Gold," following the catastrophic inflations in Austria, Germany, and a number of other countries.[83] The move back to gold had been to a gold-exchange standard, under which the primary reserves of most European nations had become the redeemable hard currencies of a small number of nations – of which the United States was the leading one. Austria was one of those countries that had added nothing to its gold reserves, only adding to its supply of hard currencies as a backing for increases in the issue of schilling notes.[84] But Mises still considered this as "the first step on the way to rehabilitating the ruined monetary situation."[85]

But what he did feel called upon to critically evaluate were the proposals being made by John Maynard Keynes in Great Britain and Irving Fisher in the United States for replacing the traditional gold standard with "managed currencies." The battle to end inflation, he argued, now was replaced with a debate over the most appropriate monetary system. Mises argued the merits of a gold standard, most especially the fact that a gold-based currency removed direct control of the printing press from the grasping hand of government. He also critically evaluated the counterproposals of Irving Fisher and John Maynard Keynes for government-managed currencies, the value of which would be the ability to manipulate them to stabilize the price level or assure a desired level of employment and output.[86]

Mises reasoned out the limits and shortcomings in all index number methods that make it near impossible to construct a measure of the purchasing power of money that is not open to disagreement about the goods to be included, the weights to be assigned to the items in the selected basket; in addition, there was the difficulty of estimating changes in the qualities of the goods whose prices are tracked through time, and the fact that new goods are constantly entering the market as old goods are being eliminated. In Mises' estimation, this meant that any monetary policy geared toward changes in "the price level" as calculated on the basis of index numbers would always be open to political manipulation on behalf of various interest groups that would benefit if the index was constructed and weighted one way rather than another.

How, then, could the world move back to actual gold-backed currencies, instead of either managed paper currencies or a gold-exchange standard? The League of Nations should be employed to use political pressure:

> Of course, in this sphere, as well as in others, it is no longer acceptable that each individual country carries on its own economic policy without any consideration for neighboring countries. In the realm of monetary systems it will be necessary to make international agreements. The goal of these international agreements must be to reintroduce the gold standard in every single country of the world, which can be achieved without difficulty if the League of Nations imposes a punitive duty on the exports of those countries that refuse to stabilize their monetary system. If the nations of the world once again agree to accept the gold standard we will once more have a monetary system that is not dependent on the influence of one or several individual governments. This monetary system would also guarantee the stability of foreign exchange rates and thereby the stability of international capital and bank transactions.[87]

It was equally in the realm of fiscal policy that Mises believed that both Austria and most other European countries desperately needed to introduce reform and retrenchment in their spending, and to narrow the arena of government activities. Once there was a time, Mises explained in a lecture delivered in Hungary on "Restoring Europe's State Finances," that conventional wisdom assumed that taxes were an evil and were to be minimized.[88] Low, indirect taxes on various items of consumption did not have to impose an egregious burden on the citizenry. "In the eyes of the older liberals, taxation of income and the interest on capital had the negative effect of slowing down the process of capital formation and hence retarded economic progress."[89]

But now the presumption was that no government spending, no matter for what or how extravagant, had a limit on it. Particularly pernicious in Mises' view was the shift from indirect to direct taxes. Under the assumption that direct taxes could be used to impose a burden only on the wealthy and the owners of property, the tax structure was shifted to weigh more heavily against those presumed to be the rich. "Feelings of envy such as this generated the belief that the impoverishment of entrepreneurs and the owners of capital was beneficial to the economy," he said. "The fact that the economy as a whole, not just the owners of capital, became poorer was completely disregarded."[90]

Equally as detrimental was the growth in government borrowing to cover the expenses and deficits of nationalized industries and municipal services. Most had been financial disasters. "The old fable about Midas has been turned on its head: whatever gold governments touch turns to dust," Mises quipped. In his view there was only one answer. "There is only one remedy for this problem. Governments and local agencies must sell off all these enterprises and turn them over to private entrepreneurs who will know how to run them at a profit." Unfortunately, Mises admitted, such a proposal ran against the entire tide of public opinion. What was needed were understanding and the will to do what was necessary. "What is needed is frugality" in government spending, he concluded. "The ability to economize, not the invention of new taxes, is the hallmark of a good finance minister."[91]

But nowhere was there a greater lack of such finance ministers and political figures than in his native Austria. In looking at "The Balance Sheet of Economic Policies Hostile to Property" in 1927, Mises stated that the deficit in the Austrian government's budget was almost totally attributable to the large losses in the state-run enterprises and the national railway system.[92] Indeed, the deficit from these two sectors of the economy was greater than the expenditures in the Austrian defense budget. Even the national forestry administration had a deficit, in spite of the profitability of timber sales and exports.

Taxes and government expenditures had to be cut back to restore balance and profitability to the Austrian economy, especially since Austria was a small country heavily dependent upon maintaining its competitiveness in a global market to which it had to adjust and conform. "Reductions in the costs of production only can be affected through a lowering of domestic wages or taxes," Mises said.

> If we cannot succeed in reducing taxes and the social burdens that the private producer has to bear, then wages will inevitably have to go down or

unemployment will have to go up. The reduction of the tax burden on our enterprises is therefore in the interest of all sectors of the population, not only in the interest of businessmen but also and especially in the interest of the labor force.

High taxes and government spending "undermines the necessary conditions for the nation's economic productivity, it is a policy of decline and destruction that must be opposed with all possible strength."[93]

But the heart of the fiscal problem was the philosophy of spending and taxing that was behind the Austrian government's budget. In an address before the Vienna Industrial Club in 1930,[94] Mises pointed out that between 1925 and 1929 spending at all levels of government in Austria had increased 31.4 percent, or almost 8 percent a year. Direct federal taxes alone had increased by 35 percent during this period. Both the Austrian federal government and the city of Vienna were budgeting for even larger increases in the years to come.

The premise behind this growth in government expenditure, Mises said, was the idea that the constraints on private individual and enterprise spending did not apply to government. Whereas in the private sector the financial means available limited the expenditures that could be undertaken, in the public sector it was presumed that taxes were to be increased to cover any desired level of expenditure with little or no thought to the opportunities foregone as a result.

> The worst of these misconceptions is the ... idea that the main difference between the state's and the private sector's budget is that *in the private sector's budget expenditures have to be based on revenues, while in the public sector's budget it is the reverse, i.e., the revenue raised must be based on the level of expenditures desired.* The illogic of this sentence is evident as soon as it is thought through. There is always a rigid limit for expenditures, namely the scarcity of means. If the means were unlimited, then it would be difficult to understand why expenses should ever have to be curbed. If in the case of the public budget it is assumed that its revenues are based on its expenditures and not the other way around, i.e., that its expenses have to be based on its revenues, the result is the tremendous squandering that characterizes our fiscal policy. The supporters of this principle are so shortsighted that they do not see that it is necessary, when comparing the level of public expenditures with the budgetary expenditures of the private sector, to not ignore the fact that enterprises cannot undertake investments when the required funds are used up instead for public purposes. They only see the benefits resulting from the public expenditures and not the harm the taxing inflicts on the other parts of the national economy.[95]

The second dangerous premise that guided Austrian fiscal policy was that direct taxation on property was always preferred to indirect taxes on consumption. The effect from following this fiscal course in Austria had been extremely damaging, Mises insisted:

Property taxes impede the creation of capital. And when the taxation of enterprises goes too far, it results in the consumption of capital. To a large extent, this has been the case here in Austria for the last 18 years. Capital consumption is detrimental not only for the owners of property but for the workers as well. The more unfavorable becomes the quantitative ratio of capital to labor, the lower is the marginal productivity of the work force and, consequently, the lower are the wages that can be paid. That the Austrian economy is only able to compete and survive on the basis of the relatively low wages that are paid today is primarily due to the fact that very significant amounts of the capital belonging to Austrian entrepreneurs have been eaten up during the past 18 years.[96]

These two premises had led to seemingly "unlimited demands … by all and sundry for access to public monies." But when the case to rein in government spending was made, Mises pointed out, the response was to say that many of these expenditures are "inevitable," since they are built into various legislative acts and entitlements. But Mises replied:

What exactly does "inevitable" mean in this context? That the expenditures are based on various laws that have been passed in the past is not an objection if the argument for eliminating these laws is based on their damaging effects on the economy. The metaphorical use of the term "inevitable" is nothing but a haven in which to hide in the face of the inability to comprehend the seriousness of our situation. People do not want to accept the fact that the public budget has to be radically reduced.[97]

The bull had to be taken by the horns. Merely dismissing public employees – as had been done under the terms of the loan agreement with the League of Nations in 1922 – did not eliminate the core of the problem. Only a reduction in government responsibilities and institutional reform could solve the problem in the long run. Mises detailed various Austrian government agencies that either were unnecessary or duplicative in their activities in the Austrian bureaucracy at the local, provincial, and federal levels that could be eliminated or streamlined to reduce taxing and regulatory burdens on business and the taxpayer. He proposed that they first be introduced in the smaller, rural Austrian provinces to see how effective they were, and when they had demonstrated their effectiveness they could then be extended to the rest of the country.

At the same time, subsidies to state enterprises and to various private sectors, such as in agriculture, had to be abolished. If the criterion of "economic hardship" continued to be the rationale for government subsidies "then probably most of the branches of production will be able to request such entitlements." The threat and existence of capital consumption due to taxes to pay for these and other expenditures were already a problem. Mises concluded that,

Corporate taxes, as well as the income tax, have to be cut, because if they are kept at their present high level, they impede industrial production and allow unemployment to grow at the speed of an avalanche. In whatever way the political situation may develop, fiscal policy in coming years,

he insisted,

> must be directed at cutting taxes on property and shifting the state's budgetary source to taxation of the general public ... In the coming years, the Public Budget Administration will have a far more difficult task. Namely to get along on less in order to adjust public expenditure to the financial capacity of an impoverished economy.[98]

The Great Depression and Austrian economic policy, 1931–1936

But living beyond its means is exactly what the Austrian government continued to do with the onslaught of the Great Depression. In 1929, the Austrian federal budget had a small surplus that was almost equal to 10 percent of tax revenues. But from 1930 on, the Austrian government's budget was in the red, with expenditures exceeding tax revenues between 1930 and 1934 in the range of 13 to 16 percent for all but one year. During this time, the deficit for all but one year was between 11.5 and 14 percent of total federal expenditures.[99]

To try to stem the tide toward greater intervention, government spending, and economic planning, Mises, along with a group of like-minded economists in Vienna attempted to influence public opinion. In the early 1930s, Mises regularly met with Gottfried Haberler, Oskar Morgenstern, and Fritz Machlup in the home of Julius Meinl, an importer of coffee and various foodstuffs, to plan out what themes were most important for them to focus on in the articles they would submit to the daily Vienna newspapers. Between September 1931 and May 1934, Machlup alone published 148 articles in the Austrian newspapers, many in a regular column he titled "Two Minute Economics."[100]

Mises applied himself in this direction as well, though to a far more limited extent, in articles and lectures. In February 1931, he delivered an address to a group of German industrialists, "The Causes of the Economic Crisis," which shortly thereafter was published as a monograph.[101] He wrote a variety of newspaper articles: "The Economic Crisis and Capitalism," "The Gold Standard and Its Opponents," and "Planned Economy and Socialism." He contributed to collections of essays in which he wrote on the themes of "The Myth of the Failure of Capitalism," "The Current Status of Business Cycle Research,"[102] and "Problems of Monetary Stabilization and Foreign Exchange Rates." And he contributed to journals such articles as "Interventionism as the Cause of the Economic Crisis" and "The Return to Freedom of Exchange."[103]

Central to Mises' argument in all of these articles was to refute the charge that the Great Depression was caused by capitalism and that more interventionism or even socialist planning was now needed to replace the market economy. The depression, Mises explained over and over again, had been caused by the monetary mismanagement of governments in the years leading up to 1929.

Interest rates had been artificially pushed below the market rate at which savings and investment would have tended toward equality. Instead, credit expansion had fed misdirections of resources and capital malinvestments that set the stage for an inevitable correction and readjustment of the economy once the money and credit expansion had slowed down or come to an end.

The duration and depth of the depression was not due to any inherent defects in the market economy. No, the severity of the depression was also the product of government interventionism that supported trade unions that resisted money wage cuts in the face of a decreasing demand for labor in the misdirected sectors of the economy; that supplied support for union resistance to wage adjustment through the "dole" that subsidized those who had priced themselves out of the labor market; and that provided subsidies and protection for industries and enterprises that used political pressure to secure their market situation from competition, capital write-offs, and lower prices that would make clear their loss-making or even bankrupt status.

The "Interventionist State" had bred corruption, "pull," and anti-market conduct throughout the economy. It had created a generation of political rather than market entrepreneurs who knew how to use the corridors of politics more than the avenues of consumer-oriented commerce. Mises explained this process concisely:

> In the Interventionist State it is no longer of crucial importance for the success of an enterprise that the business should be managed in a way that it satisfies the demands of consumers in the best and least costly manner. It is far more important that one has "good relationships" with the political authorities so that the interventions work to the advantage and not the disadvantage of the enterprise. A few marks more tariff protection for the products of the enterprise and a few marks less tariff for the raw materials used in the manufacturing process can be of far more benefit to the enterprise than the greatest care in managing the business. No matter how well an enterprise may be managed, it will fail if it does not know how to protect its interests in the drawing up of the customs rates, in the negotiations before the arbitration boards, and with the cartel authorities. To have "connections" becomes more important than to produce well and cheaply.
>
> So the leadership positions within enterprises are no longer achieved by men who understand how to organize companies and to direct production in the way the market situation demands, but by men who are well thought of "above" and "below," men who understand how to get along well with the press and all the political parties, especially with the radicals, so that they and their company give no offense. It is that class of general directors that negotiate far more often with state functionaries and party leaders than with those from whom they buy or to whom they sell.
>
> Since it is a question of obtaining political favors for these enterprises, their directors must repay the politicians with favors. In recent years, there have been relatively few large enterprises that have not had to spend very considerable sums for various undertakings in spite of it being clear from

the start that they would yield no profit. But in spite of the expected loss it had to be done for political reasons. Let us not even mention contributions for purposes unrelated to business – for campaign funds, public welfare organizations, and the like.[104]

To overcome the problem of unemployment, governments searched for indirect methods that would permit them to avoid having to confront trade union power directly. Instead, they used currency devaluation and monetary depreciation as ways to decrease the high cost of labor by raising prices through inflation in the hope that unions would accept cuts in their members' real wages by not insisting (at least not immediately) on higher money wages in the face of lost purchasing power:

> First of all, there is the problem of wages and unemployment. In many countries wages did not fall as low as the depressed state of trade required. The salaries and wages of public servants in some countries are too high relative to public revenue. It seems impossible to restore budgetary equilibrium except by a reduction of the pay roll. In trade and industry, wages in some countries are too high in comparison with the prices at which the products can be sold. The rigidity of wages has so far been successful, as real wages did not fall in the years of the slump. But on the other hand, with falling prices and unchanged nominal wages, the volume of unemployment increased as entrepreneurs were unable to employ the same number of hands as before.
>
> It is obvious that the proposals to do away with the rigidity of wages are very unpopular. But it is not fair to charge those who see no other means of escape with the accusation of hardheartedness. Those who prefer devaluation of the currency also aim, ultimately, at a reduction in real wages. All the proposals in favor of devaluation are based upon the tacit assumption that nominal wages will remain unchanged, and that with rising prices for commodities real wages will drop. Of course, they do not expressly mention this point. But when speaking of reductions in costs they mean nothing other than a reduction both in gold wages and in commodity wages while nominal wages remain unchanged at least for some time following the devaluation of the currency. The reduction in the costs of production that is meant to stimulate exports is to a large extent a reduction in the cost of labor.[105]

This policy offered no long-run solution to the problem of unemployment. First, there was no certainty that trade unions would allow the real wages of their members to decline due to inflation over time. Second, inflationary policies to reemploy a part of the work force was setting the stage for another downturn and period of necessary correction after another wave of malinvestments and misdirections of resources had been generated. Furthermore, this spelled even lower real wages for workers in the future. By taxing away capital to support the unemployed and wasting scarce capital by misdirecting it through credit expansion, real wages would be pushed down as a result of the marginal product of labor being reduced because of this consumption and squandering of capital.

Finally, Mises once again defended the gold standard and the long-run benefits from stable and certain foreign exchange rates. The gold standard was being
opposed and overthrown precisely because it stood in the way of government
manipulation of money, credit, and the purchasing power of the monetary unit.
He responded to those who warned of "imbalances" in trade, or a "scarcity" of
gold, or who wanted to give government the ability to arbitrarily manipulate
interest rates and the value of money. "Good banking policy makes well-ordered
currency relationships possible," Mises said.

> Bad banking policy jeopardizes the currency. That interest rates in Central
> Europe are extraordinarily high is the long-term consequence of the capital-
> consuming policies that have been pursued with veritable fanaticism for two
> decades. This evil cannot, however, be remedied by banking policy trickery.
> All that the policy of artificially lowering the rate of interest can achieve is
> destruction of the currency.[106]

But besides his writings to inform and influence public opinion in Austria
during the early 1930s, Mises was also working to influence economic policy
through his work at the Vienna Chamber of Commerce. As we saw earlier, the
Great Depression began to have its full impact in Austria when one of Central
Europe's most important banks, *CreditAnstalt,* was threatened with collapse due
to huge financial losses.[107]

In a series of addresses before meetings of the members of the Vienna
Chamber of Commerce in 1932, Mises persuaded them to take certain public
policy stances on a number of crucial issues, including the government system
of foreign exchange control, the gold parity, the need to rein in government
spending and taxation, and on the international loan to assist Austria in reestablishing its domestic and international finances.[108]

In a letter written to F.A. Hayek (who at this time had moved to England and
taken up a position as a professor at the London School of Economics) on
December 7, 1931, Mises reported how when he got back from a trip the previous the month,

> I was greeted on all sides upon my return to Vienna with the universal
> outcry: "We most urgently need a central authority for exchange control."
> Even today everybody is blaming the whole trouble on the delay in creating
> the central authority, it should already have been established in May, they
> say. You can see that I keep harping on this matter. I fret about it day and
> night and have to deal with it a lot in the Chamber. Unfortunately, I am also
> a member of the advisory board for foreign exchange, a totally powerless,
> hence superfluous institution.[109]

The Chamber first formally dealt with the problem of foreign exchange
control in February 1932 in a session at which Mises explained the reasons for
its imposition and the harmful, contrary-to-purpose results that already were
emerging. The decision of the Austrian National Bank to cover the losses being

suffered by *CreditAnstalt* through credit expansion required the Bank to stop redeeming schillings for foreign currencies on demand. Fearful that the schilling's value on the foreign exchanges would fall, the Bank imposed exchange control at the legally prescribed rate of exchange that had been established in 1923 at a ratio of 0.21172086 grams of gold per schilling.

What this did immediately, considering that on the foreign exchange markets in other countries the value of the schilling declined by about 20 percent, was to create an artificial stimulus for imports and an artificial barrier to exports. At the controlled rate of exchange, Austrian importers received more units of foreign money per schilling exchanged than they would at the free market rate. At the same time, since exporters had to trade in their foreign exchange earnings at an officially fixed rate they received fewer schillings for each unit of foreign exchange they traded in.

Furthermore, in an attempt to keep domestic prices from rising, the foreign exchange agency had rationed more of the foreign currencies in short supply to those importing consumer items, and less of the available foreign currencies to those needing to import raw materials and semi-finished goods for the Austrian manufacturing sectors. The latter policy undermined Austria's industrial production, weakened the country's exporting capability, and threatened increased unemployment in the manufacturing and exporting sectors of the economy. The only thing preventing an even worse deterioration in Austrian manufacturing and the exporting trade was the fact that "the system of foreign exchange control is riddled with loopholes." Indeed, Mises went as far to suggest that it was only the system of "private clearings" and "certificates" (which we explained earlier) that permitted Austria's export industry and a number of other sectors of the economy to survive at all.[110]

The Austrian National Bank, through the exchange control process, had attempted to prevent schillings held abroad from returning to Austria and adversely affect the domestic purchasing power of the monetary unit, as well as its foreign exchange value by more schillings being traded on the exchange markets in Vienna. But the latter effect had not been prevented by this policy. Schilling-denominated debt was merely transferred by consignment to be sold on foreign markets where its value was competitively determined, and at about a 20 percent discount from the officially mandated foreign exchange rate.

What then was to be done? Mises outlined "An Agenda for Alleviating the Economic Crisis" at a session of the Vienna Chamber of Commerce in March 1932. First, the official gold parity of the schilling had to be reestablished. There were too many Austrian enterprises – financial institutions, agricultural companies, and federal, state, and municipal governments – that owed debts in gold and foreign currency, and who would be shouldered with impossible costs if the schilling were to be devalued. It would also undermine international confidence in the Austrian economy, coming only a few years after the country's currency had once more been stabilized and legally placed on a fixed gold parity.

The Austrian National Bank would have to contract the supply of money and credit until the value of the schilling had been raised to a level that once more equaled the official gold parity. But this had to be done relatively quickly, Mises argued, before the domestic structure of prices had fully adjusted to the depreciated value of the schilling. Otherwise, the monetary deflation might impose too excessive a burden on the economy to bring the domestic level of prices back down. The non-neutral effects from a monetary deflation could be just as adverse as from a monetary inflation:

> The reestablishment of the legal gold parity must not be delayed until the time when the prices of all goods in general as expressed in schillings have risen into line with the decreased foreign valuation of the schilling. Otherwise the reestablishment of the gold parity would require a sharp reduction in prices, along with a period of severe adjustment.
>
> A reduction in the number of bank notes in circulation is essential for reestablishing the legal gold parity of the schilling. The note-issuing central bank must, therefore, follow a restrictive credit policy as an unavoidable necessity, even though it may create unfortunate difficulties for the economy and impose certain sacrifices on the society.[111]

The contrary policy of even greater money and credit expansion that some were calling for would only create more difficulties for the Austrian economy down the road, an economy already suffering from living beyond its means and capital consumption.

Mises then formulated the official Chamber of Commerce policy prescriptions that would enable Austria to overcome the economic crisis. Exchange controls were to be ended as soon as possible with the reestablishment of full freedom of trade. For the transition leading up to that, the Chamber advocated that all further coercive methods had to stop. All regulations that restricted foreigners from controlling and trading their schilling-denominated accounts in Vienna banks should be abolished. The prohibitions on the free exporting and importing of schilling notes should be lifted. And all existing institutions that facilitate export trade and importing of raw materials and semi-finished products used in Austrian manufacturing – the private clearings and the certificate system – should not be interfered with. "Every attempt at isolating the country from world commerce must have the most harmful effects," Mises concluded. "Things imposed on us from abroad, and which cannot be prevented through any policy of our own, must be tolerated as unavoidable. What we must not do is to promote our own isolation from the world market."[112]

Shortly after the Austrian government arranged for a new loan through the League of Nations in the middle of July 1932, the Vienna Chamber of Commerce again met in full session. Mises took the floor to discuss the case for accepting the loan. He pointed out to the Chamber representatives that most of the loan would be used to pay back the credits that had earlier been extended to the Austrian National Bank by the Bank of England and the Bank for International Settlements in Switzerland. At the most, this would leave 150 million schillings for domestic use to overcome budgetary problems. This was a relatively small amount, he said, when consideration was given to the fact that the

Federal Transportation Department had total current debts outstanding of 137 million schillings, and the overall federal deficit for the year was estimated to be 450 million schillings, with 72 million of this required to cover unemployment relief for the year. Thus, from the Treasury's perspective, the League's loan offered merely a momentary relief.

So how should the loan be viewed, then, in terms of domestic Austrian economic policy? It could serve one purpose and one purpose alone: "breathing room" for immediate implementation of long neglected but absolutely necessary domestic economic reforms.

> It is absolutely essential that all those measures of frugality that the economy has required for a long time – but which have always been delayed or sabotaged – be put into effect as quickly as possible. For this loan is nothing more than breathing room for the carrying out of those absolutely necessary reforms and retrenchments. Not for one moment should the government or the political parties assume that the loan should be looked upon as anything removing the necessity for these reforms. ...
>
> It must be stated that just as the loan has to be considered as only offering short-term breathing room for the government to introduce reforms and retrenchment measures, so too it must not be seen as a way to continue our trade, and social and budgetary policies of the past. Nor can it be assumed that the same monetary policy that has been followed for months can be continued because we have received the means to do so ...
>
> So if the National Bank were simply to continue the present system, Austrian trade would continue to contract, with all the same consequences for foreign exchange and monetary policy that have been seen in recent months. It would be a grave error to believe that the foreign exchange needed to obtain the raw materials, semi-finished products and foodstuffs that we import from abroad can simply be withdrawn from a fund that was once filled up by confiscatory measures and now is supposed to be replenished by the loan. The economy is an on-going institution, and it can only keep on receiving the needed foreign exchange by constantly replenishing the required funds through exports, foreign trade, business activity and the like. The idea that we have a certain given amount of capital upon which we can permanently operate would lead to a currency catastrophe.[113]

Failure to accept the loan and follow its stringent requirements for domestic reform and institutional change, Mises warned, would have serious international repercussions. It would undermine all confidence in the international market that Austria could again be a trustworthy trading and credit partner, with whom financial commitments could be undertaken. It was on this basis alone, Mises insisted, that the Austrian Chambers of Commerce endorsed the government's agreement to the terms of the loan. While the conditions of the loan were being imposed from abroad, the crucial reforms would "have to be carried out in Austria by Austria." Thus, the conditions specified by the League of Nations were to be supported, Mises argued, only because they would require the

Austrian government to institute the budgetary austerities that it apparently lacked the domestic will to implement without external pressure.

Near the end of 1932, at the general meeting of the Austrian Chambers of Commerce in October, Mises returned once more to the problems with the system of foreign exchange control in his remarks to the assembly. He stated that of all the damaging economic policies instituted by the Austrian government in the face of the economic crisis the most pernicious measure had been foreign exchange control. Mises again explained how the controls had artificially fostered imports and restricted exports, with an extremely negative effect on the manufacturing sectors of the economy. It served as a severely damaging "tax" on the importation of all those inputs upon which the export trade was totally dependent. "This burden is intolerable for Austrian exports and must be eliminated without delay," he insisted.[114]

What made the system especially harmful was the lack of expertise by those determining the rationing of foreign currency:

> The agents of the National Bank responsible for forming authoritative judgments about various trade policy problems appear to be totally incompetent, whether due to their educational background or their lack of prior experience. Yet these people, who most certainly cannot be considered qualified experts, have the discretionary power to finally decide whether particular export firms will be "favored" with permission to enter into a private clearing agreement or not. A refusal for this so-called "favoring" is the same thing as a prohibition on export businesses; therefore, in the final analysis, it means an increase in unemployment.[115]

The decision as to which types of transactions were permitted to be undertaken through the system of "private clearings" was completely arbitrary. Every month, for example, one million schillings were provided through the private clearings to pay the pensions of those Austrians living abroad. But payment of royalties from abroad for intellectual work by authors was excluded from the private clearings. There seemed to be no rhyme or reason to the logic of the decisions.

Furthermore, the rationing of foreign exchange served as another policy tool for economic privilege and favoritism. Foreign currency earned by an export industry had to be remitted to the foreign exchange control agency, which then allocated that foreign currency to the agricultural sector for the importing of fodder and fertilizer. "Foreign exchange control, therefore, also represents a link in the chain of economically unjustifiable privileges for agricultural producers," Mises said, "at the expense of all the other strata of the population."[116]

After critically evaluating a number of other policies connected with foreign exchange control, including the "clearing agreements" under which the Austrian government had entered into reciprocal barter trading arrangements with other countries at artificial rates of exchange that misallocated goods and resources, Mises presented the policy proposals of the Chamber of Commerce. First, no obstacles should be put in the way of the operation of the private clearings at the designated institutions. The Austrian National Bank should only prohibit trans-actions in the private clearings if it could be shown that such dealings were a cover for illegal activities. All currency transactions were to take place through the institutions assigned for private clearings, including all buying and selling of foreign exchange by the National Bank, with the latter transactions being made at the market prices established by the clearing process. And all barter "clearing agreements" entered into by the Austrian government with foreign governments should be terminated.

In additional concluding remarks Mises added that "only the shortest amount of time is suitable for the carrying out of appropriate measures. There is no reason to postpone them even for one day, measures like the ones that have been proposed." But he observed that,

> Unfortunately, when it is a question of introducing appropriate measures, the history of Austrian currency policy in recent years has provided new proof of the correctness of Grillparzer's characterization of Austrian pol-itics: "To strive halfheartedly half the way toward a half deed with half measures."[117] Only where something completely wrong is to be undertaken are we accustomed to seize it quickly and completely.[118]

The following year, Mises delivered an address on "The Return to Freedom of Exchange" at the Vienna Congress of the International Chamber of Com-merce meeting in May 1933, in which he once more explained the harmful effects of foreign exchange controls. But he also analyzed what were the precon-ditions for a permanent and successful elimination of the controls. The funda-mental problem in most countries that had introduced foreign exchange control, including Austria, was the structure of bank debt. Many banks had invested long term with short-term credits that had been extended to them by financial institu-tions abroad. Foreign exchange control gave these debtor banks an excuse to inform their foreign creditors that they could not pay because their government did not allot the funds for them to do so. But this stopgap policy device needed to be replaced with a long-term solution. This required structural changes in the debtor nations. And this could be most effectively done, Mises argued, through the participation and coordination of various international organizations:

> The restructuring of the insolvent banks must therefore precede the abolition of foreign exchange control. The banks whose balances are in severe deficit must be liquidated, and the losses that have occurred must be recognized as complete losses. It is useless to postpone the liquidation of these enterprises. The losses will only be greater by delaying a final settling of accounts. For-tunately, the balances of the majority of the banks in question are not bank-rupt but only insolvent. These banks would be in a sound condition if the maturity dates of their own debt obligations coincided with the dates when they received claims owed to them. It is necessary to make every effort to reach an arrangement through agreements between these banks and their foreign creditors, in collaboration with the governments of the various

countries involved as well as with international organizations (the League of Nations, the Bank of International Settlements, and the International Chamber of Commerce). This is all the more feasible considering that it is not in the interest of creditors that the banks in which they have placed their capital should fail and suffer further losses, only adding to the harm to themselves in the process. These arrangements should be initiated and carried out as soon as possible. Once they are, there will no longer be any obstacles, from this source, to delay the abolition of foreign exchange control.

It would be superfluous, in this regard, to provide special legislation requiring that banks maintain their own liquidity in the future. The banks will do this in their own interest, particularly if it is clear that any bank that poorly manages it own affairs can have no hope of being kept afloat by government intervention at the expense of the rest of society.[119]

In addition, Mises said, the problems of long-term debt obligations needed to be worked out as well, especially since many of these debts were owed by state and municipal governments that had sunk borrowed funds into various nationalized industries and municipal projects. These often had no long-term solution, given governments' inability to raise enough taxes to meet their obligations. Mises offered no concrete solution to this problem, other than the implicit suggestion that many of these debts would have to be completely written off. Mises concluded his remarks by emphasizing the essential importance of international trade for all nations, but especially for relatively poorer ones dependent upon foreign capital investment for their economic development, and that these benefits from international trade could never be fully taken advantage of as long as foreign exchange control stood in the way.

At the end of 1934, shortly after Mises had departed for Geneva to take up his teaching appointment at the Graduate Institute of Economic Studies, he wrote a short piece, "The Direction of Austrian Financial Policy: A Retrospective and Prospective View."[120] Democratic government had ended in Austria, a brief civil war had been fought, and the Social Democrats had been crushed. Now Mises hoped that a new calm in the country could serve as the backdrop for returning to the path of economic reform and recovery. He reviewed the course of Austrian economic policy during the preceding fifteen years since the end of the Great War. And he emphasized that what the country still needed was less government spending and taxing, more flexibility in the country's price and wage structure, a stable currency, and acceptance that as a small nation in a large global economy Austria had to adjust to the international conditions of supply and demand. Alas, in less than four years Austria's fate would be sealed for the duration of the next World War.

Conclusion: warning signs and guideposts for a future generation

From his new vantage point in Geneva at the Graduate Institute, Mises was freed from the everyday affairs of Austrian economic policy that had been the focus of his attention at the Vienna Chamber of Commerce. On March 10, 1934, William E. Rappard, the co-founder and director of the Graduate Institute, had written to Mises in Vienna offering the chair in International Economic Relations for the academic year 1934–1935.

Rappard explained to Mises that

> the professors of this Institute have only a very few formal university duties: one hour of seminar and two hours of lecture per week. We try to allow them the greatest leisure possible to continue their research work here. It is of course understood that in addition to these three hours of *ex cathedra* teaching, they will make themselves available to students who wish to consult them about their own work. If I take the liberty of asking you about the possibility of your accepting a chair here for a year, it is because we would be particularly happy to have the collaboration of one of the contemporary economists whose intellectual value we prize most highly and whose main professional interests fit best within the framework of this Institute.[121]

After an exchange of letters, Mises formally accepted on March 30, 1934, informing Rappard that he would teach his course in English, and allow the language used in the seminar (English or French) to be decided by the students. For his course, Mises chose the subject, "The International Aspects of Monetary Policy." And for his seminar, "International Finance," which he said was "sufficiently broad to allow me to treat in the seminar all problems relative to the present situation of the economic relationships among nations."[122]

In *Notes and Recollections,* Mises said,

> For me it was a liberation to be removed from the political tasks I could not have escaped in Vienna, and from the daily routine in the Chamber. Finally, I could devote myself completely and almost exclusively to scientific problems.[123]

As he said in the foreword to the first edition of *Human Action,* "In the serene atmosphere of this seat of learning … I set about executing an old plan of mine, to write a comprehensive treatise on economics."[124]

In Geneva he had no false hopes for the future of Austria. The Social Democrats had made the work of the Nazis that much easier, Mises said, because they – and especially Otto Bauer – had long made the unification of Austria and Germany one of their leading goals before their own destruction in the short-lived civil war in February 1934. If not for Mussolini's intervention during the brief Nazi coup attempt in July 1934, Austria might have been swallowed up by Germany right then. The politicians in charge of guiding Austria's foreign relations were not up to the task, Mises argued. The authoritarian government of Kurt von Schuschnigg was unable to ward off the increasing pressures from across the border in Nazi Germany that culminated in the *Anschluss* of March 1938.[125]

When Mises neared the end of his narrative in *Notes and Recollections,* he did so with romantic and heroic words: "Only one nation on the European continent attempted seriously to oppose Hitler, namely the Austrian nation."[126] However, the fact was that when Hitler arrived in Vienna, an ocean of jubilant Austrian faces filled the streets to see the man who had "liberated" them from their independence and had reunited them with the German *Volk.* At the Vienna Chamber of Commerce the employees went to work the day after Hitler had arrived and greeted each other with "Heil Hitler," with several turning out to be Nazis.[127]

Mises' despair (that we quoted at the beginning of this chapter) – that he had "set out to be a reformer, but only became the historian of decline" – is tragically understandable in the context of the course of Austrian events in the twenty years between the two world wars. But precisely because of this, his policy writings offer us a clearer understanding of why it was that in the countries of Europe between 1918 and 1938, inflation, interventionism, socialism, and economic nationalism lead to stagnation, social disruption, a Great Depression, and finally to a new world war.

In spite of his pessimism, Mises was not a fatalist. He said more than once in his writings that trends can change, that they had changed in the past, and could change again in the future.[128] With this in mind, after coming to the United States he devoted part of his time to working out the political and economic policies and reforms that could bring about a rebirth of freedom and prosperity in Europe after World War II.[129]

Likewise, from the perspective of these early years of the twenty-first century, Mises' writings from this period offer important instructions for the present and the future. Within his writings criticizing the direction of Austrian economic and social policy are also many ideas and prescriptions for free market-oriented alternatives in the areas of monetary and fiscal policy, government regulation and planning, and the social institutional order, which would move a society along the path that leads to freedom and prosperity. In fact, I would suggest that is precisely how Mises would want the modern reader to view his efforts and his writings in that period between the two world wars. He said this very clearly in the preface he prepared for the 1932 second edition of his treatise on *Socialism:*

> I know only too well how hopeless it seems to convince impassioned supporters of the Socialist Idea by logical demonstration that their views are preposterous and absurd. I know too well that they do not want to hear, to see, and above all to think, and they are open to no argument. But new generations grow up with clear eyes and open minds. And they will approach things from a disinterested, unprejudiced standpoint; they will weigh and examine, will think and act with forethought. It is for them that this book is written.[130]

His articles and essays, many of them originally penned more than seventy or eighty years ago, now, in the context of the economic and political policy controversies of those times, were, therefore, also written for us. They are warning signs and guideposts left behind by one of the greatest economists of the twentieth century to assist us in thinking about and designing better policies for our own times.

F.A. Hayek made the following remark when looking back at the events in Austria and Mises' place in them during the 1920s and 1930s: "That they had one of the great thinkers of our time in their midst, the Viennese have never understood."[131] Mises' body of writings – on theory and policy – from this period enables us to understand what they, to their great misfortune, did not.

Notes

1 Ludwig von Mises, *Notes and Recollections* [1940] (South Holland, IL: Libertarian Press, 1978), p. 115.
2 For an exposition of Mises' ideas on the theory of human action, the market economy, socialism, and intervention, see, Richard M. Ebeling, *Austrian Economics and the Political Economy of Freedom* (Northampton, MA: Edward Elgar, 2003), Ch. 3: "A Rational Economist in an Irrational Age: Ludwig von Mises," pp. 61–100.
3 Ludwig von Mises, *The Theory of Money and Credit* [1912; 1924; 1952] (Indianapolis, IN: Liberty Classics, 1981). For an exposition of the Austrian theory of money and the business cycle in the context of the Great Depression and in contrast to the Keynesian approach, see Ch. 7: "The Austrian Economists and the Keynesian Revolution: The Great Depression and the Economics of the Short Run," in the present volume; for a comparison of Mises' theory of money and the business cycle with that of the Swedish economists during this period, see Ch. 9: "Money, Economic Fluctuations, Expectations and Period Analysis: The Austrian and Swedish Economists in the Interwar Period," in the present volume.
4 Ludwig von Mises, *Nation, State and Economy: Contributions to the Politics and History of Our Time* [1919] (New York: New York University Press, 1983).
5 Ludwig von Mises, "Economic Calculation in the Socialist Commonwealth," [1920] in F.A. Hayek, ed., *Collectivist Economic Planning: Critical Studies in the Possibilities of Socialism* (London: George Routledge, 1935), pp. 87–130; reprinted in Israel M. Kirzner, ed., *Classics in Austrian Economics. A Sampling in the History of a Tradition,* Vol. 3: "The Age of Mises and Hayek" (London: William Pickering, 1994), pp. 3–30; and Mises, *Socialism: An Economic and Sociological Analysis* [1922; 1936; 1951] (Indianapolis, IN: Liberty Classics 1981). For an exposition of Mises' critique of socialist planning in the context of the critics of socialism who preceded him, see, Richard M. Ebeling, *Austrian Economics and the Political Economy of Freedom,* Ch. 4: "Economic Calculation Under Socialism: Ludwig von Mises and His Predecessors," pp. 101–135.
6 Ludwig von Mises, *Liberalism: The Classical Tradition* [1927] (Irvington-on-Hudson, NY: Foundation for Economic Education, 1996).
7 Ludwig von Mises, *Critique of Interventionism: Inquiries into the Economic Policy and the Economic Ideology of the Present* [1929] (Irvington-on-Hudson, NY: Foundation for Economic Education, 1996). For an exposition of some aspects of the Austrian ideas on interventionism, see, Richard M. Ebeling, *Austrian Economics and the Political Economy of Freedom,* Ch. 8: "The Free Market and the Interventionist State," pp. 203–230.
8 F. Kapeluch, "'Anti-Marxism': Professor Mises as a Theorist of Fascism," *Bolshevik,* No. 15 (August 15, 1925), pp. 82–87. This article has been translated from Russian and is included as an appendix to, Richard M. Ebeling, ed., *Selected Writings of Ludwig von Mises, Vol. 2: Between the Two World Wars: Monetary Disorder, Interventionism, Socialism and the Great Depression* (Indianapolis, IN: Liberty Fund, 2002), pp. 381–392.

9 Ludwig von Mises, "Anti Marxism" [1925] reprinted in *Critique of Interventionism*, pp. 71–95.

10 Ludwig von Mises, "Social Liberalism" [1926] reprinted in *Critique of Interventionism*, pp. 43–70; the quotation appears on p. 67.

11 See, Alexander Hortlehner, "Ludwig von Mises und die Österreichische Handelskammerorganisation" [Ludwig von Mises and the Austrian Chamber of Commerce] *Wirtschaftspolitische Blätter*, No. 4 (1981), pp. 141–142.

12 On the general working of the Austrian Section of the Reparations Commission, see, O. de. L., "The Reparations Commission in Austria," *Contemporary Review* (July 1921), pp. 45–50.

13 *Friedensrecht, Ein Nachrichtenblatt fiber die Durchführung des Friedenvertrages Enthaltend die Verlautbarungen des Osterreichischen Abrechnungsamtes* [The Laws for Peace, A Newsletter for the Execution of the Peace Treaty, Containing Announcements of the Austrian Office for the Settlement of Accounts] (February 1925), pp. 9–10.

14 Mises, *Notes and Recollections*, pp. 74–75.

15 Ibid.

16 See, Richard M. Ebeling, "William E. Rappard: An International Man in an Age of Nationalism," *Ideas on Liberty* (January 2000), pp. 33–41.

17 Mises, *Notes and Recollections*, pp. 76, 91.

18 Ibid., pp. 91–92.

19 Fritz Machlup in *Tribute to Mises, 1881–1973* (Chislehurst, England: Quadrangle, 1974), p. 12; from a paper delivered at The Mont Pelerin Society session at Brussels on September 13, 1974.

20 The following summary of the course of Austrian political and economic history between 1918 and 1938 is taken, mostly, from the following works: J. van Walre de Bordes, *The Austrian Crown: Its Depreciation and Stabilization* (London: P.S. King, 1924); Otto Bauer, *The Austria Revolution* [1925] (New York: Bert Franklin, 1970); W.T. Layton and Charles Rist, *The Economic Situation in Austria: Report Presented to the Council of the League of Nations* (Geneva: League of Nations, 1925); *The Financial Reconstruction of Austria: General Survey and Principal Documents* (Geneva: League of Nations, 1926); Carlile A. Macartney, *The Social Revolution in Austria* (Cambridge: Cambridge University Press, 1926); Leo Pasvolsky, *Economic Nationalism of the Danubian States* (New York: Macmillan, 1928); John V. Van Sickle, *Direction Taxation in Austria* (Cambridge: Harvard University Press, 1931); Malcolm Bullock, *Austria, 1918–1919: A Study in Failure* (London: Macmillan, 1939); David F. Strong, *Austria (October 1918-March 1919): Transition from Empire to Republic* [1939] (New York: Octagon Books, 1974); Antonin Basch, *The Danubian Basin and the German Economic Sphere* (New York: Columbia University Press, 1943); Mary MacDonald, *The Republic of Austria, 1918–1934: A Study in the Failure of Democratic Government* (Oxford: Oxford University Press, 1946); Frederick Hertz, *The Economic Problem of the Danubian States: A Study in Economic Nationalism* (London: Victor Gollancz, 1947); K.W. Rothschild, *Austria's Economic Development Between the Two Wars* (London: Frederick Muller 1947); Charles A. Gulick, *Austria: From Habsburg to Hitler*, two vols (Berkeley: University of California Press, 1948); Klemens von Klemperer, *Ignaz Seipel: Christian Statesman in a Time of Crisis* (Princeton, NJ: Princeton University Press, 1972); Eduard Marz, *Austrian Banking and Financial Policy: Credit-Anstalt at a Turning Point, 1913–1923* (New York: St. Martin's Press, 1984); David Clay Large, *Between Two Fires. Europe's Path in the 1930s* (New York: W.W. Norton, 1990); Helmut Gruber, *Red Vienna: Experiment in Working Class Culture, 1919–1934* (Oxford: Oxford University Press, 1991); and, Gordon Brook-Shepherd, *The Austrians: A Thousand-Year Odyssey* (New York: Carroll & Graf Publishers, 1996).

21 See, Edmond Taylor, *The Fall of the Dynasties: The Collapse of the Old Order, 1905–1922* (New York: Doubleday, 1963), pp. 69–96, 337–56.

22 See, Joseph Redlich, *Austrian War Government* (New Haven, CT: Yale University Press, 1929).
23 On the nationalist currents in Austria-Hungary, see, Oscar Jaszi, *The Dissolution of the Habsburg Monarchy* (Chicago: University of Chicago Press, 1929); and, Robert A. Kann, *The Multinational Empire: Nationalism and National Reform in the Habsburg Monarchy, 1848–1918*, two vols (New York: Columbia University Press, 1964).
24 On the introductions of separate currencies within the successor states of the former Austro-Hungarian Empire, see, John Parke Young, *European Currency and Finance*, Vol. II (Washington, DC: Government Printing Office, 1925), on Austria, pp. 9–25; Czechoslovakia, pp. 55–77; and Hungary, pp. 103–124.
25 Eduard Marz, *Austrian Banking and Financial Policy: Creditanstalt at a Turning Point, 1913–1923*, pp. 290–317. On the effects of rent controls in Vienna in the 1920s, see F.A. Hayek, "The Repercussions of Rent Restrictions" [1930] reprinted in *Rent Control, A Popular Paradox* (Vancouver: Fraser Institute, 1975), pp. 67–83.
26 Between 1919 and 1922 the budget deficits in nominal terms grew from 2.7 billion crowns in 1919 to 137.7 billion crowns in 1922. The deficits averaged between 40 and 67 percent, as a fraction of total federal government expenditure in Austria during this period of time. See, Kurt W. Rothschild, *Austria's Economic Development between the Two Wars*, p. 24.
27 In 1925, at a meeting of the *Verein für Sozialpolitik* [Society for Social Policy], Mises told the following story:

> Three years ago a colleague from the German Reich, who is here in this hall today, visited Vienna and participated in a discussion with some Viennese economists. Everyone was in complete agreement concerning the destructiveness of inflationist policy. Later, as we went home through the still of the night, we heard in the *Herrengasse* [a main street in the center of Vienna] the heavy drone of the Austro-Hungarian Bank's printing presses that were running incessantly, day and night, to produce new bank notes. Throughout the land, a large number of industrial enterprises were idle; others were working part-time; only the printing presses stamping out notes were operating at full speed. Let us hope that industry in Germany and Austria will once more regain its prewar volume and that the war- and inflation-related industries, devoted specifically to the printing of notes, will give way to more useful activities.

See, Bettina Bien Greaves and Robert W. McGee, eds., *Mises: An Annotated Bibliography* (Irvington-on-Hudson, NY: Foundation for Economic Education, 1993), p. 35.
28 J. van Walre de Bordes, *The Austrian Crown: Its Depreciation and Stabilization*, pp. 48–50, 83, 115–139.
29 On the provincial attempts to break away from the central government in Vienna, and the general political problems of establishing Austria's international recognition as a unified republic, see, John C. Swanson, *The Remnants of the Habsburg Monarchy: The Shaping of Modern Austria and Hungary, 1918–1922* (New York: Columbia University Press, 2001).
30 See, Joseph Redlich, "Austria and Central Europe," *Yale Review* (January 1923), pp. 243–244:

> The tendency of the old Austrian war government to suppress economic freedom and to monopolize for the state the disposition of all the economic activities of the people can easily be explained … [by] a general state of dictatorship that arose in all the belligerent countries … Yet state socialism of this kind has been preserved in republican Austria [and is] the consequence of a general and strong, but vague, idea entertained by the leading party, the Social Democrats, that economic omnipotence should be maintained by a public

administration, which must hence-forward execute only the will of the masses of the people, as a first large step towards the great Social-Democratic goal, namely, the "socialization" of the means of production and distribution of goods.

31 Carlile A. Macartney, *The Social Revolution in Austria*, pp. 94–95; David F. Strong, *Austria (October 1918–March 1919): Transition from Empire to Republic*, pp. 193–199; Charles A. Gulick, *Austria: From Habsburg to Hitler*, Vol. I, pp. 90–92; Malcolm Bullock, *Austria, 1918–1938: A Study in Failure*, p. 21; and Joseph Redlich, "The Problem of the Austrian Republic," *Quarterly Review* (July 1920), pp. 209–210.

32 Samuel Hoare, "Vienna and the State of Central Europe," *The Nineteenth Century and After* (March 1920), pp. 409–423; for pictures of the conditions in Vienna at this time – the begging on the streets, the hauling of firewood into the city by family members, of people returning from journeys to the countryside to barter for food, etc., see, Solita Solano, "Vienna – A Capital Without a State," *The National Geographic Magazine* (January 1923), pp. 77–102.

33 Friedrich von Wieser, "The Fight Against the Famine in Austria," in Lord Parmoor *et al.*, *The Famine in Europe: The Facts and Suggested Remedies* (London: Swarthmore Press, 1920), pp. 49–56; and also the contributions about the situation in Austria by, Friedrich Hertz, "What the Famine Means in Austria," pp. 17–26; and, Dr. Ellenbogen, "The Plight of German Austria," pp. 39–48. For other contemporary accounts of the starvation and general hardship conditions in Vienna in 1919 and 1920, see, Philip Gibbs, "The Tragedy of Vienna," *Living Age* (January 3, 1920), pp. 5–9; "A Dying Metropolis," *Living Age* (January 24, 1920), pp. 198–200; Ludwig Hirschfeld, "Pictures from a Shivering Vienna," *Living Age* (February 21, 1920), pp. 461–463; "Vienna Paying the Tragic Price of War, and Defeat," *Literary Digest* (March 20, 1920), pp. 83–91; Renato Ia Valle, "Two Aspects of Vienna," *Living Age* (August 7, 1920), pp. 382–386; and D.H. Loch, "Austria Revisited," *Contemporary Review* (November 1920), pp. 628–637; also, Lothrop Stoddard, "Berlin and Vienna: Likenesses and Contrasts," *Scribner's Magazine* (December 1923), pp. 651–655; one of the most detailed accounts of daily life in Vienna during this time is found in, Anna Eisenmenger, *Blockade: The Diary of an Austrian Middle-Class Woman, 1914–1924* (New York: R. Long and R.R. Smith, 1932).

34 For a detailed analysis of the Austrian constitution and changes in it during the 1920s, see Mary MacDonald, *The Republic of Austria, 1918–1934: A Study in the Failure of Democratic Government*; also W. Leon Godshall, "The Constitution of New Austria," *Current History* (May 1923), pp. 281–285; and Malbone W. Graham, "The Constitutional Crisis in Austria" *American Political Science Review* (February 1930), pp. 144–157; on the legal philosophy behind Kelsen's writing of the Austrian constitution, see Erich Voegelin, "Kelsen's Pure Theory of Law," *Political Science Quarterly* (June 1927), pp. 268–276.

35 Klemens von Klemperer, *Ignaz Seigel: Christian Statesman in a Time of Crisis*, pp. 186–219.

36 See, Helmut Gruber, *Red Vienna: Experiment in Working Class Culture, 1919–1934*; also, Anson Rabinbach, *The Crisis of Austrian Socialism: From Red Vienna to Civil War, 1927–1934* (Chicago: University of Chicago Press, 1983).

37 The tax on luxury goods imposed by the city of Vienna was abandoned in April 1923 when the federal government of Austria put into effect a general "turnover tax" of 1 percent that was raised to 2 percent in 1924. Through most of the remainder of the 1920s, it provided approximately one-third of the total that was raised in joint taxes that were divided among the provinces, cities, and towns.

38 Gulick, *Austria: From Habsburg to Hitler*, Vol. 1, pp. 354–406; Malcolm Bullock, *Austria, 1918–1938: A Study in Failure*, pp. 112–115.

39 Walter C. Langsam, *The World Since 1914* (New York: Macmillan, 1933), pp. 422–424. Mises described these private armed forces in his memoirs, *Notes and Recollections*, pp. 88, 90:

> It was even more significant that the Social-Democratic Party had at its disposal a Party Army that was equipped with rifles and machine guns – even with light artillery and ample ammunition – an army with manpower at least three times greater that the government troops, such as the Federal Forces, state and local police … The Social-Democratic Army, officially called the "Organizers," *[Ordner]* conducted open marches and field exercises which the government was unable to oppose. Unchallenged, the Party claimed the 'right to the street' … The terror caused by the Social Democrats forced other Austrians to build their defenses. Attempts were made as early as winter 1918–1919. After various failures, the "Home Guard" *[Heimwehr]* had some organizational success … I watched with horror this development that indeed was unavoidable. It was obvious that Austria was moving toward civil war. I could not prevent it. Even my best friends held to the opinion that the force (actual and potential) of the Social-Democratic Party could be opposed only by violence. The formation of the Home Guard introduced a new type of individual into politics. Adventurers without education and desperados with narrow horizons became the leaders, because they were good at drill and had a loud voice to give commands. Their bible was the manual of arms; their slogan, "authority." These adventurers – petty *Il Duces* and Führers – identified democracy with Social-Democracy and therefore looked upon democracy "as the worst of all evils." Later they clung to the catchword, "corporate state." Their social ideal was a military state in which they lone would command.

40 See Mises, *Socialism*, p. 414:

> Capital consumption can be detected statistically and can be conceived intellectually, but it is not obvious to everyone. To see the weakness of a policy that raises the consumption of the masses at the cost of existing capital wealth, and thus sacrifices the future to the present, and to recognize the nature of this policy, requires deeper insight than that vouchsafed to statesmen and politicians or to the masses who have put them in power. As long as the walls of the factory building stand, and the trains continue to run, it is supposed that all is well with the world. The increased difficulties of maintaining the higher standard of living are ascribed to various causes, but never to the fact that a policy of capital consumption is being followed.

On the theory of capital consumption, see, F.A. Hayek, "Capital Consumption," [1932] in *Money, Capital, and Fluctuations: Early Essays* (Chicago: University of Chicago Press, 1984), pp. 136–158.

41 Ludwig von Mises, Engelbert Dollfuss, and Edmund Palla, *Becht fiber die Ursachen der Wirtschaftsschwierigkeiten Österreichs* [A Report on the Causes of the Economic Difficulties in Austria] (Vienna: 1931); for a summary of some of the report's conclusions and related data on capital consumption and the shortage of capital in Austria during this time, see, Frederick Hertz, *The Economic Problem of the Danubian States*, pp. 145–168; see, also, Nicholas Kaldor, "The Economic Situation of Austria," *Harvard Business Review* (October 1932), pp. 23–34; and Fritz Machlup, "The Consumption of Capital in Austria," *Review of Economic Statistics* (January 15, 1935), pp. 13–19, especially p. 13, n2: "Professor Ludwig v. Mises was the first, as far as I know, to point to the phenomenon of consumption of capital. As a member of a committee appointed by the Austrian government … he also emphasized comprehensive factual information." The process of capital consumption due to economic miscalculation under inflation was explained by Mises immediately after the war in his work, *Nation, State and Economy: Contributions to the Politics and*

History of Our Time, [1919] pp. 161–163; also, *The Theory of Money and Credit*, pp. 234–237.

42 For accounts of Austria's experience with foreign exchange controls between 1931 and 1934, see, Howard Ellis, *Exchange Control in Central Europe* (Cambridge, MA: Harvard University Press, 1941), pp. 27–73; and Oskar Morgenstern, "Removal of Exchange Control: The Example of Austria," *International Conciliation*, No. 333 (October 1937), pp. 678–689.

43 In March 1931, the German and Austrian governments signed a protocol for the establishment of an Austro-German customs union. Under opposition from the governments of Great Britain, France, Italy, and Czechoslovakia, the customs union was prevented from operating after the World Court at the Hague found it to be inconsistent with the international agreements that Austria had signed in 1922; see, Mary Margaret Ball, *Postwar German-Austrian Relations: The Anschluss Movement, 1918–1936* (London: Oxford University Press, 1937), pp. 100–185.

44 Arnold J. Zurcher, "Austria's Corporative Constitution," *American Political Science Review* (August 1934), pp. 664–670.

45 On some of the political and cultural factors at work in bringing to an end Austria's independent existence in 1938, see, Joseph Redlich, "German Austria and Nazi Germany" *Foreign Affairs*, Vol. 15, No. 1 (1936), pp. 179–186; and, Hans Kohn, "AEIOU: Some Reflections on the Meaning and Mission of Austria," *Journal of Modern History* (December 1939), pp. 513–527; also, Oscar Jaszi, "Why Austria Perished," *Social Research* (September 1938), pp. 304–327.

46 See, Joachim C. Fest, *Hitler* (New York: Harcourt Brace Jovanovich, 1973), pp. 549–550; and Ian Kershaw, *Hitler, 1936–1945: Nemesis* (New York: W.W. Norton, 2000), pp. 84–85; Saul Friedlander, *Nazi Germany and the Jews*, Vol. I: "The Years of Persecution, 1933–1939" (New York: HarperCollins, 1997), pp. 242–244; also Getta Sereny, *The German Trauma: Experiences and Reflections, 1938–2000* (London: Penguin Press, 2000), pp. 6–8; Getta Sereny, who was a teenager in Vienna at the time of the German occupation, is the stepdaughter of Ludwig von Mises. For a more detailed account of the events in Austria following the Nazi annexation of the country, see, Dieter Wagner and Gerhard Tomkowitz, *Anschluss: The Week Hitler Seized Power* (New York: St. Martin's Press, 1971); and, Walter B. Maass, *Country Without a Name: Austria under Nazi Rule, 1938–1945* (New York: Frederick Ungar Publishing Co., 1979).

47 Ludwig von Mises, "Remarks Concerning the Establishment of a Ukrainian Note-Issuing Bank," [1918] in, Richard M. Ebeling, ed., *Selected Writings of Ludwig von Mises, Vol. 2: Between the Two World Wars: Monetary Disorder, Interventionism, Socialism and the Great Depression* (Indianapolis, IN: Liberty Fund, 2002), pp. 23–29.

48 Strong, *Austria (October 1918–March 1919): Transition from Empire to Republic*, pp. 202–203; for a detailed summary of the inflationary policies of the Austro-Hungarian National Bank during World War I, see, George A. Schreiner, "Austria-Hungary's Financial Debacle," *Current History* (July 1925), pp. 594–600.

49 See Mises, *Notes and Recollections*, p. 66:

> Toward the end of the war, I published a short essay on the quantity theory in the journal of the Association of Banks and Bankers, a publication not addressed to the public. The censor did not approve my treatment of the inflation problem. My tame academic essay was rejected. I had to revise it before it could be published.

50 Ludwig von Mises, "The Quantity Theory" and "On the Currency Question," [1918] in, Ebeling, ed., *Selected Writings of Ludwig von Mises*, Vol. 2, pp. 3–22.

51 F.A. Hayek, "Ludwig von Mises (1881–1973)" in Peter G. Klein, ed., *The Collected Works of F.A. Hayek, Vol. 4: The Fortunes of Liberalism*, (Chicago: University of Chicago Press, 1992), pp. 132–33:

There was a time then when we thought he would soon be called to take charge of the finances of the country. He was so clearly the only man capable of stopping inflation and much damage might have been prevented if he had been put in charge. It was not to be.

52 Mises, "The Currency Problem Prior to the Peace Conference," [1919] in Ebeling, ed., *Selected Writings of Ludwig von Mises,* Vol. 2, pp. 30–46.
53 The peace treaties divided the Austro-Hungarian prewar debts into two categories, secured and unsecured. Secured debts, e.g., railroads against which the property had been secured for the loan, were charged to the county in whose territory the property was now located. If the property was located across more than one of the successor states, each country was responsible for the portion of the debt corresponding to the amount of the secured property under its jurisdiction. Unsecured debt was distributed among the successor states on the basis of the fraction of the tax revenue its territory had supplied to the Austro-Hungarian monarchy. For a more detailed summary of the debt allocation process following the signing of the peace treaties, see, Leo Paslovsky, *Economic Nationalism of the Danubian States* (New York: Macmillan, 1928), pp. 42–47.
54 Mises, "On the Actions to be Taken in the Face of Progressive Currency Depreciation" [1919] in, Ebeling, ed., *Selected Writings of Ludwig von Mises,* Vol. 2, pp. 47–64.
55 Otto Bauer, *The Austrian Revolution,* pp. 105–106.
56 Mises, "On the Actions to be Taken in the Face of Progressive Currency Depreciation," p. 53.
57 Ibid., pp. 63–64.
58 Ibid., p. 60.
59 Ibid., p. 61.
60 Mises, *Notes and Recollections,* p. 87.
61 Mises, "Vienna's Political Relationship with the Provinces in Light of Economics" [1920] in, Ebeling, ed., *Selected Writings of Ludwig von Mises,* Vol. 2, p. 59.
62 Mises, "On the Actions to be Taken in the Face of Progressive Currency Depreciation," p. 62.
63 Mises, "The Reentry of German-Austria into the German Reich and the Currency Question" [1919] in, Ebeling, ed., *Selected Writings of Ludwig von Mises,* Vol. 2, pp. 65–86.
64 Ibid., p. 74.
65 Ibid., pp. 75–76.
66 Ibid., pp. 78–82.
67 Ibid., p. 86.
68 Mises, "Vienna's Political Relationship with the Provinces in Light of Economics" [1920], pp. 97–118.
69 See also Mises, "Viennese Industry and the Tax on Luxury Goods" [1921] in, Ebeling, ed., *Selected Writings of Ludwig von Mises,* Vol. 2, pp. 119–121, for his analysis of how a tax-the-rich policy undermined an essential Viennese export trade.
70 Mises, "Vienna's Political Relationship with the Provinces in Light of Economics" [1920], p. 103.
71 Ibid., p. 105.
72 Ibid., pp. 103–104.
73 Ibid., pp. 105–107.
74 Ibid., pp. 108–109.
75 Ibid., p. 114.
76 Ibid., pp. 115, 118.
77 Ludwig von Mises, "Wie könnte Oesterreich gerettet werden? Ein wirtschaftspolitisches Programm für Oesterreich" ["How Can Austria Be Saved? An Economic Policy Program for Austria"] *Die Börse* (February 17, 1921). Emphasis in the original.

78 Mises, *Notes and Recollections*, pp. 79–80.
79 Klemperer, *Ignaz Seipel: Christian Statesman in a Time of Crisis*, p. 180.
80 For Mises' analysis of the Great German Inflation, see, "Stabilization of the Monetary Unit From the Viewpoint of Theory" [1923] in, Percy L. Greaves, Jr., ed., *Von Mises, On the Manipulation of Money and Credit* (Dobbs Ferry, NY: Free Market Books, 1978), pp. 1–49; also, Mises, "The Great German Inflation," [1932] in Richard M. Ebeling, ed., *Money, Method and the Market Process: Essays by Ludwig von Mises* (Norwell, MA: Kluwer Academic Press, 1990), pp. 96–103.
81 Arthur Salter, "The Reconstruction of Austria," *Foreign Affairs* (June 15, 1924), pp. 630–643; W.T. Layton and Charles Rist, *The Economic Situation in Austria* (Geneva: League of Nations, 1925); Emil Lengyel, "Austria's Emergence from Bankruptcy," *Current History* (January 1926), pp. 539–542; and, *The Financial Reconstruction of Austria: General Survey and Principal Documents* (Geneva: League of Nations, November 1926).
82 Mises, *Notes and Recollections*, p. 83.
83 Mises, "The Return to Gold" [1924] in, Ebeling, ed., *Selected Writings of Ludwig von Mises*, Vol. 2, pp. 136–153.
84 See J. van Walre de Bordes, *The Austrian Crown: Its Depreciation and Stabilization*, pp. 219–220:

> Austria has therefore at present *a gold exchange standard,* and in the purist form-*with practically no gold* ... There is no gold in circulation, and the gold reserve of the Austrian National Bank is insignificant. At the end of 1923 the gold reserve amounted to *6.5* million gold crowns, and there was a foreign exchange reserve of 298.6 million. On several occasions during 1923 the Bank sold gold, probably because it preferred to have a reserve of interest-bearing foreign bills than of unproductive gold (E$mphasis in the original).

85 Mises, "The Return to Gold," p. 147, my emphasis.
86 Ibid., pp. 148–152.
87 Ibid., pp. 152–153; see also Mises, *The Theory of Money and Credit*, p. 434, where he repeats the idea that "[i]t would be easy to force countries into such an agreement by means of penal customs duties."
88 Mises, "Restoring Europe's State Finances," [1924] in, Ebeling, ed., *Selected Writings of Ludwig von Mises,* Vol. 2, pp. 154–159.
89 Ibid., p. 155.
90 Ibid., p. 156.
91 Ibid., pp. 157, 159.
92 Mises, "The Balance Sheet of Economic Policies Hostile to Property," [1927] in, Ebeling, ed., *Selected Writings of Ludwig von Mises,* Vol. 2, pp. 237–240; see, also, Ludwig von Mises, "Währung und Finanzen des Bundesstaates Oesterreich" ["Currency and Finances of the Federal State of Austria"] *Deutsche Wirtschaftszeitung* (September 20, 1928), pp. 913–915, where Mises emphasized that under Seipel's leadership of the government, there

> was a complete repudiation of the inflationary and capital-consuming policy that was pushed through in the first days of the war and which the government of the postwar period, being dependent as it was on the destructionist mood of the masses, had carried to an extreme ... The success of the [monetary] stabilization action can be recognized by the fact that no one any longer talks about the Austrian currency ... Hence the task that Seipel tackled in 1922 has unquestionably succeeded.

However, Austria had fiscal imbalances, Mises went on, that were almost totally due to the large deficits suffered in the state-run industries. "The financial condition of the Austrian Federation would be far more favorable," Mises pointed out, "if the Federation were not burdened with the possession and operation of the railroads, the post and telegraph system, the national forests, and the mines." The high cost of funding a bloated and redundant bureaucracy was another fiscal drag on the government. This problem was intensified in Vienna, where the Social Democrats were in power; they were determined in undertaking a wide variety of socialist experiments at the municipal level with no thought to the tax burden imposed on the private sector, or on how the regulations and controls imposed on the city's enterprises prevented improvements in the living conditions of the mass of the population. Furthermore, Austria was a capital and resource-poor country; it was heavily dependent upon exports to pay for the imported raw materials used in manufacturing and the imported consumer goods that supplemented domestic production. If Austria was to become more competitive in international markets it had to find ways to cut its costs of production. Since, "the labor unions resist a lowering of wages with all the means at their disposal," Mises concluded, "a reduction in production costs, which is an unavoidable precondition for an increase in Austrian exports and a reduction of imports, must therefore be striven for first of all through a reduction of the taxes that burden production." Hence, there was a need to find ways to decrease the activities and therefore the costs of the Austrian government on society.

93 Ibid., p. 240.
94 Mises, "Adjusting Public Expenditures to the Economy's Financial Capacity," [1930] in, Ebeling, ed., *Selected Writings of Ludwig von Mises,* Vol. 2, pp. 241–250.
95 Ibid., p. 242.
96 Ibid., p. 243.
97 Ibid., p. 243.
98 Ibid., p. 249.
99 The data is derived from the figures provided in the League of Nations' *Statistical Yearbooks* for this period.
100 Fritz Machlup, "My Early Work on International Monetary Problems," *Banca Nazionale del Lavoro Quarterly Review* (June 1980), p. 135.
101 Mises, "The Causes of the Economic Crisis: An Address" [1931] in Percy L. Greaves, Jr., ed., *Von Mises, On the Manipulation of Money and Credit,* pp. 173–203.
102 Mises, "The Current Status of Business Cycle Research and Its Prospects for the Immediate Future," [1933] in Percy L. Greaves, Jr., ed., *Von Mises, On the Manipulation of Money and Credit,* pp. 207–213.
103 Mises, "The Economic Crisis and Capitalism" [1931], "The Gold Standard and Its Opponents," [1931], "The Myth of the Failure of Capitalism," [1932], "Interventionism as the Cause of the Economic Crisis: A Debate Between Otto Conrad and Ludwig Mises," [1932], "Planned Economy and Socialism" [1933], "The Return to Free Exchange" [1933], and "Two Memoranda on the Problems of Monetary Stabilization and Foreign Exchange Rates" [1936] in, Ebeling, ed., *Selected Writings of Ludwig von Mises,* Vol. 2, pp. 169–233.
104 Mises, "The Myth of the Failure of Capitalism," pp. 188–189; Mises also pointed out that corruption was the only mechanism that permitted the economy to continue functioning, while at the same time that very corruption undermined the moral foundations upon which the market economy was ultimately based; see, Mises, "Interventionism" [1926] in *Critique of Interventionism,* p. 13.
105 Mises, "Two Memoranda on the Problems of Monetary Stabilization and Foreign Exchange Rates" [1936], pp. 224–225. At the very time in February 1936 that Mises made these criticisms of devaluation as a roundabout method to bring about a decline in real wages through a rise in prices while nominal (or money) wages are presumed to remain the same, there appeared that same month John Maynard Keynes' *The General Theory of Employment, Interest and Money* [1936] (Cambridge: Cambridge University Press, 1973). Keynes justified using just such a method for reducing real wages on the rationale that (p. 264): "In fact, a movement by employers to revise money-wage bargains downward will be much more strongly

resisted than a gradual and automatic lowering of real wages as a result of rising prices." But already in 1931, Mises pointed out in his monograph, "The Causes of the Economic Crisis: An Address," in, Percy L. Greaves, ed., *Von Mises, On the Manipulation of Money and Credit*, pp. 199–200:

> Only one argument is new, although on that account no less false. This is to the effect that the higher than unhampered market wage rates can be brought into proper relationship more easily by an inflation. This argument shows how seriously concerned our political economists are to avoid displeasing the labor unions. Although they cannot help but recognize that wage rates are too high and must be reduced, they dare not openly call for a halt to such overpayments. Instead, they propose to outsmart the unions in some way. They propose that the actual money wage rate remain unchanged in the coming inflation. In effect, this would amount to reducing the real wage. This assumes, of course, that the unions will refrain from making further wage demands in the ensuing boom and that they will, instead, remain passive while their real wage rates deteriorate. Even if this entirely unjustified optimistic expectation is accepted as true, nothing is gained thereby. A boom caused by banking policy measures must still lead eventually to a crisis and a depression. So, by this method, the problem of lowering wage rates is not resolved but simply postponed.

And, again, in 1945, Mises pointed out in his essay "Planning for Freedom" in, *Planning for Freedom and Sixteen Other Essays and Addresses* (South Holland, IL: Libertarian Press, 1980), p. 14:

> If in the course of an inflation the rise in commodity prices exceeds the rise in nominal wage rates, unemployment will drop. But what makes unemployment shrink is precisely the fact that real wage rates are falling. Lord Keynes recommended credit expansion because he believed that the wage earners will acquiesce in this outcome; he believed that "a gradual and automatic lowering of real wage rates as a result of rising prices" would not be so strongly resisted by labor as an attempt to lower money wage rates. It is very unlikely that this will happen. Public opinion is fully aware of the changes in purchasing power and watches with burning interest the movements of the index of commodity prices and of cost of living. The substance of all discussions concerning wage rates is real wage rates, not nominal wage rates. There is no prospect of outsmarting the unions by such tricks.

106 Mises, "The Gold Standard and Its Opponents" [1931], p. 180.
107 Mises anticipated the coming of a banking crisis in Austria years earlier. Fritz Machlup recounted, in his *Tribute to Mises* (p. 12), that,

> As his assistant in the University seminar which met every Wednesday afternoon, I usually accompanied him home. On these walks we would pass through a passage of the *Creditalstalt* in Vienna. From 1924, every Wednesday afternoon as we walked through the passage for pedestrians he said: "That will be a big smash." Mind you, this was from 1924 onwards; yet in 1931, when the crash finally came, I still held some shares of the *Creditalstalt,* which of course had become completely worthless.

108 Mises, "Foreign Exchange Control and Some of Its Consequences," "An Agenda for Alleviating the Economic Crisis: The Gold Parity, Foreign Exchange Control and Budgetary Restraint," "An International Loan as the 'Breathing Room' for Austrian Economic Reform," "On Limiting the Adverse Effects of a Proposed Increase in the Value-Added Tax," and "Foreign Exchange Policy" [all 1932] in, Ebeling, ed., *Selected Writings of Ludwig von Mises,* Vol. 2, pp. 251–285.
109 Letter from Ludwig von Mises to F.A. Hayek, dated December 7, 1931. Years later, Mises told about his appointment to this foreign exchange control advisory board,

and its peculiar impact on various people needing foreign exchange for travel abroad:

> I want to tell you an experience of how foreign exchange [control] interferes with everything in business, in private affairs, in religion, etc. In 1931, the Austrian government introduced overnight foreign exchange control. An advisory board was named and they immediately published the names of the men appointed to the board. My name was among them. I read it in the newspapers. I knew that the next day there would be several hundred letters from businessmen because they realized that I was the only man who was friendly to them. Then I went home and in the evening the maid told me that the Archbishop had telephoned me. Now the Archbishop doesn't telephone at all. But the maid said that he would telephone the next morning. And sure enough, the legal advisor of the Archbishop, the Canon of the University whom I knew, phoned. He told me it was important for some students from the educational institutions in Rome. He said we have to have a sum of money. I promised him that I would try to get it for him. But you see the first reaction of the foreign exchange [control] was not from business, not from people who want to flee with the capital from a foreign country, it was from a regular affair of education in a neighboring country (in Rome). You have to realize that students from Austria went to Rome to study and no authority interfered with it before. But as soon as foreign exchange control enters, at once the thing is no longer free. I want to add only that I didn't remain very long on this advisory board.

This quotation is taken from Mises' "Lectures on Political Economy" delivered at The Inn, Buck Hill Falls, Pennsylvania, June 13–24, 1955, from the stenographic notes of Bettina Bien Greaves. Other undesirable effects from foreign exchange controls were also emphasized by Mises, see, "Noninflationary Proposal for Post-war Monetary Reconstruction" [1944] in, Richard M. Ebeling, ed., *Selected Writings of Ludwig von Mises, Vol. 3: The Political Economy of International Re-form and Reconstruction* (Indianapolis, IN: Liberty Fund, 2000), p. 95:

> At any rate, foreign exchange control is tantamount to the full nationalization of foreign trade … Where every branch of business depends, to some extent at least, on the buying of imported goods or on the exporting of a smaller or greater part of its output, the government is in the position to control all economic activity. He who does not comply with any whim of the authorities can be ruined either by the refusal to allot him foreign exchange or to grant him what the government considers as an export premium, that is, the difference between the market price and the official rate of foreign exchange. Besides, the government has the power to interfere in all the details of every enterprise's internal affairs; to prohibit the importation of all undesirable books, periodicals, and newspapers; and to prevent everybody from traveling abroad; from educating his children in foreign schools; and from consulting foreign doctors. Foreign exchange control was the main vehicle of European dictatorships.

110 Mises, "Foreign Exchange Control and Some of Its Consequences" [February 1932], pp. 251–260.
111 Mises, "An Agenda for Alleviating the Economic Crisis" [March 1932], p. 262.
112 Ibid., p. 264.
113 Mises, "An International Loan as the 'Breathing Room' for Austrian Economic Reform" [July 1932], pp. 268–269.
114 Mises, "Foreign Exchange Policy" [October 1932], p. 279.
115 Ibid., 279.
116 Ibid., pp. 280–281.
117 Franz Grillparzer (1791–1872) was an Austrian dramatist considered to have written some of the greatest works ever performed on the Austrian stage.

118 Mises, "Foreign Exchange Policy," [October 1932], pp. 283–284.
119 Mises, "The Return to Freedom of Exchange" [May 1933], p. 218.
120 Mises, "The Direction of Austrian Financial Policy: A Retrospective and Prospective View," [1935] in, Ebeling, ed., *Selected Writings of Ludwig von Mises,* Vol. 2, pp. 286–293.
121 Letter from William E. Rappard to Ludwig von Mises, dated March 10, 1934; from the archive of the Graduate Institute of International Studies, Geneva, Switzerland.
122 Letter from Ludwig von Mises to William E. Rappard, dated March 30, 1934; from the archive of the Graduate Institute of International Studies, Geneva, Switzerland.
123 Mises, *Notes and Recollections*, p. 137.
124 Ludwig von Mises, *Human Action, A Treatise on Economics* (New Haven, CT: Yale University Press, 1949), p. iii. This first edition of *Human Action* was handsomely reprinted in 1998 by the Ludwig von Mises Institute of Auburn, Alabama, with an introduction by Jeffrey M. Herbener, Hans-Hermann Hoppe, and Joseph T. Salerno, which tells the history of how the volume came to be published in the United States. In Geneva, between 1934 and 1940, Mises had written the German-language forerunner to *Human Action,* titled, *Nationalökonomie: Theorie des Handelns und Wirtschaftens* [1940] (Munich: Philosophia Verlag, 1980).
125 Ibid., p. 142.
126 Mises, *Notes and Recollections*, pp. 139–141.
127 Comments of Mises' assistant at the Chamber of Commerce, Therese Wolf-Thieberger, November 26, 1971, in the notes of Bettina Bien Greaves.
128 Ludwig von Mises, "Trends Can Change" [1951] and "The Political Chances for Genuine Liberalism" [1951] in *Planning for Freedom*, pp. 173–184.
129 That is precisely the theme and purpose of the essays that he wrote in the early 1940s. See, Richard M. Ebeling, ed., *Selected Writings of Ludwig von Mises,* Vol. 3: "The Political Economy of International Reform and Reconstruction" (Indianapolis, IN: Liberty Fund, 2000); see also Ch. 6: "Planning for Freedom: Ludwig von Mises as Political Economist and Policy Analyst" in the present volume.
130 Mises, *Socialism*, p. 13.
131 Hayek, "Ludwig von Mises (1881–1973)," p. 159.

6 Planning for freedom
Ludwig von Mises as political economist and policy analyst

In May 1940, the fate of Europe seemed to hang in the balance. On August 23, 1939, Hitler and Stalin had their foreign ministers, Ribbentrop and Molotov, sign a nonaggression pact in Moscow. The pact contained a secret protocol specifying that should war break out, Nazi Germany and the Soviet Union would divide Poland between them and the Baltic States of Estonia, Latvia, Lithuania, and Finland would be recognized as part of a Soviet sphere of influence.

On September 1, 1939, Hitler's armies invaded Poland from the west and on September 17, Stalin's armies attacked from the east. Before the end of the month, Poland ceased to exist. In November 1939, Stalin attacked Finland, resulting in a protracted winter war that lasted until March 1940, when the Finns finally had to sue for peace and accept the loss of a large swath of border territory, which was annexed by the Soviet Union.

In the west, Great Britain and France had declared war on Germany two days after Hitler's invasion of Poland, but except for some minor border incursions into the Saarland, they initiated no ground offensive against Germany. Sea combat along the Scandinavian coast resulted in both the western Allies and Germany making plans to invade Norway. In April 1940, Germany's armies invaded and overran Denmark and Norway, just a few days ahead of a planned British operation.

Secure in the knowledge that Stalin was his ally in the subjugation of Eastern Europe, Hitler turned west to defeat Great Britain and France. In the early morning hours of May 10, 1940, Germany invaded the Low Countries – Holland and Belgium. By the third week of May, the German armies fully occupied Holland, most of Belgium, and portions of northern France less than seventy-five miles from Paris. The Germans had also reached the English Channel near the French town of Abbeville, thereby effectively cutting off the British Expeditionary Force from the main forces of their French allies to the south; this would result in the British evacuation at Dunkirk.

From Geneva, Switzerland, the Austrian economist Ludwig von Mises wrote a letter on May 22, 1940, to his long-time friend and colleague, Friedrich A. Hayek, a professor at the London School of Economics. Since autumn 1934, Mises had been Professor of International Economic Relations at the Graduate Institute of International Studies in Geneva. He had moved there from Vienna, where he had been employed since 1909 as a senior economic analyst for the Vienna Chamber of Commerce, Crafts and Industry. He had also taught at the University of Vienna as *a privatdozent,* an unsalaried instructor with the title Professor Extraordinary. In addition, Mises had founded and served as vice-president of the Austrian Institute for Business Cycle Research, as well as helping to revive and serve as vice-president of the Austrian Economic Society. Beginning in 1920, Mises had organized *a privatseminar* (a private seminar) at his Chamber of Commerce offices that brought together many of the best minds in economics, sociology, philosophy, political science, law, and history in Viennese society; indeed, this *Mises-Kreis* (the "Mises Circle") gained a wide international reputation during the years from its start until Mises' departure for Geneva in 1934.

Now with the high probability of the imminent fall of France in May 1940, the danger existed that neutral Switzerland might become a target for German conquest. Such an event would surely have meant Mises' arrest and deportation to a Nazi concentration camp in Eastern Europe. Besides his Jewish ancestry – his great-grandfather had been the head of the orthodox Jewish community in the Galician city of Lemberg during the days of the former Austro-Hungarian Empire – Mises was internationally known as an outspoken opponent of all forms of collectivism, including German National Socialism. The Nazis had shown their interest in him during March 1938, when, shortly after the German occupation of Austria, the Gestapo had come looking for him at his former Vienna apartment. They seized his papers and manuscripts, his family documents and possessions, his correspondence and files, and his entire library, except for the books he had taken to Geneva.

Mises had known for some time that he would have to leave a Europe increasingly threatened with Nazi control. His former student and friend, Fritz Machlup, who was then teaching at the University of Buffalo in New York, had been trying to arrange an academic appointment for Mises in California at UCLA. In a February 28, 1940, letter to Machlup, Mises stated, "Europe, unfortunately, is not a bearable place of residence anymore. I must strive to leave." But at that point in early 1940, when Germany and Britain and France were still engaged in what historians sometimes refer to as "the phony war" on the western front, Mises was reluctant to accept because of the financial terms of the appointment. Family expenses were too great for him to hope to live on the salary suggested. Mises had married in July 1938 at the age of fifty-six, and now had the financial responsibilities of a wife and her two children from a previous marriage. If the salary offer from UCLA could not be increased, then Mises stated, "Even a postponement of the appointment by one year would be financially advantageous, as I could, with my higher Swiss revenues, lessen my financial burdens. But, should this not be possible, I would have to accept the proposed salary." Mises added that, "It would be a true pleasure to see you and our other Viennese friends again. A teaching appointment alongside [Benjamin] Anderson [at UCLA] seems to be very enticing."[1]

But now in his May 22 letter to Hayek, Mises explained, "The development of events has become so worrisome, that most of my friends here in Geneva have strongly suggested that we leave Switzerland." But the decision to leave Geneva was not an easy one. Mises told Hayek:

The decision to leave is truly difficult. For me, it represents saying good-bye to a life which I have always lived, it is for me an "adieu" to a Europe which is about to disappear forever. I firmly believe that the Allies will be victorious, but I also know that the Britain of tomorrow will be sharply different from the England of the Classical Liberals of yester-years. It will resemble Seipel's Austria more than it will Victoria's Empire.

He asked Hayek to give his best wishes to all his friends in England, because, "Who knows whether, when or where we might be able to see each other again." And he hoped that Hayek and his family "will be in good hands when the last act begins."[2]

As the German armies approached the Swiss border and with an arranged offer of an academic position at Berkeley in hand, Mises went to Zurich to obtain his American visa, accompanied by his Graduate Institute colleague and friend, Wilhelm Röpke. Years later Röpke remembered that journey:

Neither of us will forget the night in May 1940 when, with the Swiss mobilization in full swing and Hitler *ante Aortas,* we took the milk train to Zurich to get the American visa from the U.S.A. consul general and when, at this dramatic moment, we tried to sum up the philosophical meaning of all this (that was happening in Europe).[3]

A month later on June 22, France surrendered to Germany, leaving all of northern and central France and the entire French Atlantic coastline down to the Spanish border under permanent German occupation. With the defeat of France, the threat of a German invasion of the British Isles starkly seemed a serious reality. And in Eastern Europe, during that same June of 1940, Stalin had ordered the Soviet military occupation of the Baltic republics of Estonia, Latvia, and Lithuania, and had annexed the Romanian province of Bessarabia and northern Bukovina. The European continent was facing a future of occupation or domination by the two totalitarian giants of Nazi Germany and the Soviet Union.

On July 4, 1940, Mises submitted his letter of resignation to William E. Rappard and Paul Mantoux, the directors of the Geneva Graduate Institute.[4] In his *Notes and Recollections,* written in the first months after his arrival in the United States, Mises said that the appointment to the Graduate Institute in 1934 had been "liberation," enabling him to "devote myself completely and almost exclusively to scientific problems." At the Institute,

There was a friendly atmosphere between teachers and students, and the spirit of genuine liberalism flourished in that unique institution. All around us the barbarian flood was rising and we all knew we were fighting with nothing but forlorn hope.[5]

Now in his letter of resignation, Mises had to express

profound regret that the premature ending of our collaboration causes me. I thank you for the honor and the confidence which you have shown in entrusting me with a chair; I have greatly appreciated in the course of these six years, the spirit which you have been able to infuse into this organization. The international roots of Geneva today seem shaken to its foundations. Nevertheless, I am convinced that the roots planted in Genevan soil still stay alive and will permit a new blossoming of international cooperation, when the time comes. For its part, the Institute will have contributed greatly to this new blossoming by the education that it has given to an elite group of students belonging to all the countries of the world. On this comforting thought I wish to take leave of you, of my colleagues, of the administrative personal, and of the students.[6]

Mises and his wife, Margit, left Geneva by bus that evening. They traveled through southern France to Barcelona, and then to Lisbon, where they booked passage on a ship to the United States. They arrived in New Jersey on August 2, where Mises' friend and former member of the *Mises-Kreis,* the sociologist Alfred Schutz, met them.[7]

All that had happened in Europe in the period between the two world wars had come as no surprise to Ludwig von Mises. Indeed, with uncanny insight he had seen where events in Germany were leading in the middle of the 1920s, during the years of the Weimar Republic. In 1925, in an essay on "Anti-Marxism," and in 1926, in an essay on "Social Liberalism," he saw the forces at work that would bring Adolf Hitler to power in 1933.[8] In these writings, Mises explained the process by which Marxian thought had come to have a stranglehold on German intellectuals during the last decades of the nineteenth and the opening decades of the twentieth centuries, and the development of divisions among these intellectuals into different anti-capitalist camps. Looking over the ideological terrain of Germany in the mid-1920s, Mises argued that the rising force in opposition to Marxian socialism was "national socialism." In post-World War I Germany and Austria a "movement has been steadily gaining significance in politics and the social sciences that can best be described as Anti-Marxism," Mises said. But "they are not attacking socialism, but Marxism, which they reproach for not being the right kind of socialism, for not being the one that is true and desirable."[9]

The great conflict in Germany, Mises said, was between those Marxian socialists who advocated class warfare and proletarian revolution and those national socialists who advocated national unity and war against foreign enemies.[10] The national socialists insisted that "proletarian interests" had to be submerged in the wider interests of the "fatherland." The strong state would also control and repress the profit motive of the private sector for the wider national good. Mises warned that, in this conflict and confusion, a growing number of Germans were "setting their hopes on the coming of the 'strong man' – the tyrant who will think for them and care for them:"[11] Thus, seven years before Hitler's ascendancy to power, Mises saw where German political currents were leading.

Mises stated that these national socialists were also determined to unite all the German-speaking people in Europe under one German state, as well as to expand the territory of such a unified German state to the point necessary to assure the living-space and resources for a German standard of living equal to or greater than the other major nations of the world. To achieve these ends they were willing to use force and risk a new world war.[12] Writing in 1925, Mises anticipated the 1939 alliance between Hitler's Germany and Stalin's Russia. Mises had asked, where would a national socialist Germany turn for an ally in this plan of conquest in Eastern Europe?

> If Germany, a nation surrounded by other nations in the heart of Europe, were to assault in accordance with this principle, it would invite a coalition of all its neighbors into a world-political constellation: enemies all around. In such a situation Germany could find only one ally: Russia, which is facing hostility by Poles, Lithuanians, Hungarians, and possibly Czechs, but nowhere stands in direct conflict with German interests. Since Bolshevist Russia, like Czarist Russia, only knows force in dealing with other nations, it is already seeking the friendship of German nationalism. German Anti-Marxism and Russian Super-Marxism are not too far apart.[13]

In 1932, when many in Germany still could not conceive that Hitler would ever really come to power, Mises clearly saw the writing on the wall. Hayek has recounted how

> in September 1932, during a committee meeting of the *Verein für Sozial-politik* [the Society for Social Policy] in Bad Kissingen, a rather large group of professional colleagues was sitting together at tea in a garden, when Mises suddenly asked whether we were aware that we were sitting together for the last time. The remark at first aroused only astonishment and later laughter, when Mises explained that after twelve months Hitler would be in power. That appeared to the other members too improbable, but more than anything they asked why the *Verein für Sozialpolitik* should not meet again after Hitler had come to power. Of course, it did not meet again until after the end of the Second World War![14]

And even earlier, in the months immediately following World War I, Mises had seen what the result would be for Germany if, out of the ashes of defeat in 1918, the German people were to harbor a thirst for revenge. In 1919, Mises published *Nation, State and Economy,* in which he analyzed, among other things, the causes and consequences of the Great War of 1914–1918. Mises warned his German readers:

> It would be the most terrible misfortune for Germany and for all of humanity if the idea of revenge should dominate the German policy of the future ... A new war that Germany might wage could easily become a Third Punic war and end with the complete annihilation of the German people.[15]

In 1945, when Germany was defeated again, the country had been reduced to rubble. Germany's cities were charred shells after years of Allied bombing, the infrastructure and industry were virtually destroyed, millions of German soldiers and civilians had been killed in the inferno of war, the surviving German population faced starvation, and the country was occupied and controlled by the United States, Great Britain, France, and the Soviet Union.

But in 1919, Mises also pointed out the direction that could bring redemption and renewal to Germany:

> The second course that the German people can take is that of completely turning away from imperialism. To strive for reconstruction only through productive labor, to make possible the development of all powers of the individual and of the nation as a whole by full freedom at home – that is the way that leads back to life ... If [Germany] is to rise again, then it can no longer strive to make the whole great at the expense of individuals but rather must strive for a durable foundation of the well-being of the whole on the basis of the well-being of individuals. It must switch from the collectivist policy that it has followed so far to an individualistic one.[16]

And, as Mises foretold, it has been the turn from totalitarian collectivism to a more individualist philosophy of public policy in the period since World War II that brought the German people greater freedom and prosperity in the second half of the twentieth century.[17]

During his six years at the Graduate Institute of International Studies in Geneva, Mises spent most of his time working on one monumental work, a general treatise on social philosophy and economic theory and policy, *Nationalökonomie, Theorie des Handelns und Wirtschaftens*.[18] It was released by the Swiss publisher in May 1940 just as Mises was preparing to leave behind the Europe he had known in the face of the rising tide of Nazi and Soviet totalitarianism.

In one of the few reviews following its publication, Friedrich A. Hayek pointed out the unique quality of the author and the work:

> There appears to be a width of view and an intellectual spaciousness about the whole book that are much more like that of an eighteenth-century philosopher than that of a modern specialist. And yet, or perhaps because of this, one feels throughout much nearer reality, and is constantly recalled from the discussion of the technicalities to the consideration of the great problems of our time ... It ranges from the most general philosophical problems raised by all scientific study of human action to the major problems of economic policy of our time ... [T]he result is a really imposing unified system of a liberal social philosophy. It is here also, more than elsewhere, that the author's astounding knowledge of history as well as of the contemporary world helps most to illustrate his argument.[19]

Nationalökonomie, which was translated and revised by Mises after his arrival in the United States and published in 1949 as *Human Action: A Treatise on Economics,* was the culmination of a twenty-year development and defense of a social philosophy of a (classical) liberal order and the market economy. There is a texture and quality to practically all of Mises' works, from this his most productive and creative period, which stands out in dramatic contrast to almost all the writings by other economists during this time.

A few months after Hayek's review, one appeared by Walter Sulzbach, a prominent German free market economist then in exile in the United States as a refugee from the ravages of war in Europe. Sulzbach, too, emphasized the uniqueness of the man and his work:

> Mises has written a remarkable book. Few economists of our generation can boast of a similar achievement. It is the work of a man who combines an immense knowledge of economic history, economic theories and present-day facts with a thoroughly logical mind.[20]

And in an interview after World War II, Oskar Morgenstern also emphasized Mises' intellectual breadth, saying that the "true value of his books is due to Mises' knowledge and experience in history. This is the real foundation of his importance."[21]

An appreciation for the historical, sociological, philosophical, and legal context of human circumstances and activities stands out as a hallmark of all Mises' writings on economic theory and policy. If it was not an often-abused phrase, it would be most appropriate to say that Mises was a "Renaissance Man" – someone who had pursued and succeeded in mastering and intellectually combining a vast array of knowledge in the worlds of both theory and practice. His work at the Vienna Chamber of Commerce required him to have a detailed and continuously updated knowledge of political events, economic statistics and legislation, and social and ideological trends, not only as they related to Austria, but to much of the rest of Europe and North America as well.

Yet he never claimed to have any special sources of inside information that were not available to others wishing to understand the stream of events, their meaning and tendencies. In an interview, Hayek explained that Mises said that it was all in the newspapers:

> He was extraordinarily well informed politically and always insisted that one need have no special source of information. Every time when I was surprised at his knowledge, he showed me that he knew it all from the newspapers. He must have been an extraordinary reader of newspapers. His knowledge of recent Austrian history, he told us, came from the obituaries. He must have had an exceptional memory to build up a really first class history of the period that we all knew least, simply from reading the newspapers. I don't know any person who knew the last twenty or thirty years largely from reading the contemporary press. The first thing every day in the office he studied the newspapers of the day, and then the second time after his nap in the afternoon he visited the coffeehouse and again studied the newspapers. He read newspapers up to the point that would be routine for most people, but he got more out of the newspapers than anyone else. He never kept files of newspaper clippings.[22]

It was "all in the newspapers" because his extraordinarily wide reading of books and journal articles, not only in economics but on various topics in history as well as on political, sociological, and philosophical trends, enabled him to see it in the contemporary press.[23] And in spite of what he may have told Hayek and others around him, Mises did have inside information. In *Notes and Recollections,* he wrote that friends and acquaintances in the Austrian business sector as well as in branches of the Austrian government kept him exceptionally well-informed about the behind-the-scenes forces at work, including the often corrupt misuse of power and position by politicians and special interest groups.[24]

Ludwig von Mises and his defense of reason in the period between the two World Wars

In his review of *Nationalökonomie,* Hayek had referred to the "intellectual spaciousness" of the work that made it resemble more the creation "of an eighteenth-century philosopher than that of a modern specialist." It was not only the breadth of integrated knowledge that made Mises' contributions appear in the same category as the writings of the Enlightenment. It was also Mises' insistence upon and devotion to reason and rational thought in all matters pertaining to the study of man and the human condition. Hayek, however, came to criticize this aspect of Mises' system of ideas, charging him with being too much "a child of the rationalist age of enlightenment."[25] He believed that Mises suffered from both factual error and an "extreme rationalism" in thinking that it was "rational insight into its general benefits that led to the spreading of the market economy."[26]

Hayek's accusation seems to be justified on the basis of the following passages, the first from Mises' treatise *Socialism:* "Society is the product of thought and will. It does not exist outside of thought and will."[27] And this one from *Human Action:* "Any given social order was thought out and designed before it could be realized."[28] What could be more glaring examples of what Hayek has called "constructivist rationalism," the idea that man has consciously created the human institutions and the social order in which he lives or that he can intentionally redesign them at will.[29] And what statements are these to be made by a leading member of a school of thought whose founder emphasized "[t]he theoretical understanding of those social phenomena which are not the product of agreement or of positive legislation, but are unintended results of historical development."[30]

That Mises should be accused of such an "extreme rationalism" is even more peculiar due to the fact that when Hayek delivered the inaugural lecture at the London School of Economics in 1933, "The Trend of Economic Thinking," and gave his first real formulation of and emphasis to the idea of society not as a planned organization but as

> the spontaneous interplay of the actions of individuals [who] may produce something which is not the deliberate object of their actions but an organism in which every part performs a necessary function for the continuance of the whole, without any human mind having devised it,

it was to Mises' own discussion of this point in *Socialism* to which Hayek referred the reader in text and footnote.[31]

And, indeed, Mises rejected a deliberative contract theory of society and its institutions, arguing that there was no historical justification for the claims that this was the origin of any society. Such institutions as law and property emerged and evolved only slowly over many generations, as did the concepts of "justice" and "rights." The advocates of natural law, Mises argued, have

> erred in regarding this great change, which lifts man from the state of brutes into human society, as a conscious process; as an action, that is, in which man is completely aware of his motives, of his aims and how to pursue them ... Because it led to present conditions, people regarded the development of social life as absolutely purposeful and rational ... Today we have other theories with which to explain the matter.[32]

Mises, no less than Hayek, emphasized the importance of Menger's explanation of the origin of money and other social institutions as "the unintended result, the unplanned outcome of specifically individual efforts of members of society."[33] In fact, he said that Menger's contribution was central "for the elucidation of the fundamental principles of praxeology and its methods of research," and quoted the same passage from Menger included in the previous sentence.[34]

How then do we reconcile the earlier passages quoted from Mises that led Hayek to criticize his "rationalism" with Mises' own appreciation of Menger on the very theme that Hayek considered crucial for any legitimate theory of society and the role and limits of economic policy?

For Mises, reason is man's unique feature and characteristic. Action, in Mises' formulation, is the conscious and purposeful pursuit of preferred ends. To undertake a course of action, the actor must believe that there are means or methods capable of reaching the desired goals. Hence, man searches for causalities in the physical and social world in which he lives that might serve as the paths to the attainment of his chosen ends. That he imagines possible preferred states of affairs and contemplates courses of action to bring them possibly into existence means that he thinks that the choices he makes, and the actions undertaken on the basis of them, can make the future different from what it might be if not for his intervention.

Thus, from the actor's point of view, the future is not predetermined or foreordained; he may be able to influence the shape of things to come. The future therefore is shrouded in a degree of uncertainty; that is, it could develop in one way or some other(s), partly based on the actor's decisions and actions. This means, as well, that the actor deliberates and acts on the basis of limited and imperfect knowledge; otherwise, he would already know (or believed he knew) beforehand, what "choices" he *had to make* and what their outcomes by necessity *had to be*. His behavior would no longer be what Mises defines as "action."[35]

Every action, in Mises' framework, is therefore an instance of reason applied to purpose:

Action is preceded by thinking. Thinking is to deliberate beforehand over future action and to reflect upon past action. Thinking and acting are inseparable. Every action is always based on a definite idea about causal relations. He who thinks a causal relation thinks a theorem. Action without thinking, practice without theory are unimaginable. The reasoning may be faulty and the theory incorrect; but thinking and theorizing are not lacking in any action.[36]

Every personal or interpersonal action, therefore, is based on thinking and willing. It is based on a theory of the relevant causality to attain an end in mind. It does not mean that the actor, with full deliberative reflection, rethinks the theoretical reasoning behind every repeated action he follows on the basis of, say, routine.[37] Nor, certainly, does it suggest that the actor has clearly thought through or even is able to comprehend all of the implications and possibilities that may reside in the implicit theory that serves as the background for the actions he has and is undertaking.

But, nonetheless, from Mises' standpoint, to enter into an exchange requires that in each of the trader's minds the actor has conceived the idea of an improvement of his respective circumstance by giving up something he values less highly for something he values more highly. He thinks that such an improvement can be obtained by giving up some quantity of what he has for some quantity of another good in the possession of another. He thinks he can communicate and bargain with this other, and that "cooperation" rather than "conflict" is possible; that the other will reciprocate in like manner. And he thinks that a bargain can be struck and the terms – the price – can be agreed upon and the goods will be transferred. The actors may have thought about all this in a highly unsystematic way in comparison to the social and economic theorist's far more formal explanation of their conduct. But for the actors to have acted in the way they did, for them to have seen this as the meaning in their actions, they would nonetheless have had to formulate the causal chains in their minds that implicitly reflect a theory of the potential method and outcome of an act of exchange.[38]

In this thought process, Mises argued, there is, though rudimentary, the essence of a formulation of a social order of mutual cooperation based on the method of agreed-upon exchange. The actor need not have thought about his own thought processes in any such consciously "system" manner; indeed, it is not required of him and is not a part of his purpose or horizon. Nevertheless, interactions of these types have within themselves the potential for results that were no part of the actor's intention. A system of thought concerning a possible form of human association is what Mises called an "ideology":[39]

This temporal and logical precedence of an ideological factor does not imply the proposition that people draft a complete plan of a social system as the utopians do. What is and must be thought out in advance is not the concerting of individual actions into an integrated system of social organization, but the actions of individuals with regard to their fellow men and of already formed groups of individuals with regard to other groups. Before a man aids his fellow in cutting a tree, such cooperation must be thought out. Before an act of barter takes place, the idea of mutual exchange of goods and services must be conceived. It is not necessary that the individuals concerned become aware of the fact that such mutuality results in the establishment of social bonds and in the emergence of a social system. The individual does not plan and execute actions intended to construct society. His conduct and the corresponding conduct of others generate social bodies.[40]

If Mises' adamant and repeated insistence that society is the product of deliberative human action is so sharply drawn that it caused a misunderstanding in someone as conversant with Mises' thought as Hayek, it should be kept in mind what were some of the leading characteristics of the German-language intellectual environment in which Mises was called to do battle in that long period between the two world wars. These years, especially in central Europe, rang with calls to the "blood" and the "race." They appealed to irrational "instincts" and primordial "drives," claims that communal entities of the "nation" or "*Volk*" or "class" not merely transcended the mind and interests of the individual, but were not intelligible by "bourgeois" or "Jewish" logic, or traditional scientific methods of discourse.[41]

Mises referred to it as the "revolt against reason." As he expressed in 1931, as the ideological forces were accelerating in Germany that would bring Hitler and primitive race-collectivism to power two years later:

> The romantic revolt against logic and science does not limit itself to the sphere of social phenomena and the sciences of human action. It is a revolt against our entire culture and civilization. [Its proponents] demand the renunciation of scientific knowledge and the return to the faith and the bucolic conditions of the Middle Ages, and all Germans ... joyfully agree with them ... We should not deceive ourselves about the fact that today not only the masses, but also the educated public – those who are called intellectuals – are not to be found on the side of science in this controversy ... It is with horror that we now witness the maturation of the fruits of the policy that results from this abdication of the intellect ... The fate of mankind – progress on the road that western civilization has taken for thousands of years, or a rapid plunge into chaos from which there is no way out, from which no new life as we know it will ever develop – depends on whether this condition persists.[42]

He was not alone in saying this. In February 1933, a week after Hitler came to power, the German free market economist Wilhelm Röpke delivered a public lecture in Frankfurt am Main, in which he said that the Germans were in the grip of a "revolt against reason, freedom and humanity." Nazism was the culmination of Germany's slide into "illiberal barbarism" based on "a longing for state slavery," an "irrationalism" calling for the German people to be guided by "blood," "soil," and a "storm of destructive and unruly emotion" and a "brutalism" in which "[t]he beast of prey in man is extolled with unexampled cynicism, and with equal cynicism every immoral and brutal act is justified by the sanctity of the political end."[43]

In 1935, Mises' friend, the French Classical Liberal Louis Rougier, referred to the phenomena as the political and economic mystiques of the age, beliefs which could not be demonstrated by reason, but which were blindly accepted for irrational reasons. The greatest of them in the interwar period, Rougier argued, was the "totalitarian mystique," in which conceptual realism was triumphant and the political collective became "real," with a purpose and destiny of its own – what the fascists called the "corporate nation," the Nazis called "the racial community of the people," and the communists called the historical laws of class conflict.[44]

In this setting, Mises clearly felt called upon to forcefully challenge and attack the mythologies of national, racial, and class collectivism, and the appeals to pure "urges," "force," and polylogisms of various types. It is possible to understand, therefore, the reasons behind his constant reminders and explanations that only individuals think and act, that reason and logic are the same for all men and in all places, that there is only one reality with its natural laws in the physical world and its economic laws in the orbit of man; and that society and the social order have no origin and existence outside the human actions of individual participants.[45]

Ludwig von Mises as political economist: a theory of society as a foundation for Classical Liberalism

In Mises' view, the greatest contribution of British Classical Economics as it developed in the eighteenth and first half of the nineteenth centuries was its demonstration of the higher productivity that arose out of human collaborative participation in a system of division of labor. Ricardo's theory of comparative advantage was really a formulation of the human *law of association,* Mises said.[46] The Ricardian insight clearly showed that both the "weak" and the "strong" benefited from exchange and a process of mutual interdependency. The earlier theories of societal order, that claimed that society was the product of contract or imposed organization by a powerful authority or divine intervention, were not only historically false or unprovable, but also created the idea that there was a potentially permanent conflict between the interests of the individual and the social group.

With the Classical Economists' contribution, it was possible to show how society had emerged and taken form over the centuries as the result of individuals discovering the mutual benefits from trade, the additional gains by individuals specializing in particular lines of production, and the resulting expanding network of human relationships that evolved from this process of growing interdependency. The theory of the division of labor, therefore, is able to serve as the analytical tool for explaining society as being the result of human action but not of any prior blueprint of human design. As Mises explained it:

> The task with which science is faced in respect of the origins of society can only consist in the demonstration of those factors that can and must result in

association and its progressive intensification. Praxeology solves the problem. If and in so far as labor under the division of labor is more productive than isolated labor, and if and as far as man is able to realize this fact, human action itself tends toward cooperation and association ... The [Ricardian] law of association makes us comprehend the tendencies which resulted in the progressive intensification of human cooperation. We conceive what incentive induced people to not consider themselves simply as rivals in a struggle for the appropriation of the limited supply of means of subsistence made available by nature. We realize what has impelled them and permanently impels them to consort with one another for the sake of cooperation. Every step forward on the way to a more developed mode of the division of labor serves the interests of all participants ... Thus we are in a position to comprehend the course of social evolution.[47]

The process that leads from narrow tribal group existence to a great society of human cooperation did not happen overnight and not without much confusion and limited understanding of the benefits of peaceful association. Nonetheless, conflicts and combat to the death are replaced with peace terms that allow the possibilities for human collaboration; from this societal evolutionary perspective, even slavery can be viewed as a step in man's social development. Belligerents slowly formulate rules of warfare that limit the terms of engagement and the procedure for settling the conflicts; men begin to think of future cooperative relationships with the "enemy," when the war is over.[48]

Not only does peace become a concept of value for furthering the interests of members of conflicting groups, it becomes the foundation for the cultural development of man. For only a few and then for a slowly widening circle of people, the greater material productivity of a peaceful division of labor provides the means for the development of what we call civilization. The means are provided that enable the leisure and the peace of mind for art, literature, and scientific and philosophic reflection. Men increasingly become differentiated from each other, but not only in the specialized tasks and skills through which they find their place in the division of labor. They differentiate also in the sense that they have the time to develop their distinct individual personalities on the basis of the use they make of the greater means that are at their disposal, and the interests and pursuits they find attractive to devote their available time to cultivate. Individualism, meaning man as distinct from a tribal mass and unique in his character and qualities as a singular human being, becomes one of the products of this evolution of society through the extension and intensification of the system of division of labor.[49]

That great achievement of the Classical Economists, Mises said, was to see the logic of this process and explain it in a systematic fashion, in a way that had not been understood before. Their theory of division of labor and comparative advantage became the basis for a "science of society."[50] A foundation was laid for the theory of market relationships, the interconnections between supplies and demands and the network of market prices for finished goods and the factors of production. Now was opened the discovery of "the inevitable laws of the market and exchange" that is "one of the great achievements of the human mind."[51] Out of the Classical Economists' theory of division of labor there developed the eighteenth-century Classical Liberal "philosophy of peace and social coopera- tion," Mises said, that became the basis "for the astonishing development of the economic civilization of that age."[52]

It was encapsulated in David Hume's famous conclusion to his essay, "Of the Jealousy of Trade," when he said, "I shall venture to acknowledge, that, not only as a man, but as a British subject, I pray for the flourishing commerce of Germany, Spain, Italy, and even France itself. I am at least certain, that Great Britain, and all those nations, would flourish more, did their sovereigns and min- isters adopt such enlarged and benevolent sentiments towards each other."[53] No longer were individuals and nations enemies in which the economic improve- ment of one requires an economic loss to another. Instead, all nations benefit from the productive capabilities of their potential trading partners by opening the opportunities for greater markets for one's own goods as the means to acquire from others what they could produce better and cheaper than if one attempted to manufacture them at home. Peace and free trade became the avenues to prosper- ity and freedom.

With the development of "the Liberal Social Philosophy the human mind becomes aware of the overcoming of the principle of violence by the principle of peace," Mises said.[54] No longer is man groping in the dark, sometimes sensing and moving in the direction of the gains from collaborative trade and associ- ation, and at other times regressing into antagonistic antisocial relations of con- quest, plunder, and violence.[55] The theory of a division of labor and peaceful trade now becomes a conscious framework for understanding, evaluating, and proposing policies in the social order.[56] Man can now purposefully take steps to move the social order in the direction of liberal association. "In Liberalism humanity becomes conscious of the powers which guide its development," Mises argued. "The darkness which lay over the paths of history recedes. Man begins to understand social life and allows it to develop consciously."[57]

For Mises, the triumph of free enterprise within nations and free trade between nations in the nineteenth century demonstrated the efficacy of the new conscious awareness of the principles of social cooperation. Indeed, it was the triumph of *Classical Liberal planning*. "[T]he British government in the liberal age certainly had a definite plan," Mises stated. "Its plan was private ownership of the means of production, free initiative and market economy. Great Britain was very prosperous indeed under this plan."[58]

A complete discussion of Mises' social philosophy would require an analysis of his conception of utilitarianism and his defense of it in his various writings, a discussion that goes beyond the limits of this chapter. But it may suffice to explain that he rejected all theories of the social good derived from and based upon theology and natural rights. World views that attempted to develop and incorporate a general cosmology of the natural order and man's place in it were considered as going beyond what either man's reason or experience could ration- ally prove and justify. Neither reason nor scientific methods of evaluating evid- ence, for example, could prove the existence of God, that any particular set of values were God's code for man to follow, or that a certain set of human institutions were the ones – and only ones – laid down as God's moral and social order for man. Mises neither denigrated nor denied the importance of such questions; indeed, the fact that man had been asking himself for all of recorded history these questions about the why of his existence and how he should live his life to give it both meaning and purpose demonstrated the importance of them. It was just that in Mises' judgment reason by itself could not provide the answer, nor could reason alone differentiate between alternative visions of these ultimate questions for the determination as to which was the true and only right one.[59]

Also a central element in Mises' social philosophy was the idea that the ends that men chose to follow – the values, final purposes, the ultimate meanings they gave to their lives – were not open to rational debate and settlement. These were based upon metaphysical beliefs, attitudes, or conceptions about which there exists no final proof or demonstrable evidence to confirm that one ultimate end or hierarchy of ends are the "objectively" correct or true ones. Reason's role, he said, is its ability to analyze the efficacy of means applied for the achievement of ends.

Mises accepted the fact that no human science, including economics, could say by itself that life was better than death, that health was better than sickness, and that material comfort and prosperity were better than poverty and hunger. He did not believe that from any conception of the "is" a particular "ought" could be directly derived. That is why economic theory might be a fundamentally important conceptual tool to aid in the analysis of social and economic policy questions, but was not on its own a justification of or an apology for laissez faire or any other notion of a desirable social order.[60]

Classical Liberalism was a vision of appropriate human relationships that had emerged in the eighteenth and nineteenth centuries out of the insights of the Classical Economists, Mises said, but was distinct from economics as a value-free science. What Classical Liberalism had learned from economics was that from the perspective of the social and economic order as a whole, there need be no long-run conflicts between the interests of the individual and the interests of society (meaning the interests of all other individual members participating in collaborative endeavors through a system of division of labor). The theory of division of labor had shown that all participants are made better off through specialization and exchange than in an existence of isolated self-sufficiency; that the quantities, varieties, and qualities of the goods and services available to people are greater and better than under autarky.

Property and property ownership, Mises argued, had been shown to play an important social function, beyond whether or not, and any degree to which, a particular property owner successfully accumulated a great amount of material wealth as a result of applying his property in productive ways. In the system of division of labor under conditions of voluntary exchange, property owners could only improve their own circumstances through their effective use of the means of production under their control or supervision. And an effective use meant directing those factors of production in the service of satisfying the wants of others, upon whom any particular property owner was dependent for the goods and services he desired to acquire from them.[61]

Classical Liberalism, distinct from economic theory, also made an empirical statement about men in general: that the vast majority of human beings throughout history had demonstrated a preference for material improvement and comfort, both for themselves and for others about whom they cared. The fundamental value judgment upon which Classical Liberalism was based, as Mises formulated it, was that such material improvement was both good and the appropriate rationale for evaluating social and economic policy.

Mises emphasized that this did not mean that Classical Liberalism ignored or discounted other values of a nonmaterial type that men desired and tried to attain – such things as peace of mind, happiness, a personal sense of meaning and purpose, or joyful and fulfilling shared experience with others. But these were things that the material goods of life by themselves could not provide. Each man had to find these things inside himself. But it was obvious, Mises stated, that the pursuit of these "higher" goals and ends were made that much easier to the extent to which man's thoughts and actions need not be crowded each day with concerns of bare human survival. The material things of life not only alleviated hunger, but also provided the means for man to have both the leisure time and the means to pursue these other – possibly higher – purposes.

The task of social policy, in Mises' view, was to determine what arrangement of the political and economic order would be most conducive to facilitating the maximum opportunity for material improvement so men may use those material means to serve any individual ends and goals they may have chosen as the ones most important, respectively, to them. This task is a form of social engineering, Mises argued:

> The organization of human society according to the pattern most suitable for the attainment of the ends in view is a quite prosaic and matter-of-fact question, not unlike, say, the construction of a railroad or the production of cloth or furniture ... [H]owever lofty may be the sphere in which political and social questions are placed, they still refer to matters that are subject to human control and must consequently be judged according to the canons of human reason. In such matters, no less than in all other mundane affairs, mysticism is only an evil ... Problems of social policy are problems of social technology, and their solution must be sought in the same ways and by the same means that are at our disposal in the solution of other technical problems: by rational reflection and by examination of the given conditions. All that man is and all that raises him above the animals he owes to his reason. Why should he forgo the use of reason just in the sphere of social policy and trust to vague and obscure feelings and impulses?[62]

In this context, no set of traditions, customs, or political institutional orders could be said to stand above rational discourse and be outside modification and change if reasoned deliberation suggested that the social good would be best served by such an alteration. This applied, Mises said, even to the U.S. Constitution:

It is rather unimportant that this pro or that con corresponds to some law or constitutional document, even if it should be as venerable and famous as the Constitution of the United States of America. If human legislation proves to be ill-suited to the end in view, it must be changed. A discussion of the suitability of policy can never accept the argument that it runs counter to statute, law or constitution.[63]

Mises did not claim that man's knowledge had reached the point at which no further progress was possible, and that it was now in his power to finally specify the social and economic institutional conditions most objectively conducive for man's material and personal improvement. Indeed, he went out of his way to insist that such arrogance would always be misplaced. After all, he reminded his readers of John Stuart Mill's claim in 1848 – twenty-five years before the emergence of the theory of subjective value – that there was nothing more of fundamental importance to explain in the theory of value. "An error of this kind on the part of such a man," Mises pointed out, "must ever stand as a warning to all theorists."[64] "Economic theory is not perfect. No human work is built for eternity. New theorems may supplement or supplant the old ones," Mises stated.[65]

Hence, Classical Liberalism, as an ideology applying the insights from economic theory to questions of social policy, may have to be modified and revised as economic knowledge improved. Indeed, his own restatement of the principles and policy implications of Classical Liberalism was based on the idea that the arguments had to be presented anew precisely because the contributions of economics, sociology, and political philosophy had not stood still since the high watermark of the Classical Economists in the early nineteenth century. And, thus, the Classical Liberal perspective was not unchanged since that earlier time either.[66]

Ludwig von Mises as political economist: evaluating possible systems of social cooperation

In early February 1933, Friedrich A. Hayek sent Ludwig von Mises a draft of the lecture, "The Trend of Economic Thinking," that he would deliver that March at the London School of Economics. A week later, Mises sent Hayek his comments, in which he said that:

There is a substantive divergence in our views in that you discuss the issue of laissez faire in the traditional manner rather than from the standpoint of the various organizational possibilities of societal collaboration (i.e., individual property, communal property, etc.), a distinction that I make in my own work. From my standpoint it is essential that the issue is not whether to choose laissez faire or an omnipotent state, but rather which of a limited number of conceivable types of organization is best suited or the only appropriate organization for allowing human cooperation in the economy.[67]

What Mises seemed to object to in this draft of Hayek's lecture was the absence of a particular ordering principle in the context of which Mises believed questions concerning economic systems needed to be investigated. Hayek emphasized the misdirection the German Historical School had given to economic reasoning by rejecting "theory" in place of a narrow study of "the facts" of history; he also focused on the failure of later economists who were influenced by these German Historicists from any longer having a full appreciation of the "spontaneous institutions" that generate an order to economic and social processes, the recognition of which demarcates economic science's distinct subject matter.[68]

Hayek suggested that socialists had slowly come to realize that many of the features they most objected to in the market economy – such as interest – would have to be incorporated in a planned economy if a rational use of resources were to occur.[69] "The best the dictator could do in such a case would be to imitate as closely as possible what would happen under free competition," Hayek said. The leading hurdle preventing the "wise planner" from doing so, in Hayek's view, was the pressures of special interest groups who lobbied for the maintenance of the status quo upon which their present income positions were dependent.[70] He also argued that appreciation of the spontaneous order of the market did not imply a "purely negative attitude" toward the role of the state in economic affairs. Indeed, he hoped that the generally critical stance toward government intervention by economists, due to the often naive and uninformed policy prescriptions of the "lay mind," would "not prevent economists from devoting more attention to the positive task of delimiting the field of useful State activity ... To remedy this deficiency must be one of the main tasks of the future."[71]

For Mises the most important contribution to economic theory in his time had been the discovery of the logical impossibility of rational economic calculation under a system of comprehensive socialist central planning.[72] The nature and requirements for economic calculation were the cornerstones for evaluating and judging the political practicability of alternative economic systems. This is the context for understanding Mises' remark in his letter to Hayek.

It would be completely incorrect, of course, to suggest that the need for an institutional method for economic calculation had never been considered before Mises' writings on the subject beginning in the 1920s. Mises himself drew attention to the fact that in the 1850s Hermann Gossen had pointed out that "only with the establishment of private property can the yardstick be found for the determination of the optimal quantity of each commodity to be produced under given circumstances" and that under a communal system of ownership "the central authority – projected by the communist – for the purpose of allocating the different types of labor and their rewards would soon find that it has set itself a task that far exceeds the power of any individual."[73] In the 1870s, Walter Bagehot had given great emphasis to the central role of a market-created money in enabling the calculation of profits and costs, without which an efficient allocation of capital among alternative productive uses could never occur.[74] And in the last decades of the nineteenth and first decade of the twentieth centuries, a number of economists demonstrated the inherent difficulties in a system of socialist planning without private property, market competition, and money prices."[75]

The development of the necessity for and methods of economic calculation, Mises argued, arose from the evolution of society. As social relationships emerged from the hegemonic, or command, type to that of an increasing circle of contract and freer exchange, and as trading relationships grew and became more complex, men began to devise the intellectual techniques for estimating whether various transactions had brought them profits or losses.[76] This process was inseparable as well from the emergence of a medium of exchange through which a common denominator was offered. On this basis, the various hetero-geneous physical goods and means of production traded on the market could now be expressed in a simplified form for easy comparison and evaluation of their value and cost in alternative uses.

Hayek has often been credited for drawing special attention to the fact that the "economic problem" is really and ultimately a "knowledge problem," in the sense that a system of division of labor carries with it a resulting division of knowledge that requires an institutional solution for coordinating the activities of multitudes of market participants.[77] Yet, in Hayek's first detailed discussion of the nature of this problem, his 1936 presidential address before the London Economic Club on "Economics and Knowledge," it was to Mises' *Socialism* that he drew the readers' attention.[78] There Mises had stated, "In societies based on the division of labor, the distribution of property rights effects a kind of mental division of labor, without which neither economy nor systematic production would be possible."[79]

Indeed, the necessity for a method enabling economic calculation arises from the finite abilities of the human mind, in Mises' view. Under fairly simple pro-duction within the primitive household and where the stages through which pro-duction must pass are extremely short and hardly roundabout at all, a decision-maker might be able to reasonably choose among alternative ways of achieving his ends among the limited possibilities. But once the methods of pro-duction become more complex and involve comparing and choosing among technologically more diverse ways of pursuing goals in mind, the task grows beyond the ability of unaided thought processes.[80] "[I]n the bewildering chaos of alternative materials and processes the human mind would be at a complete loss," Mises said.[81]

> [N]o single man, be he the greatest genius ever born, has an intellect capable of deciding the relative importance of each one of an infinite number of goods of higher order. No individual could so discriminate between the infi-nite number of alternative methods of production that he could make direct judgments of their relative value without auxiliary calculation.[82]

This intellectual difficulty is only overcome through the existence of private property, market competition, and money prices. The system of market prices provides a method of orientation for the individual in making his own choices concerning the use of the resources at his disposal, and they provide the link between the multitudes of individuals participating in the system of division of labor.[83] Through the price system for both finished goods and the factors of production, the valuations and appraisements of all market participants can be shared and brought to bear in determining what goods should be produced and the opportunity costs of applying the means of production among their possible alternative uses in the market as a whole.[84]

Each individual plays two roles in this process. As a consumer he provides information about his valuations for consumer goods, and thus assists in the formation of consumer goods prices. As a producer, he appraises the most highly valued employment for his factor services, thus contributing to the pricing of the factors of production and their allocation among alternative lines of production.[85] Central, therefore, to Mises' criticism of socialism as a viable economic system in place of the market economy was that

> [i]t must forgo the intellectual division of labor that consists in the coopera-
> tion of all entrepreneurs, landowners, and workers as producers and con-
> sumers in the formation of market prices. But without it, rationality, i.e., the
> possibility of economic calculation, is unthinkable.[86]

In Mises' view, therefore, "Monetary calculation is the guiding star under the system of division of labor. It is the compass of the man embarking upon production."[87] For whom is economic calculation important? For each and every individual, and it only has meaning from his point of view. It is the method through which the individual evaluates either the outcome of actions he has undertaken in the past, or estimates the possible results of actions he is contemplating for the future. From either perspective, any profits or losses calculated are only meaningful in the context of the actor's circumstances, his judgments concerning the meaning of actions done or actions imagined. And, thus, prices and the economic calculations made on their basis are clearly tools for evaluation in the context of the actor's knowledge of alternatives forgone in the past, or weighed in deliberating about the future.

In "Economics and Knowledge," Hayek also argued that the limits of the pure logic of choice arose from the fact that any formal conclusions concerning the consistency among actions only relate to the individual whose conduct is being analyzed, in terms of the knowledge and facts of the situation as known to him. "It is only because of this," said Hayek, "that the propositions we deduce are necessarily a priori valid and that we preserve the consistency of the argument."[88] They offer no direct solution to the problem of how interpersonal plans may be coordinated in the market when the knowledge and facts known to the various market participants may diverge. Hayek seemed to imply that the shortcoming of focusing only upon the "a priori" validity of economic theorems relating to individuals, rather than including additional and clearly empirical assumptions concerning how men can acquire knowledge about the actions of others for interpersonal coordination, was one that Mises was guilty of since the only footnote reference given in Hayek's text was to Mises' discussion of "The Scope and Meaning of the A Priori Theorems" in economics in the latter's *Epistemological Problems of Economics*.[89]

But it is also clear that, just as in Hayek's later discussion in his famous essay on "The Use of Knowledge in Society,"[90] it is the price system that Mises considers the informational tool through which individuals are able to tend toward a coordination of their actions and plans. Why else would Mises build an entire critique against the possibility of economic planning under socialism if not for the simple fact that it is the price system that assists people in rationally choosing the most economical, the least-cost methods of production, given the competing uses and demands of others in the society for the same scarce means of production through which each is trying to attain his ends? Why else would he have stated that,

> The pricing process is a social process. It is consummated by an interaction of all members of the society ... Competing in cooperation and cooperating in competition all people are instrumental in bringing about the result, viz., the price structure of the market, the allocation of the factors of production to the various lines of want-satisfaction and the determination of the share of each individual. These three events are not three different matters. They are only different aspects of one indivisible phenomenon that our analytical scrutiny separates into three parts.[91]

Furthermore, when Mises would say, for example, that "To the entrepreneur of capitalist society a factor of production through its price sends out a warning: Don't touch me, I am earmarked for the satisfaction of another, more important need," what was this but an emphasis on the informational role of prices?[92] The market price for factors of production do in fact inform that in the competitive rivalry for employing them there are alternative uses unknown to the individual decision maker, which must be taken into consideration. He then uses those prices to calculate from within his own corner of the market which of the potential combinations of the factors of production might minimize the costs of manufacture.

The distinguishing characteristic of Mises' theory of social cooperation through the market in comparison to Hayek's is that Mises developed a theory of entrepreneurship and the coordinating role of the entrepreneur in bringing about a tendency for equilibrium – for a multi-personal coordination of plans. Entrepreneurs are the

> driving force of the market process ... They approach the owners of the factors of production, and their competition sends the prices of these factors up to the limit corresponding to their anticipation of the future prices of the products. They approach the consumers, and their competition forces prices of consumers' goods down to the point at which the whole supply can be sold. Profit-seeking speculation is the driving force of the market as it is the driving force of production.[93]

"It is this competitive driving force for profit on the part of entrepreneurs, "Mises argued, "that does not tolerate the preservation of *false* prices of the factors of production."[94]

Each entrepreneur is guided by his own appraisements and expectations concerning the shape of things to come – his personal knowledge, beliefs, and imperfect information in the division of labor. But the market's "objective" test, as to whether the individual entrepreneur has formed correct expectations about the demands of the consumers and the best use of means of production, are the monetary profits or losses he gains or suffers. The continuous "selection process" of the market serves the social purpose – the "unintended" purpose from the individual actor's point of view – of constantly tending to shift control over the means of production to those who have more successfully anticipated future consumer demands and better devised ways of producing goods at the least opportunity cost of resource use in comparison to his rivals, and away from those who have demonstrated a poorer capacity to do these things in comparison to his competitors.[95]

Furthermore, while it was not as clear in his earlier works, Mises did offer an "empirical" theory of how actors formed expectations about the actions and plans of others for purposes of designing their own market-oriented plans. Adapting Max Weber's notion of the "ideal type," in *Human Action,* in *Theory and History,* and *Ultimate Foundations of Economic Science,* Mises explained that no individual has knowledge of the actions and plans of others other than on the basis of "experience." That all men do act and plan, that there is logic to their conduct, is a knowledge that could never be acquired from "experience" if we could not "look within ourselves" to comprehend what it means to plan, choose, and act through the mental act of introspection. But introspection and the formal logic of action tell nothing about the specific choices and actions undertaken by people in the past, or the choices and actions they may undertake in the future.

Through interactions with others in business and other settings, from the written word and other sources of information about the past, and from the most recent actions and activities of others and groups of others, individuals construct images in their minds of "ideal types" of the characteristics and qualities of those other men. With this experience-based information and knowledge the decision maker forms judgments concerning the possible and most likely actions and patterns of action that others may follow in those future settings over which he is constructing his own plans of action. These ideal typifications, along with all other forms and types of knowledge and information about the social situation that the actor considers relevant, serve as the method for evaluating what market prices may mean in terms of the future course of human events. Mises admitted that in comparison to the apparent exactitude and determinism of some of the methods of the natural sciences, this alternative method of "understanding" might seem imprecise and inexact; but it was, he argued, the only tool open to actors wishing to anticipate to some degree the likely conduct of others for interpersonal planning.[96]

The pivotal point around which any evaluation of the relative merits of alternative economic systems of social order had to be constructed, therefore, in Mises' framework, was the capacity for economic calculation. This was the standard for comparison by which a market economy, a socialist economy, and an interventionist economy had to be judged. The "impossibility" of socialism arose from the fact that a fully comprehensive system of central planning abolished the only institutional prerequisites for a rational use of society's means of production in terms of attempting to satisfy as many consumer ends in the best and most economical way, given the expression of those ends in the form of consumer demand on the market.

Socialist planning eliminated the institutional avenues – private property and market competition – through which individuals are able to express their estimates of the value of goods and means of production on the market on the basis of their bids and offers, and buying and selling of these scarce items. Prices could not emerge as the composite outcome and expression of these multitudes of individual valuations and appraisements. And as Mises concisely said: 'Where there is no market there is no price system, and where there is no price system there can be no economic calculation."[97] The divided knowledge of society had no mechanism under socialism for concentration into a simple and usable form for purposes of the individual planning that is essential for coordination of all the activities in the complex system of division of labor. Thus, he concluded, "Human cooperation under the system of the social division of labor is possible only in the market economy. Socialism is not a realizable system of society's economic organization because it lacks any method of economic calculation."[98]

This conclusion was one that Mises thought should have been simple to accept. Either socialism offers institutions enabling effective coordination of the actions of the participants in the system of division of labor, or it does not. As he argued:

> It is difficult to see how people can decide that Socialism is any way better than Capitalism unless they can maintain that it functions better as a social system. With the same justification it might be said that a machine constructed on the basis of perpetual motion would be better than one worked according to the given laws of mechanics – if only it could be made to function reliably. If the concept of Socialism contains an error which prevents that system from doing what it is supposed to do, then Socialism cannot be compared with the Capitalist system, for this has proved itself workable. Neither can it be called nobler, more beautiful or more just.[99]

Interventionism, on the other hand, did not abolish the market economy and its institutions of private property, market competition, and money prices. Interventionism did, however, interfere with the market's normal functioning by deflecting prices and production from the patterns they would have taken if guided and determined solely by the forces of supply and demand. The context in which Mises presented his critique of interventionism may be understood in the following passage from an article that he wrote in 1931 on the nature of market relationships and the effect from various types of government intervention:

> The structure of our society rests on the division of labor and on the private ownership of the means of production. In this system the means of production are privately owned and are used either by the owners themselves – the capitalists and landowners – for production or are turned over to other entrepreneurs who carry out the production partly with their own and partly

with others' means of production. In the capitalist system the market functions as the regulator of production. The price structure of the market decides what should be produced, how, and in what quantity. Through the structure of commodity prices, wages, and interest rates, the market brings supply and demand into agreement, and sees to it that each branch of production is as strongly supplied as corresponds to the extent and the intensity of the effective demand. Thus, capitalistic production derives its meaning from the market. Of course, a mismatch between production and demand can temporarily occur, but the structure of market prices sees to it that the balance is reestablished in a short time. Only if the mechanism of the market is disturbed by external interventions, if the effect of market prices on the regulation of production is prevented, are severe disturbances produced which can no longer be remedied by the automatic reactions of the market, disturbances that are not temporary but prolonged.[100]

A single intervention or sets of interventions introduced into the market disrupt and interfere with the interdependent relationships that are coordinated through the competitively generated structure of relative prices for finished goods and the factors of production. Mises summarized the fruits of interventionism in the period between the world wars in Europe in the same article.

For two generations now the policy of the European nations has been based on nothing else than preventing and eliminating the function of the market as the regulator of production. By duties and trade-policy measures of other sorts, by legal requirements and prohibitions, by the subsidization of uncompetitive enterprises, by the suppression or throttling of business that offers unwelcomed competition to the spoiled children of the political regime through the regulation of prices, interest rates and wages, the attempt is made to force production into paths which it otherwise would not have taken. Under the protection of import duties, which destroy the unity of the world market, production is deflected from more profitable lines of production; cartels arise which are intent on preserving even the least efficient businesses and whose artificial support often only leads to the result that investment activity is guided into the wrong directions. Under the influence of the ideology of socialism, which today affects all thinking on economic policy, numerous enterprises have been taken out of the hands of entrepreneurs and capitalists, and put in the hands of governments and public administrations. In almost all cases these public administrations have proved a failure; the majority of these enterprises require more or less large subsidies from taxes, since they operate at considerable financial loss. To raise the money for this purpose and for subsidies of every sort, including unemployment relief – which calls for the greatest expenditure – taxes are increased again and again. These taxes have long since attacked not only income but also a not inconsiderable part of capital. The most prominent characteristic of the present reigning economic system [of interventionism] is that it consumes capital. The capitalist economy has an inherent tendency to increase the stock of capital. The system of state interventionism and state socialism, in contrast, leads to capital consumption. The result of these policies is the severe economic crisis under which we suffer today. The crisis had its starting point in mistaken economic policy, and it will not end until it is recognized that the task of governments is to create the necessary preconditions for the prosperous operation of the economy, and not squandering more on foolish expenditures than the industry of the population is able to provide.[101]

If the social function of the market system of competition and prices is to direct production into those avenues that continually tend to reflect the changing patterns of consumer demand and potentials for production, then interventionism by definition brings about resource allocations and price relationships inconsistent with this end. The social system of division of labor is prevented from being coordinated into those patterns in which each participant is guided to find the place that his comparative advantage suggests would be his most highly valued use in serving the ends of others as the means by which he earns the income to demand those productions from others he desires for his own purposes.

The distortions and imbalances that are necessarily part of the results from these interventions then produce a situation in which the interventionist must decide whether or not any significant negative side effects will now serve as the justification and rationale for additional interventions to compensate and attempt to correct the earlier interventions. Thus, in Mises' construction of the logic of interventionism, a "dynamic" is set in motion that generates the potential for an ever-expanding circle of interventions due to the disruptions previous interventions may have created. Mises' conclusion was that an interventionist system could be considered "unstable," in that if new interventions kept being added to try to adjust for the distortions and imbalances resulting from preceding interventions, the logical culmination from such interventionist policies would finally be a situation in which overall government control of the economy would be reached via a piecemeal process.

Mises understood that men could be led, by the attraction of short-run benefits through intervention, to lobby for the assistance of the state to interfere with the market. He was not ignorant of what today is understood as the economics of special interest group politics.[102] After all, the core ideas of this theory were articulated by the Classical Economists,[103] and given a formulation by another Austrian, Oskar Morgenstern, in the 1930s.[104]

But the perspective from which he asked people to look at the limits and problems of interventionism was from that of the market system as a whole. In other words, that individuals had incentives to gain at other people's expense through political favor and privilege, and that others lose as a result of this, was something fairly clear and obvious. The real question was why shouldn't they try to do so? What was at stake of being lost from a longer-run view of things?

The answer to this, in essence, was the weakening and ultimate destruction of the system of peaceful social cooperation. The greater the number of interest groups that obtained privileges and favors that restricted competition, manipulated prices or wages away from their market-determined levels, or redistributed income and wealth through political means, the potentially poorer and more disorganized society could become.

Resources would be directed to uses less than their most highly valued ones (as would be reflected by their use guided by market-determined prices and competition); imbalances would be created between the patterns of supply and demand; and incentives might be weakened for capital formation and the spirit for work among the most industrious. Group antagonisms would divide society, as social interaction became less "cooperation through competition," as Mises called it, and more conflict through political collusion.

To reverse this process, it was necessary to bring about a reawakened understanding of the principles of peaceful cooperation that the Classical Economists had discovered, and the Classical Liberals had fostered in an earlier time. And it was necessary to implement economic policies consistent with those principles to create the institutional foundation for free men to interact for mutual benefit and material improvement.

Ludwig von Mises as policy advocate: the need for an agenda for economic reform and reconstruction

In June 1946, Ludwig von Mises wrote a letter to his friend and former colleague at the Geneva Graduate Institute of International Studies, Paul Mantoux, the famous economic historian of the Industrial Revolution. They had been discussing the possibilities for economic reform in Europe, and Mantoux had disagreed with some of Mises' criticisms of the "third way," a system of moderate interventionist-welfare statism that had been proposed by Wilhelm Röpke in a series of books written during the war as a "third solution" to social problems in a world not willing to accept laissez faire capitalism and that would only face disaster if socialist central planning were adopted.[105]

In his letter Mises said:

> I am fully aware of the fact that under the present ideological conditions no statesman could venture to resort to a policy of outright liberalism (in the 19th century connotation of the term, not in the sense in which the term is used in present-day America). Given the state of pubic opinion, a certain amount of interventionism cannot be avoided, at the present juncture. But one should know, that in resorting to such measures one elects an evil, although an unavoidable one. If this insight is lacking, one continues in the application of these short-run makeshifts until their undesired and undesirable long-run effects bring about chaos and general unrest ... Therefore, I think that my analysis of the necessary consequences of all kinds of interventionism is of use also for those statesmen who believe that, as the wind blows now, another policy cannot be adopted. It is not merely a secluded doctrinaire's pastime.[106]

The role of the liberal economic policy analyst, therefore, from Mises' perspective, was fairly clear: his first duty was to the truth, to state what sound and logically correct economic theory deduced as the consequences that were most likely to follow from the introduction of any particular government intervention into the market economy. The statesman who, under the pressures of the prevailing ideas and ideologies of the time, may have to acquiesce or even introduce various interventions should be able to rely upon the economist's honest analysis as a benchmark and safeguard for evaluating the implications of such interventionist policies so as to have clearly in his mind the outcomes to which they may lead if not restrained beyond certain points.

The underlying belief behind Mises taking such a position was that the only path to the establishment of a Classical Liberal order of free market capitalism was through the use of reason and persuasion. "Whoever wants to see the world governed according to his own ideas must strive for dominion over men's minds," he said. "It is impossible, in the long-run, to subject men against their will to a regime that they reject."[107] In the ideological battle that Mises saw being waged around the world between market liberalism and various forms of collectivism, he insisted that it was "the Liberal belief that power depends upon a mastery over mind alone and that to obtain such mastery only spiritual weapons are effective."[108] Subterfuge and deception could never create good outcomes in the long run.[109]

The great tragedy of the twentieth century was that reason had lost its sway as the single legitimate tool for social change. Mises stated that Europe's descent into conflict and social destruction following World War I had been due to what he called the "liberation of the demons." The real significance of Lenin and the Bolshevik Revolution, he argued, was the rejection of the entire Western tradition of rule of law, restrictions on political violence, respect for the rights of individuals, and the use of peaceful democratic means for political change. Unrestrained force for political ends became the new principle for all of the socialist regimes that had appeared out of the ashes of World War I.[110] In this context, he emphasized that it was "important to realize that Fascism and Nazism were socialist dictatorships," and that both had been "committed to the Soviet principle of dictatorship and violent oppression of dissenters."[111]

He recalled that before the Great War, Benito Mussolini had been one of the leading socialists in Italy. His major heresy from Marxian orthodoxy had been his strong endorsement of Italy's entry into that war on the Allied side as a means to "liberate" Italian-speaking areas under Austrian control in the Alps. When the war ended, Mussolini organized the fascist movement, unifying Italian nationalists, economic collectivists, and various groups from all walks of life that had come to reject traditional Marxian socialism. Mussolini took his economic agenda from the philosophy of syndicalism – the idea that trades, crafts, professions, and industries should be grouped into mandatory cartels and unions through which the nation's economic system would be planned and directed under government supervision and control.[112] Mises pointed out that fascism "began with a split in the ranks of Marxian socialism ... Its economic program was borrowed from German non-Marxian socialism" and "... Its conduct of government affairs was a replica of Lenin's dictatorship. Corporativism, its much advertised ideological adornment, was of British origin."[113]

Mises also argued that the philosophy of Nazism was "the purest and most consistent manifestation of the anti-capitalistic and socialistic spirit of our age."[114] Indeed,

> The Nazi plan was more comprehensive and therefore more pernicious than that of the Marxians. It aimed at abolishing laissez faire not only in the production of material goods, but no less in the production of men. The Führer was not only the general manager of all industries; he was also the general manager of the breeding-farm intent upon rearing superior men and eliminating inferior stock.[115]

Furthermore, Mises said,

> There were nowhere more docile disciples of Lenin, Trotsky and Stalin than the Nazis ... They imported from Russia: the one party system and the preeminence of this party in political life; the paramount position assigned to the secret police; the concentration camps; the administrative execution or imprisonment of all opponents; the extermination of the families of suspects and of exiles; the method of propaganda,

and many other techniques besides.[116]

These were the legacies that Europe was left with at the end of World War II. Fascism and Nazism had been destroyed in the firestorm of war, but the Soviet form of socialism was looked to by millions as the model and ideal for the society of the future. At the same time, the economics of interventionism dominated the thinking of all the major political parties of Europe. What were the policies that a Classical Liberal of Mises' type could espouse and articulate for the reestablishment of a peaceful, market-based system of social cooperation for the Europe that he had left behind in 1940?

During his first years in the United States, Ludwig von Mises in fact devoted a good portion of his intellectual effort to thinking about this problem. Due to the financial generosity of the Rockefeller Foundation, between 1940 and 1944, he was able to devote his time to analyzing the causes that had led to World War II and to formulating proposals for the economic reform and reconstruction of postwar Europe. While affiliated with the National Bureau of Economic Research in New York, Mises published a work that explained how Europe had fallen into the abyss of totalitarianism and war.[117] In a series of lectures and monographs written in the first half of the 1940s, Mises presented an array of policy prescriptions for Europe's economic recovery after the war.[118]

Mises' diagnosis of the causes of Europe's ills

In three lectures delivered during the early 1940s, Mises offered his diagnosis of Europe's political and economics ills. Throughout the entire twenty-year period between the two world wars, Europe had been in the grip of economic nationalism. Economic nationalism was the foreign policy corollary of the interventionist dogma that had dominated the internal economic policies of the various nations of Europe.

Everywhere in Europe, but especially in central and Eastern Europe, governments undertook to resist and prevent the workings of the market. The liberal epoch of the nineteenth century had brought about an internationalization of trade and commerce; the world was being integrated into one global system of division of labor. The elimination or significant reduction of most barriers to the free movement of goods, capital, and labor had been bringing about an equalization of returns on investment, as well as the remuneration received by workers in the form of wages. Standards of living never known before, even by the kings and princes of earlier times, were now conditions of life taken for granted by a growing number of the general population in North America, Europe, and other parts of the world. The fantastic expansion of European industry and the dramatic growth in capital accumulation had enabled the export of investment capital to the far reaches of the earth to slowly but surely bring the same benefits and improving standards of living to the more economically backward parts of the planet.[119]

This global economic order had benefited Europe immensely. The continent's expanding population, which might otherwise have experienced a decline in the wage rates for certain types of labor, had an outlet through migration to areas of the world offering employment opportunities at higher rates of pay. Europe was able to pay for the resources and raw materials it needed for its expanding industrial manufacturing through the export of finished goods to the suppliers of the means of production it imported. And its capital investments around the world generated part of the income to pay for those means of production and to finance the purchase of foods and other consumer goods that other continents could supply less expensively than their European counterparts.[120]

Even before World War I, but particularly after it, governments began to follow protectionist, interventionist, and socialist policies. Under the pressures of new competitors from abroad that were able to produce both agricultural and industrial goods less expensively then their European rivals, governments in Europe introduced trade barriers to protect domestic producers. In some countries, such as Austria, the net income transfer due to subsidies and tariff walls was from manufacturing to agriculture; in other countries, such as Hungary, the net income transfer through these types of policies was from agriculture to manufacturing. Every restraint on imports, however, also limited exports, since a nation's potential trading partners were limited in the remuneration from foreign sales that would otherwise have provided the financial wherewithal to demand what that first nation was offering to the international market.

The heightened barriers against freedom of movement in the post-World War I era had condemned millions of workers and peasants throughout Europe to work at jobs and till the fields where their marginal productivity, and, consequently, their real wage, was lower than if they had been able to freely migrate to lands where their potential earnings would have been higher. Inequalities in wages and standards of living, as a consequence, were artificially created and maintained due to the political restrictions on the free movement of people.[121]

The end result, Mises insisted, was the threatened destruction of the international division of labor with all of its benefits and the standards of living dependent upon it. As he expressed it in 1937:

> Let us take care that we do not thoughtlessly squander Europe's advantage in the world: the international division of labor is the foundation of the European economy, yea, of all of European culture. Every step away from the international division of labor is a step toward destitution.[122]

Governments had also nationalized and municipalized a significant number of industries and services following World War I. Many were so badly run that national and city governments had to constantly raise taxes to cover operating and capital expenses. As Mises had explained in 1927:

> Public enterprises have failed all over the whole world. The finances of every single European and non-European nation are in as much greater disorder as the government concerned has gone further into the field of the management of business enterprises. In view of this fact, it sounds like a mockery that only a few years ago the further expropriation of private enterprises was recommended in all earnestness for the relief of financial distress and that this policy is still looked upon by wide circles as the highest wisdom in financial policy. The real root of all of our financial difficulties lies precisely in the fact of these public enterprises; in order to cover their operational losses the private sector must be taxed enormously.[123]

The increasing tax burden that sapped the finances of the private sector, Mises argued, was based on a perverse reversal of the logic concerning the relationship between ends and means. Rather than income and revenues limiting expenditures, Mises explained that debates over public finances, especially in a country such as his native Austria, were premised on the idea that whatever the desired level of government expenditure, the private sector was to be taxed to cover it. No thought was given to the effect on incentives, and on the financial ability and opportunity costs for further investment, or even on the maintenance of capital. As Mises argued in 1930:

> The errors of our [Austria's] financial policy stem from the theoretical fiscal misapprehensions that dominate public opinion. The worst of these misapprehensions is the famous but, unfortunately, unsuccessful fight against the concept that the main difference between the state's and the private sector's budget is that in the private sector's budget the expenditures have to be based on its revenues, but that in the public budget it is the reverse: the revenues must be based on expenditures. The unsustainability of this sentence is evident as soon as one thinks it through. There is a rigid limit for expenditures, namely the limitedness of the means. If the means were unlimited, then it would be difficult to understand why one should have to curb any expenses. If in the case of the public budget it is assumed that its revenues

are based on its expenditures and not the other way around, i.e., that its expenses have to be based on its revenues, it results in that tremendous squandering, that characterizes our fiscal policy. The supporters of this principle are so nearsighted that they do not see that it is necessary that all public expenditures that are incurred have to be compared not only with the budgetary expenditures of the private sector, but they must also be confronted with the fact that enterprises cannot make investments when the funds that are needed for them are used for public expenditures; they only see the advantage resulting from the public expenditures but not the harm this taxing inflicts on other parts of the national economy.[124]

The European governments had also followed anti-employment policies after the Great Depression had begun, through acquiescence and support for trade union wage demands that kept the costs of labor above market-determined levels. Prolonged and mass unemployment was the outcome. Furthermore, the costs of maintaining the unemployed through the dole and other subsidizing techniques increased the tax burdens upon the very private sector employers who were the source of jobs in the economy. Even worse, the taxes to pay for the unemployed cut so deeply into private enterprises that capital consumption was a reality in countries like Austria, resulting in the need for even greater cuts in wages to restore full employment because of the consequent decline in the marginal productivity of labor.[125]

The pursuit of interventionist policies in each country invariably pushed them toward economic nationalism in their foreign policies. The various interest groups to be protected, shielded, and subsidized domestically could only be guarded from being undermined by foreign competition if each government acted to harm foreign suppliers attempting to sell in their markets. In a world of economic nationalism, political sovereignty came to mean the power to prevent foreign sellers and investors from freely participating in a country's domestic economic affairs. To achieve that end, governments felt free to repudiate debts, manipulate foreign exchange rates and impose exchange controls, expropriate properties within their borders owned by foreign investors, and impose special taxes on profits repatriated to the foreign investor's home country.[126]

Neither peace nor prosperity had been possible in this world of economic nationalism.[127] All of these domestic and foreign economic policies had helped bring Europe into the abyss of war. Mises reasoned that the war had been caused not only by the Nazis; it was also caused by the failure of the surrounding European nations to participate in a common policy of collective security to prevent Hitler's aggressions from the start. But beside other political factors that had prevented this from happening, "collective security was unrealizable among nations fighting one another unswervingly in the economic sphere."[128]

Mises' prescription for the political economic rebirth of Europe

War had come. Now the task was to reconstruct the foundations of the social and economic order in Europe. Said Mises:

> There is one great task in our age: to revive and to spread the economic and social mentality that makes war useless and peace durable. But, in the face of the fact that our contemporaries are far from such a mentality, we have to answer the question of what can be done to protect civilization after the war. We have to emphasize that a really lasting peace can be attained only with the universal acceptance of an ideology that could lead us to a perfect free market economy.[129]

The most fundamental changes to establish the foundations for the political and economic revival of Europe, Mises argued, involved the mentality of the people. The first of these changes in thinking, he said, required no longer focusing primarily upon the short-run gains from various economic policies. Indeed, the economic calamities of the 1930s and the war through which Europe was then passing represented the fruits of a political economy of the short run. "Of course, there are pseudo-economists preaching the gospel of short-run policies," Mises admitted. "'In the long-run we are all dead,' says Lord Keynes. But it all depends upon how long the short run will last." And in Mises' view, "Europe has now entered the stage in which it is experiencing the long-run consequences of its short-run policies."[130]

Practical politics in the earlier decades of the twentieth century had been geared to providing immediate benefits to various groups that could be satisfied only by undermining the long-run prospects and prosperity of society. In the new postwar period, Mises said, taxes could no longer be confiscatory. International debts could no longer be repudiated or diluted through currency controls or manipulations of exchange rates. Foreign investors could no longer be viewed as victims to be violated or plundered through regulations or nationalization of their property.

The countries of Europe needed to design economic policies with a long-run perspective in mind. European recovery would require capital, and this would mean attracting foreign capital investment to assist in the process. Foreign private sector investors – especially American investors – would be reluctant unless they had the surety that there would be a protected and respected system of property rights, strict enforcement of market contracts for domestic and foreign businessmen, low and predictable taxes, reduced and limited government expenditures, balanced budgets, and a non-inflationary monetary environment.

These were the institutional preconditions for the economic reconstruction of Europe, Mises argued. Once these general changes had been made, governments would have done all in their power to establish the general political environment that would be most conducive to fostering the incentives and opportunities for the people of Europe to start the recovery and rebirth of their own countries. But economic change does not just happen. It is dependent upon human action, and in the system of division of labor the crucial actor is the entrepreneur whom Mises considered central to the innovating and coordinating processes of the market.

The entrepreneurs, however, were the ones who were most despised and plundered by governments in that interwar epoch of interventionism and economic nationalism, and who had been shockingly liquidated especially in Central and Eastern Europe since a large percentage of them had been Jews. Mises estimated that before World War II, 50 percent of the business community in Central Europe and 90 percent of that community in Eastern Europe had been Jews. They were now all gone.[131] Among the thousand leading entrepreneurs in his native Austria, Mises estimated that two-thirds of them had been Jewish. Already by 1940, only two years after Hitler's annexation of Austria, Mises said these leading men of industry and trade were no more. "They were deprived of their enterprises; many of them were slain or slowly tortured to death in concentration camps," Mises lamented. "The rest were expelled from the country. They are scattered all over the world trying to start afresh."[132]

The lifeblood for European recovery had been lost, particularly in Eastern Europe. There would have to be a new respect and regard for these creative men of the market in order to foster the emergence of a new generation of such individuals. "If there is any hope for a new upswing it rests with the initiative of individuals," Mises said. "The entrepreneurs will have to rebuild what the governments and the politicians have destroyed."[133]

The second change needed in the European mentality, Mises said, was an end to special interest group politics. Governments throughout the interwar period had followed a "producer policy," in which individual manufacturers, farmers, and workers in various niches in the system of division of labor formed coalitions to gain favors for themselves at the expense of others in the society. At the behest of trade unions, governments intervened, supported, and subsidized policies that in the longer run resulted in restrictions in output, misdirections of capital, and restraints on labor markets. Such policies had to be abandoned because they work counter to the integrative role prices and competition were meant to play in assuring coordination of markets, and the incentives and ability for capital formation.[134] Producer-oriented policies were better called "production-curtailing policies," Mises said, since they serve to protect the less competent producers from the rivalry of the more competent.[135] Europe could ill afford to indulge in favors for the less efficient and less productive if the ravages of war were to be overcome quickly.

Third, Europe needed to give up the redistributive welfare state. Mises stated emphatically that,

> it is the duty of honest economists to repeat again and again that, after the destruction and the waste of a period of war, nothing else can lead society back to prosperity than the old recipe – produce more and consume less.[136]

Who would be left to be taxed in any "tax the rich and subsidize the poor" scheme in a setting in which war has made practically everyone a "have-not," when the focus of economic policy should be to foster capital formation, not wealth redistribution?[137] "There is no other recipe than this," Mises declared. "Produce more and better, and save more and more."[138]

Unless these changes occurred in people's thinking, Europe's path to reform and reconstruction would be more difficult and protracted than it needed to be. Neither the war nor its destruction stood in the way of Europe's future. Ideas would determine what lie ahead. "What ranks above all else for economic and political reconstruction is a radical change of ideologies," Mises said. "Economic prosperity is not so much a material problem; it is, first of all, an intellectual, spiritual and moral problem."[139]

In Mises' view, these were the ideological, political, and economic institutional prerequisites for Europe's escape from war and collectivism. But within this Classical Liberal political-economic framework, what specific policies and reforms were most likely to enable the survivors of war and collectivism to advance toward material prosperity and a free society? Mises spelled out what he considered these to be in several monographs. They may be viewed under three general categories:

1   economic policies for small nations heavily dependent upon international trade;
2   a political and economic union for Eastern Europe; and
3   economic policies for an underdeveloped nation wishing to industrialize and integrate itself within the international system of division of labor.

Many of the specific policy prescriptions that Mises suggested overlapped under these three headings, but these categories can still be distinguished in the studies he prepared during the early 1940s.

Economic policies for small nations: the case of Austria

Mises may have been an "international man" in the spirit of the Classical Liberal ideal, but he was also very clearly an Austrian patriot. In *Notes and Recollections,* he recounts with passion his numerous attempts to influence events in his country in the direction of economic liberalism through his theoretical and policy writings, his position with the Vienna Chamber of Commerce, and his role in Austrian public affairs. "Occasionally I entertained the hope that my writings would bear practical fruit and show the way for policy ... I set out to be a reformer, but only became the historian of decline," Mises lamented.[140] But he did not regret his participation in this battle of ideas and ideologies. "I fought because I could do no other," he said. Unfortunately, Austria's fate was doomed, not only because of the degree to which socialist and interventionist ideas permeated Austrian society, but because of Hitler's rise to power in Germany. "The enemy who was about to destroy it came from abroad. Austria could not for long withstand the onslaught of the National-Socialists who soon were to overrun all of Europe."[141]

In May 1940, as Mises was making plans for leaving Europe, he prepared "A Draft of Guidelines for the Reconstruction of Austria," at the request of Otto von

Hapsburg, the former archduke of Austria.[142] Even as Western Europe was rapidly falling under Nazi control Mises worked under the assumption that in the end Nazism would be defeated, the Allies would be victorious, and his Austrian homeland would one day again be free. There needed, therefore, to be an economic plan for Austria's political and economic restoration and recovery as an independent and prosperous member of the European family of nations.

The dilemma for a small nation such as Austria, Mises said, was that it was fairly mountainous, with relatively poor soil and limited natural resources. Interventionism and fiscal policy had undermined Austria's economic well-being even before the Nazis' arrival in 1938. In addition, a large number of the entrepreneurs of the country, as noted above, had been liquidated or expelled by the Nazis because of their Jewish background. Under the Nazi system of economic planning many of the remaining businessmen had been reduced to the status of business managers following the instructions of the National Socialist planning authorities.[143]

For a new Austria to emerge from the ashes of war, it would have to follow a clear set of economic policies. As a small country dependent on international commerce for the importation of both raw materials and numerous consumer goods, the country had to follow a strict policy of free trade. Unrestricted importation would enable Austrian manufacturers to obtain resources at the lowest cost possible to keep production expenses down, as well as enabling the purchase of desired consumer goods at the best prices possible so as to maximize the real income of the Austrian buying public. The production costs of Austrian industry needed to be minimized by keeping the resource markets open and competitive because Austrian exports were the only way to earn the income needed to pay for the importation of both raw materials and finished goods.

Were there no exceptions to the unrestricted practice of free trade? Mises argued that there were. Import duties were legitimate for those consumption goods taxed domestically and should be set equal to the internal tax on the domestic consumer product. Retaliatory tariffs would be legitimate against the products of any country that had imposed discriminatory tariffs on Austrian export goods; but such retaliation should be used sparingly so as to not undermine the general spirit of open trade, since a country like Austria was so dependent upon international commerce. The only other categories over which Mises proposed that the state have import-restricting authority were those areas concerning sanitary and veterinary matters, and the importation of weapons and ammunition. In times of extreme political international tension, import prohibitions would be permissible on military grounds as well.

Domestic industry and trade should be absolutely free of government regulation and control, with the exceptions of the production and dissemination of weapons, ammunition and explosives; medications and poisons; and sanitary and veterinary issues.[144] Mandatory trade and professional and labor associations and memberships should be abolished to permit freedom of occupation and employment.[145]

There also would have to be swift privatization of state-owned railroads, government-owned forestry properties, and government-owned or managed enterprises. This was necessary for two reasons:

1   the new Austrian government would need revenues for general operating expenses right after the end of the war when the economy would be too chaotic to generate any ordinary tax revenues; and
2   these sectors of the economy had to be transferred to competent entrepreneurial hands as soon as possible.

Fiscal policy should do everything possible to foster investment incentives and capital formation. Taxes therefore should be skewed toward consumption and not production. Government revenues, therefore, should be derived from the following types of taxes:

- excise taxes for alcoholic drinks, tobacco, and tobacco products;
- a sales tax exclusively on the sale of goods and services to the final consumer; there should be no explicit or hidden value-added tax;
- a wage tax paid by employers that was not deducted from the employee's salary to fund existing social insurance programs;
- a progressive consumption tax based on housing expenditures, but with an exemption for housing expenditures by the "less affluent";
- a tax on luxury automobiles for personal use;
- a tax on lottery winnings;
- a stamp tax on playing cards;
- administrative fees for certain services, such as issuing patent rights, brand name registrations, determination of weights and measures, and "official stamps" on documents to cover their expense;
- a moderate net profits tax on shareholders and limited liability partnerships, when annual disbursements exceed 6 percent of the enterprise's capital assets. Retained earnings by the enterprise would be exempt from taxes, so as not to discourage capital formation.

Mises stated that under such a fiscal system, all income and business earnings would be completely tax-exempt, except for the wage tax and the tax on "excess distribution of earnings." The consumption taxes under his fiscal plan, though Mises did not express it in this manner, are primarily "sin taxes" (alcohol, tobacco, and playing cards) or taxes targeting consumer items of the higher income brackets (higher priced automobiles and housing expenditures progressively scaled to impact more on the wealthier segments of the society).

The crucial element in Mises' fiscal plan was to intentionally create the greatest incentives for investment and capital formation. "The new Austria must not kill the goslings that many years hence will be laying eggs," he said. And, furthermore, Mises proposed that government spending should be strictly limited within the confines of tax revenues collected.[146]

Mises also suggested streamlining and reducing the levels of bureaucracy that have administrative responsibilities at local and provincial levels, including limits on discretionary taxing and regulatory powers at levels of government below the federal authority in Vienna. This was to reduce the potential for local favoritism, petty misuse of power, and corruption.[147]

Finally, he argued that in 1940, long before the war was won, those concerned with Austria's political and economic future, especially those implicitly working as a government-in-exile, had to start laying the groundwork for the reforms to come. Contacts had to be made with foreign businessmen to assure them that when the war was over free market principles would prevail in the country. There would have to be an attempt to entice Austrian entrepreneurs who had fled their native land to return – including Jewish businessmen. And arrangements had to be made for initiating the process of privatization for interested foreign investors immediately after the end of hostilities.

Arrangements would also have to be in process for the establishment of a note-issuing bank (a central bank), but any currency issued by this bank should be legally obligated to be backed by gold in the new Austria. The bank would be mandated to redeem all notes at legal par on demand. And the foreign exchange market would be free from all government restrictions and controls.[148]

Mises admitted that the economic plan he was proposing for Austria would be criticized by many, especially by those on the "left," and by those who represented the types of special interest groups that had benefited from the interventionist-welfare state before the war. "It is an arduous path," he said.

In the new Austria there will be no room for comfortable ministerial seats and sinecures. There will be no room for parasites who thrive on the handouts that they receive from the state at the expense of other citizens. For decades Austria has pursued a policy of capital consumption. The time has come for new capital formation and the creation of a new export industry. Only then can a new Austria take shape.[149]

Freedom from above: a political and economic union for Eastern Europe

Historical atlases containing a map of the Austro-Hungarian Empire before 1914 often have an accompanying demographic map depicting the geographical distribution of different linguistic groups throughout Central and Eastern Europe before or after World War I. It is a checkerboard of Germans, Poles, Lithuanians, Latvians, Estonians, Czechs, Slovaks, Hungarians, Slovenes, Croats, Serbs, Albanians, Italians, Romanians, Ruthenians, Ukrainians, Russians, Bulgars, Greeks, Turks, and Tartars.[150] While almost every one of these linguistic groups is concentrated in some one area on the map, demarcating that "nationality's" geographical homeland, virtually every one of these national concentrations has different colored sprinkles within its territory marking off various areas where significant numbers of linguistic minority groups reside. It is difficult to imagine any gerrymandering of national borders that would not continue to leave sizable linguistic minorities within the boundaries of some larger national group.

Mises considered this to be one of the unique problems confronting postwar Europe. As a Classical Liberal, Mises had discussed this issue in some detail in earlier works, especially in *Nation, State and Economy,* in *Socialism* and in

Liberalism.[151] In these works he had pointed out that in a truly Classical Liberal world, borders and boundary lines on maps would be reduced to purely administrative demarcations, delineating the area of responsibility belonging to different national governments for protecting within their territories the life, liberty, and property of their respective citizens. Goods, men, and money would move freely to wherever was considered most economically profitable and personally advantageous. Governments in such a Classical Liberal world would possess no legal authority to bestow privileges and favors upon some individuals and groups at the expense of others. Political discrimination on the basis of ethnicity, language, or religion would be prohibited under the impartial enforcement of the rule of law.

Yet, even in such a most perfect of Classical Liberal worlds, Mises admitted, linguistic minorities would always to some degree feel alienated from the wider society in which they lived. Political, social, and cultural discourse and debate is primarily undertaken in the language of the majority group. Even if the state's responsibilities are narrowed to the minimum required to secure life and property, there will be numerous occasions when the linguistic minority member has to appear in court, sign legal documents, and participate regularly in market activities and various social events. He may never completely feel a member of the greater society.

This alienation and isolation is magnified a thousand times when governments are not limited to impartial protection of equal rights before the law. In the interventionist state, political power can, and in Eastern Europe had been, frequently used to discriminate against minority groups for the benefit of members of the majority. Mises explained the nature of the problem:

> If, for instance, members of the minority are alone engaged in a specific branch of business, the government can ruin them by means of customs provisions. In other words, they can raise the price of essential raw materials and machinery. In these countries, every measure of government interference – taxes, tariffs, freight rates, labor policy, monopoly and price control, foreign exchange regulations – was used against minorities. If you wish to build a house and you use the services of an architect from the minority group, then you find yourself beset by difficulties raised by the departments of building, of health and fire. You will wait longer to receive your telephone, gas, electric, and water connections from the municipal authorities. The department of sanitation will discover some irregularities in your building. If members of your minority group are injured or even killed for political reasons, the police are slow in finding the culprit.[152]

The more extensive and pervasive the interventionist state in a country, Mises argued, the worse these abuses became in many of these Eastern European nations.

The solution that Mises proposed in his earlier writings had been the right of freedom of self-determination. He made it clear that he meant *individual* self-determination, and not any collectivist conception of national self-determination that argued that everyone belonging to the same ethnic or linguistic group had to be compelled to belong to the same nation-state. In principle each individual should have the right of determining to which political entity he would belong. But clearly administrative limitations precluded this below a certain level.

> One cannot place at every street-corner both a German and a Czech police-man, each of whom would have to protect only members of his own nation-ality. And even if this could be done, the question would still arise as to who is to intervene when members of both nationalities are involved in a situation that calls for [police] intervention. The disadvantages that result from the necessity of a unified administration in these territories are unavoidable.[153]

But certainly regions, districts, and even towns could have plebiscites in which a vote would be taken, according to Mises' reasoning, in which the majority in that area could decide whether they desired to remain a part of the nation-state of which they were presently connected, or to be administratively part of some other nation-state even if this entailed no direct territorial proximity (after all, Alaska is separated from the lower forty-eight states by Canadian territory), or to form their own separate political entity (Singapore became a small city-state rather than a part of neighboring Malaysia). This would not eliminate the problem of linguistic minorities, because even within these new self-determined areas invariably there would still reside some other minority, including some who belonged to what had previously been the majority group. But clearly Mises considered this to be a method that was both consistent with a degree of freedom for individuals to make their own choices about these matters and at the same time reduce many of the interlinguistic group tensions.

But by the late 1930s, however, Mises had come to the conclusion that in the political environment of aggressive economic nationalism, an alternative method for securing greater freedom and peace as well as economic well-being for the inhabitants of Eastern Europe had to be devised. He offered his own plan in 1941, in a monograph titled "An Eastern Democratic Union: A Proposal for the Establishment of a Durable Peace in Eastern Europe."[154]

The only way to eliminate both interventionism and economic nationalism among the countries of Eastern Europe was through the forging of a unified, single political state that encompassed and incorporated the entire region. Mises proposed that such an Eastern Democratic Union would include Albania, Bulgaria, Czechoslovakia, Estonia, Greece, Hungary, Latvia, Lithuania, Poland, Romania, Yugoslavia, and all German lands east of the Oder–Neisse Rivers (that is, all pre-World War II German territories that in fact were annexed by Poland and the Soviet Union after the war). Said Mises:

> The whole territory of Eastern Europe has to be organized as a political unit under a strictly unitary government. Within this area, every individual has to have the right to choose the place where he wishes to live and to work. The

laws and the authorities have to treat all natives – that is, all citizens of Eastern Europe – in the same way and on an equal footing without privileges or discrimination against individuals or groups … If we want to abolish all discrimination against minority groups and if we want to give all citizens actual and not only formal equality, we have to vest all powers in the central government.[155]

Mises had lost all hope in a federalist form of government in this part of the world. If the central government of such a Union was committed to Classical Liberal principles but some of the member states were committed to an interventionist mentality, the latter could use their degrees of legislative autonomy under a federalist system to follow discriminatory policies harmful both to minorities in their jurisdictions and to other member nations. The Union would have to have, therefore, a central authority to establish and assure absolute freedom of trade within and among the member nations as well as with the rest of the world.[156]

Mises offered a fairly detailed outline of his proposed political and economic institutional structure of such an Eastern Democratic Union. There would be a single chamber parliament with approximately 600 members, who would be elected by all the adults of the Union. The cabinet would be responsible to the parliament, and the parliament would be the only legislative body in the territory of the Union. The "governments" of the member nations would be transformed into local and provincial councils serving as advisory boards to the parliament. Standing commissions of the Union's central government would monitor the administrative conduct of the now provincial administrators of the former nation-states to guarantee that central laws were being properly enforced and that no violations of citizen's rights were occurring. The administrations of the member countries would have authority at their local levels, but only to administer the Union laws of the land.[157]

Mises even suggested the site of the capital for this Eastern Democratic Union:

> For the seat of the central offices only Vienna could be considered. The region of Vienna and its environs would then have to be separated from the territory of the Austrian state and would have to be administered after the fashion of the District of Columbia.[158]

Taxing powers would solely reside with the parliament and the central government of the Union. Funds would be apportioned by the parliament to the member countries on the basis of their respective population sizes. All bond issuances would be the prerogative of the central authority and some larger cities given special permission.

To minimize friction between the linguistic groups, all languages spoken by members of the Union would be treated equally, with all government documents translated into each. English would be the official common language for all dealings among the member groups and in the Union's documents and laws. All religions would have the same standing and protection under the law as under the United States Constitution. All schools would be private, and all citizens and groups would have the freedom to establish private educational institutions. If these private schools met certain standards set by the central government – Mises did not specify what they might be – then they would be eligible to receive a lump-sum subsidy per pupil. If circumstances warranted that a local government takes over a private school, it would have the authority to administer the school, but only with funds allocated by the central government. English language training would be mandatory in all secondary education.

Free trade was to be the guiding rule in the Union's international relations with all other countries. The only permitted exceptions being the failure of another nation to treat the Union according to the "most-favored-nation" principle or when another nation prohibited the importing of goods produced within the Union. Then limited retaliatory trade restrictions would be permissible as a tool to persuade that other nation to reverse its anti-free trade policy.

In the transition leading up to the election of the Union's first parliament, Mises proposed that the League of Nations appoint the first president and cabinet members. For a more extended transition period, foreign citizens would be eligible to hold public and judicial offices in the Union – with the exception of Germans, Italians, and Russians.[159]

Mises understood that the likelihood of any such Union was dim, considering the political and ideological currents prevailing in Eastern Europe at the time. But he argued that it was in terms of such a Union that the future political-economic institutional arrangements of the region should be considered. A single parliamentary chamber with 600 members elected in a manner reflecting each linguistic group's relative proportion in the Union would act, he believed, as a sufficiently diverse counterbalancing force to minimize the possibility of the central government being used for the discriminatory benefit of some at the expense of others. The Poles, he said, would make up the largest group by percentage of population, but only 20 percent of the total. Including so many diverse groups – Estonians to the north and Greeks to the south – would itself act as a countervailing force:

> It seems strange, indeed, that the Lithuanians should have to cooperate with the Greeks although they never before have had any mutual relations other than diplomatic ones existing among all nations of the world. But we have to realize that the [Eastern Democratic Union] has to create peace in a part of the world riddled by age-old struggles among linguistic groups ... For the smooth functioning of the [Union] it is not required that the Greeks should consider the Lithuanians as friends and brothers. (Although it seems probable that they would have more friendly feelings for them than for their immediate neighbors [with whom they would have had a long tradition of linguistic and territorial disputes].) What is needed is nothing less than the conviction of the politicians of all these peoples that it is no longer possible to oppress men who happen to speak a foreign language. They do not have to love one another, but to stop inflicting harm on one another.[160]

The task was to bury the past. "Let bygones be bygones," said Mises. "We do not have to revenge crimes of the past, but to build up a future in which people can enjoy the blessings both of peace and of freedom."[161] It is clear, however, that the establishment and successful functioning of such a Union for the maintenance of the Classical Liberal ideals of private property, market freedom, and free trade presumed that there were enough people in the area to form a sufficient intellectual and political catalyst to bring it about.

After Mises published an abridged version of his proposal for an Eastern Democratic Union in his 1944 book, *Omnipotent Government,*[162] Henry Simons, one of the leading figures of the older Chicago School of Economics, said in a review that the proposal "strikes one as both ingenuous and illiberal."[163] Its "illiberality," in Simons' view, probably came from the fact that it proposed using centralized political power to assure economic liberalism at every level of society throughout Eastern Europe. It proposed eliminating "states' rights" in the name of guarding each individual within the Union's jurisdiction from discrimination and abuse through state-level intervention. It is a dilemma and a tension that continues to confound the world, including the United States.

Economic policies for an underdeveloped nation: the case of Mexico

In December 1941, Ludwig von Mises was invited to spend most of January and February 1942 in Mexico, lecturing at the School of Economics of the National University of Mexico. There he delivered a series of lectures on "The Organization of Social Economy," and two seminar series – "The Role of Economic Doctrines in Present-day Political Antagonisms" and "Fundamental Problems of Money and Credit." He also delivered two lectures at the Independent Law School in Mexico City. In total, Mises gave twenty-three lectures over that six-week period.

The following year, in June 1943, Mises finished a monograph on "Mexico's Economic Problems," which he had prepared for a market-oriented business association in Mexico City.[164] His purpose was to develop a series of detailed economic policy proposals that a country like Mexico could follow with two underlying goals in mind: to foster that nation's industrial development and to integrate that nation's economy into the global system of division of labor.

Mises started out by emphasizing that regardless of the policies of other countries and the general international conditions, sound economic policy always begins at home and never loses sight of the long run:

> The distinctive mark of a sound economic policy is that it aims at the establishment of a durable system resulting in a continuous improvement of the nation's well-being. There can hardly be imagined a worse principle of government than that of the short-run policies of the last decades. It brought about economic depression, unemployment of millions of workers, social unrest, revolutions, and war. It led to the disintegration of world trade and the international money market ... A policy that, indifferent about tomor-

row, strives after ephemeral success and carelessly sacrifices the future is not progressive but parasitic ... There is but one means to improve the economic well-being of a whole nation and each of its individual citizens: The progressive accumulation of capital. The greater the amount of capital available, the greater the marginal productivity of labor and, therefore, the higher the wage rates. A sound economic policy is a policy that encourages savings and investment and thereby the improvement of technical methods of production and the productivity of labor.[165]

Mises presented his ideas in the context of a knowledgeable overview of Mexico's economic status as it then existed. He evaluated its major agricultural areas and potentials, considered the technical and economic possibilities of its natural resource base, including mining and oil production, and the opportunities for the development of small business and tourism. Mexico's advantages included its geographical location in the center of the western hemisphere with long coastlines facing the Atlantic and Pacific, its raw material reserves, and a population that over time had the ability to become more educated and skilled. The country's disadvantages came from its lack of capital, its relatively large and low-skilled labor supply, and its political heritage over several decades of anti-capitalist policies that had resulted in confiscation of foreign-owned properties and domestically owned large estates; heavy-handed regulations and controls; and burdensome taxes that acted as a disincentive for both domestic capital formation and foreign investment.

He explained the counterproductive consequences for Mexico resulting from the country's intellectual and political leadership having accepted many of the premises of socialist and interventionist ideology. Wrong ideas had prevented Mexico's economic development. What Mexicans had to realize was that, "The only way toward an improvement of Mexico's economic situation is economic liberalism, that is, the policy of *laissez-faire*; what Mexico needs is economic freedom."[166]

In the long run Mexico could only prosper and grow through its integration within the international division of labor. Trade would provide the markets for its natural resources, which could serve as a source of earnings to accumulate capital to develop its industrial potential and offer an improved standard of living through importation of consumer goods. Mexico need not, and could not, hope to improve its economic status through agriculture; the country did not have the cost advantages to compete with the many agricultural countries on the world market, nor could it supply all of the agricultural commodities demanded by its own population in the quantities or at the prices at which foreign producers could offer them.

Industrial processing and production would have to be the avenue to economic betterment over the long run. But here, too, many other industrial nations held a comparative advantage. Mexico, therefore, would have to search out that factor in which it had a cost advantage. That advantage was its potentially low labor costs because of its large unskilled labor force. Mexico's relative overpopulation had no outlet because of the immigration barriers that had been imposed all around the world, especially in the United States. With extremely limited freedom of movement, wage discrepancies between the United States and Mexico could not be reduced through shifts in the relative supplies of labor between the two countries. Therefore, Mexico's economic improvement pointed in the direction of lower-cost, labor-intensive lines of production.

Mises contrasted two methods for Mexico's path toward industrialization, what he called the "closed door" and the "open door" methods. The closed-door method is what became widely known in the post-World War II period as the import-substitution method of industrialization. Under this approach, industrialization was to be forced through trade restrictions and high tariff barriers behind which domestic industries would be stimulated into existence at artificially high prices, far above those in the general global market. Mises pointed out that those countries implementing such policies inevitably made their own people poorer and less productive.

Reducing imports would also reduce exports, since potential buyers of Mexican goods would lose some of the ability to earn the Mexican revenue that would have provided them with the financial wherewithal to purchase Mexican exports. Mexico would be locked out from maximizing the income it could earn from exporting those goods for which it had the greatest comparative advantage in the international market. And consumers would have to pay the cost of such a method of "hothouse" industrialization through a lower standard of living due to the higher prices and lower qualities of the domestic substitutes they would be forced to purchase on the Mexican market. Closed door, or import-substitution, methods of economic development merely represented a modern version of the eighteenth-century mercantilist fallacies that failed to appreciate that the only real benefits from exports are the imports that export-earnings enable a country to buy from abroad.[167]

Instead, Mises argued, Mexico needed to follow the "open door" approach to industrialization, initially selling mostly raw materials and resources on the world market, and thereby earning the means to import capital and so raise the standard of living of its workforce, from which domestic saving and investment would be generated over time. Many sectors of the Mexican economy could make a fairly easy and smooth adjustment to an immediate shift to a free trade policy, he estimated. But there were, admittedly, other sectors that had become significantly dependent upon the tariff walls behind which they had developed over the years.

For this reason, Mises said, "It would be inexpedient to institute the necessary reforms by the use of measures that, although beneficial in the long run, would for the immediate future bring more hardship than benefits." Of course, he went on,

> A sound industrialization program for Mexico has to repeal all import duties. But as far as products that are already produced within existing factories are concerned, the tariffs have to be abolished by a gradual process. Every year, a tariff reduction of 10 percent has to take place. Thus the enterprises will be in a position to adjust their operations to the new system.[168]

Mises' endorsement of a "gradualist approach" to tariff reform was, it can be said, nothing more than suggesting the same policy that had been often proposed by the Classical Economists when they argued for tariff reform with the goal of establishing free trade through a transition period that minimized the disruptiveness of the adjustment process, including Adam Smith, David Ricardo, Jean-Baptiste Say, and John R. McCulloch.[169]

The only exception from the free trade principle, Mises again stated, was in the case of other nations that discriminated against Mexican goods. But he also emphasized the narrow limits within which the government should have and use the authority to retaliate in this way, so as not to undermine the general rule and practice of free trade for Mexico's long-term development.[170]

However, what the Mexican government and political parties did need to do immediately was to publicly declare that henceforth economic policy would be based on:

1 no expropriation of private property;
2 no confiscatory taxation of profit;
3 no controls or restrictions on the foreign exchange market; and
4 no direct or indirect interference with the management and decision-making of private businesses.

It was important to attempt to recreate confidence in the Mexican business climate to attract foreign investors as well as creating a sense of security for Mexican entrepreneurs.[171] Said Mises:

> It is hopeless to build up a prosperous industry in a country that considers every entrepreneur as an exploiter and tries to penalize his success ... It is a common weakness of man to envy the success of luckier fellow citizens. But an honest patriot should not look askance at the wealth of efficient entrepreneurs. He must understand that in the framework of capitalist society, the only means to acquire riches is to provide the consumers in the cheapest way with all the commodities they ask for. He who serves the public best profits the most.[172]

Effective private management in the resource and infrastructure markets was essential, too. Mises clearly believed that these industries – mining, oil fields, public utilities, and the national railway system – should be privatized, but at the same time he fully appreciated that this was a delicate issue in the Mexican political climate. For example, he expressed the opinion that in reference to the Mexican national railway system,

> The best solution of the problems involved would be for the sale of the whole system to a corporation ... However, a realistic appreciation of current prejudices must recognize that public opinion is not ready to endorse such a plan. In view of this fact, a less ambitious reform must be suggested.[173]

If privatization was politically not feasible under present political circumstances, he proposed that an independent corporation should manage the railway system, while the state retained ownership. He offered an outline of a plan about how the management responsibilities should be transferred to a private corporation, how this private corporation would supply the capital for investment in the rail system in the form of a loan to the government, which would be paid back in annual installments of capital and interest. He explained the necessity for such a corporation to have full authority for operating the system and for hiring and firing, with government approval only of any plans for constructing new railway lines in the country. He proposed a profit-sharing system involving management, employees, and the government that would assure the greatest incentives for the private managers to earn a positive return through efficient operation of the rail system.[174]

He suggested that public utilities – power plants – preferably should also be run by private enterprises to attract private capital for expansion of electrification throughout the country. But whether this was possible or not, and even if public utilities remained in government hands, it was crucial that public utility prices be set at levels to fully cover all costs of production, since the country could not afford to have the treasury tax or borrow to cover losses.

The only exception to this in his view was irrigation projects, because "the agricultural population is very poor" and so "the main burden of irrigation rests on public funds."[175] For the same reason, Mises was sympathetic to the idea that the Mexican government should directly fund the formation of farming cooperatives. "The economic backwardness of a part of Mexico's agricultural population justifies intervention on the part of the government," Mises claimed.

> It is all right for the government to advise peons on how to establish and run cooperatives. Even small subsidies for newly formed cooperatives may be advocated. But it would be a mistake to subsidize them permanently or to grant them tax privileges. It does no good to mask the failure of any institution by such measures. Mexico is not rich enough to indulge in the luxury of waste.[176]

Government's only other direct infrastructure responsibility was construction of roads and airports. However, even here he advised that private enterprise should be considered an option for providing highways, with motorists paying tolls for their use.[177]

If Mexico was to succeed in its market-driven industrial development it was essential that neither government legislation nor trade union power be used to artificially raise wage rates above those set on the market, and most certainly there should be no attempt to raise them to comparable United States levels. Mexico was a capital-poor country, Mises emphasized, with a relatively large supply of unskilled labor. That necessarily meant that labor productivity was far lower than that of American workers. To be competitive Mexican workers had to specialize in those lines of production in which they had a cost-advantage in international markets.

Setting wages above market clearing levels would result in unemployment by pricing some workers out of the market, or creating "disguised" unemployment in the form of portions of the population having to remain in rural agriculture earning less than they could have if competitive job opportunities in the industrial sectors had been allowed to emerge.[178]

For similar reasons, Mises argued that the private sector should be neither taxed nor expected to directly provide workers with social insurance of any kind. If the employer is burdened with financing social insurance schemes, the cost of employing workers rises, since the full cost of hiring is both the money wage agreed to as well as the taxes for or the direct costs of providing social security, public housing, medical care, and so on. These additional labor expenses result in some workers, again, being priced out of the market or some jobs never being created.[179] Equally important, Mises said, is that mandatory social insurance limits the freedom of the employee. "It only restricts his freedom to spend his earnings *ad libitum*. It forces him to provide for illness, disability, and to spend a minimum for housing and so on," whether or not this reflects the worker's personal preferences about how best to allocate his income.[180]

Finally, on monetary and fiscal matters Mises argued that Mexico should establish a functioning gold standard that would secure a stable currency not open to direct or easy manipulation and abuse by the government. A stable, gold-based currency would also help to create a market climate more likely to attract foreign investment, without which Mexico's climb to industrial development would be that much more difficult.[181] With this goal in mind, the government had to maintain a balanced budget by keeping expenditures within the bounds of taxes collected, and with those taxes being kept generally low.

> [T]axes paralyze the spirit of entrepreneurship. No capitalist embarks upon a risky undertaking if he cannot expect sufficient compensation for the risk of losing. The system of private enterprise cannot work if there is no reward for success, only a penalty for malinvestment ... A country suffering from an insufficient supply of capital, like Mexico, must not adopt such suicidal policies. The first principle of Mexican taxation has to be the aim not to discourage saving and capital accumulation. Income taxes have to be kept, even in the upper income brackets, at a moderate level. Besides that part of a man's income which is not consumed, but invested, has to subject to an even lower rate. Moderation should be applied with regard to all taxes, too, especially corporate and inheritance taxes ... Confiscatory taxation of the wealthy citizens – a small group in every country, and a very small group in Mexico – and of corporations by preventing capital accumulation does more harm than good to the masses.[182]

Deficit spending can only be financed in one of two ways: printing money or borrowing money. The first method threatens inflationary distortions and instability that retard a country's development. The second threatens to crowd out private sector borrowing because the government absorbs portions of the country's pool of savings and prices some private borrowers out of the market by the resulting higher rates of interest.[183]

Economic development is not easy for a capital-poor country such as Mexico with its relatively large and unskilled population, especially when that country has to strive for industrialization in a world in which other nations practice economic nationalism, including immigration barriers. But, Mises said, "It is indispensable to see things as they really are, not as one would wish them to be."[184] Through free markets and free trade, Mexico could successfully traverse the path to development and material well-being for its population. But to do so it must be understood that, "Private ownership of the means of production and free enterprise are the foundations of our civilization and of political democracy. The profit motive is the vehicle of progress." Mexico, therefore, needed a reorientation in the ideas and attitudes that had been dominating its policies. "The main issue is intellectual and moral," Mises concluded, "the spirit is supreme in this field, too."[185]

Conclusion: the Classical Liberal plan for the free society of the future

Writing in the 1940s, Mises was not optimistic. He despondently commented in 1943 that, "a radical change of ideologies takes a long time. Years must elapse, generations must pass away, new ages must rise, before such a change can be expected even in the most favorable case."[186] He said, "The realization of the liberal plan is impossible because – at least for our time – people lack the mental ability to absorb the principles of sound economics. Most men are too dull to follow complicated chains of reasoning."[187]

Why did men lack this ability, "at least for our time"? Years earlier, in his study *Socialism,* Mises had suggested why he thought this was the case. In essence, the market economy had developed more rapidly and had enveloped more people than were capable of intellectually grasping the nature of this new social order and adapting to the attitudes and conduct that the system required for its proper and rational functioning. The market order first began to take on its modern form in the towns and urban areas. The problem, however, was that the more quickly the wealth of the towns and urban areas grew, the larger the number of new immigrants from the countryside who were attracted by the economic opportunities. But these new arrivals had little or no conception of the principles and ideas upon which this new emerging market order was dependent.

> Immigrants soon find their place in urban life, they soon adopt, externally, town manners and opinions, but for a long time they remain foreign to civic thought. One cannot make a social philosophy one's own as easily as a new costume. It must be earned – earned with the effort of thought ... The new inhabitants of the towns had become citizens superficially, but not in ways of thought ... More menacing than barbarians storming the walls from without are the seeming citizens within – those who are citizens in gesture, but not in thought.[188]

The difficulty of learning the nature and logic of an extended and interdependent social system of division of labor partly arises from the process of division of labor itself, Mises argued. The position that each person holds in the division of labor influences how he lives and thinks, and therefore the perspective he may hold about the social order.[189] Mises argued:

> The workman in the large or medium scale capitalist enterprise sees and knows nothing of the connections uniting the individual parts of the work to the economic system as a whole. His horizon as worker and producer does not extend beyond the process which is his task. He holds that he alone is a productive member of society, and thinks that everyone, engineer and overseer equally as well as the entrepreneur, who does not, like himself, stand at the machine or carry the loads, is a parasite. Even the bank clerk believes that he alone is actively productive in banking, that he earns the profit of the undertaking, and that the manager who concludes transactions is a superfluity, easily replaceable without loss. Now from where he stands, the worker cannot see how things hang together. He might find out by means of hard thinking and the aid of books, never from the facts of his own working environment. Just as the average man can only conclude from the facts of daily experience that the earth stands still and the sun moves from east to west, so the worker, judging by his own experience can never arrive at a true knowledge of the nature and functioning of economic life.[190]

In seeing the nature of this intellectual problem, Mises was again following in the footsteps of the Classical Economists. In *Principles of Political Economy,* John Stuart Mill drew his readers' attention to a commentary by E.G. Wakefield, in the latter's edition of Adam Smith's *Wealth of Nations*. Mr. Wakefield had pointed out that there were two forms of cooperation in a division of labor, simple and complex. A simple division of labor takes the form of men cooperating within a single enterprise, where each participant more easily sees and understands that his actions and their outcomes are dependent upon the mutual efforts of all his fellows collaborating within the same establishment. A complex division of labor takes the form of men cooperating within different enterprises, with their several contributions leading to various results, but with all their activities coordinated through the interactions of the market. The interdependency of this complex process and how the actions of each are brought into harmony with the activities of others is far more difficult to grasp.

Wakefield said that to understand this latter form of cooperation "a complex operation of the mind is required." Because "when several men, or bodies of men, are employed at different times and places, and in different pursuits, their cooperation with each other, though it may be quite as certain, is not so readily perceived" as in the case of the more simple division of labor. The difficulty of perceiving the more complex process, said John Stuart Mill in supplementing Wakefield's argument, is due to the fact that "[a]ll these persons, without knowledge of one another or previous understanding, cooperate in the production of the final result," but each does so "unconsciously on his part."[191]

But from the middle of the nineteenth century – before Classical Liberalism could complete its task of educating the average man concerning the workings of the system of division of labor, the social role of private property and the profit and loss system, the importance of the entrepreneur, and the necessity for each participant in the market order to understand why his own longer-term well-being required his willingness to adjust to changing supply and demand conditions – there arose the two new voices of socialism and interventionism. They reinforced the older habits of the pre-capitalist era, when human relationships were based on privilege and status, subjugation and obedience, power and force. In the twentieth century, socialism and interventionism brought privilege and status, subjugation and obedience, and power and force back into existence, after the early triumphs of Classical Liberalism in the first half of the nineteenth century had begun the political process of relegating those things to the past.

The task of a Classical Liberalism reborn, in Mises' view, was to articulate the new knowledge that economic theory had developed in the confrontation arising from the challenge of socialism and interventionism. A political economy of the social order, Mises believed, needed to formulate the issue of alternative economic systems in the context of asking which is best suited to foster and sustain an evermore complex system of the division of labor upon which economic progress is dependent. The insight that economic theory had given, Mises was convinced, was that only an economic system built on private ownership of the means of production, free market competition, and market-generated money prices had the capability of enabling the process of economic calculation that was required for a rational use of society's resources to best satisfy the consumer demands of its citizens.

Around this insight was constructed the "liberal plan," as Mises called it, for society and its institutional makeup. Economic theory was value-free, but Classical Liberalism was not. The Classical Liberal had a vision of the good society and how it should operate. The liberal plan, as Mises had expressed it, "was private ownership of the means of production, free initiative and market economy."[192] Within this liberal plan for society, each individual was then at liberty to design his own plans and, through the market process, orient and coordinate his plans with the plans of others through the interconnecting price system of the economy.

Classical Liberal policymaking was not neutral either, in Mises' view. In his proposals for reform and reconstruction after World War II, fiscal policy was to be designed to create the incentives and the ability for individuals to save and to devote their savings and entrepreneurial skills to the process of capital formation. The tax structure would be designed to minimize the fiscal burden of the state on investment-directed activity, while keeping taxes low and limited to the financing of those few functions that the Classical Liberal considered the duties of the government. The monetary system would be designed to create a relatively stable medium of exchange not susceptible to government manipulation. International relations would be based on the principle of free trade, but retaliatory authority would reside with government to respond to the discriminatory trade policies of other governments as a means of putting pressure on those other governments to rescind any trade barriers.

In making his proposals for economic reform Mises emphasized that the market process and economic progress were the results of human action, not blind mechanical forces. The entrepreneurs were central actors in the competitive market process: coordinating supplies with demands, innovating, and planning and directing production in the service of the consuming public. In the social system of division of labor, these individuals were the indispensable human element. They were the prime movers of economic change, adjustment, improvement, and progress.

Thus, when Mises proposed various specific policies in terms either of institutional reform or the structure of fiscal incentives, a primary purpose was to create a social and market setting which fostered the entrepreneurial spirit. Both capital formation and production required creative and guiding hands, thus the role and significance of the entrepreneur had to be fully appreciated to return to and sustain a free market economy. The task was to give as much latitude and liberty to entrepreneurial creativity as possible.

Ultimately, a sustainable and stable Classical Liberal order of economic freedom was dependent upon what Mises had highlighted as the moral and spiritual elements of social and market reform. People had to recover those essential elements of independence, responsibility, and reasoned discipline in their personal conduct and in their behavior toward others in the social, market, and political arenas, if a free and prosperous society was to be secured. This required a rebirth of character. As Mises once pointed out, when called upon to choose between bread and honor, every man of principle should have no difficulty in knowing how to act. "If honor cannot be eaten, eating can at least be foregone for honor." Only those who fear that they do not have the integrity to follow what they know they should do despise being put in the position of a free man who would have to choose between the two.[193] Society had to recover the moral and spiritual discipline to focus on the long-term principles of social cooperation within a functioning free market economy, rather than be seduced by short-run benefits obtained through political intervention in social and economic affairs.

At the same time, if a comprehensive move toward private ownership of the means of production could not be implemented immediately, Mises obviously considered it the task of the Classical Liberal policymaker to design prescriptions that would be in the direction of freer market-oriented conduct. Thus, in his proposals for Mexican economic reform he took it as a given of the political climate that natural resources and the infrastructure could not be fully privatized under the existing circumstances. As a second best, the control of these resources and infrastructure at least should be placed in the hands of autonomous private managers operating under carefully designed incentives and rules to try to assure their more rational use within the wider market economy. *The goal was a free market economy; the task, from Mises' policy prescriptions, was to move in that direction.*

But for any successful policy proposals in the form of the "second best," it was also clear from Mises' writings that the economist had to articulate to the policy implementers the limits and dangers of an economic agenda that fell short of establishing a completely free market economy. Only by doing so was there any hope of avoiding the pitfalls and harmful consequences of interventionist or non-free market proposals, as he had argued in his letter to Paul Mantoux.

Why was it important to direct policy discussions and policy prescriptions toward a freer market? Because, in spite of his despondency, Mises firmly believed that trends could change.[194] The ordinary man could be made to see the benefits and importance of establishing and maintaining a market economy.[195] Classical Liberalism had once radically changed the world and set men free. Mises devoted his life to the idea that it could do so again.

Notes

1 Letter from Mises to Machlup, dated February 28, 1940, in the Machlup Papers in the Hoover Institution archives; original letter in German. Machlup had moved to the United States in 1934, Gottfried Haberler in 1936, Oskar Morgenstern in 1938, and Alfred Schutz in 1939.

2 Letter from Mises to Hayek, dated May 22, 1940, Geneva, Switzerland, in the Hayek Papers in the Hoover Institution archives; original letter in German. Ignaz Seipel (1876–1932) was head of the Austrian Christian Social Party and twice Chancellor of Austria (1922–1924 and 1926–1929); he followed a domestic policy of social welfarism and interventionism.

3 Wilhelm Röpke, "Homage to a Master and a Friend," *Mont Pelerin Quarterly* (October 1961), p. 6. During the war years, Röpke was three times offered a position at the New School for Social Research in New York City. He chose instead to remain in Switzerland and devote his time to writing a series of books analyzing the European crisis of the twentieth century and suggesting a "third way" that he believed needed to be followed in the postwar period; see, Richard M. Ebeling, "Wilhelm Röpke: A Centenary Appreciation," *The Freeman: Ideas on Liberty* (October 1999), pp. 19–24.

4 See, Richard M. Ebeling, "William E. Rappard: An International Man in an Age of Nationalism," *Ideas on Liberty* (January 2000), pp. 33–41.

5 Ludwig von Mises, *Notes and Recollections* [1940] (South Holland, IL: Libertarian Press, 1978), p. 137.

6 Letter from Mises to Rappard and Mantoux dated July 4, 1940, from the archives of the Graduate Institute of International Studies, Geneva, Switzerland; original letter in German.

7 Margit von Mises, *My Years with Ludwig von Mises* (Cedar Falls, IA: Center for Futures Education, 2nd enlarged ed., 1984), pp. 51–56.

8 Ludwig von Mises, "Anti Marxism" [1925] and "Social Liberalism" [1926] reprinted in *Critique of Interventionism* [1929] (Irvington-on-Hudson, NY: Foundation for Economic Education, 1996), pp. 43–95.

9 Ibid., p. 71.

10 Ibid., p. 80.

11 Ibid., p. 67. Mises, of course, was not the only one during this time to sense the growing trend toward dictatorship; see, for example, the Italian historian and Classical Liberal Guglielmo Ferrero, *Words to the Deaf An Historian Contemplates His Age* (New York: G.P. Putnam's Sons, 1926), p. 143:

> Under present conditions, the aspiration to dictatorship is only one form of romantic hopelessness. The dictator dreamed of by the majority – red or white – is to be a miraculous thaumaturgist, who will know what no one knows, and find what all are vainly seeking: the remedy which will cure the ills from which the world is suffering.

Ferrero had been placed under house arrest by Mussolini's fascist government, and prohibited from teaching or lecturing in Italy. In 1930, he was given permission to leave Italy to take up a position as professor of history at the Graduate Institute of International Studies in Geneva, where he was Mises' colleague after the latter's appointment at the Graduate Institute in 1934. Ferrero died in 1942.

12 Mises, *Critique of Interventionism*, pp. 81–84.

13 Ibid., pp. 81–82.

14 Peter G. Klein, ed., *The Collected Works of F.A. Hayek, Vol. 4: The Fortunes of Liberalism, Essays on Austrian Economics and the Ideal of Freedom* (Chicago: University of Chicago Press, 1992), pp. 145–146.

15 Ludwig von Mises, *Nation, State and Economy: Contributions to the Politics and History of Our Time* [1919] (New York: New York University Press, 1983), pp. 220, 218.

16 Ibid., pp. 218–219.

17 See, Ludwig von Mises, *Omnipotent Government: The Rise of the Total State and Total War* [1944] (New Rochelle, NY: Arlington House, 1969) for Mises' developed analysis of the political, philosophical, and economic currents that led to the rise of National Socialism in Germany, and their consequences for the German people and the coming of World War II.

18 Ludwig von Mises, *Nationalökonomie: Theorie des Handelns und Wirtschaftens* [1940] (Munich: Philosophia Verlag, 1980).

19 F.A. Hayek, review of "*Nationalökonomie: Theorie des Handelns und Wirtshaftens,*" *Economic Journal* (April 1941), pp. 125, 126, 127; reprinted in Klein, ed., *The Collected Works of F.A. Hayek,* Vol. 4, pp. 149, 151, 152.

20 Walter Sulzbach, review of "*Nationalökonomie,*" *Journal of Social Philosophy and Jurisprudence* (October 1941), p. 77.

21 Interview with Oskar Morgenstern at Princeton on September 11, 1958, with Bettina Bien Greaves, p. 4 (unpublished).

22 Interview with Professor F.A. Hayek in Chicago, January 25, 1958, with Bettina Bien Greaves, p. 6 (unpublished).

23 Mises, *Omnipotent Government*, p. 14: "Whoever wishes to understand the present state of political affairs must study history. He must know the forces which gave rise to our problems and conflicts. Historical knowledge is indispensable for those who want to build a better world."

24 Mises, *Notes and Recollections*, pp. 47–52.

25 Friedrich A. Hayek, *Knowledge, Evolution and Society* (London: Adam Smith Institute, 1983), p. 18.

26 Klein, ed., *The Collected Works of F.A. Hayek*, Vol. 4, p. 142.

27 Ludwig von Mises, *Socialism: An Economic and Sociological Analysis* [1936] (Indianapolis, IN: Liberty Classics, 1981), p. 258.

28 Ludwig von Mises, *Human Action, A Treatise on Economics* (Irvington-on-Hudson, NY: Foundation for Economic Education, 4th ed., 1996), p. 188.

29 Friedrich A. Hayek, *Law, Legislation and Liberty, Vol. I: Rules and Order* (Chicago: University of Chicago Press, 1973), p. 5; and "The Errors of Constructivism" in, Hayek, *New Studies in Philosophy, Politics, Economics and the History of Ideas* (Chicago: University of Chicago Press, 1978), p. 3.

30 Carl Menger, *Investigations into the Method of the Social Sciences, with Special Reference to Economics* [1883] (New York: New York University Press, 1985), p. 139.

31 Friedrich A. Hayek, "The Trend of Economic Thinking," *Economica* (May 1933), pp. 130–131, reprinted in W.W. Bartley III and Stephen Kresge, eds., *The Collected Works of F.A. Hayek, Vol. 3: The Trend of Economic Thinking, Essays on Political Economists and Economic History* (Chicago: University of Chicago Press, 1991), pp. 27–28.

32 Mises, *Socialism*, pp. 32–33; Hayek's charge against Mises is even stranger considering that in his work on *The Constitution of Liberty* (Chicago: University of

Chicago Press, 1960), p. 57, 432, fn 15, when he discusses the "anti-rationalist" tradition among the Scottish Moral Philosophers and their theory of social evolution, Hayek footnotes and quotes this very same passage from Mises' work.

33 Menger, *Investigations into the Method of the Social Sciences, with Special Reference to Economics*, p. 155.

34 Mises, *Human Action*, pp. 405, 408.

35 For a summary of Mises' views on the meaning and logic of action and its relationship to the social order and systems of social cooperation, see, Richard M. Ebeling, *Austrian Economics and the Political Economy of Freedom* (Northampton, MA: Edward Elgar, 2003) Ch. 3: "A Rational Economist in an Irrational Age: Ludwig von Mises," pp. 61–100.

36 Mises, *Human Action*, p. 177.

37 Ludwig von Mises, "The Treatment of 'Irrationality' in the Social Sciences," [1944] reprinted in, Richard M. Ebeling, ed., *Money, Method and the Market Process, Essays by Ludwig von Mises* (Norwell, MA: Kluwer Academic Press, 1990), p. 20.

38 Mises, *Human Action*, p. 26; also, Max Weber, *Critique of Stammler* [1907] (New York: The Free Press, 1977), pp. 109, 112.

39 Mises, *Human Action*, p. 178.

40 Ibid., p. 188; also, Ludwig von Mises, *Theory and History: An Interpretation of Social and Economic Evolution* [1957] (New Rochelle, NY: Arlington House, 1969), pp. 195–196:

> History is made by men. The conscious intentional actions of individuals, great and small, determine the course of events insofar as it is the result of the interaction of all men. But the historical process is not designed by individuals. It is the composite outcome of the intentional actions of all individuals. No one can plan history. All he can plan and try to put into effect is his own actions which, jointly with the actions of other men, constitute the historical process. The Pilgrim Fathers did not plan to found the United States.

Mises, *Socialism*, pp. 466–67:

> Society is the product of will and action … But this willing sees and wills only the most immediate and direct result; of the remoter consequences it knows nothing and can know nothing. Men who create peace and standards of conduct are only concerned to provide for the needs of the coming hours, days, years; that they are at the same time, working to build a great structure like human society, escapes their notice. Therefore the individual institutions, which collectively support the social organism, are created with no other view in mind than the utility of the moment. They seem individually necessary and useful to their creators; their social function remains unknown to them.

Mises, "Anti-Marxism," p. 76:

> … liberal social theory does not explain [the] formation and progress of social ties and institutions as consciously aimed human efforts toward the formation of societies, as the naïve versions of the contract theory explain them. It views social organizations "as the unintended result of specific individual efforts of the members of society" [Menger].

And, Mises, *The Ultimate Foundation of Economic Science* (Princeton, NJ: D. Van Nostrand, 1962), p. 109:

> The market economy was not devised by a master mind; it was not first planned as an utopian scheme and then put to work. Spontaneous actions of individuals, aiming at nothing else than at the improvement of their own state of satisfaction, undermined the prestige of the coercive status system step by step. Then only, when the superior efficiency of economic freedom could no longer be questioned, social philosophy entered the scene and demolished the ideology of the status system.

41 Mises, *Human Action*, pp. 72–91, 166–169; also, Ludwig von Mises, "The Cult of the Irrational" [1935] in, Richard M. Ebeling, ed., *Selected Writings of Ludwig von Mises*, Vol. 2: *Between the Two World Wars: Monetary Disorder, Interventionism, Socialism, and the Great Depression* (Indianapolis, IN: Liberty Fund, 2002), pp. 297–301.

42 Ludwig von Mises, "The Psychological Basis of the Opposition to Economic Theory" [1931] in *Epistemological Problems of Economics* [1933] (New York: New York University Press, 1981), pp. 200–202.

43 Wilhelm Röpke, "End of an Era" [1933] in *Against the Tide* (Chicago: Henry Regnery, 1969), pp. 79–98.

44 Louis Rougier, *Modern Political Mystiques and Their International Impact* (Paris: Libraire du Recueil Sirey, 1935).

45 In the same vein, I would argue that it is possible to partly understand Hayek's emphasis on the limits of reason during the 1930s, 1940s, and after. The intellectual climate in which Hayek found himself after moving to Great Britain in 1931 and then the United States in the late 1940s was different from the one that confronted Mises in German-speaking central Europe between the wars. In England and the United States, what Hayek faced were not appeals to the irrational and calls to a common "blood" or Marxism's pseudoscientific dialectical materialism. Instead, he found an exaggerated hyper-rationalism in which social scientists from many fields confidently asserted that they had the ability to rationally reconstruct and plan entire societies. Speaking in broad terms, Mises confronted an array of tribalist forms of collectivism, while Hayek had the challenge of responding to those who represented the collectivism of the seemingly cool-headed rationalist social engineer. In this setting, part of Hayek's reply ended up taking the form of reminding his opponents not that reason was of central value, but that there were limits to what even the best of human minds could know and fully comprehend. Mises and Hayek were battling against two different – though related – manifestations of collectivism in the twentieth century. Hence, their respective emphasis and focus reflected the arguments they had to try to refute and the premises from which their opponents were basing their case for the planned society.

46 Ludwig von Mises, "The Task and Scope of the Science of Human Action," [1933] *Epistemological Problems of Economics*, p. 38; *Human Action*, pp. 159–161.

47 Mises, *Human Action*, pp. 160–161.

48 Ibid., p. 169; and *Socialism*, pp. 284–285.

49 Mises, *Socialism*, pp. 256–272; *Human Action*, pp. 157–174.

50 Mises, *Socialism*, pp. 55–56

51 Ludwig von Mises, *Interventionism: An Economic Analysis* [1940] (Irvington-on-Hudson, NY: Foundation for Economic Education, 1998), p. 24.

52 Mises, *Socialism*, pp. 268–269.

53 David Hume, "Of the Jealousy of Trade," *Essays, Moral, Political and Literary* (Indianapolis, IN: Liberty Classics, 1987), p. 331; also, in, Eugene Rotwein, ed., *David Hume's Writings on Economics* (Madison: University of Wisconsin Press, 1970), p. 82.

54 Mises, *Socialism*, p. 59.

55 Ibid., p. 268:

> History is a struggle between two principles, the peaceful principle, which advances the development of trade, and the militaristic-imperialistic principle, which interprets human society not as a friendly division of labor but as the forcible repression of some of its members by others. The imperialistic principle continually regains the upper hand. The liberal principle cannot maintain itself against it until the inclination for peaceful labor inherent in the masses shall have struggled through to full recognition of its importance as a principle of social evolution.

56 Ibid., p. 265: "The principle of the division of labor revealed the nature of the growth of society. Once the significance of the division of labor had been grasped, social knowledge developed at an extraordinary pace."
57 Ibid., p. 37.
58 Ludwig von Mises, *Planned Chaos* (Irvington-on-Hudson, NY: Foundation for Economic Education, 1947), p. 29; and reprinted in, *Socialism*, p. 493.
59 Mises, *Human Action*, pp. 179–181; *Theory and History*, pp. 35–50.
60 Ludwig von Mises, *Liberalism, The Classical Tradition* [1927] (Irvington-on-Hudson, NY: Foundation for Economic Education, 1996), pp. 4–5; *Human Action*, p. 154.
61 Mises, *Socialism*, p. 277.
62 Mises, *Liberalism*, pp. 6–7.
63 Mises, "Interventionism" [1926] reprinted in *Critique of Interventionism*, pp. 3–4.
64 Mises, *Epistemological Problems of Economics*, p. 30.
65 Mises, "The Treatment of 'Irrationality' in the Social Sciences," [1944] in, Ebeling, ed., *Money, Method and the Market Process*, p. 36; also, *Human Action*, p. 7:

> Now it is obvious that our economic theory is not perfect. There is no such thing as perfection in human knowledge, not for that matter in any other human achievement. Omniscience is denied to man. The most elaborate theory that seems to satisfy completely our thirst for knowledge may one day be amended or supplanted by a new theory. Science does not give us absolute and final certainty. It only gives us assurance within the limits of our mental abilities and the prevailing state of scientific thought. A scientific system is but one station in an endless progressing search for knowledge. It is necessarily affected by the insufficiency inherent in every human effort. But to acknowledge these facts does not mean that present-day economics is backward. It merely means that economics is a living thing – and to live implies both imperfection and change.

And *Human Action*, p. 68:

> Man is not infallible. He searches for truth – that is, for the most adequate comprehension of reality as far as the structure of his mind and reason makes it accessible. Man can never become omniscient. He can never be absolutely certain that his inquiries were not misled and that what he considers as certain truth is not error. All that man can do is to submit all his theories again and again to the most critical reexamination.

66 Mises, *Liberalism*, p. 3; *Critique of Interventionism*, p. 34.
67 Letter from Mises to Hayek, dated February 11, 1933, Vienna, Austria, from the "lost papers" of Ludwig von Mises recovered from Moscow, Russia.
68 Hayek, "The Trend of Economic Thinking," p. 129; and in Bartley and Kresge, ed., *The Collected Works of F.A. Hayek*, Vol. 3, p. 26.
69 Hayek, "The Trend of Economic Thinking," pp. 131–132; and in Bartley and Kresge, ed., *The Collected Works of F.A. Hayek*, Vol. 3, p. 29.
70 Hayek, "The Trend of Economic Thinking," p. 133; and in Bartley and Kresge, ed., *The Collected Works of F.A. Hayek*, Vol. 3, p. 30.
71 Hayek, "The Trend of Economic Thinking," pp. 133–134; and in Bartley and Kresge, ed., *The Collected Works of F.A. Hayek*, Vol. 3, p. 31.
72 Mises, "On the Development of the Subjective Theory of Value," [1931] reprinted in *Epistemological Problems of Economics*, p. 157:

> Insomuch as money prices of the means of production can be determined only in a social order in which they are privately owned, the proof of the impracticability of socialism necessarily follows. From the standpoint of both politics and history, this proof is certainly the most important discovery made by economic theory. Its practical significance can scarcely be overestimated. It alone gives us

the basis for pronouncing a final political judgment on all kinds of socialism, communism, and planned economies; and it alone will enable future historians to understand how it came about that the victory of the socialist movement did not lead to the creation of the socialist order of society.

73 Hermann Heinrich Gossen, *The Law of Human Relations and the Rule of Human Action Derived Therefrom* [1854] (Cambridge, MA: The MIT Press, 1983), pp. 254–255; see, Mises, *Socialism*, p. 117.

74 Walter Bagehot, "The Postulates of Political Economy," [1879] reprinted in *Economic Studies* [1898] (Clifton, NJ: Augustus M. Kelley, 1973), pp. 55–56:

> Profit, as we calculate, means that which is over the capital to be replaced ... [T]his comparison requires a medium in which the profits can be calculated, that is, *a money.* Supposing that in the flax trade profits are 5 percent, and that side by side in the cotton trade they are 15 percent, capital will nowadays immediately run from one to the other. And it does so because those who are making much, try to get more capital, and those who are making little – still more those who are losing – do not care how much as they have. But if there is no money to compute in, neither will they know what they are making, therefore the process of migration wants it motive, and will not begin. The first sign of extra profit in a trade – not a conclusive, but a strongly presumptive one – is an extra high price in the article that trade makes or sells; but this test fails altogether when there is no "money" to sell in. And on the debit side of the account, the cost of production is as difficult to calculate when there is no common measure between the items, or between the product, and any of them. Political Economists have indeed an idea of "exchangeable value" – that is, the number of things which each article will exchange for – and they sometimes suppose a state of barter in which people had this notion, and which they calculated the profit of a trade by deducting the exchangeable value of the labour and commodities used in its production from the value of the finished work. But such a state of society never existed in reality. No nation, which was not clever enough to invent a money, was ever able to conceive so thin and hard an idea as "exchangeable value" (Emphasis in original).

75 See, Richard M. Ebeling, *Austrian Economics and the Political Economy of Freedom*, Ch. 4: "Economic Calculation Under Socialism: Ludwig von Mises and His Predecessors," pp. 101–135, for a detailed discussion of five of these pre-World War I contributors and Mises' arguments against socialist planning in relation to theirs.

76 Mises, *Human Action*, p. 199.

77 Mises considered Hayek's writings on the "knowledge problem" of society to be:

> Hayek's valuable contribution to knowledge. The fact that knowledge exists dispersed, incomplete and inconsistent, in many individual minds, has been pointed out by Hayek and this is very important. Hayek says that if we are talking about the knowledge of our age, we are making a mistake if we think that this knowledge exists in all minds, or even that all of it exists in the mind of one man. He pointed out, for instance, in the case of the socialistic society that the progress possible is limited by the mind of one man. It is important for the capitalist economy that everybody, who has a better knowledge about some particular problem, can try to profit from this superiority and his attempts contribute to the improvement of the general conditions. In the socialistic economy, knowledge has value only insofar as it is available to the central authority, to the dictators who are making the central plan. Under capitalism, the coordination of the various bits of knowledge is brought about through the market. In a socialistic society it must be effected either in the mind of the dictator or in the minds of the members of the dictator's committee.

This quotation is from stenographic notes of Mises' NYU seminar, March 20, 1958, taken by Bettina Bien Greaves (unpublished).

78 Friedrich A. Hayek, "Economics and Knowledge" [1937] reprinted in *Individualism and Economic Order* (Chicago: University of Chicago Press, 1948), p. 50; the reference to Mises' *Socialism* was not included in the original publication of this essay in *Economica* in February 1937, but was added by Hayek when he reprinted it in his 1948 collection of essays.
79 Mises, *Socialism*, p. 101.
80 Ibid., pp. 98, 101–102.
81 Ibid., p. 102.
82 Ibid., p. 101.
83 Mises, *Human Action*, pp. 391–392.
84 Ibid., p. 99: "In the first place we are able to take as the basis of calculation the valuation of all the individuals participating in trade."
85 Ibid., pp. 103–104.
86 Mises, *Liberalism*, p. 75.
87 Mises, *Human Action*, p. 229.
88 Hayek, "Economics and Knowledge," p. 36.
89 Mises, *Epistemological Problems of Economics*, pp. 23–35.
90 Hayek, "The Use of Knowledge in Society," [1945] reprinted in *Individualism and Economic Order*, pp. 77–91.
91 Mises, *Human Action*, p. 338.
92 Ludwig von Mises, *Bureaucracy* (New Haven: CT: Yale University Press, 1944), p. 29; it is worth noting that Mises' statement about prices and what they convey to the entrepreneur was published a year before Hayek's "The Use of Knowledge in Society."
93 Ibid., pp. 328–329.
94 Ibid., p. 338; emphasis in original.
95 Mises, *Human Action*, pp. 311–315.
96 Mises, *Human Action*, pp. 59–64; *Theory and History*, pp. 309–320; Ludwig von Mises, *The Ultimate Foundations of Economic Science* (Princeton, NJ: D. Van Nostrand, 1962), pp. 46–51; for a more detailed exposition of Mises' theory of expectations, see, Richard M. Ebeling, "Expectations and Expectations Formation in Mises' Theory of the Market Process," in, Peter J. Boettke and David L. Prychitko, eds., *The Market Process: Essays in Contemporary Austrian Economics* (Brookfield, VT: Edward Elgar, 1994), pp. 83–95; and Chapter 10 in this volume, "Human Action, Ideal Types, and the Market Process: Alfred Schutz and the Austrian Economists."
97 Mises, *Socialism*, p. 113.
98 Mises, *Human Action*, p. 679.
99 Mises, *Socialism*, p. 462; *Human Action*, p. 680:

    The weight of this objection [concerning economic calculation] raised to the socialist plans is so overwhelming that no judicious man could hesitate to choose capitalism. Yet this would still be a choice between alternative systems of society's economic organization, preference given to one system as against another. However, such is not the alternative. Socialism cannot be realized because it is beyond power to establish it as a social system. The choice is between capitalism and chaos ... A society that chooses between capitalism and socialism does not choose between two social systems; it chooses between social cooperation and the disintegration of society.

100 Ludwig von Mises, "The Economic Crisis and Capitalism," [1931], in Richard M. Ebeling, ed., *Selected Writings of Ludwig von Mises*. Vol. 2: *Between the Two World Wars: Monetary Disorder, Interventionism, Socialism, and the Great Depression*, (Indianapolis, IN: Liberty Fund, 2002), pp. 169–170.
101 Ibid., pp. 170–171.

102 Mises, *Socialism*, pp. 292–313; *Human Action*, pp. 664–688; Mises, "The Clash of Group Interests" [1945] reprinted in, Ebeling, ed., *Money, Method and the Market Process*, pp. 202–214.

103 See, Jean-Baptiste Say, *A Treatise on Political Economy* [1821] (New York: Augustus M. Kelley, 1971), pp. 163–164:

> It is worth remarking, that every body thinks himself more rogue than fool; for although all are consumers as well as producers, the enormous profits made upon a single article are much more striking, than reiterated minute losses upon the numberless items of consumption. If an import duty be laid upon calicoes, the additional annual charge to each person of moderate fortune, may, perhaps, not exceed 2.5 dollars or 3 dollars at most; and probably he does not very well comprehend the nature of the loss, or feel it much, though repeated in some degree or other upon every thing he consumes; whereas, possibly, this consumer is himself a manufacturer, say, a hat-maker; and should a duty be laid upon the import of foreign hats, he will immediately see that it will raise the price of his own hats, and probably increase his annual profits by several thousand dollars. It is this delusion that makes private interest so warm an advocate for prohibitory measures, even where the whole community loses more by them as consumers, than it gains as producers.

> Also, Nassau W. Senior, "Three Lectures on the Transmission of the Precious Metals from Country to Country, and the Mercantile Theory of Wealth" [1828] reprinted in, *Selected Writings on Economics by Nassau Senior* (New York: Augustus M. Kelley, 1966), p. 4: "That if it [the trade protection] benefit the English silk manufacturer, it injures, to at least an equal amount in the whole, though the injury is less perceptible, because more widely diffused, the cotton-spinner, the cutler, or the clothier."

104 Oskar Morgenstern, *The Limits of Economics* [1934] (London: William Hodge, 1937), pp. 29–46; the relevant chapter, on "The Distribution Effects of Economic Policy" is reprinted in, Richard M. Ebeling, ed., *Austrian Economics: A Reader* (Hillsdale, MI: Hillsdale College Press, 1991), pp. 655–669.

105 For a comparison of Mises' ideas with that of Röpke's on a variety of economic policies, see, Richard M. Ebeling, *Austrian Economics and the Political Economy of Freedom* (Northampton, MA: Edward Elgar, 2003) Ch. 9: "The Limits of Economic Policy: The Austrian Economists and the German ORDO Liberals," pp. 231–246.

106 Letter from Mises to Paul Mantoux, dated June 21, 1946, from New York (unpublished).

107 Mises, *Liberalism*, p. 46.

108 Mises, *Socialism*, p. 71.

109 Ibid., p. 418:

> When nations rush blindly towards destruction, Liberalism must try to enlighten them. But even if they do not hear, whether because they are deaf or because the warning voice is too feeble, one must not seek to seduce them to the right mode of conduct by tactical and demagogic artifice. It may be possible to destroy society by demagogy. But it can never be built up by that means.

110 Mises, *Planned Chaos*, pp. 62–67; *Socialism*, pp. 518–522.

111 Mises, *Planned Chaos*, p. 68; *Socialism*, p. 523.

112 Mises, *Planned Chaos*, pp. 70–73; *Socialism*, pp. 524–527.

113 Mises, *Planned Chaos*, p. 74; *Socialism*, p. 528.

114 Mises, *Planned Chaos*, p. 75; *Socialism*, p. 528.

115 Mises, *Planned Chaos*, pp. 77–78; *Socialism*, p. 531.

116 Mises, *Planned Chaos*, p. 77; *Socialism*, p. 530.

117 Ludwig von Mises, *Omnipotent Government: The Rise of the Total State and Total War* (New Haven, CT: Yale University Press, 1944).

118 Richard M. Ebeling, ed., *Selected Writings of Ludwig von Mises: The Political*

Economy of International Reform and Reconstruction, Vol. 3 (Indianapolis, IN: Liberty Fund, 2000).
119 Mises, "Postwar Economic Reconstruction of Europe" [1940] in, ibid., pp. 21–24.
120 Mises, "Europe's Economic Structure and the Problem of Postwar Reconstruction," [1944] in, ibid., pp. 31–33.
121 Mises, "Postwar Reconstruction," [1941] in, ibid., pp. 6–7; and Mises, "The Freedom to Move as an International Problem" [1935] reprinted in, Richard M. Ebeling and Jacob G. Hornberger, eds., *The Case for Free Trade and Open Immigration* (Fairfax, VA: Future of Freedom Foundation, 1995), pp. 127–130.
122 Ludwig von Mises, "Autarky: the Road to Misery," [1937] in, Ebeling, ed., *Selected Writings of Ludwig von Mises,* Vol. 2, p. 306.
123 Ludwig von Mises, "The Balance Sheet of Economic Policy Hostile to Property," [1927] in, Ebeling, ed., *Selected Writings of Ludwig von Mises,* Vol. 2, p. 238.
124 Ludwig von Mises, "Adjusting Public Expenditures to the Economy's Cost-Bearing Capability," [1930] in, Ebeling, ed., *Selected Writings of Ludwig von Mises,* Vol. 2, p. 242.
125 Ludwig von Mises, "The Crisis and Capitalism," p. 172.
126 Mises, "Postwar Economic Reconstruction of Europe," p. 28.
127 Mises, *Human Action,* p. 832: "Interventionism generates economic nationalism, and economic nationalism generates bellicosity. If men and commodities are prevented from crossing the borderlines, why should not the armies try to pave the way?"
128 Mises, "The Fundamental Principles of a Pan-European Union," [1943] in, Ebeling, ed., *Selected Writings of Ludwig von Mises: The Political Economy of International Reform and Reconstruction,* Vol. 3, p. 44.
129 Mises, "Postwar Reconstruction," p. 14.
130 Mises, "Europe's Economic Structure and the Problem of Postwar Re-construction," pp. 40–41.
131 Mises, "Postwar Economic Reconstruction of Europe," p. 27.
132 Mises, "A Draft of Guidelines for the Reconstruction of Austria," [1940] in, Ebeling, ed., *Selected Writings of Ludwig von Mises: The Political Economy of International Reform and Reconstruction,* Vol. 3, p. 135.
133 Mises, "Postwar Economic Reconstruction of Europe," p. 30.
134 Ibid., pp. 25–26; see also, Mises, "The Clash of Group Interests," p. 207.
135 Mises, "A Draft of Guidelines for the Reconstruction of Austria," pp. 143–144
136 Mises, "Postwar Economic Reconstruction of Europe," p. 29.
137 Ibid., p. 26.
138 Mises, "Europe's Economic Structure and the Problem of Postwar Re-construction," p. 40.
139 Ibid., p. 42.
140 Mises, *Notes and Recollections,* p. 115.
141 Ibid., pp. 91–92.
142 See, Margit von Mises, *My Years with Ludwig von Mises,* 2nd enlarged ed. (Cedar Falls, IA: Center for Futures Education, 1984), pp. 68–69.
143 On the Nazi system of planning, see, Walter Eucken, "On the Theory of the Centrally Administered Economy: An Analysis of the German Experiment," *Economica* Part I (May 1948), pp. 79–100; and Part II (August 1948), pp. 173–93.
144 Mises, "A Draft of Guidelines for the Reconstruction of Austria," pp. 149–50.
145 Ibid., pp. 143–144.
146 Ibid., pp. 150–152.
147 Ibid., pp. 153–154.
148 Ibid., p. 151.
149 Ibid., 167–168.
150 William E. Shepherd, *Historical Atlas,* 8th ed. (New York: Barnes and Noble, 1956), pp. 168, 168H; and R.F. Treharne and Harold Fullard, eds., *Muir's Historical Atlas, Ancient, Medieval and Modern,* (New York: Barnes and Noble, 9th ed., 1962), p. 85.

151 Mises, *Nation, State and Economy*, pp. 9–56; *Socialism*, pp. 199–202; *Liberalism*, pp. 105–124.
152 Mises, "Postwar Reconstruction," p. 13.
153 Mises, *Liberalism*, p. 117.
154 Mises, "An Eastern Democratic Union: A Proposal for the Establishment of a Durable Peace in Eastern Europe," [1941] in, Ebeling, ed., *Selected Writings of Ludwig von Mises, Vol. 3: The Political Economy of International Reform and Reconstruction*, pp. 169–201.
155 Ibid., pp. 186–188.
156 Ibid., pp. 187–188.
157 Ibid., pp. 193–194.
158 Ludwig von Mises, "Guidelines for the New Order of Relationships in the Danube Region," [1939] in, Ebeling, ed., *Selected Writings of Ludwig von Mises, Vol. 2*, pp. 315–322.
159 Mises, "An Eastern Democratic Union: A Proposal for the Establishment of a Durable Peace in Eastern Europe," pp. 193–197.
160 Ibid., pp. 199–200.
161 Ibid., p. 186.
162 Mises, *Omnipotent Government*, pp. 271–278.
163 Henry Simons, review of *Omnipotent Government*, in *Annals of the American Academy of Political and Social Science* (November 1944), pp. 192–193.
164 Mises, "Mexico's Economic Problems," [1943] in, Ebeling, ed., *Selected Writings of Ludwig von Mises: The Political Economy of International Reform and Reconstruction*, Vol. 3, pp. 203–254. For some unknown reason, this monograph was never published in either Mexico or the United States at the time. A Spanish translation finally appeared in print in Mexico only in 1998, under the title, *Problemas Economicos de Mexico: Aye y Hoy* (Mexico City: Instituto Cultural Ludwig von Mises, 1998).
165 Ibid., pp. 203–204.
166 Ibid., p. 209.
167 Ibid., p. 221.
168 Ibid., p. 221.
169 See, Adam Smith, *Wealth of Nations* [1776] (New York: The Modern Library, 1937), Bk VI, Chap. II, p. 438; David Ricardo, *Principles of Political Economy and Taxation* [1821] in, Piero Sraffa, ed., *The Works and Correspondence of David Ricardo*, Vol. I (Cambridge: Cambridge University Press, 1962), pp. 266–267; Jean-Baptiste Say, *A Treatise on Political Economy* [1821] (New York: Augustus M. Kelley, 1971), p. 170; John R. McCulloch, *The Principles of Political Economy* [1864] (New York: Augustus M. Kelley, 1965), pp. 102–103.
170 Mises, "Mexico's Economic Problems," p. 223.
171 Ibid., p. 222.
172 Ibid., pp. 208–209.
173 Ibid., p. 231.
174 bid., pp. 230–233.
175 bid., pp. 234.
176 Ibid., p. 242.
177 Ibid., p. 233.
178 Ibid., pp. 234–238.
179 Ibid., p. 239.
180 Ibid., p. 240.
181 Ibid., pp. 242–249.
182 Ibid., pp. 250–251.
183 Ibid., pp. 249–251.
184 Ibid., p. 209.
185 Ibid., p. 253.

202   *Planning for freedom*

7   The Austrian economists and the Keynesian revolution

The Great Depression and the economics of the short run

On September 14, 1949, Yale University Press released a major new work – *Human Action* by the Austrian economist Ludwig von Mises. The following week, in his regular *Newsweek* column, Henry Hazlitt referred to this book as

> a landmark in the progress of economics … *Human Action* is, in short, at once the most uncompromising and the most rigorously reasoned statement of the case for capitalism that has yet appeared. If a single book can turn the ideological tide that has been running in recent years so heavily toward statism, socialism, and totalitarianism, *Human Action* is that book. It should become the leading text of everyone who believes in freedom, individualism, and … a free market economy.[1]

It is perhaps useful to recall the state of the world when *Human Action* first appeared in 1949. The Soviet system of central economic planning had been imposed by Stalin on all of Eastern Europe. In Asia, Mao Tse-tung's communist armies were just completing their conquest of the Chinese mainland. In western Europe, many of the major noncommunist governments were practicing what the German free market economist Wilhelm Röpke called "national collectivism" – a "combination of repressed inflation, collectivist controls, 'full employment,' exchange control, state monopolies, bilateralism, subsidies, fiscal socialism [and] 'cheap money' policies." In the United States, government policy was guided by what Henry Hazlitt had referred to in his *Newsweek* column (a few weeks before his review of *Human Action)* as "ultra-Keynesian ideology."[2]

In *Human Action,* Ludwig von Mises opposed every one of these trends and policies, plus many others in contemporary social philosophy, philosophy of science, and in economic theory and method. He challenged the foundations, logic, and conclusions of every facet of twentieth-century collectivism. In 1949, Mises' arguments were ignored or scorned as the reactionary misconceptions of a man out-of-step with the more enlightened ideas and economic policies of the postwar era. In the early twenty-first century, however, it is evident that it was Mises who understood far better than the vast majority of the contemporary economists and policy advocates the fundamental flaws in socialism, interventionism, and the welfare state.

The legacy of Keynes' "demand management" economics

But even as the twentieth century has now passed into history, one legacy of the interventionist thinking of the last one hundred years continues to dominate public policy thinking. It is the idea that government must manage and guide monetary and fiscal policy to assure full employment, a stable price level and to foster economic growth. The terms of the debate have changed considerably over the last half-century or so, but the belief that it is the responsibility of government to control the supply of money and aggregate spending in the economy persists today just as much as it did in the 1940s. As one example, in the late 1990s leading free market economists Milton Friedman and Allen Meltzer argued that the solution to possible depression problems in the United States or Japan should be a dramatic increase in the supply of money to inflate prices and stimulate "aggregate demand" as a method to restore business profitability and create employment opportunities.[3]

The modern conception of "demand management" is a legacy of perhaps the most influential variation on the interventionist theme during the past one hundred years: the Keynesian Revolution that was born out of the Great Depression and the publication of John Maynard Keynes' 1936 book *The General Theory of Employment, Interest and Money*. The impact of Keynes' book and its message should not be underestimated. Its two central tenets were the claim that the market economy is inherently unstable and likely to generate prolonged periods of unemployment and underutilized productive capacity, and the argument that governments should take responsibility to counteract these periods of economic depression with the various monetary and fiscal policy tools at their disposal. This was bolstered by Keynes' belief that policy managers guided by the economic theory developed in his book could have the knowledge and ability to do so successfully.[4]

No less important in propagating his idea of demand management economic policy was Keynes' literary ability to persuade. As Leland Yeager expressed it, "Keynes saw and provided what would gain attention – harsh polemics, sardonic passages, bits of esoteric and shocking doctrine."[5] Keynes possessed an arrogant amount of self-confidence and belief in his ability to influence public opinion and policy. Austrian economist Friedrich A. Hayek, who knew Keynes fairly well, referred to his "supreme confidence ... in his power to play on public opinion as a supreme master plays his instrument." On the last occasion he saw Keynes in early 1946 (shortly before Keynes' death from a heart attack), Hayek asked him if he wasn't concerned that some of his followers were taking his ideas to extremes. Keynes replied that Hayek need not be worried. If it became necessary, Hayek could "rely upon him again quickly to swing round pubic opinion – and he indicated by a quick movement of his hand how rapidly that would be done. But three months later he was dead."[6]

Even today, respected economists argue that Keynesian-style macroeconomic intervention is needed as a balancing rod against instability in the market economy. One example is Robert Skidelsky, the author of a widely acclaimed multi-volume biography of Keynes and director of the London-based Social

Market Foundation.[7] A few years ago Professor Skidelsky argued that capitalism has at its heart an instability of financial institutions and, "This insight by Keynes into the causes and consequences of financial crises remains supremely valuable." In any significant economic downturn, government should begin "pumping money into the economy, like pumping air into a deflating balloon."[8]

Mises and Keynes on money and monetary policy in the 1920s and 1930s

In the 1920s, Ludwig von Mises and John Maynard Keynes were among the most influential economists in their respective countries of Austria and Great Britain. Shortly before World War I Mises had published a major work on monetary theory, *The Theory of Money and Credit.* In the immediate aftermath of the Great War, Mises wrote *Nation, State and Economy,* in which he analyzed the causes and consequences of that war. Then in 1920, he published an article, "Economic Calculation in the Socialist Commonwealth," in which he argued that a fully centrally planned economy would be unable to allocate resources rationally because of the elimination of market-based prices following the nationalization of the means of production. He expanded this argument into the wider context of a comprehensive treatise in *Socialism: An Economic and Sociological Analysis* in 1922. In 1927, Mises published *Liberalism,* a forceful defense of economic and personal liberty. This was followed in 1929 by *Critique of Interventionism,* a collection of essays arguing that government regulation of prices and production in a market economy could only create imbalances and distortions that, if carried to their logical conclusion, threatened to lead to socialism via piecemeal extension of such controls. And in 1928, Mises published *Monetary Stabilization and Cyclical Policy,* in which he made the case for a gold standard, private competitive banking, and an end to inflationary policies.

During the Great Austrian Inflation of the early 1920s, Mises was a proponent of a non-inflationary monetary policy. He was primarily responsible for writing the charter and bylaws of the reconstituted Austrian National Bank once inflation was brought to an end. In his role as economic advisor to the Austrian Chamber of Commerce, Crafts, and Industry, he was also a prominent advocate of free market reforms in the Austrian economy.

In the early 1930s, Mises forcefully argued, in monographs and articles, that the Great Depression had been caused by the mismanagement of monetary policy in both the United States and Europe. And its severity and duration was the result of misguided interventions and controls introduced by governments that prevented or delayed the normal self-correcting adjustments through which the market would have restored balance and coordination, resulting in a return to full employment and a rational market-directed use of capital, resources, and labor. He restated this case for the free market in the wider context of his 1940 treatise, *Nationalökonomie,* the forerunner of his 1949 magnum opus, *Human Action.*

Shortly before World War I, Keynes, too, published a book on monetary policy, *Indian Currency and Finance.* During the Great War, he had worked in the British Treasury. In 1919 he served as an advisor to the British delegation in Versailles. But frustrated with the attitude of the Allied powers toward Germany in setting the terms of the peace, Keynes returned to Britain and published *The Economic Consequences of the Peace,* in which he severely criticized the peace settlement. In 1921, he published *A Treatise on Probability.* And in 1923, he published *A Tract on Monetary Reform,* in which he called for the end of the gold standard, suggesting a national managed paper currency in its place. He strongly opposed Great Britain's return to the gold standard in the mid-1920s at the prewar gold parity. He argued that governments should have discretionary power over the management of a nation's monetary system to assure a desired target level of employment, output, and prices.

In 1930 Keynes published *A Treatise on Money,* a two-volume work that he hoped would establish his reputation as a leading monetary theorist of his time instead of only an influential economic policy analyst. However, over the next two years a series of critical reviews appeared, written by some of the most respected economists of the day. The majority of them demonstrated serious problems with either the premises or the reasoning with which Keynes attempted to build his theory on the relationships between savings, investment, the interest rate, and the aggregate levels of output and prices. He devoted the next five years to reconstructing his argument, the result being his most famous and influential work, *The General Theory of Employment, Interest and Money,* published in 1936.

Keynes argued that the Great Depression was caused by inescapable irrationalities in the market economy that not only created the conditions for the severity of the economic downturn, but necessitated activist monetary and fiscal policies by government to restore and maintain full employment and maximum utilization of resource and output capabilities. For the next half-century Keynes' ideas, as presented in *The General Theory,* became the cornerstone of macroeconomic theorizing and policymaking throughout the Western world, and continue to dominate public policy thinking today.

The Federal Reserve policy and price level stabilization in the 1920s

Contrary to Keynes' interpretation, the Great Depression was not the result of "reckless" and "unstable capitalism" combined with "passive, indifferent government." The Great Depression was caused by monetary mismanagement by America's central bank, the Federal Reserve System. The Depression's intensity and duration were the result of government interventionist and collectivist policies that prevented the required readjustments in the economy that would have enabled a normal recovery in a much shorter period of time.

The roots of the Great Depression were laid with the establishment of the Federal Reserve System in 1913. While the American monetary system had many serious flaws before 1913 – practically all connected with federal and state regulations and controls over the banking industry – the Federal Reserve System became the mechanism for centralizing control over the monetary and banking

structures in the United States. Those controls became the mechanism for monetary central planning that generated a large inflation during World War I, the
illusion of "stabilization" in the 1920s, and the reality of the Great Depression in
the early 1930s.

In the first seven years after the Federal Reserve came into full operation in
1914, wholesale prices in the United States rose more than 240 percent. How
had this come about? Between 1914 and 1920, the currency in circulation had
increased 242.7 percent. Demand (or checking) deposits had gone up by 196.4
percent, and time deposits had increased by 240 percent.

With the establishment of the Fed, gold certificates began to be replaced
with the new Federal Reserve Notes. Unlike the older gold certificates that
had 100 percent gold backing, Federal Reserve Notes had only a 40 percent
gold reserve behind them, enabling a dramatic expansion of currency. Member
banks in the new system were required to transfer a portion of their gold
reserves to the Fed to "economize" on gold in the system. At the same
time, reserve requirements on deposit liabilities were lowered by 50 percent
from the pre-1914 average level of 21 percent to 11.60 percent; and they were
lowered even further in June 1917 to 9.67 percent. Reserve requirements on time
deposits were set at only 5 percent and diminished further to 3 percent in June
1917.

The decreased reserve requirements on outstanding bank liabilities created a
tidal wave of available funds for lending purposes in the banking industry. And,
indeed, between 1914 and 1920, bank loans increased by 200 percent. Much of
the additional lending ended up in U.S. government securities, especially after
America's entry into World War I in April 1917. Between March 1917 and June
1919, bank loans to the private sector increased by 70 percent, while investments
in government securities went up by 450 percent.[9]

As C.A. Philips, T.F. McManus, and R.W. Nelson explained in their important work, *Banking and the Business Cycle: A Study of the Great Depression in
the United States:*

> Had it not been for the creation of the Federal Reserve System, there would
> have been a [lower] limit to the expansion of bank credit during the War ...
> The establishment of the Federal Reserve System, with its pooling and
> economizing of reserves, thus permitted a greater credit expansion on a
> given reserve base ... It is in the operations of the Federal Reserve System,
> then, that the major explanation of the War-time rise of prices lies.[10]

The years 1920 to 1921 saw the postwar slump. Prices fell by about 40
percent during these two years, and unemployment rose to more than 10 percent.
But the depression, though steep, was short-lived. Why? Because the American
economy still had a great degree of wage and price flexibility. The imbalances in
the market created by the preceding inflation were soon corrected with appropriate adjustments in the structure of wages and prices to more fully reflect the new
postwar supply-and-demand conditions in the market.[11] But this postwar adjustment did not return prices to anything near prewar levels. Prices in the United

States were still almost 40 percent higher in 1922 than they had been in 1913. This was not surprising, since the money supply contracted by only about 9 to 13 percent during this period from its previous inflationary high.[12]

Following the depression of 1921, the Federal Reserve System began a great experiment with price level stabilization under the influence of Yale University economist Irving Fisher, one of the most internationally respected economists of the time. Fisher argued that unexpected changes in the general level of prices can have disruptive effects on production and employment in the economy as a whole. This was a theme that he developed in his 1911 work, *The Purchasing Power of Money,* and that he popularized in a series of books, such as *Elementary Principles of Economics, Stabilizing the Dollar,* and *The Money Illusion,* as well as in the dozens of articles he published throughout the 1920s.[13]

Fisher said that during a period of unexpected price inflation or price deflation, prices for finished goods and services and the prices for resources and labor change at different times and to different degrees. As a result, profit margins between the prices for finished goods and the means of production can be artificially and temporarily increased or decreased, resulting in fluctuations in production and employment in the economy.

Prices for finished consumer goods, Fisher explained, tend to be fairly flexible and responsive to changes in the level of market demand. On the other hand, resource prices, including the wages for labor, tend to be fixed by contract.

During periods of unexpected price inflation, the profit margins between consumer-goods prices and resource prices are artificially widened, creating an incentive for employers to expand output to take advantage of the increased return from sales. This, he argued, is the cause of the "boom," or expansionist, phase of the business cycle.

But the boom inevitably comes to an end when resource prices, including wages, come up for contractual renegotiation. Resource owners and laborers, in a market environment of heated demand for their services, bargain for higher prices and money wages to compensate for the lost purchasing power they have suffered while their money incomes have been contractually fixed in the face of rising prices. The "bust" or contractionist phase of the business cycle then sets in, as profit margins narrow in the face of the new higher costs of production and as employers discover that they have over-expanded and overextended themselves in the earlier boom period.

During periods of unexpected price deflation, profit margins between consumer-goods prices and resource prices are artificially narrowed or wiped out, as consumer-goods prices are declining while resource prices and wages temporarily remain fixed at their contractual levels. Employers have an incentive to reduce output to economize on costs and reduce losses, generating a general economic downturn. The diminished profits or losses are eliminated when resource prices (including wages) come up for contractual renegotiation. Rather than risk losing their businesses and jobs, resource owners and workers moderate their price and wage demands to reflect the lower prices in the marketplace for their products. Furthermore, since consumer-goods prices in general are declining, resource owners and workers can accept lower resource prices and money wages. In real buying terms, they will be no worse off than before the price deflation began.

If price inflations and price deflations could be perfectly anticipated, changes in the purchasing power of money could be incorporated into resource and labor contracts, with profit margins being neither artificially widened nor narrowed by the movements in the general level of prices. The business cycle of booms and busts would be mitigated or even eliminated.

Unfortunately, Fisher again argued, such perfect foresight is highly unlikely. And unless some external force is introduced to keep the price level stable – to eliminate both price inflations and price deflations – Fisher concluded that, given the monetary institutions prevailing in most modern societies during the time he was writing, the business cycle would remain an inherent part of a market economy.

Irving Fisher's solution was to advocate a stabilization of the price level. What was needed, he insisted, was a monetary policy that would ensure neither price inflation nor price deflation. In *Stabilizing the Dollar,* Fisher stated:

> What is needed is to stabilize, or standardize, the dollar just as we have already standardized the yardstick, the pound weight, the bushel basket, the pint cup, the horsepower, the volt, and indeed all the units of commerce except the dollar ... Am I proposing that some Government official should be authorized to mark the dollar up or down according to his own caprice? Most certainly not. A definite and simple criterion for the required adjustments is at hand – the familiar "index number" of prices ... For every 1 percent of deviation of the index number above or below par at any adjustment date, we would increase or decrease the dollar's weight (in terms of purchasing power) by 1 percent.[14]

How would the government do this? By changing the quantity of money and bank credit available in the economy for the purchase of goods and services. In his 1928 volume, *The Money Illusion,* Fisher praised the Federal Reserve Board – the American central bank's monetary managers – for following a policy since 1922 close to the one he was advocating. Though only a "crude" beginning, "stabilization ushers in a new era for our economic life ... adding," he claimed, "much to the income of the nation."

> The dollar ... has been partially safeguarded against wide fluctuations ever since the Federal Reserve System finally set up the Open Market Committee in 1922 to buy and sell securities, especially Government bonds, for the purpose of influencing the credit situation ... When they buy securities they thereby put money into circulation ... When they sell, they thereby withdraw money from circulation. [Along with the Federal Reserve's control over bank reserves and the discount rate at which it directly lends to banks, through Open Market Operations] the Federal Reserve does and should safeguard the country ... against serious inflation and deflation ... This power, rightly used, makes the Federal Reserve System the greatest public service institution in the world.[15]

Through the power of the Federal Reserve System, Fisher happily pointed out, America had established a "managed currency," guided by the policy goal of a stable price level.[16] That this was the Fed's goal was confirmed by Benjamin Strong, chairman of the New York Federal Reserve Bank through most of the decade and the most influential member of the Federal Reserve Board of Governors during this period. In 1925, Strong said, "It was my belief ... that our whole policy in the future, as in the past, would be directed toward the stability of prices so far as it was possible for us to influence prices." And in 1927, he once again emphasized, "I personally think that the administration of the Federal Reserve System since the [depression] of 1921 has been just as nearly directed as reasonable human wisdom could direct it toward that very policy [of price level stabilization]."[17]

Did the Federal Reserve succeed in its policy of price level stabilization? An index of wholesale prices, with 1913 as the base year of 100, shows that the average level of prices remained within a fairly narrow band: 1922–138.5; 1923–144.1; 1924–140.5; 1925–148.2; 1926–143.2; 1927–136.6; 1928–138.5; 1929–136.5. During the entire decade, wholesale prices on average were never more than about 7 percent higher than in 1922. At the end of the decade, before the Great Depression set in (1929), wholesale prices, as measured by this index, were in fact about 1.5 percent lower than in 1922.

Like Irving Fisher in his praise of Federal Reserve policy in 1928, John Maynard Keynes, in his two-volume *Treatise on Money,* pointed to the Fed's record during the decade and said, "The successful management of the dollar by the Federal Reserve Board from 1923 to 1928 was a triumph ... for the view that currency management is feasible."[18]

By how much had the Federal Reserve changed the supply of money and credit during the decade to bring about price level stabilization? The answer to this depends on how one defines the "money supply." Milton Friedman and Anna Schwartz, in their famous *Monetary History of the United States, 1867–1960,* estimate that between 1921 and 1929, the money supply increased about 45 percent, or approximately 4.6 percent a year. They used a definition of money that included currency in circulation and demand and time deposits (a definition known as "M-2").[19]

In *America's Great Depression,* Austrian economist Murray Rothbard used a broader measurement of the money supply that included currency, demand and time deposits, savings and loan shares, and the cash value of life-insurance policies. Using these figures, Rothbard estimated that the money supply had increased by 61.8 percent between 1921 and 1929, with an average annual increase of 7.7 percent.[20]

While shares owned in savings and loan banks increased by the largest percentage of any component of the money supply – 318 percent between 1921 and 1929 – it represented only 4 to 8 percent of the total money supply during the period, as measured by Rothbard. The cash value of life insurance policies increased by 213 percent during the period; and it represented between 12.5 percent and 16.5 percent of the money supply, as measured by Rothbard.

If the cash value of life insurance policies is subtracted from Rothbard's measure of the money supply, and if deposits at mutual savings banks, the postal savings system, and the shares at savings and loans are added to Friedman and Schwartz's definition (which, in fact, they do to calculate a broader money definition called "M-4"), the results practically coincide. The money supply, by both measurements, increased by about 54 percent for the period, with an average annual increase of approximately 5.5 percent.

During the decade, this monetary increase did not, however, occur at an even, annualized rate. Rather, it occurred in spurts, especially in 1922, 1924–1925, and 1927, with monetary slowdowns in 1923, 1926, and late 1928 and early 1929. These were not accidents, but rather represented the "fine-tuning" methods of the Federal Reserve Board of Governors in their attempt to counteract tendencies toward either price inflation or price deflation, with price-level stabilization as a crucial signpost of success.

The two main Federal Reserve policy tools for influencing the amount of money in the economy were open-market operations and the discount rate. When the Fed purchases government securities, it pays for them by creating new reserves on the basis of which banks can expand their lending. The sale of government securities by the Fed drains reserves from the banking system, reducing the ability of banks to extend loans.

The discount rate is the rate at which the Fed will directly lend reserves to member banks of the Federal Reserve System. Throughout most of the 1920s, the Fed kept the discount rate below the market rates of interest, creating a positive incentive for member banks to borrow from the Fed and lend the borrowed funds to the market at higher rates of interest, earning the banks a profit. Even when the Fed sold government securities at certain times during the 1920s, member banks were often able to reverse the resulting drains of reserves out of the banking system by borrowing them back from the Fed at the below-market discount rate.

Increases in currency in circulation were a negligible fraction of the monetary expansion, representing less than 1 percent of the increase. Demand deposits increased by 44.6 percent, and time deposits expanded by 76.8 percent. This fostered a major economic boom. As Philips, McManus, and Nelson explained in *Banking and the Business Cycle:*

> As a result of the plethora of bank credit funds and the utilization by banks of their excess reserve to swell their investment accounts, the long-term interest rate declined and it became increasingly profitable and popular to float new stock and bond issues. This favorable situation in the capital funds market was translated into a construction boom of previously unheard-of dimensions; a real estate boom developed, first in Florida, but soon was transferred to the urban real estate market on a nation-wide scale; and finally, the stock market became the recipient of the excessive credit expansion.[21]

Trying to rein in the stock market boom, the Fed all but froze the money supply in late 1928 and the first half of 1929. The monetary restraint finally caught up with the stock market in October 1929.

But why did the stock market downturn develop into the Great Depression? Other than the boom in the stock market, there were few outward signs of an unstable inflationary expansion that would have suggested a need for a recessionary adjustment period to reestablish certain fundamental balances in the economy. The wholesale price index, as we saw, had remained practically unchanged between 1922 and 1929.

Clearly, however, there were forces at work beneath the surface of a stable price level that were generating the conditions for a needed correction in the economy. But depressions had occurred before and recoveries had followed, usually not too long afterward. Why, then, did this downturn become the Great Depression?

The Austrian economists on the origin and the purchasing power of money

Even before World War I, a number of prominent American economists had criticized Irving Fisher's proposal for price-level stabilization through monetary manipulation by the government. Frank Taussig of Harvard University, J. Laurence Laughlin of the University of Chicago, and David Kinley of the University of Illinois had forcefully argued that implementing Fisher's scheme would generate more, not less, economic instability.

But it was the Austrian Economists who reasoned most persuasively against a price-level stabilization policy in the 1920s. To understand their criticisms, it is necessary to begin with Carl Menger, the founder of the Austrian School. In his *Principles of Economics* and in a monograph on "Money," Menger explained the origin of a medium of exchange.[22] Often there are insurmountable difficulties preventing people from directly trading one good for another. One of the potential trading partners may not want the good the other possesses. Perhaps one of the goods offered in exchange cannot readily be divided into portions reflecting possible terms of trade. Therefore, the transaction cannot be consummated.

As a result, individuals try to find ways to achieve their desired goals through indirect methods. An individual may first trade away the good in his possession for some other commodity for which he has no particular use. But he may believe that it would be more readily accepted by a person who has a good he actually wants to acquire. He uses the commodity for which he has no direct use as a medium of exchange. He trades commodity A for commodity B and then turns around and exchanges commodity B for commodity C. In this sequence of transactions, commodity B has served as a medium of exchange.

Menger went on to explain that over time transactors discover that certain commodities have qualities or marketable attributes that make them especially serviceable as media of exchange. Some commodities are in greater general demand among a wide circle of potential transactors. Some commodities are more readily transportable and more easily divisible into convenient amounts to reflect agreed-upon terms of exchange. Some are relatively more durable and scarce and difficult to reproduce. The commodities that possess the right combinations of these attributes and characteristics tend to become, over a long period of time, the most widely used and readily accepted media of exchange in an expanding arena of trade and commerce.

Therefore, those commodities historically became the money-goods of the market because the very definition of money is that it is a commodity that is most widely used and generally accepted as a medium of exchange in a market. Money, then, begins as an ordinary market commodity, but because of its particular marketable qualities, it slowly comes to be demanded for its usefulness as a medium of exchange. Over time, its use as a medium of exchange may supersede its other uses as an ordinary commodity. Gold and silver thus came to serve as the most widely accepted media of exchange – the money-goods of the market.

For Menger and later members of the Austrian School, this was a strong demonstration, both theoretically and historically, that money is not a creation or a creature of the state. In its origin, money naturally emerges from the processes of the market, as individuals search for better and easier ways to satisfy their wants through trade and exchange.

A second question that the Austrians asked was: Once a money is in use, how does one define its purchasing power or value in the market? First Menger and then Ludwig von Mises in his book *The Theory of Money and Credit* devoted careful attention to this question.[23]

In a state of barter, when every commodity directly trades for all the others, each good on the market has as many prices as the goods against which it exchanges. But in a money-using economy, goods no longer trade directly one for the other. Instead, each good is first sold for money; with the money earned from selling commodities, individuals then turn around and purchase other goods. Over time, each good comes to have only one price on the market – its money-price.

But money remains the one exception to this. Money is the one commodity that continues to trade directly for all the other goods offered on the market. As a result, money has no single price. Rather, money has as many prices as goods with which it trades on the market. The purchasing power of money, therefore, is the array or set of exchange ratios between money and every other good. The actual value of money at any moment in time is that set of specific exchange ratios that have emerged on the market.

By definition, the purchasing power or value of money is always subject to change. Anything that changes people's willingness and ability to sell goods for money or to sell money for goods will modify the exchange ratios between money and goods. If people change their preferences, such as they now want to consume more chicken and fewer hamburgers, the demand for chicken on the market would rise and the demand for hamburger would fall. This would change the relative price between chicken and hamburger: the price of chicken would tend to go up relative to the price of hamburger. But at the same time, it would also change the purchasing power or value of money, since now the money price of chicken would have increased and the money price of hamburger would have decreased. The array or set of exchange ratios between money and other goods on the market would, therefore, also now be different.

Suppose, instead, that people changed their preferences and decided to demand fewer goods and to hold a larger amount of the money they earned from selling goods as an available average cash balance for some future exchanges. The demand for goods would decrease and the demand for holding money as a cash balance would increase. The money prices of goods would tend to decline, raising the purchasing power or value of each unit of money, since at lower money prices, each unit of money would command a greater buying power over goods.

Unless people decreased their demand for goods proportionally, at the same time that the value of money was rising the relative prices among goods would change as well. Why? Because if the demand for, say, chicken decreased more than the demand for hamburger, then even at the overall lower scale of money prices, the money price of chicken will have tended to decrease more than the money price of hamburger. The structure of relative prices would have changed as part of the same process that had changed the scale or level of money prices in general.

Irving Fisher's proposal, therefore, to "stabilize, or standardize, the dollar just as we have already standardized the yardstick, the pound weight, the pint cup ..." was built on a false analogy. A yardstick is a multiple of a fixed unit of measurement – an inch. But the purchasing power or value of money is not a fixed unit of measurement. It is composed of a set of exchange ratios between money and other goods, reflecting the existing and changing valuations of the participants in the market about the desirability of and their demand for various commodities relative to the attractiveness of spending money or holding it as a cash balance of a certain amount.

In *The Theory of Money and Credit* and his later monograph "Monetary Stabilization and Cyclical Policy," Ludwig von Mises also challenged Irving Fisher's proposal for measuring changes in the purchasing power of money through the use of index numbers.[24] A consumer price index, for example, is constructed by selecting a group of commodities chosen as "representative" of the normal and usual types of goods bought by an average family within a particular community. The items in this representative basket of consumer purchases are then "weighted" in terms of the relative amounts of each good in the basket that this representative family is assumed to purchase during any normal period. The prices for these goods times the relative quantities of each bought is then defined as the cost of purchasing this representative basket of consumer items.

The prices of these goods, multiplied by the fixed relative amounts assumed to be bought, are tracked over time to determine whether the cost of living for this representative consumer-family has increased or decreased. Whether the sum of money originally required to buy the basket at the beginning of the series is able to buy a larger, smaller, or the same basket at a later period is then taken to be a measure of the extent to which the purchasing power or value of money has increased, decreased, or stayed the same.

Mises argued that the construction of index numbers, rather than being a supposedly precise method for measuring changes in the purchasing power of money, was in fact a statistical fiction built on arbitrary assumptions. The first of these arbitrary assumptions concerned the selection of goods to include in the basket and the relative weights to assign to them. Preferences for goods vary considerably among individuals, even among individuals in similar income and social groups or geographic locations. Which group of goods to include, therefore, can claim no scientific precision, nor can the judgment concerning the relative quantities be labeled "representative."

The second arbitrary assumption also concerns the "weights" assigned to the goods in the basket. It is assumed that over the periods compared, the same relative amounts purchased in the beginning period are purchased in future periods. But in the real world of actual market transactions, the relative amounts of various goods purchased are always changing. Preferences and desires for goods are constantly open to change. Even when people's basic preferences for goods have not changed, in the real world the relative prices of various goods are changing. People tend to buy less of goods that are rising in price and more of goods decreasing in price or more of those not rising in price as much as others.

The third arbitrary assumption is that new goods are not being offered on the market and that older goods are not being taken off the market. But both occurrences are common and modify the types and quantities of goods in a consumer's basket. The fourth arbitrary assumption concerns changes in the quality of the goods offered. A good that improves in quality but continues to be sold at the same price is now a cheaper good; that is, the consumer is receiving more for the same amount of money. However, the index records no increase in the value of the consumer's dollar. A good may rise in price and, at the same time, be improved, but there is no exact way to determine how much of the higher price can be attributed to the product's improvement and how much is due to other market conditions.

Mises' conclusion, therefore, was that there is no scientific way of knowing whether and by how much the purchasing power or value of money may have changed over a given period of time. Thus, the statistical method considered by Irving Fisher to be the key for guiding monetary policy to stabilize price levels was fundamentally and irreparably flawed.

But whether the construction and application of index numbers was flawed or not, stabilization of the price level became a target for the Federal Reserve in the 1920s. And that policy was a prime ingredient in creating the market imbalances that resulted in the Great Depression.

Ludwig von Mises and the non-neutrality of money

In the late 1850s, the British economist John E. Cairnes published a series of articles analyzing the sequence of events that followed the gold discoveries in Australia. He explained that the increase in gold had its initial impact on prices in coastal towns and cities, where the miners first spent their new supplies of gold as money. The increased money demand for goods and services stimulated additional imports into Australia. The Australian merchants paid for these increased stocks of goods with the new gold paid to them by the miners. As gold entered, and then was spent in, the European markets, prices for goods and services began to rise there as well. Manufacturers in Europe, in turn, increased their demand for resources and raw materials from Asia and Africa, paying for them with the new gold that had passed into their hands. Prices then began to rise in those other parts of the world.

The increase in gold supplies brought about a general rise in prices that followed a particular pattern. It began when the gold was introduced into the market, followed by a sequence of expenditures and receipts that reflected the increased demand for commodities and resources in the order of who received the new gold money first, second, third, and so on.[25]

Changes in the quantity of money have long been understood as a primary influence on the rise or decline of prices in general. But the particular method of analysis used by different economists has not only affected the explanation of money's effects on an economy, it has influenced various policy conclusions drawn from this analysis as well.

In *The Purchasing Power of Money* and many of his other works, Irving Fisher presented a rather "aggregated" analysis. As we have already seen, Fisher argued that an increase in the supply of money tended to bring about a rise in selling prices in general, relative to the costs of production. The temporary increase in profit margins between selling prices and costs (due to input prices being fixed for a period of time by contract) acted as the stimulus for attempts to increase output. But when contracts came up for renewal and were revised upward, profit margins would return to "normal" and the "boom" phase of the business cycle would end. It would be followed by a period of correction, in the wake of businessmen's discovering that their over-expansive plans were unsustainable; this was the downturn or depression phase of the business cycle.

Fisher concluded that the cause and sequence of the business cycle were the result of unanticipated increases in the money supply that made selling prices rise relative to cost prices. His policy prescription was to keep the price level stable. If that were done, he argued, price-cost relationships would be kept in proper order, at least to the extent they were influenced by monetary forces. And that, in turn, would mitigate, if not eliminate, the primary cause behind the business cycle.

An alternative method of analysis for explaining money's influence on prices and production was in the tradition represented by John E. Cairnes. In this alternative approach, the analysis is "disaggregated" into a study of money's impact on the economy and traces the path by which changes in the money supply are introduced into the economy and the sequence of events by which this change in the money supply passes from one individual to another and from one sector of the economy to another.

This alternative tradition of monetary analysis is the one followed by the Austrian Economists, their leading expositor being Ludwig von Mises. He developed this approach in *The Theory of Money and Credit,* in *Monetary Stabilization and Cyclical Policy,* and in his comprehensive treatise on economics, *Human Action.*[26]

If increases or decreases in the quantity of money brought about simultaneous and proportional increases and decreases in all prices, changes in the supply of money would be neutral in their effects on the economy. That is, neither the structure of relative prices nor the patterns of relative income shares earned by individuals and groups in the society would be affected by changes in the quantity of money. Money's effect on the economy would be nominal and not real.

Mises and the Austrians argued that money's impact on the market was always non-neutral. Economists such as Irving Fisher reasoned that the non-neutrality of money was due only to the fact that changes in the money supply were less than fully anticipated, and as a result, resource and labor contracts did not completely incorporate the actual average rate of price changes into resource prices and wage negotiations. Hence, cost prices would temporarily lag behind selling prices, creating temporary profit differentials.

The Austrians, on the other hand, insisted that money would be non-neutral in its effects even if resource prices and wages were as flexible as selling prices and even if market participants were to fully anticipate the average rate of change in the general price level as measured by a price index. The reason for that was the Austrians' method of analysis. Mises pointed out that any change in market conditions must ultimately have its beginning in the changed circumstances of one or more individuals. Nothing happens in the market that does not start with the decisions and choices of acting individuals.

If there is an increase in the supply of money, it must necessarily take the form of an increase in the cash holdings of particular people, who are at the starting point of the resulting social consequences of a change in the quantity of money. Finding themselves with a greater amount of cash than they normally hold, they proceed to spend the "surplus" cash on the goods and services they find attractive and profitable to buy.

The demand for goods and services begins to rise because of this increase in the money supply. But it is not all demands that initially increase – only the particular demands for the particular goods that the individuals with the additional cash purchase in greater quantities. In this "first round" of the process, the prices of only those goods for which there has been an increased demand begin to rise. As the money is spent on those goods, the resulting sales become additional money receipts for the sellers. Those sellers, finding their cash positions improved, increase their demands for various goods and services. This is the "second round" of price increases, but again the prices affected are only of those goods which this second group of recipients of new money wishes to purchase.

The money spent in the second round becomes additional money receipts for another group of sellers, who likewise find their cash position improved and who, in turn, increase their demands for various goods and services. That results in a "third round" increase in prices. The process will continue until the demand for all goods and services in the economy, in principle, have been affected, with all prices to one extent or another changed by the monetary expansion. Prices in general will be higher, but each will have been affected by the monetary increase in a particular sequence, to a different degree, and at different times in the process.

The fact that monetary change works its way through the economy in a particular temporal sequence means that relative price relationships in the market will have been modified. The sequential price-increase differentials modify the relative profitabilities of producing various goods, which in turn influence the demand for and the allocation of resources and labor among the various sectors of the economy. As long as the inflationary process is working its way through the market, the patterns of demand for goods and services and the distribution of the factors of production are different from what they were before the inflationary process began, and they are different from what they will be when the inflationary process has come to an end.

At the same time, the very fact that the prices for those goods and resources (including labor) are changing in a non-neutral manner means that income and wealth are redistributed among individuals and groups as an integral part of the monetary process. Those who receive increases in the money supply earlier in the inflationary process are able to purchase more goods and services before the full price effect on the economy has materialized. On the other hand, those whose demands and incomes are impacted much later in the process find themselves paying higher prices for many of the goods they buy, while their own prices and wages have either not increased at all or not to an extent equal to the general rise in prices. That inevitably creates groups of net gainers and net losers during the sequential–temporal process following changes in the money supply.

Any anticipation by the participants in the market of the increase in the average level of prices remains just that: a statistically calculated average of the individual price changes. Both during an inflationary (or deflationary) process and at its end, some prices will have increased (or decreased) more than the average and some less than the average. For money to be neutral during an inflationary (or deflationary) process, it would be necessary for each participant in the market to anticipate correctly when and to what extent the demand and the price for his particular resource (including labor services) would be affected by the monetary expansion (or contraction) in the particular temporal sequence of that historically distinct timeframe. This clearly involves a greater degree of knowledge than can ever be possessed by agents in the market.

Nor is the non-neutrality of money dependent on the fact that the prices for many resources and labor services are fixed by contract for various periods of time. Even if they were not, in the temporal–sequential stages of an inflationary (or deflationary) process, the prices for different goods are affected at different times, necessarily modifying the relative profitabilities of producing those goods. It is those price-differential effects that influence producers to change their production decisions during an inflation (or deflation) and not merely the fact that some prices and wages are fixed.

Likewise, it is not the unanticipated changes in the money supply per se that cause money to be non-neutral and, therefore, to have real output and employment effects on the economy. Rather it is the fact that monetary changes work their way through the economy in a manner that necessarily cannot be fully anticipated and that actually modifies the relative prices of goods and the relative income positions among individuals and groups as an inherent part of any inflationary or deflationary process.

If any monetary change is always non-neutral in its effect on the market, then changes in the money supply made by the government's monetary authority in an attempt to maintain a "stable" price level can themselves be destabilizing. This, in fact, was the argument made by Mises' fellow Austrian Economist Friedrich A. Hayek.

Friedrich A. Hayek and the destabilizing influence of a stable price level

One indication of rising standards of living is increases in the quantity and quality of goods available to the consuming public. For example, during the twenty-year period from 1880 to the turn of the century a dramatic increase in the productive capacity of the United States economy occurred, matched by an equally significant expansion of goods and services. In their *Monetary History of the United States, 1867–1960,* Milton Friedman and Anna Schwartz pointed out:

> The two final decades of the nineteenth century saw a growth of population of over 2 per cent per year, rapid extension of the railway network, essential completion of continental settlement, and an extraordinary increase both in the acreage of land in farms and output of farm products ... [A]t the same time, manufacturing industries were growing even more rapidly.[27]

As a result, between 1879 and 1897, real net national product increased at an average annual rate of about 3.7 percent, with per capita net national product increasing at a 1.5-percent annual average rate during this period. The improvements in productive capacity and output, of course, did not occur evenly year-by-year. During this period the United States experienced several severe economic downturns, sometimes related to the uncertainties surrounding the political battles of the time concerning whether America would remain on a gold standard or shift to a bimetallic standard of gold and silver.

But what is also interesting about this period of rapid industrial growth and rising standards of living is that it occurred during a time when prices in general were falling. Between 1865 and 1899 the average level of prices declined more than 45 percent. From 1880 to 1897 prices in general declined by more than 22 percent, or 2 to 3 percent each year. "Economic growth," as Milton Friedman later observed, "was entirely consistent with falling prices."[28]

Assuming that there is neither an increase in the supply of money nor a decrease in the demand for money, it is inevitable that increases in productivity, output, and, therefore, the quantities of goods and services offered on the market will result in the prices of those goods and services decreasing. Given the demand for any commodity, an increase in its supply will result in a decrease in its price, if all that is offered for sale is to attract enough buyers to take the good off the market.

If improvements in productivity and increases in output are occurring in many sectors of the economy more or less at the same time, then many prices will be decreasing, each one sufficiently to bring supply and demand into balance in its respective market. If statistical averages of market prices are calculated before and after these greater supplies of goods have been placed on the market, they will show that a decline in the general "price level" of goods and services has occurred. The market will have experienced "price deflation."

But it should be clear that there is nothing inherently harmful in this type of deflationary process. If an entrepreneur introduces a technological innovation to lower his costs of production, it is because he hopes to be able to make a commodity for less, so he can offer it for a lower price, yet still reap larger profits. The price decline is part of his plans. Even if competition forces him to fully lower the price to reflect his now lower costs of production, there are no negative consequences for the economy. Competition will have done its job, which is to compete prices down to the lowest level consistent with the most efficient costs of manufacturing.

It is, of course, possible that an entrepreneur may have overestimated the quantity that will be demanded at the lower price. As a consequence, his total revenue might be less than before the cost efficiencies were introduced into the operation. This means that consumers value more other goods on the market. For example, suppose that the old price was $10 and he had been selling 100 units each month. His total monthly revenues would have been $1,000. Suppose the new price is $9 but he sells 105 units per month; his total revenue would now be $945. Consumers would be buying more and economizing while doing so.

These consumers would shift those saved dollars toward other purchases. Suppose that an entrepreneur in another market has also introduced cost efficiencies into his line of production. Previously he sold 200 units of his commodity each month at a price of $16 apiece, for a total revenue of $3,200. Now he prices the good at $15 and sells 217 units each month for total revenues of $3,255. Consumers will be buying more of this second good as well, paying for the additional quantities with the $55 saved on the first good. Previously consumers spent a total of $4,200 on the two goods and obtained 100 units of the first good and 200 units of the second. After cost-efficiencies in production have lowered prices, they still spend a total of $4,200 on these two goods, but now they are able to buy 105 units of the first and 217 units of the second. Their standard of living has improved through an increase in the real buying power of their dollars.

In the jargon of the economist, the demand for the first good was inelastic (at the lower price total revenue was less), while the demand for the second good was elastic (at the lower price total revenue was more). As a result, it may be necessary for some of the resources, including labor, to be let go in the manufacture of the first good and reemployed in the market where the second good is produced. There is simply no way to get around this in the long run. Changes in demand or supply always carry the need to modify what goods are produced, where they are manufactured, or with what resources. It is part of the price people must pay in a free society for improvements in the quantities and qualities of the goods and services offered on the free market.

If there is an attempt to prevent prices from adjusting to their market-clearing levels in the face of cost-efficiencies and greater supply, the result can only be imbalances and distortions in the market. Eventually adjustments must be made to the reality of supply and demand. Delaying them only builds a backlog of needed market changes that will be more severe in their effects than if the necessary incremental adjustments been allowed to occur as they slowly manifested themselves.[29]

In the late 1920s and early 1930s, Austrian Economist Friedrich A. Hayek argued that the policy of price-level stabilization was creating such imbalances in the market by preventing a fall in prices in the face of cost-efficiencies and greater supplies of goods. He made this case in an essay, "Intertemporal Price Equilibrium and Movements in the Value of Money," and in two books, *Monetary Theory and the Trade Cycle* and *Prices and Production*.[30]

Hayek said that if a proper balance between supplies and demands was to be maintained, then the price of each good had to reflect the actual supply and demand conditions in existence in the various markets during each time period. Any attempt to "stabilize" the price of a good or a set of goods at some given "level," in spite of differing market conditions that might arise, would set in motion market responses that would be "destabilizing."

If, for example, the supply of a good would be greater in the future than today because of some innovation introduced that would lower costs, and if equilibrium existed in that future period as well as in the present period, the price of that good in the future (assuming given demand conditions) would have to be lower than the price in the present period. If this good's future price was "stabilized" at the "level" that prevailed in the present, this would result in future expected profit margins being greater than if natural market forces were at work, competing the price down to reflect the now lower costs of production. The "stabilized" higher price in the future would tend to induce an excess production of the good in comparison to what the "real" supply and demand conditions would dictate; this "surplus" would eventually have a destabilizing effect on the market.

What was true for any particular good would be true during a general expansion of output due to falling costs across markets. If each price in this situation was permitted to find its proper equilibrium level, then, as measured by some statistical averaging, the general "price level" would have declined. But the structure of relative prices will have kept the various supplies and demands in balance.

However, through most of the 1920s the Federal Reserve expanded the money supply in an attempt to prevent prices from falling in the face of increasing supplies of goods resulting from cost-efficiencies in the methods of production. The monetary expansion created a situation in which the prices for various goods and services were above what they would have been if not for the increase in the money supply.

Suppose, using our previous example, that our two entrepreneurs had each lowered their costs by $1 a unit, enabling them to lower their respective prices from $10 and $16 to $9 and $15. But now suppose that the government monetary authority increased the money supply by $322 and distributed this sum among consumers in a manner that enabled them to buy five more units of the first good and seventeen more of the second at the original prices of $10 and $16, respectively. The first entrepreneur would earn total revenues of $1,050 instead of $945, and the second would earn total revenues of $3,472 instead of $3,255. Our two entrepreneurs would be earning additional profits of $105 and $272, respectively, with total spending on the two goods being $4,522 instead of $4,200.

The artificially maintained selling prices and the larger earned profits would stimulate these entrepreneurs to expand their outputs to, say, 110 and 225 units. But for consumers to be able to buy these larger quantities at the original prices of $10 and $16, total consumer spending would have to be $4,700 ($1,100 for the first good and $3,600 on the second). If the money supply was not expanded by another $178 when the additional quantities were offered on the market, these entrepreneurs would discover that they had increased their supplies in excess of the consumers' ability to buy them at the original prices of $10 and $16.

Furthermore, in the process of attempting to expand their outputs due to the stimulus of greater profits, these entrepreneurs would have to attract resources and labor from other sectors of the economy to increase their levels of production. Part of the additional profits earned, therefore, would have to be expended as higher resource prices and wages to bid them away from their alternative employments in other parts of the economy.

But unless there were to be a change in the patterns of consumer demand, when these resource owners and workers earned these higher input prices and wages, they would spend them not on the larger quantities of these two goods that were now available, but on other goods they preferred instead. As result, it would be discovered that too much of these two goods were on the market, and too little of the other commodities.

The market would then have to go through a "correction," in which output was cut back in the two sectors of the economy that had originally experienced the cost efficiencies, and resources and labor would have to be reallocated to sectors of the economy that had greater consumer demand. The false appearance of economic stability with a stabilized "price level" would be hiding the fact that the monetary expansion that stabilized the price level was in fact distorting profit margins and creating imbalances in the relative supplies of various goods offered.

Austrian Economists such as Mises and Hayek combined their theory of the non-neutrality of money with the Austrian theory of capital and interest to develop what is known as the Austrian theory of the business cycle.

The Austrian theory of capital and interest

Time is an element inseparable from the human condition. Everything we do involves time. Reading this chapter takes time. And the time taken by reading is not available for other things. The importance of time in the processes of production and in the evaluation of choices has been emphasized by many members of the Austrian School of Economics, beginning with Carl Menger, the founder of the School.

But among the early members of the Austrian School it was Eugen von Böhm-Bawerk who developed the first detailed analysis of the role of time in the processes of production and the process of human choice. The first two volumes of his master work on this theme, *Capital and Interest,* were published in the 1880s. The third volume, which mostly replied to his critics, appeared in its final edition in 1914, shortly before his death.[31]

The other major contributor to the Austrian theory of time in the early years of the twentieth century was the American economist Frank A. Fetter. His analysis of the process of "time-valuation" was presented in two treatises, *The Principles of Economics* and *Economic Principles.*[32] During the 1930s and 1940s, additional contributions to the theory of capital and interest were made by the Austrian Economists Richard von Strigl in *Capital and Production,*[33] Friedrich A. Hayek in *Prices and Production* and *The Pure Theory of Capital*[34] and Ludwig von Mises in *Nationalökonomie*[35] and *Human Action.*

Every one of our actions requires us to think about time and act through time. Whether it is boiling an egg or constructing a spaceship, we are confronted with the necessity of waiting for the desired result. We apply the means at our disposal to the tasks at hand, and we try to bring about the desired ends. But the cause (the application of the means) always precedes the effect (the resulting end or goal); and between the initiation (cause) and its conclusion (effect), there is always a period of time, be it merely a few minutes or many, many years. Each one of our plans, therefore, contains within it a *period of production.*

Rarely, however, can our production plans be completed in one step. Usually the resources must go through various transformations in a number of *stages of production* before the consumer good is ready for use. A tree must be chopped down in the forest. The wood must be transported to the lumber mill and processed. The cut wood must be taken to the pulp factory and manufactured into paper. The paper must be boxed and shipped to the print shop. The paper must be printed and trimmed to size to produce the volume that is in your hands. What is expressed in this simple example has its analog in every line of production for the manufacture of every conceivable good.

To undertake these processes of production, however, requires a certain amount of savings. Resources and raw materials that might otherwise have been used to satisfy a more immediate want must be freed up for more time-consuming production activities. First, some resources must be available for transformation into capital goods – tools, machinery, and equipment – with which workers who are not employed in the more direct manufacture of consumer goods can combine their efforts in more time-consuming, or "roundabout," production processes. Second, resources and consumer goods must be available for use by those employed during the production processes leading up to the completion of other finished goods.

The more savings, the more and longer are the processes of production that can be undertaken and, as a result, the greater the quantities and the qualities of the goods that will be available in the future. Why? Because other things held even, the more time-consuming, or "roundabout," the production process, the more productive are the resulting methods of production.

However, the longer the periods of production, the longer we have to wait for the goods we desire. Therefore, we have to evaluate the sacrifice, in terms of time spent waiting, that we are willing to make to get a potentially greater and more desired effect.

The sacrifices of time people are willing to make differ among individuals. And these differing evaluations of time open up opportunities for potential gains from trade. Those who are willing to defer consumption and the uses of resources in the present may find individuals who desire access to larger quantities of goods than they currently have available to them. And this latter group may be willing to *pay a price in the future* for the use of those resources in the present.

An intertemporal price emerges in the market as transactors evaluate and "haggle" over the value of time and the use of resources. The rate of interest is that intertemporal price. It reflects the time preferences of the market actors regarding the value of resources and commodities in the present compared to their future value.

As the price of time, the rate of interest balances the willingness by some to save with the desire by others to borrow. But the rate of interest not only coordinates the plans of savers and investors, it also acts as a "brake" or "regulator" on the length of the production time undertaken with the available savings. For example, what are the respective present values of $100 invested for one year, two years, or three years, with a market rate of interest of, say, 10 percent? They would be, respectively, $90.91, $82.64, and $75.13. Suppose that people changed their time preferences and now chose to save more, and the resulting greater supply of savings available for lending decreased the rate of interest to 7 percent. What would be the present values of $100 invested for one, two, or three years? The present values would be, respectively, $93.46, $87.74, and $81.97.

The present value will have increased for all three potential investments, with their different time horizons. But the percentage increases in the present values of these three possible investment horizons would not be the same. On the one-year investment project, its present value will have increased by 2.8 percent. On the two-year project, its present value will have increased by 5.7 percent. And on the three-year, its present value will have increased by 8.6 percent. Clearly, the tendency from a fall in the rate of interest would be an increase in investments with longer periods of production.

If time preferences were to move in the opposite direction, with people choosing to save less, the resulting increase in the rate of interest would make longer-term investments relatively less attractive. If the rate of interest were to rise from 7 percent to 10 percent, the present values of $100 invested for one, two, or three years would decrease, respectively, by 2.7 percent, 5.4 percent, and 8 percent. This would make investments with shorter periods of production appear relatively more attractive.

In an economy experiencing increases in real income, decisions by income-earners to save a larger proportion of their income need not require an absolute decrease in consumption. Suppose income-earners' time preferences were such that they normally saved 25 percent of their income. On an income of $1,000, they would save $250. If their preference for saving were to rise to 30 percent, with a given income of $1,000, their consumption would have to decrease from $750 to $700 to increase their savings from $250 to $300. However, if income earners were to have an increase in real income to $1,100 and their savings preference were to increase to 30 percent, they would now save $330. But consumption would also rise to $770. This is why savings can increase for new capital formation and investments in even longer periods of production without any absolute sacrifice of consumption in a growing economy. Consumption increases with higher real income, it just increases less than it could have had income-earners not chosen to save a greater percentage of that income.

But if there were a decline in the demand for consumer goods and an increase in savings, what would be the incentive for producers to invest in more capital and productive capacity? An economist named L.G. Bostedo leveled this criticism against Böhm-Bawerk at the beginning of the twentieth century. He argued that since market demand stimulates manufacturers to produce goods for the market, a decision by income-earners to save more and consume less destroys the very incentive for undertaking the new capital projects that greater savings are supposed to facilitate. Bostedo concluded that greater savings, rather than being an engine for increased investment, served to retard investment and capital formation.[36]

In 1901, in "The Function of Savings," Böhm-Bawerk replied to this criticism.[37] "There is lacking from one of his premises a single but very important word," Böhm-Bawerk pointed out. "Mr. Bostedo assumes ... that savings signifies necessarily a curtailment in the demand for consumption goods." But, Böhm-Bawerk continued:

> Here he has omitted the little word "present." The man who saves curtails his demand for present goods but by no means his desire for pleasure-affording goods generally ... For the principle motive of those who save is precisely to provide for their own futures or for the futures of their heirs. This means nothing else than that they wish to secure and make certain their command over the means to the satisfaction of their future needs, that is over consumption goods in a future time. In other words, those who save curtail their demand for consumption goods in the present merely to increase proportionally their demand for consumption goods in the future.[38]

But even if there is a potential future demand for consumer goods, how shall entrepreneurs know what type of capital investments to undertake and what types of greater quantities of goods to offer in preparation for that higher future demand?

Böhm-Bawerk's reply was to point out that production is always forward-looking – a process of applying productive means today with a plan to have finished consumer goods for sale tomorrow. The very purpose of entrepreneurial competitiveness is to constantly test the market, so as to better anticipate and correct for existing and changing patterns of consumer demand. Competition is the market method through which supplies are brought into balance with consumer demands. And if errors are made, the resulting losses or less than the anticipated profits act as the stimuli for appropriate adjustments in production and reallocations of labor and resources among alternative lines of production.

When left to itself, Böhm-Bawerk argued, the market successfully assures that demands are tending to equal supply, and that the time horizons of investments match the available savings needed to maintain the society's existing and expanding structure of capital in the long run.

The Austrian theory of the business cycle

The Austrian theory of the business cycle was first developed by Ludwig von Mises. He built the theory on the earlier contributions of his Austrian teacher Eugen von Böhm-Bawerk and the writings of the Swedish Economist Knut Wicksell.

We saw that the Austrian Economists, especially beginning with Böhm-Bawerk, had emphasized that all production takes time. The Austrians also explained that for time-consuming processes of production to be undertaken, savings were needed to free up resources from more direct consumption uses for investment in the formation and maintenance of capital and for supplying goods and resources to sustain the "roundabout" production processes.

Savings come from the time preferences of market participants who are willing to forgo present uses and consumption of goods and resources and transfer them to those who wish to utilize those goods and resources in the processes of production. The market interactions of suppliers and demanders of those resources generated market rates of interest that balance savings with investment. At the same time, the available savings resulting from these intertemporal market exchanges set the limits on the periods of production that could successfully be undertaken and maintained given the fund of savings available to sustain them in the long run.

In 1898, the Swedish Economist Knut Wicksell published *Interest and Prices*.[39] He adapted Böhm-Bawerk's theory of capital and time-consuming processes of production and took it a step further. Wicksell explained that in the actual market goods do not trade directly one for the other. Rather, money serves as the intermediary in all transactions, including the transfer of savings to potential borrowers and investors. Individuals save in the form of money income not spent on consumption. They then leave that money savings on deposit with banks, which serve as the financial intermediaries in the market's intertemporal transactions.

These banks pool the money savings of numerous people and lend those savings to creditworthy borrowers at the prevailing market rates of interest, and which balance the supply of savings with the investment demand for it. The borrowers then use that money savings to enter the market and demand the use of resources, capital, and labor by offering money prices for their purchase and hire. Thus, the decrease in the money demand and the lower prices for consumer goods (the results of savings) and the increased demand and the higher money prices for producer goods (the results of investment borrowing) act as the market's method to shift and reallocate resources and labor from consumption purposes to capital-using production purposes.

But Wicksell pointed out that precisely because money served as the intermediary link in connecting savings decisions with investment decisions, a peculiar and perverse imbalance in the savings-investment process could result. Suppose that the savings in society were just enough to sustain the undertaking and completion of one-year periods of production. Now suppose that the government monetary authority were to increase the amount of money available to the banks for lending. To attract borrowers to take these additional funds, the banks would lower the rates of interest.

The lowered market rates of interest created by the monetary expansion would raise the present value of investment projects with longer time horizons to their completion. As a consequence, suppose that borrowers were to undertake investment projects with a two-year period of production. Because of the increased money demands for resources and labor for these two-year investment projects, some factors of production would be drawn away from one-year projects. Thus, at the end of the first year fewer consumer goods would be available. With fewer goods on the market at the end of this first year, consumers' goods prices would rise and consumers would have to cut back their purchases. Consumers, Wicksell said, would be "forced" to save – that is, they would have to consume less in the present and wait for the two-year investment projects to be completed to enjoy a greater supply of goods.

At the same time, the greater supply of money would tend to increase prices, and, as a consequence, society would experience a general price inflation. If the government monetary authority were to repeat its increase of the money supply time-period after time-period, it would set in motion what Wicksell called an unending "cumulative process" of rising prices.

In writing *The Theory of Money and Credit,* Ludwig von Mises accepted the general outline of Wicksell's analysis of the effect of monetary expansion on production and prices. But he took Wicksell's idea further and demonstrated the process by which a monetary expansion of this type eventually created an "economic crisis" and generated the sequence of events known as the business cycle.[40]

Mises distinguished between two types of credit offered on the market: "commodity credit" and "circulation credit." Mises' student and early follower in applying the Austrian theory of the business cycle, Fritz Machlup, called these types of credit "transfer credit" and "created credit."[41] And it is this latter terminology that we will use because it more clearly states the distinction that Mises was trying to make.

If there were no increase in the money supply, any money savings out of income would represent a real transfer of market control over resources and labor from income-earners to potential investors. Savers will have loaned a quantity of real resources represented by the monetary value of those real resources in investment activities instead of using them in the more direct and immediate manufacture of consumer goods. This "transfer credit" of real resources for investment purposes would be returned to savers when the money loans were paid off with the agreed-upon rate of interest, and that returned sum of money would then have the capacity to purchase a greater quantity of real goods and services for consumption purposes. And the investment projects undertaken with this transfer credit would have time horizons consistent with the available savings and the period over which the loans were made.

However, the government monetary authority has the capacity to disrupt this fairly tight fit between savings and investment that is kept in balance by the market-determined rates of interest. Through its ability to expand the money supply, the monetary authority has the power to create credit for lending purposes. The "created credit" is indistinguishable from transfer credit for market transactions. It represents additional units of the medium of exchange that are interchangeable with all other units of money. Thus they are as readily accepted in market transactions as the units of money in existence before the monetary expansion.

Yet, Mises argued, there is an important difference: There is no compensating decrease in consumer demand for goods, services, and resources, which normally follows from the decision to save more, to counterbalance the increased demand for the use of resources and labor by the investment borrowers who took the created credit offered on the loan market.

At this point, Mises applied his theory of the non-neutrality of money to explain the sequence of events likely to follow. With newly created credit, the investment borrowers would bid resources and labor away from the production of consumer goods and investment projects with shorter time-horizons to begin investment projects with lengthier periods of production.

To attract resources and labor to these time-consuming activities, the investment borrowers would have to bid up the prices of the required factors of production to draw them away from their alternative uses in the economy. The newly created credit now passes to these factors of production as higher money incomes. They become the "second-round" recipients of the newly created money. Unless these factors of production change their time-preferences, and therefore their willingness to save, their real demand for consumer goods would be the same as before the increase in the money supply. They would, therefore, increase their money demand for finished goods and services in the same proportion of their income as before.

As a result, the prices for consumer goods would now start to rise as well. But because of the reallocation of resources away from consumer goods production, the quantities of such goods available on the market are less than before, which intensifies the rise in the prices of consumer goods. As the "second-round" factors of production expend their higher money incomes on desired consumer goods, the sellers and producers of these goods become the "third-round" recipients of the newly created money. Producers of consumer goods now increase their demand for the same scarce factors of production to draw them back into the consumer goods sectors of the economy and into investment projects with shorter time-horizons to satisfy more quickly the greater money demand for consumer goods. The factors of production drawn back into these activities closer to the final consumer stage of production become the "fourth-round" recipients of the newly created money.

Those who initially had taken the created credit from the loan market now find it increasingly difficult to continue and complete their longer-term investment projects. A "crisis" begins to emerge as a growing number of these longer-term investment projects cannot be financially continued. The demand for additional loanable funds from banks pushes market rates of interest up, creating an even greater crisis in the investment sector. The expansionary or "boom" phase of the business cycle now turns into the contractionary or "depression" phase as a growing number of these lengthier investment projects collapse.

The only way to temporarily save some of these investment activities would be for the government monetary authority to increase the money supply again in the form of more created credit. But this would merely set the same process in motion once more with the same inevitable result. If the monetary authority were to try to prevent this inevitable result through greater and greater increases in the money supply, the end-result would be a higher and higher rate of price inflation, which would threaten destruction and collapse of the society's monetary system.

Mises' conclusion from this analysis was that the causes of the business cycle in modern society were not to be found in some fundamental flaw in the market economy. Rather its basic cause was to be found in government manipulation and mismanagement of money and credit.

Austrian business cycle theory and the causes of the Great Depression

In June 1931, British economist Lionel Robbins wrote a foreword for Friedrich A. Hayek's *Prices and Production*. Professor Robbins explained the "marvelous renaissance" that the Austrian School of Economics had experienced since the end of the Great War under the leadership of such economists as Ludwig von Mises. Among the Austrian School's most important recent contributions, he said, was its theory of the business cycle, which Hayek's small volume was meant to introduce to the English-speaking world. Professor Robbins pointed out:

> Most monetary theorists seem to have failed utterly to apprehend correctly the nature of the forces operative in America before the coming of the [great] depression, thinking apparently that the relative stability of the price level indicated a state of affairs necessarily free from injurious monetary influences. The Austrian theory, of which Dr. Hayek is such a distinguished exponent, can claim at least this merit, that no one who really understood its principle tenets could have cherished for a moment such vain delusions.[42]

History is never the result of one influencing factor, even a strongly dominating one. And this was no less true in the case of the political and economic influences at work before the Great Depression began in 1929. World War I had disrupted normal economic and political relationships around the globe. Vast quantities of physical capital and human labor were consumed and destroyed in the four years of war. Wartime and postwar inflations tore apart the social and cultural fabrics of several major countries in Europe, especially those of Germany and Austria. The institutions of civil and liberal society were severely weakened and replaced with interventionist and socialist political regimes that limited or abolished civil and economic liberties.

New nations rose up in Central and Eastern Europe with the collapse of the German, Austrian, and Russian empires. To one degree or another, all followed the path of economic nationalism, imposing protectionist trade barriers, subsidizing agriculture and various privileged industries, nationalizing entire sectors of the economy, instituting artificial foreign exchange rates and exchange controls, and establishing welfare statist programs. Germany's reparations payments were a peculiar mechanism of financial musical chairs, with the U.S. lending money to the Germans so that they could meet their payments to the Allied powers, including America. American and European trade barriers made it difficult for the Germans to earn the needed sums through exports to fulfill all their financial obligations under the terms of the peace treaty that had ended the war.

The monetary system of the world – the international gold standard – was fatally weakened by inflationary policies during and after the war. In spite of the weaknesses of the gold standard and in spite of the abuses of the gold standard by the governments that had managed it before 1914, it had brought about the high degree of monetary stability that fostered a global economic environment conducive to savings, investment, international trade, and capital formation. In the 1920s, however, the monetary systems of the major nations of Europe were increasingly fiat currencies more directly controlled and manipulated by government, even when they remained nominally "linked" to gold. In the United States, the establishment of the Federal Reserve System in 1913 created a new centralized engine for monetary expansion. In this setting, the American Federal Reserve System undertook its experiment in the monetary stabilization of the price level.[43]

In the 1920s, as we have seen, Ludwig von Mises had demonstrated the fundamental weakness in all attempts to stabilize an economy through price-level stabilization by explaining the inherent non-neutrality of money. Changes in the money supply necessarily originate through the injection of additional sums into the market. These additions to the money supply then have an impact on the rest of the economy through the particular temporal–sequential process through which the new money is spent. The result would be a change in the general purchasing power or value of money, but in the process of bringing this about the structure of relative prices, wages, and income, as well as the allocation of resources, would also have been changed. And if the monetary injections occurred through the banking system, a business cycle might very well be set in motion.

But it was Mises' young Austrian colleague Friedrich A. Hayek who detailed why stabilizing the price level could distort the structure of relative prices into setting a business cycle in motion. In *Monetary Theory and the Trade Cycle*, Hayek argued that the role of the interest rate in a market economy was to assure that the amount and the time-horizons of investment activities were kept in balance with the available savings.

In an economy experiencing increases in productivity and capital formation, cost efficiencies and increased productive capacities would, over time, put downward pressure on prices due to the increased supplies of goods offered. The price of each good would decrease to the extent required to assure that the market was kept in balance. In the markets in which consumer demand was fairly responsive (or "elastic") to the increase in available supplies, the individual prices might decline only moderately. While in other markets in which consumer demand was noticeably less responsive (or "inelastic") to such an increase, the individual prices would have to decrease to a greater extent to keep the greater supply in balance with the demand.

Over time, the average level of prices as measured by some statistical price index would record that a "deflation" of prices had occurred. But this "price deflation" was not harmful – it was essential if the market-determined structure of relative prices was to keep supplies and demands in balance.

Instead of allowing this secular downward trend in prices to occur naturally, the Federal Reserve increased the supply of money in the American economy to counteract this normal process of price deflation. In aggregate terms, the amount of money demanded for goods and services was increased just enough to match the increase in the quantity of goods and services to maintain the general statistical average of prices at a fairly "stable" level throughout most of the 1920s (as measured by the wholesale price index).

But, argued Hayek:

> [T]he rate of interest which equilibrates the supply of real savings and the demand for capital cannot be a rate of interest which also prevents changes in the price level. In this case, stability of the price level presupposes change in the supply of money: but these changes must always lead to a discrepancy between the amount of real savings and the volume of investment. The rate of interest at which, in an expanding economy, the amount of new money entering circulation is just sufficient to keep the price-level stable, is always lower than the rate which would keep the amount of available loan-capital equal to the amount simultaneously saved by the public: and thus, despite the stability of the price-level, it makes possible a development leading away from the equilibrium position.[44]

Increases in the money supply, institutionally, are introduced in the form of increased reserves supplied to the banking system by the Federal Reserve, on the basis of which additional loans may be extended. But the only way banks can induce potential borrowers to take up these increased loanable funds is to lower the rate of interest and so decrease the cost of borrowing relative to the expected rate of return. But the rate of interest is not only the measure of the cost of a loan; it is also the factor by which the prospective value of an investment is capitalized in terms of its present value. The lower rate of interest also acts, therefore, as a stimulus for undertaking longer-term investment projects.[45]

232   The Austrians and the Keynesian revolution

Thus in the 1920s, beneath the apparent calm of a stable price level, Federal Reserve policy was creating a structure of relative price and profit relationships that induced an amount of longer-term investments that were in excess of actual savings to sustain them in the long run. Why were they unsustainable in the long run? Because as new money was spent on new and expanded investment projects, it eventually passed as higher money incomes into the hands of factors of production drawn into these employments. As these higher money incomes were then spent, the demands for consumer goods increased as well, attracting resources back to consumer goods production and investment projects with shorter time-horizons. Only through further injections of additional quantities of money into the banking system was the Federal Reserve able to keep market rates of interest below their proper equilibrium levels and thus temporarily maintain the profitabilities of the longer-term investment projects set into motion by the attempt to keep the price level stable.

Finally, in late 1928, under the pressure of this monetary expansion, the price level began to rise. The Federal Reserve, fearful of creating an absolute inflationary rise in prices, reined in the money supply. But with the end of monetary expansion, interest rates began to rise to their real market levels. Some longer-term investment projects were now unprofitable at the higher rates of interest. The investment "boom" collapsed, its first major indication being the "break" in the stock market in October 1929.

In 1932, Hayek summarized the lessons of the 1920s in "The Fate of the Gold Standard":

> Instead of prices being allowed to fall slowly, to the full extent that would have been possible without inflicting damage on production, such volumes of additional credit were pumped into circulation that the level of prices was roughly stabilized ... Whether such inflation merely serves to keep prices stable, or whether it leads to an increase in prices, makes little difference. Experience has now confirmed what theory was already aware of; that such inflation can also lead to production being misdirected to such an extent that, in the end, a breakdown in the form of a crisis becomes inevitable. This, however, also proves the impossibility of achieving in practice an absolute maintenance of the level of prices in a dynamic economy.[46]

The inherent limitation in focusing upon any index of prices in general was pointed out by another of Mises' students, Gottfried Haberler, in 1928, before the beginning of the Great Depression. Haberler emphasized,

> The general price level is not a given, self-evident fact, but a theoretical abstraction ... For each purpose a separate concept of the price level must be established ... An economically relevant definition of the price level cannot be independent of the purpose in mind, and for each purpose a separate index must be computed.

Indices are constructed on the basis of selecting a particular group of prices for purposes of tracing the path of some average price trend, depending on whether one was interested in tracking changes in real income, for example, shifts in the real value of deferred payments, or in the general movements in consumer or producer prices.

Furthermore, regardless of the particular purpose for which a price index may be statistically constructed, any such average necessarily hid changes that might occur between the individual prices subsumed under the average. "The relative position and change of different groups of prices are not revealed, but are hidden and submerged in a general [price] index," Haberler emphasized. And he pointed out, "It may happen, and it would be by no means inexplicable, that a period will come when prosperity is correlated with a downward movement of the price level and depression with an upward movement."[47]

Corrective forces in the market were now set in motion in 1929, once the monetary expansion had come to an end. But the depth and duration of the Great Depression turned out to be far greater and longer than would have normally seemed to be required for economy-wide balance to be restored. The reasons for the Great Depression's severity, however, were not to be found in any inherent failing in the market economy, but in the political ideologies and government policies of the 1930s.

The great depression and the crisis of government intervention

The Great Depression of the early 1930s was the most severe in modern history. In terms of the usual statistical figures alone, its magnitude was catastrophic. Between 1929 and 1933, the gross national product in the United States decreased by 54 percent, with industrial production declining 36 percent. Between 1929 and 1933, investment spending decreased by 80 percent, while consumer spending declined by 40 percent; expenditures on residential housing declined by 80 percent. In 1929, unemployment had been 3.2 percent of the civilian work force; by 1932 unemployment had gone up to 24.1 percent, and it rose even further, to 25.2 percent, in 1933.

The wholesale price index decreased by 32 percent from 1929 to 1933, and the consumer price index decreased by 23 percent. American agriculture saw the prices paid by farmers for raw materials, wages, and interest decrease by 32 percent, while the amounts farmers received for their output decreased by 52 percent.

Between 1930 and 1933, 9,000 banks failed in the United States, and tens of thousands of people lost their savings. The money supply (measured as currency in circulation and demand and time deposits, or "M-2") decreased by more than 30 percent between 1929 and 1933. Even if a larger measurement of the money supply is calculated ("M-2" plus deposits at mutual savings banks, the postal savings system, and the shares at savings and loans, a measurement known as "M-4"), the supply of money still decreased by about 25 percent between 1929 and 1933.

Internationally, the Great Depression was also devastating. The value of global imports and exports decreased by almost 60 percent, while the real volume of goods and services traded across borders declined by almost 30 percent. The gross domestic product fell by 5 and 7 percent, respectively, in Great Britain and France between 1929 and 1933. From 1929 to 1932, industrial production fell 12, 22, and 40 percent, respectively, in Great Britain, France, and Germany. Wholesale prices fell, on average, 25, 38, and 32 percent, respectively, in Great Britain, France, and Germany. Declines in consumer prices were 15 percent on average in both Great Britain and France, and 23 percent in Germany during this period.[48]

After the 1930s, most historians and many economists interpreted these numbers as a demonstration that the capitalist system had inherent flaws and tendencies toward cumulative instability that would prevent a return to a normal economic balance within any reasonable period of time. The Great Depression, therefore, came to be viewed as a "crisis of capitalism" and proof of the failure of (classical) liberal society.

This was not how many of the free market economists of the time viewed the early 1930s. For example, when German economist Moritz J. Bonn delivered the third Richard Cobden lecture in London on April 29, 1931, his topic was "The World Crisis and the Teaching of the Manchester School." Professor Bonn told his audience:

> The free play of economic forces have been replaced everywhere, at least in part, by private monopoly or by Government monopoly, by tariffs, and by all sorts of price control, from wage fixing by arbitration boards to valorization by farm boards ... There is intervention now on a big scale, based on forecasting and bent on planning, and there is a crisis much bigger than any crisis the world has seen so far ... For in the present economic situation of the world half of its institutions are [politically] manipulated whilst the other half are supposed to be free. The prices of the goods subject to the play of free competition have fallen all over the world ... The other prices have remained fairly rigid. They are maintained by economic and political coercion, by combines of labor and capital, supported by tariffs and other manipulating legislation ... If selected prices and sheltered wages can be maintained whilst all other prices are declining, a new satisfactory level [of equilibrium] cannot be attained ... The conflict between the free play of economic forces and the manipulation by Governments and monopolies is the main cause of the long continuation of the crisis.[49]

It was for this reason that a year later, in 1932, Mises concluded, "The crisis from which the world is suffering today is the crisis of interventionism and of national and municipal socialism; in short, it is the crisis of anticapitalist policies."[50]

In the United States, the crisis of anti-capitalist policies arose from the interventions of the Hoover administration. In November 1929, President Herbert Hoover met with leading American business and labor leaders; he told them that in this period of crisis purchasing power had to be maintained to keep the demand for goods and services high. He argued that wage rates should not be cut, that the work week should be shortened to "spread the work" among the labor force, and that governments at all levels should expand public works projects to increase employment.

Under the persuasion of the president and then through the power of trade unions, the money wage rates for many workers were kept artificially high. But this merely created the conditions for more, rather than less, unemployment. In 1930, consumer prices fell by 2.5 percent, while money wages declined on average by 2 percent. In 1931, consumer prices fell by 8.8 percent, while money wages decreased by only 3 percent. In 1932, consumer prices declined by 10.3 percent, while money wages decreased by only 7 percent. In 1933, consumer prices fell by 5.1 percent, and money wages decreased by 7.9 percent. While consumer prices fell almost 25 percent between 1929 and 1933, money wages on average only decreased 15 percent. Besides money wages lagging behind the fall in the selling prices of consumer goods through most of these years, labor productivity was also falling – by 8.5 percent. As a result, the real cost of hiring labor actually increased by 22.8 percent. The "high-wage" policy of the Hoover administration and the trade unions, therefore, only succeeded in pricing workers out of the labor market, generating an increasing circle of unemployment.[51]

American agriculture was also thrown out of balance by government intervention. During World War I the demand for American farm output had increased dramatically. But after 1918 European demand for U.S. agricultural goods decreased. This was partly due to a normal re-expansion of European agricultural production in peacetime, but also because of the growth in agricultural protectionism in Central and Eastern Europe that closed off part of the European market to American exports.

In the 1920s, the U.S. government attempted to prop up American farm production and income through subsidies and federally sponsored farm cooperative programs. In June 1929, the Hoover administration established the Federal Farm Board (FFB). Once the Depression began, the FFB started to extend cheap loans to the farming community to keep output off the market and prevent prices from falling. First wheat, then cotton and wool, and then dairy products came within the orbit of government intervention. The artificially high prices merely generated increasingly larger surpluses. Then the government attempted to restrict farm output to prevent prices from falling due to the very surpluses the government's farm price support programs had helped to create. As Austrian Economist Murray Rothbard explained:

> [T]he grandiose stabilization effort of the FFB failed ignominiously. Its loans encouraged greater production, adding to the farm surplus, which overhung the market, driving prices down both on direct and psychological grounds. The FFB thus aggravated the very farm depression that it was supposed to solve. With the FFB generally acknowledged a failure, President Hoover began to pursue the inexorable logic of government intervention to the next step: recommending that productive land be withdrawn from

cultivation, that crops be plowed under, and that immature farm animals be slaughtered – all to reduce the very surpluses that government's prior intervention had brought into being.[52]

In a further attempt to protect American agriculture from adjusting prices and production to the real supply and demand conditions of the world market, Congress passed and Herbert Hoover signed the Hawley-Smoot Tariff in June 1930. Benjamin Anderson, in his financial and economic history of the U.S., *Economics and the Public Welfare,* scathingly criticized this act of aggressive protectionism:

> In a world staggering under a load of international debt that could be carried only if countries under pressure could produce goods and export them to their creditors, we, the greatest creditor nation of the world, with tariffs already far too high, raised our tariffs again. The Hawley-Smoot Tariff Bill of June, 1930, was the crowning financial folly of the whole period from 1920 to 1933 ... [O]nce we raised our tariffs, an irresistible movement all over the world to raise tariffs and to erect other trade barriers, including quotas, began. Protectionism ran wild over the world. Markets were cut off. Trade lines were narrowed. Unemployment in the export industries all over the world grew with great rapidity, and prices of export commodities, notably farm commodities in the United States, dropped with ominous rapidity.[53]

U.S. farm exports as a percentage of farm income fell from 16.7 percent in the late 1920s to 11.2 in the early 1930s. U.S. exports of farm commodities fell by 68 percent between 1929 and 1933. Never was there a clearer case of government intervention resulting in consequences that were exactly contrary to its stated purpose!

After the British government abandoned the Gold Standard in September 1931, the Abnormal Importation Act was passed, giving the British Board of Trade authority to impose duties of up to 100 percent of the value of imported goods. The very day the Act was passed, a 50 percent import duty was imposed on twenty-three classes of goods, and importation of these goods practically ceased. On March 1, 1932, a 10 percent general tariff increase was established by the British government. And in July 1932, the British government introduced preferential tariffs for countries belonging to its empire at the expense of all other nations, including the U.S.

Germany instituted import licensing and bilateral trading arrangements supervised by the government in November 1931. By 1934, with the advent of the Nazis coming to power in Germany, exchange controls and import licenses were reinforced as part of the new National Socialist system of economic planning.

In 1928, the French government had lowered the import tariff rate to 15 percent, and lowered it once more to 12 percent in 1930. But in November 1931, a foreign exchange surcharge of 1 percent was imposed on British goods. And beginning in mid-1931, the French government established quotas on many imported goods. Indeed, by 1936, 65 percent of goods imported into France were entering the country under the quota system.

Christian Saint-Etienne, in his book *The Great Depression, 1929-1938,* concluded:

> [T]ariff restrictions were increasingly complemented by administrative measures, such as prohibitions, quotas, licensing systems, and clearing agreements ... Protectionism only led to a reduction in international trade, affecting all trading nations to a comparable extent, whether they initiated the trade war or merely retaliated ... It is clear that the collapse of international trade in the Depression made international recovery virtually impossible for a decade.[54]

What, then, was the way out of the Great Depression? The Austrians argued that there was only one successful route: a return to free, competitive markets.

The "Austrian" analysis and solution for the Great Depression

In February 1931, Ludwig von Mises delivered a lecture before a group of German industrialists on "The Causes of the Economic Crisis."[55] He explained that the economic depression through which they were living had its origin in the misguided monetary policies of the 1920s. The leading central banks of the major industrial countries had followed a policy of monetary expansion that had created an artificial boom that came to an end in 1929.

But after the downturn began, the depression was much more severe and prolonged than similar business cycles in the past. A unique circumstance was present that prevented the normal process of economic recovery. The unique circumstance was the pervasiveness of government interventionist policies:

> If everything possible is done to prevent the market from fulfilling its function of bringing supply and demand into balance, it should come as no surprise that a serious disproportionality between supply and demand persists, that commodities remain unsold, factories stand idle, many millions are unemployed, destitution and misery are growing and that finally, in the wake of all these, destructive radicalism is rampant in politics ... With the economic crisis, the breakdown of interventionist policy – the policy being followed today by all governments, irrespective of whether they are responsible to parliaments or rule openly as dictatorships – becomes apparent ... Hampering the functions of the market and the formation of prices does not create order. Instead it leads to chaos, to economic crisis.[56]

To the Austrian Economists, the Great Depression had been caused in the United States by the attempt to stabilize price levels through monetary expansion. The monetary expansion had artificially lowered interest rates and this, in turn, had induced an investment boom in excess of real savings in the economy.

Capital, resources, and labor had been misdirected into longer-term investment projects that, with the end of monetary inflation, were found to be unprofitable and economically unsustainable. Capital had been malinvested, labor had been misdirected, and the structure of relative prices and wages had been distorted.

Governments in the major industrial countries, including the United States, responded to the economic crisis by introducing a vast spider's web of interventionist regulations, controls, and restrictions on both domestic and international trade, as well as numerous public works projects. Rather than alleviating the depression, the interventionist measures had only made the situation worse. Governmental attempts to maintain prices and wages at levels inconsistent with real market conditions resulted in falling production and rising unemployment as goods went unsold and workers were released from their jobs.

These imbalances soon spread. The reason for this can be found in the fundamental truth of what economists since Jean-Baptiste Say in the early nineteenth century have called "the law of markets." No one can demand what others have for sale in the market unless they have something to supply in exchange. Each potential demander, therefore, has to offer in trade some good or service that others are interested in buying and at a price they are willing to pay. Doing otherwise limits the money income that can be earned from sales; and this in turn limits the amount of goods and services that can be bought from others.

Wrong prices – "disequilibrium" prices in the jargon of the economist – resulted in products and workers being priced out of the market once the Depression began in 1929. The resulting decreased revenues from the sale of goods and the resulting falling income from loss of employment meant that both businessmen and workers had to cut back their purchases of goods and services. These others, when unwilling to lower their prices and wages sufficiently in the face of falling demand, also saw, in turn, a decrease in sales and employment. The failure of prices and wages to adjust downward in the face of changing market conditions generated a "cumulative contraction" of output and employment, which, in turn, put further downward pressure on prices and wages in a widening circle of related markets. As the famous English economist Edwin Cannan concisely put it in 1932, "general unemployment is the result of a general asking too much."[57]

In 1933, Mises summarized the nature of the problem:

> [T]he duration of the present crisis is caused primarily by the fact that wage rates and certain prices have become inflexible, as a result of union wage policy and various [government] price support activities. Thus, the rigid wage rates and prices do not fully participate in the downward movement of most prices, or do so only after a protracted delay ... [T]he continuing mass unemployment is a necessary consequence of the attempts to maintain wage rates above those that would prevail on the unhampered market.[58]

Mises explained that now that interventionist policies had resulted in mass unemployment, governments proposed to get around the consequences of their own policies by resorting to a policy of "reflation." Governments hoped that if prices were raised through a new monetary expansion, unions would not immediately demand higher money wages to compensate for any lost purchasing power due to the resulting increase in the cost of living. If money wages remained relatively unchanged while the prices of goods and services were rising, this would mean that real wages would be cut, and employers might find it once again profitable to hire the unemployed. But, Mises argued, even if money wages did not immediately increase, the new monetary expansion merely would set the stage for another "bust" after a temporary "boom."

The inevitability of this result was explained by the British "Austrian" Lionel Robbins in the pages of *Lloyd's Bank Review* in 1932:

> [I]t is perhaps natural that the wish should arise to meet deflation by a counter inflation: to get around cost rigidities by acting on prices. And no doubt if inflation simply meant the simultaneous and definitive marking up of prices, as by a Government decree, there would be much to be said for this procedure. Unfortunately, inflation does not work this way. It is the essence of inflation that it affects some prices before others, that its final effects are different from its impact effects, and that production is affected differently at different stages of the process. In an inflationary boom, it is this unequal incidence of the inflation which gives rise to the maladjustments, which eventually produce the slump. Entrepreneurs are encouraged by artificially cheap money to embark on enterprises which can only be profitable provided costs do not rise. As the new money works through the system, costs do rise, and their enterprise is thus rendered unprofitable. For the time being, trade seems good but when the full effects of the inflation have manifested themselves there comes a crisis and subsequently depression.[59]

What then was the way out of the Great Depression? For the Austrian Economists it required the reversal of the interventionist policies that had exacerbated the economic crisis, and the forgoing of any monetary manipulation as a method to overcome the dilemma of unemployment. On the latter point, Friedrich Hayek, writing in 1932, was clear:

> To combat the depression by a forced credit expansion is to attempt to cure the evil by the very means which brought it about; because we are suffering from a misdirection of production, we want to create further misdirection – a procedure which can only lead to a much more severe crisis as soon as the credit expansion comes to an end.[60]

On the issue of interventionist policies that were preventing the market from normally and competitively functioning to restore economic balance, Lionel Robbins was also clear in 1932:

> It is impossible to get back to a state of true prosperity until the real underlying causes of the present stagnation are removed – barriers to international trade, in the shape of tariffs, quota systems, exchange restrictions and the like obstacles to internal adjustments in the shape of cost rigidities and bad debts which

should be written off ... But, above all, policy must be directed to restoring the freedom of the market in the widest sense of the term. By this I mean not only the lowering of tariffs and the abolition of trade restrictions but also the removal of all those causes which produce internal rigidity – rigid wages, rigid prices, rigid systems of production ... It is this inflexibility of the economic system at the present day which is at the root of most of our troubles.[61]

For Austrian Economists such as Mises, Hayek, and Robbins, the Great Depression was the fruit of the interventionist state. Beginning with the Great War, throughout the 1920s and into the Depression years of the early 1930s, the classical liberal world of free markets, free trade, and sound money under the gold standard had been undermined, weakened, and finally broken. In its place had arisen government-imposed systems of domestic regulation, nationalistic trade protectionism, price and wage rigidities, production subsidies, and state-sponsored monopolies and cartels.

The pre-World War I gold standard, though operated by government central banks, had more or less kept monetary and artificial credit expansions within narrow bounds. By the early and mid-1930s, the monetary systems of most countries were paper money systems, or monetary systems nominally gold-based but manipulated and abused by governments to serve interventionist domestic policies.

The Austrian Economists attempted to show the dead-end to which these policies had led. Unfortunately, their logical arguments and reasoned appeal fell on deaf ears. Instead, the United States and the European nations moved further down the interventionist road. And a major force for moving the intellectual climate in that direction was John Maynard Keynes.

John Maynard Keynes and the "New Liberalism"

In 1925, John Maynard Keynes delivered a lecture at Cambridge titled "Am I a Liberal?"[62] He rejected any thought of considering himself a conservative because conservatism "leads nowhere; it satisfies no ideal; it conforms to no intellectual standard; it is not even safe, or calculated to preserve from spoilers that degree of civilization which we have already attained."

Keynes then asked whether he should consider joining the Labor Party. He admitted, "Superficially that is more attractive," but rejected it as well. "To begin with, it is a class party, and the class is not my class," Keynes argued.

When it comes to the class struggle as such, my local and personal patriotism, like those of everyone else, except certain unpleasant zealous ones, are attached to my own surroundings ... [T]he Class war will find me on the side of the educated bourgeoisie.

Furthermore, he doubted the intellectual ability of those controlling the Labor Party, believing that it was dominated by "those who do not know at all what they are talking about."

This led Keynes to conclude that all things considered, "the Liberal Party is still the best instrument of future progress – if only it has strong leadership and the right program." But the Liberal Party of Great Britain could serve a positive role in society only if it gave up "old-fashioned individualism and laissez-faire," which he considered "the dead-wood of the past." Instead, what was needed was a "New Liberalism" that would involve "new wisdom for a new age." What this entailed, in Keynes' view, was "the transition from economic anarchy to a regime which deliberately aims at controlling and directing economic forces in the interests of social justice and social stability."

In 1926, Keynes published a lecture, "The End of Laissez-Faire," in which he argued, "It is *not* true that individuals possess a prescriptive 'natural liberty' in their economic activities. There is *no compact* conferring perpetual rights on those who Have or on those who Acquire." Nor could it be presumed that private individuals pursuing their enlightened self-interest would always serve the common good.

In a period in which industry was becoming concentrated and controlled by handfuls of industrial managers, Keynes proposed "a return, it may be said, towards mediaeval conceptions of separate [corporate] autonomies." But instead of these corporate entities being left to their own profit-making purposes, Keynes' proposed semi-monopolistic structures that would operate under government approval and clearly with government supervision.

In a world of "uncertainty and ignorance" that sometimes resulted in periods of unemployment, Keynes suggested "the cure for these things is partly to be sought in the deliberate control of the currency and of credit by a central institution." It also required the government's centralized collection of statistics and data about "the business situation" so the government could exercise "directive intelligence through some appropriate organ of action over many of the inner intricacies of private business." And he believed that "some coordinated act of intelligent judgment" by the government was required to determine the amount of savings in the society and how much of the nation's savings should be permitted to be invested in foreign markets as well as the relative distribution of that domestic savings among "the most nationally productive channels."

Finally, Keynes argued that government had to undertake a "national policy" concerning the most appropriate size of the country's population, "and having settled this policy, we must take steps to carry it into operation." Furthermore, Keynes proposed serious consideration of adopting a policy of eugenics: "The time may arrive a little later when the community as a whole must pay attention to the innate quality as well as to the mere numbers of its future members."[63]

This agenda for an activist and planning government did not make Keynes a socialist or a communist in any strict sense of these words. Indeed, after a visit to Soviet Russia he published an essay in 1925 strongly critical of the Bolshevik regime.[64]

> For me, brought up in a free air undarkened by the horrors of religion, with nothing to be afraid of, Red Russia holds too much which is detestable ... I am not ready for a creed which does not care how much it destroys the

liberty and security of daily life, which uses deliberately the weapons of persecution, destruction, and international strife ... It is hard for an educated, decent, intelligent son of Western Europe to find his ideals here.

But where Soviet Russia had an advantage over the West, Keynes argued, was in its almost religious revolutionary fervor, in its romanticism of the common working man, and its condemnation of money-making. Indeed, the Soviet attempt to stamp out the "money-making mentality" was, in Keynes' mind, "a tremendous innovation." Capitalist society, too, in Keynes' view, had to find a moral foundation above self-interested "love of money." What Keynes considered Soviet Russia's superiority over capitalist society, therefore, was its moral high ground in opposition to capitalist individualism. And he also believed that "any piece of useful economic technique" developed in Soviet Russia could easily be grafted onto a Western economy following his model of a New Liberalism "with equal or greater success" than in the Soviet Union.

That Keynes had great confidence in a state-managed system of "useful economic technique" was clearly seen in the following comparison he made, also in the mid-1920s, between a regulated wage system in the name of "fairness" between social classes and market-determined wages, which he condemned as "the economic juggernaut."

> The truth is that we stand mid-way between two theories of economic society. The one theory maintains that wages should be fixed by reference to what is "fair" and "reasonable" as between classes. The other theory – the theory of the economic juggernaut – is that wages should be settled by economic pressure, otherwise called "hard facts," and that our vast machine should crash along, with regard only to its equilibrium as a whole, and without attention to the change in consequences of the journey to individual groups.[65]

By the time John Maynard Keynes wrote these essays in the mid-1920s, he was already one of the most acclaimed economists in the world. His international notoriety had been established in 1919 when he published his criticism of the Treaty of Versailles, *The Economic Consequences of the Peace*.[66] In 1924 Keynes published *A Tract on Monetary Reform,* in which he called for abandoning the traditional gold standard and establishing a government-managed currency.[67] The gold standard meant that the value of a country's money was determined by international market forces to which each country had to conform in terms of appropriate adjustments in its domestic structure of prices and wages. If trade unions were strong and would not conform their wage demands to market conditions, then adherence to a market-guided gold standard could result in unemployment if the money wages that trade unions insisted upon were above what the global market determined those wages should be.

Instead, Keynes advocated abandoning the fixed exchange rate between gold and the British pound; the foreign exchange value of the British pound should be raised or lowered by the central bank to maintain domestic prices and wages at the politically determined desired level. Or as Keynes expressed it, "When stability of the internal price level and stability of the external exchanges are incompatible, the former is generally preferable."[68] As far as Keynes was concerned "there is no escape from a 'managed' currency, whether we wish it or not ... In truth, the gold standard is already a barbaric relic."[69]

In 1930, Keynes published a massive two-volume work that he hoped would establish his reputation as one of the great economists of the twentieth century, *A Treatise on Money*. But over the next two years many of the leading economists in Europe and North America wrote reviews that demonstrated the fundamental flaws in both the assumptions and the logic of his argument. But the most devastating criticisms were made by a young Friedrich A. Hayek in a two-part review essay that appeared in 1931–1932.[70]

Hayek showed that Keynes understood neither the nature of a market economy in general nor the significance and role of the rate of interest in maintaining a proper balance between savings and investment for economic stability. At the most fundamental level Hayek argued that Keynes' method of aggregating the individual supplies and demands for a multitude of goods into a small number of macroeconomic "totals" distorted any real understanding of the relative price and production relationships in and between actual markets. "Mr. Keynes' aggregates conceal the most fundamental mechanisms of change," Hayek said.[71]

In a complex market economy, it was one function of the rate of interest – as the price for the exchange of goods across time – to bring the supply of savings into balance with the demand to borrow funds for investment purposes. Changes in the rate of interest (reflecting a change in savings) assured such a proper balance and guided potential investors into using those funds for investment projects involving a period of time consistent with the available savings needed to sustain them. Keynes' argument that this was not the case led Hayek to state:

> Mr. Keynes' assertion that there is no automatic mechanism in the economic system to keep the rate of saving and the rate of investing equal might with equal justification be extended to the more general contention that there is no automatic mechanism in the economic system to adapt production to any shift in demand. I begin to wonder whether Mr. Keynes has ever reflected upon the function of the rate of interest in ... society.[72]

If there occurred prolonged unemployment and industrial depression, Hayek argued, then the cause was to be found in prices for goods and resources (including labor) being kept too high relative to actual supply and demand conditions in various markets. The solution was a free, competitive process to bring prices and costs into proper balance, and with this a return to full employment. Keynes' emphasis on aggregates and averages hid the actual pricing problems under the cover of macro "totals."

With the coming of the Great Depression, however, Keynes once again rejected the idea of a free market solution to the rising unemployment and idled industry that intensified following the crash of 1929. His remedy was outlined in two "open letters" to Franklin D. Roosevelt in December 1933 and June 1934, as well as in some addresses and speeches he delivered in England evaluating the possibilities and results of the New Deal.[73]

Keynes considered FDR "the trustee for those in every country who seek to mend the evils of our conditions by reasoned experiment within the framework of the existing social system," and he was the leader for whom Keynes was "the most sympathetic in the world." In Keynes' view, the New Deal contained two elements: "recovery and reform." The National Recovery Administration (NRA) represented one of the reform aspects of the New Deal. While considering this a desirable shift in American industrial policy for the long run, Keynes was critical of it as a short-run policy. First, the forced cartelization of American industry would "upset the confidence of the business world and weaken its existing motives to action before you have had time to put other motives in their place" and "[i]t may over task your bureaucratic machine." Second, by coercively restricting production and pushing up industrial prices and wages by decree, it was decreasing the demand for labor and thus doing nothing to stimulate employment.

Instead, Keynes recommended monetary expansion and federal deficit spending as the avenues for overcoming the mass unemployment of the Great Depression:

> [P]ublic authority must ... create additional current incomes through the expenditure of borrowed or printed money ... When more purchasing power is spent, one expects rising output at rising prices. Since there cannot be rising output without rising prices, it is essential to insure that the recovery shall not be held back by the insufficiency of the supply of money to support the increased monetary turnover ... The increased stimulation of output by increased aggregate purchasing power is the right way to get prices up ... I put in the forefront, for the reasons given above, a large volume of loan expenditure under government auspices ... [P]reference should be given to those which can be made to mature quickly on a large scale ... The object is to get the ball rolling ... I put in the second place the maintenance of cheap and abundant credit, in particular the reduction of the long-term rate of interest.[74]

In his writings of the 1920s and early 1930s, advocating a "New Liberalism" and a deficit-spending government to "solve" the Great Depression, were the premises for the Keynesian Revolution that would be officially inaugurated with the publication of *The General Theory of Employment, Interest and Money* in 1936. With those ideas, Keynes produced one of the greatest challenges to the free market economy in the twentieth century.

Keynes and Keynesian economics

The General Theory of Employment, Interest and Money by John Maynard Keynes was published on February 4, 1936. Its influence on the economics profession was astonishing, and its impact on economic theory and policy over the last seventy years has been immense. Paul Samuelson of MIT, the 1970 recipient of the Nobel Prize in Economics and one of the most influential expositors of Keynesian Economics in the post-World War II period, contributed an essay to *The New Economics,* edited by Seymour Harris in 1948, two years after Keynes' death. In an often-quoted passage, Samuelson explained:

> It is quite impossible for modern students to realize the full effect of what has been advisably called "The Keynesian Revolution" upon those of us brought up in the [pre-Keynesian] orthodox tradition. To have been born as an economist before 1936 was a boon – yes. But not to have been born too long before! ... *The General Theory* caught most economists under the age of 35 with the unexpected virulence of a disease first attacking and decimating an isolated tribe of South Seas islanders. Economists beyond fifty turned out to be quite immune to the ailment. With time, most economists in-between began to run the fever, often without knowing or admitting the condition ... This impression was confirmed by the rapidity with which English economists, other than those at Cambridge, took up the new Gospel ... at Oxford; and still more surprisingly, the young blades at the London School [of Economics] ... threw off their Hayekian garments and joined in the swim. In this country [the United States] it was pretty much the same story ... Finally, and perhaps most important from the long-run standpoint, the Keynesian analysis has begun to filter down into the elementary textbooks; and, as everybody knows, once an idea gets into these, however bad it may be, it becomes practically immortal.[75]

Even today, when the traditional Keynesian analysis has been challenged and set aside by many economists, the Keynesian framework still haunts most macroeconomic textbooks, demonstrating Samuelson's point that "however bad it may be" it has become "practically immortal."

The essence of Keynes' theory was to show that a market economy, when left to its own devices, possessed no inherent self-correcting mechanism to return to "full employment" once the economic system has fallen into a depression. At the heart of his approach was the belief that he had demonstrated an error in Say's Law. Named after the nineteenth-century French economist Jean-Baptiste Say, the fundamental idea is that individuals produce so they can consume. An individual produces either to consume what he has manufactured himself or to sell it on the market to acquire the means to purchase what others have for sale. Or as the classical economist David Ricardo expressed it,

> By producing, then, he necessarily becomes either the consumer of his own goods, or the purchaser and consumer of the goods of some other person ... Productions are always bought by productions, or by services; money is only the medium by which the exchange is effected.[76]

Keynes argued that there was no certainty that those who had sold goods or their labor services on the market will necessarily turn around and spend the full amount that they had earned on the goods and services offered by others. Hence, total expenditures on goods could be less than total income previously earned in the manufacture of those goods. This, in turn, meant that the total receipts received by firms selling goods in the market could be less than the expenses incurred in bringing those goods to market. With total sales receipts being less than total business expenses, businessmen would have no recourse other than to cut back on both output and the number of workers employed to minimize losses during this period of "bad business."

But, Keynes argued, this would merely intensify the problem of unemployment and falling output. As workers were laid off, their incomes would necessarily go down. With less income to spend, the unemployed would cut back on their consumption expenditures. This would result in an additional falling off of demand for goods and services offered on the market, widening the circle of businesses that find their sales receipts declining relative to their costs of production. And this would set off a new round of cuts in output and employment, setting in motion a cumulative contraction in production and jobs.

Why wouldn't workers accept lower money wages to make themselves more attractive to rehire when market demand falls? Because, Keynes said, workers suffer from "money illusion." If prices for goods and services decrease because consumer demand is falling off, then workers could accept a lower money wage and be no worse off in real buying terms (that is, if the cut in wages was on average no greater than the decrease in the average level of prices). But workers, Keynes argued, generally think only in terms of money wages, not real wages (that is, what their money income represents in real purchasing power on the market). Thus, workers often would rather accept unemployment than a cut in their money wage.

If consumers demand fewer final goods and services on the market, this necessarily means that they are saving more. Why wouldn't this unconsumed income merely be spent hiring labor and purchasing resources in a different way, in the form of greater investment, as savers have more to lend to potential borrowers at a lower rate of interest? Keynes' response was to insist that the motives of savers and investors were not the same. Income-earners might very well desire to consume a smaller fraction of their income, save more, and offer it out to borrowers at interest. But there was no certainty, he insisted, that businessmen would be willing to borrow that greater savings and use it to hire labor to make goods for sale in the future.

Since the future is uncertain and tomorrow can be radically different from today, Keynes stated, businessmen easily fall under the spell of unpredictable waves of optimism and pessimism that raise and lower their interest and willingness to borrow and invest. A decrease in the demand to consume today by income-earners may be motivated by a desire to increase their consumption in the future out of their savings. But businessmen cannot know when in the future those income-earners will want to increase their consumption, nor what particular goods will be in greater demand when that day comes. As a result, the decrease in consumer demand for present production merely serves to decrease the businessman's current incentives for investment activity today as well.

If for some reason there were to be a wave of business pessimism resulting in a decrease in the demand for investment borrowing, this should result in a decrease in the rate of interest. Such a decrease because of a fall in investment demand should make savings less attractive, since less interest income is now to be earned by lending a part of one's income. As a result, consumer spending should rise as savings goes down. Thus, while investment spending may be slackening off, greater consumer spending should make up the difference to assure a "full employment" demand for society's labor and resources.

But Keynes doesn't allow this to happen because of what he calls the "fundamental psychological law" of the "propensity to consume." As income rises, he says, consumption spending out of income also tends to rise, but less than the increase in income. Over time, therefore, as incomes rise a larger and larger percentage is saved.

In *The General Theory,* Keynes listed a variety of what he called the "objective" and "subjective" factors which he thought influenced people's decisions to consume out of income. On the "objective" side: a windfall profit; a change in the rate of interest; a change in expectations about future income. On the "subjective" side, he listed "Enjoyment, Shortsightedness, Generosity, Miscalculation, Ostentation and Extravagance." He merely asserts that the "objective" factors have little influence on how much to consume out of a given amount of income – including a change in the rate of interest. And the "subjective" factors are basically invariant, being "habits formed by race, education, convention, religion and current morals ... and the established standards of life."[77]

Indeed, Keynes reaches the peculiar conclusion that because men's wants are basically determined and fixed by their social and cultural environment and only change very slowly, "The greater ... the consumption for which we have provided in advance, the more difficult it is to find something further to provide for in advance."[78] That is, men run out of wants for which they would wish investment to be undertaken; the resources in the society – including labor – are threatening to become greater than the demand for their employment.

Keynes, in other words, turns the most fundamental concept in economics on its head. Instead of our wants and desires always tending to exceed the means at our disposal to satisfy them, man is confronting a "post-scarcity" world in which the means at our disposal are becoming greater than the ends for which they could be applied. The crisis of society is a crisis of abundance! The richer we become, the less work we have for people to do because, in Keynes' vision, man's capacity and desire for imagining new and different ways to improve his life is finite. The economic problem is that we are too well-off.

As a consequence, unspent income can pile up as unused and uninvested savings; and what investment is undertaken can erratically fluctuate due to what Keynes called the "animal spirits" of businessmen's irrational psychology concerning an uncertain future.[79] The free market economy, therefore, is plagued with the constant danger of waves of booms and busts, with prolonged periods of high unemployment and idle factories. The society's problem stems from the fact that people consume too little and save too much to assure jobs for all who desire to work at the money wages that have come to prevail in the market, and which workers refuse to adjust downward in the face of any decline in the demand for their services.

Only one institution can step in and serve as the stabilizing mechanism to maintain full employment and steady production: the government, through various activist monetary and fiscal policies.

This is the essence of Keynesian economics.

Keynesian economic policy and its consequences

In a famous lecture, "National Self-Sufficiency," delivered in Dublin, Ireland, in April 1933, John Maynard Keynes renounced his previous belief in the benefits of free trade. He declared, "I sympathize ... with those who would minimize rather than those who would maximize economic entanglement between nations ... Let goods be homespun whenever it is reasonably and conveniently possible; and above all, let finance be primarily national."[80] He remained loyal to economic protectionism in *The General Theory*. In one of the concluding chapters he discovered new value in the seventeenth- and eighteenth-century writings of the Mercantilists and their rationales for government control over and manipulation of international trade and domestic investment.[81]

But Keynes expressed another sentiment in that 1933 lecture:

> We each have our own fancy. Not believing we are saved already, we each would like to have a try at working out our salvation. We do not wish, therefore, to be at the mercy of world forces working out, or trying to work out, some uniform equilibrium according to the ideal principles of laissez-faire capitalism ... We wish ... to be our own masters, and to be free as we can make ourselves from the interference of the outside world.[82]

Keynes was convinced that left to itself, the market economy could not be trusted to assure either stable or full employment. Instead, an activist government program of monetary and fiscal intervention was needed for continuing economic prosperity. If this also required a degree of state planning, Keynes was open to that kind of direct social engineering as well. In an often-quoted 1944 letter to Austrian economist Friedrich A. Hayek, Keynes said that he found himself "in a deeply moved agreement" with Hayek's arguments in *The Road to Serfdom*. But less frequently mentioned is what Keynes went on to say in that same letter:

> I should say that what we want is not no planning, or even less planning, indeed I should say that what we almost certainly want is more ... Moderate planning will be safe if those carrying it out are rightly oriented in their own minds and hearts to the moral issue ... Dangerous acts can be done safely in a community that thinks and feels rightly, which would be the way to hell if they were executed by those who think and feel wrongly.[83]

Of course, the question is: who determines which members of society think and feel "rightly" enough to qualify for the power and authority to plan for the rest of us? And how is it to be assured that such power does not fall into the hands of "those who think and feel wrongly"? Furthermore, on what basis can it be presumed that even those who claim to be "rightly oriented in their own minds and hearts" could ever possess the knowledge and ability to plan some desirable economic outcome for society?

Yet, as a number of commentators have pointed out, Keynes had no doubts about either his "rightness" or competency in claiming such authority or ability. He belonged to a British elite that viewed itself as being superior to the other members of the society in practically every way. As Keynes' sympathetic biographer Roy Harrod explained, "he was strongly imbued with ... the idea that the government of Britain was and could continue to be in the hands of an intellectual aristocracy using the method of persuasion."[84] And as the American Keynesian Arthur Smithies also pointed out, "Keynes hoped for a world where monetary and fiscal policy, carried out by *wise men* in authority, could ensure conditions of prosperity, equity, freedom, and possibly peace."[85]

As we have seen, Keynes argued that the fundamental problem with a laissez faire market economy was that as incomes went up over time the saved part of that income would grow proportionally.

Individuals were habituated and socialized into having certain types and amounts of consumer wants. When these tended to be satisfied, consumers ran out of things to demand, both in the present and the future. As a result, this would limit the amount of that growing fund of savings for which there would be private investment demand.

With a psychological limit on the propensity to consume, and with investment demand restrained by limited investment opportunities for future profits, savings would accumulate and go to waste. Since workers were presumed to be unwilling to accept any significant downward adjustment in their money wage demands because of "money illusion," aggregate demand for goods and services in the economy would be insufficient to profitably employ those willing to work at the rigid money wages prevailing on the market.

In Keynes' mind the only remedy was for government to step in and put those unused savings to work through deficit spending to stimulate investment activity. How the government spent those borrowed funds did not matter. Even "public works of doubtful utility," Keynes said, were useful: "Pyramid-building, earthquakes, even wars may serve to increase wealth," as long as they create employment. "It would, indeed, be more sensible to build houses and the like," said Keynes, "but if there are political or practical difficulties in the way of this, the above would be better than nothing."[86]

Nor could the private sector be trusted to maintain any reasonable level of investment activity to provide employment. The uncertainties of the future, as we saw, created "animal spirits" among businessmen which produced unpredictable waves of optimism and pessimism that generated fluctuations in the level of production and employment. Luckily, government could fill the gap. Furthermore, while businessmen were emotional and shortsighted, the State had the ability to calmly calculate the long run, true value and worth of investment opportunities "on the basis of the general social advantage."[87]

Indeed, Keynes expected the government would "take on ever greater responsibility for directly organizing investment." In the future, said Keynes, "I conceive, therefore, that a somewhat comprehensive socialization of investment will prove the only means of securing an approximation to full employment." As the profitability of private investment dried up over time, society would see "the euthanasia of the rentier" and "the euthanasia of the cumulative oppressive power of the capitalist" to exploit for his own benefit the scarcity of capital. This "assisted suicide" of the interest-earning and capitalist groups would not require any revolutionary upheaval. No, "the necessary measures of socialization can be introduced gradually and without a break in the general traditions of the society."[88]

This did not mean that the private sector would be completely done away with. Through its monetary and fiscal policies, the government would determine the aggregate level of spending in the economy, and then private enterprise would be allowed to operate in directing resources for the manufacture of the various individual goods to be sold on the market.

The role of fiscal policy was for the government to run deficits and inject a net increase of spending into the economy by borrowing the unused savings that accumulated as idle cash or unspent hoards of money. The key, in Keynes' view, was for the government to increase spending so that prices in general would rise. "The expectation of a fall in the value of money [a rise in prices] stimulates investment, and hence employment" because it would raise the profitability of prospective investments.

Why would rising prices stimulate investment profitability? Because, in Keynes' view, workers' "money illusion" worked both ways. Just as workers would not accept cuts in their money wages with a fall in prices, workers would not generally demand an increase in their money wages when there was a rise in prices. "[A] movement by employers to revise money-wage bargains down-ward," said Keynes, "will be much more strongly resisted than a gradual and automatic lowering of real wages as a result of rising prices."[89] The government's fiscal stimulus would raise prices in general relative to costs of production (especially the money-wage costs of labor), thus increasing profit margins and creating the incentives for private employers and investors to expand output and rehire the unemployed.

Matching the fiscal stimulus, government was to introduce any required monetary expansion to keep interest rates low. If the government's fiscal stimulus succeeded in generating greater investment spending in the private sector, this would increase the private sector's demand to borrow for the financing of expanding production activities. This increased demand to borrow would push interest rates up and dampen some of the private sector business activity that the government would be trying to stimulate. Thus, the government's monetary authority was to create enough money to satisfy both the government's and the private sector's demands to borrow, while keeping interest rates unchanged (or even lowered).

Though Keynes was suspicious of attempts to construct statistical models of the economy (indeed, in a 1939 article he forcefully criticized a leading developer of econometric techniques),[90] he clearly believed that it was within the capacity of the government to determine just the right amount of fiscal and monetary stimulus to establish and maintain a fully employed economy.

He also argued that government had to regulate and control a country's imports and exports to secure a desired level of domestic production and employment. "It will be essential for the maintenance of prosperity that the authorities should pay close attention to the state of the balance of trade ... For a favorable balance, provided it is not too large, will be extremely stimulating," Keynes said. As for the effects this would have on international trade, he stated that "the classical school [of economists] greatly overstressed ... the advantages of the international division of labor."[91]

For Keynes no aspect of economic life would remain unaffected by the activist hand of government. After all, he had said, "We each have our fancy," and his purpose was to devise the rationale and tools for government "to have a try working out our salvation."

Keynesian economics and Say's law of markets

In the preface to *The General Theory of Employment, Interest and Money,* John Maynard Keynes stated that "the composition of this book has been for the author a long struggle of escape ... a struggle of escape from habitual modes of thought and expression."[92] What Keynes struggled to escape from was the common-sense foundations of economics.

From Adam Smith in the eighteenth century to the Austrian Economists of the twentieth century, economics has developed and been refined into the study of human action and the logic of human choice. After more than two hundred years economists came to understand more clearly that nothing happens in "society" or "the market" that does not first begin with the actions and decisions of individuals. Indeed, "the market" is nothing more than a summarizing term to express the arena in which multitudes of individuals meet and interact as suppliers and demanders for the purpose of mutual gains through trade.

Each individual has various goals he would like to achieve. To attain them he must apply various means to bring those desired ends into existence through production. But man finds that, unfortunately, the means at his disposal are often insufficient to satisfy all the uses he has for them. He faces the reality of scarcity. He is confronted with the necessity to choose; he must decide which desired ends he prefers more. And then he must apply the means to achieve the more highly valued ends, while leaving the other, less valued, ends unfulfilled.

In his state of disappointment, man looks to see if there are ways to improve his situation. He discovers that others face the same frustration of unsatisfied ends. Sometimes he finds that those others have things that he values more highly than some of his own possessions, and they in turn value his possessions more highly than their own. A potential gain from trade arises, in which each party can be better off if they trade away what they respectively have for what the other has. But how much of one thing will be exchanged for another? This will be determined through their bargaining in the market. Finally, they may agree upon terms of trade, and will establish a price at which they exchange one thing for another: so many apples for so many pears; so many bushels of wheat for so many pounds of meat; so many pairs of shoes for a suit of clothes.

Trade becomes a regular event by which men improve their circumstances through the process of buying and selling. Appreciating the value of these trading opportunities, men begin to specialize their productive activities and create a system of division of labor, with each trying to find that niche in the growing arena of exchange in which they have a comparative production advantage over their trading partners. As the market expands, a growing competition arises between buyers and sellers, with each trying to get the best deal possible as a producer and a consumer. The prices at which goods are traded come more and more to reflect the contributing and competing bids and offers of many buyers and sellers on both sides of the market.

The more complex the network of exchange, the more difficult is the direct barter of goods one for another. Rather than be frustrated and disappointed in not being able to directly find trading partners who want the goods they have for sale, individuals start using some commodity as a medium of exchange. They first trade what they have produced for a particular commodity and then use that commodity to buy from others the things they desire. When that commodity becomes widely accepted and generally used by most, if not all, transactors in the market, it becomes the money-good.

It should be clear that even though all transactions are carried out through the medium of money, it is still, ultimately, goods that trade for goods. The cobbler makes shoes and sells them for money to those who desire footwear. The cobbler then uses the money he has earned from selling shoes to buy the food he wants to eat. But he cannot buy that food unless he has first earned a certain sum of money by selling a particular quantity of shoes on the market. In the end, his supply of shoes has been the means for him to demand a certain amount of food.

This, in essence, is the meaning of Say's Law. Jean-Baptiste Say called it "the law of markets": that is, unless we first produce we cannot consume; unless we first supply we cannot demand.[93] But how much others are willing to take of our supply is dependent on the price at which we offer it to them. The higher we price our commodity, other things held equal, the less of it others will be willing to buy. The less we sell, the smaller the money income we earn; and the smaller the money income we earn, the smaller our financial means to demand and purchase what others offer for sale. Thus, if we want to sell all that we choose to produce we must price it correctly, that is, at a price sufficiently low that all we offer is cleared off the market by demanders. Pricing our goods or labor services too high, given other people's demands for them, will leave part of the supply of the good unsold and part of the labor services offered unhired.

On the other hand, lowering the price at which we are willing to sell our commodity or services will, other things held equal, create a greater willingness on the part of others to buy more of our commodity or hire more of our labor services. By selling more, our money income can increase; and by increasing our money income, through correctly pricing our commodity or labor services, we increase our ability to demand what others have for sale.

Sometimes, admittedly, even lowering our price may not generate a large enough increase in the quantity demanded by others for our income to go up. Lowering the price may, in fact, result in our revenue or income going down. But this, too, is a law of the market: what we choose to supply is worth no more than what consumers are willing to pay for it. This is the market's way of telling us that the commodity or particular labor skills we are offering are not in very great demand. It is the market's way of telling us that consumers value others things more highly. It is the market's way of telling us that the particular niche we have chosen in the division of labor is one in which our productive abilities or labor services are not worth as much as we had hoped. It is the market's way of telling us that we need to move our productive activities into other directions, where consumer demand is greater and our productive abilities may be valued more highly.

Can it happen that consumers may not spend all they have earned? Can it be the case that some of the money earned will be "hoarded," so there will be no greater demand for other goods, and hence no alternative line of production in which we might find remunerative employment? Would this be a case in which "aggregate demand" for goods in general would not be sufficient to buy all of the "aggregate supply" of goods and labor services offered?

The answers had already been suggested in the middle of the nineteenth century by the English classical economist John Stuart Mill in a restatement and refinement of Say's law of markets. In an essay titled "Of the Influence of Consumption on Production," Mill argued that as long as there are ends or wants that have not yet been satisfied, there is more work to be done.[94] As long as producers adjust their supplies to reflect the actual demand for the particular goods that consumers wish to purchase, and as long as they price their supplies at prices consumers are willing to pay, there need be no unemployment of resources or labor. Thus, there can never be an excess supply of all things relative to the total demand for all things.

But Mill admits that there may be times when individuals, for various reasons, may choose to "hoard," or leave unspent in their cash holding, a greater proportion of their money income than is their usual practice. In this case, Mill argued, what is "called a general superabundance" of all goods is in reality "a superabundance of all commodities relative to money." In other words, if we accept that money, too, is a commodity like all other goods on the market for which there is a supply and demand, then there can appear a situation in which the demand to hold money increases relative to the demand for all the other things that money could buy. This means that all other goods are now in relative over-supply in comparison to that greater demand to hold money.

To bring those other goods offered on the market into balance with the lower demands for them (i.e., given that increased demand to hold money and the decreased demand for other things), the prices of many of those other goods may have to decrease. Prices in general, in other words, must go down, until that point at which all the supplies of goods and labor services people wish to sell find buyers willing to purchase them. Sufficient flexibility and adjustability in prices to the actual demands for things on the market always assure that all those willing to sell and desiring to be employed can find work. And this, also, is a law of the market.

Free market economists, both before and after Keynes, have never denied that the market economy can face a situation in which mass unemployment could exist and a sizable portion of the society's productive capacity could be left idle. But if such a situation were to arise, they argued that its cause was to be found in a failure of suppliers to price their goods and labor services to reflect what consumers considered them to be worth, given the demand for various other things, including money. Correct prices always assure full employment; correct prices always assure that supplies create a demand for them; correct prices always assure the harmony of the market.[95]

This was the reality of the law of markets from which Keynes struggled so hard to escape.

Keynesian economics and savings, investment, and interest

In the 1939 foreword to the French edition of *The General Theory,* John Maynard Keynes said that in writing the book he had broken out of the prevailing economic orthodoxy, "to be in strong reaction against it, to be escaping from something, to be gaining an emancipation.[96]

The freedom that Keynes wanted to gain was from the laws of economics, the logic of human choice, and the relationships between savings, investment, and interest. For Keynes, spending out of income was determined by his "psychological law" of people's "propensity to consume" out of any given level of income. This, we saw, was dependent on various cultural, racial, class, and religious habits that change very slowly. One thing Keynes was certain did not significantly influence people's willingness to consume was a change in the rate of interest; a rise or a fall in the rate of interest had no significant effect on people's willingness to save or spend more or less out of income earned.

What did the rate of interest influence? According to Keynes, it influenced people's willingness or "propensity" to hoard money. Given that propensity to consume out of income, the amount of income saved could either be invested in interest-earning securities or bonds or held as an idle cash balance. All the rate of interest influenced was the relative attractiveness of holding bonds or cash. No matter how low the rate of interest might go, individuals would not consume more; their consumption was determined by the "psychological law." They would merely hold more and more of their savings in idle cash.[97]

In Keynes' system, the rate of interest also had no appreciable effect on the willingness to invest. People's willingness to invest was based on their estimates of the likely profitability from a possible investment relative to the rate of interest to be paid to borrow the sums needed to undertake the project. But in Keynes' view there is no way to determine precisely what the future holds in store or what the prospective return from an investment will be. Since we all must try to make some estimate of the probable results from present actions undertaken toward a radically uncertain future, Keynes believed that people fall back on "conventional wisdom." That is, we model our beliefs about the future on the basis of what we think the majority of other people think at any point in time. "[B]eing based on so flimsy a foundation," Keynes argued, "it is subject to sudden and violent changes ... New fears and hopes will, without warning, take charge of human conduct." Being based on nothing but what each thinks the other person believes, investor expectations about investment possibilities and profitabilities are open to dramatic and unpredictable fluctuations that are far more important in influencing investment demand than any changes in the rate of interest, Keynes insisted.[98]

The great demon in the Keynesian system, therefore, was the "propensity" to save some portion of additional income earned, rather than consume it all. Savings diminished spending in the economy; diminished consumption spending decreased expected revenues from sales; lowered sales expectations made businessmen want to cut back production; lowered production meant fewer jobs; fewer jobs decreased total income earned in the economy; a decline in total income created a further falling off in consumer spending; and this additional falling off in consumer spending set the process of economic contraction in motion once again. If only everything that was earned was consumed, Keynes argued, then full employment and high production would be assured.

In explaining the fundamental error in Keynes' conception of the evils of savings, I can do no better than to quote the insightful response given by the German free market economist H. Albert Hahn, from his 1946 article, "Is Saving a Virtue or a Sin?":

> According to the classical [economic] concept of the problem of savings ... the interests of the individual and of the community are in full harmony. He who saves serves his own as well as the nation's welfare.
>
> He improves his own welfare because savings implies the transfer of means of consumption from the present, where his earnings are ample, to the future where his earnings may become scarce through old age and sickness. Furthermore, savings will increase his means through the interest he receives.
>
> The nation as a whole, on the other hand, benefits from savings since these savings are paid into a bank or some other reservoir of money from which an employer may borrow for productive purposes, for instance to buy machinery. This means a change in the direction of productive activity.
>
> Through saving, production is diverted from goods for immediate consumption to goods that cannot themselves be consumed but with which consumer goods can be produced. Production is diverted, as one puts it, from a direct to a roundabout way of production ... The roundabout way of production has the advantage of greater productivity ... The high productivity of the more capitalistic production methods has further favorable effects. Because [out of the greater cost-efficient productivity] employers can – and by competition are forced to – pay interest on the capital borrowed, to raise wages, and lower costs. The standard of living of the nation rises.
>
> This process is renewed over and over again, because increased savings permit primitive direct methods of production requiring small amounts of capital to be replaced by roundabout indirect methods requiring large amounts of capital.[99]

But doesn't the falling off of consumption from the act of saving reduce the demand for goods and thus decrease the profitability from production? Why would businessmen undertake new and time-consuming investment projects to increase production capacity in the future when demand for consumer goods shows itself to be less in the present?

The answer to this Keynesian argument, as we saw, was given by the Austrian economist Eugen von Böhm-Bawerk thirty-five years before Keynes wrote *The General Theory*. In his 1901 essay, "The Function of Savings," Böhm-Bawerk pointed out that the error in such an argument arises from the failure to remember that what people do in an act of savings is defer present consumption, not forgo consumption permanently. Income earners shift a portion of their demand for goods from the present to the future, at which point they plan to utilize what they have saved and additionally earned as interest income for some desired purposes.

The savings set aside free the resources and labor to be applied to those different, roundabout productive ways, so greater and improved quantities of the goods can be produced for some future demand. The task of the entrepreneur, as Ludwig von Mises cogently emphasized in his theory of the market process, is to anticipate the direction and timing of future consumer demand, as well as the prices those future consumers might be willing to pay for goods offered in certain quantities and qualities. The market rewards those entrepreneurs who more correctly anticipate these future market conditions with earned profits and punishes the less competent with no profits, or even losses.[100]

The market system of profit and loss through competition for the use of resources and the selling of products assures a greater rationality to investment decision-making than suggested by Keynes' references to "animal spirits" and "conventional wisdom." In the market economy, control over the investment decision-making process always tends to shift into those entrepreneurial hands that, in the division of labor, demonstrate the most ability to direct production into the avenues most consistent with present and future patterns of consumer demand.[101]

The market rates of interest are meant to bring into balance the individual plans of savers with the individual plans of borrowers and investors. They serve the same function as all other prices in the market: to coordinate the activities of multitudes of people for purposes of mutual benefit through opportunities for gains from trade. Changes in market rates of interest potentially modify consumption, saving, and investment decisions just as any other change in price may modify the amount of a good consumers find attractive to buy and sellers to offer for sale.[102]

In a developed market, with numerous consumers and producers, changes in price will, at some point, modify people's response. Each of us has a threshold that leads to what economists call "marginal decision-making." Some incremental change in price will result in some incremental increase or decrease in the amount of a good that some people are willing to purchase or sell.

By arguing that a mystical "psychological law" makes people consume a certain amount of their income independent of changes in the interest rate,

Keynes was rejecting the fundamental logic of human action and choice upon which economic understanding is based. The rate of interest not only influences the attractiveness, at the margin, of investing in bonds and securities versus holding a portion of one's income as a cash balance, the interest income to be earned from savings is also the cost of not consuming. And as with any price, as the rate of interest rises or falls, some people will find it more or less attractive to consume. It is the logic of these changes in people's willingness to consume or save in the face of a change in the rate of interest that assures that the supplies and demands for consumer goods, savings, and investment projects of particular types and durations are kept in balance.

It was this logic of human choice and the rationality of market relationships between savings, investment, and interest that Keynes said he was "reacting strongly against" and from which he wanted to gain his "freedom."

Keynesian economics and the hubris of the social engineer

In September 1936, John Maynard Keynes prepared a preface for the German translation of *The General Theory of Employment, Interest and Money*. Addressing himself to German economists, Keynes hoped that his theory would "meet with less resistance on the part of German readers than from English, when I submit to them a theory of employment and production as a whole," because the German economists had long before rejected the teachings of both the classical economists and the more recent Austrian School of Economics. And, said Keynes, "if I can contribute a single morsel to a full meal prepared by German economists, particularly adjusted to German conditions, I will be satisfied."

What were those particular "German conditions"? For more than three years, Germany had been under the rule of Hitler's National Socialist regime; in 1936, the Nazis had instituted their own version of four-year central planning.

Toward the end of this preface Keynes pointed out to his Nazi economist readers:

> The theory of aggregate production, which is the point of the following book, nevertheless can be much easier adapted to the conditions of a totalitarian state, than ... under conditions of free competition and a large degree of laissez-faire. This is one of the reasons that justifies the fact that I call my theory a *general* theory ... Although I have, after all, worked it out with a view to the conditions prevailing in the Anglo-Saxon countries where a large degree of laissez-faire still prevails, nevertheless it remains applicable to situations in which state management is more pronounced.[103]

It would be historically inaccurate to accuse Keynes of explicitly being either a Nazi sympathizer or an advocate of Soviet or fascist-type totalitarianism.[104] But Keynes clearly understood that the greater the degree of state control over any economy, the easier it would be for the government to manage the levers of monetary and fiscal policy to manipulate macroeconomic aggregates of "total output," "total employment," and "the general price and wage levels" for purposes of moving the overall economy into directions more to the economic policy analyst's liking.

On what moral or philosophical basis did Keynes believe that policy advocates such as himself had either the right or the ability to manage or direct the economic interactions of multitudes of peoples in the marketplace? Keynes explained his own moral foundations in *Two Memoirs,* published posthumously in 1949, three years after his death. One memoir, written in 1938, examined the formation of his "early beliefs" as a young man in his twenties at Cambridge University in the first decade of the twentieth-century.

He, and many other young intellectuals at Cambridge, had been influenced by the writings of philosopher G.E. Moore. Separate from Moore's argument, what are of interest are the conclusions reached by Keynes from reading Moore's work. Keynes said:

> Indeed, in our opinion, one of the greatest advantages of his [Moore's] religion was that it made morals unnecessary ... Nothing mattered except states of mind, our own and other people's of course, but chiefly our own. These states of mind were not associated with action or achievement or consequences. They consisted of timeless, passionate states of contemplation and communion, largely unattached to "before" and "after."[105]

In this setting, traditional or established ethical or moral codes of conduct meant nothing. Said Keynes:

> We entirely repudiated a personal liability on us to obey general rules. We claimed the right to judge every individual case on its own merits, and the wisdom, experience and self-control to do so successfully. This was a very important part of our faith, violently and aggressively held ... We repudiated entirely customary morals, conventions and traditional wisdoms. We were, that is to say, in the strict sense of the term immoralists ... [W]e recognized no moral obligation upon us, no inner sanction to conform or obey. Before heaven we claimed to be our own judge in our own case.[106]

Keynes declared that he and those like him were "left, from now onwards, to their own sensible devices, pure motives and reliable intuitions of the good." Then in his mid-fifties, Keynes declared in 1938, "Yet so far as I am concerned, it is too late to change. I remain, and always will remain, an immoralist." As for the social order in which he still claimed the right to act in such unrestrained ways, Keynes said that "civilization was a thin and precarious crust erected by the personality and the will of a very few, and only maintained by rules and conventions skillfully put across and guilely preserved."[107]

On matters of social and economic policy two assumptions guided Keynes, and they also dated from his Cambridge years as a student near the beginning of the century; they are stated clearly in a 1904 paper, "The Political Doctrines of Edmund Burke." First,

Our power of prediction is so slight, our knowledge of remote consequences so uncertain that it is seldom wise to sacrifice a present benefit for a doubtful advantage in the future ... We can never know enough to make the chance worth taking.

And second, "What we ought to do is a matter of circumstances ... [W]hile the good is changeless and apart, the ought shifts and fades and grows new shapes and forms."[108]

Classical liberalism and the economics of the classical economists had been founded on two insights about man and society. First, there is an invariant quality to man's nature that makes him what he is; and if society is to be harmonious, peaceful, and prosperous, men must reform their social institutions in a way that directs the inevitable self-interests of individual men into those avenues of action that benefit not only themselves but others in society as well. They therefore advocated the institutions of private property, voluntary exchange, and peaceful, open competition. Then, as Adam Smith had concisely expressed, men would live in a system of natural liberty in which each individual would be free to pursue his own ends, but would be guided as if by an invisible hand to serve the interests of others in society as the means to his own self-improvement.[109]

Second, it is insufficient in any judgment concerning the desirability of a social or economic policy to focus only upon its seemingly short-run benefits. The laws of the market always bring about certain effects in the long run from any shift in supply and demand or from any government intervention in the market order. Thus, as French economist Frederic Bastiat emphasized, it behooves us always to try to determine not merely "what is seen" from a government policy in the short run, but also to discern as best we can "what is unseen," that is, the longer-run consequences of our actions and policies.[110]

The reason it is desirable to take the less immediate consequences into consideration is that longer-run effects may not only not improve the ill the policy was meant to cure, but can make the social situation even worse than had it been left alone. Even though the specific details of the future always remain beyond our ability to predict fully, one use of economics is to assist us to at least qualitatively anticipate the likely contours and shape of that future aided by an understanding of the laws of the market.

Keynes' assumptions deny the wisdom and the insights of the classical liberals and the classical economists. The biased emphasis is toward the benefits and pleasures of the moment, the short run, with an almost total disregard of the longer-run consequences. It led F.A. Hayek to lament in 1941:

I cannot help regarding the increasing concentration on short-run effects ... not only as a serious and dangerous intellectual error, but as a betrayal of the main duty of the economist and a grave menace to our civilization ... It used, however, to be regarded as the duty and the privilege of the economist to study and to stress the long run effects which are apt to be hidden to the untrained eye, and to leave the concern about the more immediate effects to the practical man, who in any event would see only the latter and nothing else ... It is not surprising that Mr. Keynes finds his views anticipated by the mercantilist writers and gifted amateurs; concern with the surface phenomena has always marked the first stage of the scientific approach to our subject ... Are we not even told that, "since in the long run we all are dead," policy should be guided entirely by short-run considerations. I fear that these believers in the principle of *après nous le deluge* may get what they have bargained for sooner than they wish.[111]

But if every action and policy decision is to be decided in the context of shifting circumstances, as Keynes insisted, on what basis shall such decisions be made, and by whom? Such decisions are to be made on the basis of the self-centered "state of mind" of the policymakers, with total disregard of traditions, customs, moral codes, rules, or the long-run laws of the market. Their rightness or wrongness was not bound by any independent standard of "achievement and consequence." Instead it was to be guided by "timeless, passionate states of contemplation and communion, largely unattached to 'before' and 'after.' " The decision-maker's own "intuitions of the good," for himself and for others, were to serve as his compass. And let no ordinary man claim to criticize such actions or their results. "Before heaven," said Keynes, "we claimed to be our own judge in our own case."

Here was an elitist ideology of nihilism. The members of this elite were self-appointed and shown to belong to this elect precisely through mutual self-congratulations of having broken out of the straightjacket of conformity, custom, and law. For Keynes in his fifties, civilization was this thin, precarious crust overlaying the animal spirits and irrationality of ordinary men. Its existence, for whatever it was worth, was the product of "the personality and the will of a very few," like himself, naturally, and maintained through "rules and conventions skillfully put across and guilely preserved."

Society's shape and changing form were to be left in the hands of "the chosen" few who stood above the passive conventions of the masses. Here was the hubris of the social engineer, the self-selected philosopher-king, who through manipulative skill and guile directed and experimented on society and its multitudes of individuals. It is what made Keynes feel comfortable in recommending his "general theory" to a Nazi readership. His conception of a society maintained by "the personality and the will of a very few," after all, had its family resemblance in the Führer's principle of the unrestrained "one" who would command the *Volk*.

The rapidity with which Keynes' ideas captured the minds of economists was astounding. American economist Dudley Dillard began his 1948 book, *The Economics of John Maynard Keynes,* by pointing out,

Within the first dozen years following its publication, John Maynard Keynes' *The General Theory of Employment, Interest and Money* (1936) has had more influence upon the thinking of professional economists and public policy makers than any other book in the whole history of economic thought in a comparable number of years.[112]

Indeed, by the mid-1940s, especially in England and the United States, Keynes' *General Theory* had practically become a "new testament" for the economics profession. Soon after World War II, textbooks began incorporating its teachings to instruct the young, and non-technical, readable expositions of Keynes' ideas were published to indoctrinate the general public with the "wisdom" of its policy proposals.

One of the most clearly written of these expositions was *The Keynesian Revolution* by Lawrence R. Klein (who was awarded the Nobel Prize in Economics in 1980).[113] Published in 1947, it represented the growing consensus of the time among economists and government policy advocates. The final chapter outlined what should be expected from government if the Keynesian "insights" were to be fully applied for the "social good."

In the brave new world guided by the ideas of Keynes, Americans would have to accept a greater degree of government regimentation than they had in the past. Should they be afraid of this? No, Dr. Klein assured his readers: "The regimentation of unemployment and poverty is infinitely more severe than the regimentation of economic planning." He was sure that the American people would "quickly come forth with support" for the regimentation of economic planning.[114]

The government "economic planners" would have to have "complete control over government fiscal policy so that they can spend when and where spending is needed to stimulate employment and tax when and where taxation is needed to halt upward price movements." The slow, cumbersome congressional budgetary process would have to be put aside. In its place:

> We must have a planning agency always ready with a backlog of socially useful public works to fill any deflationary gap that may arise [through discretionary government deficit spending powers]; similarly, we must have a price-control board always ready with directives and enforcement officers to wipe out any inflationary gap that may arise ... Government spending should be very flexible and subject to immediate release or curtailment, in just the precise amount which will maintain full employment, no more and no less ... This is the road to the kind of full employment that we need.[115]

At the same time, government would have to see to it that the members of society were kept from saving too much and spending too little, since excessive savings would diminish the "aggregate demand" upon which "full employment" was dependent. This would require, Dr. Klein argued, an active and conscious policy of redistribution of income:

> If we redistribute income from the rich, who have a relatively high marginal propensity to save, to the poor [whose marginal propensity to save is generally lower], we will decrease the community's marginal propensity to save. Such policies of income redistribution can be carried out by taxing the rich and paying a dole or other types of contributions to the poor.[116]

Also, the motives for people privately desiring to save would have to be undermined by the government taking greater responsibility for such things as retirement planning. Dr. Klein argued:

> Most children are raised on the virtues of thrift, and high spenders are usually considered to be unworthy citizens. It is difficult to change these fundamental habits ... The people acting on individualistic principles do not know their own best interests. They must be taught to look at the system as a whole [in which consumption rather than savings is the "socially" desirable conduct] ... We must resort to indirect methods such as social-security programs which wipe out the need for savings.[117]

Here was Keynes' ideal formulated for a new American future. The constitutional procedure for legislative approval of taxation and expenditures would be thrown away; economic planners would have discretionary control over taxing and spending. Taxation would be a redistributive tool for macroeconomic policy manipulation. And since individuals "do not know their own best interests," the Keynesian planners would have to teach people to give up their old bad habits of self-reliance and savings, with the state becoming the paternalistic provider.

Keynes had understood the implications of his own ideas, after all: "customary morals, conventions and traditional wisdoms" would have to be set aside – including the American tradition of constitutional government and individual financial self-responsibility. The Keynesian planners claimed, as Keynes had expressed in his memoir, "the right to judge every individual case on its own merits, and the wisdom, experience and self-control to do so successfully," in their role as macroeconomic managers. And Keynes had clearly appreciated that, as he had told the German economists of the 1930s, his "theory of aggregate production ... nevertheless can be much easier adapted to the conditions of a totalitarian state." Thus did the Keynesian revolutionaries demand vast economic control over the private affairs and market activities of the population.

Ludwig von Mises and the economics of the long run

This was the state of Keynesian economics when Ludwig von Mises' *Human Action* was published over sixty years ago. Mises devoted little space to directly challenging or refuting Keynes and his ideas. He did not consider Keynes to be the father of a "new economics." Instead, he viewed Keynes as the most successful modern defender of the interventionist and inflationist ideas of the time:

> Keynes was not an innovator and champion of new methods of managing economic affairs. His contribution consisted rather in providing an apparent justification for the policies that were popular with those in power in spite of the fact that all economists viewed them as disastrous. His achievement was a rationalization of the policies already practiced. He was not a "revolutionary," as some of his adepts called him. The "Keynesian revolution" took

place long before Keynes approved of it and fabricated a pseudo-scientific justification for it. What he really did was to write an apology for the prevailing policies of governments. This explains the quick success of his book. It was greeted enthusiastically by the governments and the ruling political parties. Especially enraptured were a new type of intellectual, the "government economists." They had had a bad conscience. They were aware of the fact that they were carrying out policies which all economists condemned as contrary to purpose and disastrous. Now they felt relieved. The "new economics" reestablished their moral equilibrium.[118]

And as for Keynes' wit and literary style, Mises considered them to be "cheap rhetorical tricks" used to confuse, ignore, or distort the ideas of the classical economists and those of contemporary economists who opposed Keynes' policy proposals.[119]

He considered Keynes' emphasis on workers' "money illusion" to be nothing more than a rationale for not resisting the power of the unions to set money wages too high to assure full employment. In his 1931 monograph "The Causes of the Economic Crisis" and his article "The Crisis and Capitalism," Mises argued that massive unemployment was the direct consequence of wage rates being set by trade unions at a height above the market value of the workers' labor, given the available capital supply and the resulting marginal productivity of the workers desiring employment. Government funding of the unemployed in the form of the dole reduced union violence and prevented those desiring work from underbidding union wages levels, which reduced the pressure on the trade unions to modify their money wage demands. As a consequence, unemployment became a widespread and long-term phenomenon.[120]

In 1933 Mises had already criticized Keynes' idea that workers would be less resistant to a cut in their real wage if it occurred through a rise in the general price level while their money wages remained constant, than if their real wage was lowered through a fall in their money wage. Said Mises:

> [I]t is no longer denied, as it generally was a few years ago, that the duration of the present crisis is caused primarily by the fact that wage rates and certain prices have become inflexible, as a result of union wage policy and various price support activities. Thus, the rigid wage rates and prices do not fully participate in the downward movement of most prices, or do so only after a protracted delay ... [I]t is also admitted that the continuing mass unemployment is a necessary consequence of the attempts to maintain wage rates above those that would prevail on the unhampered market.
>
> ... Almost all who propose priming the pump through credit expansion consider it self-evident that money wages will not follow the upward movement of prices until their relative excess has disappeared. Inflationary projects of all kinds are agreed to because no one openly dares to attack the union wage policy, which is approved by public opinion and promoted by government. Therefore, so long as today's prevailing view, concerning the maintenance of higher than unhampered market wage rates and the

interventionist measures supporting them, exists, there is no reason to assume that money wage rates can be held steady in a period of rising prices.[121]

Mises' point was that with unions knowing that none of their money wage demands would be opposed, any attempt to reduce the real value of those money wages through an inflationary rise in the price level would be met by new and higher money wage demands to make up for any lost ground in real income. Or as Mises expressed it in *Human Action*,

> However, the success of such a cunning plan would require an unlikely degree of ignorance and stupidity on the part of the wage earners. As long as workers believe that minimum wage rates benefit them, they will not let themselves be cheated by such clever tricks.[122]

The only way the real wages and the standard of living of the general work-force could be raised in the long run was through capital formation, that is, through the processes of savings and investment to increase the marginal productivity of those employed in the production processes of the market.[123] This required secure property rights, low taxes, and a sound non-inflationary political–economic environment, not one dominated and manipulated by an "activist" government.

A recurring theme in most of Mises' writings was the idea that there does not exist any inherent conflict between the interests of the individual and that of society, and that the market process is an arena of mutually beneficial cooperation through participation in the social system of division of labor. Guided by the principle of comparative advantage – what Mises termed the universal social Law of Association – each man finds his most profitable niche in the collaborative activities of production and exchange. Through participation in the division of labor, each man increases the quantities, qualities, and varieties of goods that are at his disposal in comparison to isolated, self-sufficient production.[124]

The social system of division of labor requires a number of institutions. Private property is paramount, along with money prices generated through the competitive processes of buying and selling both finished goods and the factors of production. Market prices enable the intellectual exercise of economic calculation, through which the relative value and cost of all market-traded goods and services can be established so as to assure their rational and efficient use.

The competitive interaction of market supplies and demands, the structure of relative prices for goods and resources, the presence of entrepreneurial creativity and alertness induced through the potential for market-based profits, and a relative flexibility in the mobility and adaptability of the factors of production to changing circumstances are what assure the effective functioning of the social order.

Without them the social system of competitive cooperation is weakened and, in the extreme, threatened with collapse. Preserving the functioning of the market order, therefore, was the guiding principle for any social philosophy.

This necessarily meant that the economist's and the social philosopher's task, in Mises' view, was never to lose sight of "the long run" interest of maintaining this system of human association.[125] "All that good government can do," Mises said,

> to improve the material well-being of the masses is to establish and to pre-serve an institutional setting in which there are no obstacles to the progres-sive accumulation of new capital and its utilization for the improvement of technical methods of production ... Hence, the [classical] liberals conclude that the economic policy best fitted to serve the interests of all strata of a nation is free trade both in domestic business and international relations.[126]

This was the real basis for Ludwig von Mises' conflict with John Maynard Keynes. For Keynes, "in the long run we are all dead." The danger in the altern-ative "short run" orientation of social and economic policy was that it was likely to undermine those institutions without which a free and prosperous society could not endure. Mises reasoned:

> In the short run an individual or group may profit from violating the inter-ests of other groups or individuals. But in the long run, in indulging in such actions, they damage their own selfish interest no less than that of the people they have injured. The sacrifice that a man or a group makes in renouncing some short-run gains, lest they endanger the peaceful operation of the appar-atus of social co-operation, is merely temporary. It amounts to an abandon-ment of a small immediate profit for the sake of incomparably greater advantages in the long run.[127]

That is why Mises so forcefully opposed Keynes and his New Economics. Keynesianism was an economics of the short run that meant the end of the market economy by validating inflexible wages and prices, undermining the incentives for private saving and capital formation, threatening inflation-induced malinvestment, and weakening the institution of private property and market-guided decision-making. Thus, in Mises' view, Keynesian policy was the imple-mentation of an economic irrationality, because "unfortunately nearly all of us outlive the short run" and thus must bear the longer-run consequences.[128]

Unfortunately, many Keynesian presuppositions continue to dominate eco-nomic theory and policy. But if there ever was a voice that continues to warn against the temptations and dangers of an economics of the short run, it is Ludwig von Mises and the Austrian theory of money and the business cycle that he seminally helped to develop.

Notes

1 Henry Hazlitt, "The Case for Capitalism," *Newsweek* (September 19, 1949).
2 Henry Hazlitt, "Wrong Diagnosis, Wrong Remedy," *Newsweek* (August 15, 1949).
3 Allan Meltzer, "Time to Print Money," *Financial Times* (July 17, 1998), where he argued, "Monetary expansion and devaluation is a much better solution" to Japan's

economic difficulties; and, Milton Friedman, "Bubble Trouble," *National Review* (September 28, 1998), p.16. "We know how to stop deflation – print money. The Fed [Federal Reserve System] has plenty of ability to print money."

4 James Buchanan and Richard E. Wagner, *The Consequences of Mr. Keynes* (London: Institute of Economic Affairs, 1978), p. 14.

5 Leland B. Yeager, "The Keynesian Heritage in Economics," in John Burton, ed., *Keynes's General Theory: Fifty Years On: Its Relevance and Irrelevance to Modern Times* (London: Institute of Economics Affairs, 1986), p. 27.

6 F.A. Hayek, review of Roy F. Harrod's *The Life of John Maynard Keynes* [1952], reprinted in Bruce Caldwell, ed., *The Collected Works of F.A. Hayek, Vol. IX: Contra Keynes and Cambridge* (Chicago: University of Chicago Press, 1995), p. 232; see, also, John H. Williams, "An Appraisal of Keynesian Economics" [1948] reprinted in *Economic Stability in a Changing World* (New York: Oxford University Press, 1953), p. 60:

> In my last talk with Keynes, a few months before his death ... He complained that the easy money policy was being pushed too far, both in England and here [in the U.S.], and emphasized interest as an element of income, and its basic importance in the structure and functioning of private capitalism. He was amused by my remark that it was time to write another book because the all-out easy money policy was being preached in his name, and replied that he thought he ought to keep one jump ahead.

7 Robert Skidelsky, *John Maynard Keynes: Hopes Betrayed, 1883–1920* (New York: Macmillan, 1983); and *John Maynard Keynes: The Economist as Savior, 1920–1937* (New York: Macmillan, 1992); *John Maynard Keynes: Fighter for Freedom, 1937–1946* (New York: Macmillan, 2001).

8 Robert Skidelsky, "The Real Problem with Capitalism Is the Markets," *The Independent* (October 24, 1998).

9 The figures on the money supply, required reserves, and bank loans are primarily derived from the monumental studies by Milton Friedman and Anna Schwartz, *A Monetary History of the United States, 1867–1960* (Princeton, NJ: Princeton University Press, 1963) and *Monetary Statistics of the United States: Estimates, Sources, Methods* (New York: Columbia University Press, 1970).

10 C.A. Phillips, T.F. McManus and R.W. Nelson, *Banking and the Business Cycle: A Study of the Great Depression in the United States* [1937] (New York: Arena Press, 1972), pp. 22–23.

11 Benjamin M. Anderson, *Economics and the Public Welfare* (Princeton, NJ: D. Van Nostrand, 1949), p. 77:

> The rally in business production and employment that started in August of 1921 was soundly based on a drastic cleaning up of credit weakness, a drastic reduction in the costs of production, and the free play of private enterprise. It was not based on Government policy designed to make business good ... The depression [of 1920–1921] was, however, much less severe than that of the 1930s. This was primarily because of the very rapidity of the break in prices and the general readjustment of costs.

12 Again, these figures are drawn from Friedman and Schwartz, *Monetary Statistics of the United States*.

13 Irving Fisher, *The Purchasing Power of Money* [1911] (New York: Macmillan, revised ed., 1920); *Elementary Principles of Economics* (New York: Macmillan, 1912); *Stabilizing the Dollar* (New York: Macmillan, 1920); and *The Money Illusion* (New York: The Adelphi Co., 1928).

14 Fisher, *Stabilizing the Dollar*, pp. 82, 95–96.

15 Fisher, *The Money Illusion*, pp. 132–133.

16 Even on the eve of the great stock market crash that occurred during the last two

weeks of October 1929, Irving Fisher declared on September 5, 1929, "There may be a recession in stock prices, but not anything in the nature of a crash." And on October 16, 1929, Fisher insisted:

> Stock prices have reached what looks like a permanently high plateau. I do not feel that there will soon, if ever, be a fifty or sixty point break below present levels ... I expect to see the stock market a good deal higher than it is today within a few months.

17 Quoted in Murray N. Rothbard, *America's Great Depression* [1963] (Los Angeles: Nash Publishing, 1972), pp. 155–156.
18 John Maynard Keynes, *A Treatise on Money, Vol. II: The Applied Theory of Money* (New York: Harcourt, Brace, 1930), p. 258.
19 Friedman and Schwartz, *A Monetary History of the United States*, pp. 273–274.
20 Rothbard, *America's Great Depression*, pp. 83–89.
21 Phillips, McManus, and Nelson, *Banking and the Business Cycle*, p. 81.
22 Carl Menger, *Principles of Economics* [1871] (Glencoe, IL: The Free Press, 1950), pp. 259–285; "On the Origin of Money," [1892] reprinted inm Richard M. Ebeling, ed., *Austrian Economics: A Reader* (Hillsdale, MI: Hillsdale College Press, 1991), pp. 483–504.
23 Ludwig von Mises, *The Theory of Money and Credit* [1912, 2nd revised ed., 1924] (Indianapolis, IN: Liberty Classics, 1981), pp. 117–246; see also Murray N. Rothbard, *Man, Economy and State: A Treatise on Economic Principles*, Vol. I [1962] (Los Angeles: Nash Publishing, 1970), pp. 201–215.
24 Mises, *The Theory of Money and Credit*, pp. 215–223; "Monetary Stabilization and Cyclical Policy," [1928] inm Israel M. Kirzner, ed., *Classics in Austrian Economics, Vol. III: The Age of Mises and Hayek* (London: William Pickering, 1994), pp. 48–52; and *Human Action: A Treatise on Economics* (Irvington-on-Hudson, NY: Foundation for Economic Education, 4th revised ed., 1996), pp. 219–223.
25 John E. Cairnes, *Essays in Political Economy: Theoretical and Applied* [1873] (New York: Augustus M. Kelley, 1965), pp. 1–108.
26 Mises, *The Theory of Money and Credit*, pp. 160–168, 237–243; "Monetary Stabilization and Cyclical Policy," pp. 52–58; *Human Action*, pp. 416–422; and "The Non-Neutrality of Money," [1940] in, Richard M. Ebeling ed., *Austrian Economics: A Reader*, pp. 505–517.
27 Friedman and Schwartz, *A Monetary History of the United States*, p. 93.
28 Milton Friedman, "Inflation: Causes and Consequences" [1963] in *Dollar and Deficits* (Englewood Cliffs, NJ: Prentice-Hall, 1968), p. 26.
29 Gottfried Haberler, *The Different Meanings Attached to the Term "Fluctuations in the Purchasing Power of Gold" and the Best Instrument or Instruments for Measuring Such Fluctuations* (Geneva: League of Nations, F/Gold/74, 1931); Moritz J. Bonn and Alfred Tismer, *The Effect of Fluctuations in the Purchasing Power of Gold on the Economic Life of the Nations* (Geneva: League of Nations, F/Gold/80, 1931); Alexander Loveday, *The Instrument for the Measurement of the Purchasing Power of Gold* (Geneva: League of Nations, F/Gold/22, 1930); Fritz Machlup, "Inflation and Decreasing Costs of Production" in, H. Parker Willis and John M. Chapman, eds., *The Economics of Inflation: The Basis of Contemporary American Monetary Policy* (New York: Columbia University Press, 1935), pp. 280–287; Allan G.B. Fisher, "The Significance of Stable Prices in a Progressive Economy," *Economic Record* (March 1935), pp. 49–64, and "Does an Increase in Volume of Production Call for a Corresponding Increase in Volume of Money?" *American Economic Review* (June 1935), pp. 197–211; and George Selgin, "The 'Productivity Norm' Versus Zero Inflation in the History of Economic Thought," [1995] in *Bank Deregulation and Monetary Order* (London/New York: Routledge, 1996), pp. 163–189; and, *Less Than Zero: The Case for a Falling Price Level in a Growing Economy* (London: Institute of Economic Affairs, 1997).

268   *The Austrians and the Keynesian revolution*

30 Friedrich A. Hayek, "Intertemporal Price Equilibrium and Movements in the Value of Money," [1928] in, Israel M. Kirzner, *Classics in Austrian Economics,* Vol. III, pp. 161–198; *Monetary Theory and the Trade Cycle* [1929; 1933] (New York: Augustus M. Kelley, 1966); *Prices and Production* [1932; revised ed., 1935] (New York: Augustus M. Kelley, 1967).
31 Eugen von Böhm-Bawerk, *Capital and Interest* (South Holland, IL: Libertarian Press, 1959).
32 Frank A. Fetter, *The Principles of Economics* (New York: The Century Co., 1910); *Economic Principles* (New York: The Century Co., 1915).
33 Richard von Strigl, *Capital and Production* [1934] (Auburn, AL: Ludwig von Mises Institute, 1995).
34 Friedrich A. Hayek, *The Pure Theory of Capital* (New York: Macmillan, 1941); and "The Mythology of Capital," [1936] reprinted in Stephen Littlechild, ed., *Austrian Economics,* Vol. II (Brookfield, VT: Edward Elgar, 1990), pp. 63–92; also, Fritz Machlup, "Professor Knight and the 'Period of Production,'" [1935] reprinted in Israel M. Kirzner, ed., *Classics in Austrian Economics, Vol. II: The Interwar Period* (London: William Pickering, 1994), pp. 275–315.
35 Ludwig von Mises, *Nationalökonomie: Theorie des Handelns und Wirtschaftens* [1940] (Munich: Philosophia Verlag, 1980).
36 L.G. Bostedo, "The Function of Savings," [1900] reprinted in, Ebeling, ed., *Austrian Economics: A Reader,* pp. 393–400.
37 Eugen von Böhm-Bawerk, "The Function of Savings," [1901] reprinted in, Ebeling, ed., *Austrian Economics: A Reader,* pp. 401–413.
38 Ibid., pp. 406–407.
39 Knut Wicksell, *Interest and Prices: A Study of the Causes Regulating the Value of Money* [1898] (New York: Augustus M. Kelley, 1965).
40 Mises, *The Theory of Money and Credit,* pp. 377–404; "Monetary Stabilization and Cyclical Policy," pp. 69–87; *Human Action,* pp. 538–586.
41 Fritz Machlup, *The Stock Market, Credit and Capital Formation* [1931] (London: William Hodge & Co., revised ed., 1940), p. 224.
42 Lionel Robbins, "Foreword" in F.A. Hayek, *Prices and Production* (New York: Macmillan, 1932).
43 On the economic policies between the two world wars, see my "Introduction" to, Richard M. Ebeling, ed., *Selected Writings of Ludwig von Mises, Vol. 3: The Political Economy of International Reform and Reconstruction* (Indianapolis, IN: Liberty Fund, 2000), pp. xvii–xxii.
44 Hayek, *Monetary Theory and the Trade Cycle,* pp. 113–114.
45 Fritz Machlup, "The Rate of Interest as Cost Factor and as Capitalization Factor," *American Economic Review* (September 1935), pp. 459–465.
46 F.A. Hayek, "The Fate of the Gold Standard," [1932] in *Money, Capital and Fluctuations: Early Essays* (Chicago: University of Chicago Press, 1984), p. 129.
47 Gottfried Haberler, "A New Index Number and Its Meaning," [1928] reprinted in Anthony Y.C. Koo, ed., *The Liberal Economic Order, Vol. II: Money, Cycles and Related Themes* (Brookfield, VT: Edward Elgar, 1993), pp. 107–108, 113–114; the same criticism was made by, Benjamin M. Anderson, "Commodity Price Stabilization: a False Goal of Central Bank Policy," *The Chase Economic Bulletin* (May 8, 1929), p. 20.

> The general price level is, after all, merely a statistician's tool of thought. Businessmen and bankers often look at index numbers as indicating price trends, but no businessman makes use of index numbers in his bookkeeping. His bookkeeping runs in terms of the particular prices and costs that his business is concerned with ... Satisfactory business conditions are dependent upon proper relations among groups of prices, not upon any average of prices.

48 Christian Saint-Etienne, *The Great Depression, 1929–1938* (Stanford, CA: Hoover Institution Press, 1984), pp. 3–33.

49 Moritz J. Bonn, *The World Crisis and the Teaching of the Manchester School* (London: Cobden-Sanderson, 1931), pp. 13–14, 26–27.
50 Ludwig von Mises, "The Myth of the Failure of Capitalism," [1932] in Richard M. Ebeling, ed., *Selected Writings of Ludwig von Mises,* Vol. 2 (Indianapolis, IN: Liberty Fund, 2002), p. 191.
51 Richard Vedder and Lowell Gallaway, *Out of Work: Unemployment and Government in Twentieth Century America* (New York/London: Holmes & Meier, 1993), pp. 79–97.
52 Rothbard, *America's Great Depression,* p. 209.
53 Anderson, *Economics and the Public Welfare,* pp. 224–225.
54 Saint-Etienne, *The Great Depression,* p. 29.
55 Ludwig von Mises, "The Causes of the Economic Crisis: An Address," [1931] reprinted in, Percy L. Greaves, ed., *Von Mises, On the Manipulation of Money and Credit* (Dobbs Ferry, NY: Free Market Books, 1978), pp. 173–203.
56 Ibid., pp. 201–202.
57 Edwin Cannan, "Not Enough Work for All," [1932] in, *Collected Works of Edwin Cannan, Vol. VII: Economic Scares* (London: Routledge/Thoemmes Press, 1997), p. 38.
58 Mises, "The Current Status of Business Cycle Research and Its Prospects for the Immediate Future," [1933] reprinted in, Percy L. Greaves, ed., *Von Mises, On the Manipulation of Money and Credit,* p. 211.
59 Lionel Robbins, "The Ottawa Resolutions on Finance and the Future of Monetary Policy," *Lloyds Bank Limited Monthly Review* (October 1932), p. 432.
60 Hayek, *Monetary Theory and the Trade Cycle,* pp. 21–22.
61 Robbins, "The Ottawa Resolutions … " pp. 435, 437.
62 John Maynard Keynes, "Am I a Liberal?" [1925] in, *Essays in Persuasion* [1932] (New York: W.W. Norton, 1963), pp. 323–338.
63 Keynes, "The End of Laissez-Faire," [1926] in, *Essays in Persuasion,* pp. 312–322.
64 Keynes, "A Short View of Russia," [1925] in, *Essays in Persuasion,* pp. 297–311.
65 Quoted in, D.E. Moggridge, *Maynard Keynes: An Economist's Biography* (London/New York: Routledge, 1992), pp. 433.
66 John Maynard Keynes, *The Economic Consequences of the Peace* [1919] (New York: Harper & Row, 1971).
67 John Maynard Keynes, *A Tract on Monetary Reform* (New York: Harcourt, Brace, 1924).
68 Ibid., p. 177.
69 Ibid., p. 187.
70 F.A. Hayek, "Reflections on the Pure Theory of Money of Mr. J.M. Keynes," [1931–1932] in, Bruce Caldwell, ed., *The Collected Works of F.A. Hayek, Vol. IX: Contra Keynes and Cambridge, Essays and Correspondence,* pp. 121–146, 174–197.
71 Ibid., p. 128.
72 Hayek, "A Rejoinder to Mr. Keynes," ibid., p. 162.
73 Donald Moggridge, ed., *The Collected Writings of John Maynard Keynes, Vol. XXI: Activities 1931–1939, World Crises and Policies in Britain and America* (New York: Cambridge University Press, 1982), pp. 289–339.
74 Ibid., pp. 291–297.
75 Paul A. Samuelson, "The General Theory," in, Seymour E. Harris, ed., *The New Economics: Keynes' Influence on Theory and Public Policy* (New York: Alfred A. Knopf, 1947), pp. 146–147.
76 Piero Sraffa, ed., *The Works and Correspondence of David Ricardo, Vol. I: On the Principles of Political Economy and Taxation* [1821] (New York: Cambridge University Press, 1951), p. 290.
77 John Maynard Keynes, *The General Theory of Employment, Interest and Money* [1936] (New York: Macmillan, 1973), pp. 89–112.

78   Ibid., p. 105.
79   Ibid., p. 161.
80   John Maynard Keynes, "National Self-Sufficiency," *Yale Review* (June 1933), p. 758.
81   Keynes, *The General Theory*, pp. 333–351.
82   Keynes, "National Self-Sufficiency," pp. 761–762.
83   Quoted in, Roy F. Harrod, *The Life of John Maynard Keynes* (London: Macmillan, 1951), pp. 436–437.
84   Ibid., pp. 192–193.
85   Arthur Smithies, "Reflections on the Work and Influence of John Maynard Keynes," *Quarterly Journal of Economics* (November 1951), pp. 493–494.
86   Keynes, *The General Theory*, p. 129.
87   Ibid., p. 164.
88   Ibid., pp. 376–379.
89   Ibid., p. 264.
90   John Maynard Keynes, "Professor Tinbergen's Method," *Economic Journal* (September 1939), pp. 558–568.
91   Keynes, *The General Theory*, pp. 337–338.
92   Ibid., p. xxiii.
93   Jean Baptiste Say, "On the Demand or Market for Products," reprinted in, Henry Hazlitt, ed., *The Critics of Keynesian Economics* (Princeton, NJ: D. Van Nostrand, 1960), pp. 12–22.
94   John Stuart Mill, "Of the Influence of Consumption on Production," [1844] reprinted in Henry Hazlitt, ed., *The Critics of Keynesian Economics*, pp. 24–45.
95   Ludwig von Mises, "Stones into Bread, the Keynesian Miracle," [1948] and "Lord Keynes and Say's Law," [1950] in *Planning for Freedom* (Grove City, PA: Libertarian Press, 4th ed., 1980), pp. 48–68; W.H. Hutt, *A Rehabilitation of Say's Law* (Athens, OH: Ohio University Press, 1974); and, Steven Kates, *Say's Law and the Keynesian Revolution: How Macroeconomic Theory Lost Its Way* (Northampton, MA: Edward Elgar, 1998). For an application of this understanding of Say's Law, or that rightly balanced production is the source of purchasing power, and therefore, demand, to the situation in the American economy in the early 1920s, see, J. Laurence Laughlin, "The Industrial Outlook" *Journal of Political Economy* (April 1926), pp. 209–218; and, Benjamin M. Anderson, "Equilibrium Creates Purchasing Power vs. Artificial Purchasing Power" *The Chase Bulletin* (June 1931), for an application to the situation of the early 1930s.
96   Keynes, *The General Theory*, p. xxxi.
97   Ibid., pp. 165–174, 194–209.
98   Ibid., pp. 147–164.
99   L. Albert Hahn, "Is Saving a Virtue or a Sin?" in *The Economics of Illusion: A Critical Analysis of Contemporary Economic Theory and Policy* (New York: Squire Publishing, 1949), pp. 93–95.
100 Mises, *Human Action*, pp. 257–326.
101 Carl Landauer, "A Break in Keynes' Theory of Interest," *American Economic Review* (June 1937), pp. 260–266.
102 Dennis Robertson, "Mr. Keynes and the Rate of Interest," [1940] reprinted in William Fellner and Bernard F. Haley, eds., *Readings in the Theory of Income Distribution* (London: George Allen and Unwin, 1950), p. 440, suggested that Keynes seemed to have "a curious inhibition against visualizing more than two margins at once."
103 Keynes, "Foreword to the German Edition," translated in James J. Martin, *Revisionist Viewpoints* (Colorado Springs CO: Ralph Myles Publisher, 1971), pp. 203–205; the translation of this foreword in the edition of *The General Theory*, pp. xxvi–xxvii, issued by the Royal Economic Society, is incomplete and inexact if compared to the original German, which is included in Martin's book.

104 It is, however, the case that in May 1936 Keynes delivered a talk for BBC radio's "Books and Authors" series in which he reviewed Sidney and Beatrice Webb's pro-Stalinist book, *Soviet Civilization*, and praised the Soviet experiment. See, Donald Moggridge, ed., *The Collected Writings of John Maynard Keynes, Vol. XXVIII: Social, Political and Literary Writings* (New York: Cambridge University Press, 1982), pp. 333–334:

> Until recently events in Russia were moving too fast and the gap between professions and actual achievements was too wide for a proper account to be possible. But the new system is now sufficiently crystallized to be reviewed. The result is impressive. The Russian innovators have passed, not only from the revolutionary stage, but also from the doctrinaire stage. There is little or nothing left which bears any special relation to Marx and Marxism as distinguished from other systems of socialism. They are engaged in the vast administrative task of making a completely new set of social and economic institutions work smoothly and successfully over a territory so extensive that it covers one sixth of the land surface of the world. The largest scale empiricism and experimentalism which has ever been attempted by disinterested administrators is in operation. Meanwhile the Webbs have enabled us to see the direction in which things appear to be moving and how far they have got ... It leaves me with a strong desire and hope that we in this country may discover how to combine an unlimited readiness to experiment with changes in political and economic methods and institutions, whilst preserving traditionalism and a sort of careful conservatism, thrifty of everything which has human experience behind it, in every branch of feeling and of action.

On the general issue of Keynes' sympathy and flirtations with planned economies and state-managed societies, see, Ralph Raico, "Was Keynes a Liberal?" *The Independent Review* (Fall 2008), pp. 165–188.

105 John Maynard Keynes, *Two Memoirs: Dr. Melchior A Defeated Enemy and My Early Beliefs* (London: Rupert Hart-Davis, 1949), pp. 82–83.

106 Ibid., pp. 97–98.

107 Ibid., pp. 98–99.

108 Quoted in, Donald E. Moggridge, *Maynard Keynes: An Economist's Biography* (London/New York: Routledge, 1992), p. 125.

109 Adam Smith, *An Inquiry into the Nature and Causes of the Wealth of Nations* [1776] (New York: The Modern Library, 1937), p. 651.

110 Frederic Bastiat, "What is Seen and What is Not Seen," [1850] in *Selected Essays on Political Economy* (Princeton, NJ: D. Van Nostrand Co., 1964), pp. 1–50.

111 Hayek, *The Pure Theory of Capital*, pp. 409–410.

112 Dudley Dillard, *The Economics of John Maynard Keynes: The Theory of a Monetary Economy* (Englewood Cliffs, NJ: Prentice-Hall, 1948), p. 1.

113 Lawrence R. Klein, *The Keynesian Revolution* (New York: Macmillan, 1947).

114 Ibid., p. 79.

115 Ibid., p. 180.

116 Ibid., p. 177.

117 Ibid., pp. 178–179.

118 Mises, "Lord Keynes and Say's Law," p. 66; also, *Human Action*, p. 793.

119 Mises, "Stones Into Bread, the Keynesian Miracle," pp. 53–55.

120 "The Causes of the Economic Crises," pp. 186–189; and "The Crisis and Capitalism," [1931] in, Richard M. Ebeling, ed., *Selected Writings of Ludwig von Mises*, vol. 2, p. 172.

121 Mises, "The Current Status of Business Cycle Research ...," p. 211.

122 Mises, *Human Action*, p. 777; also, "Wages, Unemployment, and Inflation," [1958] in *Planning for Freedom*, p. 149:

Inflation can cure unemployment only by curtailing the wage earner's real wages. But then the unions ask for a new increase in wages in order to keep pace with the rising cost of living and we are back where we were before, i.e., in a situation in which large scale unemployment can only be prevented by a further expansion of credit.

123 Mises "Capital Supply and American Prosperity," [1952] and "Wages, Unemployment and Inflation," [1958] in, *Planning for Freedom*, pp. 188–205, 146–147; "The Economic Role of Savings and Capital Goods," [1963] in, Bettina Bien Greaves, ed., *Economic Freedom and Interventionism: An Anthology of Articles and Essays by Ludwig von Mises* (Irvington-on-Hudson, NY: Foundation for Economic Education, 1990), pp. 26–30.
124 See, Richard M. Ebeling, *Austrian Economics and the Political Economy of Freedom* (Northampton, MA: Edward Elgar, 2003), Ch. 3: "A Rational Economist in an Irrational Age: Ludwig von Mises," pp. 61–100.
125 Mises, *Human Action*, pp. 673–688; "Economics as a Bridge for Interhuman Understanding," [1945] in *Economic Freedom and Interventionism*, pp. 223–235; and "The Clash of Group Interests," [1945] in, Richard M. Ebeling, ed., *Money, Method and the Market Process: Essays by Ludwig von Mises* (Norwell, MA: Kluwer Academic Press, 1990), pp. 202–214.
126 Mises, "Planning for Freedom" [1945] in *Planning for Freedom*, pp. 5–6.
127 Mises, "The Clash of Group Interests," pp. 209–210.
128 Ludwig von Mises, *Omnipotent Government: The Rise of the Total State and Total War* (New Haven, CT: Yale University Press, 1944), p. 252.

8 Two variations on the Austrian monetary theme

Ludwig von Mises and Joseph A. Schumpeter on the business cycle

Mises and Schumpeter at the University of Vienna, and after

Ludwig von Mises entered the University of Vienna as a student in 1900. A year later, Joseph A. Schumpeter began his matriculation there as well. Both received their doctoral degrees in Roman and Canon Law in 1906.

These were exciting years to be a student at the University of Vienna for anyone interested in economics, especially Austrian Economics. Following is a very abridged selection illustrating the faculty and course offerings in economics during this time:[1]

> Eugen von Böhm-Bawerk (returned to teaching summer semester 1905, after serving as Finance Minister of Austria-Hungary)
>> Introduction to Economics
>> Investigations into Political Economy
>> Topics on Themes in Economic Theory (for advanced students only; began summer semester 1906)
> Karl Grunberg
>> Introduction to Economics
>> History of Economics
>> Economic History of Recent Time
>> On Socialism
> Johann von Komorzynski
>> Fundamental Principles of Economics
>> The Theory of Prices
>> Credit and Banking
>> Direct Personal Income Tax in Austria
> Victor Mataja
>> Investigations into Social Policy
> Carl Menger (retired summer semester 1903)
>> Introduction to Economics
>> Public Finance with Special Consideration to Austrian Tax Law
> Robert Meyer
>> Investigations into Public Finance
> Eugen von Philippovich
>> Introduction to Economics

    Economic Policy
    Public Finance with Special Consideration to Austrian Tax Law
Richard Schaller *(Privatdozent)*
    International Trade Policy
Friedrich von Wieser (replaced Menger winter semester 1903)
    Introduction to Economics
    Economic Policy
    Public Finance with Special Consideration to Austrian Tax Law
    Theory of Money

In 1906, both Mises and Schumpeter participated in Böhm-Bawerk's advanced seminar, along with Otto Bauer (a leading Austrian socialist of the postwar period), Rudolf Hilferding (a leading Marxist), Emil Lederer (a socialist and later co-founder of the Graduate Faculty at the New School for Social Research in New York), and Felix Somary (later a prominent banker and diplomat).

Mises, in his *Notes and Recollections,* described the seminar:

> When Böhm-Bawerk opened his seminar it was a great day in the history of the University and the development of economics. As the subject matter of the first seminar, Böhm-Bawerk chose the fundamentals of the theory of value. From his Marxian position, Otto Bauer sought to dissect the subjectivism of the Austrian value theory. With the other members of the seminar in the background, the discussion between Bauer and Böhm-Bawerk filled the whole semester. Bauer's brilliant intellect was very impressive; he was a worthy opponent of the great master whose critique had mortally wounded Marxian economics. I believe that in the end Bauer had to admit to himself also that the Marxian labor theory of value was untenable.[2]

Mises does not tell of his own contributions to the discussions in that seminar, but in his memorial essay on Schumpeter's life and work, Gottfried Haberler reported,

> A member of that seminar told the author of the present essay that in the heated debates between Böhm-Bawerk and the Marxists, Schumpeter attracted general attention through his cool, scientific detachment. The seemingly playful manner in which he took part in the discussion ... was evidently mistaken by many for a lack of seriousness or an artificial mannerism.[3]

In 1909, Schumpeter was given the status of *Privatdozent* at the University of Vienna. In the summer semester 1909, he taught an "Introduction to the Study of Political Economy for Beginners," and in the winter semester 1910, he offered "The Entrepreneur and the Capitalist (An Analysis of the Modern Economy, with Special Consideration to the Capitalistic Tendency Towards Concentration and Its Relation to the Money Market)." In 1909, he was also appointed professor of political economy at the University of Czernowitz in the eastern part of the Austro-Hungarian Empire. And in 1911, he accepted a position on the faculty at the University of Graz, 150 miles southwest of Vienna, which he held until 1921. In late 1918–early 1919, he served on a commission for the socialization of industry in Berlin. From March to October 1919, Schumpeter was Finance Minister of Austria. In 1921 he became president of the Biedermann Bank in Vienna, which went bankrupt in 1924. In 1925, he accepted a chair at the University of Bonn, Germany. During 1927–1928 and 1930, he was a visiting professor at Harvard University. He accepted a permanent position at Harvard in 1932 and remained there until his death in 1950.[4]

Mises received his status as *Privatdozent* at the University of Vienna in 1913. For the winter semester 1913–1914, he taught a course on "Money and Banking." For the summer semester 1914, he taught "Bank Credit." Then in the late summer of 1914, his army reserve unit was called up for active duty, and Mises spent the next three and half years as an artillery officer, a good part of the time on the eastern front. In summer 1918, he was called back to Vienna to serve as an economic analyst for the Austrian General Staff, after having been the officer in charge of Military Currency Control in Austrian-occupied Ukraine following the Treaty of Brest-Litovsk in March 1918.

In 1919, he resumed his teaching as a *Privatdozent* at the University of Vienna and continued to do so every semester until he moved to Geneva in October 1934 as Professor of International Economic Relations at the Graduate Institute of International Studies. He had been employed, beginning in 1909, at the Austrian Chamber of Commerce as an economic advisor and analyst, a position he formally held until 1938. In 1920, he organized his famous *Privatseminar,* which continued until the late spring of 1934. He left Geneva in July 1940 and moved to the United States, where he lived until his death in 1973. From 1945 to 1969, he was a visiting professor in the Graduate School of Business Administration at New York University.

(An interesting commonality between Mises and Schumpeter is that both were offered visiting professorships in Japan in the mid-1920s, and both turned the offers down.)

Was Schumpeter an Austrian?

To suggest that both Mises and Schumpeter offered variations on the "Austrian" monetary theme in some of their writings implies that both were in some sense members or adherents or users of the methods of the Austrian School of Economics. There would be little dispute about Ludwig von Mises' credentials in this context, but Schumpeter is a different matter. Mises stated in no uncertain terms,

> Because Austrian economics is a theory of human action, Schumpeter does not belong to the Austrian School ... Economics, to him, is a theory of "economic quantities," and not of human action. Schumpeter's *Theory of Economic Development* is a typical product of the equilibrium theory.[5]

Friedrich A. Hayek, too, argued that while having been trained at the University of Vienna under Wieser and Böhm-Bawerk, "In the course of time he moved further away from the characteristic tenets of the Austrian School so that it became increasingly doubtful later whether he could still be counted as a member of that group."[6]

One has only to refer to Schumpeter's own words on this matter. In his first book, *The Nature and Essence of Theoretical Economics,* published in 1908, Schumpeter declared, "From a methodological and epistemological viewpoint, pure economics is a 'natural science' and its theorems are 'laws of nature.'"[7] In the same year that his first book appeared, he wrote a letter to Leon Walras in which he said, "I shall always try to work on the foundations that you have laid and to continue your efforts."[8] And there are, of course, the famous passages from his *History of Economic Analysis,* in which he said that

> as far as a pure theory is concerned, Walras is in my opinion the greatest of all economists. His system of economic equilibrium, uniting, as it does, the quality of "revolutionary" creativeness with the quality of classic synthesis, is the only work by an economist that will stand comparison with the achievements of theoretical physics.[9]

While the Austrians had found the right starting point in the concept of marginal utility, they could not climb all the way up the analytical ladder that led to Walrasian general equilibrium because of their "defective technique" that prevented them from understanding "the meaning of a set of simultaneous equations."[10]

The Austrians' defective technique, in Schumpeter's view, was their insistence on a "causal-genetic" theory in economic analysis.[11] Indeed, Böhm-Bawerk had taken Schumpeter to task for rejecting the causal-genetic approach, saying,

> Under the admitted influence of a certain epistemological school of the natural sciences, Schumpeter, for instance, wants to avoid the concepts of cause and effect and substitute for them the "more perfect" mathematical concept of "function" ... The *cirulus vitiosus* and the *petitio principii* lose their logical fear if we no longer distinguish between cause and effect, between which causality proceeds in a certain direction, but if we merely recognize mutual interdependency.[12]

On the other side, Israel Kirzner, in his own expositions on the Austrian theory of entrepreneurship, has pointed out many similarities between his own conception of the entrepreneur and that of Schumpeter's, while still making it clear that the emphases in the two conceptions of the role of the entrepreneur in the market process are not the same.[13] And Erich Streissler, in an essay on "Schumpeter and Hayek: On Some Similarities in Their Thought," argued that in the early part of the twentieth century, Schumpeter

> took up so many of the ideas then current only in the Austrian economic tradition that any hypothetical historian of economic thought, not knowing

Schumpeter to be an Austrian, could immediately trace him to this school ... [T]he innovative "Schumpeterian" entrepreneur, the glorified figure of the capitalist process, is actually one of Wieser's ideas, which Schumpeter merely amplified and embellished.[14]

And on the topic of credit expansion and the business cycle, Streissler even went so far as to say that he considered Schumpeter's version to be more "Austrian" in some ways than the formulations developed by either Mises or Hayek![15]

The books by Mises and Schumpeter most relevant for such a comparison are, of course, Mises' *Theory of Money and Credit* and Schumpeter's *Theory of Economic Development.* Schumpeter's book first appeared in 1911. Mises' was published the following year in 1912. Both issued revised editions at about the same time, with the second edition of Mises' *Theory of Money and Credit* appearing in 1924, and Schumpeter's second edition of *The Theory of Economic Development* in 1926. The English translations of *The Theory of Money and Credit*[16] and *The Theory of Economic Development*[17] both appeared in 1934.

Schumpeter presented briefer, English-language expositions, first in "The Explanation of the Business Cycle," published in *Economica* (December 1927)[18] and then again in "The Instability of Capitalism," which appeared in the *Economic Journal* (September 1928).[19] Mises published a restatement of his theory of the business cycle in the monograph *Monetary Stabilization and Cyclical Policy* in 1928.[20] (An English translation of Mises' monograph had been sent to T.E. Gregory of the London School of Economics in 1930 for assistance in finding a British publisher; unfortunately, no publisher could be found and this earlier translated manuscript is now lost.)

It is in the context of these writings (and a few others) that we will discuss their theories of credit expansion and the business cycle. What are the common elements that can be seen in their expositions? I would suggest they are:

1 the non-neutrality of money;
2 that credit expansion has the ability to create a discrepancy between savings and investment;
3 that such a credit expansion can bring about a redirection of investment activities through a process of "forced savings"; and,
4 the "boom" phase of the business cycle eventually results in a depression, and this depression phase is a "normal" and "healthy" process that brings the market economy back to equilibrium.

But the "stories" they tell in using these ideas are quite different.

Schumpeter's theory of economic development and the business cycle

In his famous essay "Money and the Social Product," published in 1917/1918, Schumpeter attempted to formulate a theory of the value of money using a variation of the equation of exchange.[21] He points out that his analytical framework is built on the earlier writings of such economists as Menger, Wieser, Knut Wicksell, Walras, Alfred Marshall, Irving Fisher, and Edwin Kemmerer. But he adds in a footnote, "A book whose power and originality the critics have over-looked because of some minor points, is that of von Mises," referring to *The Theory of Money and Credit*.[22] In *The Theory of Economic Development*, Schum-peter accepted the Austrian causal-genetic theory of the origin of money and its value and referred to Mises' *Theory of Money and Credit* for a demonstration that the theory did not suffer from circular reasoning in explaining the value of money.[23] And he credited Mises with having coined the "extremely happy expression 'forced saving.' " Mises later denied that he had either invented or even used the term, but he did say, "To be sure, I described the phenomena" in *The Theory of Money and Credit*.[24] Our interest is not with the particular theoret-ical construction Schumpeter developed for his theory of the value of money (other than to point out parenthetically that he did not develop his framework in a way that would be totally consistent with his own vehement defense of meth-odological individualism).[25]

But in the latter part of the essay he turns to a discussion of the "dynamic" aspects that result from changes in the quantity of money. Though at several points in the analysis he emphasizes that in the long run the general effect of an increase in the supply of money is a rise in prices, with no necessary change in the total quantity or composition of goods and services produced, he then dis-cusses the non-neutral manner in which changes in the quantity of money can in fact influence "real relationships" in the market.

> To begin with, increases in the quantity of money never occur uniformly for all people. Further, people are never completely aware of the nature of the process, so that, at least for some time, they act as if they received higher incomes, when the sum of incomes remains constant. For both reasons, prices never rise uniformly – neither the prices for consumer goods relative to each other nor the prices of consumer goods relative to those of the means of pro-duction. Thereby the price rise ceases to be merely nominal. It means a real shift of wealth on the market for consumer goods and a real shift of power on the market for the means of production, and it affects the quantities of com-modities and the whole productive process. No doubt, not all these effects are permanent ... But very frequently such re-establishment of the status quo is impossible. Newly-won positions may be permanently held and old ones permanently lost, and much in the life of the economy may thereby change – forms of business organization, direction and methods of production, etc.[26]

Schumpeter analyzes the pattern of events that are likely to arise from increases in the quantity of money when its origin is:

1   an increase in the quantity of gold-money entering the economy, either as additional consumer demand for final output or an increase in specie reserves in the banking system as some of that deposited gold becomes a basis for new loan-making;

2   an increase in fiat money for financing government spending, such as in wartime;

3   the creation of additional bank credit without additional gold reserves as backing, and the accompanying lowering of the interest rate to induce additional borrowing for investment purposes;

4   an increased demand for investment borrowing by entrepreneurs, which is satisfied through an expansion of bank credit without a prior lowering of the interest rate.

The initial impact that occurs when new money enters the economy depends on how that additional money is used to increase the money demand for goods and services. The effect then sequentially spreads through the rest of the economy, influencing the pattern of relative demands, the allocations of real resources among sectors of the economy, and the relative income positions of various groups in the society. The specific consequences will depend precisely on the paths by which the money spreads itself through the economy.[27]

The importance of the non-neutrality of money was clearly an aspect of monetary analysis that Schumpeter never abandoned. In his *History of Economic Analysis,* which was his last major enterprise, he pointed out that

> the Austrian way of emphasizing the behavior or decisions of individuals and of defining exchange value of money with respect to individual commodities rather than in respect to a price level of one kind or another has its merits, particularly in the analysis of an inflationary process; it tends to replace a simple but inadequate picture by one which is less clear-cut but more realistic and richer in results.[28]

But it is in *The Theory of Economic Development* that Schumpeter constructed his conception of the role of credit expansion, forced savings, and the business cycle. The starting point of his analysis is an explanation of the circular flowing economy in which the patterns of consumer demand, the methods of production, and the quantities and distribution of the means of production are assumed to be unchanging. Thus the processes of production and the streams of expenditures as payment for factor services repeat themselves in the same relative patterns period after period. Likewise, the finished goods created by the processes of production meet the same relative structure of demand for that output, with the same stream of receipts from sales of final output. In the circular flow, the prices of the factors of production fully reflect their imputed value from the value of consumer goods. As a result, cost prices equal sale prices in this equilibrium throughout the entire economy.[29]

Since production is perfectly synchronized with consumption and is repeated period after period, Schumpeter reaches his peculiar conclusion that in the stationary economy labor and land absorb all income, with no implicit interest income earned by savers (or capitalists), because savings is not required in the equilibrium of the circular flow.[30] Each period the owners of the firms that produce goods earn receipts equal to the sums they need to purchase the same relative quantities of factors of production to repeat the production processes in the next period. Hence, "waiting" appears not to be required; and if waiting is not required, then what "premium" is needed since no time-sacrifice is incurred?

Of course, it is the very focus on the repetition of the production processes in an equilibrium that led Schumpeter to the false notion that in the circular flow an implicit interest return for forgoing present consumption seems unnecessary. Even in the stationary economy, the owners of the firms who direct the means of production in their repeated productions have the choice to continue their production processes or withhold a portion (or even all) of the receipts from rehiring and repurchasing the factors of production they employed last period, and instead utilize those receipts for other more immediate purposes. Schumpeter said that the owners of the firms receive a "wage" for managing the production processes, and therefore their wages are part of the full imputation of the value of final output to labor and land. But hidden in these managerial wages must, therefore, be a premium for not consuming any portion of the receipts needed to continue the production processes in the same way each period. The owner-managers are, in fact, acting as their own capitalists in providing the factors of production with income until the next period's production processes are completed.[31]

Schumpeter does not argue that no change occurs in his conception of the circular flow. There can be changes in population and resulting modifications in the structure of relative demands and the availability of capital and labor, for example, that require adjustments in the types of goods produced and even in the combinations of labor and capital with which they are manufactured. But what is crucial for him in this process of adjustment and change within the circular flow is that they do not involve "revolutionary" changes in the methods of production. They are merely adaptations of the given resources and technological knowledge to moderate or incremental shifts in the relative demands for goods and combinations of the factors of production. They require nothing more from the managers of the production processes than marginal adjustments within the existing order of things in the market economy. As such, they introduce no inherent instabilities or difficulties of productive transformation within the economic system.[32]

Development, as understood by Schumpeter, involves something quite different:

> Development in our sense is a distinct phenomenon, entirely foreign to what can be observed in the circular flow or in the tendency towards equilibrium. It is a spontaneous and discontinuous change in the channels of the flow, disturbance of equilibrium, which forever alters and displaces the equilibrium state previously existing.[33]

What types of changes, then, represent "development"? They are:

1   a new good or a significant change in the quality of the good marketed;
2   new methods of production with which goods are produced;

3   the opening up of new markets, that dramatically transforms economic activities;
4   the discovery and utilization of new resources; and
5   radical changes in the organizational structures of industry.[34]

For these developmental changes the means of production must be combined in new, revolutionary ways. It involves withdrawing the means of production from their routine and repeated processes of production in the circular flow and redirecting them into new channels not known or utilized before. Eventually these radically new ways of doing productive activities will be absorbed and routinized, and be made part of a new pattern of a circular flow. But in the period between their initiation and their integration, the market economy is thrown into a setting in which the preceding production and equilibrium conditions no longer serve as a benchmark from which to evaluate the economic relationships of the market.

"Enterprise" is the name Schumpeter assigns to this process. And "entrepreneurs" are those who bring about these transformations. In Schumpeter's circular flow, however, neither enterprise nor entrepreneurship exists. In the circular flow there are neither profits nor losses and no new methods of production. The businessman is merely the overseer of standardized processes. "[E]veryone is an entrepreneur only when he actually 'carries out new combinations,' and loses that character as soon as he has built up his business," Schumpeter argued, "when he settles down to running it as other people run their businesses."[35]

For Schumpeter, the circular flow, the stationary state, market equilibrium are not merely analytical tools of thought, conceptual points of reference, with which to theoretically understand and logically explain the workings of the market order: they are actual conditions the market not only hits upon but operates within for observable periods of time.[36] There are times when neither entrepreneurship nor development may be occurring within a market to any significant degree, and the economy can be referenced as being so much more or less from the actual equilibrium state conforming to the established routinized processes of production.[37]

Now logically if the market economy is in a state of equilibrium and the conditions that have generated that equilibrium continue and are expected by the market participants to continue, then there is no place for the entrepreneur as the adjuster of production to new circumstances, because there are no new circumstances. But since Schumpeter admits that even in the circular flow of the stationary state, changes can and do occur in the form of changes in population and changes in the patterns of consumer demand, it logically follows that those who direct the processes of production must attempt to redirect the factors of production under their control to reflect these potential changes. They must attempt to anticipate when these changes will occur, to what degree, and what adjustments are needed in the uses and combinations of the factors of production (even in a setting in which the technological knowledge about how resources might be combined does not change to any significant degree).

If those who control the means of production fail to do so, profit opportunities will be missed and losses will be incurred that, in principle, might have been avoided. Thus, though Schumpeter tries to deny the title of "entrepreneur" to those who "merely" adjust the given production techniques to changing circumstances in the circular flow, their task is no less entrepreneurial. They, too, bring about "new combinations" to meet new market situations, and in the process, they inevitably think of and imagine new and different ways of bringing about a "harmony" between the wants of the consuming public and the application of the means of production to satisfy those wants.[38]

The entrepreneur is the leader who breaks out of the routine, Schumpeter says, who has the will, authority, and "weight" to bend the routinized processes of production out of the inertia and rationality of the existing knowledge and ways of doing things. But his image of the entrepreneur is not the image of the "heroic" leader of military combat or political struggle. Instead, Schumpeter argues,

> He "leads" the means of production into new channels. But this he does, not by convincing people of the desirability of carrying out his plan or by creating confidence in his leading in the manner of a political leader ... but by buying [the means of production] or their services, and using them as he sees fit.[39]

How precisely does the entrepreneur lead the means of production into new avenues in Schumpeter's analysis? This brings us to his theory of the process by which credit expansion can create a discrepancy between the equality of savings and investment in the circular flow, and the phenomenon of "forced saving."

The difficulty for the entrepreneur in the circular flow is that all the receipts earned from the sale of finished consumer goods are "spoken for" in the sense that each unit of money is earmarked as expenditure for particular production factors in the repetition of existing production processes. There are no financial means available to the entrepreneur for bidding away factors of production for revolutionizing "new combinations."[40]

Schumpeter gives negligible attention to the possibility that those entrepreneurs who conceive of new, more profitable ways to apply the means of production could enter the financial markets and bid the required monetary resources away from those who, until now, have been receiving loans to continue their routinized processes of production. In his schema of the circular flow, banking as normally thought of hardly exists. The manufacturers of goods receive the required means for continuing production in the next period from the sale of finished goods in the previous period. In this sense, Schumpeterian entrepreneurs have no one to bid against, since existing producers of goods have no intention of parting with the financial resources needed to maintain their own enterprises. Banking, the use of credit, and credit creation come into existence and take on a real role in the market process only in the context of the entrepreneurs' demand for access to the means of production.

Hence, entrepreneurs have only one source for the funding required for their revolutionizing enterprises: the additional credit created for them by the banks to which they apply for loans. Schumpeter distinguishes between "normal" and "abnormal" credit:

Normal credit creates claims to the social dividend, which represent and may be thought of as certifying services rendered and previous delivery of existing goods. That kind of credit, which is designated by traditional opinion as abnormal, also creates claims to the social product, which, however, in the absence of past productive services could only be described as certificates of future services or of goods yet to be produced ... Both serve the same purpose as means of payment and are externally indistinguishable. But the one embraces means of payment to which there is a corresponding contribution to the social product, and the other means of payment to which so far nothing corresponds – at least no contribution to the social product.[41]

In other words, normal credit represents savings out of past production, and thus reflects monetary claims against quantities of goods or of factors of production that are not being utilized for a present consumption or current uses, but which are instead being made available for the production of future goods in their repeated and routinized patterns. Abnormal credit, on the other hand, represents monetary claims that do not flow from any past production and current savings of goods or factors of production; instead, these additional money claims are introduced into the market economy, and then can compete for the use of those same goods against those whose existing money holdings reflect contributions to previous production.

The essential function of credit in our sense consists in enabling the entrepreneur to withdraw the producers' goods which he needs from their previous employments, by exercising a demand for them, thereby to force the economic system into new channels ... [I]n so far as credit cannot be given out of the results of past enterprise or in general out of reservoirs of purchasing power created by past development, it can only consist of credit means of payment created ad hoc, which can be backed neither by [specie] money in the strict sense nor by products already in existence. It ... consists in creating a new demand for, without simultaneously creating a new supply of, goods.[42]

Thus, "abnormal" credit creation has as its purpose precisely to bring about a redirection of the means of production out of those channels representing an equilibrium nexus of consumption choices and production decisions. The entrepreneur enters the market for factors of production and bids them away from those who have been using them for those routinized processes of production, and "he takes his place beside the previous producers and his purchasing power beside the total previously existing."[43]

This generates a rise in prices, first for the factors of production, for it is through the entrepreneurs' act of bidding up factor prices that those factors are induced to leave their present employments. But this is followed by a rise in consumer goods prices, as those factors of production attracted to these new entrepreneurial enterprises spend their higher money incomes on various finished goods and services. But the essential element in this process, Schumpeter argues, is the phenomenon of "forced savings."

> The price-raising effect of bank money gives rise to the phenomenon of "forced savings." Without wishing to save, people are forced to do so by the reduction in real income through the rise in prices. This releases means of production and the stock of goods at the disposal of the economy for productive purposes is increased, its fund for immediate consumption is diminished ... "[B]anking operations" can make possible an enrichment of the productive apparatus of the economy. They cause a shift in purchasing power among individuals and, if this shift favors the expansion of production, a transfer of means of production to those individuals to whom credits are granted by means of newly created credit ... New men and new plans come to the forefront that otherwise would have always remained in the background ... The banking world constitutes a central authority of the economy whose directives put the necessary means of production at the disposal of innovators in the productive organism ... The essence of modern credit lies in the creation of such money. It is the specifically capitalistic method of effecting economic progress.[44]

What sets the limit on the amount of "abnormal" credit the banking system can create to feed the demands of entrepreneurs for the factors of production? Originally writing in the period before the demise of the gold standard, Schumpeter argued that the more new credit is created and the higher prices rise, the greater the pressures brought about for potential domestic withdrawals of specie reserves and the greater the likelihood of gold redemption and export of gold for importation of less expensive foreign goods. Thus the limits of credit expansion are set by the resulting inflation being only temporary and moderate.[45]

How long does the upswing of the inflationary boom last? In Schumpeter's scheme of things, the natural end to the inflationary stage of the business cycle comes when those entrepreneurial innovations and transformations of the means of production are completed, with new supplies of goods coming onto the market, bringing with them a deflationary reversal of the rise in prices.[46] A "self-deflationary" process now sets in, that is, a fall in prices inevitably follows the previous inflationary boom. From the revolutionized methods of production come increased quantities of goods and services, manufactured in new ways that enable their sale at lower prices because of the introduction of improved cost-efficient techniques of production. But reinforcing the decline in prices due to the increase in goods offered on the market is the fact that the entrepreneurs who previously borrowed those quantities of "abnormal" credit for their enterprises now repay their loans; thus, the total quantity of circulating media returns to what it had been before the entrepreneurs received the new credits.[47]

Furthermore, during the upswing the rising costs induced by the competitive bids of entrepreneurs pushes many businesses into economically untenable positions, with a widening circle of business failures or at least narrowed profits. When these greater quantities of more and improved goods arrive on the market and sell at lower prices, more established firms find themselves unable to withstand the new market pressures. They are driven into losses and even bankruptcy.

Then, the depression phase of the business cycle sets in. But for Schumpeter the resulting depression is to be neither bemoaned nor interfered with. The depression, he stated, "we may call the 'normal' process of reabsorbion and liquidation."[48] It is the process through which the market economy searches for a new equilibrium, given the dramatic changes in the directions and methods of production introduced permanently into the market as a positive result of the innovations financed during the boom phase. Not only must entrepreneurs find their proper relationships within the new situation their activities have brought into existence, the "mere businessman" of the circular flow must adapt to the changed circumstances.

At the same time, the very disruption of the previous equilibrium, since it has overthrown many routinized relationships of the earlier circular flow, creates uncertainties, hesitations, and rigidities of various sorts that hinder adjustment to the new circumstances. These hesitations and rigidities can only delay recovery and intensify the duration and depth of the depression period.[49]

Any attempts to mitigate the depressionary phase of the business cycle will only prolong the period of normal liquidation and adjustment. The essence of the depression is the need for an adjustment in the "real factors," for example, modifications in the allocation of resources among sectors of the economy, the adaptation of new methods of production, and changes in the structure of relative prices among finished consumer goods and among the factors of production. Political interventions would only retard the finding of a new set of equilibrium relationships. Monetary expansion to bolster older industries and artificially maintain cost-price relationships that are no longer relevant would only delay the final outcome. Schumpeter argued:

> [O]ur analysis led us to believe that recovery is sound only if it does come of itself. For any revival which is merely due to artificial stimulus leaves part of the work of the depression undone and adds, to an undigested remnant of maladjustment, new maladjustment of its own which has to be liquidated in turn, thus threatening business with another crisis ahead. Particularly, our story provides a *presumption* against remedial measures that work with money and credit. For the trouble is fundamentally *not* with money and credit, and policies of this class are particularly apt to keep up and add to, maladjustment, and to produce additional trouble in the future.[50]

Though he classes the credit expansion that finances his entrepreneurial process "abnormal," Schumpeter considered it the very foundation for economic progress. It is an alien element introduced into the market order that breaks the economic system of the constraint of "given" structures of production. It is a revolt against the wishes of consumers as expressed in their decision to consume so much of their income and not less in the form of additional savings to voluntarily fund the innovations of routine-breaking would-be entrepreneurs.

Instead, they are "forced" to save a greater portion of their income through restricting their consumption due to the higher prices brought about by the entrepreneurs who have bid away resources and labor for their "revolutionizing" projects. A greater scarcity of final goods and services is created due to the inability of the established firms to continue to employ the same requisite quantities of factors of production to maintain their respective levels of final output. The consumers are finally "rewarded" for their imposed frugality when the new methods of production undertaken by the entrepreneurs bring forth an enlarged horn of plenty.

Before the full benefits of that forced savings can be enjoyed by consumers, the market order must pass through a wrenching adjustment to the new possibilities in the form of a depression. The maladjustments must be cleared away for the economy to return to a state of balanced relationships between expenditures and receipts, consumption and production, consumer prices and the cost-prices of the factors of production. What are the "maladjustments" that the market must "liquidate" to return to the equilibrium of the circular flow? The maladjustments are the remaining older modes and methods of production, the preceding distributions and combinations of the factors of production, the past relative amounts of various consumer goods and services produced by existing firms that are now inconsistent with the new conditions that the entrepreneurial changes have created and imposed upon the market-order-that-was and are incompatible with the market order that now will-be and must-be.

Crucial to Schumpeter's "story" is the confidence that nothing will interfere with the entrepreneurs' ability to bring new methods of production to completion and begin to produce the larger quantities of better quality and less costly goods and services that are their goal. The "abnormal" credit expansion that sets the entrepreneurial processes in motion operates by providing those entrepreneurs with the financial means to bid factors of production away from their prior employments. As a consequence, factor incomes rise for those employed in the new ways; those factors of production utilize their enhanced money incomes to increase their demands for various consumer goods and services; the prices of those final goods are pushed up as well, which increases the receipts of the manufacturers of those finished goods.

But the implicit assumption is that the old-method producers of consumer goods are not able to match and out compete the new entrepreneurs, even if money receipts have increased and therefore improved their capacity to bid anew to retain or draw back into their sectors of the economy the resources required to continue their levels of production. The entrepreneurs must be "fed" with ever greater quantities of "abnormal" credit so that their monetary positions are always sufficient to maintain their demands for the factors of production to complete their projects. The "periods of production" necessary to bring these new projects to completion must be shorter than the period of time over which prices will have been pushed up sufficiently from these counter-bids for the employment of the factors of production, and before the banks would be threatened with sufficiently large losses of reserves that they would have to bring the "abnormal" credit expansion to a halt. If that point is reached before the new entrepreneurial "combinations" are completed, they will be "starved" for cash and left in various incomplete states. The "malinvestments" would then be the entrepreneurial projects for which the necessary credit was unavailable.[51]

Schumpeter in designing this particular "story" of the business cycle seems to have followed too closely Wicksell's analysis of the results from a credit expansion.[52] In *Interest and Prices,* Wicksell constructs a model in which a lowering of the "money rate" of interest below the "natural rate" (or equilibrium rate) induces a shift in investment plans from a one-year period of production to a two-year period of production. At the end of the first year, consumers find that the quantities of consumer goods are less than expected, and they are "forced" to save more than they had planned; but they are rewarded with a greater quantity of goods at the end of the two years. As Wicksell explained:

> The real savings which is necessary for the period of investment to be increased [to two years] is in fact *enforced* – at exactly the right moment – on consumers as a whole; for a smaller quantity than usual of consumption goods are available for the consumption of the second year. At the end of the [second] year ... when the two years period of production comes to an end and the available quantity of consumption goods has increased correspondingly, the consumers will receive some reward for their abstinence.[53]

Mises, like Schumpeter, was greatly influenced by Wicksell's analysis. But Mises reached very different conclusions about the nature and the phases of the business cycle.

Mises' monetary and malinvestment theory of the business cycle

While Schumpeter attempted to construct a theory of economic development, in the context of which he presented a theory of the business cycle as part of the development process, Mises' purpose was different. In *Notes and Recollections,* Mises explained that Karl Helfferich's claim, made in his 1903 book, *Money,*[54] that the theory of marginal utility was unable to serve as a successful framework for analyzing the value of money, was the stimulus for his own investigation into the problems of money and banking.[55] The culmination of that study was *The Theory of Money and Credit.*

In his reminiscences, Mises described the tasks he had set for himself in that work. First, he wished to show the applicability of marginal utility theory for explaining the value of money, starting with Carl Menger's theory of cash balance holdings by individuals.[56] Rather than operating purely within an equilibrium framework, Mises developed a dynamic sequence analysis (which he called "the step-by-step method") for demonstrating the following processes:

1   the emergence of money from the arena of directly exchanged commodities;
2   the "regression theorem," by which he applied marginal utility analysis to the value of money, by showing the temporal sequence through which the purchasing power of money yesterday, today, and tomorrow are interconnected;

3   how changes are brought about in the general value, or purchasing power, of money through increases or decreases in the demand for or supply of money; and
4   the determination of the exchange ratios between different kinds of money (his formulation of the purchasing power parity theory).

Second, he wished to demonstrate, by using the same sequence analysis, the influence of credit expansion in generating the business cycle, or more precisely:

1   the development of two different types of credit in banking: commodity credit (based on fully backed reserves) and circulation credit (fiduciary media, not fully backed by reserves);
2   how the existence of circulation credit influences the purchasing power of money on the market;
3   the relationships between money, credit, and market rates of interest; and
4   the effect of increases in circulation credit in bringing about a temporary lowering of the market rate of interest below a Wicksellian "natural rate" that induces unsustainable, more "roundabout" processes of production that culminate in crisis and depression.[57]

Our concern, as with Schumpeter, is in focusing on those aspects of Mises' analysis that will enable us to understand his theory of credit expansion and the business cycle.

Taking his lead from Menger's work on the origin of money,[58] Mises applied the Austrian "causal-genetic" process analysis to explain the emergence of money from the field of directly exchanged commodities and its resulting value in the arena of exchange. Difficulties that often block successful barter exchanges lead individuals to search for other, indirect avenues for consummating their desired transactions. The differing qualities and degrees of marketability among goods result in individuals using particular commodities as the money goods that combine the features most useful to facilitate indirect exchange.[59]

The distinct "value of money" originates at that point in time when a particular commodity is no longer valued purely for its usefulness as either a consumer or producer good, but as a medium of exchange as well. From that point on, that good's exchange value is made up of two components: its subjective value for use as an ordinary good and its subjective value for use as a medium of exchange. Over time, as that good's role as money increases through a widening circle of transactions, its market value as a medium of exchange may supersede or even totally supplant its importance as an ordinary commodity.

Since the subjective value of the medium of exchange to any potential holder or user of the money-good is dependent upon its estimated real purchasing power over other goods in the market, Mises demonstrates that the present valuation of money is derived from a "historical component": its objective exchange-value in the preceding period. This preexisting purchasing power of money serves as the starting-point in the present period for the (marginal) evaluation of money's usefulness to market participants. In turn, the resulting interactions of demanders and suppliers of money generate a new array of price ratios between money and the goods against which it exchanges. The new objective exchange value of money then serves as the starting point for the subjective (marginal) valuations of money's utility to individuals in the next period. This does not result in "circular reasoning," as some critics charged, because Mises showed that money's value in the market can always be "regressed" to the point at which its value as a money began (that is, that point in the past at which the good was first used and valued not only as an ordinary commodity, but as a medium of exchange as well).[60]

Every change in either the demand for or supply of money brings about a modification in the value of the medium of exchange. But true to Mises' insistence upon a rigorous adherence to methodological individualism, he argues that any theoretical understanding of how such changes in the purchasing power of money are brought about must start with the specific individuals whose particular new demand for or supply of money sets in motion the process leading to a changed value of money on the market.[61] From this starting point in the market, the effects of the change in the demand for or supply of money work their way through the entire economic system in a temporal-sequential process, culminating in a decrease or increase in the general purchasing power of the monetary unit.

The shift from one value of money on the market to another, however, will not be neutral in its effects: That is, it will bring about a change in the relative income and wealth positions of various individuals and it will modify the structure of relative prices and the allocation of resources among competing sectors of the economy.[62] Mises' exposition of the non-neutrality of money was clear and concise:

> Changes in money prices never reach all commodities at the same time, and they do not affect the prices of the various goods to the same extent. Shifts in the relationships between the demand for, and the quantity of, money for cash holdings generated by changes in the value of money from the money side do not appear simultaneously and uniformly throughout the entire economy. They must necessarily appear on the market at some definite point, affecting only one group in the economy first, influencing only their judgments of value in the beginning and, as a result, only the prices of commodities these particular persons are demanding. Only gradually does the change in the purchasing power of the monetary unit make its way throughout the entire economy.
>
> For example, if the quantity of money increases, the additional new quantity of money must necessarily flow first of all into the hands of certain definite individuals – gold producers, for example, or, in the case of paper money inflation, the coffers of the government. It changes only *their* incomes and fortunes at first and, consequently, only *their* value judgments. Not all goods go up in price in the beginning, but only those goods demanded by these first beneficiaries of the inflation. Only later are prices of the remaining goods raised, as the increased quantity of money progresses

step by step throughout the land and eventually reaches every participant in the economy. But even then, when finally the upheaval of prices due to the new quantity of money has ended, the prices of all goods and services will not have increased to the same extent. Precisely because the price increases have not affected all commodities at one time, shifts in the relationships in wealth and income are affected which affect the supply and demand of individual goods and services differently. Thus, these shifts must lead to a new orientation of the market and of market prices ...

It is only because changes in the purchasing power of money never affect all commodities everywhere simultaneously that they bring with them ... still other shifts in wealth and income. The groups which produce and sell commodities that go up in price first are benefited by the inflation, for they realize higher profits in the beginning and yet they can still buy the commodities they need at lower prices, reflecting the previous stock of money ... At the same time, those whose incomes remained nominally the same suffered from the inflation, as they were forced to compete in making purchases with those receiving ... inflated incomes ... For some time they had to pay prices already affected by the increase in the quantity of money, with money incomes related to previous conditions.[63]

Mises' theory of the business cycle begins with his distinction between money proper and money-substitutes. Transactions may be facilitated in one of two ways: through the buying and selling of goods for quantities of the actual money good or the buying and selling of goods for quantities of perfectly secure claims to an equivalent sum of the actual money good. The latter are treated in market transactions as being, say, as "good as gold," if market participants are confident that the substitutes are redeemable "on demand" at full face value. They are viewed in market transactions as being perfectly interchangeable with the sum of the commodity-money they represent since they are supposed to be receipt-claims for the actual specie. A unique quality to money-substitutes, unlike other claims to various commodities, is that they may in principle circulate indefinitely, passing from hand-to-hand, never being redeemed for the commodity money they represent. They may be as widely used and generally accepted as a medium of exchange as the actual commodity money. Indeed, if they carry sufficient confidence, money-substitutes can, in principle, completely replace the actual commodity money in most market transactions.[64]

Mises argued that such money-substitutes could be of two types: "We may use the term Money-Certificates for those money-substitutes that are completely covered by the reservation of corresponding sums of [commodity] money, and the term Fiduciary Media for those which are not covered in this way."[65] Both are accepted in market transactions and are indistinguishable from each other. Within an economic community, changes in the quantity of money-certificates need not have any impact on the purchasing power of money from "the money side" of the economy. An increase in the number of money-certificates is matched by an equivalent decrease in the quantity of commodity money held as cash balances and utilized in facilitating transactions; a decrease in the number of money-certificates is matched by an increase in the quantity of commodity money held as a cash balance and utilized in facilitating transactions. (This assumes, of course, no net increases in the supply of commodity money within the economic system.)

In the case of fiduciary media, on the other hand, the result is potentially different. Banks of deposit and money-substitute issuance can increase the quantity of less than fully covered money-substitutes with no corresponding decrease in the quantity of commodity money in circulation. They can do so by extending loans to potential borrowers in the form of money-substitutes (notes, check-money, etc.) without a matching increase in commodity money deposits with their institutions.

To explain the nature of this process, Mises distinguished between what he called "commodity credit" and "circulation credit." But for purposes of clarity, we will use the terminology offered by Fritz Machlup for the same categories, and which Mises endorsed: "transfer credit" and "created credit."[66]

In the case of transfer credit, one of the two parties to a transaction makes a "sacrifice" in the present. Specifically, he defers his access to and use of a portion of his income or real resources for a period of time. His sacrifice is matched by the opportunity the other party now has to use that income or those resources until such a time as he is expected to return what he has borrowed, plus any interest agreed upon as the price for having had use of those "present goods." In the case of "transfer credit," the act of "savings" must precede or be simultaneous with the act of "investment."

In the case of "created credit," the borrower is given a sum of money-substitutes representing a degree of purchasing power over a quantity of goods in the market, with no corresponding "sacrifice" on the part of another member of the economic community.[67] The bank's ability to issue money-substitutes that are as readily accepted and are viewed as interchangeable with either commodity money or money-certificates enables the recipient to have access in the market to goods that no one has voluntarily chosen to set aside for use by the borrower. An act of new "investment" can occur that is independent of any increased voluntary "savings."

This possibility developed, Mises argued, because of the blending of two separate functions within the banking industry:

[t]he depository function and the lending function. An individual who deposits a sum of commodity money in a bank in exchange for money-substitutes redeemable on demand (notes or checks that may be written against his account) has made no decision to defer consumption and save. The money-substitutes are merely a more convenient form in which to hold ready cash in anticipation of possible acts of exchange. The claim that he has acquired by his deposit is also a present good for him. The depositing of the money in no way means that he has renounced immediate disposal over the utility that it commands ... [T]his is not a credit transaction, because the essential element, the exchange of present goods for future goods, is absent.[68]

But banks began to act as if these deposits were in fact savings against which they could extend loans in the form of money-substitutes. Real savings would have involved individuals depositing sums of money with a bank for a stipulated period of time during which those depositors could not withdraw those sums "on demand." On the basis of the purchasing power represented by those deposits, loans could be made for periods of time synchronized with the period of time the "savings" are to remain in the bank.

Instead, banks began to pyramid issuance of money substitutes in the form of loans on top of the already outstanding money-substitutes that represented claims on demand by depositors of commodity money. This necessarily meant that some portion of the banks' outstanding money-substitutes could not be fully covered by existing reserves if a sufficient number of holders of those money-substitutes were to demand payment within the same narrow timeframe. "Consequently the chief rule to be observed in the business of credit-issuing banks is quite clear: it must never issue more fiduciary media than will meet the requirements of its customers for their business with each other." It therefore falls upon the banks to maintain a ratio of reserves relative to outstanding claims of money-substitutes that assures their everyday ability to meet potential withdrawals on demand.[69]

This sets an upper limit on the ability of any one bank to issue fiduciary media. Issuing money-substitutes in excess of the economic community's willingness to hold them will result in a drain on reserves though direct withdrawals or by claims from other banks through the clearing-house mechanism. This is no less true for a bank that has control over the centralized reserves within the banking system; it, too, would be threatened with the loss of commodity money to those demanding redemption of their money-substitutes.[70] Only a central bank that renounced redemption of money-substitutes would be free from this threat. But then the collapse of the monetary order would be threatened if continual issuance of greater and greater amounts of money-substitutes generated an increasing rate of inflation, which would finally result in money-substitute holders escaping into a "flight for real goods."[71]

In Mises' framework, therefore, credit creation by the banking system had evolved in a manner that exceeded the bounds in which investment would be limited to actual savings. And it had introduced an element in the market order that had the potential to influence the purchasing power of money beyond the limits that would have been set by the demand for commodity money and money-certificates, on the one hand, and the supply of commodity money and money-certificates on the other. Fluctuations in the purchasing power of money, from the "money-side," now could be influenced by an additional factor other than the profitability of the production of the commodity money relative to the demand for it.[72]

Furthermore, the introduction of "created credit" into the market order, Mises argued, set the stage for the business cycle – with few of the positive effects that Schumpeter considered so praiseworthy in the process.

Banks have the capacity to expand the quantity of fiduciary media in the market, but only by making it profitable for potential borrowers to take a greater number of loans. If uninfluenced by "created credit," the rate of interest that tends to prevail on the market is Wicksell's "natural rate." This would be the rate of interest at which savings and investment would be equal if not for the intervention of disruptive monetary factors. Investments undertaken only would be those whose anticipated rate of return was greater than the rate of interest at which the borrowed funds may be obtained. And the "roundaboutness," or time structure of the investments undertaken would be confined to the savings available to sustain the projects to completion and maintain the factors of production during the "period of production." Additional investment would be dependent on an increase in savings, which would provide the income and resources to initiate more "roundabout" production projects and sustain the factors of production during a longer production period. The shift in time-valuations toward greater savings would decrease the "natural rate" of interest, and the resulting lower interest rate for loans would now make profitable potential investment projects not economically justifiable at the previous higher "natural rate."[73]

However, banks can set the money rate of interest at which they actually extend loans to a level below the Wicksellian natural rate:

[T]he number and extent of these [loan] requests are not independent of the credit policy of the banks; by reducing the rate of interest charged on loans, it is possible for the banks indefinitely to increase the public demand for credit ... If it is possible for the credit-issuing banks to reduce the rate of interest on loans below the rate determined at the time by the whole economic situation (Wicksell's *naturlicher Kapitalzins* or natural rate of interest), then the question arises of the particular consequences of a situation of this kind. Does the matter rest there, or is some force automatically set in motion which eliminates this divergence between the two rates of interest? ... Our task now is merely to discover the general economic consequences of any conceivable divergence between the natural and money rates of interest, given uniform procedure on the part of the credit-issuing banks.[74]

With the new "created credit," investment borrowers bid resources and labor away from the manufacture of consumer goods and from production processes with shorter time horizons (a lesser degree of "roundaboutness") to undertake investment projects with lengthier periods of production. To attract resources and labor into more time-consuming investment activities, the borrowers of "created credit" have to bid up the price of the required factors of production to draw them from their alternative uses in the economy.

The new "created credit" now passes to those factors of production as higher money incomes. They become the "second-round" recipients of the credit expansion. Unless those factors of production were to undergo a change in time-valuations, and therefore in their willingness to save, their real demand for consumer goods will be the same as it was before the increase in the supply of money-substitutes. Therefore when they increase their money demand for finished goods and services, it is more or less in the same proportion of their income as before.

As a result, consumer good prices start to rise as well. But because of the reallocation of resources away from consumer good production, the quantities of such goods available are smaller than they had been, which intensifies their price rise. As the factors of production expend their higher money incomes on desired consumer goods, the sellers and producers of those goods became the "third-round" recipients of the new "created credit." Producers of consumer goods now increase their demand for the same scarce factors of production to draw them back into the consumer goods sectors of the economy and into investment projects with shorter time horizons. The factors of production drawn back into the final consumer stages of the production processes become the "fourth-round" recipients of the new "created credit."

Those who initially had taken the "created credit" off the loan market now find it increasingly difficult to complete some longer-term investment projects in the face of the rising costs created when factors of production move back to the consumer good sector of the economy. A "crisis" begins to emerge as the numbers of such affected longer-term investment projects grow. The demand to the banks for additional "created credit" by some entrepreneurs to continue these longer-term projects pushes market interest rates up, creating an even greater crisis in the investment sectors of the economy. The expansionary or "boom" phase of the business cycle now turns into the "depression" phase, as some of those more long-term investment projects collapse, are left unfinished, or are restructured to operate on a smaller scale with less profits than anticipated. The result is malinvestments of capital in economically unsustainable processes of production.

The only way some of these investment activities could be temporarily saved would be for the banks to increase the quantity of "created credit" again. But this would merely set the same process in motion again, with the same inevitable result. If the banks were to try to prevent this inevitable outcome through ever-greater increases in "created credit," the result would be higher prices in general, with a threatened collapse of the society's monetary system.[75]

What is the role of "forced savings" in this process? During the early phase of the business cycle, the prices of consumer goods rise as labor and resources are drawn from consumer goods production into longer-term, more roundabout investment projects. Some members of society are "forced," through the higher prices and smaller quantities of finished goods, to provide the means of production required to begin the new investment activities by an imposed reduction in their level of consumption. But the imposed frugality need not last until the more roundabout processes of production are completed. The very rise in consumer goods prices, which restrains the buying habits of those whose money incomes have not yet increased in line with the prices of the goods they normally purchase, also brings about a counter-shift toward increased profitability for processes of production closer to the consumer goods sectors of the economy. Resources are drawn back to consumer goods production, increasing their supplies to some extent and, thus, reducing the intensity of the enforced saving.

But this very reversal toward "less roundabout" processes of production and periods of investment undermines the ability and opportunity to complete the very longer-term investment projects "created credit" initially fostered. The crisis phase of the business cycle shows that many processes of production were misdirections of society's scarce resources, rather than stepping-stones to economic progress and development. Entrepreneurs have not led the market order to a higher plane of technical and productive capability; they have been misled by the distortion of a central market signal – the rate of interest – into beginning projects that cannot be completed or maintained in operation, or which fail to earn anticipated returns.

> Sooner or later, the crisis must inevitably break out as the result of a change in the conduct of the banks. The later the crackup comes, the longer the period in which the calculations of the entrepreneurs are misguided by the issue of additional fiduciary media. The greater this additional quantity of fiduciary money, the more factors of production have been firmly committed in the form of investments which appeared profitable only because of the artificially reduced interest rate and which prove to be unprofitable now that the interest rate has again been raised. Great losses are sustained as a result of misdirected capital investment. Many new structures remain unfinished. Many of those already completed, close down operations. Still others carry on because, after writing off losses that represent a waste of capital, operation of the existing structure pays at least something.[76]

Mises also argued that there may be some permanent improvements in this process of attempted capital formation and the creation of more productive roundabout methods of production. But rather than an inherent and inevitable positive result of the business cycle, any permanent benefits brought forth by the forced savings of the "boom" would be side effects, resulting from the redistribution of wealth caused by the non-neutral manner in which individuals, industries, and income groups had been affected during the credit expansion. If income is permanently redistributed toward individuals inclined to save, then the "natural rate of interest" will be lowered; some troubled projects may find the savings required to sustain them. But to the extent that this was to happen, Mises argued, there is no way to anticipate it or estimate its magnitude, since it would be totally dependent on the particulars of the historical circumstances. Just as conceivably, there could be a change in the opposite direction – that is, a decline in the amount of savings – intensifying the degree to which investment projects are categorized as malinvestments (i.e., misallocations of scarce resources and capital).[77]

Like Schumpeter, Mises considered the depression a healthy phase of liquidation and adjustment, an elimination of maladjustments left over from the boom period of the business cycle. But Mises' interpretations of "maladjustments" and needed "adjustments" were not the same as Schumpeter's. What the depression reveals, in Mises' analysis, is the misdirection and overextension of investment projects begun under the stimulus of "created credit" expansion and artificially lowered interest rates. The misallocations of resources created during the "boom" must now be rearranged for consistency with the underlying "real" relationships of available savings, consumer demand, and the limited availability of scarce factors of production for use among competing present and future-oriented processes of production.

> Credit expansion ... diverts capital investment away from the course prescribed by the state of economic wealth and market conditions. It causes production to pursue paths which it would not follow unless the economy was to acquire an increase in material goods. As a result, the upswing lacks a solid base. It is not *real* prosperity. It is *illusionary* prosperity ... Sooner or later it must become apparent that this economic situation is built on sand.[78]

But Mises' view of the need for market-directed readjustment of production, employment, wages and prices was similar to Schumpeter's. In 1931, as the Great Depression was becoming worse, Mises argued:

> If everything possible is done to prevent the market from fulfilling its function of bringing supply and demand into balance, it should come as no surprise that a serious disproportionality between supply and demand persists, that commodities remain unsold, factories stand idle, many millions are unemployed, destitution and misery are growing and finally, in the wake of these, destructive radicalism is rampant in politics ... With the economic crisis, the breakdown of interventionist policy ... becomes apparent. Hampering the functions of the market and the formation of prices does not create order. Instead it leads to chaos, economic crisis.[79]

The conclusions of Mises and Schumpeter on the business cycle

Credit creation through the banking system was the essence of the phenomenon of the business cycle for both Joseph Schumpeter and Ludwig von Mises. It was the motor that set the engine in motion. "Normal credit" for Schumpeter and "transfer credit" for Mises represent resources set aside from past production to support demands for investment in market equilibrium. "Abnormal credit" for Schumpeter and "created credit" for Mises represent media supplied by the banks that enabled the undertaking of investments in excess of the existing savings in the market.

Both "abnormal credit" and "created credit" provided the monetary means through which some entrepreneurs were able to enter the market and bid away resources and labor from existing employments for their new enterprises and new investment projects. This reallocation of factors of production toward these new projects was made possible because the credit expansion initially increased the buying power of these entrepreneurs relative to the other members of the society who had not received such additions to their supply of money substitutes. Precisely because money was non-neutral in its effects in both Schumpeter's and Mises' analyses, those involved in the undertaking of some existing processes of production would be unable to compete successfully with those whose monetary positions has been enhanced through the increase in bank credit. The new investments in excess of "real savings" were partly financed through a rise in prices that imposed reduced purchases for goods and services on others in the society. The resources and labor required for these entrepreneurs were squeezed out of the market through "forced savings." And both Schumpeter and Mises concluded that the boom phase of the business cycle must end in a depression and a period of adjustment and liquidation.

But here the similarities ended. The initiator of the boom phase in Schumpeter's conception is the innovative entrepreneur; he is the one who possesses the vision of transforming the fields of production. The banks are essential but merely accommodative responders to the financial needs of the entrepreneur. The initiators of the boom in Mises' conception are the banks, who are guided either by the motive of financial gain from extending loans or by the influence of ideological forces,[80] to lower interest rates and stimulate borrowers' demand for investment funds in excess of real savings. The entrepreneurs are induced by the banks to start new investment projects they would not have undertaken if the higher "natural rate" of interest had continued to prevail on the market. (Mises added that the same process is set in motion even if the rate of interest is not lowered below its "natural" level, but instead any greater demand for borrowing by entrepreneurs is fed through an increase in "created credit" rather than allowing the market rate of interest to rise in the face of this greater demand to borrow.)

In Schumpeter's scheme of things, the boom comes to an end when the new investment projects and processes financed by "abnormal credit" have been completed; greater quantities of goods now appear on the market, prices fall, and entrepreneurial loans are repaid (resulting in a contraction of the then-existing quantity of credit on the market). In Mises' scheme of things, the boom comes to an end when consumer goods prices rise due to the greater scarcity of finished goods and the higher money demand for consumer goods resulting from increased money incomes earned by factors of production in the investment goods sectors of the economy; in addition, interest rates start to rise back toward the "natural rate." Many of the new, more roundabout investment projects are now found to be unsustainable and cannot be completed, and financial losses are suffered.

In Schumpeter's view, the depression is a period of adjustment and liquidation. The existing market order and processes of production must conform to the new methods and techniques of production introduced by the entrepreneurial innovators. In Mises' view, the depression is also a period of adjustment and liquidation; the resources, labor, and capital goods drawn into the new investment projects that now are seen as unprofitable and misdirected, must be revalued and reallocated for application in alternative uses consistent with the underlying "real" conditions in the market.

In spite of these differences, however, there is one final thing that Schumpeter and Mises share: the mainstream economics profession has chosen to ignore their theories of the business cycle. But what both attempted to do, each in his own way, was to formulate a dynamic microeconomic temporal-sequence analysis in which the monetary elements were interconnected with the allocation and investment of the "real" factors of production. Their macroeconomic theories were grounded in microeconomic processes. In this, both Mises and Schumpeter still remain ahead of our time.

Notes

1 This list is taken from, Kiichiro Yagi and Yukihiro Ikeda, *Economics Courses at Vienna University, 1849-1944*, Vol. 1 (Kyoto, Japan: Faculty of Economics, Kyoto University, Working Paper No. 1, Feb. 1988), pp. 65–78. I have listed only those professors to whom Mises referred as significant economists at the University of Vienna during this period in Ludwig von Mises, "The Historical Setting of the Austrian School of Economics," [1969] reprinted in Bettina Bien Greaves, ed., *Austrian Economics: An Anthology* (Irvington-on-Hudson, NY: The Foundation for Economic Education, 1996), p. 74, or in Ludwig von Mises, *Notes and Recollections* [1940] (South Holland, IL: Libertarian Press, 1978).
2 Mises, *Notes and Recollections*, pp. 39–40.
3 Gottfried Haberler, "Joseph Alois Schumpeter, 1883–1950," *Quarterly Journal of Economics* (August 1950), pp. 338.
4 Haberler, "Joseph Alois Schumpeter," pp. 338–339.
5 Mises, *Notes and Recollections*, pp. 36–37.
6 F.A. Hayek, "Joseph Schumpeter (1883–1950)" in *The Collected Works of F.A. Hayek, Vol. 4: The Fortunes of Liberalism* (Chicago: University of Chicago Press, 1992), p. 160.
7 Quoted in, Richard Swedberg, *Schumpeter: A Biography* (Princeton, NJ: Princeton University Press, 1991), p. 28.
8 Ibid., p. 31.
9 Joseph A. Schumpeter, *History of Economic Analysis* (Oxford: Oxford University Press, 1954), p. 827.
10 Ibid., p. 918.
11 Ibid., p. 908.
12 Eugen von Böhm-Bawerk, *Capital and Interest,* Vol. 3 (South Holland, IL: Libertarian Press, 1959), pp. 228–229; on the Austrian causal–genetic theory of price formation, see Hans Mayer, "The Cognitive Value of Functional Theories of Price," [1932] in, Israel M. Kirzner, *Classics in Austrian Economics: A Sampling in the History of a Tradition, Vol. 2: The Interwar Period* (London: William Pickering, 1994), pp. 55–168.
13 Israel M. Kirzner, *Competition and Entrepreneurship* (Chicago: University of Chicago Press, 1973), pp. 72–73, 79–81, 125–131; *Perception, Opportunity and Profit: Studies in the Theory of Entrepreneurship* (Chicago: University of Chicago Press, 1979), pp. 111–112, 115–119.
14 Erich Streissler, "Schumpeter and Hayek: On Some Similarities in Their Thought," in, Fritz Machlup, Gerhard Fels, and Hubertus Muller-Groeling, eds., *Reflections on a Troubled World Economy: Essays in Honor of Herbert Giersch* (New York: St. Martin's Press, 1983), p. 358; see also Erich Streissler, "The Influence of German and Austrian Economics on Joseph A. Schumpeter," in Yuichi Shionoya and Mark Perlman, eds., *Schumpeter in the History of Ideas* (Ann Arbor: The University of Michigan Press, 1994), pp. 13–38.
15 Ibid., pp. 360–361.
16 Ludwig von Mises, *The Theory of Money and Credit* [1912; 2nd revised ed., 1924; 3rd revised ed., 1953] (Indianapolis: Liberty Classics, 1981).
17 Joseph A. Schumpeter, *The Theory of Economic Development* [1911; 2nd revised ed., 1926] (Cambridge, MA: Harvard University Press, 1934).

18 Joseph A. Schumpeter, "The Explanation of the Business Cycle," [1927] in Richard V. Clemente, ed., *Essays on Entrepreneurs, Innovations, Business Cycles, and the Evolution of Capitalism by Joseph A. Schumpeter* [1951] (New Brunswick, NJ: Transaction Publishers, 1991), pp. 21–46.

19 Schumpeter, "The Instability of Capitalism," [1928] in, ibid., pp. 47–72.

20 Ludwig von Mises, "Monetary Stabilization and Cyclical Policy," [1928] in, Percy L. Greaves, ed., *Von Mises, On the Manipulation of Money and Credit* (Dobbs Ferry, NY: Free Market Books, 1978), pp. 57–171; reprinted in, Israel M. Kirzner, ed., *Classics in Austrian Economics: A Sampling in the History of a Tradition, Vol. 3: The Age of Mises and of Hayek* (London: William Pickering, 1994), pp. 33–111.

21 Joseph A. Schumpeter, "Money and the Social Product," [1917/1918], *International Economic Papers*, No. 6 (1956), pp. 148–211; for a critique of Schumpeter's framework by another Austrian economist, see Gottfried Haberler, "Critical Notes on Schumpeter's Theory of Money – The Doctrine of the 'Objective' Exchange Value of Money," [1925] in Anthony Y.C. Koo, ed., *Selected Essays by Gottfried Haberler* (Cambridge, MA: The MIT Press, 1985), pp. 531–552.

22 Schumpeter, "Money and the Social Product," p. 149.

23 Schumpeter, *The Theory of Economic Development*, p. 48; though he added that in contrast to when he wrote the first edition of the book, "he would not now consider this way of introducing the element of money to be satisfactory."

24 Ibid., p. 109; Mises, "Monetary Stabilization and Cyclical Policy," p. 121; see also, the interesting survey article by, Fritz Machlup, "Forced or Induced Saving: An Exploration Into Its Synonyms and Homonyms," [1943] in *Essays in Economic Semantics* (New York: New York University Press, 1975), pp. 213–240.

25 See Joseph A. Schumpeter, "On the Concept of Social Value," [1909] in *Essays*, pp. 2–6, 19.

26 Schumpeter, "Money and the Social Product," p. 191.

27 Ibid., pp. 192–198.

28 Schumpeter, *History of Economic Analysis*, p. 1090.

29 Schumpeter, *The Theory of Economic Development*, pp. 3–56.

30 Ibid., p. 46.

31 See, Eduard März, *Joseph Schumpeter: Scholar, Teacher & Politician* (New Haven, CT: Yale University Press, 1991), Chapter 8, "Schumpeter and the Austrian School of Economics," pp. 131–143, for a discussion of Böhm-Bawerk's criticisms of Schumpeter's theory of interest. On the general topic of the illusion of synchronized production eliminating the idea of a "period of production," see, Fritz Machlup, "Professor Knight and the 'Period of Production,'" [1935] in, Kirzner, *Classics in Austrian Economics*, Vol. II, pp. 275–315; F.A. Hayek, "The Mythology of Capital," [1936] in, William Fellner and Bernard F. Haley, eds., *Readings in the Theory of Income Distribution* (London: George Allen and Unwin, Ltd., 1950), pp. 355–383; and, Murray N. Rothbard, *Man, Economy and State*, Vol. I [1962] (Los Angeles: Nash Publishing Co., 1970), pp. 385–386.

32 Schumpeter, "The Instability of Capitalism," pp. 47–60; "The Explanation of the Business Cycle," p. 25.

33 Schumpeter, *The Theory of Economic Development*, p. 64.

34 Ibid., p. 66.

35 Ibid., p. 78.

36 See, for example, his discussion of the idea and uses of the "equilibrium" concept in Joseph A. Schumpeter, *Business Cycles: A Theoretical, Historical, and Statistical Analysis of the Capitalist Process*, Vol. I (New York: McGraw-Hill Book Co. Inc., 1939), pp. 31–71.

37 Ibid., p. 69.

38 Rothbard, *Man, Economy and State*, Vol. II, pp. 493–494; on Böhm-Bawerk's criticisms of Schumpeter's distinction between the innovator and the imitator (or adapter) in the processes of production, see, Eduard März, *Joseph Schumpeter*, pp. 140–141.

A primary distinction that Kirzner tries to draw between his notion of the entrepreneur and that of Schumpeter is that in the latter's conception entrepreneurship involves disrupting the prior equilibrium state, while in Kirzner's view, the task of the entrepreneur is to discover disequilibrium discrepancies that have arisen independent of any innovation. In Schumpeter's framework, the Kirznerian "entrepreneur" would be those directors of the means of production in the circular flow who adjust productive activities to marginal changes in market circumstances within the given market organizational structures and techniques of production. Of course, in actuality, entrepreneurs do both.

39 Schumpeter, *The Theory of Economic Development*, p. 89.
40 Ibid., p. 108.
41 Ibid., pp. 101–102.
42 Ibid., p. 106.
43 Ibid., p. 108.
44 Schumpeter, "Money and the Social Product," pp. 205–206; "The Explanation of the Business Cycle," p. 40; "The Instability of Capitalism," pp. 67–68.
45 Schumpeter, *The Theory of Economic Development*, p. 113; "The Explanation of the Business Cycle," pp. 36–37.
46 Schumpeter, *The Theory of Economic Development*, p. 233:

> The average time which must elapse before the new products appear – though of course actually dependent upon many other elements – fundamentally explains the length of the boom … This time is determined first technically, then by the tempo in which the multitude follows the leaders … This appearance of the new products causes the fall in prices, which on its part terminates the boom, may lead to a crisis, must lead to a depression, and starts all the rest.

47 Schumpeter, *The Theory of Economic Development*, pp. 232–233; "The Explanation of the Business Cycle," p. 38.
48 Schumpeter, *The Theory of Economic Development*, p. 236.
49 Ibid., pp. 238–239; "The Explanation of the Business Cycle," pp. 34–35.
50 Schumpeter, "Depressions: Can We Learn from Past Experiences?" [1934] in *Essays*, p. 117.
51 For a general critique of Schumpeter's theory of the business cycle by a prominent Austrian, see Murray N. Rothbard, *Man, Economy and State,* Vol. II, pp. 747–751; and, Rothbard, *America's Great Depression* [1963] (Los Angeles: Nash Publishing Co., 1972), pp. 69–71.
52 In saying this, there is no direct textual evidence that Schumpeter was guided by Wicksell in constructing his theory of the business cycle. Yet the similarity is close enough to suggest the conclusion that, perhaps, a Wicksellian influence was at work on him, since Schumpeter was well versed in Wicksell's writings.
53 Knut Wicksell, *Interest and Prices* [1898] (New York: Augustus M. Kelley, 1965), pp. 155–156, emphasis in the original; see also, Ch. 9: "Money, Economic Fluctuations, Expectations and Period Analysis: The Austrian and Swedish Economists in the Interwar Period," in the present volume.
54 Karl Helfferich, *Money* [1927] (New York: Augustus M. Kelley, 1969), pp. 525–534.
55 Mises, *Notes and Recollections*, p. 43.
56 Carl Menger, *Grundsätze der Volkswirtschaftslehre,* 2nd ed. (Vienna: HolderPichler-Tempsky A.G., 1923), pp. 241–331.
57 Mises, *Notes and Recollections*, pp. 57–62, 107–110.
58 Carl Menger, "On the Origin of Money," [1892] reprinted in Richard M. Ebeling, ed., *Austrian Economics: A Reader* (Hillsdale, MI: Hillsdale College Press, 1991), pp. 483–504, and in Israel M. Kirzner, ed., *Classics in Austrian Economics,* Vol. I, pp. 91–106.
59 Mises, *The Theory of Money and Credit*, pp. 42–46.
60 Ibid., pp. 117–146; see also Ludwig von Mises, *Human Action, A Treatise on Eco-*

nomics (Irvington-on-Hudson, NY: The Foundation for Economic Education, 1996), pp. 408–411; Rothbard, *Man, Economy and State,* Vol. I, pp. 160–165, 231–237; and, Murray N. Rothbard, "The Austrian Theory of Money," in, Edwin G. Dolan, ed., *The Foundations of Modern Austrian Economics* (Kansas City, KS: Sheed & Ward, Inc., 1976), pp. 160–171.

61 Mises, *The Theory of Money and Credit*, pp. 153–160.

62 Ibid., pp. 160–168, 237–243; and Mises, "The Suitability of Methods of Ascertaining Changes in the Purchasing Power of Money for the Guidance of International Currency and Banking Policy," [1930] in, Richard M. Ebeling, ed., *Money, Method and the Market Process: Essays by Ludwig von Mises* (Norwell, MA: Kluwer Academic Press, 1990), pp. 79–81; *Human Action*, pp. 412–413, 416–422.

63 Mises, "Monetary Stabilization and Cyclical Policy" [1928], pp. 95–96; also Ludwig von Mises, *Nation, State and Economy* [1919] (New York: New York University Press, 1983), pp. 156–158; and, Ludwig von Mises, "The Non-Neutrality of Money," [1940] in, Ebeling, ed., *Money, Method and the Market Process*, pp. 69–77.

64 Mises, *The Theory of Money and Credit*, pp. 67–73; Mises, "The Position of Money Among Economic Goods," [1932] in, Ebeling, ed., *Money, Method and the Market Process*, pp. 63–64; *Human Action*, pp. 432–434; Murray N. Rothbard, *What has Government Done to Our Money?* (Auburn, AL: The Ludwig von Mises Institute, 1990), pp. 43–45.

65 Mises, *The Theory of Money and Credit*, p. 133; *Human Action*, p. 433.

66 Fritz Machlup, *The Stock Market, Credit and Capital Formation* [1931] (London: William Hodge and Co., Ltd., 1940), p. 224; and Fritz Machlup, *Führer durch die Krisenpolitik* (Vienna: Julius Springer, 1934), p. 137; see Mises, *Notes and Recollections*, p. 60:

> Fritz Machlup very capably translated the two distinct concepts with the terms, "transfer credit" and "created credit." Only by the making of this distinction ... can the way be paved for understanding how the creation of fiduciary credit explains the business cycle phenomena.

67 Mises, *The Theory of Money and Credit*, pp. 296–297.

68 Ibid., p. 301.

69 Ibid., p. 362.

70 Ibid., pp. 363–364.

71 Mises, "Monetary Stabilization and Cyclical Policy," p. 129; Mises, however, admits the possibility that the purchasing power of the monetary unit could continue to decrease even at an increasing rate, without an abandonment of that type of money in the society, *The Theory of Money and Credit*, pp. 256–257.

72 However, Mises considered that there were important differences between the issuance of fiduciary media under a system of competitive free banking and under a regime of monopoly central banking. See, Richard M. Ebeling, *Austrian Economics and the Political Economy of Freedom* (Northampton, MA: Edward Elgar, 2003), Ch. 5: "Ludwig von Mises and the Gold Standard," pp. 136–158.

73 Mises, *The Theory of Money and Credit*, pp. 393–394, 399; "Monetary Stabilization and Cyclical Policy," pp. 122–123.

74 Mises, *The Theory of Money and Credit*, pp. 398–399.

75 Ibid., pp. 401–403; "Monetary Stabilization and Cyclical Policy," pp. 118–130.

76 Mises, "Monetary Stabilization and Cyclical Policy," pp. 129–130.

77 Mises, *The Theory of Money and Credit*, pp. 385–387; "Monetary Stabilization and Cyclical Policy," pp. 121–122, 126–127.

78 Ludwig von Mises, "The Causes of the Economic Crisis," [1931] in, Greaves, ed., *von Mises, On the Manipulation of Money and Credit*, p. 183, emphasis in the original.

79 Ibid., pp. 201–202.

80 Mises, "Monetary Stabilization and Cyclical Policy," pp. 136–138.

9   Money, economic fluctuations, expectations and period analysis
The Austrian and Swedish economists in the interwar period

In the mid-1970s, I once asked Fritz Machlup if any of the Swedish Economists had ever visited Vienna in the 1920s or 1930s. He thought a moment and said, "Yes, once Bertil Ohlin came for a visit, with his wife." I then asked if he remembered anything of Ohlin's visit. Again, Machlup thought a moment, and then he smiled and replied, "His wife wore a very beautiful dress." That seemed to be all that Fritz Machlup recalled of any Austrian–Swedish contacts in Vienna during the period between the wars.

In fact, the Austrians and the Swedes were closely connected during this period.[1] Indeed, their approaches originated from the same sources. In monetary and business-cycle theory, both schools viewed themselves as building on the contribution of Knut Wicksell, and, in turn, Wicksell built his own theory of money and production on the earlier writings of Eugen von Böhm-Bawerk. In 1911, Wicksell pointed out that even after reading all the critical evaluations of Böhm-Bawerk's theory of capital over the years

> my long-standing admiration for Böhm-Bawerk's achievement has not been diminished thereby ... [I]t is now possible, so long after its appearance [*The Positive Theory of Capital*], to venture the statement that it is, and will remain, one of the milestones on the road to progress in political economy. It seems difficult to say anything about the general concept of capital or its mode of operation which is not to be found completely elucidated in that excellent and thought-provoking work.[2]

In turn, in the 1914 edition *of Capital and Interest,* Böhm-Bawerk referred complementarily to Wicksell's *Value, Capital and Rent* and his *Lectures on Political Economy.*[3]

In 1912, in the preface to the first edition of *The Theory of Money and Credit,* Ludwig von Mises referred to Wicksell as one "to be counted in the first line of those who developed the new ideas" most promising in the monetary and banking theory, though Mises believed that Wicksell's solutions were not entirely successful. Neither did he consider it an accident that Wicksell's "work is standing on the foundations laid by Böhm-Bawerk's theory of capital and interest."[4] Wicksell reviewed Mises' book two years after it was published. He believed that there were several grounds upon which to criticize it, but began the review by saying that "This is a very studiously written, serious book". He also pointed out to the reader that Mises "follows very closely my views regarding the relationship between interest and capital prices."[5]

In the late 1920s and the 1930s, Wicksell's ideas were taken up by both Austrian and Swedish economists. The writings of members of these two schools, while in many ways parallel, were not identical. They asked many of the same questions, though their methods and conclusions were not always the same. In the 1930s they were both interested in understanding the processes and sequences of industrial fluctuations, but in ways that often differed in essentials from what, by the late 1930s and 1940s, came to be known as the Keynesian approach. The Austrian and Swedish approaches often overlapped because, in many of their writings, their starting point was the Austrian, or Böhm-Bawerkian, emphasis on the "roundaboutness" of production and the time element in that roundabout process. The fact that production takes time leads to the concept of a "period of production." "Waiting" for the period of production to be completed opens up analysis to consideration of the quantities and characteristics of the resources and commodities that are "tied up" during the duration of the production period.

Once the analysis goes beyond the Crusoe level, questions begin to emerge concerning the degree to which the investment and savings plans of interdependent transactors are consistent with each other during the waiting period. The analytical horizon opens for inquiring as to what the market conditions are for intertemporal plan coordination, what may cause discoordination of intertemporal plans and, if such plans do not match, what the sequential effects and consequences may be of the adjustment process that leads (perhaps) back to a condition of coordinated plans. Thus, what became the distinctive hallmarks in much of the writings of both the Austrian and the Swedish Schools during this period were what came to be known as "period analysis," "plan analysis," and "process analysis."

Böhm-Bawerk and Knut Wicksell

For Böhm-Bawerk, causality controls all the processes in the world in which man lives. If he is to control or reshape his world to fit his purposes, man must understand the laws of causality and make his actions conform to them. He can then use those laws to serve his own ends. One of the fundamental laws, Böhm-Bawerk argued, was the greater productivity (other things held given) of processes that are more "roundabout." Looking at the production process from a technological point of view, every product that comes into existence has its beginning centuries ago.

> The boy who whittles a willow whistle with his pocket knife is, strictly speaking, only continuing an operation begun by the miner who centuries ago dug the first shovelful of earth for the sinking of the mine shaft that was used to bring up the iron for the blade of the boy's pocket knife.

But to give to each of these long-gone steps in the production process their proper weight, Böhm-Bawerk invents his notion of an "average period of production." It is meant to measure the average time interval between the expenditure of the first primary factors of production and the point at which a finished product is available for use. The average period of production is Böhm-Bawerk's *backward-looking* estimate of the period of time over which physical inputs have been invested for the production of a finished commodity. The longer the average period of production, the more "roundabout" the production process.[6]

The period of production also has an economic meaning for Böhm-Bawerk, defined by the constraint of available savings. For production there must be capital, but capital has several meanings. In Böhm-Bawerk's schema, capital is defined as intermediary or produced means of production. They come into existence, are maintained, replaced or increased only through the application of the primary means of production: resources and labor. Resources and labor must be shifted from their potential use for immediate satisfaction and be directed, instead, for the making of capital goods. Resources must also be applied for the manufacturing of consumption goods for those whose labor (along with resources and the produced means of production) will be applied during the production period, at the end of which the finished product (resulting from their endeavors) will be available for sale and use. Consequently, part of the savings available for investment is an advance of present goods to workers during the period of production.[7]

In the aggregate, the chosen investment projects that may be undertaken, with their respective periods of production, are limited by the available savings to successfully sustain and maintain them. The amount of savings will depend upon the subjective valuations of the participants in the market concerning prospective gain (in terms of the value of the future greater productive output) relative to the cost of deferring the use of factors of production that could otherwise be utilized in the present for current consumption. The rate of interest emerges from the interaction of people's time preferences.[8] Thus, the rate of interest acts as the "brake" on which of the alternative investment projects are undertaken and therefore on the selected time horizons out of the technologically possible periods of production.

Böhm-Bawerk argues that the plans of market participants are intertemporally coordinated and modified through changes in the interest rate and the cost of factors of production used in investment projects containing different production periods. If savings were to increase, the demand for final goods would decrease (or in a growing economy, would not increase to the level that would have been possible if all the additional higher real income had been devoted to consumption). The corresponding decline in the interest rate would increase the present value of investment projects with longer time horizons and this would, in turn, bring about a change in the relative prices for factors of production; their prices would decline in those activities with a shorter time horizon and rise in those with longer time horizons. The allocation of factors of production among projects with alternative production periods is determined by their relative prices, and these reflect their value in alternative investment projects. The profitability of these investment projects and their corresponding periods of production are limited by the interest rate, and this reflects the time preferences of the market agents who evaluate the attractiveness of future goods over present goods.[9]

Wicksell used Böhm-Bawerk's capital theory as a framework for pursuing his own problem of the distinction between 'natural' and 'money' rates of interest. Wicksell argues that in a condition of barter where present goods trade both for each other and for future goods, there would be a tendency for market forces to establish an interest rate that balances the supply and demand for real capital.

> The rate of interest at which the demand for loan capital and the supply of savings exactly agree and which more or less corresponds to the expected yield on the newly created capital, will then be the normal or natural real rate.[10]

If, instead, money (rather than goods directly) is loaned at an equivalent rate of interest, money would then be serving as "nothing more than a cloak" over a process that could, conceptually, have been carried out just as easily without it.[11]

However, the intercession of money into the intertemporal exchange process does make a difference:

> [W]e are concerned with precisely what occurs, in the first place, with the middle link in the final exchange of one good against another, which is formed by the demand of money for goods and the supply of goods against money.[12]

In the monetary economy, "Liquid real capital (i.e. goods) are never lent ... it is money which is lent, and the commodity capital is then sold in exchange for this money." In Wicksell's view, "It is not, as is often supposed, merely the form of the matter that is just altered, but its very essence."[13]

Since money is lent, and not real capital, the monetary authority is able to increase the supply of money available for lending and to lower the money interest rate. Anticipated yields or profits on potential investments will now seem greater than before the fall in the money rate, meaning that at the margin production projects will appear attractive to undertake that did not at the previous higher money rate of interest.[14] However, not all types of investment are affected equally by the change in the interest rate. Those with longer time horizons will be influenced to a greater degree because of the present value effect.[15] To analyze the consequences from a divergence between the natural and money rates of interest, Wicksell constructs two models.

In Wicksell's first model, the period of production is one year for all firms. At the beginning of the year, entrepreneurs borrow money from capitalists (indirectly through a bank). The borrowed funds are then dispersed to the factors of production as money income, and the money income is used to purchase commodities during the year from commodity dealers (whom Wicksell assumes to be the capitalists). At the end of the year, entrepreneurs sell their finished output to the capitalist dealers for a sum just sufficient to repay the principal and interest on their loans, and the interest payments are assigned to the respective accounts held by the capitalists at the bank.[16]

A fall in the money rate of interest, due to a monetary expansion, induces an attempt by entrepreneurs to expand output. Money wages and other factor prices begin to rise as entrepreneurs bid against each other for scarce means of production, with the additional money borrowed at the lower rate.[17] If, as Wicksell assumes, entrepreneurs have expectations that the final goods prices at the end of the period will be the same as at the beginning of the period, factor bidding can only go as far as the fall in the interest rate has increased the anticipated profit margins, and competition among entrepreneurs will, in fact, eliminate those anticipated gains. Entrepreneurial disappointments, however, will be reversed when, at the end of the one-year production period, they are surprised to find that the money prices for their goods are also higher (assuming that money demand for final output rises in proportion to the increase in factor incomes). In the next period, with all factor and final output prices having risen proportionally, and assuming the monetary authorities continue to follow the same policy, entrepreneurs will once again face a situation in which the money rate of interest is below the equilibrium "natural" rate (with entrepreneurs taking the present prices as their expectations for the coming period). This sets in motion Wicksell's cumulative process.[18]

In this one-year production period, all changes are purely nominal effects. However, Wicksell then constructs a second two-year production period model. Now, when the money rate of interest is lowered, the capitalization effect creates a higher profitability for investment products requiring two years for completion instead of one. Resources are drawn into two-year investment projects from one-year production processes. This results in less finished output at the end of the first year and, due to their greater scarcity, consumer prices now rise. Entrepreneurs successfully complete their two-year investment projects, at which point a greater quantity of goods is available on the consumer market.

In this second model, *real* as well as *nominal* changes are set in motion. Based on the lower money rate of interest, entrepreneurs begin two-year investment projects in excess of the planned savings of consumers. The incompatibility between them becomes evident when, at the end of the first year, consumers demand a larger portion of final output than has been provided for. Consumers are 'forced' to save via the higher consumer goods prices, and the entrepreneurs are able to successfully complete their two-year period of production. No mechanism is suggested by Wicksell as to how the disappointed consumer spending plans, which materialized through higher final output prices, could in any way bring about a negative feedback on to entrepreneurial investment decisions. All that Wicksell offers is the possibility that when the two-year investments are finished, consumers may benefit from their forced savings through the availability of a greater quantity of final products at that point in time.[19]

Ludwig von Mises

Ludwig von Mises' *The Theory of Money and Credit* interweaves several theoretical schemata. His first task is to develop a theory of the value of money that overcomes the "Austrian circularity" problem. He does this through his "regression theorem" and, at the same time, he also derives the demand for money in the context of a "cash balance" approach.[20] Mises' second task is to develop a theory of variations in the value of money, which he does by elaborating a theory of the non-neutrality of money. His third task is to develop a theory of fiduciary media (or money substitutes) on the basis of which he then uses Böhm-Bawerk's capital theory and Wicksell's theory of the natural and money rates of interest to present a theory of the business cycle.[21]

For Mises, there is no dichotomy between the structure of relative prices and the general purchasing power of money (or the general 'price level'). In his view, money has no single price on the market. Instead, the value or purchasing power of money is represented by the set or array of exchange ratios between the monetary unit and all the goods against which money trades on the market.[22] Any change in the structure of relative prices necessarily means a change in the general exchange value, or purchasing power, of the monetary unit – as represented by that array of exchange ratios between the money and market commodities. At the same time, any change in the general value of money involves a change in the structure of relative prices, because it is only through changes in the individual supplies and demands for goods that market participants can demonstrate any changes in their desire to demand or supply money (the interaction and equilibrium between which establishes the value of money).

Mises' theory of the non-neutrality of money is a sequence, or process, analysis. Consistent with his strict adherence to methodological individualism, Mises argues that any change in the conditions of the demand for or supply of money always originates in the circumstances of the individual participants on the market. Their changed circumstances are transmitted to the market through modifications in their respective demands for or supplies of specific goods.[23] Mises' classic examples are of increases in the supply of money:

> The additional quantity of money does not find its way at first into the pockets of all individuals; not every individual of those benefited first gets the same amount and not every individual reacts to the same additional quantity in the same way. Those first benefited – in the case of gold, the owners of the mines, in the case of government paper money, the treasury – now have greater cash holdings and they are now in a position to offer more money on the market for goods and services they wish to buy. The additional amount of money offered for them on the market makes prices and wages go up. But not all the prices and wages rise, and those which do rise do not rise to the same degree ... Thus, price changes which are the result of the inflation start with some commodities and services only, and are diffused more or less slowly from one group to the others. It takes time till the additional quantity of money has exhausted all its price changing possibilities.

But even in the end the different commodities are not affected to the same extent. The process of progressive depreciation has changed the income and the wealth of the different social groups. As long as this depreciation is still going on, as long as the additional quantity of money has not yet exhausted all its possibilities of influencing prices, as long as there are still prices left unchanged at all or not yet changed to the extent that they will be, there are in the community some groups favored and some at a disadvantage. Those selling the commodities or services whose prices rise first are in a position to sell at the new higher prices and to buy what they want to buy at the old still unchanged prices. On the other hand, those who sell commodities or services whose prices remain for some time unchanged are selling at the old prices whereas they have to buy at the new higher prices ... As long as the inflation is in progress, there is a perpetual shift in income and wealth from some social groups, to other social groups. When all price consequences of the inflation are consummated, a transfer of wealth between social groups has taken place. The result is that there is in the economic system a new dispersion of wealth and income and in this new social order the wants of individuals are satisfied to different relative degrees, than formerly. Prices in this new order can not simply be a multiple of the previous prices.[24]

Mises' theory of the business cycle is a particular application of this temporal-sequence theory of the non-neutrality of money. Accepting the Böhm-Bawerkian framework, Mises argues that the degree of roundaboutness is determined by the point at which investment profitability at the margin is tending to equality with the prevailing natural interest rate; that is the point at which the periods of production which are undertaken and which are profitable to undertake are sustainable on the basis of the amount of savings available in the economic community. Lowering the money rate of interest below the natural rate acts as the inducement for undertaking longer, more roundabout periods of production. Factors of production, as a consequence, are drawn into these more roundabout projects. However, Mises takes issue with Wicksell at this point. Wicksell presented his thesis under the assumption that, if projects of a two-year duration were to supplant some of the one-year investment projects, the smaller quantity of consumer goods at the end of the first year merely raises their prices, with no change in consumer goods available until the end of the second year. Mises, however, sees a self-reversing set of forces that may come into work.

Consistent with his emphasis on the wealth and income redistributive effects that a monetary expansion tends to generate, Mises argues that the lowering of the money interest rate resulting from an expansion of bank credit may bring about shifts in wealth between social groups, and specifically from those with lower to those with higher saving preferences. This can bring about a situation in which some of the longer roundabout processes may be sustainable, since the redistribution of income and wealth has been in such a direction that some of the additional savings needed to sustain them have been generated through money's non-neutral impacts on members of the society.[25]

But while this may occur to one degree or another, Mises argues that the rise in the factor money incomes during the expansionary process will usually tend to put upward pressure on the price of consumer goods. The increased money demand for final goods and services will now reverse the profitabilities of investment projects, from those with longer periods of production to those with shorter periods of production. The scarcity of the factors of production must mean that if one sector of the economy is to utilize more of them, other sectors will have fewer factors available for use.[26] The longer, more roundabout investment projects are not all completed (as Wicksell assumed they would be in his two-period model). Rather, the scarcity of resources precludes the satisfying of the demand for present goods (as reflected in the actual savings/consumption ratio of income earners) and the plans of entrepreneurs undertaking these more roundabout projects. This, in Mises' view, is the basis for the emergence of the 'crisis' point of the business cycle.[27] The longer the period during which monetary expansion has continued and the money rate has been kept below the natural rate, the more severe may be the crisis:

> The greater this additional quantity of fiduciary money, the more factors of production have been firmly committed in the form of investments which appeared profitable only because of the artificially reduced interest rate and which prove to be unprofitable now that the interest rate has again been raised. Great losses are sustained as a result of misdirected capital investments. Many new structures remain unfinished. Others, already completed, close down operations. Still others are carried on because, after writing off losses which represent a waste of capital, operation of the existing structure pays at least something.[28]

The money rate of interest is pressured upwards back towards what would now be the relevant "natural rate," not only because of the rising demand for present goods, but also because of the emerging inflation premium on interest rates. While critical of Irving Fisher's version of the quantity theory of money, Mises did endorse his theory of the influence of inflation expectations on the nominal, or money, rate of interest. Thus, as the general value of money declines, creditors demand compensation for the anticipated depreciation of the purchasing power of lent funds during the period of the loans.[29]

If the monetary authority continues to increase the supply of fiduciary media in an attempt to maintain or increase the number of roundabout projects inconsistent with the actual real supply of savings, the increasing demand for present goods and the emerging inflation premium may be delayed or prevented from fully returning the rate of interest to the appropriate natural rate. The price of such a policy would be an unending inflationary spiral with the potential to eventually destroy the monetary system. Mises was convinced that he had presented a complete theory of the business cycle.[30]

Gunnar Myrdal and Erik Lindahl

In the interwar period, several Swedish Economists took up the Wicksellian theme. This chapter focuses on two of the leading Swedish figures during this time, Gunnar Myrdal and Erik Lindahl. Both devoted attention to the problems of "periods," "plans," and expectations.

When, in 1926, Bertil Ohlin contributed an essay on "Tendencies in Swedish Economics," for a festschrift in honor of Lujo Brentano (a leading member of the German Historical School), no mention was given to the role of expectations in economic analysis. Instead, he held that the focus of Swedish economic thought in the years following World War I had been the refinement of the existing body of "marginalist" equilibrium theory, the application of theory to contemporary and historical situations, and debates over Wicksell's analysis of the influence of change in the money interest rate on prices in general (in light of the great inflations experienced during and after the war). He suggested that the next step in the development of economics would be a "description of a time-consuming process, the real dynamics of economic science."[31]

The shift in emphasis apparently occurred a year later, in 1927, with the publication of Gunnar Myrdal's dissertation, *The Problem of Price Formation and Change*. Economic dynamics had two tasks, he argued. The first concerned an analysis of the sequential process by which one "price situation is transformed into another price situation" due to the fact that any change in the "data" and market prices during one period would be the causal elements in influencing new pricing configurations in following periods. Thus, a study of the forces creating a pricing pattern at *a moment of time* would give directional meaning to price movements *over time*. The task concerned an analysis of expectations, for it is expectations held about future events at a moment in time that would determine the present prices prevailing on the market. Since the sequence of price movements was dependent upon the expectations held at various points over the time sequence, "an investigation of the former problem [price movements over time) requires the latter (formation of expectations over time) to be solved."[32]

The next development of this train of thought came in Myrdal's *Monetary Equilibrium*.[33] Myrdal says there were two primary purposes behind his analysis: first, to determine the conditions of a "non-cumulative price situation," that is a position of equilibrium in which money serves as an intermediary for both present and intertemporal exchanges; second, to "include anticipations in the monetary system." because it is discrepancies between actual and expected values in the market that are the source of the economic disturbances usually associated with a Wicksellian-type cumulative process. The tool Myrdal believed appropriate for analyzing divergences between real and anticipated events is the distinction between *ex ante* and *ex post*.[34]

Wicksell laid down three requirements for a monetary equilibrium:

1   The natural rate was the rate of interest at which the marginal technical productivity of real capital equaled the money rate.

2   The supply of and the demand for savings were equal.
3   The price level (as measured in terms of consumer goods) was "stable."

For the first condition – the equating of the marginal technical productivity of real capital to the money rate of interest – Myrdal shows that once there is more than one factor of production, it is necessary to express the relationships between the factors in value terms. However, when so expressing marginal productivities in value terms, the next step is to realize that the only relevant value expressions for capital-investment decision-making are "anticipated values." Because it is "expected profitability of an undertaking" which "is decisive for entrepreneurs' programmes, not the profitability actually experienced during a past period." The latter is important only "indirectly as evidence of future profitability." In equilibrium, the expected rate of profit on real investment must equal the money rate of interest for each firm, otherwise any *ex post* positive (negative) discrepancies between the two rates would, in the next *ex ante* period, set off a cumulative expansion (contraction) in economic activities, as entrepreneurs' actions tend to bring the two rates back to equality.[35]

The second Wicksellian condition stated that, in equilibrium, the rate of interest must equalize the supply of and demand for saving. Since in non-stationary conditions the distinction between merely replacing existing capital and new investment becomes *hazy,* Myrdal reformulates the thesis in more general terms. Here "the money rate is normal, i.e., at its 'natural level', if it brings about an equality between gross real investment on the one side and saving plus total anticipated value-change of the real capital ... on the other side."

These first two conditions, when they hold, assure that a cumulative process would not occur.[36]

Cumulative processes can occur, Myrdal argues, under any of three conditions:

1   Where expectations of entrepreneurs rise (fall), with a given money rate of interest. With an elastic currency system, more (less) funds will be borrowed and incomes will rise (fall). This will result in higher (lower) prices for consumer goods and the raising (lowering) of profit expectations.
2   Where, given entrepreneurial expectations, the money rate of interest falls (rises). The rate of profit expected would tend to increase (decrease), again stimulating (retarding) investment. Incomes would rise (fall), with consumer goods prices then rising (falling) soon after, tending to reinforce the optimistic (pessimistic) expectations.
3   Where savings increased (decreased) but the rate of interest did not quickly adjust to reflect the new underlying conditions, consumer demand would have fallen (increased), lowering (raising) prices and profit margins than would be expected. Entrepreneurial investment activity would decline (expand), incomes would fall (rise) and consumption demand would fall (increase) even further, thus reinforcing the initial change.[37]

As for Wicksell's third equilibrium condition (that the rate of interest must be such that the "price level" is kept "stable"), Myrdal argues that if the "equilibrium price relations ... are fulfilled, any movement of the absolute money prices consistent with them will leave monetary equilibrium undisturbed."[38]

Equilibrium requires appropriate relative prices, and as long as relative prices are "correct" and retained, the "price level" and its height is secondary. However, as a practical matter Myrdal also says changes in the "price level" can disturb the equilibrium price relationships if all prices, particularly wages, do not show easy and smooth flexibility. A falling price level in which some prices, such as wages, did not decline to the appropriate degree would generate cost-price discrepancies that would disturb monetary equilibrium. His conclusion was that a "monetary policy aimed to preserve the equilibrium relations must ... adapt the flexible prices to the absolute level of the sticky ones" if there was a danger of falling prices.[39]

Finally, there is Myrdal's analysis of *ex ante* and *ex post* and their relation to "periods." For accounting purposes, *ex post*, there must always be a balance between savings and investment, but there is no reason for the *ex ante* savings and investment decisions to balance, and it will be the *ex ante* calculations and plans that will always be "driving the dynamic process forward."[40] *Ex ante* calculations relate to the point in time at which they are made and to a period of time for which the calculation and plan is constructed. Any full analysis would contain two parts: an analysis of plans and expected values at one point in time, which are then compared with the *ex post* values at another point at the end of the specified period; and an analysis of the development of events between these two points in time, which are the factors that would generate a discrepancy between the *ex ante* estimates and the *ex post* results. A focus on the *ex ante* plans at the beginning of the period highlights the "tendencies which must be studied as a preparatory step to the dynamic analysis proper which refers to the causal development in time up to the next point studied."[41]

Our critical remarks will focus on three points: the meaning of "periods" in Myrdal's approach; his analysis of investment patterns in the cumulative process; and his assumptions about the "neutrality" of price level movements in the face of flexible prices and wages. First, concerning Myrdal's "periods."[42] His comparison of the *ex ante* plans with the *ex post* results set rigid limitations on consumption and production decisions during the period. All plans for the coming period – investment, production and consumption plans – must be made at the same moment at the beginning and must extend over the entire period. None of these plans can be revised during the period so that, for instance, what may happen during the first half of the period is not allowed to influence or modify any of the plans for the second half. Thus, what Myrdal constructs is not actually a sequence or process analysis through periods of time, but an analysis of outcomes in comparison to expectations that may change plans between periods.

When Myrdal outlines Wicksell's schema, he emphasizes that an integral aspect of the cumulative process is the shifting of factors of production from shorter to longer time-consuming investments. Indeed, he goes so far as to state that the shift in production thus brought about is the essential and necessary change keeping the cumulative process going as long as there is the drive for capital values enhanced by a discrepancy between the money rate of interest and the "natural rate."[43]

Yet, in his exposition of the cumulative process, Myrdal almost totally ignores this influence, discussing instead the incentives for investment in general by emphasizing the larger rate of profit available. The essential ingredient in Wicksell's sequence of events – based as it is on Böhm-Bawerk's theory of roundaboutness – is that interest rate changes do not affect the profitability of all investments equally, i.e., changes in the money rate of interest can influence the structure of production because of the increased profitability of investments possessing a longer "time-shape."[44] Parts of Myrdal's analysis, therefore, collapse into a simple "derived demand" process. Changes in expectations about the demand for consumer goods either stimulate or retard investment demand, *in general*. The Wicksell-Mises approach, on the other hand, recognized the influence of changes in and expectations about consumer goods, but offered a richer analysis precisely by pointing out that not all investment activities would be affected in the same way or to the same degree, and that as a result the "structure of production" would be modified during and was inseparable from the cumulative process.

Finally, there is Myrdal's assumption that as long as institutional rigidities did not prevent wages and prices from changing so as to maintain "equilibrium values." Monetary policies that "stabilized" the "price level" or moved it in a particular direction need have no distorting effect. This might be true under either of two conditions:

- all changes in aggregate monetary expenditures to influence the "price level" occur proportionally and simultaneously in all sectors of the economy (thus assuring that money was "neutral" in terms of the structure of relative prices)
- while a change in aggregate monetary expenditures does not affect the various sectors simultaneously, expectations on the part of the market participants are such that each one can correctly anticipate when, how and to what extent the change in monetary expenditure will impinge on his respective activities, so each individual is able to successfully distinguish "real" from "monetary" forces at work, and adjust their market actions accordingly.

As neither of these two conditions is likely ever to be present, monetary policies that change the aggregate expenditure streams will necessarily affect the structure of relative prices – even when the policy goal is only "price level" stabilization.

In *Monetary Equilibrium*, Gunnar Myrdal gave credit to Erik Lindahl for being one of the first to "give a more systematic representation of certain parts of Wicksell's monetary theory."[45] In his early studies, *The Aims of Monetary Policy*

(1929) and *Methods of Monetary Policy* (1930), Lindahl offered an extended elaboration of Wicksell's cumulative process by postulating alternative assumptions about perfect and imperfect knowledge, production periods and the existence of full or less-than-full employment, as well as the consequences of pursuing various "price level" goals. In his later monograph, "The dynamic approach to economic theory," Lindahl developed his more detailed theory of "period" and "plan" analysis.[46]

In both the earlier and later expositions, a common assumption is the idea of periods of time so short that the factors directly affecting prices, and therefore also the prices themselves, can be regarded as unchanged in each period. All such changes are therefore assumed to take place at the transition points between periods. Prices in these "short periods" are set at the beginning of the period and supply and demand are determined by them.[47]

We will first consider Lindahl's analysis in his 1930 study. Following Wicksell, Lindahl emphasizes that, if starting from a position of equilibrium, the money rate of interest is lowered, there "will be an increase in all capital values, which will of course be proportionally greater for relatively long-term investments than for relatively short-term ones."[48] The actual working of the cumulative process, he continues, will depend upon the subsidiary assumptions.

For our purposes we will consider two of Lindahl's cases, those that start with full employment and others that begin with idle resources. Under conditions of full employment, the lowering of the money rate of interest brings about a

> lengthening of the investment period which is now profitable ... Factors of production will be transferred from direct production of consumption goods to the production of capital goods, the relative prices of which have increased. And in the capital goods industries the newly constructed equipment will be more durable than the old while the production process will itself occupy a longer period.[49]

Furthermore, the shift of resources to capital goods production will tend to reduce the supply of consumer goods; the prices of consumer goods will begin to rise because of the smaller supply and because of the higher money demand for goods due to the additional income generated via the borrowing at the lower money rate. The rising consumer prices raise entrepreneurial expectations further "since capital values are partly determined by the anticipated prices of consumer goods."[50] The savings necessary to enable longer production processes to be undertaken is obtained through "forced savings": the bidding of resources towards investment activity lowers the supply of consumer goods and "forces" consumers to consume less (at higher prices) than they would if the lower money rate of interest had not acted as an investment stimulus.[51] The cumulative process continues as long as the money rate is kept below the natural rate.

The other alternative is to assume that initially unemployed resources are available. The sequence of events will depend upon where in the economy the unemployed factors are located. If unemployment is in the capital goods sectors, the unemployed will be absorbed into investment activity, without having to diminish the supply of consumer goods. But consumer goods prices will still tend to rise because a given quantity of consumer goods will now be demanded by a larger work force. If resources are mobile between the consumer goods and capital goods sectors, when all idle resources have been finally absorbed in the investment sector, input factors will, finally, be bid away from consumer goods industries and consumer goods prices will rise even further as their supply diminishes.

If unemployment is initially in the consumer goods sectors, greater investment activity will result in a transfer of some of those unemployed factors into capital goods production; but as consumer goods demand begins then to rise, the prices for final output need not rise significantly at first, since the idle factors can be used to expand supply. Only when all unemployed resources are finally utilized will the continuing transfer of factors to capital goods production result in significant price increases for consumer goods.

Finally, if unemployment exists in both investment and consumer goods sectors both will be able to expand, with the upward pressure on prices initially slowed. When one or the other becomes fully employed, the sequence of events will follow along the lines of the previous two cases.[52] A money rate of interest above the "natural" rate would set in motion a reverse set of events, with the additional complications that may arise from any wage or price rigidities that might prevail.[53]

We see that in this early 1930 study, Lindahl had an income-expenditure framework; income is generated through the sale of factor services and influenced by the terms at which funds can be borrowed on the loan market. Earned income is then translated into savings and consumption expenditures in which it is discovered that the savings and consumption patterns of factor-income earners is incompatible with the attempts of entrepreneurs to carry through with various investment plans. The income-expenditure pattern, however, is also linked with the distribution of the real factors among their alternative uses and the effect of that distribution on the availability of consumer goods. In other words, Lindahl attempts to contain in one analysis both the *patterns of monetary expenditures* that appear as incomes with the *patterns of resource allocations* that generate those incomes. What is found to be insistent is the *ex post* availability of consumer goods in relation to capital goods, compared to the *ex ante* planned expenditures stream on consumer goods. This *ex ante-ex post* incompatibility has been caused by the way in which the real factors were initially allocated in the structure of production.

In his 1939 monograph, "The Dynamic Approach to Economic Theory," Lindahl directs his attention to the changing pattern of plans and actions due to disappointed *ex post* results. The analysis attempts to explain future changes in planned actions in a determinant fashion based upon events in past and future periods. Lindahl argues that if we know the respective plans of the individuals at the beginning of the period; if we know how the individuals would change their plans under different future conditions; and if we have the knowledge of external conditions so that we know what events will impinge on individuals and make them revise their plans in particular ways, "then it should be possible to provide a theoretical construction of the developments that will be the outcome of the initial position."[54]

A theory of planning is developed in which it is shown how present period plans act as constraints on future choices, while at the same time the different successful steps in each imagined plan would open future options that the alternative plans might exclude. Lindahl summarizes his approach in the following way: "The dynamic process is divided into fairly short time periods, e.g., a day. All decisions about the business and consumption plans to be adopted, and all price changes, take place at the transition points between these periods." For example, at the beginning of the "day" sellers set their prices. Entrepreneurs and consumers combine this price information with their expectations of the future profitability or anticipated utility from alternative courses of action. They choose the ones that offer the highest returns, entrepreneurs proceed to purchase factors of production and consumers to buy various finished commodities. At the end of the "day" each individual sums up his experiences based on the outcome of the period just passed (of either unexpected unsold inventories or unexpected orders in excess of supply), then sets the prices for the next "day," given the quantities each now decides to supply.[55]

A dynamic, ongoing process is thus created in which past period events influence present period expectations and plans, and, in turn – depending upon the compatibility of the interpersonal plans – set up the conditions under which future plans in future periods will have to be revised. Lindahl assumes no tendency for interpersonal plan coordination or equilibrium. Instead there is only a sequence of periods in which there may be temporary equilibrium or a pattern of disequilibrium situations. If equilibrium occurs it happens only "sporadically."[56]

In the earlier 1930 study, Lindahl attempted to unify an analysis of expenditure patterns with an analysis of the pattern of the distribution of the factors of production. However, in this later monograph the focus shifts almost completely to income and expenditure flows during periods, and to their influence on changes in planned pricing and quantities supplied in the next "short period." Gone is any concern with the "time-shape" of the structure of production and its importance for the stream of available goods *over periods*.[57]

A cumulative process in this new framework would take the general (and rather superficial) form of an excessive increase in aggregate money demand for quantities available at present period prices. The next period would see a rising of prices and the cumulative process would be continuing if, at these higher prices, money demands again exceed the quantities demanded. In terms of the Wicksellian framework that Lindahl used in 1930, this later approach passes over without discussion the very elements of the cumulative process that Wicksell considered to be crucial.

Finally, while claiming to offer a more realistic analysis of dynamic processes, it is important to remember that the determinant steps in Lindahl's sequential periods are dependent upon the assumption of knowing not only the initial plans of the individuals, but how they will form concrete expectations when faced with a particular circumstance. What Lindahl does not offer is a theory of expectations formation that could serve as a guide to how individuals decide on a plan of action, when the actions they undertake must incorporate some anticipation of the likely actions of others if their own plans are to have a chance to succeed.

Friedrich A. Hayek

Friedrich A. Hayek was the most prominent proponent and refiner of the Wicksell–Mises business-cycle theory. Indeed, it is no exaggeration to say that the theory gained world renown among economists through him.[58] Yet Hayek's use of the Wicksell–Mises theory has a uniquely distinct twist to it. Both Wicksell and Mises had been interested in explaining how a discrepancy between the natural and money rates of interest set in motion a cumulative process of a general rise or fall in prices. The essential accompanying process through which this rise (fall) in prices is brought about is a distortion of the intertemporal allocation of resources from a shorter (longer) period of production to a longer (shorter) one.

Hayek makes his primary task that of analyzing discrepancies between the natural and money rates of interest as an explanation of how changes in the supply of money must bring about modifications in the structure of relative prices, with any changes in the general value of money as an incidental result of this process. This is explained in his first book, *Monetary Theory and the Trade Cycle* (1929) and in *Prices and Production* (1931), as well as in his articles on "Intertemporal Price Equilibrium and Movements in the Value of Money" (1928) and "On 'Neutral Money'" (1933).[59] Hayek's criticisms of "price level" stabilization were an analytical tool to demonstrate that stability or movement in the general level of prices was neither an indicator nor a benchmark for equilibrium in the economy.

In the later 1930s and 1940s, Hayek's research in this area led him to rethink what "equilibrium" meant, and what its existence required in terms of coordinating interpersonal plans in and across time. This theme was taken up especially in his essays on "Price Expectations, Monetary Disturbances and Malinvestments" (1933), "Economics and Knowledge" (1937), and "The Use of Knowledge in Society" (1945), and in the chapter on "Equilibrium Analysis and the Capital Problem" in *The Pure Theory of Capital* (1941).[60]

In "Intertemporal Price Equilibrium and Movements in the Value of Money," Hayek attempted to demonstrate that equilibrium through time required prices of goods at each moment across time to consistently reflect the supply and demand conditions of those respective moments. Any attempt to "stabilize" the price of a good or a set of goods at the same "level" across time, in spite of differing market conditions across that time, must set in motion market reactions that would be "destabilizing." If, for example, the supply of a good was going to be greater in the future than today because of some productive innovation being introduced that would lower costs, and if equilibrium is to prevail in that future period as well as in the present period, then the price of that good in the future period (assuming given demand conditions) must tend to be lower than the price in the present period.

If this good's future price was to be "stabilized" across time at the "level" that prevailed in the present, this would result in future expected profit margins being greater than if natural market forces normally were at work competing the price down to reflect the now lower costs of production. The stabilized higher price in the future period would tend to induce an excess production of the good in comparison to what the "real" supply and demand conditions would dictate, and this "surplus" would eventually create a destabilizing effect in this market.[61]

What was true for any particular good would be true for a situation in which there was a general expansion of output due to falling costs across many markets. If each price in this situation was permitted to find its equilibrium level, the general "price level" (as measured by some statistical averaging) would have declined, though the structure of relative prices will have been kept in equilibrium across time. However:

> if the money supply is increased just sufficiently to prevent a fall in prices, it must have basically the same effect on the structure of production as any other expansion in the quantity of money not "justified" by an increase in output. By preventing the temporal gradation of prices determined by the "goods situation" from being established, it gives rise to shifts in production which prevent the necessary equalization of the supply of goods as between different points in time. Moreover, at a later stage, when some of these shifts have already been irrevocably completed, it obliges much greater changes in prices which must result in the loss of some portion of the expenditures made.[62]

Thus, "price level stabilization" through a policy of monetary expansion (contraction) can in fact be destabilizing. Stability on the monetary surface can hide disequilibrating forces beneath that surface.[63]

The task that Hayek saw for monetary theory was to analyse how the presence of money in the exchange process had the potential to undermine the "normal" forces in the market that should tend to establish and maintain equilibrium relationships across the economy. Whereas in barter every change in any supply or demand tended directly to bring about the appropriate reciprocal actions from other suppliers and demanders, these direct links and reciprocal actions were not present in the same way in a money economy.[64] Instead:

> The necessary starting point for any attempt to answer the theoretical problem seems to me to be the recognition of the fact that the identity of demand and supply, which must necessarily exist in the case of barter, ceases to exist as soon as money becomes the intermediary of the exchange transactions. The problem then becomes one of isolating the one-sided effects of money ... which will appear when, after the division of the barter transaction into two separate transactions, one of these takes place without the other complementary transaction. In this sense, demand without corresponding supply, and supply without a corresponding demand, evidently seem to occur in the first instance when money is spent out of hoards (i.e.,

when cash balances are reduced), when money received is not immediately spent, when additional money comes on the market, or when money is destroyed.[65]

The influence of money on "real" factors is inseparable from the presence of money in the market process. Conceptually, "monetary" forces can be distinguished from "real" forces, but in a money-using economy any real changes are only transmitted in the form of money demands for and supplies of goods and services. Furthermore, a change in the supply of money that increases (decreases) individuals' cash balance positions directly influences the capacity for individuals to demand real goods and services. This modifies the actual structure of relative prices for as long as a change in the supply of money continues, or while its effects are still working through the economy.[66] So, like Mises, Hayek considers the non-neutrality of money to be the cornerstone for analyzing money's influence upon and relationship to the real economy. The primary task of monetary theory consequently becomes, in Hayek's view, the study of money's influence on relative prices and the structure of production.[67]

Hayek's Austro-Wicksellian theory of the trade cycle is an application of this monetary approach to a particular problem, but with the following difference. Unlike some of the Swedes, Hayek's analysis never strays far from an emphasis on money's influence on the intertemporal structure of prices and production. The Hayekian triangles highlight the intertemporally interdependent relationships which permeate the economic order. The stages of production are connected and coordinated with each other through the network of prices which encapsulate the demand and supply for the various "higher" and "lower" order goods. The rate of interest is the governor mechanism. It ensures that the period of production and the flow of consumer goods from it over time is effectively coordinated with the patterns of consumer preference for consumption goods per period and the preference for savings sufficient to maintain production processes of particular time durations.[68] Hayek argued that

An equilibrium rate of interest would then be one which assured correspondence between the intentions of the consumers and the intentions of the entrepreneurs ... [T]his would be rate of interest arrived at on a market where the supply of money capital was of exactly the same amount as current savings. If the supply of money capital is increased, by monetary changes, beyond this amount, the result will be that the rate of interest will be lowered below the equilibrium rate and entrepreneurs will be induced to devote a larger part of the existing resources to production for the more distant future than corresponds to the way in which consumers divide their income between savings and current consumption. At the time when entrepreneurs make this decision the consumers have no possibility of expressing their wishes with sufficient emphasis since their money incomes are as yet unchanged while the expansion of credit has increased the funds available for investment. The investment of these funds, however, must in the course of time increase total income by nearly the full amount of these funds, either because wages are raised in order to attract people away from producing consumers' goods towards producing capital goods, or because the funds are used to employ formerly unemployed workers. This will certainly tend to increase the intensity of the demand for consumers' goods ... The entrepreneurs who have begun to increase their productive equipment in the expectation that the low rate of interest and the ample supply of money capital would enable them to continue and to utilize these investments under the same favorable conditions, find these expectations disappointed. The increase in the prices of all those factors of production that can be used also in the late stages of production will raise the costs of, and at the same time the rise in the rate of interest will decrease the demand for, the capital goods which they produce. And a considerable part of the newly created equipment designed to produce other capital goods will stand idle because the expected further investment in these other capital goods did not materialize.[69]

The question of the compatibility of expectations and intertemporal plans led Hayek in the mid-1930s to pursue the meaning of equilibrium and the level of knowledge that market participants would need for a coordination of plans to be possible.[70] In "Economics and Knowledge," Hayek defined equilibrium as meaning that

the foresight of the different members of the society is in a special sense correct. It must be correct in the sense that every person's plan is based on the expectation of just those actions of other people which those other people intend to perform and that all these plans are based on the expectation of the same set of external facts, so that under certain conditions nobody will have any reason to change his plans.[71]

This conception of equilibrium, he argues, does not require any assumption that the knowledge of the agents is either perfect or extending into an infinite future. All that is required is that the agents have all the "relevant" knowledge to assure that their plans are mutually compatible. The relevant knowledge in this case is all the knowledge that each of them "is bound to acquire in view of the position in which he originally is, and the plans which he then makes."[72] In other words, given that the agent may discover in the process of undertaking a plan that his expectations about the actions of others with whom he is interdependent is incorrect, the direction in which the inconsistency exists will provide the agent with the additional, new knowledge concerning how he should revise his plans so they are more compatible with the actions of those with whom he is interacting.[73] In elaborating some of the types of knowledge used by participants in the social system of division of labor, Hayek explains how the price system helps economize on the detailed information required by agents when coordinating their activities with others.[74] Furthermore, agents each coordinate their action with that of others to the greatest extent possible by continually adjusting their conduct to the changing price conditions in their respective corner of the market.

This conclusion brought Hayek back to where he started from in 1929 when he said that "in the exchange economy, production is governed by prices, independently of any knowledge of the whole process on the part of individual producers."[75] As long as individuals allow themselves to be guided in their actions by prices and any changes in prices "relevant" to their particular activities, there need be no forces that can bring about systematic mistakes by a large number of market participants, especially entrepreneurs. This is likely to occur only if an exogenous disturbance is introduced into the system – such as a change in the supply of money that brings about a deviation of the money rate of interest from the natural rate.

This in no way solves the question of how individuals are to use the price information that comes their way. Either an actual price which is different from the one that was expected, or a quantity of some good actually sold which is greater/smaller than was expected to sell at that price, are both forms of knowledge that show plans need to be revised. But the plan revisions to be undertaken in these cases are ambiguous. The information provided by a frustrated plan in the present must be interpreted in the context of what it is suggesting about the shape of new plans oriented towards the future. In other words, Hayek's analysis of equilibrium and knowledge fails to provide a theory of expectations.[76]

Ludwig von Mises – again

By the late 1930s and 1940s, members of the Swedish School like Myrdal and Lindahl, and Austrians like Hayek, had reached the point at which periods, plans and expectations had come to be seen as central questions to be answered if economic analysis was to be taken further. Each had come to this point from a similar starting point: Wicksell's theory of a cumulative process induced by a discrepancy between the money and natural rates, which set in motion intertemporal misallocations of resources and output mixes. Each had understood this process as the product of mutually inconsistent plans between consumers and producers, savers and investors; and these inconsistencies only manifested themselves at sequentially different times as different participants discovered that their respective plans could not be successfully consummated.

This led the Swedish Economists to formulate various types of "plan" and "period" analyses. Lindahl, for example, postulated that prices are set at the beginning of the period, transactions are carried out during the period, and at the end of the period the registered quantities bought and sold at those prices are tabulated. Based on any disappointed expectations, revisions are made in pricing and production plans and these serve as the starting point for the events of the next period. Lindahl divides the sequential periods into arbitrarily "short periods" during which the individual plans are postulated as unchanged.[77]

The Swedes were no better at solving the problem of expectations than Hayek. To say that plan disappointments in one period serve as the basis for plan revisions in the next period tells little about how individuals form expectations about what they should do in the next period. If, at the end of the present period, sales of a product are less than expected (because demand was not as great as had been anticipated), does it naturally follow that in the next period the planner should revise the production level downwards? Well, it depends. Is the level of sales experienced in the first period a temporary or a permanent change in demand? How might one's competitive rivals on the supply-side be reacting to this actual level of demand? The answers not only influence the choice of the next period's output level, they may also influence investment decisions planned for several future periods. Hayek's emphasis on market price as an economizer of information – to which individuals should adjust their actions when price changes are experienced – has the same problem. An actual price different from an expected price informs the planner that plans should be changed, but expectations must still be formed on the basis of that price information so as to specifically know what to do.

In his later work, Ludwig von Mises suggested his own version of what "periods" should mean in economic analysis and offered a theory of expectations formation.[78] In his earlier writings, there was an explicit sequence analysis: Mises' theory of the non-neutrality of money is, what he called, a "step-by-step" analysis of the diffusion of a monetary change throughout the economy, during which relative demands, price relationships and resource allocations are sequentially and temporally impacted upon. It is only in his later writings that the problem of the meaning of periods and expectations are explicitly dealt with; and they can only be understood in the context of his wider theory of human action.

In Mises' view, man is above all else the being who acts. Man has intentionality and he pursues purposes. He designs plans to succeed in his endeavors and he applies means to bring them about. Possessing consciousness, man mentally projects himself into the future and imagines conditions or states of affairs that he would prefer to his actual or other potential circumstances. He tries to discover causal relationships and connections in the world in which he lives and selects the ones he thinks would be most effective for achieving his goals. In selecting between alternative courses of action, man must choose, and choice implies uncertainty: the actor believes that his actions can influence the future and thus the future, from his perspective, is not "preordained." At the same time, what individuals view as "ends" to pursue, what they classify as "means" for various tasks, what are the "benefits" and "costs' in the context of choices being weighed – these have intelligibility and meaning only when understood from the actor's perspective. It is a human mind that contemplates possibilities, that classifies, orders and arranges the physical things of the world into categories of meanings and relationships. As a result, it is how the human actor assigns meanings to various things that determines what they are (in the context of the purposes and plans the actor has constructed) and which then guides his conduct towards those things in his environment. Looking at man in this manner is what Mises referred to as the "subjectivist method"; the analyst understands the world from the actor's point of view.[79]

In this methodological subjectivist perspective, all action occurs in and is inseparable from time. All action implies a before and an after, a sooner and a later, a becoming and a became. This means that it is impossible, Mises says, for man to be indifferent to the passing of time. Indeed, it is in the contemplation of action that man becomes most conscious of time. And, in Mises' view, it is the potential for action that delineates the past from the present and the present from future.[80] He argued:

That which can no longer be done or consumed because the opportunity for it has passed away, contrasts the past with the present. That which cannot yet be done or consumed, because the conditions for undertaking it or the time for its ripening have not yet come, contrasts the future with the past. The present offers to acting opportunities and tasks for which it was hitherto too early and for which it will be hereafter too late. The present qua duration is the continuation of the conditions and opportunities given for acting. Every kind of action requires special conditions to which it must be adjusted with regard to the aims sought. The concept of the present is therefore different for various fields of action. It has no reference what ever to the various methods of measuring the passing of time by spatial movements. The present contrasts itself, according to the various actions one has in view, with the Middle Ages, with the nineteenth century, with the past year, month, or day, but no less with the hour, minute, or second just passed away. If a man says: Nowadays Zeus is no longer worshipped, he has a present in mind other than that of the motorcar driver who thinks: *Now* it is still too early to turn. And as the future is uncertain it is always undecided and vague how much of it we can consider as *now* and present. If a man had said in 1913: At present – now – in Europe freedom of thought is undisputed, he would have not foreseen that this present would very soon be a past.[81]

In this conception of time, individuals pursuing various goals invariably operate simultaneously in terms of "periods" of varying length. Each action has its own time horizon. For some plans, the actor is in the middle of the "present" period; for other plans, the "present" period is coming to a close; for yet other plans the "future" period is just becoming the "present." For still other plans, the potentials for action are still in a "future" period. Nor are these periods of equal length. For some actions, the "present" period is an instant as measured by the movement of the clock, and then is gone; for other actions, the "present" extends far into the future as measured by the clock. Each planning period would have its sub-periods divided into "past," "present" and "future" (for instance, "Right now I'm working on my undergraduate degree" would have the sub-period "Right now I'm in my first year," which would have the sub-period "Right now I'm having lunch in between my morning and afternoon classes").

In the market changes usually do not impact simultaneously on all transactors. Instead, a change in market conditions originates at some point in the economic system. From this "epicenter" the consequences of the change, in terms of changes in the actions and plans of those initially impacted, emanates out in a particular path-dependent sequential and temporal order. Some individuals in the social system of division of labor will be affected by this – to a greater or lesser extent – at a different time than others; some individuals may be impacted at the same time; some will be impacted sooner, others later. At each of those moments at which the change reaches each individual, each of them will have to weigh the meaning and significance of the change in terms of requiring a "change in plans," that is in terms of when, how and how much.

How precisely shall the change be interpreted for deciding how plans should be modified? This brings us to Mises' theory of expectations formation.[82] In developing his theory of expectations formation, Mises was influenced by Max Weber and by one of his young Viennese contemporaries, Alfred Schutz. Max Weber had defined action as "all human behavior ... insofar as the acting individual attaches a subjective meaning to it." Social action was defined as action in which the actor "takes account of the behavior of others and is thereby oriented in his course."[83] Social actions, including market interactions, are actions of mutual orientation, in which each participant is aware of others whose activities are relevant to one's own goals or purposes.[84]

Mises states that the fundamental problem for the "acting man" in the social arena is the problem of anticipating the future actions of others:

> How can a man have any knowledge of the future value judgments and actions of other people? ... The task with which acting man, that is, everybody, is faced in all relations with his fellows does not refer to the past; it refers to the future. To know the future reactions of other people is the first task of acting man. Knowledge of their past value judgments and actions, although indispensable, is only a means to this end.[85]

The historian reconstructs the past by sorting and arranging the preceding actions of human actors. Everyday acting man, however, must anticipate the future actions of other men, without which the success of his own action may be impossible. This is done, Mises explains, on the basis of the knowledge we collect about other individuals and groups of individuals from our past interactions or accumulated information about them. This knowledge is "acquired either directly from observing our fellow men and transacting business with them or indirectly from reading and from hearsay, as well as our special experience acquired in previous contacts with the individuals or groups concerned." With this knowledge, "we try to form an opinion about their future conduct."[86]

Mises' young associate and friend, Alfred Schutz, conceptualized the method that men use to form expectations in the idea of the "ideal type."[87] First we are all born into a common world of intersubjective meaning. These intersubjective meanings, which we learn from childhood, specify and define the meanings of actions and objects in the social world around us. They enable us to identify certain actions and things in most "typical" situations as meaning one thing rather than another. They enable us to understand and mutually orient ourselves in the social arena. But besides these general meanings that define situations and activities as usually or "typically" meaning "this" or "that," when a person is seen doing something or using something, there are also "ideal types" we create in our minds of particular individuals or groups of individuals. The ideal type, in other words, is a composite image of an individual or a group of individuals created in an individual's mind for understanding other's actions in the past or anticipating them in the future. Or as Mises puts it:

> The characteristic mark of an "ideal type" ... is that it implies some proposition concerning valuing and acting. If an ideal type refers to people, it implies that in some respects these men are valuing and acting in a uniform or similar way. When it refers to institutions, it implies that these institutions are products of uniform or similar ways of valuing and acting or that they influence valuing and acting in a uniform or similar way.[88]

Ideal types, Mises argues, enable an acting man to be "the historian of the future."[89] Forming composite pictures or images of individuals in terms of characteristics, qualities, motives and meanings, ideal types enable an individual decision maker to project himself into the future, imagine that another individual or individuals is confronted or faced with a particular situation or change in circumstances, and then ask: "How might these individuals respond?" on the basis of the behavioral typifications the decision-maker has in his mind of them.

It is a peculiar fact that this part of Mises' writings – his suggestion for defining "periods" in terms of "potentials for action," and his theory of expectations formation on the basis of "ideal types" – has received little attention by Austrian Economists. If integrated into the Austrian theory of entrepreneurship and the market process, intertemporal exchange and the structure of production, as well as the Austrian theory of money and the business cycle, it could potentially go a long way towards improving the internal consistency of the Austrian system, as well as increasing our practical knowledge about how the "real world" works.

Notes

1 For summaries of the "Austrian" approach to economics, see, Ludwig M. Lachmann "The Significance of the Austrian School of Economics in the History of Ideas," [1966] reprinted in, Richard M. Ebeling, ed., *Austrian Economics: A Reader* (Hillsdale, MI: Hillsdale College Press, 1991), pp. 17–39; and, Richard M. Ebeling, *Austrian Economics and the Political Economy of Freedom* (Northampton, MA: Edward Elgar, 2003), Ch. 2: "The Significance of Austrian Economics in 20th Century Economic Thought," pp. 34–60. On the "Swedish" approach to economics, see, Richard M. Ebeling, "The Stockholm School of Economics: An Annotated Bibliography," *The Austrian Economics Newsletter,* Vol. 3, No. 2 (1981), pp. 1–12.

2 Knut Wicksell, "Böhm-Bawerk's Theory of Capital," [1911] in *Selected Papers on Economic Theory* (London: George Allen & Unwin, 1958), pp. 176, 178.

3 Eugen von Böhm-Bawerk, *Capital and Interest,* Vol. 3, (South Holland, IL: Libertarian Press, 1959), pp. 360, 476.

4 Ludwig von Mises, *Theorie des Geldes und der Umlaufmittel* [1912] (Munich/Leipzig: Duncker & Humblot, 2nd revised ed., 1924), p. x.

5 Knut Wicksell, "Review: Theorie des Geldes," [1914] translated and reprinted in, Bettina Bien Greaves and Robert W. McGee, eds., *Mises: An Annotated Bibliography,* (Irvington-on-Hudson, NY: Foundation for Economic Education, 1993) pp. 197–199.

6 Böhm-Bawerk, *Capital and Interest,* Vol. 2, pp. 3–15, 85–88.

7   Ibid., pp. 95–101.
8   Ibid., pp. 290–341.
9   Ibid., pp. 112–115; Böhm-Bawerk, "The Function of Savings," [1901] reprinted in, Richard M. Ebeling, ed., *Austrian Economics: A Reader*, pp. 401–413, rejects the later Keynesian-type arguments that the greater profitability of longer-term investment project will be counteracted by the decline in effective demand for final output that results from an increase in savings. He also responds to the argument that, since consumers do not specify the future benefit they want from their acts of saving, the uncertainty of what might be profitable to produce for future consumption may counteract the incentives for long-term investment.
10 Knut Wicksell, *Lectures on Political Economy*, Vol. 2 [1911] (London: George Routledge & Sons, 1935), p. 193. Wicksell's use of the concept of the "natural rate" was not without ambiguity. Arthur W. Marget, *The Theory of Prices*, vol. 2, [1942] (New York: Augustus M. Kelley, 1966), pp. 201–204, for example, distinguished at least eight different meanings that Wicksell assigns to the "natural" rate. The difficulties of calculating a "natural" rate in barter (that is, one without a unit of account with which to convert productive capabilities into value terms) was also emphasized by a number of Wicksell's followers; see, Ludwig von Mises, "The Position of Money Among Economic Goods," [1932] in, Richard M. Ebeling, ed., *Money, Method and the Market Process, Essays by Ludwig von Mises* (Norwell, MA: Kluwer Academic Press, 1990), p. 65; Erik Lindahl, *Studies in the Theory of Money and Capital* [1939] (New York: Augustus M. Kelley, 1970), pp. 247–249; and, Gunner Myrdal, *Monetary Equilibrium* [1939] (New York: Augustus M. Kelley, 1962), pp. 49–51.
11 Knut Wicksell, *Interest and Prices* [1898] (New York: Augustus M. Kelley, 1969), p. 104; *Lectures on Political Economy*, Vol. 2, p. 193.
12 Wicksell, *Lectures on Political Economy*, Vol. 2, p. 159.
13 Wicksell, *Interest and Prices*, pp. xxvi, 135.
14 Wicksell, ibid., p. 89; *Lectures on Political Economy*, p. 186.
15 Wicksell, *Interest and Prices*, pp. 91–92, 143, 149, 155; *Lectures on Political Economy*, pp. 195–196.
16 Wicksell, *Interest and Prices*, pp. 137–141. A detailed breakdown of the Wicksellian "periods" process under both "stationary" and "cumulative" conditions, as well as an analysis of some of the internal inconsistencies to be found in Wicksell's exposition, is given by, Carl Uhr, *Economic Doctrines of Knut Wicksell* (Berkeley: University of California Press, 1962), pp. 235–245.
17 Wicksell, *Lecture on Political Economy*, p. 195, points out that it is "not impossible for the rise in prices to be counteracted to a certain extent by an increase in production ... if previously there had been unemployment."
18 Wicksell, *Interest and Prices*, pp. 141–149. Wicksell was under no illusion that "constant price" expectations would long be in effect under these circumstances. The series of rising prices would, as he expressed it, "create its own drought." Entrepreneurs would begin making decisions not purely on present prices but based on anticipated future prices. Factor prices, in turn, would spiral upwards to reflect the expected higher final goods prices (ibid., pp. 96–97). In a criticism of those who have advocated a gently rising price level as a beneficial stimulus to economic activity, Wicksell remarks that

> if a gradual rise in prices, in accordance with an approximately known schedule, could be reckoned on with certainty, it would be taken into account in all current business contracts; with the result that its supposed beneficial influence would necessarily be reduced to a minimum.

(Ibid., pp. 3–4)

19 Wicksell, *Interest and Prices*, pp. 155–156.
20 For an exposition and elaboration of Mises' regression theorem, see George Selgin, "On Ensuring the Acceptability of a New Fiat Money," *Journal of Money, Credit and*

Banking (November 1994), pp. 808–826. For a comparison of Mises' cash balance approach with A.C. Pigou's Cambridge "k" cash balance approach, see, Richard M. Ebeling, "Variations on the Demand for Money Theme: Ludwig von Mises and Some Twentieth-Century Views," in, John W. Robbins and Mark Spangler, eds., *A Man of Principle: Essays in Honor of Hans Sennholz*, (Grove City, PA: Grove City Press, 1992), pp. 127–138.

21 See, Richard M. Ebeling, *Austrian Economics and the Political Economy of Freedom*, Ch. 5: "Ludwig von Mises and the Gold Standard," pp. 136–158.

22 Ludwig von Mises, *The Theory of Money and Credit* [1953] (Indianapolis, IN: Liberty Classics, 1981), p. 216. In defining the purchasing power of money in this manner, Mises was following some of the classical economists. Jacob Viner, *Studies in the Theory of International Trade* [1937] (New York: Augustus M. Kelley, 1965), pp. 311–314.

23 Ludwig von Mises, "Monetary Stabilization and Cyclical Policy" [1928] in *On the Manipulation of Money and Credit* (Dobbs Ferry, NY: Free Market Books, 1978) pp. 95–103; Mises, *The Theory of Money and Credit*, pp. 160–168.

24 Ludwig on Mises, "The Non-Neutrality of Money," [1940] in Richard M. Ebeling, ed., *Money, Method and the Market Process, Essays by Ludwig von Mises*, (Norwell, MA: Kluwer Academic Press, 1990) pp. 72–73.

25 Mises, "Monetary Stabilization and Cyclical Policy," pp. 126–127; *The Theory of Money and Credit*, pp. 384–388.

26 Mises, like Wicksell before him, accepted that the availability of unemployed resources at the start of the sequence would delay this counteracting process from setting in as soon as would otherwise tend to be the case; see, Mises, "Monetary Stabilization and Cyclical Policy," pp. 125:

> At times, even on the unhampered market, there are some unemployed workers, unsold consumers' goods, and quantities of unused factors of production, which would not exist under "static equilibrium." With the revival of business and productive activity, these reserves are in demand right away. However, once they are gone, the increase in the supply of fiduciary media necessarily leads to disturbances of a special kind.

See, also, Ludwig von Mises, *Interventionism: An Economic Analysis* [1941] (Irvington-on-Hudson, NY: Foundation for Economic Education, 1998), p. 42.

27 Mises, "Monetary Stabilization and Cyclical Policy," pp. 118–130; *The Theory of Money and Credit*, pp. 396–404.

28 Mises, "Monetary Stabilization and Cyclical Policy," pp. 129–130.

29 Ibid., pp. 93–95; and *The Theory of Money and Credit*, pp. 225–234.

30 Ludwig von Mises, *Notes and Recollections* [1940] (South Holland, IL: Libertarian Press, 1978), p. 110. However, see, Simon Kuznets, "Monetary Business Cycle Theory in Germany," *Journal of Political Economy* (April 1930), p. 14.

31 Bertil Ohlin, "Tendencies in Swedish Economics," *The Journal of Political Economy* (June 1927), pp. 343–363.

32 Erik Lindahl, "Review: Dynamic Pricing," *Economic Journal* (March 1929) pp. 89–91.The quotations appear in Tord Palander, "On the Concepts and the Methods of the 'Stockholm School,'" *International Economic Papers* (1953), Vol. 3, p. 9; see, Brinley Thomas, *Monetary Policy and Crises: A Study of Swedish Experience*, (London: George Routledge & Sons, 1936), pp. 66–74, and, for a detailed summary of Myrdal's analysis in this work, see, Bert Hansson, *The Stockholm School and the Development of Dynamic Method* (London: Croom Helm, 1982), pp. 29–46.

33 It originally appeared as an article in *Ekonomisk Tidskrift* (1931) and was enlarged in a revised version two years later, appearing under the title, "Der Gleichgewichtsbegriff als Instrument der Geldtheoretischen Analysis" [The equilibrium concept as a tool of analysis in monetary theory]. It was this essay, slightly revised, that was finally published in English in 1939 as *Monetary Equilibrium* (New York: Augustus M. Kelley, 1962).

328 *Money, economic fluctuations, expectations*

34 Myrdal, *Monetary Equilibrium*, pp. 30–32, 47.
35 Ibid., pp. 49–69. It is not always easy to follow and summarize Myrdal's exposition. This is partly because, while he says that there are two ways of thinking about these problems – as purely theoretical problems and as practical problems requiring "operational" content – he in fact shifts back and forth, sometimes combining and confusing the two.
36 Ibid., pp. 95–96.
37 Ibid., pp. 101–112.
38 Ibid., p. 132.
39 Ibid., pp. 134–135.
40 Ibid., pp. 45–46.
41 Ibid., pp. 44–45, 55.
42 The following remarks on this point rely heavily upon the arguments made by Palander, "On the Concepts and the Methods of the 'Stockholm School.'" See also Hansson, *The Stockholm School and the Development of Dynamic Method*, pp. 103–155.
43 Myrdal, *Monetary Equilibrium*, p. 26.
44 Thus, I do not agree with the view of either Howard Ellis, "Review: Monetary Equilibrium," *Journal of Political Economy* (June 1940), pp. 434–436, or Joan Robinson, "Review: Monetary Equilibrium," *Economic Journal* (September 1939), pp. 493–495 that Myrdal's analysis is plagued by the "Austrian" notion of a "period of production." Quite to the contrary. Nor do I share Ellis' and Robinson's preference to see the concept of a "period of production" dropped from economic theory.
45 Myrdal, *Monetary Equilibrium*, p. 7.
46 *The Aims of Monetary Policy* appeared only in Swedish. *Methods of Monetary Policy*, on the other hand, was condensed and translated as Part II of Erik Lindahl, *Studies in the Theory of Money and Capital* [1939] (New York: Augustus M. Kelley, 1970), pp. 139–268, under the title "The Interest Rate and the Price Level." The 1939 volume opens with a long monograph on "The Dynamic Approach to Economic Theory," and it is in this essay that the "period analysis" for which Lindahl is famous was given its most elaborate exposition. It also shows a definite change in Lindahl's approach to "process analysis." In the earlier work, Lindahl moved along strongly Wicksellian lines, focusing on changes in the production structure during the phases of the cumulative process. In the 1939 monograph, Lindahl abandons this mode of exposition for what is primarily an income-expenditure model in terms of periods and the influence of the results in previous periods on present and future periods.
47 Lindahl, ibid., pp. 158–159. The assumption that during "the period" prices are fixed and quantities demanded and supplied adjust to them distinguishes Lindahl's "period analysis" from John R. Hicks, *Value and Capital* (Oxford: Oxford University Press, 1939), pp. 115–140, who assumes quantity as fixed and prices the adjusting factor in the period. See Hicks' contrast between his own approach and that of Lindahl in John R. Hicks, "Methods of Dynamic Analysis," in *Twenty-Five Essays in Honor of Erik Lindahl* (Stockholm: Ekonomisk Tidsskrift, 1956), pp. 139–151. See also Karl Bode, "Plan Analysis and Process Analysis," *American Economic Review* (June 1943), pp. 348–354.
48 Lindahl, *Studies in the Theory of Money and Capital*, p. 154.
49 Ibid., pp. 170–171.
50 Ibid., p. 171.
51 Ibid., pp. 173–176.
52 Ibid., pp. 169–179.
53 Ibid., pp. 183–186.
54 Ibid., pp. 37–38.
55 Ibid., pp. 62–63.
56 Ibid., pp. 64–69.
57 Lindahl's use of "fairly short periods," in which prices are set at the beginning and a

summing up of plan successes or failures is not done until the end of the period, is open to criticisms raised by Myrdal: it ignores the fact that necessary adjustments may require more time than an analytical "short period" allows for, and the outcomes of the process may well depend upon the "time order" of the actual events in the period, and which are ignored by focusing only on beginning and end "points of registration." At the same time, Lindahl is open to the criticisms raised by Tord Palander against Myrdal. While it is true that Lindahl's approach offers a "sequence analysis" over time that Myrdal's did not offer in his "dynamic analysis," Lindahl's "points of regis-tration" at the point between periods take on little meaning once we realize that the relevant points and times for plan re-evaluation will depend upon the individual's par-ticular plans and the time horizons in them. An appropriate time for comparing *ex ante* plans with *ex post* may, for some people, be some point within the "short period," while for others the time for comparing *ex ante* plans with *ex post* outcomes may be outside the "short period."

58 Of course, Hayek was not the only proponent; there was a wide circle of economists in Austria, and especially in England, who accepted the theory and used it in their analyses of cyclical phenomena. Among the more important of them were, Gottfried Haberler, "Money and the Business Cycle," [1932], in Richard M. Ebeling, ed., *The Austrian Theory of the Trade Cycle and other Essays* (Auburn, AL: The Ludwig von Mises Institute, 1990); Richard von Strigl, *Capital and Production* [1934] (Auburn, AL: The Ludwig von Mises Institute, 1995); Fritz Machlup, *The Stock Market, Credit, and Capital Formation* [1931] (London: William Hodge, 1940) and, *Führer durch die Krisenpolitik* (Vienna: Julius Springer, 1934); Lionel Robbins, *The Great Depression* (London: Macmillan, 1934); and, C.A. Phillips, T.F. McManus, and R.W. Nelson, [1937] *Banking and the Business Cycle* (New York: Arno Press, 1972). For a listing of many other books and articles in the Austrian monetary tradition published during this period, see Ebeling "Ludwig von Mises and the Gold Standard," p. 156.

59 Friedrich A. Hayek, *Monetary Theory and the Trade Cycle* [1929; 1933] (New York: Augustus M. Kelly, 1966); *Prices and Production* [1931; 2nd ed., 1935] (New York: Augustus M. Kelley, 1961); "Intertemporal Price Equilibrium and Movements in the Value of Money" [1928] and, "On 'Neutral Money,'" [1933] in *Money, Capital and Fluctuations: Early Essays* (Chicago: University of Chicago Press, 1985).

60 Friedrich A. Hayek, "Price Expectations, Monetary Disturbances and Malinvest-ments," [1933] in *Profits, Interest and Investment* (New York: Augustus M. Kelley, 1969), pp. 135–156; "Economics and Knowledge" [1937] and "The Use of Know-ledge in Society" [1945] in *Individualism and Economic Order* (Chicago: University of Chicago Press, 1948), pp. 33–56, 77–91; and *The Pure Theory of Capital* (London: Macmillan, 1941), Ch. 2: "Equilibrium Analysis and the Capital Problem," pp. 14–28.

61 Hayek, "Intertemporal Price Equilibrium and Movements in the Value of Money," pp. 91–93.

62 Ibid., p. 94. See, additionally, Hayek, *Prices and Production*, p. 28. See, also, Gott-fried Haberler, *The Different Meanings Attached to the Term 'Fluctuations in the Pur-chasing Power of Gold' and the Best Instrument or Instruments for Measuring Such Fluctuations*, official no. F/Gold/74, (Geneva: League of Nation, 1931); Allen G.B. Fisher, "The Significance of Stable Prices in a Progressive Economy," *Economic Record* (March 1935), pp. 49–64, and "Does an Increase in Volume of Production Call for a Corresponding Increase in Volume of Money?" *The American Economic Review* (June 1935), pp. 197–211; Fritz Machlup, "Inflation and Decreasing Costs of Production," in H.P. Willis and J.M. Chapman, eds., *Economics of Inflation*, (New York: Columbia University Press, 1935), pp. 280–287; and Richard M. Ebeling, "Stable Prices, Falling Prices and Market-Determined Prices," in, Richard M. Ebeling (ed.) *Austrian Economics: Perspectives on the Past and Prospects for the Future*, (Hillsdale, MI: Hillsdale College Press), pp. 481–499.

63 Gottfried Haberler, "A New Index Number and Its Meaning," *The Quarterly Journal of Economics*, May 1928, pp. 434–449.

64 Hayek, "Price Expectations, Monetary Disturbances and Malinvestments," pp. 93, 108.
65 Hayek, *Prices and Production*, p. 130.
66 Hayek, *Monetary Theory and the Trade Cycle*, pp. 104, 124–125.
67 Ibid., pp. 116–117; and *Prices and Production*, p. 29.
68 Hayek, *Prices and Production*, pp. 32–100; and Murray N. Rothbard, *Man, Economy, and State: A Treatise on Economics*, Vol. 1 [1962] (Los Angeles: Nash Publishing Co. 1970), pp. 273–386.
69 Hayek, "Price Expectations, Monetary Disturbances and Malinvestments," pp. 145–146, 148.
70 In fact, Hayek stated that his thoughts turned in this direction because of the criticisms by Swedish economists, like Gunnar Myrdal, that he had failed to incorporate expectations and uncertainty into his theory of the trade cycle; see, F.A. Hayek, "Price Expectations, Monetary Disturbances and Malinvestments" [1933] in *Profits, Interest and Investment* (New York: Augustus M. Kelley, [1939] 1966), pp. 155–156. Having turned his attention to these matters, when Hayek reviewed Lindahl's *Studies in the Theory of Money and Capital*, he said that

> the strongest impression [the volume] leaves with the reader is one of intense regret that Professor Lindahl's ideas should not have become more widely accessible when they were first outlined in Swedish some ten years ago ... [Y]et, when at last they are made available to us in full, we find that not only have they lost most of the attraction of novelty but even that what might have been a revelation to us now mostly represents a stage through which we ourselves have passed, although considerably later than Professor Lindahl, yet some time ago.

See, F.A. Hayek, "Review: Studies in the Theory of Money and Capital," *Economica* (August 1940), pp. 332–333. Hayek also admitted that it was the earliest essays included in the volume that had most attraction for him, in which

> Professor Lindahl remains closest to the views of his master Wicksell ... Since then Professor Lindahl has taken an active part in the general movement away from "real" problems towards almost exclusive concern with the monetary aspects of economic problems, and indeed has become a leader in that movement.

71 Hayek, "Economics and Knowledge," p. 42.
72 Hayek, "The Use of Knowledge in Society," p. 53.
73 Hayek, *The Pure Theory of Capital*, p. 23.
74 Hayek, "The Use of Knowledge in Society," and "Economics and Knowledge," pp. 77–91.
75 Hayek, *Monetary Theory and the Trade Cycle*, pp. 84–85.
76 See, Richard M. Ebeling, "What is a Price? Explanation and Understanding," in, Don Lavoie, ed., *Economics and Hermeneutics* (London: Routledge, 1990), and also, Ebeling, "Toward a Hermeneutical Economics: Expectations, Prices and the Role of Interpretation in a Theory of the Market Process," in David L. Prychitko, ed., *Individuals, Institutions, Interpretations: Hermeneutics Applied to Economics* (Brookfield, VT: Avebury, 1995), pp. 138–153, where I have discussed this shortcoming in Hayek's writings in another context.
77 It would be a false impression to assume that Lindahl's particular period analysis was one that all, or even most, Swedish economists during these years accepted or used. Other Swedish economists gave different meanings to "periods." Erik Lundberg, *Studies in the Theory of Economic Expansion* [1937] (New York: Augustus M. Kelley, 1964), stated that the relevant period depended upon the nature of the theoretical exercise. One had to first specify whether the focus of the analysis concerned "production periods," or "periods of contract" or "reaction or adjustment periods," and to analyse the total effect of a change it would be necessary to have a period long

0
0

0

enough for everyone in the economy to have been affected. Bjorn Hansson, "The Stockholm School and the Development of Dynamic Method," in, B. Sandelin, ed., *The History of Swedish Economic Thought* (London: Routledge, 1989), pp. 168–213, summarizes several of the alternative period and process models developed by different members of the Swedish School.

78 Ludwig von Mises, *Human Action: A Treatise on Economics* [1949] (Irvington, NY: Foundation for Economic Education, 4th revised ed., 1996); *Theory and History: An Interpretation of Social and Economic Evolution* (New Haven, CT: Yale University Press, 1957); *The Ultimate Foundations of Economic Science: An Essay on Method* (Princeton, NJ: D. Van Nostrand, 1962).

79 On Mises' theory of action and some of its implications, see, Richard M. Ebeling, "Austrian subjectivism and phenomenological foundations," in, Peter J. Boettke and Mario Rizzo, eds., *Advances in Austrian Economics, Vol. 2A*, (Greenwich, CT: JAI Press, 1995), pp. 39–53. See also my introduction to, Richard M. Ebeling, ed., *Money, Method and the Market Process, Essays by Ludwig von Mises*, (Norwell, MA: Kluwer Academic Press, 1990), pp. ix–xxvi.

80 Mises, *Theory and History*, pp. 202–203, 287.

81 Mises, *Human Action*, pp. 100–101.

82 Richard M. Ebeling, "Expectations and Expectations-Formation in Mises' Theory of the Market Process," in, Peter J. Boettke and David L. Prychitko, eds., *The Market Process: Essays in Contemporary Austrian Economics* (Brookfield, VT: Edward Elgar, 1994), pp. 83–95; and, Richard M. Ebeling, "Cooperation in Anonymity," in, Prychitko, ed., *Individuals, Institutions, Interpretations: Hermeneutics Applied to Economics*, pp. 81–92.

83 Max Weber, *The Theory of Social and Economic Organization* [1922] (New York: Oxford University Press, 1947), p. 88.

84 Max Weber, *Critique of Stammler* [1907] (New York: The Free Press, 1977), pp. 109, 112; Mises, *Human Action*, p. 195, refers to the exchange relation as "the fundamental social relation," in which there is "intentional mutuality."

85 Mises, *Theory and History*, p. 311.

86 Ibid., p. 313.

87 Alfred Schutz, *The Phenomenology of the Social World* [1932] (Evanston, IL: Northwestern University Press 1967); *Collected Papers, I: The Problem of Social Reality* (The Hague: Nijhoff, 1962).

88 Mises, *Theory and History*, p. 316.

89 Ibid., p. 322.

10 Human action, ideal types, and the market process

Alfred Schutz and the Austrian economists

Alfred Schutz and the Vienna *Miseskreis*

Alfred Schutz studied at the University of Vienna with legal philosopher, Hans Kelsen, and Austrian Economist, Friedrich von Wieser.[1] Among his classmates were Friedrich von Hayek (who was awarded the Nobel Prize in Economics in 1974) and Fritz Machlup. Schutz first met Ludwig von Mises in 1920. Though Schutz never attended Mises' seminar at the University, he had to pass a three-hour oral examination before a governmental commission of economists to receive his law degree. The students did not know who would be on the examining panel ahead of time. When they saw Mises coming up the staircase, they realized they were not in for an easy time; he was known to be a demanding examiner.[2]

By then, Mises was already well-known in Europe as a leading monetary theorist, based on his 1912 volume, *The Theory of Money and Credit*.[3] He was a senior economic advisor to the Austrian Chamber of Commerce, and had published a well-received book entitled, *Nation, State and Economy* (1919), in which he analyzed the causes and consequences of the Great War.[4]

Just about the time Schutz took his examination, Mises had published an article on, "Economic Calculation in the Socialist Commonwealth," which soon caused a firestorm of controversy.[5] He argued that socialism was an economically unworkable system; with the nationalization of the means of production and the resulting abolition of market prices and competition, the socialist central planners would have eliminated the only method for rationally estimating the relative value of scarce resources in alternative productive uses. Thus, rather than offering a more efficient and wealth-generating economic order, socialism in practice would lead to economic waste and stagnant standards of living.[6]

Mises tried to trick Schutz during his University examination. He asked Schutz if he had ever read *The Distribution of Wealth* by American economist, John Bates Clark. Schutz replied that he had. Mises then asked in what language he had read the book. Schutz answered that he had read it in the original English. Mises responded by saying, "It is good you answered as you did, because there *is* no German translation."[7]

Shortly after passing his own examination, Fritz Machlup told Schutz that Mises had organized *a Privatseminar,* and that it would be possible for him to attend. At first Schutz was not especially enthusiastic, having explained to Mises that his main interest was sociology, and not economics. But Mises began to give him topics for seminar presentations, and soon Schutz was finding the meetings interesting and stimulating. In fact, Schutz's first assignment for the *Miseskreis* (the Mises Circle), as it soon became known, was a presentation on Max Weber's methodology.[8]

Mises' private seminar met every other Friday from October to June. The membership varied over the years and was made up of about twenty to twenty-five scholars from a wide variety of disciplines, including economics, sociology, philosophy, history, political science, law, and psychology. The seminar continued from 1920 through the spring of 1934, shortly before Mises moved to Geneva, Switzerland, where he took up a position as Professor of International Economic Relations at the Graduate Institute of International Studies.

Mises' own description of the private seminar shows its focus and quality:

> All who belonged to this circle came voluntarily, guided only by their thirst for knowledge. They came as pupils, but over the years became my friends. Several of my contemporaries joined the circle. Foreign scholars visiting Vienna were welcome guests and actively participated in the discussions … We formed neither school, congregation, nor sect. We helped each other more through contradiction than agreement. But we were agreed and were united on one endeavor: to further the sciences of human action. Each went his own way, guided by his own law … We never gave thought to publishing a journal or a collection of essays. Each worked by himself, as it befits a thinker. And yet, each one of us labored for the circle, seeking no compensation other than simple recognition, not the applause of his friends. There was greatness in this unpretentious exchange of ideas; in it we all found happiness and satisfaction.[9]

One of the members of the *Miseskreis* was Martha Steffy Browne, who later taught at Brooklyn College. She remembered the seminar as follows:

> Professor Mises proved his intuition as well as his judgment of perception in the choice of the participants of his seminar. In the beginning, it was a small circle of economists only … But it was only a few years later that Mises invited people of various intellectual capacities. Scholars like Eric Voegelin, Felix Kaufmann, and Alfred Schutz pioneering in the fields of sociology and philosophy, enriched the level of the economic discussions. Highly gifted economists of the so-called younger school of Austrian economics like [Friedrich] Hayek, [Gottfried] Haberler, [Fritz] Machlup, [Oskar] Morgenstern, and many others were stimulated and challenged through the speeches and discussions. Professor Mises never restrained any participant in the choice of a topic he or she wanted to discuss. I have lived in many cities and belonged to many organizations. I am sure there does not exist a second circle where the intensity, the interest and the intellectual standard of the discussions is as high as it was in the Mises Seminar.[10]

Fritz Machlup observed that among the many topics discussed in the seminar, "Of special interest was the year of methodological discourse, partly thanks to the affiliation of Alfred Schutz and Felix Kaufmann with the ideas of Edmund Husserl and Kaufmann's with the Schlick Circle."[11] Indeed, the last semester of the private seminar, in spring, 1934, was entirely devoted to "methodological problems," with papers delivered by Mises, Felix Kaufmann, Ewald Schams, Robert Walder, and Oskar Morgenstern.[12]

Austrian economics as a science of human action

From its beginning in 1871, with the publication of Carl Menger's *Grundsätze der Volkswirtschaftslehre*,[13] the members of the Austrian School were critical of any unreflective adoption of the methods of the natural sciences in the social sciences in general and in economics in particular. They began, instead, with the concept of intentionality. Consistent with this starting-point, the Austrian Economists saw the human mind as the primary source of knowledge about man, i.e., the logical relationships on the basis of which men made their choices, and from which were derived the "Laws of Economics"; these were discoverable through the use of introspection and the method of mental experiments.[14]

In the period between the wars, members of the Austrian School of Economics generally focused on the following types of theoretical problems:

1   The methodological foundations of the social sciences in general and economics in particular.
2   Formalization of the logic of human action and choice.
3   The theory of price formation and market equilibrium.
4   The problem of imperfect knowledge and the formation of expectations.
5   The theory of entrepreneurship and market coordination.
6   The theory of capital formation, the processes of production, and the rate of interest.
7   The theory of money and economic fluctuations (business cycles).[15]

Especially because of Mises' influence, the focus of attention for many of the discussions among the Austrians revolved around the significance and applicability of Max Weber's methodology to the problems of economic theory. In the 1920s and early 1930s, Mises wrote two essays in which he discussed the possibilities and limits of the Weberian approach as a foundation for economic science.[16] He fundamentally accepted Weber's idea of "action" as the foundational concept for economic theorizing. What separated the natural sciences from the social sciences was that the latter dealt with phenomena in which the subject matter possesses purposefulness and intentionality. Man above all else is the being who acts. He imagines possibilities more to his liking, he conceives of ways of using the objects of the world as "means" to his "ends," and he plans courses of action to bring those desired ends to fruition. The domain of all social sciences, including economics, Mises argued, was the subjective world of acting man. The meanings that men assign to their purposes and plans define objects, situations, and social relationships.[17]

Emphasis on the subjectivist quality of the subject-matter of economics immediately draws attention to the fact that men look out at the world and plan their actions on the basis of knowledge that is necessarily imperfect, a knowledge that is derived from their local circumstances in a social system of division of labor. The question then arises how men, mutually dependent upon each other in that system of division of labor, can successfully coordinate their activities for assurance of a balance between the multitudes of demands and supplies for various goods and services in a complex and developed market order. Since all production processes embody various periods of time for their completion, investments must be undertaken "today" if finished consumer goods are to be available at some point in the future. Hence, if future supplies are to match "tomorrows" demands, expectations must be formed by those who direct the production processes geared towards the future demands of the consuming public.[18]

This lead the Austrians to investigate the significance of prices as a coordinating mechanism in market relationships, as well as the role of the entrepreneur as the "undertaker" and director of production in a system of private enterprise. Friedrich Hayek, in particular, addressed the significance of prices in a market economy. He argued that prices do not merely act as incentives for productive activities, but they also serve to disseminate information about changing demand and supply conditions throughout the market; guided by the information those prices convey, each can then try to adjust his own activities as seems most appropriate, given his local situation and circumstances in his corner of that system of division of labor.[19]

The role of the entrepreneur as the central figure in the market process was emphasized by Joseph Schumpeter in his seminal work, *The Theory of Economic Development*.[20] And an equal significance was placed on the entrepreneur by Mises, especially in his treatise, *Human Action*.[21] Since all social processes begin with the actions of individuals, there must be an agent in the market economy who imagines, organizes and directs the production processes for purposes of coordination with the prospective demands of consumers. In the social system of division of labor that role belongs to the entrepreneur. The market "rewards" successful entrepreneurship with profits and "penalizes" unsuccessful entrepreneurship with losses. The competitive openness of a free market tends to bring about a situation in which financial control over resources and the factors of production are shifted into the hands of those entrepreneurs who demonstrate their superior ability in correctly anticipating future directions of consumer demand through profits earned, and who offer desired products and services at prices and with qualities better than the next closest supply-side rivals. Those who perform this entrepreneurial role more poorly experience diminished profits or suffer actual losses; over time they lose financial control over the means of production and the direction of the production processes of the market. Hence, the competitive market is continuously shifting ownership and productive control over the factors of production into those hands that demonstrate a greater comparative advantage in the knowledge and ability of serving the consuming public.

Clearly, such coordination of a vast number of interpersonal plans, in which the market actors are separated from each other in terms of both time and space, requires some mechanism through which expectations can be formed concerning the likely intentions of "others" for purposes of constructing one's own plans. In other words, there is Weber's problem of "social action," in which each must in some way be able to successfully "orient" himself to the actions of others, when the actions of those others have a bearing on the outcomes of one's own designs.

One attempt at explaining the process of mutually-oriented social action in economics has been "the theory of games," first developed by the Austrian Economist, Oskar Morgenstern, and the mathematician, John von Neumann.[22] Another was made by Ludwig von Mises, through an adaptation of Max Weber's concept of ideal typification.[23]

Yet is it a peculiar fact that economists in general and even members of the Austrian School have devoted little effort to develop a realistic theory of expectations and intersubjective fields of mutual orientation. The failure to do so for mainstream or Neo-Classical Economics is partly understandable as due to the strong Positivist influence on Neo-Classical Economists during the past hundred years. A method that emphasizes that only the quantifiable is to be considered appropriate "facts" for scientific investigation, and which rigorously strives to reduce human action to the status of a "dependent variable" in a system of interdependent mathematical equations, leaves little room for a study of "meanings" and "intentions." As Fritz Machlup has observed,

> For [the] method of imagined introspection, curves and equations are poor substitutes. Sliding down a smooth curve until it intersects another curve is a healthy mental exercise; and solving a set of simultaneous equations is too; but neither of these will ensure our understanding of the way a man makes up his mind when he ponders a business decision.[24]

It is stranger that most Austrian Economists have failed to try their hand at this either,[25] especially since Alfred Schutz's writings offer an analytical framework that can serve as an important guide for doing so.[26] Before suggesting how Schutz's system of ideal typifications in a field of intersubjective meanings and relationships can assist in constructing a theory of expectations and entrepreneurial decision-making, it will be useful to contrast the Neo-Classical Economic conception of the logic of choice with Schutz's analysis of choosing among projects of action.

The Neo-Classical economist's logic of choice and Schutz's choosing among projects of action

At one end of the ideal typification spectrum, Schutz explains, is the anonymous other. This "other" is conceived as having only the most abstract and general qualities and characteristics that can be said to be found in any man, and therefore can be considered to be representative and true of all men.[27] In this typification, man is viewed only in the context of that most universal image of a "purposeful being," i.e., a chooser of ends, an applier of means, and a performer of acts. Here man is representative of what Neo-Classical economists have come to call "the logic of choice." Given a set of ends that have been ranked in order of preference, and given a quantity of means with which those ends may be pursued, and given a set of prices at which alternatives may be traded one for the other, the chooser applies the principle of marginal decision-making to select that combination of ends that maximizes his utility or satisfactions. It also means that in this framework, human choices are open to prediction. If the chooser's preference structure is given and known and if the actual terms of trade are "objectified" in the form of market prices, then the individual's decisions can be reduced to the status of a set of "reactions" to external changes in relative prices.[28]

Alfred Schutz was impressed with the analytical force of the economist's schema of decision-making. But what he believed to be a fundamental shortcoming in the economist's approach is the confusing of the "because" motive with the "in-order-to" motive. That is, the confusing of an *ex post* reconstruction (by actor or analyst) of the situation in which a particular choice was made (or planned) with the *ex ante* process by which elements out of which a choice may be made are constructed by the potential chooser.[29] For most economists, once the order of the ends and relative means available are clearly specified, the choice-problem becomes "unproblematic." The solution to an efficient allocation of scarce means among competing ends is purely a matter of mathematical techniques for utility maximization. For Schutz, when the ends and means are being specified and clarified by the chooser in his own mind, the "unproblematic" becomes "problematic." Now the problem of choice confronts the actor.

Why what is "unproblematic" for Neo-Classical Economics is "problematic" in Schutz's analysis is understood when the role of time is studied in the two approaches. In Neo-Classical Economics, time as real, temporally-lived experience does not exist; even when "choice" involves the allocation of either resources or actions through time, it is a choice "out of time."[30] The reason for this is the "retrospective" perspective from which "choice" is evaluated by the Neo-Classical Economist. With the assumption of a prior creation and constitution of the ends, a designation of the quantities and qualities of the means, and delimitation of the time horizons over which choice alternatives are to be compared, the analyst is confronted with a "timeless" moment in space in which he "observes" an actual or hypothetical decision. As consequence, it is a "choice" that is *not a real choice*. From this conceptual *ex post* or "because-motive" perspective, the analyst explains why, given the agent's preferences and means-constraints, this particular "choice" was the only (and therefore the inevitably) logical one that the "chooser" had to or would have to make in the specified circumstances.

In Schutz's analysis, on the other hand, ends and means, and any resulting choices made, only emerge out of a temporal process of imagination. Out of the actor's general field of interests, an interest of a particular relevance at a moment in time comes to the foreground. He concentrates on this interest by projecting in his mind a future moment in time when a state of affairs representing the fulfillment of that interest would be accomplished. The actor then mentally traces out the means and methods he believes would be required "in-order-to" bring that state of affairs to actual fruition. Other alternative states-of-affairs, and the actions believed necessary for their accomplishment, may be projected in a similar fashion in the actor's mind.

Appreciation of this mental process by which ends and means are constructed integrates the temporal dimension into an understanding of choice. This is so not merely in the sense that this process of imagination itself occurs in time, but also concerns the construction of competing or complementary plans of future states-of-affairs only potentially realizable by various actions *through time*. It is *the futurity of ends and means* in a plan that creates its "problematic" character. For there is no present certainty concerning the results of a project undertaken over time. Furthermore, the process by which selection may be made among the alternative projections is problematic: having created the alternatives, the actor must compare them; he possibly modifies them after thinking about the others; he weighs the relative likelihood of their success; and ranks them in relative orders of importance, until one (or some) is (are) finally chosen over the other(s).

The analyst, as a result, cannot know with predictive certainty what the actor's choice will be, *ex ante,* because the actor does not even know what the alternatives are or how he shall evaluate and rank them independent of the temporal "fantasizing" process out of which a choice may emerge. What is determinate and "predictable" for Neo-Classical Economics is, therefore, open-ended, "problematic," and unpredictable in a Schutzian framework.

Thus, what the Neo-Classical Economist takes as the "givens" from which he begins his analysis of the "logic of choice," and on the basis of which he predicts how men will "act," are not "givens" at all at a more fundamental level. The "givens" of the logic of choice are created by the actors themselves who do the actual, eventual choosing. It is the actors who create their own "ends" through fantasizing about possible preferred states of affairs; it is the actors who design their own "means" by fantasizing about possible means and methods to bring those states of affairs into possible existence; it is the actors who construct their own trade-offs by fantasizing about what might be worth giving up to obtain something else that they decide they value more highly, and therefore what might be the maximum and minimum "prices" they would, respectively, pay or accept to do one thing rather than another.

This is why creativity, innovation, and change ultimately cannot be predicted. Creativity, innovation and change arise out of modifications in people's conduct, i.e., out of new and different choices they make and the actions they undertake. And these choices, as we have seen, emerge out of the fantasizing processes of the human mind; but those human minds do not know ahead of time what their choices and actions will be until they have run through their own projecting processes of imagined possibilities and alternatives. In this sense, our future choices are not only hidden from the social and economic analyst, but from ourselves as well. We can never really know our choices until we make them. Thus knowledge about our own choices always awaits us in our own futures, whether that future is a moment from now or decades away.[31]

Structures of intersubjective orientation and process of market coordination

If full knowledge was possessed of the objective conditions and circumstances of the market by both actors and analysts, no problem of economic coordination would exist. Given the assumptions upon which they construct their models of man, it is not surprising, therefore, that Neo-Classical Economists have tended to focus their analysis on states of economic equilibrium, and found it difficult to develop theories of market processes.[32] The most fully developed of the theories of market processes and coordination among the Austrian Economists has been that of Ludwig von Mises. How can the actors, and especially the entrepreneurs, anticipate the future conditions of the market? We have already seen that in the Austrian theory of competition, it is through the rivalry of the market for consumer business that entrepreneurs either earn profits or suffer losses. How can they anticipate the future patterns of consumer demand as the point on the horizon of tomorrow for directing their production activities today?

Following Max Weber, Mises said that a primary tool for the historian is the construction of various ideal types for the stylization and conceptualization of the motives, ideas, and goals of the individuals and groups of individuals the historian is trying to understand. But Mises also argued that ideal types are the primary tool by which acting men anticipate the possible future actions of others with whom they may interact in the social arena. Acting man must be an "historian of the future," who projects himself forward from the present and imagines the likely conduct of others in various settings and situations for purposes of forming expectations of the shape of social things to come.

He constructs such images of possible futures on the basis of ideal types that he builds up in his mind from our "experience, acquired directly from observing our fellow men and transacting business with them or indirectly from reading and hearsay, as well as out of our special experience acquired in previous contacts with the individuals or groups concerned." And on this basis "we try to form an opinion about their future conduct." On the nature of ideal types, Mises said:

> If an ideal type refers to people, it implies that in some respect these men are valuing and acting in a uniform or similar way. When it refers to institutions, it implies that these institutions are products of uniform and similar ways of valuing or acting, or that they influence valuing and acting in a uniform or similar way.

The difficulty in anticipating future actions by the method of ideal types is that the "historian of the future" must construct them on the basis of: (a) an inclusion of the institutional or behavioral characteristics considered present and relevant that may influence and guide the conduct of the others he is interested in anticipating; (b) and a relative "weighting" assigned to the institutional or behavioral factors that will determine the actual outcome of future actions of others that the decision-maker is trying to anticipate.[33]

But no one has taken the Weberian ideas of "social action," "mutual orienta- tion," and ideal typification and developed them with as much rigor and consist- ency as has Alfred Schutz for a theory of structures of intersubjective meaning for purposes of understanding the social world.

Schutz argued that each individual is born into a preexisting "intersubjective world of daily life." As we grow up, we are incorporated into this world of inter- subjective meaning; through repetition or reappearance and reinforcement we come to understand the meaning of gestures and facial expressions, bodily movements, and words and sentences. The nuances of social life, about which each of us begins knowing nothing, become "objectified" as the meanings of words, movements, objects, and actions. We come to understand both ourselves and others because the medium through which we express our own intentions and comprehend those of others is against this background of learned, socially given structures of meanings. While each of the institutional structures of meaning could be reduced to an historical process through which they have evolved out of human conduct, at any moment in time they exist as a "given" into which the individual fits and orients himself. At the same time, these mean- ings, themselves, are evolving over time. The structures of intersubjective meaning slowly change as individuals experience new thoughts and express new ideas; these are then conveyed back to others through the shared "given" meaning structures. Thus a dynamic process of mutual dependency emerges in which the "given" meaning structures serve as points of individual and social orientation for "understanding," while being themselves modifiable through their use for the expression of new meanings by individuals.

At the opposite end of the ideal typification spectrum from the abstract and general anonymous "other" is the specific "face-to-face" relationship where indi- viduals share a common environment of place, time and experience. They observe each other's facial expressions; they ask and respond to questions; they grow older together. Here the individuals do not construct a composite typifica- tion of a universal "any other," and therefore of all men; instead they create a typification of the particular other individual, on the basis of which each in the interaction forms judgments and expectations about the other's typical attitudes ("He is a liberal"), his typical response to situations ("He is always cool under fire"), the typical interests that guide his actions ("He is only interested in sports").[34]

In between the anonymous any other and the particular individual other, Schutz argued, was a range on the ideal typification spectrum made up of any number of specific others whose behavior is constructed on the basis of various "courses-of-action" and "personal types." Here the typical behavior expected is based on the type of purpose or function and role an individual takes on in a spe- cific setting in the social world. We identify him and anticipate forms of conduct from him on the basis of the typical meanings that are taken for granted for actions with a particular goal in mind, or a particular form of activity associated with any "other" performing a specific function or role within the social order.[35] These kinds of ideal types, composed of mental pictures of others in varying degrees of anonymity and intimacy in various settings, serve as the background knowledge for "understanding" and interpreting the past actions of others, and as the anticipatory framework for the projection of possible actions in the future.

Oddly enough, even though Schutz was well acquainted with the writings of the economists of his time, especially with the writings of the leading members of the Austrian School, and in spite of the fact that he spent a major part of this life in the world of business, his published writings contain few concrete applications of his ideas to economic and market processes.[36] Schutz's close friend, Fritz Machlup, on the other hand, believed that his ideas had great relevance to economic theory-construction and analysis.[37]

We have seen that what Schutz calls the "other" of total anonymity, to whom only the most general and generic properties of any human actor can be assigned, is none other than the economist's old friend, Robinson Crusoe. The Crusoe construction enables us to deduce those attributes in human activity so broad and abstract in their nature that they would have to be found in any conscious human being undertaking the process of choice under conditions of scarcity. They represent the core principles of the logic of any and all human action. Indeed, Schutz considered the logic of action and choice guided by the principles of marginal utility as the "regulator" on the basis of which economists, on postulated conditions, can derive the "laws of economics."[38]

An example in economics nearer the other end of Schutz's spectrum – the face-to-face relationship – is to be found in the economist's theory of bilateral monopoly. Here two potential trading partners confront each other, and a wide range exists within which the price at which trade may occur can fall. The traders haggle; they size each other up concerning their respective bargaining skills; they form judgments as to the other's intensity of desire for trade and how long the "other" may be willing to continue the bargaining process before breaking off discussion and forgoing any transactions. Each agent, in other words, constructs in his mind an ideal type of the other as face-to-face interaction proceeds; and this serves as the basis for the consummation of any transactions that may result.

At the opposite extreme would be the case that economists often classify under the heading of "perfect competition." Here, rather than only two particular traders confronting each other on opposite sides of the market, the theory postulates a large number of buyers and sellers; each seller contributes such a small portion to the total supply of the good in the market in which he operates, that any variation in the quantity offered by him is not large enough to influence the market price for that good, given the consumer demand for it; each seller offers a good exactly like his rivals, so each is marketing a commodity that is a perfect and interchangeable substitute for the goods offered by his competitors in his market; and there is absolute openness and ease of entry and exit from each market in the economy. Every seller is therefore assumed to be a "price taker," who adjusts the quantity he sells to maximize his net revenue given the price he finds to be prevailing in the market, and which his individual supply-side decisions cannot influence.

Numerous inconsistencies and contradictions can be found in this conception of a "perfectly competitive" market.[39] But regardless of this, for the sellers to be "price takers," it requires each of them to hold a particular set of ideal typifications of themselves and others in the market, such that each passively adjusts his quantities offered for sale at whatever price he finds offered to him; nor does he attempt to differentiate his product relative to the ones being sold by his rivals. They each must have an ideal type in their minds of the "typical" consumer in their market, who will immediately stop all their buying from any one of them and purchase this good from other sellers in the market if the price he charges were raised by him even by the smallest amount. He must believe that these consumers *think of* his commodity as being exactly no different from the ones sold by his competitors, and therefore the consumers are indifferent as to whether they buy from him or someone else. Each seller must *believe* that their actual and potential rivals have the ability to adjust their production methods and activities so rapidly to any change he may try to introduce to cut costs or improve the quality of his product, that any profits that he hoped to reap from such innovation would be immediately competed away by his rivals instantaneously matching whatever he does.

Only *if* the sellers in this "perfect" market view themselves and their rivals in this way, will they *act like* price takers. Regardless of the "objective" conditions, *if* any of the sellers think they can influence the price by modifying the quantity they bring to the market; *if* they think they can make consumers view their product as being different than the ones offered by their competitors; *if* they believe they can reap profits for some period of time by introducing cost-saving techniques, then they will act in ways inconsistent with what the "objective" conditions lead the economist to expect from them. Merely adding up the numbers of sellers in a market, merely comparing the physical characteristics of the goods sold, and merely estimating the ease with which a new cost-cutting technique could be physically introduced into all the sellers' production facilities, tells us nothing about how sellers will act or how consumers will react to a change in any one or more sellers' behavior. This depends upon how actors in the market have typified their own circumstances and the "courses of action" they think most likely to be forthcoming from buyers and rivals for sales.[40]

Without understanding how actors understand intersubjective relationships in the markets in which they do business, there is no way to successfully analyze and anticipate their likely courses of action. It is a clear example of what Schutz meant when he said that the social scientist must realize that his analytical constructs must be "constructs *of* the second degree, namely constructs *of* the constructs made by the actors on the social scene, whose behavior the scientist observes and tries to explain."[41]

It is in the wide intermediate range of Schutz's spectrum of ideal typification that most of the problems of economics and market coordination fall. "The Market" represents an arena in which traders neither function in atomistic Crusoe isolation nor intimately know all the "others" with whom they either cooperate or compete in the far-flung and complex system of division of labor. Yet, for such a division of labor to emerge and extend across time and space, actors must have the means to anticipate the intended actions of others both in the present and the future.

When looked at through Schutzian glasses, the regularities of the market place that enables "Paris to be fed," that opens the possibility for future demands to be gleaned from past consumption patterns as a guide for directing present production, and that allows prices to convey information to the respective actors in the processes of production, all have their basis in the interlocking structure of ideal typifications for mutual orientation. A building contractor must judge the state of the housing market to make decisions about the types, quantities, and price ranges of houses that he could construct. Any such decisions will be made on the basis of his experience, knowledge, and "feel" for the various types of consumers who might be willing to purchase the homes he could offer for sale. Unable to personally know all those who may in the future want to buy his housing output, he must be guided in his decisions by the mental constructions he implicitly creates in his mind of, e.g., the typical consumer who may desire a ranch-style home; how that ideal typical consumer will respond if the price of the house is lowered by five hundred dollars; or if the rate of interest increases by 1 percent.

Economists often speak of human behavior guided by market prices. To the extent that actors modify their behavior in response to shifts in market prices, however, it is because prices are, themselves, serving as ideal typifications of an abstract sort. If the market price of a commodity declines, should one buy more or less of it? That decision will depend upon, among other things, whether it is believed that the price will or will not go even lower in the near future. But this judgment will be dependent upon the ideal types that potential buyers of the commodity construct concerning the potential sellers' future pricing decisions. Market prices, by themselves, do not speak; like words on a page they must be interpreted. And the way actors make judgments concerning interpretations of market conditions is on the basis of ideal types of the patterns of other actors' behavior (both individuals and groups under typical and atypical circumstances).

The competitive rivalry of the market is ultimately a clash of different inter-pretations of meanings in men's actions. Entrepreneurial rivalry is based on each of those entrepreneurs having constructed an alternative set of ideal typifications of the subgroup of the consuming public towards which they are directing their productive activities. The market test of who among these entrepreneurs was more right in their earlier projected "fantasies" concerning consumer demand will only be found out when the products they have produced are offered to the market in competition with those of their rivals. And the consumers, now con-fronted with the wares offered to them, will then make their choices, or decide to direct their purchases to different markets, or to abstain from some of their pur-chases until a future date.

Another ingredient in this playing out of the market process will be the extent to which in designing and selecting their production plans, entrepreneurs will have successfully constructed ideal typifications of their rivals' conduct. For it will not have been enough to form expectations about the possible buying decisions of some subgroup of consumers, if their expectations do not incorpo-rate typifications of the likely characteristics of goods to be offered by potential rivals and the prices at which they may be sold.

But all of these decisions can be made only against a background of other "courses of action" and "personal" ideal types. Each entrepreneur must have expectations about the reliability of suppliers of raw materials and other resource inputs if production processes are to be undertaken with degrees of confidence that the supplies will be delivered on time and according to the terms of agreement and contract. They must form expectations about whether the political order is stable, property rights are secure, that contracts will be enforced, and that war or civil war is not imminent. All such expectations are dependent on the stability and reliability of various social institutions and the conduct to be expected from those who administer the law and who protect life and property. Rarely, however, have economists paid attention to the structures of intersubjective meaning and ideal typification that are necessary for a market order to function properly, and upon which the social order of civil society ultimately rests.[42]

Nobel economist, Ronald Coase (a leading contributor to the theory of the economics of property rights and transaction costs), has expressed the concern that economists have imperialistically moved into neighboring social sciences, and imposed their own method of analysis on political science, sociology and anthropology. Coase does not deny that the "economic way of thinking" may have useful and indeed valuable applications in other surrounding disciplines. But he reminded his fellow economists that economics has potentially as many interesting things to learn from those other social sciences as it has to contribute to them.[43]

The advantage of Schutzian-type sociology as a first step in economists learning from one of their neighboring disciplines is that it draws attention to what lies behind and significantly determines the structures of the market processes: the patterns of intentional behavior of acting men through lived, historical time. Luckily, in beginning this interdisciplinary process there is one school of economists, the "Austrians," who already construct their conception of men and markets on the basis of meaningful conduct and realize that the social order is grounded in the intersubjective world of acting men.

Notes

1 Helmut Wagner, *Alfred Schutz: An Intellectual Biography* (Chicago: University of Chicago Press, 1983), pp. 11–13.
2 Bettina Bien Greaves, "An Interview with Dr. Alfred Schutz" (unpublished, 1958).
3 Ludwig von Mises, *The Theory of Money and Credit* (Indianapolis, IN: Liberty Classics, 1981). For a discussion of Mises' contributions to monetary theory and policy and their relationship to the writings of other Austrians on the same themes, see, Richard M. Ebeling, *Austrian Economics and the Political Economy of Freedom* (Northampton, MA: Edward Elgar, 2003), Ch. 5: "Ludwig von Mises and the Gold Standard," pp. 136–158.
4 Ludwig von Mises, *Nation, State, and Economy* [1919] (New York: New York University Press, 1983).
5 Ludwig von Mises, "Economic Calculation in the Socialist Commonwealth," [1920] in F.A. Hayek, ed., *Collectivist Economic Planning: Critical Studies on the Possibilities of Socialism* (London: George Routledge & Sons, 1935), pp. 87–130, reprinted in Israel M. Kirzner, ed., *Classics in Austrian Economics: A Sampling in the History of a Tradition*, Vol. 3 (London, William Pickering, 1994), pp. 3–30.

6 For a more thorough discussion of Mises' critique of socialist central planning, see, Richard M. Ebeling, *Austrian Economics and the Political Economy of Freedom*, Ch. 4: "Economic Calculation Under Socialism: Ludwig von Mises and His Predecessors," pp. 101–135; also, Richard M. Ebeling, "Why Socialism is 'Impossible,'" *The Freeman: Ideas on Liberty* (October 2004), pp. 8–12.
7 Bettina Bien Greaves, "An Interview with Dr. Alfred Schutz."
8 Ibid.
9 Ludwig von Mises, *Notes and Recollections* (South Holland, IL: Libertarian Press, 1978), pp. 97–98.
10 Margit von Mises, *My Years with Ludwig von Mises* (Cedar Falls, IA: Center for Futures Education, 1984), p. 207.
11 Ibid., p. 203.
12 These papers were found by the present writer among the "lost papers" of Ludwig von Mises in a formerly secret archive in Moscow, Russia. In March, 1938, the Gestapo came looking for Mises in Vienna following the annexation of Austria by Nazi Germany. Mises was in Geneva, Switzerland at the time, but the Gestapo seized all of his papers, documents, unpublished monographs, articles and correspondence that he stored in his Vienna apartment. At the end of the war, Mises' papers, along with millions of pages of other documents, papers and archival materials the Nazis looted in occupied countries, were captured by the Soviet Army in Czechoslovakia; see, Richard M. Ebeling, "Mission to Moscow: The Mystery of the 'Lost Papers' of Ludwig von Mises," *Notes from FEE* (Irvington-on-Hudson, NY: Foundation for Economic Education, July, 2004), available online at: www.fee.org/pdf/notes/ NFF_0704.pdf.
13 Carl Menger, *Principles of Economics* [1871] (New York: New York University Press, 1981).
14 See, Richard M. Ebeling, "Austrian Subjectivism and Phenomenological Foundations," in, Peter J. Boettke and Mario J. Rizzo, eds., *Advances in Austrian Economics*, vol. 2A (Greenwich: JAI Press, 1995), pp. 39–53, for the relationship between the Austrian approach to theory-formation and Husserl's phenomenological method for deriving essentialist properties of concepts.
15 For summaries and overviews of the ideas of the Austrian School of Economics, see, L.M. Lachmann, "The Significance of the Austrian School of Economics in the History of Ideas," in, Richard M. Ebeling, ed., *Austrian Economics: A Reader* (Hillsdale, MI: Hillsdale College Press, 1991), pp. 17–39; and, Richard M. Ebeling, *Austrian Economics and the Political Economy of Freedom*, Ch. 2: "The Significance of Austrian Economics in Twentieth-Century Economic Thought," pp. 14–33.
16 The most significant ones from this period are "Sociology and History" (1929), and "Conception and Understanding" (1930); they were reprinted in, *Epistemological Problems of Economics* [1933] (New York: New York University Press, 1981), pp. 68–145.
17 Ibid., pp. 1–67; also, Ludwig von Mises, *Nationalökonomie: Theorie des Handelns und Wirtschaftens* (Munchen: Philosophia Verlag, 1980) and, *Human Action: A Treatise on Economics* (Irvington-on-Hudson, NY: Foundation for Economic Education, 1996).
18 On some aspects of this problem, see, Oskar Morgenstern, *Wirtschaftsprognose* (Wien: Julius Springer, 1928); also, "Perfect Foresight and Economic Equilibrium," [1935] in, Andrew Schotter, ed., *Selected Economic Writings of Oskar Morgenstern* (New York: New York University Press, 1976), pp. 169–183.
19 See F.A. Hayek, "Economics and Knowledge," [1937] as well as his "The Use of Knowledge in Society," [1945] in, *Individualism and Economic Order* (Chicago: University of Chicago Press, 1948), pp. 35–56, 77–91. For a critical evaluation of Hayek's writings on this theme, partly from a Schutzian point of view, see, Richard M. Ebeling, "Toward a Hermeneutical Economics: Expectations, Prices, and the Role of Interpretation in a Theory of the Market Process," in, David L. Prychitko, ed.,

Individuals, Institutions, Interpretations: Hermeneutics Applied to Economics (Brookfield, VT: Avebury Publishing, 1995), pp. 138–153.

20 J.A. Schumpeter, *The Theory of Economic Development* (Cambridge, MA: Harvard University Press, 1934).

21 On the differences in the conception of the entrepreneur in Schumpeter's and Mises' writings, see, Israel M. Kirzner, *Competition and Entrepreneurship* (Chicago: University of Chicago Press, 1973).

22 See John von Neumann and Oskar Morgenstern, *The Theory of Games and Economic Behavior* (Princeton, NJ: Princeton University Press, 1944).

23 For a summary and critical analysis of Mises' use and application of the Weberian Ideal Type for purposes of developing a theory of expectations, see, Richard M. Ebeling, "Expectations and Expectations-Formation in Mises' Theory of the Market Process," in, D.L. Prychitko, ed., *Individuals, Institutions, Interpretations: Hermeneutics Applied to Economics*, pp. 83–95.

24 Fritz Machlup, *The Economics of Sellers' Competition* (Baltimore, MD: The Johns Hopkins Press, 1952), p. 370.

25 For more expositions by Austrian Economists on economic processes of adjustment, coordination and discovery, see, Robin Cowan and Mario J. Rizzo, "The Genetic-Causal Tradition and Modern Economic Theory," *Kyklos* 49, no. 3 (1996), pp. 273–317; and, Israel M. Kirzner, "Entrepreneurial Discovery and the Competitive Market Process: an Austrian Approach," *Journal of Economic Literature* (March 1997), pp. 60–85 and *How Markets Work: Disequilibrium, Entrepreneurship and Discovery* (London: Institute of Economic Affairs, 1997).

26 I have attempted to suggest how such a theory of expectations and intersubjective market orientation can be applied using Schutz's ideas in several writings. See, Richard M. Ebeling: "What is a Price? Explanation and Understanding," in Don C. Lavoie, ed., *Economics and Hermeneutics* (New York: Routledge, 1990), pp. 177–194; "Cooperation in Anonymity," in D.L. Prychitko, ed., *Individuals, Institutions, Interpretations: Hermeneutics Applied to Economics*, pp. 81–92; "Toward a Hermeneutical Economics," pp. 138–153. The following section draws upon these earlier writings and extends the analysis and applications.

27 Alfred Schutz, *The Phenomenology of the Social World* [1932] (Evanston, IL: Northwestern University Press, 1967), pp. 137, 245.

28 Gary Becker, "De Gustibus Non Est Disputandum," in *Accounting for Tastes* (Cambridge, MA: Harvard University Press, 1996).

29 Alfred Schutz, "Choosing Among Courses of Action," *Collected Papers I: The Problems of Social Reality* (The Hague: Martinus Nijhoff, 1962), pp. 67–97.

30 As an example of this Neo-Classical analysis of the allocation of time, see, Gary Becker, *The Economic Approach to Human Behavior* (Chicago: University of Chicago Press, 1976), pp. 89–130; for an Austrian critique of the Neo-Classical conception of time, see Gerald P. O'Driscoll Jr. and Mario J. Rizzo, *The Economics of Time and Ignorance* (New York: Routledge, 1996), pp. 52–70.

31 On the limits of knowing and making predictions about the future in terms consistent with this analysis, see, Bertrand de Jouvenel, *The Art of Conjecture* (New York: Basic Books, 1967); and, John Jewkes, *A Return to Free Market Economics?* (London: Macmillan, 1978), pp. 12–38; also, Richard M. Ebeling, "Freedom and the Pitfalls of Predicting the Future," *The Freeman: Ideas on Liberty* (June, 2006), pp. 2–3.

32 For a detailed critique of the founding theories of Neo-Classical equilibrium analysis by an Austrian Economist, see, Hans Mayer, "The Cognitive Value of Functional Theories of Price," [1932] in Israel M. Kirzner, ed., *Classics of Austrian Economic,* Vol. 2 (London: William Pickering, 1994), pp. 55–168.

33 Ludwig von Mises, *Theory and History: An Interpretation of Social and Economic Evolution* [1957] (Auburn, AL: Ludwig von Mises Institute, 1985), pp. 312–320.

34 Alfred Schutz, *Collected Papers II: Studies in Social Theory* (The Hague: Martinus Nijhoff, 1974), pp. 27–33.

35 Ibid., pp. 25–26.
36 For an exception to this, in which Schutz discussed "The Basic Assumption of Economic Theory for Dealing with the Problem of Choice," see Alfred Schutz, "Choice and the Social Sciences," in Lester Embree, ed., *Life-World and Consciousness: Essays for Aron Gurwitsch* (Evanston, IL: Northwestern University Press, 1972), pp. 584–588. There have been published in English four previously unavailable papers by Schutz on aspects of the nature and application of economic theory for understanding the social world, see Alfred Schutz, *Collected Papers*, Vol. 4 (Boston: Kluwer Academic Press, 1996), pp. 75–105.
37 Fritz Machlup, *Methodology of Economics and Other Social Sciences* (New York: Academic Press, 1978), pp. 211–301.
38 Alfred Schutz, *Collected Papers*, Vol. 4, p. 102.
39 For a discussion of some of these contradictions and inconsistencies, see, Richard M. Ebeling, *Austrian Economics and the Political Economy of Freedom*, Ch. 8: "The Free Market and the Interventionist State," pp. 203–230; and Hayek, "The Meaning of Competition," pp. 92–106.
40 Machlup, *The Economics of Sellers' Competition*, pp. 418–424.
41 Alfred Schutz, "Choosing Among Courses of Action," p. 6.
42 A few of the rare exceptions in which aspects of this problem have been analyzed include, H. Schuman, *The Promises that Men Live By* (New York: Random House, 1938); S.H. Frankel, *Money and Liberty* (Washington DC: American Enterprise Institute, 1980); F. Fukuyama, *Trust: The Social Virtues and the Creation of Prosperity* (New York: The Free Press, 1995). On some of the institutions and social relationships essential for a functioning market order and how the Classical Economists of the eighteenth and nineteenth centuries understood them, see, Richard M. Ebeling, *Austrian Economics and the Political Economy of Freedom*, Ch. 1: "How Economics Became the Dismal Science," pp. 1–13.
43 Ronald H. Coase, *Essays on Economics and Economists* (Chicago: University of Chicago Press, 1994), pp. 34–46.

Index

Abnormal Importation Act 236
American Institute for Economic Research (AIER) xviii
Anderson, Benjamin M. 142, 236, 266, 268, 270
Anschluss 46, 47, 92, 99, 100, 106, 127
anti-Semitism 5, 33, 36, 40, 41, 45, 46, 49, 52, 53, 54, 63
Association of Austrian Economists 107
Austrian Colloquium xv, xvii
Austria 5, 6, 7, 33, 36, 41, 42, 45, 46, 47, 48, 51, 52, 53, 54, 58, 59, 60, 62, 63, 65, 67, 68, 70, 74, 75, 76, 78, 80, 81, 83, 84, 85, 88, 89, 90, 91, 92, 93, 94, 95, 96, 97, 98, 99, 100, 103, 105, 106, 107, 109, 110, 111, 112, 113, 114, 115, 120, 121, 122, 123, 125, 126, 127, 129, 131, 132, 133, 134, 136, 137, 138, 139, 142, 143, 144, 147, 169, 170, 171, 173, 174, 175, 176, 177, 192, 196, 205, 230, 273, 275, 329, 345
Austria-Hungary 5, 38, 44, 58, 59, 61, 62, 64, 66, 67, 70, 72, 73, 74, 75, 77, 81, 86, 87, 92, 100, 131, 273
Austrian economists xvi, 2, 19, 212, 222, 223, 226, 237, 240, 251, 334, 336, 339, 346
Austrian economics xv, xvi, xvii, xviii, 4, 11, 12, 273, 275
Austrian Institute for Business Cycle Research 22, 142
Austrian National Bank (Austro-Hungarian National Bank) 37, 64, 65, 73, 93, 96, 99, 101, 103, 107, 120, 121, 122, 123, 124, 125, 134, 136, 205
Austrian School of Economics xvi, xvii, 1, 11, 12, 13, 19, 23, 33, 48, 66, 80, 81, 83, 212, 213, 222, 223, 229, 257, 275, 276, 334, 336, 341, 345

Bagehot, Walter 158, 197

Bank of England 99, 122
barter 124, 125, 132, 151, 197, 213, 252, 288, 305, 318, 326
Bastiat, Frederic 259
Battalana, John xvii
Bauer, Otto 103, 105, 127, 274
Bismarck, Otto von 23, 33, 60, 61
Becher, Joachim 87
Block, Walter xvii
Boettke, Peter xvii
Bolshevism 25, 93, 96, 100, 145, 167, 241
Böhm-Bawerk, Eugen von 1, 7, 15, 66, 74, 77, 80, 81, 86, 87, 223, 225, 226, 256, 273, 274, 276, 299, 302, 303, 304, 305, 307, 308, 313
Bonn, Moritz J. 234
Bostaph, Samuel xvii
Brentano, Lujo 310
Brest-Litovsk, Treaty of 100, 275
Brody 36, 37, 50
Browne, Martha Steffy 48, 333
business cycle xv, xviii, 4, 6, 7, 8, 11, 28, 88, 129, 208, 209, 216, 222, 226, 227, 229, 230, 237, 265, 266, 277, 279, 284, 285, 287, 288, 292, 294, 295, 296, 297, 300, 301, 302, 307, 308, 309, 317, 325, 334
Butos, William xviii

Cairnes, John E. 215, 216
Calcagno, Peter xviii
Caldwell, Bruce xvii
Cannan, Edwin 238
capital consumption 98, 116, 122, 133, 165, 171, 177
capital investment 126, 169, 172, 225, 295, 296, 309
capitalism 4, 11, 23, 29, 42, 53, 76, 81, 89, 117, 163, 166, 167, 197, 198, 203, 205, 206, 234, 248, 266
cartels 23, 118, 164, 167, 240, 244

350   *Index*

For Product Safety Concerns and Information please contact our EU
representative GPSR@taylorandfrancis.com
Taylor & Francis Verlag GmbH, Kaufingerstraße 24, 80331 München, Germany